The Construction Project

PHASES • PEOPLE • TERMS • PAPERWORK • PROCESSES

SECOND EDITION

Marilyn Klinger and Will Beasley, Editors

ABA
AMERICAN BAR ASSOCIATION
Tort Trial and Insurance
Practice Section

Cover design by Mary Anne Kulchawik/ABA Design

Printed in the United States of America.

27 26 25 24   5 4 3 2

ISBN 978-1-63905-408-4

Discounts are available for books ordered in bulk. Special consideration is given to state bars, CLE programs, and other bar-related organizations. Inquire at Book Publishing, ABA Publishing, American Bar Association, 321 N. Clark Street, Chicago, Illinois 60654-7598.

www.shopABA.org

CONTRIBUTORS

EMORY G. ALLEN • Senior Attorney in the Frisco, Texas office of Clark Hill, PLC. He is licensed in Alabama, Colorado, and Texas as well as admitted in multiple U.S. District and Bankruptcy Courts across the country. Mr. Allen represents clients in litigation and contract matters with an emphasis on surety, construction, and contract claims. After graduating with honors with a Bachelor of Business Administration from Mississippi State University, Mr. Allen completed his Juris Doctorate from University of Mississippi School of Law.

TODD BAUER • President of Guardian Group, Inc., a national surety and construction firm. He received his Bachelor of Science in Business Administration from the University of Southern California and received his Masters in Business Administration from the University of Texas. Mr. Bauer holds a B California general contractor license and is president of Guardian Group, Inc.'s subsidiary, Completion Contractors, Inc. He is affiliated with numerous industry organizations and is a frequent speaker at industry conferences and events.

WILL BEASLEY • Senior claims attorney and contract claims manager at Merchants Bonding Company. Mr. Beasley is a graduate of the University of Tennessee, Knoxville, B.A., and SMU Dedman School of Law. His practice focuses on finding creative solutions to complex issues in the construction and surety industries.

RON E. BOYLE, CPA CGMA, CCA, CCP • President of Boyle Consulting, Inc., a forensic accounting firm. He received his B.A. degree in business administration from Mid-America Nazarene University in 1980. Mr. Boyle is a certified public accountant with licenses in Kansas and Florida. He is also a charted global management accountant, a certified construction auditor and a construction control professional. He has served in the surety industry since 1986.

SHANNON J. BRIGLIA • Shannon J. Briglia is a partner at the national construction law firm Smith, Currie & Hancock, LLP where she concentrates her practice in the resolution of public and private construction disputes. Elected to the American College of Construction Lawyers in 2016, Ms. Briglia has a thriving practice representing sureties, owners, contractors, and subcontractors and is a certified construction arbitrator. Ms. Briglia received her B.S. from Virginia Tech and her J.D. from George Mason University School of Law. She served as the pro se law clerk for the judges of the United States District Court for the Eastern District of Virginia, Alexandria Division. She is married and has two sons.

MICHAEL BURKHARDT • Michael Burkhardt is Senior Surety Claims Counsel for Liberty Mutual Surety in the Northeast Region Claims Office in Plymouth Meeting, PA. He has over 25 years of experience in the risk management, insurance, and surety industry, and has been managing surety bond claims as a surety company claims attorney for the past 17 years. Michael graduated with a B.B.A. degree in Risk Management and Insurance from Temple University in 1994 and a J.D. degree from the University of Pittsburgh in 2000. He is a frequent presenter on numerous topics at various surety claims conferences and meetings.

BENJAMIN CHAMBERS • Director, Bond Claims and Credit and Political Risk Insurance, for The Hartford. He graduated from Western Washington University in 2000 with a B.A. in Philosophy and received a J.D from Seattle University School of Law, magna cum laude, in 2004. He is admitted to practice law in Washington State.

CHRISTINA CRADDOCK • Senior Surety Claims Counsel for Liberty Mutual Insurance Company. She has over 30 years of surety claim experience, both as outside counsel and in-house claims counsel. She is a graduate of the University of Georgia, BBA, International Business, magna cum laude, 1979 and the University of Georgia School of Law, Juris Doctor, cum laude, 1982. Ms. Craddock is a Vice Chair of the ABA/TIPS Fidelity & Surety Law Committee and Co-Chair of the Law Division and the Women's Involvement Committee of the ABA/TIPS Fidelity & Surety Law Committee.

BRYCE HOLZER • Technical Director & Counsel with Travelers Bond & Specialty Insurance. He joined Travelers in August 2012 and primarily handles complex performance and payment bond claims. He graduated from Washington State University summa cum laude in 2007, and from the University of Washington Law School in 2011. Mr. Holzer is a member of the Washington State Bar Association.

MICHAEL HUHN • Principal of JHS Tax & Consulting in northern California. He is a graduate of California State University, B.S. magna cum laude, and is a Certified Public Accountant, Certified Fraud specialist and Certified in Financial Forensics by the American Institute of CPAs. Mr. Huhn has been consulting for surety and fidelity companies since 1986 and often provides consultation and expert testimony regarding economic damages associated with construction contract disputes and bond losses.

MATTHEW R. JOY • Director and certified Planning and Scheduling Professional with Civic CM. Mr. Joy received his B.S. in Construction Management from Brigham Young University in 2002 and has over 20 years of experience in the construction industry. Mr. Joy provides construction consulting and expert services specializing in areas of project scheduling, delay, time impact analysis, construction management, surety, payment and performance bond claims, and project completion oversight. Mr. Joy has prepared and defended numerous delay, disruption, acceleration, and change order claims on behalf of general contractors, subcontractors, and sureties throughout the Western United States.

MARILYN KLINGER • Office Managing Partner of the Los Angeles office of SMTD Law LLP, a construction, surety, and commercial law boutique. After years practicing in all aspects of construction law, representing the full spectrum of the construction industry, from owners, contractors, subcontractors, and sureties, Ms. Klinger is now focusing her practice in the neutral world—arbitration and mediation. She is a graduate of the University of Santa Clara, B.S., cum laude, 1975, and University of California, Hastings College of the Law, Thurston Society and Order of the Coif, 1978. Ms. Klinger is a past Chair of the ABA/TIPS Fidelity & Surety Law Committee and a recipient of the ABA/FSLC Martin Andrews Award as well as the Los Angeles County Bar Association James Acret Award for construction legal writing.

DAVID KOTNIK • Surety claim leader, responsible for leading Westfield's surety claim operations. In his current role, Mr. Kotnik oversees five claim attorneys and one support staff. David additionally focuses on resolving the most complex contract surety performance and payment defaults and disputes. He has 25 years of surety claim experience in various roles. Prior to joining Westfield, Mr. Kotnik practiced surety and construction litigation at Frantz Ward LLP. While in private practice, he represented sureties, contractors, subcontractors and suppliers in all phases of law and litigation. Prior to practicing law, Mr. Kotnik was a claims analyst for a third-party adjusting firm, dealing primarily with contract surety bond claims. This experience provided him with unique insight and knowledge of issues involving construction dispute and resolution. Mr. Kotnik is a member of the American Bar Association (Fidelity and Surety Law Committee), the Defense Research Institute, and is on the board of the National Bond Claims Association. He is a frequent lecturer on surety and construction law topics. He earned his B.S.B.A.

degree from The Ohio State University and his J.D. degree from Cleveland-Marshall College of Law.

AMANDA L. MARUTZKY • Partner at the Irvine, California office of Watt, Tieder, Hoffar & Fitzgerald, LLP, a firm specializing in construction and surety for 45 years. She has over 13 years of litigation, construction, and surety experience and handles all aspects of construction and surety bond claims. She graduated from the University of Texas at Austin with Honors in 2006 and attained her J.D. in 2010 from Pepperdine University School of Law.

LAUREN P. McLAUGHLIN • Partner at Smith, Currie & Hancock, LLP, one of the oldest construction and government contracts law firms in the country. She has over 23 years of experience handling surety matters, including during her time as founding partner of BRIGLIA MCLAUGHLIN, PLLC, a construction and surety law firm servicing clients with disputes in Virginia, Maryland, and D.C. She is a member of the American College of Construction Lawyers, graduated Phi Beta Kappa and magna cum laude from Trinity University, and received her J.D. cum laude from Catholic University in Washington D.C.

JACK NICHOLSON, CPA, CFF, CGMA • President of Nicholson Professional Consulting, Inc., based in Atlanta, Georgia, with various other office locations throughout the United States. The firm provides Accounting, Engineering, and Construction Management expertise, primarily to the surety and fidelity industry. Mr. Nicholson is a Certified Public Accountant and a member of the Georgia Society of Certified Public Accountants and the American Institute of Certified Public Accountants. He is a graduate of Georgia State University, a former construction company controller, and a former national bank accountant. He has over 30 years of experience in the surety, fidelity, and banking industries. He has been accepted as an expert witness on accounting matters related to those industries on numerous occasions, in various courts.

TAYFUN "TY" OKSUZLER • Director at J.S. Held, LLC. a global consulting firm providing technical, scientific, and financial expertise. Mr. Oksuzler earned his B.S. in civil engineering from the University of Texas at Austin in 1994 and is LEED AP BD+C accredited. He accrued over twenty years experience as a cost estimator and project manager for Texas based contractors before becoming a construction industry consultant. He serves in JS Held's construction advisory practice with a focus on serving surety industry clients.

DENNIS P. O'NEILL • President of Beacon Consulting Group, Inc., a national surety, and construction consulting firm. He received his B.S. in Civil Engineering from the University of Maine and received his M.S. in Real Estate Development/Finance from New York University. Mr. O'Neill has over 25 years of extensive construction consulting and management expertise related to construction management, complex surety bond claims consulting, and dispute resolution matters. He specializes in assessing the condition of troubled construction projects and recommending /implementing corrective actions to successfully complete these projects. Mr. O'Neill is a licensed Construction Supervisor, a Member of the New York Building Congress and American Society of Professional Estimators along with several other industry trade organizations. Mr. O'Neill is also on the board of the Surety Claims Institute and frequently provides presentations related to construction management and completion of troubled construction projects.

CYNTHIA E. RODGERS-WAIRE • Partner with the law firm of Wright Constable & Skeen, L.L.P. She received her B.A. from the University of Virginia in 1989 and her J.D., with honors, from the University of Maryland School of Law in 1992. Ms. Rodgers-Waire practices in the areas of surety and fidelity law, construction law, bankruptcy, and general litigation.

JORDAN S. ROSENFELD, CPA • Senior Director with Imperium Consulting Group, in Bellevue, Washington. Mr. Rosenfeld graduated from the University of Massachusetts in 1976 with a BA in Accounting. He is a Certified Public Accountant with over 48 years' experience, including 40 years specializing in the construction and surety industries.

MICHAEL W. SPINELLI, AIA • Principal at Cashin Spinelli & Ferretti, LLC, a nationwide surety consulting and construction management firm headquartered in New York. Mr. Spinelli is a registered architect and attorney. He received his B.S. in Architectural Technology from the New York Institute of Technology, and his Juris Doctor, summa cum laude, from the Touro Law Center. He is past president of the Long Island Chapter of the American Institute of Architects, and past vice-chair of the Fidelity & Surety Law Committee. Over his 30-year career, Mr. Spinelli has been a graduate school professor, frequent lecturer, and author on surety and construction claims. He has been recognized as an expert in these areas in numerous state and federal jurisdictions.

DAVID J. STRYJEWSKI, CPA • Partner in the Philadelphia office of Matson Driscoll & Damico, LLP. He practices in the area of forensic accounting with a focus on surety, construction, and fidelity related matters. Mr. Stryjewski is a graduate of Lehigh University, BS, 1994. He is a Certified Public Accountant licensed in the Commonwealth of Pennsylvania, a Certified Construction Accountant, and is a member of the American Institute of Certified Public Accountants, Pennsylvania Institute of Certified Public Accountants, American Bar Association, as well as Treasurer for the National Bond Claims Association.

DOUGLASS F. WYNNE JR. • Partner at Simon, Peragine, Smith & Redfearn, LLP. Mr. Wynne graduated from Loyola University New Orleans College of Law. Mr. Wynne practices in the areas of surety and construction law and is a frequent lecturer and author on surety and construction issues.

TABLE OF CONTENTS

Chapter II

INTRODUCTION

Beyond every construction contract and contract surety bond, there is a physical construction project. This book, which is an update of the original book published in 2006, provides its readers with an overview of that construction project. It offers a step-by-step primer to understand how the construction project flows from the initial design through the final project "close-out."

This book does not attempt to describe the building process for structures. Nor does it explain architectural or engineering processes or terms. Rather, it provides a general overview of the construction project's phases and the people involved. It focuses more on the contractual aspects of the construction project - the paperwork, the process, and the unique terms encountered in project-related documents.

Our hope is that this book will provide its reader with a clear understanding of the people and paperwork involved in a construction project, which may serve as a handy resource for anyone approaching a construction project for the first time. To do so, this primer is broken into five chapters:

- Chapter One, ***Phases***, provides an overview of the construction phases from the project's conception, to its physical construction, and ultimately its closeout. In discussing these phases, this chapter touches on the project's design and bid, contractor selection/award, progress and final payments, and certain post-construction activities.
- Chapter Two, ***People***, describes the people one might encounter throughout the phases of a project. This includes the Construction Manager, Superintendent, Inspector, Owner, and Contractor. The chapter explains each participant's involvement and role in the project, and identifies their relationship with the other parties.
- Chapter Three, ***Terms***, describes and explains key words and phrases used in construction. Terms include contract delivery systems, contract documents, contract administration, and payment-related terms. It also includes some of the important legal terms found in the contract documents and provides definitions for key players/persons in construction projects.
- Chapter Four, ***Paperwork***, examines the paperwork associated with a construction project and identifies the significance of various documents. This chapter is especially helpful should

you be in a position of analyzing a failed construction project or dispute.

- Finally, Chapter Five, ***Processes***, provides greater detail about certain key processes that occur during the various construction phases. Processes include items such as the bidding and award processes, the contract administration processes, and the contract close-out processes.

Every construction project is unique, so please be mindful that this book deals with generalities and describes typical construction projects and documents. Where possible, the exhibits in the appendix provide examples of the documents and paperwork encountered during the various phases of the construction project.

We thank all of the contributors for their efforts to bring these materials together to create this primer. We hope you find it helpful.

Co-Editors

Marilyn Klinger
Los Angeles, California

Will Beasley
Dallas, Texas

CHAIR'S MESSAGE

The Fidelity and Surety Law Committee of the American Bar Association, Tort Trial & Insurance Practice Section (TIPS) is pleased to publish the long-awaited second edition of this unique book. Unlike the many available books that address technical aspects of construction projects and/or the complex legal issues that arise related to construction projects, this book provides an essential primer on the basics of a construction project, focusing, as the title suggests, on the phases, people, terms, paperwork, and processes involved. This book is perfect as a starting point for someone just starting in the construction or surety industries. Familiarity with the basics of how a construction project runs and the relevant terminology, which this book provides, is an essential first step. When young lawyers begin their career as surety/construction lawyers at my firm, it is one of the first resources I point them to. That said, this book is not just intended for those that are new to the construction industry. It also provides an excellent reference source for seasoned practitioners that helps succinctly and simply explain complex construction concepts that can be used in briefing to courts or otherwise. It is a must in every construction library!

The Committee extends its special thanks to Marilyn Klinger, co-editor of both the first and second editions of this publication, and Will Beasley who co-edited this edition. Another thanks is in order for Marianne Susong, the creator and co-editor of the first edition. And, last but not least, thanks to the seasoned construction/surety practitioners that contributed to each of the chapters.

This publication continues the tradition of quality publications by the Fidelity and Surety Law Committee.

Christopher R. Ward
Frisco, Texas
Chair, Fidelity and Surety Law Committee
American Bar Association
Tort Trial & Insurance Practice Section

CHAPTER I

PHASES OF THE CONSTRUCTION PROJECT

By: Will Beasley, Michael R. Huhn,
Ty Oksuzler, and Douglass Wynne, Jr.

A. Introduction

Construction is an art, not a science. To deliver a project it takes a team working together through each phase of construction—from the owner's planning and budgeting phase, through the design stage when the drawings and plans are created, to the contractor selection stage, and through the physical construction phase of the project when the project is complete and turned over to the owner for use. It is an art of coordination and management to keep a project on time and on budget throughout each phase.

Andrew Carnegie said, "[t]eamwork is the ability to work together toward a common vision. The ability to direct individual accomplishments toward organizational objectives. It is the fuel that allows common people to attain uncommon results." Taking ideas and turning them into end products of well-built, useful structures is a remarkable feat. It requires coordinated teamwork among all the players involved, throughout all the phases of the project, to attain the successful delivery of a completed construction project. This chapter describes and discusses the many steps that occur in each phase of the construction project. While there are only three main sections, Pre-Construction, Construction, and Post-Construction, the activities that occur during each phase of a construction project are anything but simple.

This chapter's overview of the construction project phases will provide a better understanding of the many processes and elements of teamwork that need coordination on every construction project for successful completion.

Recognizing the uniqueness of every construction project, this chapter describes the phases of a typical, general building project, focusing on state/local public works rather than private or federal projects. Where appropriate, the chapter adds comments related specifically to private or federal works.

B. Pre-Construction Phase

Starting with a hammer and no plan is a recipe for disaster. A successful construction project starts with a well-thought-out pre-construction phase. Good pre-construction includes (a) planning, budgeting, and permitting; (b) pre-construction consulting; (c) contractor selection; (d) bidding; and (e) the pre-con meeting.

1. Planning, Budgeting, and Permitting

a. Initial Project Planning and Feasibility

Every project starts with a conceptual plan and budget. The planning process for major development projects can often take years and be very complex, especially when public funds are involved. The process will often involve the preparation of a lengthy feasibility or development report. Thus, a public agency will often contract with planning firms to help with this process. For major projects, the process typically starts with a facility or needs analysis to forecast future demand against current supply. For example, a school district forecasts the need for a new grade school in a community based on enrollment projections and availability in existing surrounding schools. The planning process typically involves many public agencies, including building officials, public utility engineers, planners, and elected officials, as well as community participation.

In the planning process, the planner will also investigate site constraints, which may dramatically affect the usefulness or the cost of the project. For example, in selecting the site for a new school, the district determines that the school needs to be near multiple modes of transportation such as streetcar, rail, bicycle lanes, and bus routes. A project can earn "Leadership in Energy and Environmental Design" (LEED) Location & Transportation Credits for providing "Access to Quality Transit" and "Bicycle Facilities." The planners also need to weigh the effect of the development on the local community, such as noise, traffic, aesthetics, use of local utilities, cultural/historical impacts, and future growth.

Budget constraints often limit the planning of a major development project. In the public arena, a governmental agency will often place major projects on a priority list, which will then involve legislative approval before funding. Governmental agencies will often set the budget before they arrange for the production of detailed designs. Therefore, to perform an accurate cost estimate, the planners need to include an adequate contingency fund in their preliminary budgets. Frequently, because of budget constraints, the governmental agency needs to completely redefine the basic conceptual plan. Therefore, it is uneconomical to proceed with environmental permitting or architectural design until the agency sets the conceptual plan and budget.

While the first stage of any project involves planning and budgeting, environmental constraints are becoming an increasingly limiting factor in development. For many projects, the environmental review process can take years, sometimes longer than the actual design and construction process. In addition, the environmental review process often will set the design constraints for the project, such that no detailed design can take place until after the process is completed.

Typically, an environmental consultant performs the management of the environmental review process. That process could include studies on the impact on local endangered species, traffic, cultural or archeological sites, erosion or sediment control, visual impacts, and impacts on tourism and local businesses. The goal of the study is to prove that the project has little or no impact on each of the areas of concern; or, if it does have some impact, to offer mitigation factors. For example, if the study finds that the project will impact a cultural resource, the impact report may propose an offsetting benefit to the community in terms of environmental, visual, tax base, or other gain. In some cases, the study will recommend mitigation of the impact. For example, if the report finds that the project will impact a certain habitat, the developer may offer mitigation by converting another site into one that will support the lost habitat. The proposed mitigation is typically at an equal or greater size and at the developer's expense.

Generally, the developer/applicant prepares an Environmental Impact Review (EIR) or Environmental Impact Statement (EIS) for the local governing agency's review. An EIR is a simplified version of an EIS. Legislation determines the governing agency that has jurisdiction and could include local review (such as a city or county environmental/planning board); state review (such as a state environmental review board); federal review, such as the Environmental Protection Agency (EPA) or U.S. Army Corps of Engineers (USACOE); or special jurisdictional review, such as a coastal commission or regional planning commission. The magnitude and anticipated impact of the project determines whether there needs to be an EIR or EIS.

b. Design Team and Approach

The selection of a designer is a major factor in a project's success and takes place once the owner establishes the project's design criteria. The owner creates the project design criteria once it knows its budget, environmental restrictions, and other needs. The project design criteria describe the project's purpose, architectural goals, applicable codes, and special requirements. See Exhibit 1 for an example of project design criteria.

These project design criteria govern the architect and engineer in their project design and often determine the final project budget. Upon the owner's approval of the design, the designers formalize the design into plans and specifications suitable for construction.

Designers are typically engineers or architects, and they are often involved through final completion of the project. The quality of their design, preparation of contract documents, and assistance in the construction management process is critical to a project's success. The decision as to whether to have an architect or engineer lead the design effort is a function of the project's needs. If the project is a building, an architect often takes the lead. If the project is infrastructure-based, such as a road, bridge, or treatment plant, typically an engineer takes the lead.

The increasing complexity of modern projects requires a multi-discipline approach to design. Therefore, several specialty designers or sub-consultants will also need to perfect the design. As illustrated in the below chart, under a conventional design approach, an owner will contract directly with a geotechnical engineer (often before the jobsite is acquired), an architect, and a commissioning agent if building commissioning is part of the owner's project program. The architect will contract with engineers and other consultants, including structural, mechanical, and electrical, as well as consultants to assist with interior design, landscaping, lighting, acoustics, and building envelope.

Conventional Design Team

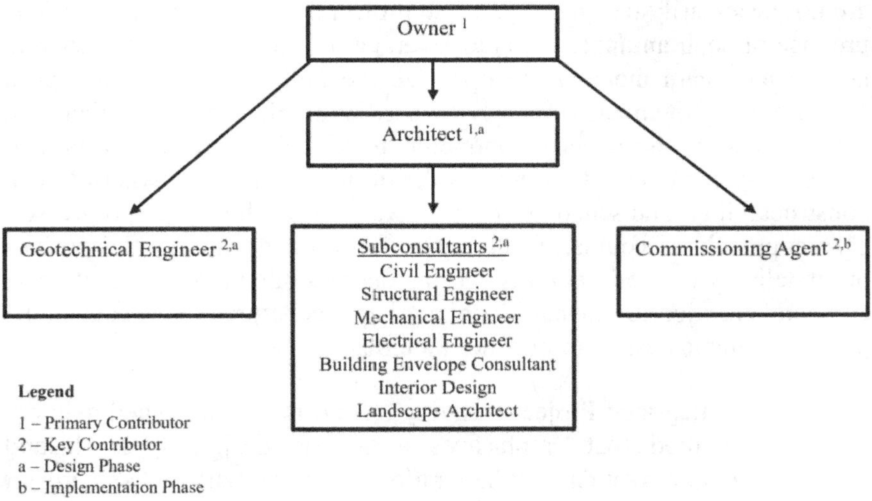

In contrast, illustrated below is a typical organization chart for an engineering project such as a bridge or a water treatment facility.

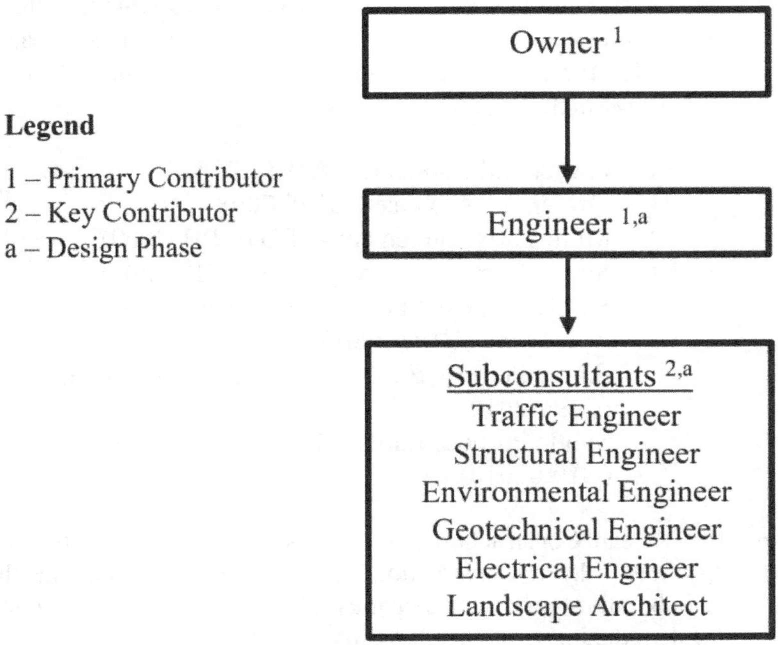

The construction industry is gradually evolving towards a more holistic design approach incorporating more project team members (who are not necessarily designers) into the project design process earlier. The premise of such an approach is to leverage the expertise of primary and key project team members to optimize the building design. In such a scenario, team members primarily focused on implementation rather than design, such as the general contractor, major trade subcontractors, and special systems contractors, inform the designers and the owner of cost, constructability, and schedule issues in real-time as the design progresses. This approach, of course, which varies from a conventional design-bid-build delivery method, requires varying degrees of contract commitments and compensation for the additional participants before they engage in the project. Holistic design approaches include:

- "Integrated Project Delivery" (IPD) is an established delivery method that emphasizes a holistic design approach and emphasizes early collaboration among primary and key project contributors. This approach, applicable to complex, high-performance buildings and structures, relies heavily on the use of Building Information Modeling (BIM) technology. Key features of IPD include the early involvement of all major team members, the use of a single contract for all major team members, and the use of a shared project management system. The American Institute of Architects (AIA) has created multiple forms of agreements titled "Integrated Project Delivery" including:

    - Owner and Contractor (A195-2008)
    - Owner and Architect (B195-2008)
    - Multi-Party Agreement – IPD (C191-2009)
    - Single Purpose Entity – Owner (C196-2008)
    - Single Purpose Entity – Non-Owner Member Agreement (C197-2008)
    - Single Purpose Entity – Consultant Agreement (C198-2010)
    - Single Purpose Entity – Contractor Agreement (C199-2010)

- The "Lean Construction Institute" is an organization that has promoted "Lean Construction" as a technique to facilitate the collaborative goals and demands of more modern construction while reducing waste resulting in a "leaner" process.

- Leadership in Energy and Environmental Design (LEED) is the preeminent organization in sustainable building construction. It heavily promotes the "Integrative Process" approach to successful sustainable designs and awards a standalone credit under the LEED Rating System for projects that implement the "Integrative Process" approach to the project design. The gravitation towards holistic project designs with integrated project teams, sustainable design, and construction is likely to advance hand-in-hand into the future of the construction industry.

During the pre-construction phase of a project, the owner may include a requirement for the contractor and its major trade subcontractors to use BIM, which is a digital representation of a building or structure, and the processes and systems within it. Although first required at the contracting phase, the parties to the construction contract use BIM throughout the construction project, from design and planning to construction, operation, and maintenance. As noted above, BIM uses 3D modeling software to create a virtual model of a building or structure, in order to visualize and analyze design options, simulate building performance, and plan and coordinate construction activities. Additionally, the parties can use the BIM model to extract information, such as dimensions, in order to create construction documents, schedules, and cost estimates. A very sophisticated BIM model can include more than three dimensions, such as money, time, and safety. BIM also assists in the management and maintenance of the building after project completion by providing access to accurate and up-to-date information about the building's systems and components.

The organizational chart below reflects a holistic building design team.

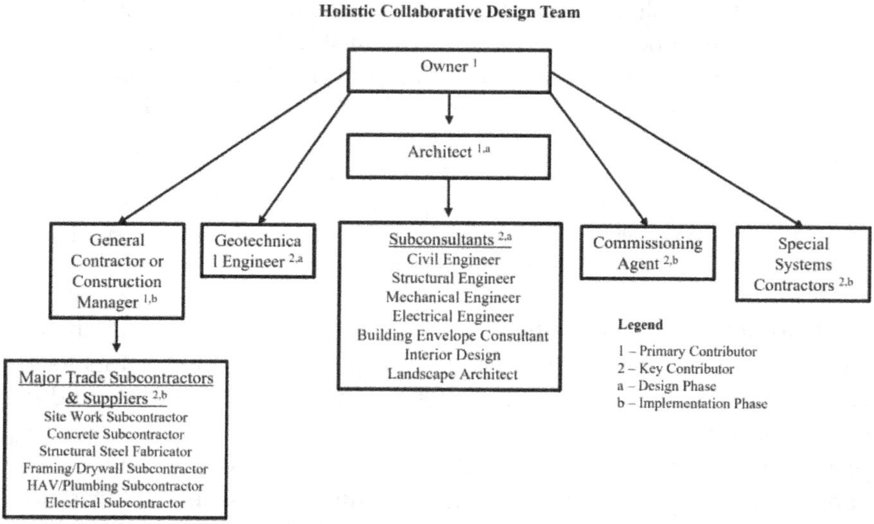

The selection of a design firm typically proceeds through a Request for Proposal (RFP) process. Interested firms will prepare proposals, which will include their proposed sub-designers, their experience, and an estimate of their costs and fees. The RFP may also request the prospective designers to include a write-up of their design approach to the project or request the designers to provide preliminary sketches.

The selection process could also involve an interim step, known as a design charrette. In a design charrette, the owner asks a short-listed group of designers to present their preliminary designs before a selection board. The selection board will then combine the best ideas from all groups and make a final selection for the designer.

The selection of a designer is a time-consuming and laborious process that can often take months to complete. However, it is an important process in determining the success of the project. The owner must weigh the experience, creativity, and cost of the designer's services in making its final selection.

After selecting the designer, the owner and designer will execute a contract for services. The most common and standard contract that designers and owners use is an AIA contract. Typically, the determining factor for the type of contract is the method of payment. Payment methods include lump sum, time and material (T&M), or percentage of the cost of construction. Because the owner does not typically know the ultimate project scope at the time of contracting with the design firm, it is often difficult to determine an accurate lump sum price. As a result, most design contracts are either T&M or a percentage of the cost of construction. In a T&M contract, the designer will bill the owner, pursuant to a predetermined rate sheet, the actual staff hours spent on the project. In addition, the designer will also bill the cost of materials provided for the project. In some contracts, there is an established cap or not-to-exceed (NTE) amount. When the designer reaches its cap, it cannot continue to bill for services rendered under its contract.

Alternatively, the designer bases its fee on a percentage of the ultimate cost of construction. However, because the owner does not know the ultimate cost until project completion, the parties estimate an amount based on the contract value and then add allowances for adjustment when they know the ultimate cost.

For a designer to fully meet an owner's needs, the design process will need to involve close interaction between the designer and the owner. It is important that the owner fully understands the proposed design as changes during the construction phase are orders of magnitude more expensive than changes during the design phase. As such, the designer must present the design in such a manner that the owner can visualize the designer's intent. To facilitate this interaction and provide opportunities for focus on specific issues, there may be a phased approach to the design process. During each phase, the design team will develop more evolved drawings, which will then allow for the owner's further review and modification. As phasing can vary by project, the design contract typically spells out the phasing specifics in the design contract.

c. Three Phases of a Common Project:

A common project approach involves three phases: (i) the Schematic Design Phase, (ii) the Design Development Phase, and (iii) the Construction Drawings Phase. The purpose of a phased design approach is to clearly layout the procedure for which the designer will complete intermediate design presentations to allow for owner comment and interaction.

The purpose of a phased design approach is to clearly layout the procedure for which the designer will complete intermediate design presentations to allow for owner comment and interaction.

(i) Schematic Design Phase

The schematic design phase is also called the preliminary design phase or 20% design phase because these drawings represent the project at 20% of the design effort. In this phase, the designer and owner will formalize and document the program requirements, develop a site survey (or an as-built drawing set if the project is a remodel of an existing structure), complete the review of local building code restrictions, and conduct preliminary meetings with local planning commissions. The designer will develop drawings and/or sketches which will include a preliminary site plan, a preliminary exterior elevation, a preliminary floor plan, and preliminary building sections. The sketches will include only approximate dimensions, usually detailed to the nearest foot. The designer typically develops these drawings to a level by which it can determine parameters, such as coverage, building height, floor area, and overall architectural concept. The designer may even present a physical model. The design contract should spell out the specific details of the expected work product of the designer.

Upon completion of this phase, the owner will review and comment upon the work product produced. In order for the project design phase to stay on schedule, the design contract should set clear deadlines and milestones that outline when the designer will complete each design phase and the allowable time for the owner to provide comments.

(ii) Design Development Phase

In the Design Development phase, the designer will incorporate the owner's comments received during the schematic design review. The designer will then develop detailed site plans, floor plans, and building sections. Incorporated into these drawings are the structural, electrical, and mechanical requirements, as well as interior design and lighting, including the various designers' and/or sub-consultants' designs. In addition, the designer will propose and incorporate preliminary material and color selections.

Upon completion of the design development phase, the designer will have produced a more detailed drawing set, which should include floor plans, interior and exterior elevations, a site plan, furniture layout plans, and preliminary electrical, mechanical, foundation, and structural framing plans. The designer develops these drawings to a stage to allow for the preparation of a preliminary construction estimate.

The design development phase will also include a draft of the specifications. "Specifications" outline submittal requirements, allowable products and materials, installation constraints, allowable tolerances, inspection and testing requirements, and warranty requirements. The specifications (combined with the construction drawings) should cover every item of work that the contractor will encounter. The specifications will also reference applicable standards that a contractor must follow.

Well-written specifications should divide the work into chapters or divisions in the same manner that trade subcontractors would logically divide the work—a work breakdown structure. A good division of work defined in the specifications will allow for clear communication of issues between the design team, contractor, subcontractors, and suppliers. The parties often use the Construction Specifications Institute Master Format list of Divisions as their organizational basis for their specifications. See Exhibit 2 for a listing of the traditional 16 divisions.

In some cases, color renderings and/or three-dimensional computer graphic representations accompany the completion of the design development phase. These drawings are 50% design drawings.

As in the completion of the first design phase, the Schematic Design Phase, the owner will review and comment on the work produced during the Design Development Phase. Again, the design contract should define the work product that the designer will produce upon completion of the Design Development Phase. In addition, the design contract should specify the timeline for both completion and the owner's review.

2. Construction Drawing Phase

After including the owner's comments, the designer will develop the final construction drawings and specifications. The construction drawings will include complete and accurate dimensions on the site plan, floor plan, and elevations; complete and detailed selection of materials; and complete mechanical, electrical, lighting, foundation, and structural drawings. The final specification book will detail materials, inspections, and the level of workmanship.

The goal of the construction drawing phase is to develop drawings and specifications that are thorough enough for a contractor to accurately estimate the cost to construct and construct the project. These are the 100% drawings.

The designer typically first transmits these construction drawings in draft form—the final draft drawings. Upon the owner's review and acceptance, the designer produces the final construction drawings.

The completion of the final construction drawing is not the end of the designer's involvement with the project, however. At a minimum, the designer will need to be involved in the construction process to answer questions [typically in the form of RFIs (requests for information)] and provide interpretation. In addition, state or local statutes often require the designer to provide a final certification. In some projects, the owner will also retain the designer to manage the project, approve monthly payment applications/requisitions, approve change orders, conduct claims review, and/or provide inspections. The design contract should detail the designer's involvement in construction administration services during the construction phase.

a. Preconstruction Consulting

During the design process, the owner will often incorporate pre-construction consulting activities in an attempt to minimize future construction problems. These activities include preliminary cost estimating, constructability reviews, and value engineering. The owner sometimes adds these tasks to the designer's scope; however, a separate design or construction professional should handle these tasks in order to provide for an impartial review of the designer's work—sometimes referred to as a "peer review." Construction or cost engineering consultants often perform these reviews or, in some cases, another architectural or construction firm will perform them.

Under more holistic design approaches, cost estimating, constructability reviews, and value engineering are performed as the design progresses. The general contractor or construction manager, depending on the delivery method, will provide preliminary cost estimates at various stages of design, material availability feedback, real-time market feedback, construction sequencing, preliminary scheduling, and early procurement of long lead materials and equipment.

b. Preliminary Cost Estimating

The goal of performing a preliminary cost estimate is to determine the approximate project cost early in the process so that the owner can either make adjustments to the design or allow for budget changes. The owner or its design professional typically performs the preliminary cost estimate upon completion of the Design Development Phase, but they can perform the estimate upon the completion of the Schematic Design and Construction Drawing Phases. While preliminary cost estimates are typically done at the Design Development Phase, one advantage of performing a cost estimate upon completion of the Construction Drawing Phase is that the owner has at least one benchmark to determine if a bid, which is based on the Construction Drawings, is reasonable if it is the only one received.

c. Constructability Review

A constructability review addresses the practicality of building the project as designed. When performed early in the design process, a constructability review can help identify trade coordination issues, potential logistical challenges, availability of materials, spatial conflicts, or material use problems. For example, the project may include the use of prefabricated large-span beams in its preliminary design. However, a constructability review may reveal that the site may be constrained such that the erection of such large beams is impossible or economically unfeasible. If the parties discover the problem early in the process, the designer can then research alternative solutions, such as a cast-in-place concrete beam, field welding, or adding a column.

d. Value Engineering

The purpose of value engineering is to evaluate the design on a cost-benefit basis. When executed properly during the pre-construction phase, the value engineering process can yield the greatest savings to the owner in terms of both time and money.

In the value engineering process, the contractor or a third-party is called upon to evaluate the design and determine whether a different design for certain items may achieve the same or similar goals but in a more cost- or time-efficient manner. For example, the designer may have specified a poured-in-place concrete retaining wall; however, a more cost-effective solution may be concrete block, given the local market conditions.

The use of value engineering in construction has proven so effective in achieving cost savings for owners that some have provided incentives to contractors who achieve value engineering. An example is the United States government, which on some contracts will allow the contractor to keep 50% of the cost savings on approved value engineering proposals.

Both the designer and the owner need to review the acceptability of a value engineering proposal. As the designer is still typically responsible for the overall design, it needs to ensure that the proposed change will not adversely affect the project. For example, a contractor could offer to substitute a masonry-faced earth retaining wall in lieu of a concrete earth retaining wall for a cost savings and a more aesthetically pleasing look. However, the masonry-faced wall solution could require mechanical stabilization of the earth behind the masonry-faced earth retaining wall through the use of geogrids. This would mean that the subsurface for quite some distance behind the face of the wall would need to be clear of underground utilities. The design team would, therefore, need to evaluate if any underground utilities originally intended to be placed adjacent to the former concrete retaining wall could be relocated within the constraints of the jobsite.

One of the benefits of a holistic approach to design, such as Integrated Project Delivery (IPD), is that value engineering is provided at the earliest stages of design such that contractor feedback results in a more seamless design as opposed to an afterthought that requires a less than optimal design revision at later stages in design.

3. Contractor Selection and Timing of Selection

After the selection of the designer, contractor selection is the next most important step for an owner to ensure a successful project. The contractor selection process can vary greatly depending on the project and legislative constraints. However, some delivery methods (CMAR and Design-Build, discussed below) select the contractor before the design is complete in order to integrate the contractor's knowledge of concepts such as current market conditions and constructability factors into the design. Early inclusion of the contractor achieves more seamless value engineering efforts sooner rather than later in the design.

a. Contracting Method

First, the owner will need to decide on which method of contracting to use. This decision is best made early in the design process, as the method will often alter the design process itself. If the owner intends to leverage the expertise of the general contractor and other entities responsible for the implementation of the design into the construction, the owner may select a delivery method that selects the general contractor or construction manager during the design phase. At a minimum, a public owner who is obliged to select a contractor via the competitive bidding process, must finalize the form of the contract and make it a part of the bidding documents prior to the bid date. Examples of contracting options include:

- Lump Sum Contract – a fixed price agreement for a finite scope of work, which complete or very near complete construction documents define. Major trade scopes provide the breakdown of the value of work. Payments are based on the completion percentage of individual work line items.
- Unit Price Contract – a unit price-based agreement where the bidder quotes unit rates inclusive of overhead and profit against estimated quantities of discrete scopes of work in a work breakdown structure with lump sum line items. The estimated contract value is the sum of all unit-priced line items. Payments are based on actual measured quantities installed which may exceed or underrun the estimated contract value.
- Cost Plus (T&M—time and material) – an agreement based on actual recorded costs for labor and material incurred as work progresses plus a fee. The contractors must maintain and submit cost records with payment applications for reimbursement.

- Multi-Prime – an agreement where the owner contracts directly with multiple prime contractors or trades for various aspects of the construction project.
- Design-Build – a single (non-owner) entity assumes responsibility for both the design and construction of the project. In one design-build format, the design-build contract segregates preconstruction/design fees from construction services fees, which the owner then pays as the design-builder performs the services. The design-builder's construction costs are not committed until the parties execute a cost amendment to the agreement at a stage when both the owner and design-builder agree that the design is sufficiently advanced to commit to a price. In other design-build scenarios, the design-builder and the owner enter into a lump sum contract. The design-builder is typically a general contractor who subcontracts with a design professional who designs the project that the design-builder then constructs.
- Construction Manager At Risk (CMAR) – The construction manager acts as the builder, and provides both preconstruction services in support of the owner and design team, and construction services, again paid as separate sequential tasks with their own respective fees. The CMAR's construction costs are not committed until the parties execute a cost agreement at the stage when both the owner and the CMAR agree that the design is sufficiently advanced to commit to a price.
- Integrated Project Delivery – a contract between the owner, designer, builder, and, often, trade contractors, the goal of which is to promote collaboration and innovation and deliver a high-quality project.

b. Potential Contracting Constraints

In addition to the selection of the contracting method and form of contract, the owner will need to decide on several other contracting constraints prior to the selection of the contractor. These include:

- Time for Completion
- Liquidated Damages
- Insurance Requirements
- Bonding Requirements and Bond Form
- Union vs. Open Shop
- Prevailing Wage Restrictions
- Minority and Women-Owned Contracting Incentives or Requirements (MBE/WBE)

- Minimum Experience and/or Qualifications
- Subcontracting Requirements
- Green Building Rating Program (The LEED – Leadership in Energy and Environmental Design – is a voluntary, consensus-based national standard for developing high-performance, sustainable buildings. Members of the U.S. Green Building Council representing all segments of the building industry developed LEED and continue to contribute to its evolution).

The General or Special Provisions section of the Specifications should clearly address these contracting constraints. Several of these constraints are requirements of local, state, or federal statutes, such as prevailing wage and minority- or women-owned contracting requirements. The owner should clearly indicate in the bidding documents the statutes that apply to the project. In that way, prospective bidders can accurately evaluate and estimate the project.

4. Bid Phase

Bidding procedures vary greatly on projects, especially between private and public projects. In the private sector, for which bid collusion statutes do not apply, owners have greater flexibility in selecting a contractor and often will simply negotiate with one or several entities. For public agencies, the selection process must follow guidelines and laws developed to prevent favoritism and corruption and allow for fair competition.

In either case, the goal of the bid phase is to select the lowest qualified bidder to allow for project completion to the owner's satisfaction at the most competitive price.

Depending on which delivery method the owner employs, the timing of bid solicitations can vary from early in the design process to after issuance of construction documents under a traditional design-bid-build approach. Methods requiring or leveraging early contractor involvement could require an alternative selection process such as a competitive Request for Proposal (RFP) process by which candidates submit their firm's qualifications and proposals for overhead and profit, only leaving candidates to establish their direct costs further into the design process. The owner selects the contractor based on the selection criteria applied to the proposals that it receives.

The owner and contractor entering into an agreement with a cost commitment before the design process has advanced into the construction document phase exacerbates cost overrun risks. The owner can reduce that risk by establishing the contract value in the more advanced stages of design as illustrated in the following:

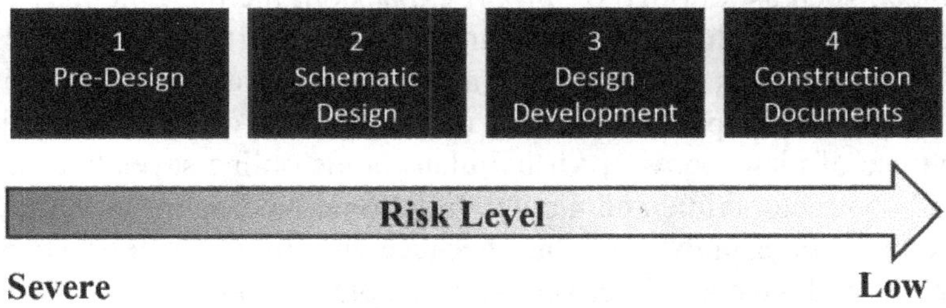

The parties should establish a cost commitment when design documents are sufficiently advanced to detail the contractor's assumptions in preparing an estimate. If there is a significant gap between the contractor's perception of the final design, the designer's vision, or the owner's expectations of the finished product, conflicts will surface in later stages, particularly during construction.

The bid phase for a design-bid-build approach typically involves the following stages:

a. Advertisements

By law, public agencies must advertise a project to ensure equal and fair competition, but private developers also use project advertisements to attract qualified contractors. Typical advertisement publications include local newspapers or trade journals like *Engineering News and Record, Reed Construction Data,* and *McGraw Hill.* Contractors frequently upload bid documents to their own FTP sites and provide weblinks to their site within their bid solicitations to subcontractors, which solicitations are distributed electronically by email and/or advertised on their company websites. In addition, there are many online services such as www.bidclerk.com and www.construction.com offering project-listing services. Large agencies, which procure many projects, frequently have their own publications, such as the United States government's *Commerce Business Daily.* Contractors will subscribe to these publications and review them weekly, if not daily, to learn about bidding opportunities. A project advertisement or solicitation will typically describe the project, provide a rough order-of-magnitude estimate or cost range, describe where to obtain plans and specifications, detail the bid time and location, the pre-bid meeting time, and location, and explain any unique aspects of the project, such as MBE/WBE requirements. The advertisements will typically run up until bid date. The time allowed for bidding on a project will vary on the project size, complexity, and scheduling constraints, though a period of 30 days for projects under $1 million is normal. For a large project, such as a bridge or airport expansion, the bid time may be several months. See Exhibit 3 for an example of an advertisement for bids.

One of the benefits of listing with an agency is that the agency will provide the plans and specifications for review in plan rooms up until bid time. The use of plan rooms or virtual plan rooms online saves both the owner and contractors time and money. Electronic bidding, or e-bidding, has become increasingly popular because it improves efficiency, transparency, and the cost-effectiveness of the bidding process. E-bidding can significantly streamline the bidding process by allowing contractors to quickly and seamlessly submit their bids online, and helping to reduce errors. Additionally, the use of e-bidding can encourage and facilitate collaboration through joint ventures and partnerships on larger projects.

b. Pre-Bid Meeting

The owner will conduct a pre-bid meeting on most public projects to facilitate a better understanding of the nuances of the project. Attendance at the pre-bid meeting mandatory is often mandatory. Typically, the contractor's estimator attends these meetings as the contractor's representative. The meeting, preferably held at the project site, allows the owner to introduce the project, discuss the bidding documents, and conduct a site walk. At the conclusion of the meeting, there is usually a short question-and-answer period. Most owners require the attendees to sign-in so that the owner can then send answers to any questions asked at the meeting to all bidders by way of a written addendum so that all bidders are working with the same information in preparing their bids.

c. Addenda

Written addenda change or clarify the bidding documents between the time the owner issued the documents and the bid date. The owner generates addenda and then issues them to all bidders. They then become part of the bid package and, ultimately, part of the contract. Typically, for an owner to consider a contractor's bid responsive, the contractor must acknowledge receipt of all addenda. As an owner, it is important when reviewing bids to confirm that the contractor has acknowledged receipt so that bids are judged on equal footing. See Exhibit 4 for an example of a bid addendum.

d. Bid Bonds

With most public bids, the bidder is required to include a bid bond or other form of security to ensure that, as the lowest responsive bidder, the bidder/contractor will enter into a contract with the owner. The value of the bond is typically equal to 10% of the bid amount. See Exhibit 5 for an example of a bid bond.

Alternately, in lieu of a bid bond, the owner may allow the bidders to provide a cashier's check or irrevocable letter of credit as the bidder's security. If a bidder fails to provide adequate bid security, the bid is non-responsive and the owner can reject the bid.

e. Preparation of the Bid

The contractor's estimator, cost engineer, or sometimes the intended project manager prepares the contractor's bid. As to the intended project manager as the person preparing the bid, it incentivises the project manager to ensure that costs of construction align with the bid price at the conclusion of the project. The process of developing a bid varies greatly among contractors and they often guard the process as proprietary. In general, the process involves determining the quantities and types of the various building components by studying the plans and specifications. Based on these quantities, the estimator will then estimate the cost of the materials, labor, and equipment needed to construct a particular component. The estimator will evaluate means and methods, site conditions, schedule, safety, and environmental constraints. Finally, the estimator will determine profit and overhead, which involves a complex evaluation of risk, market conditions, competitiveness, and experience. Contractors need to ensure that they have included all the proper and relevant costs they will incur in the construction of the project, as the owner will hold them to their bid amount incorporated into the contract.

f. Selection of the Lowest Responsible Bidder

Historically, the collection of bids for most public projects is at a set time and place with the submission of bids in sealed envelopes. The process was often frenzied, with contractors having a bid runner arrive at the location prior to the bid opening. Improvements in technology have allowed for the bidding process to become electronic. No longer is a bid runner required because contractors can now submit their bids electronically. Depending on the platform, bidders can upload their bidding documents individually or all at once. Once the bidding window closes, the owner or their representative will review the submitted bids.

The owner will often publicly open and read all bids having invited contractors, subcontractors, and the general public to attend the opening. However, the awarding agency does not select the lowest responsive bidder until it determines that the contractor complied with the bidding instructions, provided all required bid documentation, is properly licensed, has met the bonding and insurance requirements, has met, or exceeds qualification and experience minimums, and has met the project's special requirements, such as MBE/WBE participation. The period for the bid evaluation process may be as long as 30 to 60 days and during that period, the contractors' bids remain irrevocable, and the bidders cannot withdraw them, with limited exception (i.e., clerical error or error in calculation/compiling figures). Under certain circumstances, the public entity can extend this period, though the number of extensions allowed is often limited. Once the public agency confirms all these elements, by law it must award the project to the lowest responsive and responsible bidder.

Once the owner determines the lowest responsive and responsible bidder, the awarding agency will then publicly announce and/or publish the results. The award will typically follow the announcement, allowing for a short period for which another bidder may protest the results. See Exhibit 6 for an example of a notice of award.

After the notice of award, the contractor and owner formally execute the contract, and the contractor will need to provide its surety bonds (performance and payment) and insurance certificates as required under the bid documents. The failure or refusal to enter into the contract after notice of award could result in forfeiture of the contractor's bid bond or other bid security.

Alternatively, under a more holistic design approach, the owner and/or designer will select the contractor based on its relationship with the contractor or through a competitive Request for Proposal (RFP) process before the parties even start or complete the design process. The project owner will establish selection criteria for the best qualified contractor based upon the contractor's experience and responsiveness to the RFP in the proposed fee, project personnel, and approach to the project. Such an approach requires a more rigorous qualitative decision-making process on the part of the owner than a strictly low bid criterion.

g. The "Pre-Con" Meeting

Once the parties have executed the awarded contract, a pre-construction meeting (commonly referred to as the "Pre-Con") occurs. The purpose of the Pre-Con is to discuss the administration and communication methods for the project to ensure effective coordination and cooperation among the many parties involved in the construction process. The Pre-Con meeting may be at the owner's offices, at a hotel meeting space near the jobsite, or at the site itself.

The Pre-Con meeting participants include the owner and/or owner's representative, the construction manager (referred to as the CM) if the owner is using one, the inspector of record, the project manager and superintendent for the general contractor, and the project manager and superintendent for each subcontractor.

At the Pre-Con meeting, the owner introduces the various parties and reviews the project systems that the owner will utilize to maintain project control. The control systems provide the means and methods for effective administration of all the project's paperwork and allow a communication flow between the owner, contractor, and all the parties involved in the construction process. These project control systems typically involve document control, schedule control, and meeting schedules, and include the processes involving certified payroll, daily reports, and submittals. If the owner's project control systems are effective, they can help to control the time and cost of performance of the construction work for all the parties.

C. Construction Phase

A construction project can be a complex and multifaceted process involving a wide range of activities.[1] It is essential to have effective management of the construction process, careful and strategic planning of activities before construction begins, and an understanding of the key milestones in the construction process. This section will explore these topics and provide insight and detail for a better understanding of the construction phase.

1. Managing the Process

There are many different methods to manage the construction process via different delivery systems. The most common is to contract with a general contractor, also known as a prime contractor, who will then enter

---

1 "[E]xcept in the middle of a battlefield, nowhere must men coordinate the movement of other men and all materials in the midst of such chaos and with such limited certainty of present facts and future occurrences as in a huge construction project.... Even the most painstaking planning frequently turns out to be mere conjecture, and accommodation to changes must necessarily be of the rough, quick and ad hoc sort, analogous to ever-changing commands on the battlefield. *Blake Const. Co., Inc. v. C.J. Cookley Co., Inc.,* 431 A.2D 569, 675 (D.C. 1981).

into subcontracts with trade contractors to perform certain aspects of the project while performing certain other aspects with its own forces. Other forms of delivery include multi-prime, in which multiple trade subcontractors enter into contracts directly with the owner. The owner hires a construction management firm to manage the multiple "prime" contractors. Another form of delivery is a Construction Manager at Risk (CMAR), where the owner hires a CM, who then enters into subcontracts. Sometimes, the CM awards its subcontracts to subcontractors through a competitive bid process such that the underlying costs are based on market conditions. The CMAR contract is often administered on a cost-plus-fee basis with a guaranteed maximum price. This chapter discusses the management of a typical general contractor delivery approach.

For efficient and productive management of the construction process, the contractor, owner (or owner's representative), and designer must establish a communication and decision-making process (i.e., the project control system). In addition, the contractor, subcontractors, suppliers, and field workers must establish this communication and decision-making process down the chain. The processes established provide the mechanism by which the contractor and subcontractors can receive answers to their design questions. These processes also facilitate processing progress payments, resolution of unforeseen conditions or changes, managing schedules, controlling the quality of work, documenting delays and disruptions, and identifying extra or additional work to the contract.

a. RFIs (Requests for Information)

To document questions and responses to informational inquiries, the parties use requests for information (RFIs). The appropriate decision-maker may not be onsite at the time a question arises and the matter may impact more than one trade. Accordingly, the parties use the RFI form to document and log the communication to permit all affected parties to know about the inquiry and response. It is not unusual for RFIs to be the genesis of ASIs (architect supplemental instructions), PCOs (proposed change orders), or COs (change orders), but most often they represent clarifications to the plans and specifications where there may be some conflicts or ambiguities.

b. ASI (Architect Supplemental Instruction)

The architect's supplemental instructions often clarify ambiguities, provide detail that the contractor cannot readily ascertain from the drawings, or make minor changes based on field conditions. The instructions may represent a change that is not significant enough to warrant a change order and does not change the contract sum or contract time. Supplemental instructions may also provide a detailed description of the work or particular construction methods that the contractor is to perform or specifications of materials or equipment that the contractor is to use. The contractor typically indicates its acceptance of the instructions by signing the ASI form and returning a copy to the architect. Alternatively, the contractor may insist that the architect's supplemental instruction warrants a change order and submits a change order request in response to the ASI.

c. Notice of Delay

The contractor documents an owner's act or disruption that the contractor perceives as the cause for a delay or potential delay as a formal notice of delay. A subcontractor that does not arrive on the site to accomplish a task that is on the critical path on a given day may become the subject of a delay notice as well. Sanctions for causing a delay are typically included in the general conditions or specifications. Most often, the notice of delay serves to document the party that may eventually be held responsible for the economic costs associated with the delay.

d. Notice of Changed Conditions/Differing Site Conditions

Although the owner quite often conducts site inspections and test bores in the early preconstruction stage, it is nearly impossible to predict the exact nature of all site conditions that a contractor might encounter, especially when excavating or driving piles. Therefore, when the contractor encounters differing site conditions, such as impenetrable bedrock at a shallow depth, a notice of changed conditions is prepared to document the obstacle encountered. The notice initiates the study of the unanticipated conditions to allow for alternative construction methods or, at least, documents the cause of potential increased costs associated with additional time or material modifications necessitated by the conditions.

e. Notice of Potential Claim

If a contractor is unable to obtain satisfaction via the change order process for additional compensation, it may initiate the claims process by filing a notice of potential claim to document the event, changed conditions, or the owner's actions that is negatively impacting the contractor. The notice serves the purpose of notifying the owner and design professionals that the contractor is contemplating making an affirmative claim against the project, yet also allows the contractor to continue working on the project to avoid disruption.

f. Changes

Changes are modifications of an original contract that effectively change the provisions of the contract, including changes in specifications or design, method or manner of performance, facilities, equipment, materials, site, and completion of work. Change orders are typically in writing and signed by the owner and construction manager, engineer, or architect as well as the contractor, indicating its acceptance of the change order. Change orders may award additional compensation and additional time to complete the project. An owner may also issue deductive change orders, reflecting the elimination of a scope of work from the project or the incorporation of an alternative material or construction method into the project at a lesser cost.

g. CORs/PCOs (Change Order Requests/Proposed Change Orders)

Contractors, including subcontractors, may communicate a desire for a contract change via a change order request (COR) or proposed change order (PCO) that they submit to the owner, construction manager, or general contractor, depending on which party is originating the request.

h. Change Order Process

The construction manager or owner's representatives evaluate whether change order requests are meritorious. If they determine that the referenced work is outside of the scope of the original contract, they likely will authorize a change order. Typically, the owner's representative, architect, project engineer, construction manager, and contractor all approve and sign change orders.

i. Unilateral Changes

Unilateral changes, sometimes referred to as construction change directives (CCDs) are changes that the owner initiates, which require the contractor to perform modified or additional work that the contractor did not request. CCDs may be issued in a time-sensitive situation when the contractor must immediately address the issue. The owner may issue a CCD instructing the contractor to proceed with the necessary work, and the parties will discuss or negotiate the costs and schedule impacts after the contractor completes the work. A CCD can cause conflict between the owner and contractor because of unanticipated increased costs or delays which can affect the contractor's cash flow and profit margins.

j. Unbilled Change Orders / Unfunded Directives

Often, the parties initiate change order work and the contractor completes the work based upon a written directive to proceed or a verbal approval from an owner's representative. The parties use this method of achieving changes to the work for scheduling and efficiency reasons as it would often be more disruptive to the workflow to stop work and wait for the signing of a formal change order. Unfortunately, absent an executed change order, the contract may not permit the contractor to invoice for the work. The term, therefore, has evolved to recognize the cost incurred to complete change order work that is undisputed and that the parties fully anticipate will receive approval. For accounting purposes, the contractor recognizes the revenue for unbilled changes to match the cost of that work on its income statement in the category of under billings.

k. Claims

Claims are amounts in excess of the agreed contract price that a contractor seeks to collect from the owner for owner-caused delays, errors in specifications and designs, unapproved change orders, or other causes of unanticipated costs. Sometimes called affirmative claims, they typically arise when the owner denies the contractor's CORs and the contractor is unable to obtain the compensation or relief to which it believes it is entitled from the owner. Meeting contract deadlines is critical to preserving claims because most construction contracts contain specific timeframes for a contractor or subcontractor to submit claims for additional compensation or time extensions. The timeframes are included in contracts to ensure conflicts or disputes are resolved promptly. Failing to meet contract deadlines can lead to disputes, which may result in costly arbitration or litigation.

l. Dispute Resolution Process

In addition to contract provisions mandating mediation and arbitration, alternatives to traditional litigation have become more prevalent over the past few years. It is not uncommon on large projects to utilize a dispute resolution panel, entitled DRBs (dispute resolution boards), comprising independent construction professionals to mitigate the potential harmful effects of contract disputes and resolve the matters quickly at the jobsite rather than in the court system.

m. Partnering

In recent years, some contractors and owners have entered into partnering agreements in which the parties agree to communicate throughout the construction project and attempt to resolve differences amicably. Some public agencies have instituted annual excellence in partnering awards to promote the concept and adherence to minimally disruptive and cooperative working relationships.

n. Quality Control Inspection

Public officials, owner's representatives, and design professionals inspect construction work to ensure adherence to contract plans and specifications and appropriate local building codes. Inspectors typically issue notices of defects or non-compliance shortly after inspection, if not on the spot. In rare instances, inspectors have determined the project site to be hazardous or unsafe and have even ordered a work stoppage.

Another form of inspection that the owner and project lender conducts focuses on the construction progress and the completion percentage to determine the appropriate amount for the contractor's periodic payment applications/requisition.

o. Correction of Defects

If a defect is discovered, the owner typically allows the contractor a reasonable amount of time to cure or correct the defect and proceed with the remainder of the construction.

p. Critical Path Method (CPM) – Scheduling for Schedule Control

Contractors utilize Critical Path Method network scheduling to show the sequences and interdependences of activities. The critical path is the sequence of activities that indicates the shortest time path for completion of the project and determines the optimum sequence and duration of operations. Many construction contracts contain provisions that limit the recovery of damages only to situations that affect the critical path. The purpose of limiting damages is to ensure that damages are only recoverable in situations where a delay or disruption significantly impacts the project. Activities that the contractor does not need to complete prior to the next critical activity are "off the critical path."

The construction industry also sometimes refers to scheduling by the acronym PERT (Program Evaluation and Review Technique). Contractors will typically use commercially available computer-based programs such as Primavera P3, Suretrak, and Microsoft Project to prepare their CPM schedules.

q. Updated Schedules

Throughout the construction project, as the contractor completes activities at times different from the originally anticipated schedule, the parties typically amend the original schedule to reflect the actual timing and status of activities.

r. Delay/Impacted Schedules (Fragnets)

Delays to a construction project result from occurrences that impact the schedule or critical path. Delays can result from weather, material delivery delays, labor inefficiencies, and owner influences including unilateral changes.

s. Recovery Schedule

A revised schedule may be prepared, which includes overtime or other streamlined procedures, and that represents the contractor's best effort to recover from the delay and still complete the project within the originally anticipated completion date.

t. Budget Control

Construction cost accounting is critical to contractors' financial success. Not only should the parties account for the actual costs by project, but they should also provide a comparison to the original budget to facilitate tracking of potential cost savings and recognition of cost overruns—preferably in time to react and apply corrective measures. The contractor should review change orders, changed conditions, and changed circumstances such as material price variances that cause fluctuations in anticipated contract costs, updated cost estimates, and budgets throughout the project. Using available scheduling and contractor accounting software programs, which include budgeting modules, contractors can easily compare actual cost accumulation and time consumption to their original estimates.

Proper cost recognition and projected completing cost estimates are critical to contract revenue recognition under the percentage of completion cost method of accounting. Adequate and comprehensive cost accounting can also provide contractors with a historical cost perspective when estimating new projects.

u. Payment Process

Because of the long-term nature of most construction projects, contractors would suffer undue financial and cash flow hardship if the owner withheld payment until completion of the work. Contractors typically must pay for labor weekly and compensate vendors for materials delivered to the site. Accordingly, the parties use progress payments to compensate contractors for work completed within incremental, primarily monthly, periods of the project. This practice typically provides sufficient cash flow to the contractor to cover direct costs and overhead incurred throughout the project.

v. Monthly Payment Applications/Requisitions/Estimates

Also referred to as payment estimates, monthly construction invoicing is typically on a percentage-of-completion basis by contract line item. Contractors estimate the cumulative progress to date on each line item and then submit estimates to the owner's representative for review. After modification, if appropriate, and approval, the owner issues payment for the current portion of the contract amount calculated from the total completed to date less prior payments.

w. Releases

As a condition precedent to receipt of progress payments, contracts often require that contractors provide releases that constitute signed statements that the contractor has completed all work represented in the payment application and has paid all subcontractors, suppliers, and laborers for costs incurred during that pay period. The intent is to bar future claims for additional compensation for the work during the period. Partial releases coincide with progress payments, and, upon final payment of contract funds, it is common to obtain full and final releases.

x. Retainage/Retention

In addition to releases, another form of protection for the owner is withholding retainage, also called retention. Typically, retainage is 5-10% of the total amount of the contract. The owner withholds retainage in accordance with the contract provisions until accepting the work.

2. Activities Before Construction Starts

a. The Notice to Proceed

After the parties execute the contract, hold the Pre-Con meeting, and establish the project control systems, the owner provides a written notice to proceed to the contractor. This notice to proceed, which places the contractor on notice to commence its scope of the construction work, generally requires the contractor to mobilize to the project site within a set amount of time, such as within ten days from the date of the notice, and to commence performance.

The notice to proceed is the trigger that starts the clock on the contractor's time for completion as specified in its contract. For example, if the contract time for completion is 450 calendar days, the contractor has 450 calendar days to complete its scope of work from the date stated in the notice to proceed. Subject to excusable delay and extensions of contract time, which occur on most construction contracts, if the contractor fails to complete within the contract's specified time, the owner may assess liquidated damages or actual delay damages, depending upon the terms of the contract.

b. Submittals

Before the contractor performs any actual building, the contractor complies with the contract-specified submittal process. The submittal process outlined in the specifications will require the contractor to submit detailed information about the means, methods, and materials that the contractor proposes to use on the project. The designer and owner review the submittals to determine whether the selected materials or methods meet the contract's intent. Because the contractor's submittals provide important details to the owner, requiring the owner's approval, the submittal process should occur very early during the construction phase of the project so as not to delay construction.

For example, a contractor installing cabinets and countertops would submit a sample of the intended countertop material, as well as a shop drawing indicating how the hardware will attach to the cabinetry. The owner reviews the quality, texture, color, size, and finish of the submittal and will approve or reject the submittal based on the criteria of the contract specifications and the plans. Sometimes, the contractor provides a mock-up, model, or sample for the designer's and owner's approval. If the designer or owner's representative rejects any submittal, the contractor must find different materials or revise methods of installation to reflect the contract's specifications and resubmit the information. If the contractor disagrees with the rejection and altering the approach causes increased costs, the issue may eventually become a claim. Typical contractor submittals include:

- Shop Drawings (detailed fabrication or construction drawings of specific items of a project)
- Catalog Cut Sheets (detailed product information copied from the manufacture's catalog)
- Samples (small pieces of the actual proposed material, for example, a single 4-inch x 4-inch tile)
- Mockups (typically, a full-size sample to demonstrate what the final installed product will look like, i.e., a 2 feet x 2 feet board, with tiles and grout installed, or, if required, a full-size demonstration of the exterior finishes (See photo example below).

A contractor must also submit many other documents to outline the contractor's overall plan, most of which must receive owner approval. These submittals typically include:

- Baseline Schedule (the contractor's original intended schedule for performance)
- Schedule of Values (the contractor's total contract value broken down per the schedule or divisions of work)
- Safety Plan (the contractor's methods for complying with safety laws and regulations, such as OSHA [Occupational Safety and Health Administration] regulations, along with any special safety requirements of the owner)
- Quality Control Plan (a written plan that outlines the contractor's method of inspection and ensures the work installed meets the contract requirements).

Depending on the type of project, submittals may also include special plans for items such as storm water erosion protection, demolition, erection, or traffic control.

3. Key Construction Milestones

Certain milestones apply to general building construction to identify key stages of the construction process, from mobilization through the finish stage. The key building milestones are below (Note: roadways, canals, hydroelectric dams, and bridges have their unique measurements of partial completion).

a. Mobilization

After receiving a notice to proceed, but prior to actual construction, a contractor and its subcontractors mobilize resources and physically occupy the construction site. Depending upon the nature of the project, the contractor may need to transport heavy equipment onto the site. The contractor relocates its labor forces, establishes temporary housing for them, secures jobsite trailers and sanitary facilities, and connects temporary utilities. Mobilization can represent a significant investment that contractors often itemize as a line item in the bid to provide compensation for costs incurred that may otherwise be perceived as not contributing to the completion percentages.

b. Out of Ground

With a few exceptions, new construction (versus renovations) occurs from the ground up. Site clearing and grubbing occur first, followed by site excavation that may involve cutting and filling to move dirt from high elevations to lower elevations. After completion of final grading and the project layout and staking occur, the contractor drills piles (if appropriate), installs underground utilities, and constructs forms, and the project is made ready for the concrete foundation pour. The work may use masonry in the construction of foundation walls, particularly on sloped sites and in the construction of underground parking or basements.

After the contractor constructs the foundations, it pours the concrete slabs—referred to as "flat work." Quite often, plumbing and utility conduit are embedded within the concrete slab as well as reinforcing steel bars or screens, and anchoring devices such as j-bolts tie the walls to the foundation. The layout of these items is critical, because relocation after the pour is difficult and expensive, at best.

After the foundation is in place, the project is "out of ground" and construction of structural members begins. These structural members may range from simple wood or lightweight steel studs in homes or small buildings to heavy steel I-beams for larger structures. Structural members are the "skeleton" of the building, upon which all other pieces are supported or hung.

c. Topping Out

The placement of the highest structural member, roof truss, or rafter is "topping out." At that point, the building's structural framing is complete and the exterior enclosure, window installation, roofing, interior framing, rough plumbing, and rough electrical may begin. The placement of a Christmas tree on the apex of the structure during holiday periods may signify the topping out of a building or other structure. The evergreen symbolizes that the project went up without the loss of life, or it may be a good luck charm for future occupants. Another popular adornment, especially at union labor projects, is the United States flag. The flag may signal the use of federal funds or it may merely suggest patriotism.

d. Dry-In

A structure is "dried-in" upon the installation of the roof system and exterior waterproofing and temporary or permanent doors and windows. Most likely, exterior trim, lighting, finish masonry, painting, and perhaps even roof shingles are not yet complete. However, the structure is sufficiently weather or watertight to allow interior work to commence on electrical and HVAC (heating, ventilation, and air-conditioning) systems without posing a threat to the safety of the workers or interior surfaces, such as drywall, cabinetry, and wood trim.

e. Rough-In & Cover-Up

This stage is often referred to as the completion of rough-in. The contractor has completed and inspected all framing, rough electrical such as conduit, boxes, and buried fixtures, rough plumbing such as water and waste, communication systems such as telephone, computer, and cable, and HVAC ducting inside the walls and ceiling. Often owners require a rough-in inspection and sign-off at this time.

These tasks typically represent a relatively large amount of work that may translate into significant time and cost depending upon the complexity of the project. A hospital or high-technology manufacturing facility will generally contain more systems and represent a greater percentage of the total project cost in this area than a tilt-up warehouse, for example. Upon completion of this stage, the contractor can close in the interior walls, which typically involves the installation of insulation and/or drywall.

Coordination is most critical at this time. With numerous trades working on the site at the same time, it is not uncommon, for example, to have plumbers interfering with electricians and mechanical subcontractors, or vice versa. This phenomenon is known as "stacking of trades" and often causes delay damages, which a subcontractor will include in a claim for additional compensation.

f. Finish Stage

After cover-up and drywall fastening to the interior studs, the contractor typically tapes and textures the walls and prepares them for painting. Following the painting of the interior wall surfaces, next comes the installation of carpentry, cabinets, wood trim, electrical fixtures, outlets, switches, HVAC registers, and plumbing fixtures. Typically, the contractor installs the interior finish flooring last to avoid damage from construction traffic. If applicable, exterior scope items such as exterior painting, parking lot striping, and landscaping are also completed in the finish stage.

D. Post-Construction Phase

The post-construction phase of a project is a critical period that involves several key milestones, including achieving substantial completion, obtaining a certificate of occupancy, and making final payment. It is also a time for the protection of unpaid parties and the resolution of any disputes.

1. Completion of the Project

At the finish stage milestone, the project moves into the post-construction phase, where the project moves towards its end completion. The completion of the project will not occur at a single point in time. Rather, it is a process unto itself, with the completion of numerous project management and contract administration processes, along with the performance of any remaining physical work items.

This completion stage is often called the closeout process, consisting of its own key milestones. The first completion milestone is "substantial completion," which is concurrent or followed by the "certificate of occupancy." The last milestone is "final completion." The stage between substantial completion and final completion is the punch list stage. Some contracts establish separate timetables and valuations for liquidated damages for the late achievement of substantial completion and final completion. The time following final completion is the "warranty period." Each milestone has specific contractual significance in the construction process and, as such, a formal certification process usually accompanies each milestone. The details of these key completion milestones and their interim phases are below.

2. Substantial Completion

The contract usually defines "substantial completion," but some state statutes governing works of improvement also define it. The AIA documents define substantial completion as occurring when construction is sufficiently complete per the contracts so that the owner can occupy or utilize the work or designated portion thereof for its intended use (See AIA Document A201-2017™ Exhibit 7). Under the AIA documents, the architect determines the date of substantial completion by issuing a certificate of substantial completion.

At the point of substantial completion, the contractor, owner, and/or architect conduct an inspection to determine a list of items, the punch list, for completion or correction before final completion. Upon completion of the punch list items, the contractor then requests a final inspection. The owner performs the final inspection to determine if the contractor has completed all the punch list work to the owner's satisfaction.

3. Commissioning

Commissioning is a process that assures the owner's project requirements are fulfilled from design through start-up of building systems and post-occupancy. A third-party agency frequently performs commissioning working directly for the owner that collaborates with the building designers as to functional systems such as HVAC, plumbing, electrical, and passive systems such as building envelope systems. In some instances, during construction, the commissioning agent performs a quality assurance role in observing, recording, measuring, testing, and verifying the proper start-up of functional and passive systems. The commissioning agent may verify and document that the owner and contractor have performed proper training of building maintenance personnel. The commissioning agent may also monitor warranty responses and sustained optimization of functional systems post-occupancy.

LEED requires "Fundamental Commissioning and Verification" as a pre-requisite for the pursuit of Energy & Atmosphere credits and offers credits for "Enhanced Commissioning." Commissioning has become standard practice in building construction regardless of whether it is part of a formal sustainable design program or not.

4. Certificate of Occupancy

A certificate of beneficial occupancy, or certificate of occupancy, is a document that a governmental authority issues certifying that all or a designated portion of a building complies with the provisions of applicable statutes and regulations and permitting occupancy for its designated use. Although receipt of the certificate of beneficial occupancy is a separate milestone from substantial or final completion, the contract sometimes ties it to achieving either substantial or final completion.

5. Submission of Closeout Documents

The contractor submits its final project closeout documents either concurrently with final completion or soon after. The contract documents define the project closeout documents and typically include the following:

a. As-Built Drawings

Drawings that the contractor has prepared that incorporate all change orders and modifications to make a final set of plans, depicting dimensions, locations, and materials as the contractor actually installed them. These are often called "red-lines" because the method often used to document changes and dimensions on an as-built is to physically write over the contract documents with a red pencil.

b. Operation and Maintenance Manuals (O&Ms)

The contractor will compile and organize user manuals from the various manufacturers that provided goods and operating systems on the project which require routine oversight and/or maintenance. These are critical for building maintenance personnel and end users to properly maintain building functionality.

c. Product Warranties

Product warranties depend on the product's manufacturer. The contractor sometimes submits these warranties with submittals at the beginning of the project or at the close-out phase.

d. Labor Warranties

Contractors provide labor warranties and generally state that they have performed the work in a good and workmanlike manner according to the plans and specifications. The owner and general contractor often obtain a warranty/guarantee from subcontractors and suppliers warranting that all materials and equipment furnished under the subcontract, field work orders, and/or change orders are new unless otherwise specified, and that all work is of good workmanship, free from defects, and in strict conformance with the requirements of the project documents, subcontract agreement or purchase order, and all building codes. The subcontractor/supplier warrants to the owner and general contractor that, for a period, usually one year following the date of punch list completion, the subcontractor/supplier agrees to repair or replace any or all work, together with any work or property that it damages, which is defective in materials or workmanship.

The subcontractor/supplier warranty is in addition to any other warranties that may be available to the owner and general contractor from a manufacturer or otherwise. It usually does not modify or limit the rights or actions that the owner or general contractor may otherwise have against the subcontractor/supplier by law, statute, or in equity.

e. Special Instructions and Training Records

The contractor is required to conduct training for the owner's building maintenance personnel as to the operation and maintenance of mechanical, electrical, fire alarm, security, and other functional building systems.

Training sessions are often documented with attendee sign-in sheets and are sometimes video recorded for building maintenance personnel's future reference.

f. System Start-Up and Testing

The contractor also does system start-up and testing as part of the project closeout. This system start-up and testing includes all activities needed in order to ensure that systems are operating as specified. The contractor documents start-up, testing, and monitoring activities for future reference as well.

6. Attaining Final Completion

The "final completion" of a project constitutes the owner's occupation of a work of improvement accompanied by a cessation of labor; the owner's acceptance of the work of improvement; or the completion of all work pursuant to the contract documents, including the punch list. Remaining corrective or repair work does not prevent the final completion of the project. However, if the project lacks any significant items that the contract documents require, such as painting, fixtures, or landscaping, then the project has not reached final completion until the contractor has furnished those items.

In many states, the owner files or records a notice of completion. In California, the owner records the notice of completion in the office of the county recorder of the county in which the site is located. If recorded properly, the notice of completion serves to shorten the time deadlines for contractors to serve stop payment notices, record mechanics liens, serve notices to sureties, and file lawsuits on stop notices, mechanics liens, and payment bonds. Other jurisdictions have similar provisions and notice requirements or provide alternative methods for defining the time of project completion and deadlines for pursuing claims.

Once the contractor achieves all the completion milestones, and final completion, whether determined through the issuance of an architect's certificate or by statutory definition, the responsibility for security, maintenance, utilities, insurance, and similar items shifts from the contractor to the owner. The owner's payment of retainage to the contractor is also linked to either achieving substantial or final completion. Additionally, the warranty periods and, in some instances, job rights periods, such as stop notices and claims on payment bonds, begin to run based on achieving either substantial or final completion, or receipt of the certificate of occupancy. A well-written construction contract will outline the conditions for meeting the completion milestones and will define the rights or obligations that each milestone triggers.

a. Retainage/Retention Payment and Contract Reconciliation

Retainage is an amount the owner or general contractor withholds from each of the payments due. The owner or general contractor does not pay the contractor or subcontractor retainage until a specified time, usually upon achieving either substantial or final completion of the project. Almost all construction contracts provide for retainage, and the purpose of retainage is to preserve a fund of money to be available to ensure final completion and to correct defects in work. Retainage is an added incentive to complete the work on a timely basis. The owner can use this fund of money to satisfy unexpected claims that may arise, or it may apply it against contractor default. Generally, an owner/general contractor withholds an amount of retainage, typically 5-10%, from the amount owed to a contractor/subcontractor on each progress payment to guarantee the contractor's completion of the work. The contract and/or applicable statutes determine the time for the owner or general contractor to pay retainage to a contractor or subcontractor. When the owner releases the retainage upon achieving substantial completion, it will often nonetheless retain a portion of the retainage to cover any incomplete or defective items described on the punch list.

b. Final Contract Reconciliation

The owner or contractor performs the final contract reconciliation to calculate the final contract price. It includes a final determination as to change orders, final adjustment for unit price items or allowances, and final adjustments for back charges from the owner for liquidated damages, defective work, or other credits.

c. Unit Price Adjustments

For unit price contracts, the contractor has agreed to specified unit prices for specific items of material and labor. Parties use these contracts for construction projects for the construction or installation of one or a few specified materials, such as laying pipelines or the construction of sidewalks. The parties make a final quantity adjustment at the end of the project so that the final total contract price becomes the total of the number of "units" of that material and labor used on the project.

d. Allowances

Many contracts provide "allowances" as part of the contract price. An allowance is an amount that the contractor has allocated to a particular item, or portion of the work, for which it did not provide a detailed bid or estimate. The amount specified is the maximum that the contractor commits to spend for the item. If the item costs more, the owner must pay more. In other words, if the actual cost of providing or performing that work exceeds the allowance, the parties will typically increase the lump sum or guaranteed maximum price of the contract by the overage via a change order.

For unexpected or unforeseen costs, some contracts may include a "contingency allowance." A contingency allowance is a budget set aside for unforeseen or unanticipated expenses at the time the contract is executed. This type of allowance provides a buffer for unexpected costs, which may occur because of design changes, unforeseen site conditions, or changes in requirements. These funds are not a guaranteed amount of money for a contractor to use for the project, but rather an emergency account for the unexpected. On the other hand, some contracts may include owner contingencies exclusively for the owner's use. The contract should set forth how the contractor can use the contingency for such unexpected expenditures and to whom unspent contingency should accrue at the end of the project.

e. Liquidated Damages

These are time-related charges for the failure of the contractor to achieve certain predetermined milestone dates as defined in the contract. Generally, when a contract includes liquidated damage provisions (LDs), the LDs are the owner's sole recourse for a delay in completion of the project and the owner is unable to recover its actual damages for the delay.

f. Defective Work Back Charges

Most contracts give the owner the option to accept a credit for unacceptable or defective work in lieu of having the contractor repair the work. This option usually applies where repair of the defect will cause more harm than if it is left alone or if it is simply economically unreasonable to perform the repair.

7. Final Payment and Final Releases

Before the architect issues the final certificate for payment and the owner releases the final payment, the owner typically requires the contractor to provide proof that it has paid all invoices owed. The contractor must submit its payment applications/requisitions to the owner on a timely basis and include all the work performed through the date of the invoice. Many subcontractors and suppliers are thinly capitalized and depend upon a timely and steady stream of payments in order to meet payroll and procure materials. Therefore, any disruption to this income could lead to a work stoppage, payment bond claims, stop notices, mechanic's liens, and, in some cases, bankruptcy or project abandonment.

Therefore, the contractor must promptly disperse payments received from the owner to subcontractors. When the contractor pays subcontractors and suppliers for their work, contractors typically obtain releases/waivers of the subcontractors' and suppliers' job rights, including bond claims, in exchange for payment. Generally, subcontractors and suppliers execute a conditional final release and send it to the contractor with the final billing. Subcontractors and suppliers execute unconditional final releases once the contractor makes the final payment and the subcontractor or supplier receives that payment. The release forms are often statutory.

8. Rights of Unpaid Parties

a. Stop Notices

Some jurisdictions may provide unpaid contractors, subcontractors, or suppliers with "stop notice" or "stop payment notice" rights to stop or "freeze" construction funds before the owner disburses those funds to the contractor by giving a notice of claim to the person holding the funds—typically the project owner or lender who is financing the project. Contractors need to obtain stop notice releases from any subcontractor or supplier who served a stop notice in order to obtain final payment from the owner.

b. Mechanic's Liens

Virtually all states protect contractors, subcontractors, suppliers, and laborers on private works projects in the form of mechanic's liens. An unpaid contractor, among others, can record a mechanic's lien against the project's real property. Thereafter, the mechanic's lien claimant can file an action to foreclose the mechanic's lien if not paid.

c. Claims on Payment Bonds

Publicly owned property is not subject to mechanic's liens. Accordingly, the law gives protection to those who furnish labor and materials for public construction projects either through stop notices or public works payment bonds, either under the Federal Miller Act, 40 U.S.C. § 3131 et seq. on federal projects or under state "Little Miller Acts" or public works payment bond statutes on state or local-owned projects.

d. State "Little Miller Acts"

State "Little Miller Acts" often mirror the Federal Miller Act in protecting subcontractors, suppliers, and laborers on state and local public work projects. Because of the similarity of terms and provisions, this discussion will focus primarily on the Federal Miller Act. However, in practice, a particular state's Little Miller act may contain specific prerequisites for asserting a claim on a payment bond in that state.

e. The Federal Miller Act

The Federal Miller Act, 40 U.S.C. § 3131, et seq., requires the general contractor on a federal construction project to furnish a payment bond guaranteeing payment to subcontractors, suppliers, and laborers if the general contractor defaults. The amount of the payment bond is equal to the contract price unless the contracting officer awarding the contract determines, in writing, that a payment bond in that amount is impractical upon which the contracting officer can set an alternative amount.

A Miller Act payment bond only covers the following parties: (1) material suppliers who contract with the general contractor; (2) first-tier subcontractors who contract with the general contractor; and (3) second-tier subcontractors and material suppliers who contract with first-tier subcontractors. 40 U.S.C. § 3131(a)(2); see also Clifford F. MacEvoy Co. v. United States, 322 U.S. 102 (1944)). Miller Act payment bonds do not cover material suppliers who contract with other material suppliers.

A claimant need not prove the actual incorporation of materials. *United States ex rel. Lanahan Lumber Co. v. Spearin, Preston & Burrows, Inc.*, 496 F.Supp. 816 (M.D. Fla. 1980). Instead, the material supplier must only prove "four elements: (1) the materials were supplied in prosecution of the work provided for in the contract; (2) the supplier has not received payment; (3) the supplier had a good faith belief that the materials were intended for the specified work; and (4) the jurisdictional requisites were met." *U.S. ex rel. Graybar Elec. Co. v. Team Construction,* 275 F.Supp. 3d 737, 749 (E.D.N.C. 2017); *U.S. ex rel. Polied Env't Servs., Inc. v. Incor Grp., Inc.,* 238 F.Supp. 2d 456 (D. Conn. 2002); *U.S. ex rel. Steel Constructors v. Avanti Constructors,* 750 F.2d 759, 761 (9th Cir. 1984). A claimant may recover for all materials it supplied when it has a good-faith belief that the contractor used the materials on the project or that the contractor intended to use the materials on the project. *United States ex rel. Balzer Pacific Equipment Co. v. Fidelity & Deposit Co.,* 895 F.2d 546 (9th Cir. 1990).

The Miller Act provides that a claimant not in privity with the general contractor must give written notice by registered mail to the general contractor of any non-payment, including the amount claimed and the name of the party to whom the claimant furnished the materials. The claimant must give this notice within 90 days from the date on which it last furnished the labor and materials. 40 U.S.C. § 3133(b)(1).

A claimant must institute legal action against the Miller Act payment bond no later than one year from the date it last performed labor or supplied materials. 40 U.S.C. § 3133(b)(4). Failure to comply strictly with statutory deadlines can result in the loss of bond rights. Jurisdiction and venue for actions on Miller Act payment bonds lay exclusively in the United States District Court for any district in which the contract was to be performed and executed and not elsewhere. 40 U.S.C. § 3133(b)(3)(B).

f. Dispute Resolution

By the time the project reaches final completion, disputes may exist between the owner and contractor as to the amount of final payment due to the contractor. To resolve these post-construction disputes, the parties often turn to, or the contract requires that they use, a form of alternative dispute resolution prior to, or in lieu of, litigation. Many forms of alternative dispute resolution are available and are finding favor in the construction industry. These include arbitration, mediation, and partnering.

(i) Arbitration

Binding arbitration is a method of settling claims or disputes between parties to a contract outside of the litigation process, where an arbitrator or panel of arbitrators hears the evidence and renders a decision. When the parties arbitrate their disputes, typically it is because the contract requires arbitration. Arbitration tends to utilize decision-makers who are involved in and are familiar with the construction process and construction law. Its goal is to move faster than the judicial system and to be less costly than litigation. Sometimes it achieves its goal; sometimes it does not. Because arbitration is binding, the parties waive their right to appeal. The parties to arbitration also waive their right to a jury trial. In addition, similar to litigation, the arbitration provision in the subcontract sometimes forces subcontractors with small claims into lengthy multi-party arbitration.

(ii) Mediation

Mediation is a method of dispute resolution involving a neutral third party who tries to assist the disputing parties in reaching a mutually agreeable solution. However, the mediator's decision is not binding on the parties, and one party may reject the mediator's input and assistance and decide to utilize an alternative dispute resolution method or traditional litigation.

(iii) Partnering

Partnering involves the parties to the construction project agreeing to be involved in a process that starts before the work begins. Generally, a neutral third party, a facilitator, leads the process intending to avoid problems or minimize the number and severity of problems.

CHAPTER II

THE PEOPLE INVOLVED IN THE CONSTRUCTION PROJECT

By Emory G. Allen, Benjamin Chambers, Michael W. Spinelli, and David Stryjewski

A. Introduction

Coming together is a beginning,
Keeping together is progress,
Working together is success.
— Henry Ford

Henry Ford's motivational words provide a good description of the framework for any successful construction project. Ultimately, it is the people involved during each phase that determines whether a project will be successful. This chapter discusses the various categories of people involved in construction projects. First, is a discussion of the people who come together at the beginning of a project. Next, is a discussion of the people involved on a project who work together to progress the project through the various stages of construction to completion. Unfortunately, even when the required people work together, success does not always come easy. Financial struggles, misunderstandings, and/or changing circumstances sometimes result in claims and disputes. As such, this chapter concludes with a discussion of the people involved in the process of addressing disputes and claims incident to a project.

Construction projects come in various shapes and sizes. The size, complexity, and type of project (including whether a project is private, local, state, or federal) allow significant variations in the people involved.

B. People Involved in Site Selection

When an owner has a clear and concise idea of the type and extent of the construction project, the owner typically begins the process of selecting the location of the project. In order to accomplish this goal, the owner may seek assistance from a real estate broker or agent to obtain a list of potential project sites that meet the size, land use, and location requirements of the project.

As a part of the site selection process, a project owner may contract with a land surveyor and real estate appraiser. The owner may employ an environmental engineer to conduct tests to rule out environmental hazards.

1. Real Estate Broker/Agent

The real estate broker/agent often can provide a select list of properties that fall within an owner's pre-determined price range. A real estate broker is a licensed professional who knows the real estate market in the selected locale. A real estate broker typically can ascertain those locations that best fit the owner's needs and budget. Real estate brokers are typically familiar with local zoning and tax laws and can direct the owner to sources of financing. Real estate brokers often act as intermediaries in price negotiations between buyers and sellers. A real estate agent, an independent party, provides services to licensed real estate brokers on a contract basis. In return, the broker pays the agent a portion of the commission earned from the agent's sale of the property.

2. Land Use Counsel

A land use attorney is a legal professional who specializes in zoning and other regulations related to land development and usage. Their role is to provide legal advice to clients who are seeking to develop, buy, or sell real property. Land use lawyers help clients navigate often complex zoning laws, environmental regulations, and other legal requirements related to land use. They advise clients on issues related to land development, such as zoning, permitting, and compliance with environmental regulations. They also assist clients in negotiating with government agencies and other parties involved in land development projects. In addition, land use lawyers may represent clients in disputes related to land use, such as zoning appeals, boundary disputes, and eminent domain cases. They may also work with other professionals, such as architects, engineers, and surveyors, to ensure that development projects comply with all legal requirements.

3. Land Surveyor

A land surveyor is a professional who specializes in measuring and mapping land. The surveyor frequently determines the boundaries, shape, and contours of a piece of real property and provides an accurately dimensioned survey map that includes the property's boundary lines. Their work is crucial for a variety of purposes, including construction, land development, and property management. A surveyor measures distances, directions, and angles between points and elevations of points, lines, and contours on, above, and below the earth's surface. In the field, a surveyor selects known survey reference points and determines the precise location of important features in the survey area. The surveyor researches legal records, looks for evidence of previous boundaries, and analyzes the data to determine the location of boundary lines. The surveyor also records the results of the survey, verifies the accuracy of data, and prepares necessary plots, maps, and reports. Typically, states license the surveyors who establish real property boundaries.

4. Real Estate Appraiser

A real estate appraiser also provides information about the land's market value and any pre-existing structures. Several factors such as recent comparable properties' sale prices, the property's proximity to highways and transit, prior use of the land, and environmental issues determine market values.

A real estate appraiser prepares written descriptions of the property and provides an estimate of its value. A real estate appraiser often completes standardized checklists for the property and the surrounding area in which it is situated. Appraisers typically obtain land values from county sources and sales information about nearby properties. They also examine the income records and operating costs of income properties. Appraisers estimate building replacement costs using building valuation manuals and professional cost estimators. They also verify legal descriptions of properties with county records, measure the property, and compare the measurements with the legal descriptions. They draw land diagrams and note conditions and special features of buildings. After an appraiser analyzes and evaluates the pertinent data, the appraiser prepares a written report outlining the methods by which the appraiser estimated the fair-market value.

C. Design Professionals

After the owner has decided to begin a construction project, one of the most important steps to make the owner's vision a reality is the selection of design professionals (architects and engineers) to prepare the plans and specifications for the project.

Every project presents its own unique problems requiring unique solutions. One of the most important roles of the design team is to anticipate the problems that may arise as the project progresses. To the extent the design team anticipates such problems in the initial planning phase, it can minimize later unanticipated delays and expenses. That being said, however, a design team's role on a construction project often does not stop at the initial planning phase. Frequently, projects progress through schematic design and design development stages before the design team has finalized the design or completed the final construction documents. As a result, the design team often has a continuing role on a project that is integral to successful completion.

Just as construction projects come in various shapes and sizes, so do the various forms of contract management and design. In the traditional arrangement, an owner will contract separately with a design team and with a contractor/builder. Under the traditional design-bid-build project delivery method, the design team contracts with the owner to provide a design and the general contractor contracts with the owner to implement the design. As a part of its contractual agreement with the owner, the design team will often also agree to stay involved in the administration of the project through completion to ensure appropriate implementation of the design. Below is an illustration of this traditional relationship.

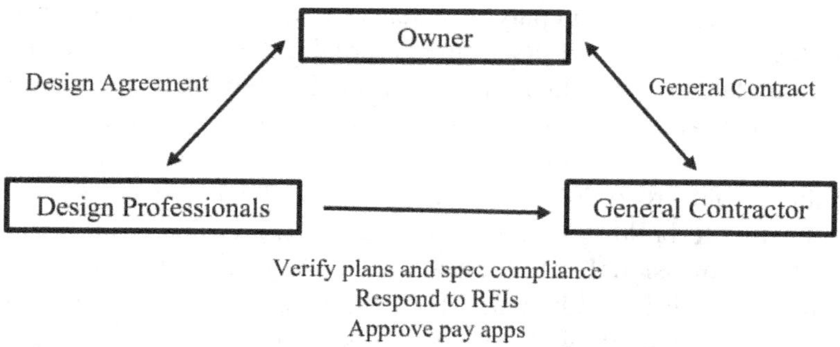

However, the traditional model depicted above is by no means the only method of project delivery, design, and management utilized on construction projects. The expansion of construction management, multi-prime contracts, public/private partnerships (P3), and/or utilization of a design-build arrangement can lead to numerous variations in the contractual relationships with, and role of, the design professionals. The following illustrates examples of design-build as possible variations in the traditional model. The example where the design-builder is the contractor is much more prevalent than where the design-builder is an architectural or engineering firm.

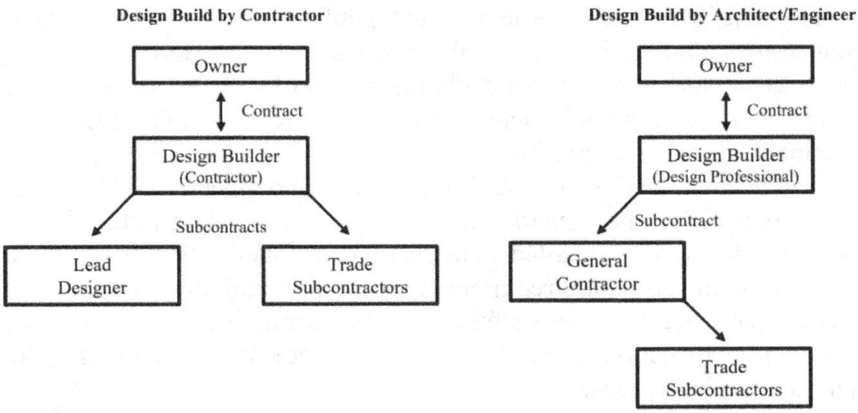

By adding a construction manager into the mix, there are even further possibilities

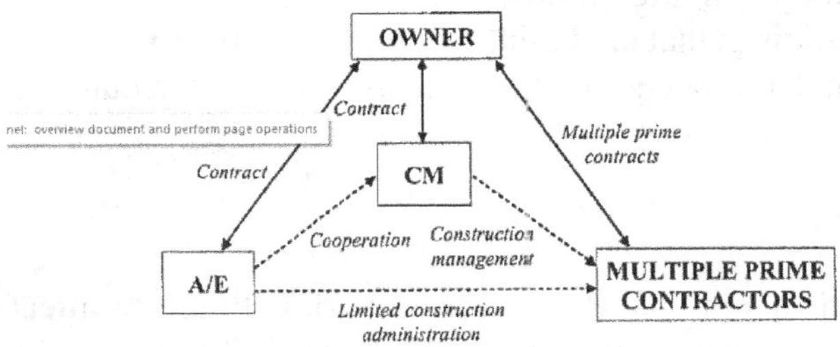

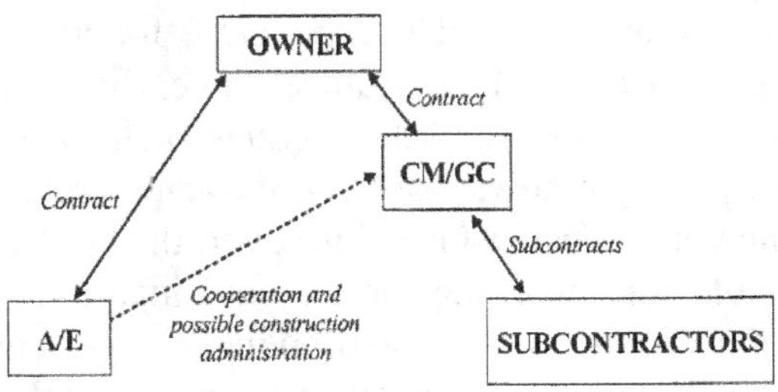

Steven G.M. Stein, Construction Law ¶ 3.01[4][a] (2005)

1. Architect

The role of an architect is to design buildings and other structures that are functional, safe, and aesthetically pleasing. Architects are trained professionals who use their knowledge of art, science, and aesthetics of design and construction, including their component parts and the spaces around them, to create buildings that meet the needs of their clients, while safeguarding life, health, property, and public welfare. These services frequently include consultation, planning, preliminary studies, designs, construction documents, and the administration of construction contracts while also considering factors such as site location, materials, sustainability, and energy efficiency.

The responsibilities of an architect may include meeting with clients to understand their needs and goals for a project, creating initial design concepts, developing detailed construction documents that incorporate engineering and structural requirements, selecting building materials and finishes that meet the project's functional and aesthetic requirements, and observing construction to determine if the project is built according to the plans and specifications.

Architects may work on a wide range of projects, from small residential homes to large commercial buildings, manufacturing facilities, and power plants and with hospitals, schools, hotels, warehouses, and multi-residential buildings in the middle. Ultimately, the role of an architect is to create buildings that are both functional and beautiful, while also taking into account the needs of their clients and the surrounding environment.

2. Civil/Site Engineer

The owner often hires a civil/site engineer to work with the architect to prepare site plans and, if necessary, zoning plans. The civil/site engineer typically handles issues connected with zoning approval. In addition, the civil/site engineer is often responsible for any design issues outside a building's perimeter. For instance, the civil/site engineer will address, in coordination with the architect, issues such as storm water management, drainage piping, roadway design, landscape design, parking lot design, etc. Working with a licensed land surveyor, the civil/site engineer may also be responsible for surveying the site and identifying all existing structures and proposed construction on drawings for presentation to the appropriate local municipality and/or other governmental agencies for approval. Working with land use counsel and the project architect, the civil/site engineer may also assist in the application for any zoning variances or other changes that the governmental agency may require.

For infrastructure projects, such as roads, bridges, dams, etc., architects may not be involved at all, and only civil engineers handle the design and contract administration.

3. Landscape Architect

When a project includes interior or exterior landscape areas, the owner may hire a landscape architect to design appropriate landscaping for the project. As discussed above, a civil/site engineer may participate in the landscape design in order to ensure that the landscape designer has appropriately addressed issues such as zoning, drainage, and site management. The owner may ask a landscape architect, often working in conjunction with the civil/site engineer, to address the aesthetic aspects of the landscape design to ensure that the look of the project meets the owner's expectations, while also addressing the specific needs of the plants included in the landscape design. For instance, the owner may ask the landscape architect to recommend the types of plants that the owner should include based on the amount of sunlight, moisture, erosion controls, and the desired aesthetic look of the project. In addition, the landscape architect can also recommend a landscape design that minimizes the owner's later upkeep.

4. Geotechnical Engineer

A geotechnical engineer (often called a "soils engineer") is frequently an essential participant on the design team. The geotechnical engineer investigates the subsurface conditions at the project site before the structural engineer designs the structural foundation. The geotechnical engineer fulfills the essential role of determining the bearing capacities and stability of the soils present at the project site. This function allows other members of the design team, who typically design a building from the roof down, to determine the appropriate loads for the building. If a geotechnical engineer determines that the soils at the site are unstable or that inappropriate fill material is present on the site, such findings may ultimately weigh against continuing with the project on the selected site altogether. Although the owner can modify most sites to support a structure irrespective of the soil conditions, the expense required to do so may dictate against proceeding. An owner's failure to appropriately consider these issues before proceeding with the rest of the design obviously can have serious consequences.

The geotechnical engineer typically drills borings at various locations on the site and/or digs test pits to obtain information regarding the type of soil, the water table, and the locations of existing rock. After performing these tests, the geotechnical engineer prepares a report describing the findings obtained from the borings and provides recommendations for the design of the proposed structure's foundation and structural system. This soils report that the geotechnical engineer provides is typically one of the starting points for the structural engineer. The owner may also ask the geotechnical engineer to stay involved in the project to inspect the footing base and compaction levels before the contractor pours footings and monitoring the subsequent pour of the footings.

5. Structural Engineer

The structural engineer is the person who designs the building or other structure so that it will serve its intended purpose and withstand the loads that the owner's usage will place on it. The structural engineer designs the footings and structural system and determines whether certain portions of the project should be steel, wood, or concrete. A structural engineer typically performs this work in conjunction with the architect or lead civil engineer for infrastructure projects to ensure the structural integrity of the structure, while maintaining the design concept.

6. Environmental Engineer

The owner sometimes retains an environmental engineer to perform a study of the project site to determine whether there will be any environmental concerns. Many financial institutions will not finance a project unless the owner has arranged for an appropriate environmental assessment of the project site. Many governmental entities require environmental studies before allowing construction. The type of land often determines the type of study that the environmental engineer will perform. For instance, raw land may only require a Transaction Screening Process.

On the other hand, previously used land may require a more complex Phase I Assessment. In a Phase I Assessment, an environmental engineer researches the site history, past uses, current uses, and any known contamination of surrounding properties that may affect the property in question. The goal of an environmental engineer in such a study is to identify problems that may trigger liability for cleanup, present health hazards, or impact protected lands or wildlife. The environmental engineer's report typically includes information regarding EPA, state, and regional records of contamination at the project site. The environmental engineer will also visually inspect the site to determine whether there appear to be any environmental concerns. For instance, the environmental engineer may need to determine whether there are any asbestos concerns in existing buildings.

If a Phase I Assessment reveals any potential environmental concerns, a Phase II Assessment may be required, including drilling and test pits. Depending on the findings, the environmental engineer may also need to provide recommendations and specifications for the remediation and clean-up of the project site.

7. Mechanical Engineer

A mechanical engineer is responsible for preparing the plans and specifications for any needed HVAC (Heating, Ventilation, and Air Conditioning) systems, plumbing systems, and, if required, fire and smoke sprinkler systems.

8. Electrical Engineer

The electrical engineer is responsible for all issues relating to the design and coordination of light and power on a project. In addition, an electrical engineer will design and coordinate other systems on a project such as "smart" building systems, computer system wiring, and communication systems.

9. LEED or Sustainability Consultant

LEED (Leadership in Energy and Environmental Design) is a certification program for green building worldwide, though it is primarily used in the U.S. An owner or design professional may retain a LEED Consultant (or sustainability consultant for any other green building certification) to manage compliance with the requirements of the LEED certification program. The current certification is based on design and construction, rather than energy usage outcomes, and state or local authorities may provide incentives for obtaining green building certification as part of the construction of some projects.

10. BIM Modeler

BIM (Building Information Modeling) is a way of generating a digital representation (often in three dimensions) of a building. Prior to construction, the designer, contractor, and/or MEP (mechanical, electrical, and plumbing) subcontractor(s) may use BIM to aid in the design process, including locating places for cost savings, as well as identifying and addressing conflicts between different trades whose work needs to go into shared spaces—examples including ductwork, piping, and electrical conduits housed between a ceiling and the floor above. A BIM Modeler is someone trained to work in the chosen BIM software platform and can work for the architect/engineer, the contractor, and/or subcontractors.

11. Permit Expeditor

A Permit Expeditor is someone familiar with local codes and zoning requirements who an owner may retain to work with the design and construction team to ensure that the design meets those requirements. They will also handle the permit application and work with the building department to obtain permit approval.

12. Other Design-Related Professionals

As stated above, different projects give rise to different problems/concerns that directly relate to or affect the design and/or engineering of a project and that may require the expertise of several different design professionals. For instance, if a project includes the rehabilitation of an existing structure that has historical significance or is in a historically significant area, it may be necessary to design the project to meet the requirements of the National Park Service (which regulates many historical districts) or local and/or state historical societies. Where there is historical significance on a project site, the National Preservation Review Act triggers a historical review of the particular site, requiring the involvement of a historical consultant. These individuals will typically advise and/or assist the owner/architect in coordinating with the National Park Service and any local and/or state historical societies.

In addition, an archeologist may be required in specific situations where buried remains are, or may be, found. For instance, where there are Native American burial grounds or areas of long-standing history, there may be requirements that a specific site be "dug" prior to beginning work. In those cases, the owner will retain an archeologist to perform the necessary "dig."

Depending on the various complexities of a given project and/or the specific desires/budget of the owner, the project may include additional specialists. For instance, under mechanical engineers, there may also be (1) heating, ventilation, and air-conditioning (HVAC) engineers; (2) plumbing engineers; (3) sanitary (public health or wastewater) engineers, (4) fire protection engineers; and/or (5) electrical and electronics engineers. In addition, there are interior designers, lighting designers, and certified planners who may be included on the design team. There could also be specialized equipment consultants depending on the project needs, including A/V (audio visual), IT (information technology), or solar.

D. Participants In Contract Formation/Construction Bidding

After completion of the design, the next step on a project is to locate and bring together the contractors and/or individuals with the expertise necessary to complete the project. This phase of a project may take various forms depending on the goals and desires of the owner. In some instances, primarily on private projects, an owner may decide to forgo competitive bidding and simply enter into contract negotiations with a contractor (or contractors if it is a multi-prime contract) as to the time and price to complete the project. However, the more frequent method utilized for purposes of contract formation on a large construction project is through some form of competitive bidding. Generally speaking, the owner's goal in competitive bidding is to locate a responsible bidder at the lowest possible price. The contractors placing bids with an owner for a construction project will likewise negotiate with and/or seek bids from subcontractors and suppliers necessary to complete the work.

1. Owner Representatives

On private projects, the individual(s) who solicit and consider bids and/or negotiate the terms of a construction contract on behalf of an owner varies from project to project depending on the desires of the owner. In many instances, private owners utilize their architect/engineer to put a project out to bid. In other situations, private owners may utilize a construction manager or other designated individual(s), such as a clerk of the works, to solicit and evaluate bids.

Private owners may also elect to seek the assistance of a bid management group. Bid management groups are companies that provide services to assist in the bidding process, including locating potential contractors for a project and coordinating the bidding process. Such bid management groups often provide centralized document repositories for plans, specifications, addenda, notifications, transmittals, and so forth. They may also provide a secure environment for communication regarding the bidding and may coordinate the distribution of bid invitations and documents, act as the repository for bids, monitor the bidding process, and provide a bid analysis.

Unlike a private project, statutory or administrative regulations often pre-determine the identity of the owner's representatives on a public project. Those representatives solicit bids, negotiate contracts, and administer the performance of the construction contract.

On federal projects, the individual responsible for soliciting bids, entering into contracts, terminating contracts, and making necessary determinations and findings on behalf of the federal agency is the

"Contracting Officer." The Code of Federal Regulations further specifically spells out the responsibilities of the Contracting Officer to include bid solicitation. For instance, concerning bid solicitation, the Contracting Officer must submit "pre-solicitation notices" to prospective bidders prior to the submission of formal invitations for bids on any project exceeding $100,000. The Contracting Officer is also responsible for submitting formal invitations for bids and considering protests regarding the bidding process and/or documents.

2. Bidders

a. Pre-Qualified Bidders/Lowest Bona Fide Bidder

Generally speaking, there are two types of bidding methods, closed bidding and open bidding. With closed bidding, which is the primary method used on private projects, an owner invites several "pre-qualified" bidders to bid on a project. In such situations, the owner, often with the assistance of its design professional(s) or construction manager, pre-determines which contractors will receive invitations to bid on a particular project. (See Exhibit 8) for a sample notice inviting bids.) Which contractors the owner invites to bid as "pre-qualified" depends on various criteria that the owner deems important. When the owner has pre-qualified the bidders, the owner will typically award the contract to the lowest responsible, responsive bidder.

Although owners on private projects have a large amount of discretion to determine what bidders to accept, statutes exist in many states that require contractors to be appropriately licensed before undertaking a construction project, be it private or public. The ramifications to an owner of having an unlicensed contractor perform construction include the risk of defective construction and/or contract default. The ramifications for an unlicensed contractor are much more severe. For instance, in California, an unlicensed contractor may not sue for payment of the construction work performed and is liable to repay an owner for payments already received for work performed because of the lack of licensure.

b. Lowest Responsible Bidder

With open bidding, an owner (typically on public works projects) publicly advertises to receive bids from qualified contractors. Because the owner does not undertake to "pre-qualify" bidders, the owner's objective is to identify the "lowest responsible, responsive bidder." After receiving the bids, the owner determines the lowest responsible, responsive bidder by considering the characteristics of each bidder, including factors such as the bidder's expertise, financial capacity, general reputation, past performance on similar jobs, and/or other comparable factors. The owner's goal in considering these factors is to determine which contractor can appropriately complete the job at the lowest price with the least administrative cost to the owner. On a private project, the owner can consider these factors subjectively. On public projects, however, often statutes and/or regulations establish the particular qualifications needed to be a "responsible bidder." For instance, on federal projects, the Code of Federal Regulations, specifically the FAR (Federal Acquisition Regulations) spells out the characteristics needed to be a "responsible" contractor. On state public projects, many states have likewise established characteristics that determine whether a contractor is "responsible."

Public owners may also require special criteria on certain projects. For instance, on federal projects requiring particular expertise, a Contracting Officer may establish certain "special standards of responsibility" that contractors must meet in order for the owner to consider them a "responsible" contractor. Also, disbarment may automatically disqualify certain contractors as "responsible" bidders. The Code of Federal Regulations sets forth the various reasons for disbarment. The General Services Administration Office maintains a list of disbarred contractors.

c. Special Classes of Bidders (MBEs, DBEs, WBEs, and SDBs)

Certain state and federal statutes encourage and/or require that a "fair proportion" of public contracts include small, socially, and economically disadvantaged business concerns or women-owned businesses. MBE stands for minority-owned business enterprise. DBE stands for disadvantaged business enterprise. WBE stands for women-owned business enterprise. SDB stands for socially and economically disadvantaged business enterprise. Statutes and regulations establish the criteria for "socially and economically disadvantaged small business concerns" on federal projects.

For federal projects, the Small Business Administration (SBA)'s contracting programs identify which projects are reserved for small businesses or other SBA socio-economic program participants. For larger projects that are not set aside for small businesses, the SBA may require some portion of the subcontracts for that project to include SBA program participants. Those programs include 8(a) Business Development, HUBZone, Women-Owned Small Business, and Service-Disabled Veteran-Owned Small Businesses. The 8(a) program is designed to provide training and technical assistance to firms controlled by socially and economically disadvantaged individuals. The HUBZone program encourages development in certain areas based on the location of the small business's office and the percentage of employee residences.

Where there is an objection during the bidding process on a federal project challenging a contractor's status as a small business, typically an SBA Government Contracting Area Office in the area where the protested party is located will investigate the protest. Furthermore, when a Contracting Officer questions the qualifications of a small business entity to bid on a project, the SBA is responsible for considering the contractor's qualifications and issuing, if appropriate, a Certificate of Competency. The SBA's size determinations are subject to appeal to the Office of Hearing and Appeals.

3. Estimators/Contract Sales

Large contractors and subcontractors frequently have a specialized team of individuals, often including people referred to as estimators, senior estimators, or contract sales representatives who review bid packages and prepare bids on behalf of the contractor or subcontractor. Many contractors have "Get Work" teams for locating potential projects and pursuing those projects through the estimating and/or negotiating process.

E. People Involved in the Procurement of Bonding and Insurance

Every worthwhile endeavor involves a certain measure of risk. Construction projects, whether large or small, simple or complex, are no exception and, indeed, some consider construction a higher risk endeavor than many others because of both the personal injury and property damage risks and the financial risks. Owners, contractors, and other construction professionals use insurance and surety bonds to manage the risks inherently associated with construction projects. Following is a description of the various people often involved in the procurement of insurance and bonding for a construction project.

1. Contractor Representatives

Larger contractors typically assign the responsibility to obtain insurance and bonding to a particular individual, or group of individuals, within the company. In many instances, the Chief Financial Officer (CFO) or Controller for a construction company is responsible for procuring the insurance and bonds required to bid on and construct projects as either a general contractor or a subcontractor. Large construction companies may have a Risk Manager whose primary function is to consider and obtain appropriate coverages.

2. Agents/Brokers

Contractors typically develop relationships with bonding/insurance agents or brokers who provide the contractor with insurance and bonding programs that fit their needs. The insurance and bonding companies that place the policies and bonds for the contractor pay these agents' and brokers' fees and/or commissions. Agents/brokers can be small local or regional firms or firms with a large geographical or nationwide presence. Regardless of the size of the agent/broker or the size of the contractor, the relationship between them should result in an understanding of the limits as to the size and type of projects that a contractor can undertake with the maximum probability of success and profit.

3. Surety

Sureties (also "bonding companies") are companies that provide bonds or guarantees that the construction company will perform per the terms of the construction contract or subcontract. The entity for whom the surety issues a bond is the "bond principal." The entity that is the named beneficiary on a bond is the "bond obligee."

4. Underwriters

Concerning surety bonds, a bond broker requests surety bonds (e.g., bid bonds, performance bonds, and payment bonds, etc.) from an area or regional surety underwriter. That underwriter gains knowledge of the contractor through meetings with the construction company's leaders, reviewing the construction company's past projects, and analyzing the company's financial condition. The bond broker's and regional surety underwriter's review of the bond request is the initial stage in approving the issuance of a bond.

If the bond underwriter determines that the contractor is qualified for a bonding line, the bond underwriter will then forward the bond request and a recommendation to the surety's home office underwriting managers. The home office will then review the request and make the final decision, sometimes requesting additional information from the contractor. Large and complex construction projects sometime require the surety's additional review and analysis prior to agreeing to issue bonds. Joint venture projects, design/build projects, and fast-track or turnkey projects are examples of several types of contracts that often demand the surety's additional scrutiny. Sureties may obtain assistance from specialized consulting services, such as construction and accounting consultants, to assist them when additional underwriting is necessary. Often, the size of a construction project may dictate that several sureties join together on a bond as co-sureties.

Surety bonds (performance and payment) provide guarantees that their principals will complete the construction contracts and will pay for labor, materials, subcontractors, and vendors. Surety is different from insurance. Surety bonds do not protect the contractor or owner from the risks inherent in the physical activities required to construct a project.

Various insurance policies and programs provide protection from these risks. Typically, the construction contract will spell out the minimum coverages required. As with surety bonds, a broker/agent requests the issuance of necessary policies (whether a general liability policy, builder's risk policy, workers' compensation policy, etc.) to an area underwriter for approval. That underwriter may also need to obtain home office approval. Once the underwriter receives approval, the broker/agent will typically provide certificates of insurance to the contractor.

The process for obtaining subcontractor default insurance (SDI), an insurance product available to larger contractors, is similar in the sense that the contractor obtains the insurance through brokers/agents who specialize in subcontractor default insurance. Generally, subcontractor default insurance provides coverage for potential economic losses a general contractor may incur due to a subcontractor's default. Essentially, the issuing company indemnifies the general contractor from any costs (direct and indirect) related to the subcontractor's default.

5. Owner Controlled Insurance Program Managers

In most cases, the general contractor obtains the primary insurance coverages that the owner requires for a given construction project pursuant to the terms of the contract. Additionally, subcontracts will typically require subcontractors to obtain their own insurance covering the project, often listing the general contractor and owner as additional insureds. However, some owners elect to obtain the necessary project insurance for the entire project. For instance, owner-controlled insurance programs (OCIPs) are a type of wrap-up insurance program, an increasingly popular insurance procurement option that allows coverages for multiple insureds to be bundled (or wrapped up) into one consolidated program. Owners typically use OCIPs on very large construction projects involving many contractors and subcontractors. They provide the owner with certain cost savings. As with a large contractor, an owner typically identifies a particular individual or individuals within its organization (e.g., the CFO or a risk manager) to obtain and manage such insurance programs or any other insurance the owner obtains for a project.

F. The Owner's Construction Representatives

1. Owner

The owner is the entity or individual who initiates the construction project. It is for the owner's purpose that the project is designed and built. Public owners are typically agencies of federal, state, or local government. The construction of a public project meets a specifically defined public need. Private owners can be individuals, businesses, partnerships, or any combination thereof. The owner may construct a private project to occupy it or to lease or sell it to others.

2. Owner's Representative

The owner itself can supervise the actual field construction or the owner can assign that responsibility to another entity or individual. The entities and/or individuals that supervise a project on behalf of an owner are commonly referred to as the "owner's representative" because they represent the owner's interests often with the authority to act on behalf of and make decisions for the owner. There may be no distinction between an "owner's representative" and a construction manager (CM) if the owner retains a third party to manage the project's construction.

3. Federal Contracting Officer

The Code of Federal Regulations defines "Contracting Officer" as the person with the authority to enter into, administer, and/or terminate contracts and make related determinations and findings. The term includes certain authorized representatives that the Contracting Officer has delegated to act within the express limits of their authority. "Administrative Contracting Officer" (ACO) refers to a contracting officer who is administering contracts. "Termination Contracting Officer" (TCO) refers to a contracting officer who is settling terminated contracts. A single contracting officer may be responsible for duties in any or all of these areas.

4. Construction Manager

Owners may enter into a contract with a construction management firm to oversee the actual construction. A construction management firm typically possesses a staff of experienced construction specialists including, but not limited to, construction managers, cost estimators, project managers, project superintendents, professional engineers, cost engineers, architects, and surveyors.

Synonyms for a "construction manager" working on behalf of an owner include owner's representative, construction superintendent, general superintendent, project engineer, general construction manager, or executive construction manager.

An owner may engage a construction manager, as its agent in lieu of or in addition to a general contractor. As the owner's agent, the construction manager is responsible for scheduling and coordinating the design and construction activities of the construction project but does not have a contractual relationship with subcontractors, generally does not perform any construction work on the project, and usually undertakes no risk of performance. A construction manager plays a managerial role, ensuring that the contractor completes the work per the architect's and engineer's drawings and specifications. Often, the construction manager verifies that the contractor performs the work in conformance with local building codes. Other duties often include, but are not limited to, the preparation of budgets, schedules, and daily work force reports.

A construction manager's coordination and supervision of a project often begins at the conceptual development stage of a project and continues through final construction, making sure that the contractor completes the project on time and within budget. A construction manager very often works closely with other owner representatives, engineers, architects, and others who are involved in the construction process. At the initial planning stage, a construction manager may evaluate and assist in determining the appropriate construction delivery systems and the most cost-effective plan and schedule for completing the project.

After the initial planning is complete, a construction manager may oversee the selection of general contractors and trade contractors to perform specific aspects of the project—which aspects could include everything from structural metalworking and plumbing to painting and carpet installation. A construction manager may also determine the labor requirements and, in some cases, supervise or monitor the hiring and dismissal of workers. In short, a construction manager often oversees the performance of all trade contractors to ensure that they appropriately complete all of the work and do so in a timely fashion.

There is a growing movement towards certification of construction managers to ensure that a construction manager has a certain body of knowledge, ability, and experience. Although certification is not required to work in the construction industry, voluntary certification can be valuable because it provides evidence of competence and experience. Both the American Institute of Constructors (AIC) and the Construction

Management Association of America (CMAA) have established voluntary certification programs for construction managers. Requirements combine written examinations with verification of education and professional experience. AIC awards candidates the Associate Constructor (AC) and Certified Professional Constructor (CPC) designations if they meet its requirements and pass the appropriate examinations. CMAA awards the Certified Construction Manager (CCM) designation to practitioners who meet its requirements through work performed in a construction management organization and by passing a technical examination. The CMAA certification requires the completion of a self-study course that covers a broad range of topics central to construction management, including the professional role of a construction manager, legal issues, and allocation of risk.

5. Construction Cost Estimator

The project's architect or owner may employ a construction cost estimator to estimate costs or to track actual costs relative to bid specifications as the project develops. In large construction companies that employ more than one estimator, it is common practice for estimators to specialize. For example, one may estimate only electrical work and another may concentrate on excavation, concrete, and forms.

An estimator determines the quantity of materials and labor the contractor will need to complete the project on behalf of the owner. This process, called the quantity survey or "take-off," involves using various estimating software, completing standard estimating forms, filling in dimensions, numbers of units, etc.

Regardless of the industry in which they work, estimators compile and analyze data on all of the factors that can influence costs, such as materials, labor, location, and special machinery requirements, including computer hardware and software. Job duties vary widely depending on the type and size of the project.

Some construction companies have their project managers estimate the prospective construction projects, the theory being that the project manager will have a vested interest in insuring that the project comes in on time and on budget, substantiating their own estimate in those regards.

6. Clerk of Works

The project's architect or owner may also employ a clerk of works to ensure that the quality of both materials and workmanship are compliant with the design specifications and drawings. The clerk of works is responsible for detailed and oftentimes rigorous inspection throughout the building process to protect the owner's interests. Generally, the clerk of works performs a visual inspection of the work as it progresses with a responsibility of reporting back any discrepancies or noticed concerns to the owner or architect as its client.

7. Resident Engineer

The owner, project architect, or project engineer may engage a resident engineer, with the responsibility of assuring that the contractor performs the project's construction work pursuant to the contract's requirements – specifically, with respect to quality, time, and cost requirements. A resident engineer oftentimes acts as a liaison or intermediary between the project engineer and contractor, reporting to the project engineer regarding the status of the project, work progress, and records of the same. A resident engineer will have the level of authority or responsibility that the owner, architect, or project engineer has delegated to it. That authority and responsibility typically include monitoring the performance of subcontractors, supervising work activities, and ensuring materials meet plans and specifications.

8. Architect / Engineer as Construction Administrator

It is quite common that the owner will appoint the architect or the engineer for the project to manage and administer the contract. In such a role, the architect/engineer performs observatory inspections of the work in place, construction practices, and materials provided to the site to confirm that all meet the quality and conditions that the plans and specifications require. Further, the architect or engineer in such a role may confirm that the project's progress is consistent with the contractor's representations in its pay applications, review and make independent recommendations regarding the contractor's requested changes, and oversee schedule compliance during construction.

9. Facility Manager

A facility manager plans, designs, and manages buildings and grounds in addition to people. This task requires integrating the principles of business administration, architecture, and behavioral and engineering science. Although the specific tasks assigned to facility managers vary substantially depending on the organization, the duties fall into several categories, relating to operations and maintenance, real estate, project planning and management, communication, finance, quality assessment, facility function, technology integration, and management of human and environmental factors. Tasks within these broad categories may include space and workplace planning, budgeting, purchase and sale of real estate, lease management, renovations, or architectural planning and design. Facility managers monitor the facility to ensure that it remains safe, secure, and well-maintained. Often, the facility manager is responsible for directing staff, including maintenance, grounds, and custodial workers.

G. General Contractor Personnel

1. Contractors

Companies or individuals who an owner engages to perform the work, are classified generally as one of the following:

a. Highway Contractors

A highway contractor is typically involved in the construction, maintenance, repair, and improvement of highways and other transportation infrastructure, including bridges, tunnels, roadway markings, lighting and signage, drainage, and airport runways and taxiways. Highway contractors are also involved in maintaining and repairing existing highways and infrastructure.

b. Heavy Construction Contractors

Heavy construction contractors primarily construct large earth-moving projects such as foundations, dams, tunnels, bridges, and power plants. Highway contractors and heavy construction contractors come under the category of "horizontal" construction in the vernacular of the industry.

c. General Building Contractors

This largest category of contractors erects or remodels virtually every kind of residential, industrial, and commercial building or shelter. General building contractors come under the category of "vertical" construction in the industry's vernacular.

2. General Contractor ("Prime Contractor")

The general contractor or prime contractor contracts with the owner and is responsible for all the work on a project. Typically, general contractors subcontract out a substantial part of the work while maintaining overall control through project managers and on-site supervision, although they may perform some "self-performed" work. Prime contractor is often synonymous with general contractor except for a delivery method entitled Multi-Prime Contractors where the owner contracts directly with specialty trade contractors, typically subcontractors, and hence the term "Multi-Prime."

3. Home Office Personnel

The backbone of a successful construction project is a well-organized home office. A contractor's home office staff plays an integral role in ensuring that all record-keeping duties are met, that all project laborers are paid, that all customers are invoiced, and that all costs are properly recorded and analyzed. On a large construction project, the contractor's home office staff may be quite specialized. The following depicts a typical home office:

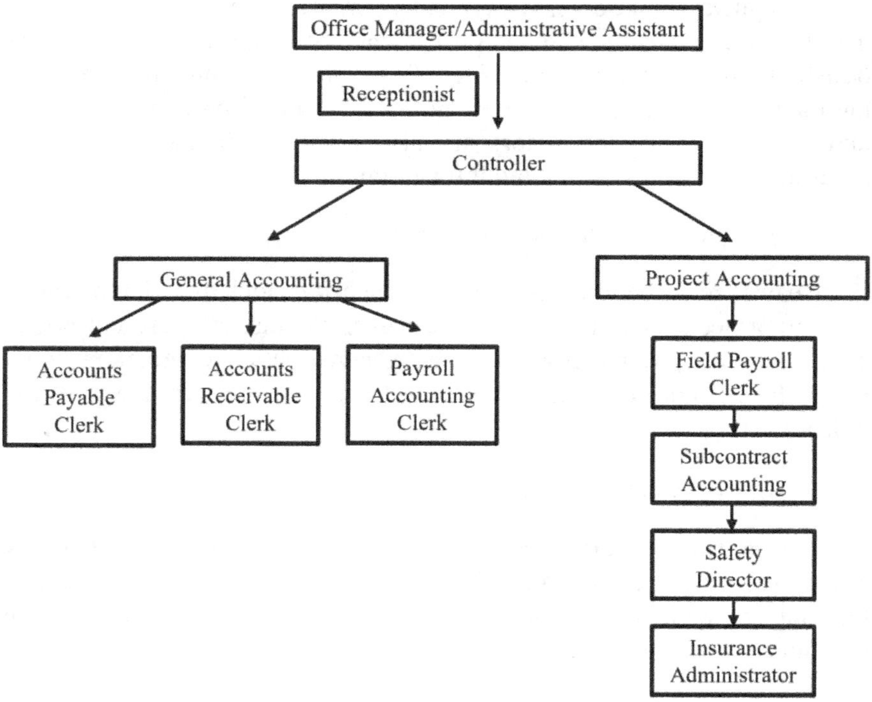

a. Office Manager

An office manager is responsible for performing and/or coordinating an office's administrative activities and storing, retrieving, and integrating information for dissemination to staff and clients. An office manager often has overall responsibility for information and communication management in the office — planning and scheduling meetings and appointments, organizing and maintaining paper and electronic files, conducting research, and disseminating information. Other terms for office managers include administrative managers, administrative assistants, and administrative service managers. Some office managers have business development/"get work" responsibilities.

b. Receptionist

A receptionist is often the first representative of the contractor that a visitor encounters. The receptionist answers telephones, routes and screens calls, greets visitors, responds to inquiries from the public, and provides information about the organization. Some receptionists are also responsible for the coordination of all mail into and out of the office. With the advent of virtual offices, voicemail, and electronic mail, the future of the construction company receptionist is in question.

Chief Financial Officer

The Chief Financial Officer ("CFO") is the top-level financial executive of a company. The CFO is responsible for managing both the finance and accounting divisions of the company as well as approving and issuing financial statements. In addition to issuing financial statements, they often play a role in strategic initiatives, which include bank financing and surety credit. They are also responsible for cash flow, financial planning, and taxation. The CFO will assist the Chief Operating Officer ("COO") on business matters relating to budget management and planning, cost-benefit analyses, and forecasting. CFOs generally report to the Chief Executive Officer ("CEO") of a company.

c. Controller

A controller directs the preparation of financial reports that summarize and forecast the organization's financial position, such as income statements, balance sheets, cash flow statements, and analyses of future earnings or expenses. Often, controllers oversee the daily accounting operations of a company. This oversight includes heading up the accounting department, which may include accounting personnel, accounts payable, accounts receivable, payroll, and cost accountants. In smaller companies, the controller may be responsible for cash management and risk management which typically are responsibilities of the treasurer and CFO in larger companies. The controller generally reports to the CFO.

d. Management Accountants

Management accountants—also called cost, managerial, industrial, corporate, or private accountants—record and analyze financial information of the companies for which they work. Among their other typical responsibilities are budgeting, performance evaluations, departmental audits, cost management, and asset management. Usually, management accountants are part of executive teams involved in strategic planning and/or development of new products. They analyze and interpret the financial information that corporate executives need in order to make sound business decisions. They also prepare financial reports for other groups, including stockholders, creditors, regulatory agencies, and tax authorities. Within accounting departments, management accountants may work in various areas, including financial analysis, planning and budgeting, and cost accounting.

In a construction environment, an accountant may produce reports projecting total construction costs and cash flow requirements, as well as interim reports on cost overruns or anticipated surpluses. They also prepare financial reports that other entities such as banks, sureties, insurance companies, and government agencies may require and rely upon.

e. Treasurers and Finance Officers

Treasurers and finance officers direct an organization's financial goals, objectives, and budgets. They oversee the depositing and investment of funds, manage associated risks, supervise cash management activities, execute capital-raising strategies to support a firm's expansion, and deal with mergers and acquisitions. The treasurer is also responsible for ensuring that any financial transaction is compliant with applicable laws and regulations. A treasurer's productivity is often overseen by the CFO, who is typically the highest-ranking financial executive.

f. Timekeeping Clerk/Payroll Clerk

The fundamental task of a timekeeping clerk is to distribute and collect timecards each pay period. The timekeeping/payroll clerk reviews employee work charts, timesheets, and timecards to ensure the proper recording of payroll information and the appropriate signatures of authorized officials. The timekeeper/payroll clerk often reviews computer reports listing timecards that contain errors and contacts the employee or the employee's supervisor to resolve problems. In addition, a timekeeping clerk may be responsible for informing managers and other employees about procedural changes in payroll policies. In addition to calculating employee compensation, the payroll clerk is responsible for updating internal payroll databases and ensuring timely payments. The payroll clerk will also support compliance with payroll. This support includes assisting in the preparation of weekly, monthly, and quarterly tax filings and payments such as 941's and W-2's.

A payroll clerk, also sometimes referred to as a payroll officer or technician, will review timecards for calculating, coding, or other errors. The payroll clerk computes pay by subtracting from gross earnings allotments, including federal and state taxes and contributions to retirement, insurance, and savings plans. On public projects, a payroll clerk may prepare required certified payroll submissions. Increasingly, computers perform the necessary calculations and alert payroll clerks to problems or errors in the data. In small organizations or for new employees, clerks may need to perform the necessary calculations manually. In some small offices, clerks or other employees in the accounting department process payroll.

g. Accounts Payable Clerk

The duties of an accounts payable clerk include receiving and processing vendor invoices, including recording vendor bills, and coding expenditures. The accounts payable clerk should verify and investigate discrepancies in invoices, vendor accounts, and monthly vendor statements. They will also process payments. The accounts payable clerk often provides certain financial reports to the controller. These reports often include information concerning total accounts payable, aged accounts payable, unpaid bills, and accounts payable sorted in various ways, including by project and vendor. The accounts payable clerk will ensure compliance with the receipt of W-9s, processing of 1099s, sales tax reporting, and remittances.

h. Accounts Receivable Clerk

The duties of an accounts receivable clerk include all aspects of customer invoicing. The accounts receivable clerk is typically responsible for preparing payment requisitions, pay applications, or invoices to the owner. The accounts receivable clerk may also provide certain financial reports to the controller. These reports often include information concerning total accounts receivable, aged accounts receivable, open invoices, and accounts receivable sorted in various ways including by project and by customer. Oftentimes, the accounts receivable clerk will follow up with customers for the collection of outstanding invoices.

i. Subcontract Accounting Clerk

A contractor may have a subcontract accounting clerk position when the number of subcontractors, or the complexity of the procedures involved, require a separate division to properly maintain control of the subcontractor paperwork. A subcontract accounting clerk may assist with preparing and reviewing subcontract agreements. In addition, the subcontract accounting clerk may be responsible for obtaining all necessary subcontractor insurance certificates and other paperwork as required by subcontracts, such as waivers and lien releases as well as creating and maintaining various databases to log and control subcontractor documents.

j. Insurance Administrator/Risk Manager

The insurance administrator or risk manager is responsible for procuring all necessary contractor insurances such as general liability insurance, worker's compensation insurance, automobile insurance, umbrella insurance, builder's risk, and any other specialized insurance that the contract documents require. This individual is also responsible for maintaining records regarding coverage limits, premiums, and terms of coverage so that the company remains compliant.

k. Safety Director

The safety director is responsible for developing, preparing, and/or maintaining the company health and safety manuals, which set forth all policies, procedures, and reporting requirements. The safety director is typically responsible for maintaining a record of all accident reports, scheduling safety meetings, and addressing employee concerns regarding job safety issues. The safety director is often responsible for providing subcontractors with information regarding the safety program and obtaining written agreements to ensure compliance with the safety regulations. Safety directors may also perform safety audits and conduct training sessions.

4. Field Personnel

Field personnel, simply stated, are those individuals who typically perform the majority, if not all, of their duties at the construction project site. Among this group are individuals who interact with both those actually constructing the project and the office personnel. The chart below provides an overview of the typical organization of the field project management and personnel for a large general contracting firm.

Understandably, this is only a basic model and variations occur from one firm to another.

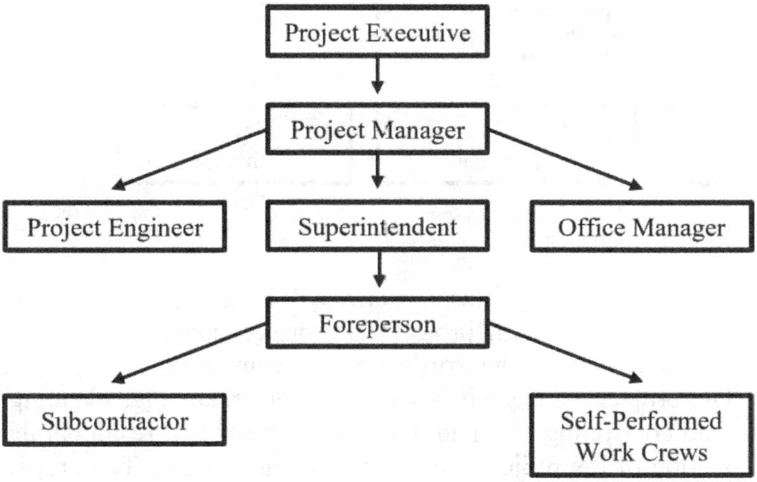

a. Project Executive

A project executive for a large general contracting firm assumes the leadership position within the organization for the development, coordination, facilitation, and execution of major project activities. Similar titles for this position may be director of operations or vice president of operations. Generally, the project executive will supervise and facilitate the entire project procurement process for more than one project at a time. The procurement process includes the bidding, scoping, negotiating, and awarding of subcontract packages. The project executive often works closely with the owner and the overall design team through project completion. The project executive must develop and maintain positive relationships with owners, project managers, subcontractors, and staff.

Although the project executive spends considerably less time in the "field" than others, the project executive interacts with the project manager and leads project teams toward quality control, timely completion of projects, and management of risk and safety issues. Other duties include visiting project sites and participating in project team meetings. The project executive also interacts with home office personnel, such as finance and human resources directors. The project executive is responsible for the integration of the lessons learned from project successes and failures into standard operating practices of the firm.

The president or other officers of small to medium-size general contracting firms may perform the duties of a project executive.

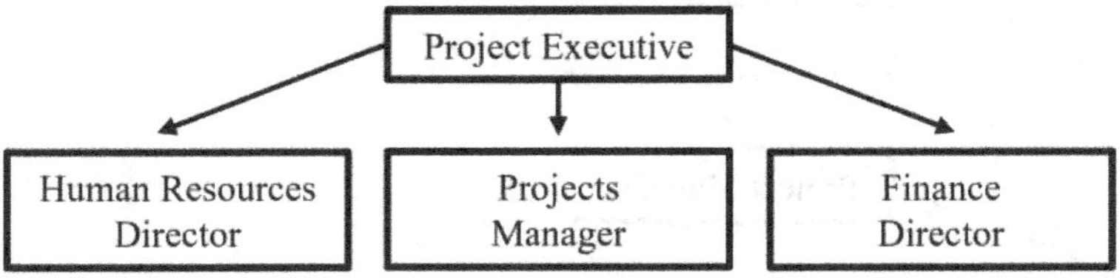

b. Project Manager

Large general contracting firms normally will have a full-time project manager on every construction project. The project manager typically reports either to a member of the firm's top management or to the project executive. The project manager is responsible for organizing, planning, scheduling, and controlling the field work in a manner that results in the timely completion of the project within the cost limitations. The project manager works closely with the owner and design team through project completion. The project manager typically has an on-site project team consisting of various personnel to assist in the day-to-day field operations and also relies upon the support of home office management personnel.

The qualifications of an effective project manager include, but are not limited to, (1) a considerable background of practical construction experience; (2) the expertise and experience in the application of specialized management techniques in the industry, i.e., computer knowledge or access to computer support personnel; (3) the capacity to step back from the complex details of daily construction operations in order to plan for upcoming events, material deliveries, and manpower requirements and identify possible changes to the work; and (4) having the personality and insight to work with other people under very stressful circumstances.

Specific duties of a project manager include assisting in the creation, implementation, and control of the project construction schedules, cost monitoring and control, project engineering, subcontract agreements and management, labor union relations, material requisitions, manpower requirements, equipment requirements, shop drawings and material submittal review, and quality control. The project manager may have the direct authority to execute contract documents, including the contract and owner change orders, subcontract agreements and subcontractor change orders, payment applications/requisitions, and material purchase orders. However, the project manager typically delegates the day-to-day tasks on the project to a project superintendent, project foreperson, project engineer, labor union liaison, and the office management and accounting departments.

c. Project Superintendent

Under the direction of a project manager, a project superintendent (sometimes referred to as a general superintendent) is responsible for managing, coordinating, scheduling, and directing the daily details of a construction project, including, but not limited to, project planning, project scheduling, project documentation, and overall on-site project coordination. Additionally, a project superintendent is responsible for the coordination of subcontractors, with the assistance of a foreperson, and the procurement of materials.

Specific duties of a project superintendent typically include, but are not limited to, attending pre-construction and construction meetings, maintaining documents such as daily reports and timecards, inspecting construction and installation progress to ensure conformance to plans and specifications, and assisting the project manager in the preparation of data for monthly payment applications/requisitions, and periodic percent completion data reports.

d. Project Foreperson

Under the direction of a project manager and/or superintendent, a foreperson is typically the overseer of specific trade(s) and/or self-performed work of the general contractor. The project foreperson works closely with and directs the production and coordination of subcontractors' work and that of their crews. A foreperson maintains records of day-to-day construction operations, including daily logs, delivery logs, daily production numbers, and time sheets. The size of the construction project and/or the complexity of the specialized work may necessitate multiple forepersons, a lead foreperson, and/or a general foreperson.

e. Scheduling Engineer

The scheduling engineer plays a critical role in construction projects by developing and maintaining a detailed project schedule. The primary responsibilities of a scheduling engineer include the sequence of activities required to complete the project, identifying critical path activities, dependencies, and constraints, and updating the project schedule regularly to reflect changes in the project timeline, scope, or resources.

The scheduling engineer may also work with the project team to allocate resources, such as labor, equipment, and materials, to ensure that the project schedule is realistic and achievable. Overall, the role of a scheduling engineer is to ensure that the contractor completes the construction project on time and within budget by developing and maintaining an accurate and achievable project schedule.

f. Cost Control Engineer

A cost control engineer plays an important role on the construction project by ensuring that the project stays within budget. The primary responsibilities of a cost control engineer include developing the project budget, monitoring project expenses, forecasting future costs, managing change orders, and preparing regular reports on project expenses, including the status of the project budget and any variances. Working with the project team and the original bid estimate, the cost control engineer develops a detailed project budget that includes all anticipated costs, such as labor, materials, and equipment.

g. Project Engineer

A general contractor may also have a project engineer on the field team to assist in the construction of the project. A project engineer often coordinates efforts related to scheduling, costing, surveying, quality assurance and control, and field inspections. Project engineers may not have engineering degrees notwithstanding the title. Also, on very large projects, project engineers are often responsible for the management of one or more specific trade subcontractors.

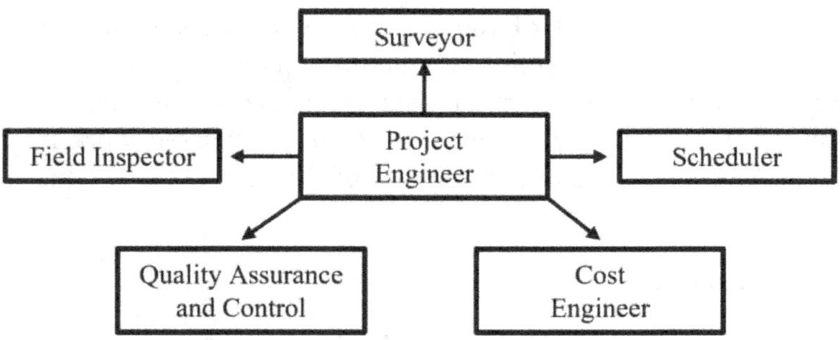

H. Subcontractor/Supplier Personnel

The general contractor, multi-prime contractors, and subcontractors on a project often subcontract portions of their work to lower-tier subcontractors or sub-subcontractors. The key specialty trades, electrical, plumbing, and HVAC subcontractors, maintain organizations of skilled mechanics, making it possible to perform certain parts of the contracted work more efficiently and cost effectively. Subcontracting is the device that spreads both the risk and the financial burdens of a large construction project. In that no contractual relationship exists between the owner and the subcontractor, the general contractor remains responsible under its contract with the owner for the subcontractor's faulty performance or lack of performance.

Key field personnel for the subcontractor would include a part-time or full-time project manager, superintendent, foreperson, and crew (journeyperson and apprentice laborers). The roles and responsibilities of these individuals are very similar to those of the corresponding employees of a general contractor. However, they typically have a more limited scope depending on the applicable subcontract. The home office personnel of a subcontractor are also very often the same type of individuals and positions described above with respect to a general contractor, although often with various positions and roles consolidated depending on the size and sophistication of the subcontractor. Considering the specialty of work that the subcontractor offers, many employees of the subcontractor may be members of labor unions and, as discussed below, may have very different titles depending on their experience and the particular work performed.

Suppliers are the entities that supply materials or equipment from off the site for incorporation into the project, including specially fabricated material and equipment. Suppliers often have similar personnel as subcontractors although, just as often, suppliers function more like manufacturers or jobbers outside of the construction arena. Accordingly, their personnel would be more akin to the personnel found in the manufacturing industry.

I. Laborers and Labor Unions

1. Laborers

Estimating the manpower requirements or laborers needed on construction projects is one of the most difficult tasks for the general contractor and subcontractors. Meeting these requirements with sufficient manpower with the specialized skills needed to perform the contract or subcontract are other challenges they encounter.

Prevailing wage laws, including the Davis-Bacon Act applicable to federal projects and various state labor laws (often referred to as "Little Davis-Bacon Acts") in place for state public work, require contractors working on a public project to pay workers current rates in the community where the publicly funded project is under construction. On each project subject to prevailing wage statutes, just as the estimators establish local prices for materials and equipment, they also advise the bidding contractors about local wage and benefit norms. The U.S. Department of Labor determines the prevailing wage rate for each job classification required for federal construction projects by surveying current wages and fringe benefits paid in the locality. Prevailing wage standards exist on federal/public construction projects whether the labor force is non-union, union, or both.

The various classifications of employees under the Davis-Bacon Act (contained in a Davis-Bacon wage decision obtained for a federal project) and Little Davis-Bacon Acts (which are often already set forth in applicable statutes) are numerous. A listing of the various classifications applied to workers in the various trades depending on their experience and job duties fills up many pages. A failure of a contractor to pay the appropriate wages to its laborers can have serious consequences. While the professionals and management personnel described in this chapter are critical to the completion of a project, it is, of course, the actual trade laborers who "get the work done."

2. Labor Unions

Many subcontractors for the key specialty trades employ members of labor unions. The labor union will represent workers of a particular craft, e.g., electrical, plumbing, and HVAC, or function such as operators, carpenters, and laborers, and focus on improving and defending wages, benefits, and working conditions. In the United States, a labor union may acquire the status of a legal entity called a "collective bargaining agent," whose mandate is to negotiate with employers to maintain and improve wages and working conditions for the workers it represents.

The chart below illustrates the typical progression for skilled laborers in the specialty trades:

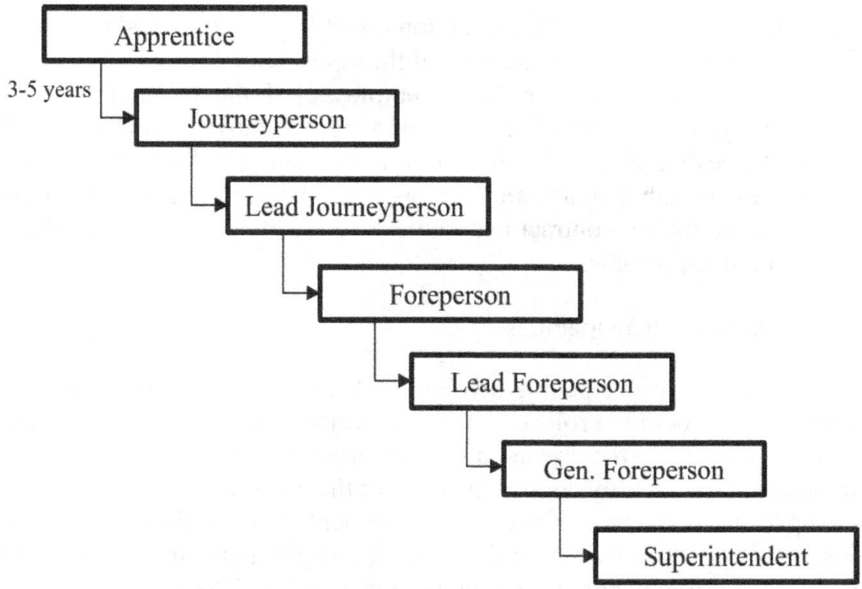

Apprenticeship is a training program that produces skilled workers by combining on-the-job training with related classroom instruction. Private and public sponsors, including employers and joint labor union/management organizations, operate these programs. The program must register with the U.S. Department of Labor.

The unskilled laborer starts as an apprentice. Most do not incur costs for their training but rather actually earn while they are learning. The programs vary in length. The building and construction trade union-sponsored programs generally take three to five years to complete. For example, union electricians spend five years in an apprenticeship program, as opposed to three years for a union roofer. During the apprenticeship period, health insurance, pension, vacation, and other benefits come with union membership. Apprentices' wages increase over the life of the three-to-five-year program.

Upon completion of the program, they become certified journeypersons, skilled and competent in their trade. A journeyperson can further advance to lead journeyperson, foreperson, lead foreperson, general foreperson, and superintendent as prescribed by the individual craft or trade organization.

A union steward represents the individual members of the labor union, from apprentice to superintendent, in the event of any investigatory interview as a result of any labor dispute. The union steward, along with the member, would meet with a project superintendent and a labor relations representative or liaison of the general contractor. In the event the issue is not resolved, further action could involve the president of the local union and upper management of the contracting firm.

A union business agent is an employee of the union that union members elect or appoint. They serve as a representative to the larger body of employees/members. The business agent manages the daily business matters of the labor union and acts as a liaison between the union and management during contract negotiations. They also inform the media of labor union happenings.

J. Construction Inspectors

There are various people involved in the inspection of the work on a typical construction project. On most projects, there is an inspection process that both the owner and contractor implement to ensure the maintenance of quality control throughout the contract period. The lender on a private works project may also implement an inspection process. The inspector for a lender will provide recommendations regarding construction draws based on construction in place. The owner then uses the construction loan funds to pay its contractor(s) and/or vendor(s) performing the work and supplying the materials.

The inspection process is as simple or complex as the type of project. Regardless of the size or complexity of the project, the common goal is final acceptance and beneficial use and occupancy of the project.

The inspection process, be it by the owner, contactor, or various local, state, and/or federal officials, involves the examination of buildings, building components, highways and streets, sewer and water systems, dams, bridges, and other structures. The goal of the inspection is to ensure that the construction, alteration, or repair complies with laws, regulations, building codes and ordinances, safety standards, zoning regulations, labor and wage laws, and contract specifications. Building codes and standards are the primary means to regulate building construction in the United States for the health and safety of the general public.

Needless to say, the inspection requirements for the construction of a nuclear power plant would be much more demanding than for the construction of a roadway. Each type of project will generate its inspection requirements based on complexity and the owner's degree of concern. In addition, whether the project is public or private, the intended end use of the project and particular jurisdictional requirements can influence the required and/or desired inspection processes and individuals involved in such inspections. Below is a general description of the various people often involved on a project whose role is, at least in part, to inspect the work performed.

1. The Contractor's Quality Control (QC) Team

QC refers to a contractor's efforts to ensure that the contractor and its subcontractors and suppliers perform the work in accordance with plans and specifications. The contract documents usually specifically spell out the contractor's responsibility with respect to QC. The general contractor has overall responsibility for QC and should ensure that specific QC requirements are included in all subcontracts and purchase orders issued as part of the work. The following is a list of the general categories of people typically involved in QC on behalf of a contractor.

a. Construction Manager or Executive

A construction manager/executive is the individual with overall responsibility for the quality of the finished project. This person provides the highest level of communication with the owner and/or the owner's designated representative(s).

b. General Superintendent

A general superintendent is the individual responsible for the daily inspection requirements and quality of workmanship at the jobsite. The superintendent will assign specific quality control tasks to others in control of the various aspects of the work, including subcontractors.

c. Craft Superintendents

Craft superintendents are responsible for the quality of the work of the various trades and subcontractors. Their responsibility may include inspection of particular aspects of the work, such as site work, mechanical, electrical, excavation, compaction, plumbing, structural steel, concrete, and/or any other appropriate aspects of the work depending on the size and complexity of the task.

d. Foreperson

A foreperson is the individual on the front line who is responsible for the quality of the work of the work crews.

e. Project Engineer/Office Manager

Project engineers and/or office managers usually oversee and direct the field office staff who, in turn, administer the paperwork and any reports that document the contractor's adherence to the QC requirements.

f. QC Inspector

Certain contracts, frequently in connection with public projects, will require designated QC officers who ensure that the work complies with the technical requirements of the project. Once familiar with the plans and specifications, the QC officer is responsible for performing or arranging for the performance of those tests and inspections that building codes, industry standards, or governmental regulations require.

g. Third-Party Inspectors

QC inspections extend to all aspects of the contractor's activities. In some situations, a project's complexity and/or the contract specifications will require the owner or contractor to utilize the expertise of independent firms for materials testing, steel fabrication, structural design, compaction, or other needs. These services are readily available through consulting firms and testing labs throughout the country.

2. The Owner's Quality Assurance (QA) Team

QA is the method of inspection that the owner implements to oversee the contractor's QC and to provide assurance that the contractor is constructing the project as designed. The contract plans and specifications describe what the owner expects in a finished project. The owner will employ its own inspection program with the type and complexity of the project and its budget dictating the number and type of individuals involved.

Owners utilize various measures to provide QA to projects. The owner's in-house personnel, architectural and engineering professionals, independent testing labs, and/or other specialized firms administer quality assurance to varying degrees depending on the type or complexity of the project. Although in-house expertise may sometimes exist with an owner, they generally use the services of design professionals, architects, construction managers, and/or third-party inspection professionals to provide required quality assurance.

The owner's inspectors have the authority and responsibility to protect the owner's interests in the construction process. They identify work that is out of compliance with the contract and require correction of that work prior to authorizing payment for the value of the work. They review for any safety violations and report any incidents of safety violations to the individual that the contractor has designated as responsible for safety issues. The inspector may call for a work shutdown if a dangerous situation occurs.

Beyond the owner's need for quality workmanship and safety on a project, other aspects of the work often will interface with entities outside of the contract between the owner and the contractor. Depending on the contract's scope of work, interfacing with various municipal utilities (water, electric, sewer, etc.), transit systems, or waterways may increase the inspection requirements of a contract.

Typically, the specific expertise of the inspectors is as follows:

- Site Work and Landscaping, including Erosion Control
- Foundations
- Structural Excavation
- Concrete Mix, Design, and Placement
- Structural Steel Design, Fabrication, and Erection
- Electrical Systems
- Mechanical Systems
- Plumbing Systems (water, sewer, etc.)
- Fire Systems
- Elevators
- Communication Systems

Inspectors conduct final inspections to ensure the project is compliant with all applicable regulations, codes, and permits before the agencies can issue certificates of substantial and final completion or beneficial occupancy.

3. Public Inspectors

On many construction projects, various public officials must inspect specific aspects of the project to ensure compliance with all applicable building codes and regulations before beneficial occupancy can occur. This inspection requirement is especially true on public projects or projects constructed for the general public's use. Local building officials are often involved in inspecting a construction project to ensure compliance with applicable local codes and regulations.

A local government office will often have various people involved in the inspection and approval of the different scopes of work at various phases, starting with a review and approval of the plans and continuing periodically as the contractor completes various systems on the project. (See below for a sample organizational chart.)

In addition, the state or local fire marshal's office will also often be involved, reviewing the plans and the finished construction. The fire marshal's office's inspection will typically include an inspection of the fire alarm system, smoke evacuation system, and fire protection system to ensure that those systems comply with state and local fire codes and regulations and are operational. The fire marshal also inspects building egress so that occupants may safely exit a building during a fire or other emergency.

Other public officials may also inspect/monitor certain aspects of the performance of the work during construction. For instance, a compliance officer with the Occupational Safety and Health Administration (OSHA) may inspect the project, or a portion thereof, to ensure compliance with applicable OSHA standards. In addition, representatives of the state or federal departments of labor with jurisdiction over a project may inspect the project and relevant payroll records during construction to ensure that the contractors are appropriately paying prevailing wages to their laborers including properly categorizing them. On a federal project, the United States Department of Labor may send out an inspector to ensure compliance with the Davis-Bacon Act.

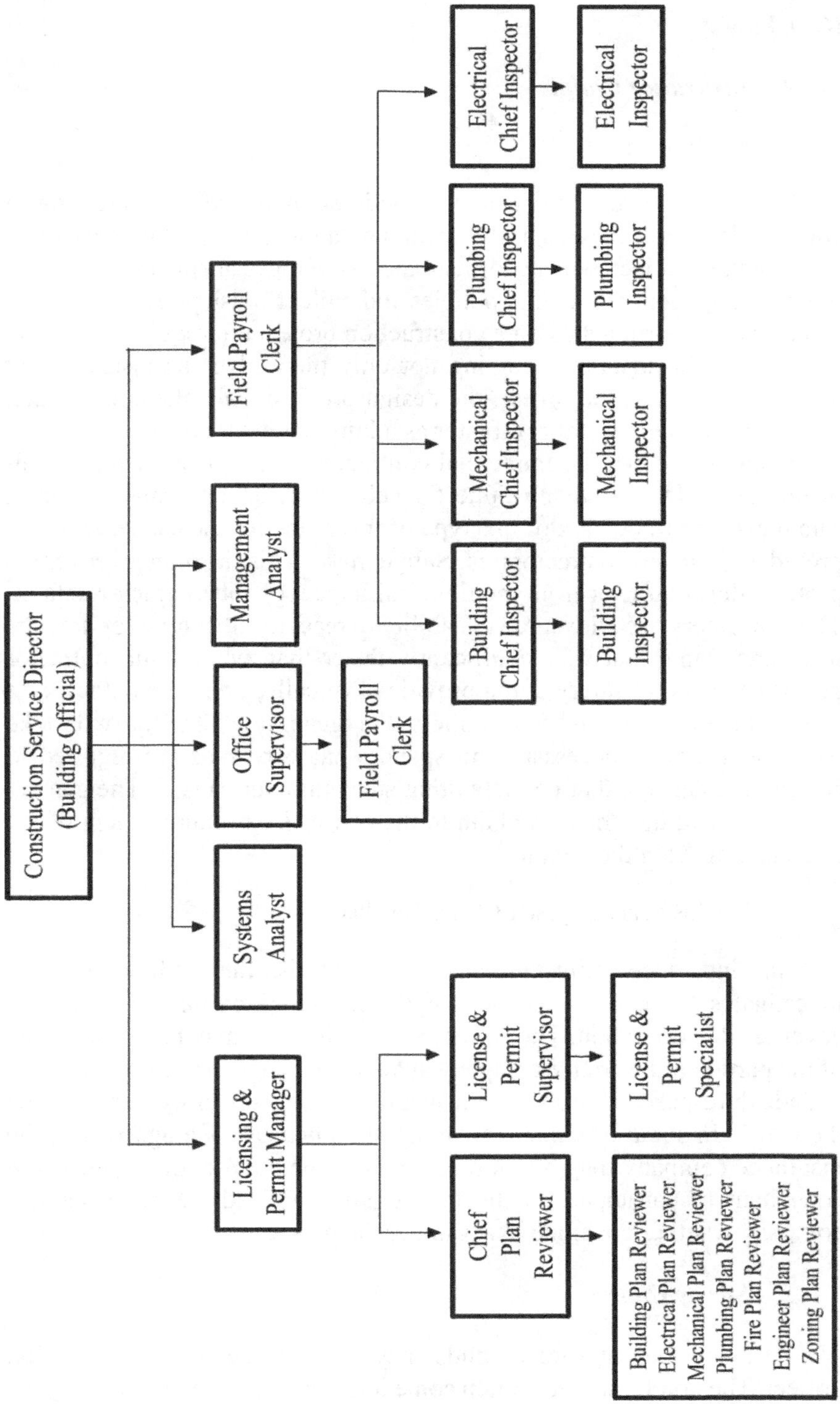
Construction Service Director
(Building Official)
Licensing & Permit Manager
Systems Analyst
Office Supervisor
Management Analyst
Field Payroll Clerk
Field Payroll Clerk
Chief Plan Reviewer
Building Plan Reviewer
Electrical Plan Reviewer
Mechanical Plan Reviewer
Plumbing Plan Reviewer
Fire Plan Reviewer
Engineer Plan Reviewer
Zoning Plan Reviewer
License & Permit Supervisor
License & Permit Specialist
Building Chief Inspector
Building Inspector
Mechanical Chief Inspector
Mechanical Inspector
Plumbing Chief Inspector
Plumbing Inspector
Electrical Chief Inspector
Electrical Inspector

K. Claims

1. Insurance Claims

a. Insured

Numerous types of insurance policies may be in place on a construction project. Generally speaking, almost all participants on a construction project will have insurance coverages in place, including, most notably, general liability policies and builder's risk policies. In many instances, the participants on a construction project are required to obtain project-specific insurance naming not only themselves as insureds, but also others such as the owner, the design professionals, the construction manager, and the general contractor as additional insureds.

Some of the larger commercial contractors use subcontractor default insurance ("SDI") as a substitute for subcontractor performance bonds. The registered trademark of this type of insurance for the carrier that first provided SDI to contractors is Subguard®. This insurance coverage protects the contractor from the financial impact of subcontractor default. The consumers of SDI wanted the ability to react to subcontractor defaults in a time frame that was significantly faster than what a subcontractor performance bond surety could provide. Typically, upon the default of a subcontractor under an SDI policy, the general contractor will take whatever action is necessary and spend whatever funds are required to remedy the damage that the defaulting subcontractor caused. The general contractor will then make a claim to the carrier for reimbursement of the costs arising from the default.

b. Insurance Adjuster/Claims Handler

An insurance adjuster/claims handler is the individual who investigates the claim on behalf of the insurance carrier and makes a coverage determination. The adjuster/claims handler may be an employee of the particular insurance company against which the claim is made or an outside third-party adjuster that the insurance company hires to investigate the claim. In some instances involving complicated coverage issues, the insurance company may retain outside coverage counsel or a specialized consultant to participate in the investigation and advise the insurance company whether coverage exists under the policy.

2. Surety Claims

Various types of surety bonds may be in place on a construction project. The bonds that most often come into play on a construction project are payment and performance bonds that the general contractor has provided to the owner and that subcontractors have provided to the general contractor.

Generally speaking, a performance bond is a written guarantee that a named principal (contractor) will perform in accordance with the terms and conditions of an underlying bonded contract with an obligee (owner). The performance bond protects the obligee from financial loss should the principal fail to perform the contract. A payment bond guarantees that the principal will pay certain claimants, such as subcontractors or material suppliers furnishing labor or material to the principal for use in the performance of the bonded contract. Other than the surety representatives, the participants in a surety claim are the same subcontractors, contractors, and owners discussed above. However, in a surety claims context, the participants have special labels applied to them, such as "principal," "obligee," and "claimant."

a. Principal

The principal can be the contractor or a subcontractor and is the entity with the primary or principal obligation on the bonded contract—the entity whose performance the surety guarantees to the obligee, whether under a payment or performance bond.

b. Obligee

The obligee is the party with whom the principal has contracted and to whom the principal's obligations run. Essentially, the obligee is the party protected by a performance bond—the beneficiary. The obligee appears as such in both the performance and payment bond, although it typically can make a claim only against the performance bond, not the payment bond. The subcontractor and suppliers are the beneficiaries of the payment bond. With respect to a general contractor, the obligee is the project owner. With respect to bonds issued on behalf of subcontractors, the obligee is the immediate upstream contractor, usually the general contractor.

c. Surety

A surety is a company licensed to provide surety bonds to third parties guaranteeing the performance of a principal. In many instances, sureties will be insurance companies. However, suretyship is fundamentally distinct from insurance. As such, certain states do not consider suretyship to be insurance.

d. Claimant

Generally speaking, a claimant is a party who has a right to make a bond claim. The language of the bond itself and/or any applicable statute governs whether a party has a right to make a bond claim. With respect to a performance bond, the issue of who is a claimant is not typically an issue. Typically, it is the obligee who will be the claimant. On private projects, a lender may be a co-obligee with the owner and be able to make a claim against the performance bond. However, the term "claimant" has more prevalence when referring to someone who has a claim against a payment bond. With respect to payment bonds, who qualifies as a claimant may be a more difficult issue to answer (for instance, a downstream subcontractor not in direct privity with the principal may or may not qualify as a claimant).

e. Surety Personnel

A claims handler, claims adjuster, claims examiner, and/or surety claims counsel or attorney typically handles surety claims. In many instances, the surety claims handler will be an attorney. The role of the claims handler in most cases will be to acknowledge the claim, investigate the claim, communicate with the claimant regarding the claim, make the determination of whether the claimant has perfected a valid claim (i.e., adjust the claim), and take the steps necessary to resolve the claim, if appropriate.

In many instances once there is one surety bond claim on a project, many more will follow. As such, it is not uncommon for claims handlers to obtain the assistance of specialized surety consultants (both construction and financial) and/or outside counsel to assist in investigating and adjusting claims, whether performance or payment bond claims.

There are typically others within a surety company who may be involved in the claim process behind the scenes. For instance, there are often claims managers who have claim authority above a claims handler's limited authority. In addition, many sureties have claims committees to which claims handlers and/or claims managers are required to report regarding claims.

f. Participants in a Surety's Completion Effort

When a general contractor or subcontractor defaults on a bonded construction project, the bond obligee (the owner or general contractor) may call upon the performance bond surety to complete the project or the subcontract scope of work. There are various options available to a performance bond surety in responding to a performance bond claim. One of those options is to arrange the completion of the project.

(i) Surety/Construction Consultant

In instances where a surety has received a demand on its performance bond, the surety will often retain a surety/construction consultant to investigate and document the status of the project, determine the scope of work remaining to be completed, estimate the potential cost to complete, and assist in locating a qualified contractor to complete the work, including creating a new bid package and putting the scope of remaining work out for competitive bid. Those individuals who function as surety/construction consultants typically have construction and/or engineering backgrounds or prior surety claims-handling experience.

(ii) Surety Attorneys

In many instances, outside surety counsel will also be involved in negotiating various agreements with the owner and a completion contractor. There is a surety bar in the United States that specializes in surety and construction law and provides advice and counsel to the surety claims industry.

(iii) Surety/Accounting Consultant

When a surety invokes its right to perform a books and records review of the principal, it may elect to retain or involve a surety/accounting consultant. These individuals will request financial information to assist in determining the financial condition of the principal as well as to review, verify, and determine the reliability of financial information. General financial information may include verification of accounts receivables, accounts payable, and the status of payroll tax and union obligations. The accounting consultant may also identify assets and the status of the principal's indebtedness. The accounting consultant can often work to secure project-specific information such as billings and job cost information. In certain instances, a surety may use the accounting consultant to establish a third-party escrow account for the collection of progress billings and payment of subcontractor and vendor invoices, often referred to as "funds control."

(iv) Takeover Surety

When the surety arranges for the completion of a defaulted contract and enters into a takeover agreement with the obligee, the surety becomes the "takeover surety." At the point that a surety becomes a takeover surety, it typically gains certain additional rights and responsibilities.

(v) Completion Contractor

The contractor who the surety retains to complete the bonded work is the "completion contractor." The completion contractor enters into a contract with the surety to complete the remaining work and to address any existing defects in the work. On some occasions, the surety will tender the completion contractor to the obligee and the completion contractor and the obligee will enter into their own separate construction contract.

(vi) Ratified Subcontractors

Prior to or after retaining a completion contractor, the surety often undertakes to enter into ratification agreements with certain subcontractors and suppliers who had contracts with the bonded principal for the performance of certain scopes of work on the project. Sureties and others often refer to these subcontractors and/or suppliers as ratified subcontractors. By ratifying the subcontractors, the surety hopes to maintain continuity on the project (including securing existing warranty obligations) and, in many instances, obtains a cost benefit by locking in the price of performance and/or material at the time of the original subcontract, which very well may have increased. In arranging a completion contractor to complete the remaining scope of work, the surety often identifies the ratified subcontractors in its completion bid package and allows the bidding contractors to decide whether they will use such ratified subcontractors, via assignment from the surety, or obtain new subcontractors.

3. Construction Litigation

Unfortunately, litigation is an all too frequent occurrence in connection with construction projects.

a. Mediator/Facilitator/Dispute Resolution Board (DRB)

Many construction contracts and subcontracts require that before the parties arbitrate their claims or submit them to the court system, they follow an alternative dispute resolution procedure. Typically, this takes the form of a non-binding mediation (referred to in some jurisdictions as facilitation). In these situations, a mediator (or a facilitator) attempts to broker a negotiated settlement.

Other contracts have set up DRBs typically made up of people with specialized knowledge in the construction industry. A DRB will hear both sides of an issue and render a decision. Some DRB decisions are binding on the parties; others are not, although the parties often may use the decisions as evidence in future arbitrations or court proceedings.

b. Arbitrator(s)

Where mediation fails, the parties may submit their claims to arbitration. Often, the construction contract dictates arbitration as the dispute resolution mechanism for any disputes arising out of the construction project. Where the parties submit their claims to arbitration, they will present their claim to one or more neutrals. Several arbitration associations provide both neutrals and rules to govern arbitration, the best known of which include the American Arbitration Association (AAA) and Judicial Arbitration and Mediation Services (JAMS).

c. Judge and/or Jury

Where the parties submit their claim to the court system, the participants will present the controversy to a judge and/or jury.

4. Bankruptcy

There is one particular forum that often raises its ugly head in connection with a construction project — bankruptcy.

a. Chapter 7 (Liquidation) Bankruptcy

(i) Debtor

The debtor is a person, defined as an individual, partnership, or corporation concerning which a case under this title has been commenced. 11 U.S.C. § 101(13); 11 U.S.C. § 101(41).

(ii) Debtor's Counsel

The debtor's counsel is an attorney that the debtor has retained to file the bankruptcy petition/schedules and to represent the debtor in the bankruptcy proceeding. In a Chapter 7 case, the debtor's counsel has a very limited role once the debtor has filed the petition because the only goal of a Chapter 7 case is liquidation of the company and distribution to creditors.

(iii) Chapter 7 Trustee

The Chapter 7 trustee is an agent of the court who liquidates the property of the debtor for the benefit of the creditors. The court appoints a trustee in most Chapter 7 cases. This type of trustee is different from the U.S. Trustee, who plays an administrative role in all bankruptcy cases. A Chapter 7 trustee is the official representative of the bankruptcy estate and can sue and be sued. 11 U.S.C. § 323.

(iv) Trustee's Counsel

The trustee's counsel is an attorney hired to represent the trustee and assist with the administration of the bankruptcy estate and is usually the primary contact for parties needing to communicate with the trustee.

(v) United States Trustee

The U.S. Trustee is an agent of the U.S. Department of Justice appointed to assist in bankruptcy cases. The U.S. Trustee administers many of the duties of the court including appointing committees, appointing trustees and examiners, and scrutinizing bankruptcy documents, etc. The U.S. Trustee "may raise and may appear and be heard on any issue in any case or proceeding" under the Bankruptcy Code. 11 U.S.C. § 307.

(vi) Creditors

Creditors include persons or organizations to whom the debtor owes money or has some other form of legal obligation that arose at the time of or before the filing of the bankruptcy petition. 11 U.S.C. § 101(10).

(vii) Class

A class consists of each of the different categories of creditors who have claims against a debtor.

(viii) Secured Creditors

Secured creditors are one of two general types of creditors of a debtor. Secured creditors have a lien on the property of the debtor.

(ix) Unsecured Creditors

Unsecured creditors are the other of the two general types of creditors of a debtor. The unsecured creditors have no liens on the property of the debtor.

(x) Administrative Expense Claimant

Administrative expense claimants are creditors holding claims incurred, with court approval, after the bankruptcy filing including necessary costs of preserving the estate, wages, salaries, court costs, attorney's fees, accountants' fees, trustees' expenses, etc. 11 U.S.C. § 503.

(xi) Auctioneer

An auctioneer is a person that the trustee hires (with court approval) to conduct a sale of the debtor's assets.

b. Chapter 11 (Reorganization) Bankruptcy

(i) Debtor

See above.

(ii) Debtor-in-Possession (DIP)

The debtor-in-possession is the bankruptcy debtor, which remains in control of operations as opposed to having a trustee operate the debtor. 11 U.S.C. § 1101(1). The debtor in possession in a Chapter 11 is a fiduciary for the creditors, owing loyalty to the creditors and not the shareholders of the debtor.

(iii) Debtor's Counsel

The debtor hires the debtor's counsel to file the bankruptcy petition/schedules and continues as counsel for the debtor-in-possession to represent the debtor after the filing of the petition. In a Chapter 11 case, the debtor's counsel has an involved role in the post-petition dealings as the stated goal of Chapter 11 cases is to reorganize the debtor's business.

(iv) United States Trustee

See above.

(v) Chapter 11 Trustee

See above regarding Chapter 7 trustee. The court appoints a trustee in a Chapter 11 case when it determines that the debtor-in-possession's management should not remain in control. 11 U.S.C. § 1104.

(vi) Chief Restructuring Officer

Oftentimes, a debtor may elect to appoint a Chief Restructuring Officer or CRO. The CRO is an appointed officer of the company and frequently becomes the main point of contact for the debtor. The CRO will work with lenders to secure additional financing or to restructure existing debt. The CRO will also prepare budgets and cash flows for the debtor to monitor financial progress and results. The CRO can become essential in negotiating changes to vendor terms, leases, etc. to improve the liquidity of the debtor.

(vii) Creditors, Class, Secured Creditors, Unsecured Creditors, Administrative Expense Claimants

See above.

(viii) Creditors Committee

A creditors committee is comprised of the debtor's creditors that the U.S. Trustee appoints. 11 U.S.C. § 1102. The committee acts on behalf of all creditors in a particular class or in all of the classes on negotiating a plan of reorganization with the debtor-in-possession and other major actions. 11 U.S.C. § 1103.

L. Conclusion

The success of a construction project depends on many factors. However, it is undeniable that one of the most important factors is the quality of the people involved. As illustrated above, there are numerous people with varying degrees of experience, expertise, knowledge, and responsibilities on any given construction project.

CHAPTER III

TERMS

By Shannon J. Briglia, Michael F. Burkhardt, Christina Craddock, and Matt Joy, Lauren P. McLaughlin, and Jack Nicholson

A. Contract Delivery Systems

Construction Management Contract - A written agreement assigning responsibilities for coordination and accomplishment of overall project planning, design, and construction to a construction management firm. The building team generally consists of the owner, the contractor, and the designer or architect.

Construction Manager Agency ("CMA") - A project delivery method under which the construction manager legally represents the owner and makes project-specific decisions on behalf of the owner but is not in privity of contract with contractors and subcontractors and is not financially at risk for not meeting the project budget.

Construction Manager at Risk ("CMAR") - A project delivery method under which the construction manager commits to oversee the project from design to construction for a guaranteed maximum price ("GMP"), usually involving preconstruction services to help balance costs, schedule, quality, and scope of the project. The CMAR will generally be financially liable for any costs in excess of the GMP and will be in privity with contractors and subcontractors. *See also*, Guaranteed Maximum Price Contract.

Cost Plus Fee Agreement ("Cost-Plus") - A written agreement with the owner under which the contractor or the architect/engineer is reimbursed for its direct and indirect costs and, in addition, is paid a fee for its services. The fee may be fixed or it may be calculated as a percentage of cost.

Design-Bid-Build - The traditional method of construction contracting, where the design is completed first pursuant to a contract between an owner and a design professional (architect or engineer), bids are then solicited from contractors, and the construction follows. There is no overlap between any of the three activities.

Design-Build - A delivery method involving an agreement to perform both design and construction under one contract between and owner and a design-build contractor. The benefits include single point responsibility for design and construction and faster delivery of the project.

Fast Track Construction ("Fast Tracking") - A method of construction management that involves a continuous design-construction operation. The general contractor starts the construction work before the plans and specifications are complete and the design professionals refine and complete the design as construction proceeds.

Fixed Fee - A set amount added to a contract for overhead and profit.

Fixed Price Contract (or Lump Sum Contract) - The contractor agrees, except to the extent errors are encountered in the plans and specifications, to complete the project for an agreed upon price including all labor, materials, equipment, and services plus the contractor's overhead and profit, regardless of the problems or difficulties that the contractor may encounter. The owner and contractor may increase the contract price by change orders for various reasons.

Force Account Work - Work done and paid for on an expended time and material basis.

Guaranteed Maximum Price ("GMP") - A form of contract delivery system where the contractor guarantees to perform the work up to a ceiling price for the cost of construction.

Guaranteed Maximum Price with a Fee - A form of contract delivery system where the contractor guarantees to perform the work for the cost of the work for construction plus a fee for the contractor's profit.

IDIQ (Indefinite Delivery Indefinite Quantities) - A type of government contract delivery system (typically federal) where a contractor agrees to provide an indefinite quantity of goods or services at agreed upon prices for a finite period of time.

Integrated Project Delivery ("IPD") - A project-specific form of contract delivery where the owner, designer, constructor, and sometimes major trade contractors are parties to a single contract usually including limited financial risk and reward sharing (*i.e.*, savings splits), waivers of liability between team members, and an operating system and philosophy based on a high degree of collaboration.

Lump Sum Contract (or Fixed Price Contract) - *See*, Fixed Price Contract.

Progressive Design-Build – A project delivery system where a design-builder selected based upon qualifications delivers the project in two phases: (1) preliminary or preconstruction services under which budget level design development occurs, preconstruction services are provided to refine cost, schedule, quality, operability, life cycle, and other considerations, and negotiation of a firm contract (either lump sum or guaranteed maximum price); and (2) final design or construction services which includes final design, construction, and commissioning.

Public Private Partnership ("PPP" or "P3") - A long-term agreement between a government and private entity under which the private entity finances the design, construction, and operation of a public project in exchange for sharing of the risk and a promised stream of payments for a specified time, received either directly or indirectly from the government or users of the asset. Initially used to construct toll roads but now also used for bridges, power generation projects, water services, health infrastructure, and even courthouses.

Purchase Order - A written document from a buyer to a seller to purchase materials, services, equipment, or supplies with acceptable purchase terms indicated.

Multiple Prime Contracts or Multi-Prime Contracts - Contracts with work-scope/trade contractors, that the owner individually awards under a multiple contracting format. Under this project delivery method, the owner is in a direct contractual relationship with each work-scope/trade contractor for a specific portion of the work of improvement. The construction industry often uses general, prime, and direct contractor interchangeably but when an owner contracts directly with work-scope/trade contractors, the industry refers to that relationship as a Multiple or Multi-Prime Contract.

Time and Materials ("T&M") - A written agreement between the owner and the contractor where payment is based on the contractor's actual cost for labor, equipment, materials, and services plus a fixed add-on amount, or fee, to cover the contractor's overhead and profit. The fee is often a percentage figure.

Unit Price Contract - A written contract where the owner agrees to pay the contractor a specified amount of money for each unit of work successfully completed as set forth in the contract. A unit price contract is essentially a fixed price contract with the only variable being units of work performed.

B. Contract Documents-Definitions

Addendum (Addenda) - Written information adding to, clarifying, or modifying the bidding documents. The owner/design professional generally issues an addendum to all prospective bidders during the bidding process and as such, addenda are intended to become part of the contract documents upon execution of the construction contract.

Allowance – An estimated price included in a bid or proposal that serves as the placeholder for a material or service that the contractor cannot determine the exact quantity or price at the time of the bid. The actual cost of that material or service is reconciled at the time the contractor is to provide it, usually resulting in an increase or reduction in the value of the contract amount via change order.

Alternate Bid - Amount stated in the bid to be added or deducted from the base bid amount proposed for alternate materials and/or methods of construction.

Architect's Supplemental Instruction ("ASI") - Additional instructions, sketches, or clarifications that the architect issues during construction to refine, define, or change the design.

Authority Having Jurisdiction – Governmental body or individual in a given jurisdiction responsible for developing and/or enforcing building codes, fire codes, safety or other regulations or for approving materials, installation, or procedures.

BIM (Building Information Modeling or Building Information Management) – A highly collaborative process that allows architects, engineers, real estate developers, contractors, manufacturers, and other construction professionals to plan, design, and construct a structure or building within one 3D model. Sometimes referred to by its tradename, AutoDesk Revit®, BIM integrates structured, multi-disciplinary data to produce a digital representation of an asset across its lifecycle, from planning and design to construction and operations.

Bid Bond (aka Tender Bond) - A bond that a contractor provides with its bid submission to demonstrate the contractor's ability to enter into the contract and to obtain final (payment and performance) bonds upon the owner's award of the contract. An owner requires bid bonds to provide a level of security should the successful bidder fail to proceed with the contract for any reason. Bid bonds are typically a fraction of the bid amount (2.5, 5, or 10% are common). Primarily, a bid bond provides the owner a means to recover the cost of having to repeat the bidding process when the awarded bidder cannot or does not execute the contract. Some bid bonds are forfeiture bonds whereby the owner can recover the full amount of the bond regardless of its costs to repeat the bidding process or award the contract to the next lowest bidder. A bid bond does not guarantee any portion of the construction, it only provides some assurance that the project can progress at no additional expense to the owner.

Bid Spread – The dollar amount difference between the lowest bidder's price and the second lowest bidder's price.

Borings – Soil sample data providing the characteristics of the soils on which the project will be built obtained by drilling or digging into the ground. The owner's civil or geotechnical engineer usually conducts the borings. The extracted soils are analyzed in a laboratory to determine moisture content, expansivity, collapsibility, compressibility, density, and any number of other aspects of the soils, which assist the structural and civil engineers in establishing design parameters for the design and construction of the building, infrastructure, and other aspects of the construction that depend on the soils for support.

Boring Logs - The boring logs, when plotted and analyzed, provide the design engineers with a three-dimensional picture of the subsurface conditions of a specific site and assist in accounting for the varying thickness of the layers. Borings on large projects are normally accomplished in a grid pattern. The nature of the soils and the testing results can then provide a geotechnical map of the soils conditions of a specific site. The soil layers are rarely the same size and dimension over a large area.

Commercial Terms - A document establishing the terms and conditions under which the work will progress and defining all ancillary services related to the actual work to be accomplished. Payment terms, the scope of the contractor's warranty obligation, the extent of the owner's representations and warranty concerning the plans, specifications, or the site conditions, procedures for changing the scope of the work and submitting claims, the prevailing law, and dispute resolution procedures are some of the many terms contained in the commercial terms. In addition, commercial terms may include items such as materials, fittings, and fixtures to be left on site for maintenance and repair, procedures for requesting and accomplishing warranty work, and post-project expectations of the owner, contractor, and occupants.

Construction Administration Services – Services that the architect provides during the construction phase to ensure the contractor builds in compliance with the plans and specifications. The architect conducts periodic site visits, reviews and responds to submittals from the contractor, attends project meetings with the contractor and owner, aids in problem-solving, reviews payment applications, and usually documents the progress of the work through periodic reports to the owner.

Construction Drawings ("Drawings" or "Plans") - The construction plans, normally reproductions (full size 24" x 36" when in paper format) of the illustrations that the architect and its consulting engineers create illustrating and describing the work for the general contractor and the trade subcontractors to accomplish, the materials to use in accomplishing the work, the intended final location of all elements of the construction project, dimensions for the layout of the construction, and the horizontal and vertical placement of building components.

Design Development Drawings ("DD Drawings") - The drawings that come in the middle phase of the design process, occurring after schematic design and before construction documents, containing significant, but not yet final information such as structural systems, building systems, dimensions, materials, and other details necessary to construct the project in compliance with applicable building codes and requirements.

General Conditions - The guts of a contract, usually establishing every requirement and procedure required. Typical contents include project-related definitions, applicable ordinances, laws and regulations, non-discrimination parameters, owner and contractor bonding and insurance requirements, project schedules, jobsite regulations, procedures for securing information, supervision, access to the work, a schedule of values and methods for submitting bills and securing payment, project close-out, change orders, termination and suspension of work, and many other critical elements of the project.

General Contractor – Contractor engaged by the owner or developer to manage the construction process. The General Contractor may self-perform some of the work but more commonly subcontracts all or a portion of the scope of work to subcontractors, vendors, and material suppliers, reserving only the overall coordination and management of the work required by the contract documents. Also known as the Prime Contractor.

Geotechnical Report - A document produced by the geotechnical engineer accounting for the underground investigation, testing, analysis, and findings of the field and laboratory personnel, often called the "Soils Report." The document identifies the results of the borings, the characteristics of the soils, and the anticipated ability of the soils to perform as the project requires. The report may also include recommendations for foundation bearing, point loading, preparation of soils for loading, requirements for supplementing the existing soils with other materials that will assist it its performance, and, where required, the need to excavate the native soils materials due to total incapacity to perform as required.

IFB (Information for Bidders) - An instructional document intended to provide all of the necessary information regarding the scheduling, processing, and administration of the bid process, including procedures for completing the bid proposals, informing potential bidders of procedures, procedures for acquiring answers to questions, scheduled project viewings, requirements for bonds, method to be used in selecting and awarding contracts, and all deadlines applicable to the bidding process. An IFB often accompanies an IFB (Invitation for Bid). The goal is to accomplish a fair bidding procedure, assuring that all bidding parties receive the same information in preparing their bids.

IFC (Issued for Construction) Drawings - The last stage of the design process, IFC drawings are complete, detailed, and coordinated construction drawings that the design professional (architect or engineer) issues with the intent that the contractors and its subcontractors can rely on them for project construction.

LEED (Leadership in Energy and Environmental Design) – The U.S Green Building Council's (USGBC) environmentally oriented building certification program, which aims to improve building and construction project performance across seven areas of environmental and human health. The rating system evaluates, in a holistic way, the design and use of integrative processes, location and transportation, sustainable building site development, water efficiency, energy efficiency, and materials and resources selection to assign a rating from Certified, Silver, Gold, to Platinum.

Letter of Credit ("LOC") - A letter from a bank or financial institution guaranteeing that payments will be made to the contractor, on time, in established amounts or percentages of the total, in intervals over the life of a construction project. If the buyer is unable to complete the project, the bank will cover the full or remaining balance of the construction costs to the limit of its letter of credit, typically only 10% of the contract price.

Notice to Proceed ("NTP") - Upon the execution of the contract, the owner issues the NTP to instruct the contractor that it is to commence work (often with a stipulation of a specific date to commence) and by reference, in accordance with specific documents, plans, specifications, etc. The notice normally requests a signature and response verifying the receipt of the notice and intention to comply with the requested start date.

Payment Bond - The payment bond provides security for payment to laborers, material suppliers, and subcontractors for labor and materials incorporated into the project in the event the contractor on the bond fails to pay for such labor and materials received for the project. In that public property is not subject to mechanic's liens, the payment bond may be the only protection claimants working on a public project have if they do not receive payment for the goods and services they provide to the project. Payment bonds are nearly universally required on public projects or those financed with public funding.

Performance Bond - A performance bond guarantees that, in the event of a contractor's default, the surety will complete the project or provide the funds necessary to finish the construction. Performance bonds are nearly universally required on public projects or those financed with public funding. From the local government's point of view, a contractor's default during construction will most likely result in delayed project completion and additional expenses for a completion contractor to finish the work. For this reason, it is common for public entities to require contractors to provide a bond from an independent surety company so that the local government can secure the completion of the work and/or recover damages it may sustain as a result of the contractor's default up to a stipulated limit, the penal sum of the bond.

Pre-bid Conference – Used for competitively bid procurements, the pre-bid meeting helps bidders gain a better understanding of the bid documents, scope of work, and any project requirements as they prepare and submit their bids. Bidders are permitted to ask questions and the owner typically provides written responses to those questions to all prospective bidders.

Prequalification - The procedure, often established in the IFB or RFP, whereby the owner can evaluate and acquire a reasonable sense of security that only those parties demonstrating a history of successful projects, skill, ability, financial resources. and integrity will submit bids.

Prime Contractor - *See*, General Contractor.

Request for Proposal ("RFP") or Quote ("RFQ") - The RFP is the procurement document that governmental entities often use. It is a resource for securing bids or proposals. The RFP includes specifications identifying the methodology for completing the work. Owners use RFPs to acquire architectural, quality control, waste disposal, landscape, and other professional services. The RFP usually leaves the means and methods up to the parties submitting the proposals. Other terms for an RFP are an invitation to bid ("IFB") or solicitation.

Scope of Work ("SOW") - An explanation or listing of construction obligations, work activities, and/or deliverables that the contractor is to provide. The SOW may be very detailed, including a project overview, specific objectives and deliverables, quantifiable goals, a schedule for all required tasks, including the overall expected project duration, any restrictions or limitations, and details about the timing of payments, change orders, and contract and legal requirements.

Schematic (or Conceptual) Drawings – The first step in the design process, schematic drawings are often freehand or simplistic drawings that designers such as architects, engineers, and interior designers use as a way of exploring initial ideas for project design. The goal of the conceptual design phase is to establish the scale, form, and basic relationships of different parts of the project – that is, how the project basically looks and operates.

Special Conditions - Document that identifies contractual requirements unique to the project, accounting for site conditions, weather, vendor requirements, and generally any terms or conditions out of the ordinary regarding the project.

Specifications ("Specs") - The specifications are written documents intended to supplement the information contained and illustrated in the plans. On smaller projects, the architect will include pages in the plans that contain project specifications. On larger projects, the specifications are normally prepared and presented on standard paper and compiled in one or more volumes or electronically in a similar format. Regardless of the format, each specification accounts for each element of the construction and instructs the contractor as to what materials, manufacturers, standards, and/or procedures are to be followed in the procurement and assembly of the materials of construction. Specifications can account for everything from the factory coating applied to nails and screws, to the mixture components used in the foundation concrete, to the paint used to stripe the parking lot. Specifications commonly follow a standard index developed by the Construction Specification Institute which divides the work into divisions by discipline. *See*, www.csinet.org/s_csi/docs/9400/9361.pdf.

Supplemental General Conditions - Document that identifies special conditions, bonding procedures, documentation required of the contractor, and any other procedural requirement not contained in the General Conditions. Often the Supplemental General Conditions will amplify, amend, or supersede provisions in the General Conditions.

Underwriting - The process of evaluating, defining, and pricing insurance, bonding, and reinsurance risks. The insurance entity or surety will look at many factors in assessing the past performance and financial condition of the contractor seeking coverage and will attempt to anticipate the future performance of that contractor. Often, an insurance entity may determine that because of the level of risk, assuming the responsibility for that risk may be too great a gamble for it and deny coverage.

Unit Prices - A method of estimating the cost of construction when either time or information is in limited supply. Often accurate construction plans may not be available, time may be a factor, and the parties must estimate certain elements of construction based on the cost per segment or cost per quantity to determine anticipated costs for the work. This process is usually more accurate when the amount of work is known.

C. Contract Administration Terms

Activity - A scheduling term describing the smallest work unit within a project; the basic building block of a project schedule.

As-Built Drawings ("Record Drawings") - Construction drawings updated and revised to show significant changes made during the construction process. May be completely revised or may be marked up in colored ink, or "posted" in the form of drawings, sketches, prints, or other data provided by the architect or contractor. As-Built Drawings are also used at the beginning of a project and in connection with the design process for remodels, renovations, or new construction over old construction sites.

Bar Chart - A type of scheduling methodology that graphically shows the various activities necessary to complete the work charted with reference to time. The horizontal axis of the chart is scaled to increments of time; the various activities are charted vertically. A horizontal line or bar depicts the duration of an activity beginning at the start date of the event and the ending date for event completion. The bar chart presents the status of all the activities required to complete the project simultaneously at any point in time.

Bill of Quantities ("BOQ") – Document in which materials, parts, and labor are itemized. The BOQ details the terms and conditions of the construction contract and itemizes all work to enable a contractor to price the work for which they are bidding. The owner typically issues the BOQ to bidders for them to prepare a price. The BOQ assists bidders in the calculation of construction costs for the bid as it allows for all bidding contractors to price the same quantities.

Building Code - The legal requirements of the prevailing governmental authority (usually a state or local government) identifying the minimum acceptable requirements for all types of construction.

Building Permit - The governing governmental authority's written document permitting construction to begin on a specific project in accordance with drawings and specifications that the governmental authority approved.

Bulletin - A document issued to memorialize clarifications or changes to the construction documents. The owner uses the bulletin process to formally issue changes to the construction documents, drawings, and specifications after the contract is in place.

Change Estimate ("CE") - A forecast of construction cost for a particular new or changed item of work based on a detailed analysis of materials and labor necessary to construct that item of work.

Change Order ("CO") - A written order to the contractor that the owner and/or architect has signed, issued after contract execution, authorizing a change in the work and/or an adjustment in the contract sum or contract time. The contractor typically signs a change order to memorialize its consent to the change. A contractor may sign the change order but include a reservation or exclusion of claims. Most contracts state that the parties can only modify the contract by written change order.

Change Order Request ("COR") or Proposed Change Order ("PCO") - The contractor's request to the owner for approval to adjust the construction contract's value and/or duration due to changes in the scope of work. This contractor-generated document describes a change in the scope of work, including a detailed description, drawings, and specifications, and a request for changes to costs or time, as necessary, to inform the owner of the nature of the requested change to the contract.

Changes to the Work - Changes that the owner or architect ordered after contract execution consisting of additions, deletions, or other revisions within the general scope of the work, the contract sum, and the contract time. Most contracts require a written, executed change order for all changes in the work, except those of a minor nature not involving an adjustment to the contract sum or the contract time.

Computer-Aided Design ("CAD") - Software that engineers, architects, designers, subcontractors, and/or construction managers use to create designs. These designs are precise drawings or illustrations of plans and can be either two-dimensional or three-dimensional. Construction drawings are often referred to using the commercially available software, AutoCad®, or simply, as CAD drawings.

Construction Change Directive ("CCD") - A technique that owners, architects, or construction managers use on some projects to accomplish minor changes within the general scope of the contract without the contractor's agreement. The owner, architect, or construction manager issues a written order, directing a change to the work prior to agreement on the adjustment, if any, to the contract sum or time. The contractor performs the work and the contract dictates the adjustment, if any, to the contract sum or time.

Construction Estimate - Cost estimate for the completion of the work which includes all components of the cost of the work, as well as the contractor or construction manager's fee or markup for the project.

Cost Item – A specific item which, when aggregated with other items necessary to perform the work, aggregates to the cost of the work. Typically itemized on a Schedule of Values, cost items can be the entire cost of specific scopes, such as excavating, concrete, fireproofing, plumbing, or the more discrete items that comprise the various scopes, such as rental earthmoving equipment, concrete finisher field labor, a particular material consumed in the project, fuel, rented items, overhead, etc.

Critical Path - The shortest path in a CPM schedule; the order of events (each of a particular duration) that results in the least amount of time required to complete a project. Activities on the critical path have no slack or "float" time.

Critical Path Method ("CPM") Schedule - A planning, schedule, and control technique that contractors use on construction projects to break down into individual activities all the actions necessary to construct a project, defining the duration of each activity, the relative timing of each activity, and then interconnecting all the activities. It permits the determination of the timing of and relative significance of each event and establishes the optimum sequence and duration of operations. The contractor can update the CPM to account for actual progress, to adjust for changes in the work or the sequencing of the work, and to determine responsibility for delays.

Daily Reports – A report that the contractor prepares daily to reflect activity on the project site, including the weather conditions, number and type of workers, materials delivered, work performed, visitors to the site, and any issues encountered or areas of concern.

Detail – An element of construction drawings that provides more comprehensive design information for a particular feature, including more precise information than drawings intended to portray more expansive scopes of work such as overall site plans, floor plans, and elevations. Drawings that present more expansive, less detailed perspectives utilize symbols and notations to refer the reader to detail sheets that effectively enlarge specific plan elements to communicate more enhanced design information and requirements. Details can address unique elements of the project or communicate information about typical scenarios applicable anywhere the detailed condition occurs.

Error and Omission – Mistake, conflict, or omission of design detail in construction drawings. An error and omission frequently occurs as a conflict between the architectural drawings (which depict how the finished work should look) and a detail drawing created for a specific discipline (*i.e.*, structural drawing). An error and omission may also occur when there is an issue of constructability of the design.

Extra or Extra Work – An additional construction item that is not included in the original scope of the contract. Extras usually entail an item of work involving additional costs.

Field Order or Field Work Order – A written order that the architect issues during contract performance effecting a minor change in the work not involving an adjustment to the contract sum or contract time.

Final Inspection - The final inspection and construction closeout process consists of site walkthroughs that the architect conducts verifying that the contract has completed everything in accordance with the contract documents. Once confirmed, the building is ready for its intended use or occupancy.

Float - A scheduling term describing extra or slack time associated with an activity or multiple activities.

Fragnet - A contemporaneous, fragmentary scheduling network that graphically identifies the sequencing of all critical and non-critical new activities and/or activity revisions arising from a compensable or excusable delay. A fragnet includes logic ties to all affected existing activities noted on the schedule isolates and quantifies a time impact of a specific issue, determines and demonstrates any such specific delay in relation to past and/or other current delays, and provides a method for incorporating all contract adjustments to the contract time into an update of the approved schedule.

Gantt Charts - A Gantt chart is a project management tool that graphically represents activity against time, useful to assist project professionals plan, monitor, and schedule projects of all sizes.

General Conditions - The part of the contract document that sets forth many of the rights, responsibilities, and relationships of the parties involved in the contract. The parties to a construction project also use the term "general conditions" to refer to the variable indirect costs associated with performing the work, i.e., the costs of supervision, the cost of a jobsite trailer, temporary electricity, jobsite office supplies, water, ice, small tools, etc.

Log - A listing of items with relevant dates such as date of submission, approval, rejection, or other disposition used to manage the work. Log examples: Submittal Log, Change Order Log, Requests For Information Log, etc. See Exhibit 39 (Submittal Log), Exhibit 40 (Change Order Log), and Exhibit 41 (RFI Log).

Means and Methods - Colloquial reference to the contractor's right (usually reserved in the contract) to perform the work using whatever techniques and sequencing that it chooses. If the owner or architect requires the contractor to perform the work in a certain way and contrary to or in addition to its typical means and methods, the owner may be liable for any increased cost over the contractor's estimated cost to perform as extra work.

Modification ("Mod") – *See*, Change Order.

"Or Equal" - A product, material, or piece of equipment offered in place of a specified product, material, or piece of equipment.

Predecessor Activity - A discrete schedule activity that the contractor or owner must complete before the contractor can start a later or successor activity.

Proposed Change Order ("PCO") - A proposal that a contractor or subcontractor submits as to the cost and/or time estimated to perform a proposed new item of work. Another term for PCO is a request for change order ("RCO").

Punch List - A list made near the end of construction identifying items that the contractor or a subcontractor needs to furnish or work to correct or complete in order to complete the project. Creation of the punch list or satisfaction of the items on the punch list may be a condition to achieve substantial completion or final acceptance or to receive final payment. The contract may designate one party to be the drafter of the list, otherwise, typically the architect performs this duty.

Quality Assurance/Quality Control ("QA/QC") - Quality Assurance is a system of procedures for selecting the levels of quality desired for a project to perform the functions intended and for assuring that the contractor and its subcontractors meet these levels. Quality Control is a system of procedures and standards by which a contractor, manufacturer, or material supplier monitors the properties of the finished work.

Record Drawings - *See*, As-built Drawings.

Reports - Many documents generated on a construction project are labeled "Report," including Daily Report (contractor-prepared to reflect the weather conditions, number of workers, materials delivered, and work performed); Inspection Report (architect- or inspector-created to reflect the results of a particular inspection); QA/QC Report (contractor-prepared to demonstrate what was done to monitor and ensure the quality of construction); Progress Report (contractor-prepared for the owner on a monthly or other periodic basis to report on the overall project status); and Job Cost Report (accounting summary of all direct costs incurred on the project as of a specific date).

Request for Information ("RFI") - A written request issued either in connection with the bid process or after contract award during construction from a contractor to the owner or architect for clarification or information about the contract documents.

Shop Drawing - Drawings that trade contractors, suppliers, and manufacturers of materials and equipment furnish in order to provide the details for the construction, fabrication, or installation of the components of the work, that trade contractor, supplier, or manufacturer is providing. The owner or architect typically approves shop drawings before work commences.

Sole Source - A specific manufacturer, brand, model, item, or type of material or equipment that the specifications require the contractor to furnish. Sometimes, the specifications will identify a specific manufacturer, brand, model, item, or type of material or equipment but add "or equivalent," eliminating the sole source requirement.

Submittal - A sample, manufacturer's data, shop drawing, or other item that the contractor or subcontractor submits to the owner or architect for approval and subsequent incorporation into the work.

Takeoff - A listing of the type and quantity of the materials necessary to execute the work. The materials takeoff is the first step in the estimating process, which involves determining the total cost of the materials, labor, and equipment that will form the proposal or bid to perform the work.

Value Engineering - Analysis of the design and functions of various components and materials to identify alternative materials, products, or methods of performing the work at a reduced cost with no or a minimal, acceptable reduction in design, quality, or performance.

Warranty - Assurance that the providing party furnished the work, material, and equipment under warranty and will perform as promised or pursuant to the requirement of the contract for a defined period. Also, the actual document that sets forth the assurance and describes what actions are needed to call on the warranty and satisfy it.

Window of Time Analysis - Measures labor productivity losses on a project by comparing labor productivity achieved during a period when work activities are subject to disruptive or delaying events or conditions compared to productivity during a period with no interruptions.

Work - Usually a defined term in the contract. Generally, it includes the entire scope of the work the contractor is to perform at the construction project site including labor, materials, equipment, transportation, and such other facilities as are necessary to fulfill all the obligations under the contract.

Work Authorization or Extra Work Authorization ("EWA") - The owner's or architect's written order directing the contractor's performance of a specified scope of work.

Work Order or Extra Work Order ("EWO") - See, EWA.

D. Payment Related Terms

Application for Payment - A contractor's or subcontractor's formal written request for payment for work completed on a contract and, if allowed under the contract, materials stored on the jobsite or in a warehouse. An Application for Payment is essentially the contractor's invoice for work performed during a specific period of time, typically monthly.

Back Charges - Charges for work performed or costs incurred by one party that another party should have performed or incurred. Disputed back charges are accounted for as a claim.

Backlog - The amount of revenue that a contractor expects to realize from work it has yet to perform on uncompleted contracts, including new contractual agreements on which work has not begun.

Budget (Construction Budget) - An itemized summary of estimated or intended expenditures for a given period or the total sum of money allocated for a specific project.

Certificate of Payment - An architect's or other design professional's statement, based on professional judgment, notifying the owner of the amount due to a contractor for work completed and/or the delivery or storage of building materials to be incorporated into the project.

Certified Payrolls - A contractor's or subcontractor's written representations as to the actual total costs of labor expended in the completion of a construction project. Certified payroll records often include employee names, wage rates, wages paid, wage deductions, and a representation under oath that the contractor has paid all amounts included.

Claims/Equitable Adjustments - Disputes as to amounts more than the original contract price that a contractor tries to collect, such as a disputed change order. A claim may result from unanticipated additional costs that the contractor incurs for work or issues impacting construction that are not part of the existing contract and are not reasonably included as part of the existing contract.

Contract Item ("Pay Item") - An element of work, specifically described in a contract, for which the contract provides either a unit or lump sum price.

Consent of Surety - A written document obtained from the surety confirming notice to the surety when a bonded contract is changed. A Consent of Surety also applies to the surety's consent for payment to the bond principal. A Consent of Surety obtains the surety's acknowledgement that a bond given in connection with the original contract or subsequent modification continues in effect even after the change(s) or payment(s) are made.

Contract Overrun/Underrun - The amount by which the original contract price, as adjusted by change orders, differs from the total cost of a project at completion. If the total cost of the project at completion exceeds the original contract price, there is a Contract Overrun. If the total cost of the project at completion is less than the original contract price, there is a Contract Underrun.

Costs to Complete - An estimate of the costs required to complete an ongoing project. See Estimated Costs to Complete.

Direct Costs (or Hard Costs) - Costs including material, labor, equipment, and subcontracting costs that are clearly related to the project and are consumed in the physical construction of the project.

Draw - The amount of progress billings on a contract that is currently available to a contractor under a contract with a fixed payment schedule.

Equipment and Tools - A cost item where the contractor generally allocates equipment based on a use rate, such as dollars per hour of use. A contractor normally charges small tools to a contract as they are consumed.

Estimate - The amount of labor, materials, and other costs that a contractor anticipates for a project, as summarized in the contractor's bid proposal for the project.

Estimated Costs to Complete - The anticipated additional cost of materials, labor, and other items required to complete a project at a scheduled time.

Extras - Additional work, not included in the original plan, that the owner or architect requests from a contractor that the contractor will bill separately and will not alter the original contract.

Front-end Loading - A common practice that contractors use to assist them in the financing and cash flow of their projects. It is a method of unbalanced bidding reflected in a contractor's Schedule of Values and used to accelerate the collection of cash at the beginning of a project.

General Condition Items - A popular term used to describe items that are part of the project's overhead costs of construction (for example, the premium for a performance bond or the monthly lease cost of the contractor's construction trailer).

Hard Costs - *See*, Direct Costs.

Incentives - A bonus paid to a contractor for completing the project before the scheduled completion date. The contract identifies incentives. They are most frequently used when tied to the date a tenant is willing to move in upon partial or full completion of a project.

Indirect Costs ("Soft Costs") - Costs incurred to construct a project which are not consumed in the physical project, including indirect labor, contract supervision, tools and equipment, supplies, inspection, insurance, repairs, and maintenance. Indirect/soft costs are typically included in general conditions.

Line Items - The elements, systems, items, or other subdivisions of the Work, with a value attached to each, the total of which equals the contract sum and often the components of the Schedule of Values. the Continuation Sheets of Application and Certificate for Payment AIA Documents. See Exhibit 9 for an example of a pay application and continuation sheet.

Overbillings (also known as "Billings in Excess of Cost and Profit") - The dollar amount of work that the contractor has billed on a project in excess of what the contractor has actually completed or earned. If the owner pays these overbillings, then the contractor may get so far ahead in billings on a project that it may need to use cash from another source to finish the project.

Precontract Costs - Costs incurred before the contract is awarded, for example, engineering, architectural, or mobilization costs.

Progress Billings - Amounts that the contractor bills periodically in accordance with the provisions of a contract based on the percentage of progress to date under the contract. See also Application for Payment.

Progress Payments - Amounts that an owner pays in accordance with the provisions of a contract based on approved progress as of that date.

Retainage - The amount of money that the owner withholds or retains from earned progress payments due to the contractor until project completion, typically established in the contract as a percentage (most commonly 5% or 10%). The contractor, in turn, retains a portion of the payment due to subcontractors. The purpose of retainage is to provide the owner security for costs incurred to repair defective work, to settle third-party claims that are the contractor's responsibility, and to ensure that work is completed in accordance with the contract. Statutes often establish limitations on the amount of retainage on public projects.

Retention – See Retainage.

Schedule of Values (or Cost Breakdown) - A listing of elements, systems, items, or other subdivisions of the work, usually in the form of a table, establishing a value for each, the total of which equals the contract sum. Contractor-prepared and typically owner-approved, a contractor attaches the Schedule of Values to its periodic payment applications submitted as part of the payment process on construction projects. The Schedule of Values allows the parties to keep track of the project's progress, including the budget and the percentage of completion. Commonly presented on the Continuation Sheets of Application and Certificate for Payment. See Exhibit 9. Schedule of Values often follows the Construction Specification Institute's divisions by discipline. *See*, Exhibit 2 and www.csinet.org/s_csi/docs/9400/9361.pdf.

Soft Costs - *See*, Indirect Costs

Stored Materials - Materials intended for use in the completion of a construction contract not yet incorporated into the project. The contractor may store these materials on the construction site or at another location.

Unapproved Change Orders - A payment request when the contractor has incurred costs for changes in or additional work performed after the execution of the contract that the owner has not yet approved as to either scope or price.

Underbillings (also known as "Costs in Excess of Billings and Profit") - Costs that a contractor has incurred on a project that exceed amounts billed to date to the owner. Concerns arise when underbillings are the result of disputes or unapproved change orders.

E. Accounting Terms

Accrual Basis of Accounting - The method of accounting whereby the contractor identifies revenues and expenses with the specific periods of time, such as a month or year, and records those revenues and expenses as incurred, along with acquired assets, without regard to the date of receipt or payment of cash.

Cash Basis of Accounting - A basis of keeping accounts whereby the contractor records revenue and expense on its books of account when received and paid, respectively, without regard to the period to which they apply.

Completed Contract Basis of Accounting - An accounting method that recognizes revenue upon completion of the project. More conservative than the percentage of completion method, it is acceptable if the contractor cannot develop reasonable estimates of total project cost and each period's progress. Although the contractor might receive cash from interim billings, it postpones recognizing revenue to the period in which the contract is substantially complete.

Depreciation Expense - That portion of the cost or other basis of a fixed asset or fixed asset group charged against the operations of an accounting period.

Extended General Conditions - Additional indirect costs associated with a specific project as a result of the extension of the project completion date for reasons other than the contractor's fault.

Extended Overhead - Home or field office overhead incurred as a result of the extension of the project completion date for reasons other than the contractor's fault. Under certain conditions, extended overhead can be a compensable item of damage and in certain cases it is subject to calculation based upon the *Eichleay* formula. *See*, Eichleay Formula.

Field Office Overhead – That portion of contractor business costs necessary to operate the contractor that is specifically related to the project but do not constitute the "work" of the project. Not to be confused with home office overhead.

Furniture, Fixtures & Equipment ("FF&E") - Assets the accounting industry classifies as personal property rather than real property. A contractor may provide FF&E as a part of its scope of work, or the owner may control and schedule the FF&E, which then will require the contractor's scheduling and coordination to prepare the project for occupancy and normal daily operations for which the project is intended.

FF&E most commonly appears in hotel, retail store, and office construction. Also, FF&E can be an abbreviation associated with interior design and planning of retail stores or office facilities.

Generally Accepted Accounting Principles ("GAAP") - The conventions, rules, and procedures that define accepted accounting practices at a particular time and provide a standard by which auditors form their professional opinions about financial presentations. GAAP includes not only broad guidelines of general application but also detailed practices and procedures.

Home Office Overhead – That portion of contractor business costs necessary to operate the business entity that is not specifically related to the project work. Not to be confused with field office overhead.

Idle Equipment Time - The period a machine, equipment, or asset is waiting to do its task. As it is yet to complete the assigned task, the equipment is not available for use for any other project – it is essentially rendered idle in waiting.

Job Costing - A cost accounting method that accumulates the costs of doing a separately identifiable portion of the project. The total cost of the project includes raw material, labor, and other costs, which are directly traceable to that project and, usually, a share of the non-traceable or indirect production costs.

Margin - Gross profit; the excess of the payments that the contractor receives from the owner over the costs of performing the work.

Markup - The amount added to an established selling price to determine a new and higher selling price, the percentage of markup is based on the previously established selling price, or the amount established in the contract. Typically, when pricing a change order, general contractors add a markup to their subcontractor's price.

MCAA Factors (Mechanical Contractors Association of America) - Labor-related factors that the MCAA has developed to identify the major causes of labor productivity loss that contractors involved in the heating, air conditioning, refrigeration, plumbing, piping, and mechanical services experience. Contractors use the MCAA factors not only to estimate the adverse effects of productivity factors on labor productivity levels but also to measure the extent to which a contractor has incurred damages as a result of estimated losses of labor productivities encountered over the course of a project.

Notes to Financial Statements - A medium for imparting additional information, usually a narrative, indexed to a particular item reported in a financial statement. Notes are required wherever the title customarily attached to a monetary item is inadequate for an informed understanding of the financial statement.

Operating Cycle - The elapsed time between the purchase of inventory items (raw materials or merchandise) and their conversion into cash. The typical succession of transactions involved is (a) the purchase, offset by accounts payable; (b) the liquidation of the payables; (c) the manufacturing operation with its added costs, of the warehousing in the case of merchandise; (d) the sale of the finished product or merchandise; and (e) the liquidation of the amount receivable from the customer. A normal operating cycle is generally regarded as one of the determinants of the character of items classified as current assets. It is also important in establishing working capital requirements. The operating cycle can also refer to the time it takes for a business to receive payment for goods and/or services performed and/or sold.

Overhead - Any cost of doing business other than a direct cost of an output of a product or service.

Overrun - Time or expenses beyond or above an expected or allowed duration or cost. An instance of something exceeding an expected or allowed time or cost.

Percentage of Completion Method of Accounting - A method for allocating revenues and costs (with related net income or loss) to projects in proportion to completion, which method is commonly on long-term contracts, such as construction projects, where the payments are based on a pro-rata share of progress, usually measured by costs incurred or engineering estimates.

Qualified Opinion - An auditor's exception to one or more specified items in the financial statements, including an explanation of the reason for the qualification.

Time Related Overhead ("TRO") - Overhead costs, including field and home office overhead, that are in proportion to the time required to complete the work.

Work in Progress ("WIP") - An accounting concept meaning the value of the work completed but not yet invoiced. WIP can be important to understand the current profitability of a project, especially if the percent completion of a line item is ahead of or lagging the estimated number of labor hours included in the budget for that line item. WIP reports can also help manage cash flow since they provide a sense of what billings are likely to be at the end of the month, which is vital for keeping a gauge on financial health.

Working Capital - Capital in current use in the operation of a business: the excess of current assets over current liabilities; net current assets.

F. Insurance and Surety Terms

Additional Insured - Anyone other than the insurance policyholder, which the insurance policy covers.

Additional Insured Endorsement - An addendum to an insurance policy that alters the named insured section of the policy to add additional insureds to the policy and extend coverage under the policy to those additional insureds. The endorsement will also detail the extent and limits of coverage provided for the additional insureds.

Bond Penalty - The monetary amount for which the surety may be liable under the bond. The amount appears on the face of the bond and is otherwise referred to as the bond penal sum.

Bonding Capacity - Refers to the ability of a contractor to obtain surety bonds. It may refer to both the maximum aggregate dollar amount of bonds that a contractor can obtain from a surety at any given time and/or the highest individual dollar amount of an individual bond that a contractor can obtain from its surety during that same time.

Builder's Risk Insurance - Insurance coverage on a construction project during construction, including extended coverage that the contractor or the owner may add to the contract for the owner's protection. Builder's Risk provides insurance against loss to the buildings or structures during construction.

Certificate of Insurance ("COI") - A document that the insurance company issues detailing the insurance coverages and limits of those coverages that the insurance company is providing to the insured.

Commercial General Liability ("CGL") - Insurance policy covering a variety of general liability exposures, including Premises and Operations (OL&T or M&C), Completed Operations, Products Liability, and Owner's and Contractor's Protective coverage. The CGL policy may also include Contractual Liability and Broad Form coverages. "CGL" now means commercial general liability forms and has replaced the earlier "comprehensive" general liability forms.

Contractor Controlled Insurance Program ("CCIP") - An insurance policy that the general contractor purchases, which consolidates insurance coverage for all parties on a construction project into one blanket policy. The program generally provides CGL insurance, excess liability insurance, and/or workers' compensation insurance for all enrolled participants working on the specific construction project under a single policy.

Construction Wrap Insurance - A single umbrella policy issued to provide general liability insurance coverage for the owner, general contractor, and subcontractors on a specific construction project. There are two types of wrap insurance – Owner Controlled Insurance Programs (OCIP and CCIP). The primary difference between the two is the party that purchases the policy, either the owner (OCIP) or the general contractor (CCIP).

Environmental Remediation Liability - The amount of liability resulting from or arising out of the duty to remediate any hazardous substances that are or might be present or are threatened to be released from real property or a facility and/or natural resource damages associated with the presence or threatened release of hazardous substances in the environment.

Funds Control - Process in which an independent third party (the functional equivalent of an escrow agent) receives contract proceeds on behalf of the contractor and disburses those contract proceeds to subcontractors and/or suppliers on a specific construction project. Sureties and lenders are the entities that may require funds control to ensure that the contractor uses the contract proceeds from a specific construction project to pay for labor and/or material supplied to and incorporated into that project.

Owner-Controlled Insurance Programs ("OCIP") - A type of wrap-up, an increasingly popular insurance procurement option, that bundles (or wraps up) coverage for multiple insureds into one consolidated program that the owner administers. See Construction Wrap Insurance.

Performance Obligations - A promise to perform or deliver a specific product or service pursuant to a contract or bond.

Professional Liability Insurance - Insurance that design professionals and construction managers obtain that protects them from the owner's claims of the insured's errors and omissions or negligent acts. Often referred to as Errors and Omissions (E&O) insurance.

Takeover Agreement - An agreement between the surety and the owner and sometimes the defaulted contractor outlining how the surety will perform under the performance bond to complete the remaining scope of work under the contract.

Tender - Process by which the surety, following the default termination of its principal, obtains bids, identifies a qualified completion contractor, and submits the successful bidder to the owner for completion of the work with whom the owner will enter a new contract. If the bid for completion exceeds the remaining contract funds, the surety will generally tender funds to make up the difference between the remaining funds and the new bid. The new contractor provides bonds, and the owner releases the surety from the surety's obligation to complete although the owner may reserve other claims it might have against the surety such as delay damages resulting from the bonded contractor's default.

Workers' Compensation Insurance - Insurance providing coverage for worker's injuries or death occurring on a construction project. The workers' compensation insurance carrier charges premiums based on the insured's payroll, multiplying the labor dollars by a rate to determine the total premium.

G. Technical Terms

Aggregate - A granular material usually composed of rock, gravel, or sand for an engineered purpose. Common uses of aggregate include use as base material on which to build roads or other structures, use as a component of concrete or asphalt mixed in with cement or bitumen to bind the mix together, or as fill to allow for improved water drainage and to prevent erosion.

American Society of Mechanical Engineers ("ASME") - A professional organization that maintains a body of codes and standards that are commonly relied upon in project specifications to establish performance requirements for materials, products, and systems for project construction. For example, rather than dictating the use of a specific product, brand, or manufacturer, project specifications may instead require that specified components and services meet referenced ASME standards.

ASTM (ASTM International, formerly the American Society for Testing and Materials) - An international standards organization that maintains a body of codes and standards that design professionals commonly rely upon in project specifications to establish performance requirements for materials, products, and systems for project construction. For example, rather than dictating the use of a specific product, brand, or manufacturer, project specifications may instead require that specified components and services meet referenced ASTM standards.

Backfilling - The process of filling in an excavated area that has been dug out for construction purposes to restore or replace the excavated material and bring the area back to a planned grade level. Backfill can consist of restoring the originally removed material or replacing the original material with new material designed to suit the needs of the project.

Backing - Added support or bracing built into a structure to bear or distribute the weight of other elements of a project. For example, the design may require the installation of backing within a wall to support finish elements such as handrails or shelving that will attach to the backing through the wall, or it could refer to a layer of material installed underneath flooring to stabilize or insulate the finish flooring.

Ballast - A term with multiple uses that generally describes a heavy or stabilizing material. In reference to aggregate material, it describes large angular rock that forms a stable water-draining base for structures such as railroad ties. In reference to temporary site signage and enclosures, it describes heavy support material such as concrete blocks that form a solid temporary foundation. Ballast also describes temporary means of holding or weighing down lighter materials to prevent displacement by wind or other disturbance, or an electrical component that stabilizes the flow of energy through an electrical fixture.

Balustrade - Balusters are the vertical posts of a handrail, low wall, or low fencing/enclosure system. Balustrade refers to a system or row of such balusters, including a top or cap rail, and is often used for decorative architectural railing and enclosure systems.

Building Envelope (or Building Shell) - The structure and systems that separate a building's interior and exterior, separating climate-controlled and conditioned space from unconditioned space and exposure to the elements. The building envelope can consist of the structural frame, insulation, and weather barriers including windows, doors, roofing, and exterior finishes.

Caisson - A hollow watertight structure that is submerged in a body of water such as a river to create an open-air environment for construction activity below water level. A caisson can be constructed above ground and submerged into place or constructed in place and pumped out for further foundation work. Caissons commonly feature an open top, open to the air above water level, but can also be fully enclosed and pressurized below water level. Caissons are employed in the construction of projects that require underwater foundations, such as bridges and piers.

Cantilever - A structure that is supported on only one end (or at a midpoint), with portions of the structure extending out into unsupported space. As an example, a shade structure or balcony that extends into horizontal space without the aid of vertical supports at its perimeter is said to be cantilevered. In bridge construction, a span that visually appears to be supported on both ends may consist of multiple balanced cantilevers connected end to end. Consider for example the letter 'T' as a visual representation of a balanced cantilever with unsupported ends projecting into horizontal space, with a series of T's, 'TTTTT', forming a representation of a cantilever bridge.

Conduit - Tubing or piping providing a determined route for other flexible material to travel through, most commonly electrical wiring. Conduit can protect its contents from damage or exposure to the elements, protect other components from exposure to its contents, allow for repair and replacement of its contents without destructive processes, and increase flexibility in the planning and sequencing of construction activities.

Curtain Wall - A lightweight non-structural outer shell of a building that provides for weather protection and exterior finish aesthetics, such as the glass shell of a commercial or public building. As curtain walls are not load-bearing, they feature fewer and smaller structural members than load-bearing window walls, allowing for more extensive glazing and increased light infiltration.

Feasibility Review – Evaluation of a project's probable success, usually by the project owner or investors, taking into account the proposed schedule, costs, operational or legal challenges, and projected return on investment.

Flashing - Material used to direct and control the flow of water over different elements of a structure to prevent water penetration into the structure. Where different elements of a structure intersect, such as walls, doors, windows, roofing, and other roof and wall penetrations, rain and other elements have an increased likelihood of seeping into the building. Flashing generally consists of thin, waterproof, corrosion-resistant materials that can be layered or lapped to guide water away from such penetrations.

Geographic Information Systems ("GIS") - Computer-based tools used to store, visualize, analyze, and interpret geographic data. Geographic data (also called spatial, or geospatial data) identifies the geographic location of features. Map applications used on smart phones or tables rely on GIS to maintain updated maps and to provide navigation. Overlaying construction plans on a base map will show where everything is not only within the structure under construction but also in the context of the asset's physical location.

Girder - Larger, horizontal, primary structural support beams designed to bear heavy weight loads and distribute those weight loads within a structure. Girders are generally bigger and less flexible than other beams and often support multiple smaller beams that transfer load to the girder. Usually made of steel in large buildings or reinforced concrete for bridges, girders can be wood or other materials for smaller, lighter applications.

I-beam - I-beam describes the shape and design of a common type of beam as seen at a cross-section, such that if one were to look at the end of an I-beam, or cut it in two, the section would appear like the shape of the letter 'I'. Most commonly constructed of steel or reinforced concrete, the 'I' shape of the beam allows it to weigh much less than a solid beam would, while still maintaining great strength and rigidity. 'H' beams are similar in shape but generally thicker and heavier. Other beam shapes include 'U', 'L', and 'T' profiles along with a hollow tube and solid bar or plate shapes.

Interior Finish - Generally refers to most surfaces that are visible after the completion of construction; surfaces that overlay a project's structural components for utility and visual appeal. Interior finishes can include such elements as paint, ceiling tile, flooring, casework, trim, countertops, HVAC grilles and registers, outlet covers, light fixtures, toilets, sinks, and other hardware.

Laser Technology - The construction industry uses laser technology for purposes of leveling, aligning, plumbing, squaring, and other traditional manual processes. Lasers or laser levels uses include installing sewer pipe, site grading, grades for drainage, masonry, ceiling tiles, chair railings, and receptacles for power, just to name a few.

Mechanical, Electrical, and Plumbing ("MEP") - A common grouping of the largely non-structural disciplines that support a conditioned, functioning, and habitable building. Most frequently "MEP," it can also be "MPE," indicative of a commonly preferred sequence of construction wherein the project calls for the plumbing trade contractor to install larger elements such as ductwork before the electrical trade contractor installs smaller or more flexible elements like electrical lines to prevent and navigate pathing conflicts.

Parapet - Commonly shorter walls found on the top level of a structure that extend up beyond the level of a flat roof or elevated bridgeway but do not support another level, roof, or ceiling above the parapet wall. They serve as a barrier against potential falls and as an architectural feature obscuring the view of unsightly roofing and rooftop equipment from lower levels.

Plan Check – Review of plans, drawings, and documents for compliance with the building codes by the Building Code Official or AHJ (Authority Having Jurisdiction).

Precast - Concrete components that are fabricated prior to installation, rather than poured in place with wet concrete at their intended location. Precast has a large variety of applications such as concrete wall panels to be hoisted into position, concrete girders and beams often visible in bridge work and parking structures, and drainage structures used for storm water management.

Rough-In - Refers to the stage of construction that generally follows structural work and precedes finish work (see "Interior Finish"). In vertical construction such as buildings for example, rough-in work would generally follow foundation and structural construction, after which mechanical, plumbing, high and low voltage electrical, and fire protection systems would be "roughed-in" and routed through the structure.

Following inspections to ensure the integrity of the systems and any effect on the structure, materials such as drywall and ceiling tile could then cover the rough-in work.

H. Legal Terms

Armed Services Board of Contract Appeals ("ASBCA") - Authorized under the Contract Disputes Act, the ASBCA is a neutral, independent forum whose primary function is to hear and decide post-award contract disputes between government contractors and certain government agencies, including the Department of Defense, the Corps of Engineers, National Aeronautics and Space Administration, and the Central Intelligence Agency. The ASBCA's decisions provide precedential authority for contracting officers and government contractors to complete their contracts.

Assignment - The transfer to another person the contract rights of a party to the contract. In the construction context, contractors may assign to a bank, factor, or other creditor the right to receive contract funds. However, most contracts permit assignment only with the consent of the other party to the contract. Frequently, the owner includes a provision in the contract that allows it to assume subcontracts by assignment upon termination of a general contract.

Affirmative Claims - Usually a written demand for recovery of costs, time, or other compensatory damages arising out of the contract's performance.

Beneficial Occupancy - Use of a project or portion of a project for the purpose intended.

CBCA (Civilian Board of Contract Appeals) - An independent tribunal housed within the General Services Administration to hear and decide Contract Disputes Act disputes between government contractors and civilian executive branch agencies (except for the Department of Defense, National Aeronautics and Space Administration, the United States Postal Service, the Postal Regulatory Commission, and the Tennessee Valley Authority).

Condition precedent - An act or event that must happen or be performed before a right dependent upon it accrues. An example in the payment context is where the contractor must perform the work and submit a fully completed and acceptable payment application before its right to receive payment accrues.

Contract Disputes Act ("CDA") - A federal statute (41 U.S.C. §7101, et seq.) creating a comprehensive system for resolving claims and disputes between a contractor and a procuring federal agency arising from the procurement or performance of contracts to procure property, services, construction, alteration, repair, or maintenance of real property.

Design Specification - Specifications that set forth precise measurements, tolerances, materials, in-process and finished product tests, quality control measures, inspection requirements, and other specific information about how the contractor is to build the project or a portion of the project. The owner is responsible for the correctness and adequacy of the design and engineering included in the design specification. Compare with Performance Specification.

Differing Site Condition ("DSC") - An unanticipated physical condition at the site that differs materially from those set forth in the contract or ordinarily encountered in work of the same nature. In federal construction contracts and many other governmental and private contracts, DSCs are Type I, subsurface or latent physical conditions at a construction site that differ materially from the conditions indicated in the contract documents; or Type II, unknown physical conditions at the site, of an unusual nature, that differ materially from conditions ordinarily encountered and generally recognized as inherent in work of the kind provided for in the contract. Most construction contracts set forth provisions for the treatment, notice requirement, and compensation for DSCs encountered.

***Eichleay* Formula** - A method of calculating unabsorbed home office overhead damages in construction delay cases based on the decision in *Eichleay Corp.*, ASBCA 5183, 60-2 BCA ¶ 2688. In cases where the contractor is entitled to compensation for unabsorbed home office overhead, the *Eichleay* formula computes the daily amount of unabsorbed home office overhead allocable to the contract based upon the ratio of billings of the subject contract to total firm billings, multiplied by the total overhead during the contract period, divided by the actual days of performance. That daily amount is then multiplied by the number of days the contractor was delayed to generate the amount of recoverable home office overhead resulting from the government's delay.

Escalation Clause - A contract provision that provides for adjustments of the price of specific items as conditions change. For example, a provision that requires wage rates based on wage levels included in collective bargaining agreements with labor unions will allow for escalation if the union wage rates increase. Escalation clauses can also apply to materials and equipment.

Excess Costs of Reprocurement - Costs that the owner incurs exceeding the contract price of a contract that it has terminated for cause or that the contractor has abandoned. The owner must mitigate its losses and may not recover costs for work or materials in excess of the scope of the terminated or abandoned contract.

False Claim - A demand for money or property that knowingly presents a false or fraudulent claim for payment or approval or the false or fraudulent avoidance of an obligation to pay the government under either the federal False Claims Act, 31 U.S.C. § 3729-3732, or a corollary state False Claims Act.

Final Acceptance - The owner's acceptance of the project from the contractor upon the architect's or engineer's certification that the project is complete and in accordance with the contract requirements. Final payment often confirms final acceptance unless otherwise stipulated in the contract.

Final Completion - The time when the work is complete, and the contractor has fulfilled all contract requirements.

Financing Statement (a/k/a, "UCC-1") - A legal form that allows a lender (or surety) to announce and record a lien on a specific personal property asset or more generally on all of an entity's personal property assets (a blanket lien) to secure a debt. By filing the UCC-1, the lender (or surety) gains the right to potentially receive the personal property of the debtor identified as collateral in the event of a default. The filing also establishes a hierarchy among creditors should the debtor default or declare bankruptcy.

Force Majeure - A superior or irresistible force, such as lightning, earthquakes, storms, hurricanes, floods, extreme heat, and freezing that occurs without any human intervention. Some contracts include war, labor strife, pandemics, or governmental action in their definition of force majeure. Contractors commonly use Force Majeure clauses to protect them if they cannot perform the contract or a part of the contract because of causes outside of their control and which they could not have avoided even with the exercise of due care.

Joint Check Agreement - An agreement between an owner and contractor, by which the owner can make payments jointly to the contractor and a subcontractor, without creating a contract between the owner and the subcontractor or further obligating the owner in any way. Joint Check Agreements also apply one tier down where the contractor issues a joint payment to a subcontractor and a supplier or lower-tier subcontractor.

Joint Ventures - A business arrangement in which two or more companies agree to pool their resources to obtain and construct a particular project pursuant to an agreement under which they agree on who is responsible for the management, profits, losses, costs, and other aspects necessary for the performance of the work.

Latent Defect - A defect in materials, equipment, or work that is not apparent through reasonably careful observation during the performance of the contract or thereafter.

Letter of Intent - Written confirmation that the owner has accepted a bid and the parties will execute a contract to perform the work in due time. This agreement serves as a placeholder until the parties execute the contract and is typically enforceable under state law.

Liquidated Damages - Contracts often include completion dates to which the contractor agrees. In the event a contractor fails to achieve the contract completion date, the liquidated damage clause obligates the contractor to pay the owner a daily rate that compensates the owner for estimated damages arising from late completion.

Liquidating Agreement - An agreement between a general contractor and its subcontractor to jointly pursue claims arising from the owner's or architect's acts or omissions and holding in abeyance any claims between the general contractor and subcontractor pending the outcome of the claims against the owner. The essence of the agreement is that the subcontractor conditionally releases the claims it has against the general contractor pending recovery from the owner. Liquidating agreements can provide that the subcontractor can revive its claim against the general contractor if there is no recovery from the owner. The agreement typically outlines how the parties will manage the litigation against the owner, how the parties will negotiate and agree to settlements with the owner, the disbursement of any funds collected, and other matters.

Mechanic's Lien - A lien on real property, created by statute or even constitutional protections in many jurisdictions, in favor of persons supplying labor or materials for a building or structure for the value of the labor or materials supplied. Although a mechanic's lien may be available, it requires action on the part of the person claiming payment to establish and, once that person initiates action, the lien will create a debt against the project. Absent very unusual circumstances, mechanic's liens are not usually available on publicly owned property.

Minority Business Enterprise ("MBE") - A business or enterprise where one or more ethnic minorities own, manage, and control at least 51% of the business enterprise. Typically, the statute defines which ethnic minority groups are eligible for MBE status.

No-damages-for-delay clause - A provision contained in some contracts prohibiting the contractor (or subcontractor) from seeking or recovering damages for delays. Some states have legislatively banned the use of no-damages-for-delay clauses in public contracts, finding them void and against public policy.

Novation - The substitution of a new contract in place of an old one—similar to but not the equivalent of assignment. The process involves the rights and obligations of one of the original parties to the contract being transferred ("novated") to a third party; that third party "steps into the shoes" of one of the original parties for all purposes.

Order of Precedence - The order of hierarchy of various parts of the contract. Commonly defined in the contract, the order of precedence clause can resolve conflicts and omissions in the contract drawings and documents by defining which part of the contract controls over another conflicting part.

Patent Defect - A defect that is open or obvious or which a person may discover by reasonable observation.

Pass-Through Claims - Claims for time or money that a subcontractor incurs in the performance of its work resulting from the owner's actions, which the general contractor may or should pursue against the owner on the subcontractor's behalf. They are called pass-through claims because the general contractor must pass the subcontractor's claim through to the owner, as there is no privity of contract between the subcontractor and the owner permitting the subcontractor to directly pursue the claim against the owner. Typically, there has been no conduct on the part of the general contractor that contributed to the subcontractor's claim. Liquidating agreements are the mechanism by which the parties pursue pass-through claims.

Pay-if-Paid Clause - Clause contained in some subcontracts conditioning the general contractor's payment obligation to the subcontractor upon receipt of payment from the owner. In some states, these clauses are an absolute defense for the general contractor against subcontractor claims if the clause clearly and unequivocally shifts the risk of owner non-payment to the subcontractor. In the states enforcing such clauses, the words "payment by the owner to the general contractor is a condition precedent to payment from the general contractor to subcontractor" or similar language is often required. Some states have determined that pay-if-pay clauses are against public policy and view such contractual provisions as timing mechanisms only. *See*, Pay-When-Paid Clause.

Pay-when-Paid Clause - Clause contained in some subcontracts conditioning the general contractor's payment obligation to the subcontractor upon receipt of payment from the owner. A Pay-when-Paid clause does not provide the general contractor an absolute defense to the subcontractor if the owner never pays because it does not shift the risk of owner non-payment to the subcontractor. The general contractor's obligation to pay is suspended for a reasonable time but, ultimately, the general contractor must pay the subcontractor. Some courts view all efforts to condition payment to a subcontractor upon payment by the owner as timing mechanisms only. Courts have been slow to define what is "reasonable" in connection with Pay-When-Paid Clauses. *See*, Pay-If-Paid Clause.

Performance Specification - Technical requirements that set forth the operational characteristics desired for the work or a portion of the work. The contractor accepts general responsibility for product design and engineering and for achievement of the stated performance requirements. Compare with Design Specification.

Related Parties - Parent companies, subsidiaries, associate firms, joint ventures, or a company or entity that a related party controls or significantly influences or manages.

Service Disabled Veteran Owned Small Business/Veteran Owned Small Business ("SDVOSB/VSOB") - A certification obtained through a program that the United States Small Business Administration ("SBA") administers to assist small businesses which are 51% or more unconditionally and directly owned by one or more Service-Disabled Veterans allowing access to federal contracting, including sole source and set-aside contracts.

***Severin* Doctrine** – Based upon *Severin v. United States*, 99 Ct.Cl. 435 (1943), the doctrine allows a prime contractor who has contractual privity with the government to sue the government on behalf of its subcontractor for damages that the subcontractor has incurred as a result of the government's actions. Also known as "pass-through" claims, this doctrine allows the prime contractor to serve as an intermediary to pursue the subcontractor's claims against the government. Pass-through claims can be successful only if the prime contractor remains liable to the subcontractor for the claimed damages.

Small Business Enterprise ("SBE") - A race and gender-neutral certification program that the SBA established and manages to help small companies compete for small business set-aside federal government contracts. Limited to businesses whose annual gross receipts are within the standards that the SBA defines and which are at least 51% owned by individuals whose personal net worth falls within defined limits.

***Spearin* Doctrine** - The legal theory that *United States v. Spearin*, 248 U.S. 132 (1918) pronounced imposing responsibility under an implied warranty on the government that the plans and specifications it furnishes for construction are suitable for their intended purpose. The contractor who is bound to build according to the owner's plans and specifications will not be responsible for the consequences of defects in the plans and specifications.

Subrogation - The substitution of one person for another with respect to legal rights, such as a right of recovery. Subrogation occurs when a third person, such as an insurance company or surety, pays a debt of another or claim against another and succeeds to all the legal rights which the debtor or person against whom the claim was asserted may have against other persons.

Substantial Completion - The date that the architect certifies when the work or a designated portion thereof is sufficiently complete and in accordance with the contract documents, so the owner may occupy or utilize the work or designated portion thereof for the use for which it is intended. Some contracts have very specific definitions and conditions that the contractor must satisfy to achieve substantial completion.

Suspension of Work - Owner delay, either by order or constructively, of a contractor's work. Many contracts contain a suspension of work provision which allows the owner to order the contractor, in writing, to suspend, delay, or interrupt performance of all or any portion of the work for a designated time. Delays or suspensions over a certain number of days may entitle the contractor to additional compensation or even contract termination.

Tax Credits - A wide variety of tax-related incentives for owners and developers to construct projects, ranging from sales tax exemptions, property tax abatements, energy credits, low-income housing tax credits, research and development tax credits, and historic rehabilitation tax credits.

Termination for Cause (or Default) - The right of the owner (or contractor) to terminate or cancel the performance of work under a contract (or subcontract), in whole or in part, because of the contractor's (or subcontractor's) actual or anticipated failure to perform its contractual obligations. Termination for cause clauses usually define the type of failures justifying termination for cause and will require the owner (or contractor) to provide notice and an opportunity to cure the default before termination can occur. Termination for default clauses also usually state that the terminated contractor is liable for damages resulting from the termination, including the costs of excess reprocurement.

Termination for Convenience - The right of the owner (or contractor) to terminate or cancel the performance of work under a contract (or subcontract), in whole or in part, at the owner's (or contractor's) sole discretion. Termination for convenience clauses nearly always provide for the appropriate payment to the contractor (or subcontractor) in the event of a termination for convenience.

CHAPTER IV

PAPERWORK USED IN A CONSTRUCTION PROJECT

By Todd Bauer, Bryce D. Holzer, Jordan S. Rosenfeld, and Amanda L. Marutzky

A. Introduction

On any construction project, if the phases are the chapters, the people the characters, and the terms the language, then the paperwork tells the story. A careful reading of the paperwork will provide at least a partial understanding of what will happen and what did happen on a project, with all of its twists, turns, and pit stops. Especially when a project fails or a construction dispute arises, the savvy project analyst will obtain and review as much of the digital record and information ("paperwork") from the project as possible to identify and understand the issues in dispute.

This chapter provides an overview of the often-voluminous paperwork associated with a construction project and indicates which party is likely to have custody and control of specific documents. Additionally, this chapter provides an understanding of the significance of various documents for an analysis of a failed project or construction dispute. The chapter is divided into various files based on types of documents, most of which will be in the custody and control of the contractor and many of which will also be in the custody and control of other project participants, such as the design professional, the owner, and/or subcontractors.

We do not live in an ideal world, and construction project files are often incomplete or non-existent. Thus, the process of reviewing and analyzing project paperwork is typically concurrent with the process of searching for the project paperwork.

Thanks to the benefits of modern technology, the volume of paperwork on construction projects is primarily stored electronically or "in the cloud." The types of electronic "paperwork" applicable to a construction project include nearly all of the project documents: contracts, plans and drawings, specifications, project records, photographs, and daily reports generated during construction, emails, texts, payment applications, releases, and schedules, just to name a few. Contractors, designers, and owners have duties under federal and state law and applicable rules of procedure to retain such electronic information. Thus, most of the "paperwork" on a construction project will be in a paperless, electronic format. In this chapter, any references to "paperwork" refer to both paper and electronic versions of documents.

B. Standard Contract Forms

The construction industry has produced many standard form contract documents that delineate the rights and obligations of the various parties to a construction project. In particular, several professional and trade organizations have promulgated "families" of contract forms available for use depending on the type of construction project or the relationship of the contracting parties. Such forms include those that the American Institute of Architects (AIA), the ConsensusDocs®, the Associated General Contractors of America (AGC), the Engineers Joint Contract Documents Committee (EJCDC), the Construction Management Association of America (CMAA), and the Design-Build Institute of America (DBIA) have produced. The sample standard contract forms used in this book are AIA and ConsensusDocs®.

The AIA has published the most widely used of these standard forms including design and construction contracts, as well as other forms to facilitate the design and construction process, having started as early as 1888, well over 100 years ago. The AIA periodically updates and publishes these documents in successive versions or "editions," coming out with new editions roughly every 10 years, with the most recent update in 2017. Once the AIA publishes an updated document, it replaces the prior version.

The AIA has six series of agreements divided by document use or purpose: A-Series, Owner/Contractor Agreements; B-Series, Owner/Architect Agreements; C-Series, Other Agreements; D-Series, Miscellaneous Documents; E-Series, Exhibits; and G-Series, Contract Administration and Project Management Forms. The AIA also groups its documents into "families" according to project type or delivery method. The documents within each family attempt to provide consistent structure and text to support major relationships on design or construction projects. These families include the following:

- The Conventional family, used for the traditional delivery approach of sequential design-bid-build;
- The Construction Manager-Advisor (CMa) family, used when the project owner retains a construction manager (CM) to act as an independent advisor on construction management matters;

- The Construction Manager-Constructor (CMc), used when the project owner merges the functions of a contractor and construction manager to complete the construction and provide CM services;
- The Design-Build family, used when the project delivery method is design-build.

AGC is the largest trade association in the United States that represents contractors and industry-related companies. In 2007, AGC was a founding endorsing organization to the ConsensusDocs® Coalition which created ConsensusDocs® contracts. ConsensusDocs® includes over 100 standard form contract documents that cover all major project delivery systems including design-bid-build, design-build, construction management, and program management. Like the AIA forms, the ConsensusDocs® apply to the relationships among the various parties to and tiers of a construction project: the owner, the contractor, the surety, the subcontractor, the architect/engineer, the design-builder, the construction manager, and the program manager.

The advantage of using such standard form contract documents is that they help achieve a certain degree of efficiency and predictability in both contract negotiation and in analysis and resolution of construction disputes. The documents all contain significant risk shifting and exculpatory language that assigns risk regarding various aspects of the project to one party or another. While each organization touts the fairness and objectivity of its form documents, the respective organization's members have generally prepared each form document to protect their interests.

Of course, it would be impossible for a preprinted form to respond to all of the complexities of specific construction projects, without modifications. Thus, even though a standard form contract might be the basis of a project document, the parties may have modified the contract form, sometimes substantially, to meet the needs of the parties to the specific project. Accordingly, most contracts that appear to be a standard form contract are actually manuscripted contracts, customized to meet project-specific issues.

C. Bid File

The paperwork included in a bid file is generally the same regardless of whether the file is for a general contractor who is soliciting bids or a subcontractor who is submitting bids. The difference in the files lies in the purpose behind the paperwork. The general contractor will use the bid file paperwork to set forth the scope of work and analyze bids received to determine the most qualified subcontractor. The subcontractor uses the bid file paperwork to prepare its bid for submittal. The bid file will continually be updated over the course of a project as additional or revised bids and/or bid information are submitted. The bid file can be retained at the contractor's office or the project site but often is retained in a document management program specialized for construction projects. Examples include Procore, Autodesk Construction Cloud, e-Builders, PlanGrid, and Bluebeam Revu, just to name a few.

1. Request for Proposal (Bid)/Notice Inviting Bids

The request for proposal (RFP) and other related documents -- such as a request for bid, notice inviting bids, invitation to bid, and solicitation for offer -- define the scope of work, requirements, and terms for submittal of a qualified bid. The request for proposal will typically provide a general description of the project and incorporate all plans, specifications, schedules, and other addenda needed to prepare and submit a pricing proposal. See Exhibit 8 for an example of a Notice Inviting Bids.

2. Bid Documents

The bid documents are typically included in the RFP. Bid documents are all of the documents used during the bid process. They define the work and the requirements for submitting a successful bid.

3. Permits

Most bid files will include either the actual permits required for construction or specify the permits required and the party that is responsible for procuring them. Depending on the type of construction project, different permits may be required. A general contractor may be responsible for securing federal, state, or municipal permits; and subcontractors may also be responsible for securing permits for their work, such as grading, concrete, or electrical. The bid file will often include a permit log that tracks the owner of the permit, the location of the permit, and the time period that the permit is valid.

4. Easements and Rights-of-Way

Easements and rights-of-way provide the holder with certain rights regarding the usage of the property. They often allow access through property owned by a third party. The owner of the property continues to own the land and has only given up defined rights on the portion of land used for the right-of-way or easement. Typically, the project owner is responsible for obtaining any easements or rights-of-way needed for construction.

An easement and right-of-way agreement defines all the rights and obligations of the holder of the easement or right-of-way and the restrictions placed on the property subject to the agreement. Easements and right-of-way agreements are often necessary for a contractor to complete its work. The contractor typically retains these agreements in the bid file. See Exhibit 34 for a sample Easement of Right-of-Way Agreement.

5. Bid Summary/Bid Spread Summary

The bid summary is the log identifying the bids received on a project, either the general contractor bids that the owner has received or the subcontractor bids that the general contractor has received. Typically, it will list the name of the bidder, the specification section that the bid addresses, the date of the bid, the price of the bid, and, occasionally, any exceptions to the original request for proposal. The bid summary tracks and records bid information, sets forth the difference between the bids, and assists in the analysis of bids received. See Exhibit 10 for an example of a bid summary.

6. Take-off Sheets

Take-off sheets are internal working documents that the contractor develops during the process of estimating and calculating a bid price for a scope of work. The contractor develops the take-off sheets as it reviews plans, specifications, and other project criteria for bid purposes. Take-off sheets can come in almost any shape and size and are typically different for each particular type of work on a project. The contractor often updates the take-off sheets throughout the life of a project in order to determine the initial versus changed scope of work and to identify cost variances and change orders. If a question ever arises internally whether a contractor has included a particular component of work in its bid, the take-off sheets are one of the primary documents to review and analyze.

7. Subcontractor/Supplier Quotes/Proposals

The contractor will use Subcontractor/Supplier quotes/proposals in preparing bids. The contractor typically lists subcontractor/supplier quotes/protocols on a log sheet.

D. Owner File

1. Owner-Design Professional Agreement

The terms of the agreement between the owner and the design professional (architects and engineers) govern the design professional's rights and responsibilities in relationship to the owner.

Two of the most widely used forms are the AIA Standard Form of Agreement between Owner and Architect, often referred to by its AIA document number, B101™, and the ConsensusDocs® Agreement Between Owner and Design Professional, or ConsensusDocs® 240. These agreements define the design professional's duties and responsibilities and the services it will provide. In addition to a design professional's design responsibilities, owner-design professional agreements address the design professional's responsibilities during the construction such as submittal reviews, evaluation and processing of change orders, work site visits, processing contractor payment applications/requisitions, and assistance with inspections to determine the dates of substantial completion and final completion of the contractor's work.

However, the AIA B101™ and the ConsensusDocs® 240, as well as other owner-design professional agreements, differ in several respects. For instance, one traditional design professional role noticeably absent in ConsensusDocs® 240 is that of initial arbiter of claims and disputes between the owner and the contractor. This omission is a departure from AIA B101, which gives a role to the design professional in resolving project disputes. See Exhibit 11 AIA B101™-2017, Standard Form Agreement Between Owner and Architect.

2. Schematic Design

The schematic design of the design professional's work involves the development of the project "program" into more detailed "schematic" or preliminary plans for the project. As part of this process, the design professional will prepare the preliminary design of the project -- the schematic drawings. These drawings usually illustrate the size and configuration of the building or structure, its elevation, and its relationship to other components of the project, such as site layout and the surrounding areas.

On an infrastructure project, this phase of service is often referred to as "preliminary engineering" and consists of the engineer's activities, such as topographic surveys of the project area, investigations of existing utilities, environmental, and geotechnical conditions, and detailed engineering calculations.

E. Contract File

1. Contract Documents

Unlike many commercial contracts, a construction contract is not a single document but consists of a group of construction documents. These contract documents typically include the following:

- Agreement between the owner and contractor, which sets forth the basic provisions and obligations of the parties;
- General Conditions, which describe the legal terms and conditions of the contractor's work for the owner in much greater detail than in the agreement;
- Supplementary and/or Special Conditions, which modify the terms of the General Conditions;
- Plans or Drawings, which describe in graphic terms the construction that the contractor is to perform;
- Specifications, which contain detailed technical instructions and descriptions of the materials from which the contractor is to construct the project;
- Addenda, which are modifications that the owner issues before the parties sign the agreement and often in conjunction with the bid process;
- Change Orders, which are subsequent modifications to the agreement; and
- Geotechnical/soils reports or other engineering data.

One or more of the contract documents, usually the agreement and/or the General Conditions, defines what documents comprise the "contract" and refer to them as the "Contract Documents."

One important issue is the order of hierarchy between and among the various items comprising the Contract Documents in order to resolve inconsistencies and contradictions among the various contract documents. This hierarchy provision is typically called a "precedence clause."

A notable difference between the form of the AIA contract documents and the ConsensusDocs® contract documents is that AIA documents have General Conditions separate from the agreement between owner and contractor. In contrast, the ConsensusDocs® contract documents have both the General Conditions and the agreement between owner and contractor in one document. The General Conditions of the Contract for Construction, AIA Document A201™, is the central document in AIA's family of contract forms. It is frequently incorporated into construction contracts. See Exhibit 7 for a sample of AIA A201™.

Larger public and private owners often prepare their own contract documents, but many smaller to mid-sized contractors will use the standard form contracts that the various industry organizations provide. When the parties use a standard form, there are often case law or learned articles available that have addressed the specific language of a standard form contract to assist the contracting parties in determining how a court in a particular jurisdiction will construe that language.

Whether the parties use a standard form contract or a manuscripted form, most of those contracts will include contract provisions addressing the following key provisions: scope of work, project start and completion dates, price, payment terms, termination, change orders, and extra work, delays, claims and disputes and dispute resolution, insurance and bonding requirements, project safety, testing/inspection, and correction of defective work. Within these broad contract provisions will be language addressing, if not necessarily resolving, frequently litigated provisions such as notice requirements, change orders, differing site conditions, no-damage-for-delay, liquidated damages, indemnity, default, and termination.

2. Agreement between Owner and Contractor

The agreement between the owner and the contractor is the primary document to which the other documents are attached in order to form the universe of contract documents. The agreement between the owner and the contractor describes the type of construction contract and will identify the method of payment to the contractor. The most common types of construction contracts are lump sum, cost-plus-a-fee (cost plus), guaranteed maximum price, and unit price.

A lump sum or stipulated sum contract is one in which the contractor agrees to build the project, including supplying all labor and materials, whether the contractor performs the work with its own forces or via subcontractors, for a specified dollar amount (or lump sum). The owner must pay the contractor the fixed amount no matter what it costs to finish the work. Government contracts often use this method as do owners who want to competitively bid the contract. AIA Document A101™ - 2017, Standard Form of Agreement between Owner and Contractor Where the Basis for Payment Is a Stipulated Sum, is a relatively simple, straightforward lump-sum agreement. See Exhibit 12 for an AIA A101™ - 2017. AGC's baseline owner/contractor agreement is ConsensusDocs® 200, Standard Form of Agreement and General Conditions between Owner and Contractor (Lump Sum). See Exhibit 13 for the ConsensusDocs® 200.

Another payment method is the cost of the work plus a fee, in which the owner reimburses the contractor for the actual costs of performing the work and also pays the contractor a fee. The concept of actual costs is synonymous with time and materials (T&M) while the fee is usually some percentage of the cost of the work. In this payment method, the owner reviews the costs that the contractor has incurred, and the contract must define what costs are reimbursable. There is often much negotiation concerning what is reimbursable and what is not. There is no cap on the costs that the owner could potentially be obligated to pay under this payment method. Owners most often use this method when the plans and specifications are incomplete, and the bidders cannot establish a lump sum or guaranteed maximum price. These types of projects include "fast-track" projects that are under construction while the owner and design professionals are producing the construction documents.

In a guaranteed maximum price contract (GMP), the owner will pay the contractor the costs of the work, plus a contractor's fee, the total of which will not exceed a guaranteed maximum dollar amount. Under a GMP contract, the theory is that the owner will know at the time of contracting that it may pay less than, but never more than, the GMP. Owners use GMP contracts on large, sophisticated projects in the private sector. Most owners negotiate the terms of a GMP contract with a pre-selected contractor, rather than bidding out the project. The AIA GMP agreement is AIA A102™ - 2017, Standard Form of Agreement between Owner and Contractor, Where the Basis of Payment Is the Cost of the Work Plus a Fee with a Negotiated Guaranteed Maximum Price. The AGC GMP agreement is ConsensusDocs® 230, Owner and Constructor Agreement (Cost of Work Plus a Fee with GMP). See Exhibits 14 and 15 for samples of cost plus GMP agreements, AIA A102™ - 2017 Agreement, and ConsensusDocs® 230 Agreement.

Unit prices are not usually the basis for an entire contract; however, owners use the unit price method in construction projects that construct or install one or several specified items, such as laying pipelines or constructing sidewalks. In a unit price contract, the contractor agrees to specified unit prices for specific items of material and labor, and the total contract price becomes the total of the number of "units" of that material and labor required to complete the project. Some contracts are a hybrid between unit price and lump sum contracts, with the contractor furnishing or performing some items at unit price while performing the rest of the work as a lump sum.

ConsensusDocs® has an additional addendum used on projects on which the owner and others intend to use Building Information Modeling (BIM) or virtual design and construction (ConsensusDocs® 301 BIM

Addendum). This three-dimensional design or modeling software is typical for larger, complex construction projects. The BIM Addendum can be used with all types of contracts but is common for those that include preconstruction services. See Exhibit 16 for ConsensusDocs® 301.

3. General Conditions

The General Conditions expands upon the information provided in the agreement and provides more complete contract terms governing the parties. The General Conditions include such items as the owner's obligations to the contractor, the services that the contractor will provide, insurance and bonding requirements, changes in the work, payment procedures, and the construction administration services that either the architect or a construction manager will provide.

As discussed above, the General Conditions in ConsensusDocs® documents are included in the owner/contractor agreement. AIA A201™ - 2017, General Conditions of the Contract for Construction, the baseline AIA General Conditions, is in wide use as a construction project document and courts frequently discuss it. Exhibit 7 is a sample of A201.

As the courts have widely used and interpreted A201, any variations from that document will suggest a different intention and potentially a different legal outcome. There are fifteen articles in the AIA General Conditions, and each suggests its subject matter:

- General Provisions;
- Owner;
- Contractor;
- Architect;
- Subcontractors;
- Construction by Owner or by Separate Contractors;
- Changes in the Work;
- Time;
- Payments and Completion;
- Protection of Persons and Property;
- Insurance and Bonds;
- Uncovering and Correction of Work;
- Miscellaneous Provisions;
- Termination or Suspension of the Contract;
- Claims and Disputes.

Other standard form General Conditions and those that are manuscripted vary the rights and responsibilities of the parties.

4. Supplemental and Special Conditions

Supplemental and special conditions of the contract modify or supplement the agreement and General Conditions of the contract. These may clarify, delete, or otherwise amend standard contractual provisions.

5. Plans

Plans are the drawings that the design professional has prepared and that are the graphic expressions of the work that the contractor is to perform. The plans may be in electronic (i.e., CAD [Computer-Aided Design] or BIM [Building Information Modeling]) format as well as printed on paper. Disputes on failed construction projects often involve questions as to whether the plans and/or specifications were defective.

6. Specifications

Specifications are the written technical requirements for the materials, equipment, systems, and standards for the work. Typically, the owner and/or owner's design team issue the specifications and provides them to potential bidders as part of the RFP.

7. Submittals and Shop Drawings

While the plans and specifications set forth how the contractor is to perform the work, the contractor is responsible for confirming with the architect or engineer, through shop drawings and submittals, the materials and equipment that the contractor intends to use and how the contractor will fabricate and install those materials and equipment. The contractor will prepare, process, and transmit submittals and shop drawings to the design professional for almost every material or product on the project. Exhibit 17 is a sample of a material submittal. The contractor first reviews submittals, many of which originate with subcontractors and suppliers, and then transmits them to the design professional for review and approval. If rejected, the design professional returns the submittal to the contractor for revision and resubmission. Depending on the nature of the submittal, the review process can take weeks, sometimes resulting in a dramatic delay to the construction schedule. On large and complex projects, shop drawings and submittals can number in the thousands. If a bottleneck occurs in the process, the construction schedule is likely to suffer. This situation is not uncommon on industrial projects requiring specialized equipment or on projects where there are several different design firms with differing responsibilities.

The review process often leads to disputes between the contractor and the design professional(s) concerning the timing of the submittal and review of shop drawings and submittals as well as who has ultimate responsibility and liability for approved shop drawings containing errors and omissions.

8. Submittal Logs and Shop Drawing Logs

Submittal logs and shop drawing logs show the movement of each submittal and shop drawing through the review process in order for the parties to track submittals and approvals. These logs also assist in tracking procurement and any delays that might disrupt the construction schedule.

9. Notice to Proceed

A notice to proceed is a written notice from the owner to the contractor that directs the contractor to begin working on the construction project. The contract time for completion of the project usually begins to run from the date of the notice to proceed. Exhibit 18 is a sample of a Notice to Proceed.

10. Schedule of Values

A schedule of values is a breakdown of the total contract amount into activity costs to serve as a basis for the owner's progress payments to the contractor or the general contractor to a subcontractor. The schedule of values in conjunction with the project schedule determines the amount of each progress payment. Exhibit 9 is a sample of a Schedule of Values.

11. Bid, Performance, and Payment Bonds

The contract documents, the bonds, and any applicable statutes determine a surety's liability. As with other construction documents, industry organizations have prepared bid, performance, and payment bonds as part of their family of documents. For instance, widely used, almost omnipresent, in the construction industry are the AIA A312™ performance and payment bonds and their predecessors, the AIA A311™ performance and payment bonds. See A312™ Performance Bond at Exhibit 19; A312™ Payment Bond at Exhibit 20, a manuscripted Subcontract Performance Bond at Exhibit 35, and a manuscripted Subcontract Payment Bond at Exhibit 36.

The AIA bond forms, A311™ and A312™, are the most widely used bond forms. A311 has been in existence since 1970 and many courts have reviewed and interpreted it. There is also significant case law construing its younger and lengthier sibling, A312.

The ConsensusDocs® family of documents includes bond forms as well: ConsensusDocs® 262, Bid Bond; ConsensusDocs® 260, Performance Bond; and ConsensusDocs® 261, Payment Bond. In addition, ConsensusDocs® has produced performance and payment bond forms for design-build projects: ConsensusDocs® 470, 471, 472, and 473. The language of these bond forms varies regarding risk and liability for design costs and services.

Federal projects use Miller Act bonds. The federal Miller Act requires the general contractor on most federal public works projects to furnish Miller Act performance and payment bonds. See Exhibits 21 and 22, Miller Act Performance and Payment Bonds, Standard Form 25. All states have a "Little Miller Act" or otherwise require performance and payment bonds on public projects.

Notwithstanding the myriad of standard bond forms that the various organizations such as the AIA and ConsensusDocs® have prepared, many project owners and general contractors, when in the role of bond obligee, require the use of their own bond forms. They sometimes contain onerous provisions that attempt to increase the risk to the surety.

A bidder provides a bid bond to guarantee that the bidder, if the owner awards it the contract, will enter into the contract. If the successful bidder does not proceed after the contract award, the surety's liability is limited to the amount of the bid bond and some bid bonds require the forfeiture of the entire amount of the bond. See Exhibit 5 AIA Document A310™ - 2017 Bid Bond.

The bond language dictates the rights and obligations of the surety along with the statutory provisions that require the bonds. For instance, some bonds require that the obligee declare the bond principal in default before the surety has any liability on the bond. Some performance bonds, such as the A312™, require the obligee to terminate the principal pursuant to the terms of the underlying bonded construction contract before the surety can be liable.

12. Co-Obligee Rider

A co-obligee or dual obligee rider, applicable to the payment and performance bond, names a lender or other party as an additional obligee, which will have a direct right of action under the bond. On its face, a co-obligee rider, absent language to the contrary, does no more than add a party with standing to bring a bond claim, without extending the potential liability of the surety. Construction lenders, with an interest in the completion of a project, often require such riders. Exhibit 23 is a sample of a co-obligee rider.

13. Certificates of Insurance

A certificate of insurance is a standard form that provides proof of insurance coverage. An insured contractor or subcontractor can obtain from its broker a certificate of insurance describing the type and amount of insurance coverage that the insured maintains, as well as any "additional insureds" under the policy. An insurance agent or broker will issue a certificate of insurance for informational purposes only: it is not the actual policy itself. The policy itself sets forth the scope of coverage. See Exhibit 24 for a sample certificate of insurance.

F. Subcontract File

The subcontract file is the depository for all information related to a specific subcontractor. General contractors typically maintain a distinct file for each subcontractor.

1. Subcontract

The subcontract memorializes the agreement between the general contractor and the subcontractor. Subcontracts come in many forms; some are standard forms and some manuscripted. There are a few widely used and commonly accepted subcontract forms including the AIA A401™ - 2017 Standard Form of Agreement between Contractor and Subcontractor; and the ConsensusDocs® 750 (2018) Standard Agreement between Constructor and Subcontractor. See Exhibit 25 for an example of AIA Document A401™ - 2017.

2. Subcontractor Quotes/Proposals

Subcontractors submit quotes in response to a request for proposal or request for bid on a particular component of work. See Exhibit 26 for an example of a subcontractor quote.

3. Subcontract Change Orders (SCO/CO)

SCOs or COs memorialize agreements between the general contractor and the subcontractor entered into subsequent to the signing of the subcontract. A general contractor can issue a SCO/CO for a variety of reasons and the SCO/CO can be either additive or deductive. They address some type of change to the original subcontract, such as time, scope of work, and compensation. They are typically numbered and filed chronologically.

4. Subcontractor Bonds

Copies of the performance, payment, stop notice release, warranty, and all other bonds required under the subcontract are located in the subcontract file for each particular subcontractor.

5. Subcontractor Certificates of Insurance

Contractors require their subcontractors to provide copies of certificates of insurance covering all lines of insurance verifying that the required insurance coverages are in force. Typically, the contractor enters insurance certificates into an insurance log that identifies the type of insurance and dates that the policies will expire. See Exhibit 24 for a sample of a certificate of insurance.

6. Subcontractor Payment Application/Requisition

Contractors typically retain a copy of each payment application/requisition that a subcontractor submits. The payment application/requisition indicates the amounts earned and paid for each pay period by line item in the bid schedule of values. See Exhibit 27 for an example of a subcontractor payment application.

7. Subcontractor/Supplier Invoices

Contractors typically retain a copy of each subcontractor/supplier invoice received and paid. See Exhibit 28 for an example of a supplier invoice.

8. Subcontractor Certified Payroll Reports

Primarily on public works projects, prior to approving and paying any subcontractor payment application or invoice, the general contractor obtains and reviews the subcontractor's certified payroll reports to ensure compliance with federal, state, local, and project requirements. Certified payroll reports are typically located in the subcontractor file in chronological order. Certified payroll reports are typically required on public works projects and include an employee's name, social security number, job description/category, wages paid, hours worked, and pay period. The certified payroll reports are accompanied by a subcontractor's sworn statement that the reports are accurate and that the subcontractor has paid all wages in accordance with the report. See Exhibit 37 for a Certified Payroll Report for the federal government.

9. Subcontractor Release Forms

Prior to approving progress or final payments to any subcontractor on a project, general contractors typically obtain the proper release forms. Although various types of release forms are used, generally there are four different types:

- Conditional progress payment release;
- Unconditional progress payment release;
- Conditional release upon final payment;
- Unconditional release upon final payment.

Most releases provide the subcontractor signing the release the opportunity to reserve rights to any disputed funds that the release does not cover. A release is considered conditional if the document states that is not effective until funds are made available by the issuer's bank. Upon the issuer's bank releasing the funds, the subcontractor or supplier should provide an unconditional release.

Releases can also release a subcontractor's rights to additional compensation, stop notice and lien rights, and other affirmative claims. See Exhibit 29 for a sample of the four types of releases listed above.

10. Consent of Surety

The consent of surety form is applicable only where the subcontractor has provided surety bonds to the contractor. Some, but not all contractors request or obtain consent of surety for the release of progress and/or final payments to bonded subcontractors. The consent of surety form provides the subcontractor's payment/performance bond surety with the opportunity to review the records of its principal and determine whether the surety has any reason to request that the obligee withhold payment from the bond principal. Obtaining consent of surety provides the contractor with some protection from potential surety claims after the contractor has released those funds. See Exhibit 30 for an example of a consent of surety form.

11. Preliminary Notices

Preliminary notices provide the contractor and, sometimes, the owner with knowledge of the names of the subcontractors that the general contractor is using on the project and the suppliers that are furnishing material and equipment for use on the project. With this information, the owner can ensure that the contractor has paid its subcontractors and suppliers prior to the owner's release of payments to avoid stop notices and mechanic's liens. Preliminary notices are also required in certain cases to protect certain rights under payment bonds and other laws. See Exhibit 31 for an example of a preliminary notice from California.

12. Subcontractor Correspondence

General contractors typically retain correspondence to and from the subcontractor in chronological order in their subcontractor files, although with the advent of email, contractors typically store their communications with their subcontractors in their email systems or electronic project folders.

G. Purchasing Process Files

The purchasing process includes the purchase, receipt, payment, and costing of materials, equipment rentals, or other miscellaneous items for a project. The paperwork that the contractor generates or receives in this process includes purchase orders, delivery tickets, invoices, and checks.

1. Purchase Orders

Many contractors' (although certainly not all) systems include the requirement purchase orders for all purchases from outside vendors or at least all purchases over a given dollar amount. Purchase orders provide the quantity and pricing details of the purchased item(s), along with job costing information. As with subcontracts, purchase orders indicate the contractor's committed costs.

Traditional paper purchase orders are often three-color triplicate forms. The original goes to the vendor; a colored copy is for the project files; and the accounting or purchasing department keeps the other one. The process for filing purchase orders varies among contractors. The contractor might file it numerically or alphabetically in a vendor file. The contractor might file the accounting copy alphabetically pending subsequent match with the appropriate invoice.

Digital purchase orders have greatly simplified and enhanced the purchase order process. In a digital system, an electronic purchase order is automatically created containing the details of the transaction through the software system. The digital purchase order system directs the purchase order electronically to the appropriate person(s) for approval. Once approved, the purchase order is sent to the vendor for acceptance. The acceptance of the electronic purchase order is communicated through email and becomes a legally binding document.

2. Delivery Tickets

A contractor receives delivery tickets or "packing slips" from a vendor upon delivery of materials to the contractor. The delivery ticket states the actual quantity and description of the materials. It is the responsibility of the contractor to verify upon delivery that the goods actually received match the delivery ticket. The accounting (or purchasing) department matches purchase orders and invoices. See Exhibit 32 for an example of a delivery ticket.

In a digital system, the quantity of materials received is entered into the purchasing system for electronic matching with the appropriate purchase order.

3. Invoices

The system for processing invoices from vendors varies with each contractor and depends on the specific stage of invoice processing. The following is a summary of a typical invoice processing system:

- Upon receipt, the accounting department sorts the invoices alphabetically.
- The accounting department then matches them with purchase orders and delivery tickets applicable to the invoice.
- The accounting department often writes job cost posting information derived from the purchase order on the invoice.
- The accounting department forwards the invoice with attachments to the project manager for approval. (Some companies do not require project management approval if there is an appropriately completed purchase order attached.) Frequently, the project manager just stacks the to-be-approved invoices in a pile in no apparent order. Typically, the contractor does not enter the invoices into the accounting system until the project manager returns them "approved."

- Upon return of the approved invoices, the accounting department files them alphabetically by vendor in the accounts payable files.
- Upon payment, the accounting department attaches a copy of the check to the invoices and files them alphabetically by vendor in the paid invoice files. The contractor usually keeps these files for the current fiscal year and, after a year, transfers them to a permanent storage location.

In a digital system, much of the above is handled automatically. Upon receipt, an invoice is scanned and entered into the system with the appropriate purchase order reference. The purchase order should already contain the job cost posting information. In lieu of a stack of hard copy invoices, the project manager or designated authorized person can electronically review a listing of open invoices and, if needed, the scanned invoices. As the three-way matching of purchase orders, delivery tickets, and invoices is done electronically, the system eliminates delays in the invoice approval process. The project management approval process can focus more on issues with a particular purchase.

4. Equipment Rental Tickets/Invoices

Contractors frequently have a file with equipment rental tickets and invoices. Equipment rental tickets and invoices will reveal whether there has actually been a sale rather than a rental. They will also reveal whether the charges include repairs in addition to rental fees.

H. Billing Process Files

The contractor/subcontractor files related to the company's billings to owner/general contractors for work performed are at the project site (or project manager's files in the home office) with the company's accounting department also keeping a copy. The billing file documents provide important information concerning the cash status of the contract and the estimated stage of completion. The billing files include the following:

1. Invoice/Payment Application Log

Many contractors keep a log of the billings submitted on each contract. The log includes the invoice or payment application number, date, gross billing amount, retainage withheld and net billing amount, and the date and the amount of payments received.

2. Invoices

Invoices summarize the payment application as of a certain cut-off date. The contractor generates the invoices following a standard format that facilitates the input of the billing information into the company's accounting system. The information on an invoice commonly includes the following:

- Invoice number;
- Invoice date;
- Job name and number;
- Current gross earnings;
- Current retainage withheld;
- Net amount due.

It may also include:

- Contract amount;
- Change orders to date;
- Earnings to date;
- Retainage;
- Payments to date.

Not all contractors prepare invoices. Some contractors simply input the billing information into their accounting systems directly from the payment application.

3. Payment Applications/Requisitions

Payment applications/requisitions are the periodic (typically monthly or bi-monthly) schedules that provide a detailed summary, by line item, of the contractor's earnings to date on the project. The owner often dictates the format of payment applications, which vary widely. The payment application detail typically provides the following information by line item within the schedule of values:

- Line item number;
- Description;
- Total amount;
- Earned to date;
- Percent complete to date;
- Previous payment application earned to date;
- Previous payment application percent complete;

- Current payment application earned;
- Unearned balance.

For unit-priced contracts, the payment application will also include:

- The contract quantity;
- The unit price;
- The quantities to date (in lieu of the percent complete).

See Exhibit 9 for a sample of a payment application and a continuation sheet.

The payment application summary provides a summary of the current billing amount (current gross earnings, current retainage withheld, and net amount due). Most payment application summaries also include a summary of the contract (original contract amount, change orders, and miscellaneous other adjustments, such as liquidated damages assessments or stop notice withholdings) and the total-to-date billing status (total earned to date, retainage to date, net earnings, and payments to date).

4. Payment Application/Requisition Drafts

Payment application/requisition drafts, also referred to as "pencil drafts," are the preliminary detail sheets created in the determination of the payment application. The preliminary detail includes handwritten notes of quantity or completion percentage estimates determined during the general contractor's or subcontractor's month-end jobsite walk-through with the owner's or general contractor's representative.

5. Subcontractor and Supplier Releases

The contractor should have received and filed releases from subcontractors and suppliers, including all known lower-tier subcontractors and suppliers as payment proceeds. See Exhibit 29 for a sample subcontractor release. While the releases apply to more than just a subcontractor's or supplier's lien rights, such as stop notice and payment bond rights, these releases are generically called "lien releases." They are statements that a subcontractor or supplier has released its stop notice, payment bond, and mechanic's lien rights, among others, for work performed or materials supplied. Lien releases can be either conditional or unconditional. A conditional lien release states that the subcontractor or supplier releases its various rights upon actually receiving payment. An unconditional lien release means that the subcontractor or supplier has received full payment and unconditionally releases all rights regarding the project for the pay period at issue. General contractors collect conditional lien releases from subcontractors and suppliers monthly, prior to paying them. The contractor must require subcontractors and suppliers to provide lien releases from lower-tier subcontractors and suppliers that should have submitted "preliminary" or supplier notices to ensure that those lower-tier entities have received proper payment.

6. Check Copies

Many companies keep a copy of the checks received.

7. Stop Notices

The billing file should include copies of stop notices (sometimes called stop payment notices) that subcontractors or suppliers have submitted to the owner indicating that they have not received payment for amounts due from the contractor. The owner will withhold payment in the amount of the stop notice, plus some percentage (often 25%), until the parties resolve the payment issue.

8. Stop Notice Releases

Stop notice releases are the forms that subcontractors or suppliers submit to an owner indicating that the previously submitted stop notice issue has been resolved and the owner no longer needs to withhold funds from the contractor for that issue.

I. Process Management Files

During a construction project, the parties maintain several files to document the progress of the work as well as issues that arise during construction, generically referred to as the process management files.

Many contracts require the contractor's and owner's representative, usually an architect or construction manager, to maintain specific files in a particular manner. The contract will expressly identify the types of files required (for example, "Correspondence to Architect") and the documents to be included in that file (for example, all communications the general contractor sends to the architect that do not relate to any other identified category). In those cases, the parties will identify each document on its face with an acronym identifying the party and document number. For example, ABC Contracting's first letter to the architect would be located in the Correspondence to Architect file and identified as ABC-1.

Where the contract does not require the maintenance of the project files in a particular manner, there are nonetheless certain general categories of files that the contractor's and owner's representative regularly maintain. Project management files include the following.

1. Request for Information File (RFI)

The owner and the contractor generally maintain RFIs and responses to the RFIs in a separate RFI file. The RFIs and responses to RFIs are often in standard form to facilitate communication between the owner's representative and the contractor. Sometimes, rather than using forms, an RFI from the contractor may be no more than a transmittal letter forwarding a concern that a subcontractor has raised to the owner's representative.

The owner and the contractor may also include a copy of the RFI in the particular sub-file related to the subject of the request. For example, an RFI that asks a design question regarding the ventilation system may also be included in the HVAC subcontractor's file. However, the parties should maintain a copy of each RFI and the corresponding response in a separate RFI file. Each RFI file should include an RFI Log. The RFI log is a running index of each RFI submitted on the project, along with its response.

The RFI log commonly records the following:

- The number of the RFI;
- The location of the RFI in the file (usually by document number as explained above);
- The RFI date;
- The general subject of the RFI;
- The date of the response to the RFI.

Another document that may be included in the RFI file is the Architect's Supplemental Instructions (ASIs), which may be a direct response to a contractor's RFI. The parties may also store the ASIs in a separate file containing a separate log. An ASI is a document that the architect or owner's representative issues to the contractor providing supplemental instructions for the performance of the work. The ASI generally involves a minor change to the work that does not impact the contract price or time of performance. The contractor signs the ASI to indicate its receipt and acceptance.

2. Changes File

During the course of construction, it often becomes necessary to make changes to the original design or scope of work included in the contract. The parties accomplish these changes in several ways. Consequently, various types of files and documents memorialize the changes to the design or scope of work On a less complicated project, the parties may maintain all of these change documents in one file simply identified as "Scope of Work Issues" or "Changes." On a more complex project, each type of change would likely result in a separate file.

a. Change Order Request (COR)

When a contractor perceives the need for the owner to issue a change order, as discussed below, the contractor will submit to the owner a COR. Depending upon the circumstances, the owner may then issue a change order.

b. Change Orders (COs)

In general, a CO is a written change to the contract that the owner's representative prepares and the owner and contractor sign, documenting a change to the contract scope of work resulting in a revision to the contract price and/or time for contract performance. For the owner to issue a CO, the owner and contractor must agree on the change to the work and the contract price and time revisions. COs usually appear on a standard form. See Exhibit 33 for a sample CO--AIA Document G701™ - 2017. The owner's representative completes the form and includes a description of the work, the price adjustment, the time adjustment, and the reason for the change.

Often the owner's representative will request that the contractor submit a proposal for a contract price and/or time adjustment related to the change in the design or scope of work prior to issuing the CO. The CO proposal generally includes all of the background information that the contractor used in reaching its projected contract price and/or time adjustment, including any drawings, product and price information, and calculations. The owner's representative may incorporate the proposal, along with all of the background information related to it, into the CO by reference.

The parties usually maintain COs in a separate file with a separate, running CO log. The parties could also maintain a copy of the CO in the subfile related to the content of the request. For example, the contractor could include a copy of a CO related to the type of flooring for the project in the CO file as well as the flooring subcontractor's file.

c. Force Account or Extra Work

Sometimes an owner's representative will direct the contractor to perform certain work on a force account or extra work basis. In that case, the contractor will record daily the labor, equipment, and material used related to the work on a form called an extra work bill, extra work daily report, or extra work ticket. The contractor and the owner's representative will sign the form daily indicating agreement on the information included on the form, such as labor and equipment hours and quantities of materials put in place. However, no price is included on the form because the contract specifications or special provisions include the labor, equipment, material, overhead, and profit rates. Both the contractor and the owner's representative maintain a copy of the form. Generally, the contractor maintains the extra work forms in a separate file so that the contractor can easily verify the hours and quantities applicable to the extra work.

d. Construction Change Directives (CCDs)

A CCD is a written order directing a change in the work within the general scope of work of the contract. The owner's representative will use a CCD where the owner's representative and contractor do not agree on the terms of a change order, such as the contractor's proposed price. The owner's representative prepares the CCD, generally on a standard form that includes revisions to the contract, including adjustments to contract price and time, if applicable. Both the owner's representative and the owner, but not the contractor, execute the CCD. The owner's representative then gives a copy of the CCD to the contractor. Both the contractor and the owner's representative generally maintain the CCDs in separate files with separate logs. If the CCD relates to a particular subcontractor's work, the contractor will often keep a copy of the CCD in that subcontractor's subfile as well.

e. Field Orders

A field order is a written order that the owner or the owner's representative issues to the contractor as a directive to clarify a specification, resolve a site access difficulty, deal with technical execution problems, or change the contract documents. The owner's representative often writes the order after giving a verbal directive. A field order itself cannot change the contract price or time. If, however, the field order increases costs or time, it should lead to a change order. This issue is often a source of dispute between contractors and owners.

f. Claims

The claim procedure, including requirements for claim documentation, is generally contained in the contract. The claim procedure allows a contractor to submit the basis for its disagreement with the owner's representative as to whether a particular item of work results in a change to the contract price or time. The contractor and owner's representative usually maintain the claim documents in a separate file. The contract dictates the types of documents required and the time requirements for the submission of a claim.

(i) Notice of Claim

On many projects, prior to a formal submission of a claim, the contractor must first give the owner and/or owner's representative a notice of claim. The notice of claim may be a standard form that the owner's representative has provided. The notice of claim will include a brief description of the basis for the claim; it usually will not include specific information regarding increases to contract price and time. The contractor will usually provide the notice of claim to the owner and the owner's representative.

(ii) Claim

The claim itself is the contractor's written request for an increase in the contract price and/or time in excess of that set forth in the construction contract and that the owner's representative has rejected. The claim should include the exact amount of the requested price and/or time adjustment, along with all documentation supporting the contractor's position. The supporting documentation might include copies of cost estimates, subcontractor invoices, subcontractor bills, citations to industry guides/standards, and correspondence between the contractor and owner's representative. The owner's representative provides a written response to the claim, including an explanation of the basis for its response. At that point, either the parties resolve the claim, and the owner issues a change order or the matter proceeds to the additional dispute resolution procedure outlined in the contract.

3. Schedule File

On most construction projects, after the owner awards the contract, the contractor must prepare and submit its anticipated schedule integrating all work within the time allotted in the contract. This initial schedule is often referred to as the "baseline schedule." The contractor, owner's representative, and the owner maintain the schedule in a separate file. Often, the owner will dictate the information that the contractor is to include in the schedule or provide a standard form. The owner's requirements or form will generally include the following items:

- General description of the project;
- Contract working days;
- Start date;
- Proposed sequence of work (often depicted by a horizontal bar graph);
- "Controlling" or "critical path" items (often identified on the horizontal bar graph);
- Projected number of working days for each item (often shown on the horizontal bar graph);
- Proposed progress of the work.

The contractor usually provides a separate "schedule of submittals" that coordinates with the construction schedule. This schedule of submittals is important so that the approval of the contract submittals progresses along with the construction work progress. The contractor and owner's representative often maintain the "schedule of submittals" with the schedule file.

As the work progresses, the contract time adjusts, by change order or another method, such that the contractor must make revisions to the schedule. The contractor will revise the original schedule and submit a copy of the revised or updated schedule to the owner's representative often due with each pay application. The contractor and owner's representative will maintain the revised schedule in the same file as the original schedule.

Additionally, it is common for the owner's representative to prepare weekly reports to the owner regarding the contractor's actual performance of the construction work as compared to the contractor's construction schedule. This report is commonly called the weekly statement of working days, or the weekly report. The owner's representative usually prepares it on a standard form and includes the day, date, hours worked, "controlling" or "critical path" item, number of working days charged, and a brief statement of whether the contractor's performance is consistent with the construction schedule. The owner's representative gives a copy of the report to the contractor. The contractor and the owner's representative generally maintain the report in a separate file entitled weekly reports.

On many construction projects, the contractor provides a two- or four-week "look ahead" schedule. As its name implies, it provides a prospective of the work the contractor plans to perform in the next two or four weeks, typically in more detail than the schedule itself. The contractor and owner's representative handle the look-ahead schedule in the same manner as the weekly reports described above.

4. Meeting Minutes Files

Throughout the life of a construction project, the parties hold many organized meetings to discuss project issues. The meetings are generally phase-specific and relate to matters at issue during that construction phase. The meetings are often entitled OAC meetings, standing for Owner, Architect, and Contractor. At each meeting, one party is responsible for recording the official meeting minutes and circulating the minutes to the attendees. The format of the meeting minutes, regardless of which construction phase is involved, is generally the same and usually resembles a business memorandum although with boxes that include each particular facet of construction at issue, what was discussed, what is planned, and who has responsibility for that particular facet. The recorder will provide a copy of the meeting minutes to all of the meeting's attendees. The recorder will address the minutes "to" the attendees.

Usually, the recorder obtains the attendees' contact information through an attendance form that each attendee at the meeting signs providing name, company, and contact information. The recorder is identified in the "from" line of the heading. The recorder will date the meeting minutes on the date they are prepared; in many cases, the meeting minutes are prepared on the same day as the meeting. In the subject line of the meeting minutes memorandum, the recorder will indicate the name of the project and the date of the meeting, at a minimum. See Exhibit 38 for an example of the agenda for the preparation of meeting minutes.

a. Pre-Bid Meeting Minutes

Some projects may require that contractors interested in bidding on the project attend a "pre-bid" meeting. The purpose of the meeting is to ensure that those contractors interested in submitting a bid understand the project well enough to provide a responsible and responsive bid. A "pre-bid meeting" will not generally involve a discussion of construction methods or project progress. The owner's representative, often the architect or construction manager, directs the meeting and records the meeting minutes.

b. Pre-Construction Meeting Minutes

Before construction begins, the parties attend a "pre-construction" meeting, which includes the owner, the owner's representatives, the design professionals, the contractor, and the subcontractors. The owner's representative typically directs the meeting and records the meeting minutes. The owner may review and/or approve the meeting minutes before the owner's representative issues them to the other attendees.

c. Progress Meeting Minutes

Most contracts require regularly held progress meetings during construction. These meetings are sometimes called OAC (Owner-Architect-Contractor) meetings. Depending on the complexity of the project, these meetings will be held weekly or monthly on the same day of the week or month and at the same time. In more recent times, the meetings are often hybrid with some people attending in person, some virtually, and some via telephone. The meeting attendees generally include the owner, the owner's representative, certain design professionals, the general contractor, and any major subcontractor or supplier working on the project at the point in time of the progress meeting. Either the owner's representative or the general contractor conducts the meeting and records the meeting minutes. The recorder then distributes the meeting minutes to all attendees with sufficient time to allow those attendees to review them and suggest revisions prior to the next meeting.

d. Safety/"Tool Box" Meeting Minutes

Many contracts also require the general contractor to ensure that its subcontractors conduct regular safety meetings. These meetings are sometimes referred to as "toolbox" meetings. The purpose of these meetings is to provide safety and health training and information to the laborers on the project. Attendees of these meetings include the superintendent or foreperson for the particular subcontractor and the subcontractors' employees on the site and may include a representative of the owner and general contractor. The subcontractor's superintendent or foreperson conducts the meeting and records the minutes. The subcontractor generally provides a copy of the meeting minutes to the general contractor, regardless of whether the general contractor's representative was in attendance at the meeting, as evidence of its compliance with the contract's safety requirements.

5. Work Performance File

During construction, various parties write several reports to document the installation of materials, the quality of safety employed on the site, and the quality of work put in place and to record generally the work in progress and the site conditions on any given date. These documents, prepared contemporaneously with the work, are often pivotal in gaining a later understanding of what occurred on the project and which parties were involved in work performance and decision-making.

a. Material Inspection Report/Material Release Summary

A material inspection report or material release summary is a document that the owner's representative prepares to record materials delivered to the site. For example, a steel supplier might deliver all of the steel beams for the project at one time. The contractor will not install the steel beams on the day of delivery. Therefore, the parties inspect the materials for compliance with the plans and specifications, inventory them, identify them by number, and store them. Later, when needed, the contractor releases the materials to the steel erector for installation.

The material inspection report or material release summary is the document that records all information related to these materials. This report or summary is typically a form document prepared that the owner's representative has prepared. It includes the following information:

- The type of material;
- The contract item to which the material relates;
- The name of the supplier;
- The date of receipt of the materials;
- The quantity delivered;
- The lot or identification number.

Later, when it is time for the contractor to release some or all of the materials, the owner's representative records, on either the same form or an attached form, the following information:

- The release date of the materials;
- The quantity released;
- The lot or identification number of the released quantities.

The owner's representative retains a copy of the form and usually provides a copy to the supplier and the general contractor.

b. Approved Quantity Reports

An approved quantity report or quantity sheet is a document that the owner's representative prepares that documents the materials put in place on a particular date. This report applies to "unit price contracts and serves as the basis for determining the number of units installed on a particular date to allow payment to the contractor for the work performed. The owner's representative may prepare more than one form on a project as the work typically progresses over several pay periods. Certain items appear in every report:

- The contract item to which the material relates;
- The total planned quantity of the material;
- The unit of measure (for instance, yards);
- The contract unit price;
- The authorization of the owner's representative that the contractor performed the work.

The report may also include:

- The date of material installation;
- The location of the material installation (for example, if a roadway, the point of installation on the road);
- The quantities put in place on that specific date;
- The total quantity in place as of that date.

The owner's representative will retain a copy of the report and will provide a copy to the general contractor and, if applicable, to the subcontractor.

c. Safety Reports

Occasionally, the federal or state Occupational Safety and Health Administration (OSHA) will conduct safety inspections. OSHA will provide its observations on a form report and note items of concern that the parties must address. The contractor, in turn, provides a copy of the report to any subcontractors involved and requires the subcontractor to correct any issues. If a safety concern is serious, OSHA may "tag" the project site and prohibit any work on the site until the contractor corrects the problem. The owner's representative and the general contractor each receive a copy of the OSHA report and/or tag in order to remedy the concerns.

d. Owner's Representative Daily Report

The owner's representative on the project site, typically a construction manager, resident architect, or engineer keeps a log generally recording all activities on the project site each day. The report includes the following information:

- The date;
- The day of the week;
- The time(s) of the day the owner's representative was at the site;
- The temperature and other weather conditions.

The narrative of the report will identify the subcontractors present on the site and describe generally the work they are performing. The narrative may also include any significant conversations or questions. Often, the owner's representative keeps the daily report in a bound diary-often the only copy. Sometimes, the daily report is a loose sheet, in which case the party writing it usually signs it and keeps it in a file or binder. In any event, the owner's representative usually maintains the daily reports on the project site until the close of the project. In today's day and age, many of these reports are kept in digital format, often on tablets that facilitate handwriting directly to the tablet.

e. General Contractor's Daily Report

The general contractor's representative on the project site, usually the project manager or project superintendent, also keeps a daily log or diary. The general contractor's report also includes the date, the day of the week, the time(s) of the day that he or she was at the site, and the temperature and other weather conditions. The narrative of the report will identify the subcontractors present on the site and generally describe the work being performed; it may also note whether the owner's representative is present on the site. The general contractor's log may also include any significant conversations or questions. It may also include issues to address with the owner's representative in the future or other items related to construction. Usually, the general contractor maintains the report in a bound diary at the project site until the close of the project. Again, these reports are often now prepared and stored digitally.

6. Certified Payroll Report File

The terms of public contracts will usually require that the general contractor and subcontractors submit labor compliance documentation

(Certified Payroll Reports) for those forces that are subject to prevailing wage requirements. The contract documents will identify the forms and information that the general contractor and subcontractors must provide. The general contractor keeps a copy of the Certified Payroll Reports and also provides copies to the owner's representative and any governmental authorities that require them.

The Certified Payroll Reports, provided weekly, typically include the following:

- The name of each employee;
- The social security number for each employee;
- The employees' work classification or craft;
- The day, date, and hours worked per day;
- The total hours for the period, including overtime;
- The rate of pay;
- The gross amount earned for the specific project;
- The total that the employee earned for the period;
- The tax and other deductions;
- Fringe benefits;
- Travel and subsistence payments;
- The net wages paid;
- Check number.

The general contractor must provide an affidavit with the Certified Payroll Reports testifying that the information included in the reports is accurate and that the contractor has paid all employees as indicated on the reports. That affidavit is why they are called Certified Payroll Reports. Certified Payroll Reports are typically produced automatically through the company's payroll software system or by a third-party payroll service if the general contractor or its subcontractors utilize such a service for processing payroll.

Another common labor report often required of a contractor is a "Fringe Benefit Statement." The statement verifies payrolls and will apply to any force account work done on the project. For each employee, the general contractor provides the dollar amount of vacation time, health and welfare benefits, pension, any apprentice or other fees, and the name and address of the fund (usually, a union trust fund) to which the benefits are paid.

7. Correspondence Files

Oftentimes a project will have correspondence or documents that do not relate to any other category of documents used in maintaining the construction project records. To address this issue, the contractor will usually create "general correspondence" files. Because the general contractor will maintain most of the project correspondence on the project in the file of the particular issue to which it relates (for example, RFIs, COs, ABC subcontractor), there are often few general correspondence files. However, the volume of these files frequently grows exponentially throughout a project, particularly if there are disputes. It is common that the contractor maintains separate "'to" and "from" files. Such general correspondence files typically include the following:

- To Architect;
- From Architect;
- To Construction Manager/Resident Engineer;
- From Construction Manager/Resident Engineer;
- To Inspector(s) of Record;
- From Inspector(s) of Record;
- To Utility Companies;
- From Utility Companies;
- To Owner/Contracting Officer;
- From Owner/Contracting Officer.

Included in the general correspondence file of the owner's representative are any documents related to the owner's contention that the contractor is in default. Therefore, the correspondence file may include:

- The owner's notice(s) of default and right to cure;
- Notice(s) of cure (See Exhibit 42 for a sample of Notice to Cure);
- Notice of termination either for convenience or for cause.

These documents often take the form of correspondence rather than form documents. The owner's representative, however, may create a separate "default file" and maintain those documents separately from the general correspondence.

J. Close-Out File

Project close-out is the process of completing all the construction and paperwork required to finish a contract. It is often the work that project managers like the least and perform the worst. Contractors should have set procedures, documented by a checklist or log, for closing out a project and compiling all the necessary documents. Those documents are discussed below.

1. As-Planned and As-Built Schedules

Sometimes, the contract will require the contractor to provide an as-built schedule at the conclusion of the project. Also, if the contractor has a dispute with the owner, the contractor will prepare an as-planned/as-built schedule that compares the schedule that the contractor anticipated when it started the project to what actually happened during construction.

2. Inspection and Deficiency Reports

The owner's representative receives inspection reports throughout the project as various governmental inspectors review the work of the contractor and the subcontractors. Deficiency reports describe aspects of the work that are defective or not in compliance with applicable codes. Ultimately, the contractor should receive signed-off permits from the authority having jurisdiction over the project.

3. Punch Lists

The architect or owner's representative typically develops the punch list based on a walk-through of the project at or near the end of construction. The punch list is a list of items that the contractor needs to complete or correct for the project to be 100% complete. Once the contractor completes the punch list work, all of the responsible parties should sign off on the punch list.

4. Operations and Maintenance Manuals (O&Ms)

O&Ms are the collection and organization of data on "what" and "how to" regarding all of the operational equipment on a project. The contractor collects the O&Ms from all appropriate subcontractors and suppliers and organizes them in hard copy or electronic binders for the owner.

5. Warranties

Written and signed warranties and guarantees from all subcontractors and suppliers, including lower-tier subcontractors and suppliers, should be included in the close-out file. These warranties are in addition to any express warranties in the construction contract by which the contractor agrees to correct defective work within a certain period of time.

6. As-Built Drawings

Contract specifications usually require the contractor to provide as-built drawings detailing the design as actually built. The general contractor and the major trade subcontractors note the actual dimensions and conditions of installed work on the contract drawings. The parties often attach the field questions and sketches to the drawing. From this information, the general contractor will prepare as-built architectural, structural, and, sometimes, civil drawings.

7. Certificate/Notice of Substantial Completion

According to the AIA 201™ General Conditions, and other contract General Conditions, once the work on a project is substantially complete, the architect or the owner's representative is to prepare and issue a "certificate of substantial completion," which indicates that the contractor has "substantially" completed the work with minor exceptions, such as remaining punch list items. It is an important document in that it often signals the end of the contractors' liquidated damages exposure and may also indicate the date of the owner's beneficial occupancy. The date of substantial completion also is the time when the owner becomes responsible for maintenance items and when warranties commence, although certain material warranties commence upon delivery or installation and not upon substantial completion.

8. Certificate of Occupancy

In some locales, prior to the owner's taking possession of the property upon substantial completion, the applicable inspector must certify that the property is fit for occupation. Once the inspection is complete, the local inspector will issue a "certificate of occupancy" attesting that it has accounted for all code-related issues and that the project is sufficiently complete for the owner to safely occupy it. In contracts that do not require a "certificate of substantial completion," the "certificate of occupancy" can establish the date of substantial completion.

9. Consent of Surety to Release Retainage/Retention

Once the owner's representative issues the certificate of substantial completion, the contractor and owner's representative may request that the general contractor's surety issue a consent to the owner to reduce the retainage that the owner is holding and make payment to the contractor. Such a consent of surety may be a requirement of the contract, or it may simply be the business practice of the owner to obtain a consent of surety. The consent of surety typically indicates that the surety has not received any payment bond claims.

CHAPTER V

PROCESSES UNDERTAKEN DURING A CONSTRUCTION PROJECT

A. Introduction

Throughout a construction project, from conceptual planning through completion, some processes are used to efficiently and successfully complete a construction project. These processes can assist in organizing project documentation, collaboration between team members, and managing the project budget. These processes have evolved, and, in this chapter, we are going to discuss them and when the parties may implement them. In particular, we are going to discuss the most significant processes, which the parties use during different phases of the construction project.

As one might expect, the construction of roads and bridges, facilities for handling waste and wastewater products, large infrastructure, prisons, court facilities, schools, and other such facilities tend to be public projects. Therefore, procurement statutes, regulations, and policies, such as competitive/sealed bidding requirements and participation prerequisites related to disadvantaged business entities (DBEs) often govern vendor procurement (both design and contracting).

By contrast, residential single and multi-family home-building, office buildings, private hospitals, private schools, manufacturing facilities, retail outlets, hotels, and other such projects tend to be privately owned construction. Private construction procurement is largely free of regulatory restrictions and, therefore, best business practices, personal preferences, and the owner's financial constraints typically govern the procurement process.

In recent years, there has been a significant increase in construction performed through public-private partnerships (PPPs), which is an arrangement whereby private entities collaborate with government agencies to design, finance, build, and operate new construction. Typically, PPP arrangements feature a long-term contract in which the private entity finances some or all of the initial building costs of the public project, which are commonly infrastructure projects such as roads, bridges, or parks. The project is almost always revenue-bearing. The private participant enters into a PPP under the expectation that it will recoup its construction and operation/maintenance costs, and, ideally, realize future profit by collecting an agreed percentage of the revenue stream from the completed project.

B. Processes During the Pre-Construction Project Phase

Utilizing pre-established and well-defined processes during the pre-construction phase will assist the owner/developer in making an informed decision regarding the feasibility of the project. Those processes will also enable the owner/developer to efficiently develop conceptual plans and materials to review with investing parties. Good pre-construction processes will also ensure the efficient development of detailed design/construction documents that will ideally reduce unforeseen conditions and change orders during the construction phase. In the following sections, we will discuss the pre-construction process and some of the technology that is used during that process.

1. Project Planning and Feasibility Analysis

a. Project Objectives and Scope of the Project

Among the first steps in the pre-construction process is the development of objectives as well as the scope of the project. Logically, the owner/developer drives this process. In the private sector, this process could entail looking at the needs of a community and developing initial objectives that will satisfy those needs. For example, the community may need more housing, more retail, more lab space, or all of the above. In this scenario, the owner/developer will identify project objectives and a scope for the project that would satisfy these objectives. Similarly, in the public sector, the commencement of a project could be driven by public needs or demands. Does the community need a new school with upgraded technology? In this case, the objective would be to do just that - provide the community with a new school with up-to-date technology to enhance the students' learning experience. In both the private and public sectors, the owner/developer will first develop the objectives and then the scope of the project. Although early in the planning stage, the owner may prepare schematic drawings and a three-dimensional rendering to demonstrate the magnitude and functionality of the project.

b. Market Research and Demand Analysis

The next step in the pre-construction process is gathering data to support the demand for the development of the project. This data gathering could involve retaining a market research firm to gather necessary information regarding the needs of the area, future development in the area, and future economic factors related to the area. For example, a pharmaceutical company opening a manufacturing facility in the area may require more housing, service industries, and retail for employees. The goal of this due diligence process is to determine both the demand for the proposed construction project and the related needs surrounding the potential project. In the public sector, political concerns such as the community's need for a new school or a new park may drive this demand.

c. Other Due Diligence Considerations

Along with market research, during this due diligence process, the developer/owner will also review other factors that may affect the project. For example, there may be environmental factors that could affect the community, such as how this proposed development will affect traffic in the area. The owner/developer should also be familiar with the local politics in the area. In other words, will the community accept this project? Although there is a demand, there may be other factors impacting the project. The owner/developer will need to assess how the other factors will affect the feasibility of the project.

d. Presenting a Plan to the Finance Team

Once the demand analysis and the community due diligence process are complete, the next step in the pre-construction process is to develop a plan to present to financing entities. This plan will include a package for both equity and debt lenders. In the public sector, this package could be presented to a local building committee or state or federal agencies that are providing funds. Private developers often work with certain equity partners and then work with lending institutions for debt financing. Others collaborate with brokers that will line up both debt and equity financing. For this process, the owner/developer usually presents a narrative describing the scope of the project; the demand for the project; a background of the development team's experience; schematic drawings; and a three-dimensional rendering that demonstrates the functionality and visual magnitude of the project. Most importantly, the narrative may include a proforma of the project illustrating its financial feasibility.

2. The Design and Architectural Planning Process

The next step in the pre-construction process is the design and architectural planning phase. This phase starts by retaining a lead designer to manage the design process. There may be a request for proposal (RFP) process by which the owner solicits qualification packages and fee proposals from potential architects (design leads) to prepare the design. In preparing a response to the RFP, the architect will team with other design professionals to demonstrate their experience in designing a project of this size and scope.

a. The Design Team

The architect's design team is made up of several team members. Along with the lead architect, there will be several other design disciplines working on the design team. Some of the major design disciplines on a typical design team are as follows:

(i) Architect (usually the design team lead)

(ii) Mechanical, Electrical, Plumbing, and Sprinkler Engineers (also known as MEPS)

(iii) Structural Engineer

(iv) Civil Site Design Engineer

(v) Landscape Designer

(vi) Interior Designer

(vii) Specialty Designers

b. Technology Used in the Design Process

To integrate the numerous design disciplines, many designers use a collaborative design process utilizing building information modeling (BIM) software. For the design team professionals, BIM enables the design disciplines (Architect, MEP Engineers, Structural Engineer, Civil Site Engineer, Landscape Designer, and other Specialty Designers) to share a virtual model. Each professional adds discipline-specific data to the shared model, commonly known as the 'federated' model. Combining models enables visualization of all models in a single environment and enables the designers to work out "clashes" as well as providing for a more coordinated process. Resolving these clashes in the design phase saves time and money when it comes to the construction phase.

The professionals typically have design collaboration meetings during the design phase where they review clashes between the models and other issues within the federated model. At these meetings, after reviewing any clashes between discipline models, the professionals decide what changes they must make in order to resolve the clashes. This process catches any potential conflict in the design drawings which hopefully substantially reduces change orders due to design deficiencies during the construction process. It also improves the procurement process by calculating the exact quantity of certain materials.

Along with the three-dimensional BIM model, the design team can also use this information to provide three-dimensional renderings of the project. These project renderings provide an accurate visual model of the project as designed. In some instances, the design teams also use augmented reality with a headset to visualize a myriad of views of the construction including, for example, how furniture and room finishes will look in a designed space. The use of technology has advanced exponentially over the past decade, and, through artificial intelligence and other advancements, technology will continue to change and benefit the pre-construction process.

c. Programming and Planning

Once the design team is assembled, the programming process commences. This process includes taking the project concept objectives and reviewing them against the functionality of the project. In some instances, this review could involve meetings with the end user or stakeholders. For example, in the construction of a new research laboratory, the design team will likely meet with several managers of the laboratory to discuss the needs and functionality of the workspace. Similarly, with the construction of a new school, the design team may meet with the principal and several department heads to review objectives and functionality. These practical meetings are an important part of the process that enables the design team to combine objectives and functionality to create a favorable design.

d. Architectural Plans and Design Options

During the design process, the design team will use information and data obtained in the programming and planning process to prepare design documents that address design objectives, functionality, and owner preferences. The design team will then present design options to the owner, highlighting design necessities/functionality and design preferences. Based on budget concerns, the owner can work with the design team on the most favorable design.

e. Cost Estimation and Budgeting

Along with design options, the design team will collaborate with the owner and develop various budgets for the different design options. These budget estimates may consider historical costs, current market condition costs, risk factors, and contingencies. Utilizing the BIM model, the cost estimator can obtain precise material take-offs. With this data, the estimator will utilize cost-estimating software to provide the owner with budgets for different design options. The cost estimator will also work with the design team on value engineering for the project. This includes evaluating design options with similar functionality that can reduce the project budget. Depending upon the delivery method, the contractor may be involved in the cost estimating and value engineering process. We will discuss delivery methods in the upcoming sections. Examples of commonly used construction estimating software are Buildxact, PlanSwift, and Stack.

3. Procurement Strategy and Contracting Process

There are several procurement/delivery models for a construction project. Regardless of the model, the process will entail the preparation of bid documents such as the invitation to bid, instructions to bidders, a bid form, and contract documents. The procurement process for public and private projects contains similar documents; however, the bidding procedures for public projects may differ drastically. Public projects often require participation from a Woman- and Minority-Owned Business Enterprise (WMBE) and/or a Small Business Enterprise (SBE). They may also have "set aside projects" for veteran-owned companies or other classifications. Certain municipalities may also have a "filed sub-bid" process where only qualified subcontractors can bid on the project. Each public entity will have its own specific requirements.

Some of the most common procurement models are design-build, design-bid-build, construction management, CM/GC (Construction Manager/General Contractor), and unit cost. The procurement process for some of these models is discussed below:

a. Procurement Delivery Models

(i) Design-Build Delivery Method Process

Utilizing the design-build procurement model, the owner will prepare a request for a proposal (RFP) for an entity to design and build the project. The bid documents usually contain a performance specification, a conceptual drawing, and the qualification parameters of the bidding design-build entity. This package enables the bidders to respond to the owner with a qualified design-build team. As part of its proposal, the bidder may also provide schematic drawings and preliminary specifications. The design-build model gives a single point of responsibility for delivering the entire project and can help ensure good buildability, cost control, and speed. In a design-build project delivery scenario, the design-builder is obviously involved early in the process and either self-performs the design preparation or retains the design team directly (rather than the owner doing so directly). The general contractor may retain certain subcontractors that are critical to the project earlier than is typical in other project delivery methods to assist with fine-tuning the design, securing pricing, reviewing constructability issues, and other related matters.

(ii) Design-Bid-Build Delivery Method Process

In the design-bid-build arrangement, the owner contracts with the design team, and the general contractor is typically not involved until the design team has largely completed the design and the owner has released the resulting plans and specifications for competitive bidding or negotiated pricing. After the design is complete, the owner will provide the bidders with detailed specifications, drawings, and general conditions. The bidders will respond typically with a lump sum price to complete the defined scope illustrated in the contract documents. The design-bid-build project delivery method is the most commonly used in the United States public works construction market due to competitive bidding requirements. While this method is usually the most economical, it is rigid. If the construction documents are not clearly defined, unforeseen change orders could occur that could cause the budget to unexpectedly increase.

(iii) Construction Management

The construction management (CM) procurement method solicits a contractor to provide general conditions to manage the project and work with the owner on an open-book basis to scope and buy out the project. The RFP will typically request a lump sum for general conditions and a fee to buy out and manage the construction. Another version of the CM model is the construction manager at risk (CMAR) model. Under this delivery model, the CM typically bids a guaranteed maximum price (GMP) for the project. If the project costs exceed the budget, the CM is at risk for the additional cost. If the project budget is under, the CM would make more profit unless the bid provides for a shared-saving contingency. This model improves and requires communication between the owner, the designer, and the contractor.

(iv) Unit Cost

In the unit cost procurement method, the owner provides the bidders with a schedule of quantities to be installed, delivered, or removed for the project, and the bidders bid unit costs for each of the quantity line items. This method of procurement is typical for roadway and site work. These bid quantities are estimated, and actual quantities will go up or down based on the actual quantities installed. Another version of unit cost contracts is continuing contracts used primarily for maintenance. Continuing contracts are similar to unit price contracts except that the owner will request a bid price for maintaining a building on a square foot basis, building out or demolishing interior portions of a building on a square foot basis, etc. The contract runs for a specific duration of time and the ultimate quantity of work that the contractor will perform is uncertain.

(v) Multi-Prime Delivery Method Process

The procurement process for a multi-prime bid is similar to the design-bid-build method, but the owner uses individual bid packages for trade contractors, not general contractors. Rather than the general contractor selecting the subcontractors, the owner bids each package of trades as a prime contract. In this scenario, the owner usually has a construction manager manage all of the multi-prime contractors. This process is common with public construction and provides for competitive bidding at the subcontractor level. It also provides the owner with more control over the subcontractors.

There are several other delivery methods, but, the above-referenced are the most common. Other, less-common procurement methods include public-private partnerships (PPP or P3) and integrated project delivery (IPD). Regardless of the structure, the pre-construction documents are similar; however, the bid package requirements can have some significant differences.

b. Bidding Procedures

Regardless of the procurement model that the owner chooses, the owner and its design team will prepare a bid package that is intended to include sufficient information to allow prospective contractors to determine both their initial interest in participating in the project and to prepare a viable bid or proposal. A typical bid package includes contract drawings (detailed plans), specifications, information on the project location and surrounding buildings, and, the various required forms that the contractor must use such as an initial bid form and lien waiver forms. In recent years, the detailed plans may include three-dimensional plans of the proposed building developed through BIM, which, as explained earlier, is a useful tool that promotes collaboration among the members of the design and construction teams and helps identify and resolve design conflicts (particularly related to MEP work in confined spaces) at an earlier stage.

In some circumstances, particularly on public projects, the bid package will also include information about statutory or regulatory requirements such as wage and hour requirements and related labor reporting requirements. The bid information will also describe any project participation/set-aside requirements for various types of Disadvantaged Business Enterprises (DBEs).

To generate interest in projects subject to competitive and sealed bidding, the owner usually publishes the bid package in bulletins forwarded to contractors who are on bidding lists. Bid documents for both public and private works projects are also published in "Dodge" rooms, other bid depositories, and through organizations having contractor-members. Of course, the digitization of construction documents has now made it easier to access and transmit bid documentation in electronic format.

(i) Invitation for Bid

An invitation for bid (IFB) is typically used in a competitive, sealed bidding scenario where the scope of the project is known and well-defined. The IFB package should enable interested bidders to put together a detailed estimate, know the specific materials and equipment for procurement, and be aware of any statutory requirements that may impact the availability and cost of required labor and the nature of the permitting and inspection processes. As long as the bidder meets qualified criteria, pricing determines the successful bidder in the IFB process.

Typically, statutes or regulations requiring a construction project to be competitively bid through an IFB govern public projects, although certain exemptions, such as for emergency work, do apply. Public projects will have open bidding procedures for any qualified contractor wishing to bid, and the owner may express minimum qualifications for bidding contractors. Public owners usually do not have the legal discretion to select the pool of bidders and must entertain bids from any qualified bidder. In nearly all cases, a public entity must accept the lowest bid from a qualified bidder unless certain statutory bidder preferences or other exceptions apply.

(ii) Request for Proposal

A request for proposal (RFP) procurement process is more frequently used in a design-build scenario where an owner knows what it wants as the final product and can provide generic specifications, sometimes called "performance specifications," as distinguished from "design specifications," with a pre-determined design. This form of negotiated procurement is mostly limited to private-sector construction. The RFP process is still competitive but tends to look at factors beyond just price. It may involve continuing negotiations between the owner and several prospective contractors after the submission of initial responses in addition to a request for a final and best offer from each contender.

In the private sector, factors that may influence an owner's decision to reject the lowest price proposal include the contractor's experience with the type of work involved, prior favorable business dealings with the contractor, personal loyalties, or simply a belief that the personality of a specific contractor will work better with the owner's design team. Typically, a private owner can select and reject bidders without fear of allegations that the owner has acted improperly or illegally.

(iii) Fully Negotiated Contracts with Chosen Contractor

Fully negotiated, non-competitive bidding scenarios can follow almost any process the owner desires. It is common, however, for the owner to disclose to a pre-approved select group of bidders a list of qualifying issues to be negotiated. Each contractor may then address the specific issues and the owner has full discretion to continue negotiations with one or more contractors as it sees fit.

(iv) Process of Choosing the Form of Contracting

When not bound by procurement regulations, the owner's preferred form of project delivery may influence the bid process that the owner selects. IFB processes are best suited for design-bid-build lump sum contract forms, whereas RFPs are best suited for design-build contracts. As discussed earlier in this chapter, there are several different procurement delivery models including lump sum contracts, unit price contracts, guaranteed maximum price contracts, and continuing contracts such as for routine maintenance, as-needed repairs, or similar projects. Depending on the delivery model, the owner will tailor the bid package to obtain its desired response.

For lump sum contracts, the owner's bid package is looking for the lowest qualified price from bidders to construct and complete the entire project as designed and shown in the contract bid documents. For unit price contracts, where the owner can only estimate the total quantity of work at bid time, the owner is looking for unit costs for certain quantities of work. This type of bid package is common with roadway and infrastructure work. For guaranteed maximum price contracts, the owner's bid package will be structured to obtain from qualified bidders a reasonable general conditions fee and markup on direct costs, all subject to a guaranteed maximum price. This structure may also include a shared cost-savings component if the project is under budget.

(v) Processes Used for Addressing Outstanding Design and Other Price-Sensitive Issues at Time of Bidding

In all contract bidding scenarios, circumstances such as budgetary constraints or outstanding design decisions may result in the owner needing to carve out certain construction components as contingent items for the contractor to price as add/deduct alternates in its bid or proposal. The alternates may relate to the possible use of different qualities or quantities of materials, furnishings, finishes, or a variation in the scope of work. The owner will accept or reject each alternate based on its desires and budgetary limits.

c. Contractor Bidding Response Process

A contractor prepares a bid or proposal by reviewing the bid documents contained in the IFB or RFP, conducting site investigations as necessary, attending pre-bid meetings that the owner and design team conduct, and seeking clarification of various items in the bid documents. How a contractor presents its bid or proposal often depends on what parameters are set forth in the bid documents. Because of competitive bidding requirements on public projects, bidding contractors must strictly comply with the bid documents, submit all required insurance certificates, qualification statements, and bonds, and properly fill out the bid form. These strict requirements ensure that every contractor is bidding on the same project on the same basis. Any deviation may result in the owner disqualifying the bid as non-responsive. Many bid packages on public projects require the bidding contractors to provide certain bid alternates and allowances. A formal request for information or clarification addresses any questions about the bid documents. The owner then provides a public response, often via addendum, rather than private communications between the owner and prospective bidder, because private communications could give one bidder an unfair advantage.

In contrast, the rigidity of a private project's bidding requirements, or lack thereof, depends on the owner's discretion, with lender input where appropriate and applicable. In general, the private owner is free to negotiate terms with prospective contractors throughout the bid process and may disregard bid non-conformities if it chooses to do so. A contractor may also modify its bid after submission if this practice is acceptable to the owner.

d. Owner Bid Review and Contract Award

On public projects, the contract documents included in the bid package typically dictate the time, date, and place of bid openings. All bidders must meet those specific requirements unless there is an addendum to the contract documents changing that information. Bidders who do not respond timely or completely are disqualified from consideration.

Once the owner opens the bids, public project contract deliberations are typically of short duration unless the bids come in over budget or contain significant deficiencies. In these circumstances, the owner will likely rebid the project with modifications to the contract documents to avoid problematic issues. The bidding process then begins again with a new bid date. In the case of IFB bids for proposed lump sum contracts, analysis of competing bids is usually straightforward. Because all contractors bid the same contract documents and the owner provided the same information to all contractors, the owner simply awards the contract to the lowest responsive bid from a responsible bidder. A public bid award is usually formal and may be governed by statute. The notice of award is generally available for public inspection.

Given the more complex nature of the RFP process, analysis of RFP responses is usually more intensive and takes more time. The "qualification" response in an RFP can be more in-depth than evaluating a "low bid" scenario.

Private bid openings may be accomplished in the same fashion as public bid openings; however, there is no requirement for such. Private bid openings take many forms, and a bidder may be allowed to submit a late bid or subsequently correct omissions in its bid. Frequently, the owner negotiates with more than one bidder before awarding a contract to achieve the best price.

e. General Contractor and Subcontractor Negotiation Process before and after General Contract Award

Unlike the restraints on direct contract communications between owners and general contractors on public projects, there are typically no such restrictions on subcontractors or supplier negotiations with prospective general contractors or construction managers. Prior to bid day, subcontractors may revise their pricing for any number of reasons, including receipt of new pricing from downstream vendors or pressure from upstream contractors to reduce proposals.

It is not unusual for large general contractors in the construction industry to submit bids without the benefit of advance subcontractor pricing because they have in-house estimators who price out the entire project. These contractors negotiate with subcontractors after contract award, allowing the contractor to negotiate more favorable terms because the subcontractor is bidding to the successful contractor or construction manager rather than just to a prospective bidder.

Although many subcontractors and some general contractors consider it unethical to re-negotiate pricing after bids have been turned in, the practice, known as bid shopping, still occurs. Although general contractors are frequently required to submit a list of proposed subcontractors as a part of the bid process, some owners allow the general contractor to provide an amended list even after the owner has opened the bids. In general, this process enables general contractors to exert pressure to obtain lower pricing from subcontractors.

At least one state has taken steps to prevent subcontractor bid shopping. California's Public Contract Code sections 4100 to 4110 entitled Subletting and Subcontracting requires a bidder on a public works project to list most of its subcontractors in its bid and requires a significant process for then substituting out its listed subcontractors, thereby preventing bid shopping once the owner awards the project to the contractor.

f. Bid Challenge Procedures

Unsuccessful bidders on a public project may challenge an award or a bid if they determine that there is evidence of bias or unfair advantage and those circumstances were under the owner's control. Examples include permitting one contractor to substitute materials while not making that information available to all other bidders; providing one contractor with inside information on alternates that the owner desires; and disqualifying a bidder on a marginal violation of the bid package. Unsuccessful bidders may also challenge bids involving public contracts on the basis that a contractor or its designated subcontractors are not legitimate DBEs. Although rare, a successful bid challenge process may result in an owner throwing out an award or scheduling a rebid of the project, or the unsuccessful contractor may receive compensation as a result of the improper bid process.

Contractors bidding on private projects have little recourse available to them if the owner chooses to use someone else. A private owner is free to contract how it wishes, even if it winds up paying more because it chose not to use the lowest bidder. The same scenario applies to subcontractors and suppliers bidding on both public and private projects.

C. Processes During the Construction Phase

Processes during the construction phase play a pivotal role in the successful execution of any construction project. They provide the framework that guides every aspect of the project, from start-up to final completion. These processes facilitate coordination, effective resource allocation, cost control, and time management. Furthermore, well-defined construction processes enable clear communication among team members, stakeholders, and subcontractors, reducing the likelihood of errors, delays, and misunderstandings. In essence, these processes form the backbone of a project, enabling it to progress efficiently, stay on track, and achieve its intended objectives.

1. Various Communication Processes

The communication process is of paramount importance in the construction industry as it serves as the bedrock for successful project execution. Clear and effective communication ensures that all stakeholders, including architects, engineers, contractors, and clients, are on the same page regarding project goals, timelines, and expectations. It helps prevent misunderstandings, minimizes errors, and facilitates problem-solving. Regular communication among team members promotes collaboration and coordination, leading to efficient resource allocation and timely decision-making. Whether it is relaying design changes, addressing safety concerns, or adapting to unforeseen challenges, open communication enhances transparency and fosters trust, ultimately resulting in the smooth progression of construction projects and the delivery of high-quality outcomes.

a. Partnering Arrangements

Though it may have originated as an owner-initiated concept, owners, general contractors, and subcontractors all play a key role in the partnering process. Partnering is a rather recent phenomenon in the construction industry going back only to the 1980s. The concept of partnering is for all project stakeholders, owner, architect, engineers, general contractor/construction manager, and key subcontractors to work together as a cooperative team rather than as adversaries to achieve the common goal of successful completion of the construction project. Partnering proponents assert that successful partnering agreements result in less project delay due to more frequent and honest communication among the parties and better problem-solving techniques. Communication and problem-solving techniques result in less formal dispute resolution processes, thus reducing overall project costs.

Partnering activities commence before construction begins with a pre-construction meeting or workshop involving representatives of all proposed partners. The purpose of such a session is to set common goals and standards for the project, delineate clear responsibilities and risk allocations, establish strategies for better communication and dispute-resolution techniques, and attempt to create an atmosphere that fosters teamwork. In many cases, the parties sign a formal partnering agreement. During construction, the partners hold periodic meetings to review goals established at the initial meeting, check progress against those goals, implement further procedures agreed to at the initial meeting, and ensure that the parties are living up to their commitment to proceed through teamwork. In some circumstances, the parties use a partnering facilitator to guide the partnering process.

b. Protocols for Electronic Transmission of Project Communications and Contract Documents

With the universal use of technology, the parties digitally create and convey to other project participants nearly all project documentation from the initial design through the final payment application. Many routine project communications are also made via email and text messages. As a result, newer contract forms or contract exhibits, such as the AIA G201™-2013 Project Digital Data Protocol Form, establish protocols among the project participants for the electronic transmission of project information. See Exhibit 43.

One area of particular concern is the extent of authorized use of electronically shared documents. For example, the AIA G202™-2013 exists to regulate the sharing and use of BIM work product. It addresses whether the parties should consider the BIM work product as useful background information for coordination or as a formal contract document, and it also covers how to protect the intellectual property rights of the party creating the modeling for a specific project.

Additionally, project management software platforms tailored specifically to the construction industry, such as Procore, enable different project participants to collaborate and share information electronically across a single software platform. These platforms include contracts, bulletins, change orders, payment applications, requests for information

(RFIs), schedules and schedule updates, plans and specifications, meeting minutes, daily reports, and other tracking logs.

c. Periodic Progress/Coordination Meeting Obligations

Even on construction projects without formal partnering agreements, the project participants hold periodic meetings, called "progress meetings" or OAC (Owner, Architect, Contractor) meetings, which foster communication among the various parties, identify and attempt to resolve problems and delays, and maximize efficiency in the scheduling and performance of the work. Progress meetings are so important that contract documents often require them at certain stated minimum intervals.

On a large-scale construction project, more than one type of progress meeting may occur. Owner or OAC progress meetings may take place between the owner, some of its representatives (particularly the architect), and the general contractor (and possibly other co-prime contractors or key subcontractors) to discuss various issues that could potentially cause problems on the project. The meetings typically address a variety of issues intended to coordinate work, identify and resolve problems, and maximize safety, quality, coordination, and timeliness in the performance of the work. The owner's representative will normally prepare an agenda for the parties to follow and take notes during the meeting. Typical agenda items include payment status, project performance, and schedule status, coordination with the owner and other trades, performance deficiencies, outstanding requests for information and other design issues, inspection scheduling, any outstanding submittals/samples needed from the general contractor, any submittal/sample responses needed from the owner, change order status, and conditions on the project site. See Exhibit 38 for an example of an agenda for project meetings. On larger projects, there may also be separate "subcontractor" progress meetings that take place between the general contractor and subcontractors to discuss, among other things, work progress and obstacles thereto, coordination of current and future work among various trades, and scheduling of future work.

Most progress meetings are documented through written meeting minutes that are formalized and distributed to the parties and serve as a contemporaneous diary of construction progress. Typically, one party is designated to draft the proposed meeting minutes, subject to the other meeting participants' review. They may request edits before the meeting minutes become an official part of the project record. The party in charge of the meeting minutes typically updates the minutes at each subsequent meeting: removing completed items, discussing "old business" to determine the progress toward completion, and raising "new business" added to the minutes for review at future meetings.

d. Processes for Dispute Resolution

Like most conflicts, it is more productive to resolve construction disputes quickly rather than allow them to linger and fester, threatening project goodwill, productivity, and camaraderie. Various mechanisms are available to encourage or compel early dispute resolution processes while work is ongoing. The process could be the project architect's or other designated initial decision maker's immediate review of a contested change order, a mandatory meeting of upper-level management of the involved parties, or the use of a neutral third-party—either a dispute review board or a mediator.

Although these early dispute resolution methods resolve most disputes, some remain intractable. Typically, the specific methods for formal dispute resolution and any limitations thereon are set forth in the parties' contract, in the parties' separate partnering agreement, or in the case of public projects, in an applicable statute or regulation. The contract may mandate litigation, arbitration, or an administrative hearing before a public body in the case of a claim against a public owner.

Because of the technical and complicated issues involved in many construction disputes, it is common for contracts to contain jury trial waivers, though such waiver provisions are not universally enforceable. Contracts may also mandate venue for the formal dispute resolution proceeding; however, these are also not universally enforceable as some states have statutes that require the resolution of a construction project dispute in the state where the construction takes place and courts may find that the statute takes priority over a conflicting contractual venue provision.

Finally, as discussed in more detail below, the claimant party may have both a claim for breach of contract and a legal right to pursue the same claim against third parties, as in the case of a performance or payment bond claim or the right to pursue a mechanic's lien. Depending on the law of the jurisdiction and the nature of the claim, contractual dispute resolution processes may or may not bind the third party. Some courts hold that sureties are bound to participate in construction contract-mandated arbitration rather than separate bond litigation if the bond incorporates the contract by reference; other courts disagree. Some claimants wish to pursue the surety or real property owner independently of their breach of contract claim, but the surety or landowner may be able to secure a stay of the bond or mechanic's lien litigation pending completion of the separate breach of contract adjudication.

e. Contractual/Legal Notice Requirements

The purpose of any contractual or legal notice requirement is to give the recipient (whether the owner, general contractor, or subcontractor) the opportunity to correct a perceived problem or at least mitigate the damages that the problem caused. Most construction contracts require a general contractor or a subcontractor to give notice of any issue, condition, change in work, etc. that would give rise to a claim for additional time and/or compensation. Owners tend to have very few contractual notice obligations. On public projects, such notice requirements may appear as contractual provisions referencing applicable statutes or regulations.

Examples of issues that may require contractor compliance with a contractual notice provision include discovery of a differing or hidden site condition, delays or disruptions to the contractor's work from causes outside the contractor's control, and necessary work that the contractor considers to be outside the agreed scope of work. Some contractor notice provisions are rather onerous as the failure to provide notice of an occurrence or proof of entitlement to additional time or compensation by the stated deadline may result in a waiver of any future claim.

Owners rarely have a contractual obligation to provide notice of an intent to assert backcharges or assess liquidated damages, though as a practical matter, they often provide such notice to spur improved performance from the contracting team. Some contract forms require an owner to provide notice of default to allow the general contractor the opportunity to cure the default, as discussed in detail below. Public construction contracts may simply incorporate by reference statutes or regulations that require the owner to provide various notices, including notice of intent to terminate the contractor for default.

Other notice requirements may apply but lie outside the construction contract itself. For example, state mechanic's lien statutes generally require notice to the property owner and other parties of a contractor's participation in the construction project as well as a contractor's intent to claim a lien for non-payment. Likewise, the federal Miller Act and various state "Little Miller Acts" require a party not in contractual privity with the general contractor to provide notice to certain parties of non-payment and the intent to assert a claim against the general contractor's payment bond. Private bond forms may also contain their own formal notice requirements.

2. *Processes Involving Performance or Scope of Work*

a. Shop Drawings, Samples, and Submittals

An owner wants assurance that the work for which it is paying conforms to the project plans and specifications and all applicable laws. Accordingly, most construction contracts require the general contractor to submit a variety of documents to the owner, design team, and in some cases, regulating authorities detailing the work it will perform. The required submissions are typically identified in contract documents and may include detailed structural, electrical, and/or mechanical plans, shop drawings, and product samples. Other required documentation includes proof that the general contractor and subcontractors maintain the required insurance coverages, bonds, licenses, and permits. On public projects, these documentation requirements often expand to regulatory compliance forms and certified payroll records.

The owner or one of its representatives (typically the architect and/or engineer) will review the general contractor's and subcontractors' submissions for compliance with the contract documents and applicable law. For example, the general contractor will submit shop drawings describing in detail how it will construct a particular element of the construction. After reviewing the shop drawing, the owner or architect will either approve the shop drawing or request revisions and re-submission. Approval of shop drawings and/or submittal is a prerequisite to starting the related fabrication/installation of the submitted construction component.

General contractors may provide physical samples to the owner to allow the owner and its design team to give final approval of a particular product or make a final selection of items such as paint, carpeting, and cabinetry. Sometimes, the contractor will provide a mock-up of a particular feature of the project for owner and architect approval. The general contractor and the owner typically track the status of all required digital and physical sample submittals. Due to the large number of submittals on a complex project, one or more of the parties may prepare, routinely update, and share a formal submittal log. See Exhibit 39 for a sample of a Submittal Log. The log will note any items that are not in compliance or that the contractor has not timely submitted. If critical to project completion, the parties will likely address any submittal issue both in correspondence and at the regularly scheduled progress meetings.

Many projects include a schedule as part of the contract documents, either that the parties have included as a contract exhibit or that the general contractor submits for owner approval at some agreed time shortly after contract execution. Sophisticated scheduling software now exists, and most projects of any complexity require the submission of a form of critical path method (CPM) schedule and periodic updates, as discussed in more detail below. These schedules allow the parties to monitor delays, identify the cause(s) of such delays, and determine the impact, if any, on meeting the project completion deadline. Primavera and Microsoft Project are two of the most prominent CPM scheduling software used in the construction industry.

b. Coordination and Clarification

Project coordination involves two phases: coordination of design drawings and coordination of the various workforces. In a typical design-bid-build project, the design team is responsible for the coordination of the various drawings, which different members of the design team, including the architect and various engineers depending on the nature of the project, may have prepared. Once work commences, construction contracts often require the general contractor to coordinate the performance of its own forces, those of its subcontractors, and sometimes those of the owner's other contractors. A construction manager is often utilized to coordinate the work of multiple trade contractors depending on how the owner has structured project staffing. Proper coordination of various trade contractors all working in the same relatively small space is critical to schedule efficiency, labor productivity, and overall project safety. There is an increase in the use of BIM and other technology in the design and coordination of a construction project. BIM software has been an effective tool for coordinating trades and uncovering design conflicts prior to the commencement of construction activities. This process saves time and money in the construction phase. Nonetheless, failure to coordinate different design drawings or staffing of the project may cause delay or disruption costs to the owner and/or one or more of the other contractors, which delay or disruption may result in backcharges and claims against the offending party(ies).

When the contract documents lack certain information, are not properly coordinated, or the parties encounter unexpected circumstances during the work, the general contractor can formally seek guidance from the owner and design team by way of the request for information ("RFI") process. Typically, the contract provides for the architect to provide a formal response to RFIs, as RFIs commonly implicate questions of design or design changes. If the contractor cannot proceed forward until it receives an RFI response, the owner and design team are motivated to respond timely. Delays caused by untimely responses to valid RFIs can result in the general contractor seeking extensions of time for completion of the work and delay damages including additional overhead costs that result from the extended schedule.

The general contractor and the owner typically track the status of all RFIs by keeping an RFI log. See Exhibit 40 for an example of an RFI Log. The RFI log notes the status of the RFI's resolution and open RFIs are regularly the subject of progress meetings. An RFI response resulting in a change in the contractor's scope of work typically results in a contract amendment.

c. Scope Changes

Virtually all general contracts contain a clause allowing the owner to make changes to the scope of work so long as the requested changes are consistent with the general scope of the project and do not constitute a cardinal change to the nature of the contract. The contract will outline the specific procedures for making requests for changes to the scope of work and time for completion, including deadlines for notice of a change, submission of a change order request, quantification and documentation of any cost or time impact, and response to the change request. Of course, the parties to a contract are free to agree to add or delete scope of work or even terminate the contract, in whole or in part.

Numerous project participants including the owner, architect/engineer, contractor, subcontractor, supplier, or applicable regulating authority (i.e., changes driven by code compliance issues) can instigate changes during a construction project. However, owners and contractors are the primary sources of change order requests. Construction changes arise for a multitude of reasons, including hidden or differing site conditions, local inspection authority demands, statutory or regulatory changes enacted after contract execution, unusual adverse weather conditions, significant supply chain issues, value engineering initiatives, cost-saving material or process changes, credits for the owner's acceptance of non-conforming work, or simply an owner's change of design preferences. As discussed above, many project changes have their roots in the RFI process.

(i) Owner-Initiated Changes

Owner-initiated changes occur because of evolving design decisions, the owner's decision to use other contractors for certain scopes, funding issues, new tenant requests, value engineering, and a variety of other issues. Because the owner initiates these changes, there is no dispute that the contractor is entitled to a change order, but the parties may not agree on the value/cost and time impact of any change.

If the proposed changes are time-sensitive, the owner may first issue a full or partial "stop work order" directing the general contractor to refrain from performing work that is either no longer desired or that may need to be delayed. The general contractor (and its affected subcontractors) may be entitled to additional compensation for the impact of the stop work order if its issuance was not due to any fault of the general contractor or its subcontractors.

If proposed changes are purely optional or not time-sensitive, the owner will typically issue a request for proposal ("RFP") to the general contractor that outlines the issue/proposed change and requests a proposal that includes the general contractor's proposed price for making the changes, including any anticipated impact on the schedule. The owner may elect not to proceed with the proposed change after evaluating the contractor's RFP response.

In other instances, if the contract permits it, the owner may issue a construction change directive ("CCD") to the general contractor instructing the contractor to perform as directed, which in some cases may be a directive to omit certain base contract scope of work. The general contractor must adhere to the CCD unless it is such a significant alteration to the agreed scope of work that it is a "cardinal change." As there is no advance agreement among the parties as to price or time in the CCD scenario, the general contractor is entitled to receive the reasonable value of any new or altered work performed as well as the reasonable value of the impact on other areas of the work.

Finally, the owner may also change the scope of work or manner of performance by way of a "field directive." An owner, owner's representative, or architect, who verbally initiates the changed scope at the project site, should only use a field directive for minor changes.

Nearly all construction contracts have language that the owner is not responsible for paying for changes that it has not authorized in advance in writing. However, in practice, construction projects move quickly under schedule constraints and contractors often perform change order work based on verbal orders with little to no formal advance notice and approval. Often, the general contractor and the owner can reach an agreement on fair compensation for the additional work at a later point. If coming to an agreement after-the-fact on changed work is the common practice on a project, courts may disregard contract language to the contrary and find that the parties have waived the requirement of compliance with the formal contractual change order process and will treat the verbal order as a change directive.

If a subcontractor's work is affected by the changes, the general contractor must undergo largely the same change order processes with each subcontractor in order to gather the necessary information to pass through the subcontractor's claims as part of its own change order request. Frequently, the general contractor protects itself by including provisions in its subcontracts that require the subcontractor to comply with the general contract change order provisions and bar a subcontractor from receiving any more compensation for a change order than the general contractor has received from the owner on that subcontractor's behalf.

(ii) Contractor-Initiated or Subcontractor-Initiated Change Requests

General contractor or subcontractor-initiated changes most often occur because of disagreements with the owner over the exact base contract scope of work or other unforeseen events or conditions that the parties did not factor into the contractor's original pricing such as force majeure delays or owner-caused delays, differing site conditions, design errors, and time impacts associated with the work of other contractors. These change order requests may result in disputes with the owner as to both entitlement and value. The general contractor may initiate a change request by submitting what may be referred to on a particular project as a change order request (COR) or proposed change order (PCO) reflecting the contractor's proposal for resolving the time and/or cost impact of an alleged added scope or changed condition. CORs typically include both the general contractor's proposed costs and those of any affected subcontractors. These change orders will also illustrate any time impacts to the contract schedule.

Change orders are on either a lump sum basis (value known prior to work beginning) or a cost-plus basis (value unknown until completion of change). The specific type of change order normally determines the level of documentation that the general contractor and affected subcontractors will need to prove for entitlement and amount. For example, when the owner approves a lump-sum change order in advance of the performance of the new work, the contractor does not need to track or keep specific cost records applicable to the changed work. If the owner disputes the change order request, or the change order is to proceed on a cost-plus basis, the contractor needs to keep specific records to support the costs associated with the change (i.e., establish a cost code and compile invoices and supporting labor, materials, and equipment tracking records to quantify the value of the changed condition.) Accordingly, the contractor must establish and maintain controls and procedures to track costs and the impact associated with each specific change during the project's life.

Many construction contracts do not contain clear guidance for quantifying changed or added work. Unclear and vague contract provisions fuel further disagreements when it comes to valuing or pricing the changed or added work. Terms such as "direct cost," "actual costs," "overhead and profit markups," and "direct labor," among others, give rise to creative interpretations of their meaning if the contract does not specifically define them. Accordingly, differing opinions as to the way to value changes and extra work cause many of the disputes related to change orders.

(iii) Tracking of Changes

Like other construction project paperwork, the contractor typically sequentially numbers change order proposals for tracking purposes. A COR should include both the cost and time impact, if any, of the proposed change. The party receiving the change order proposal may assign its own internal tracking number to the COR.

Contractors and owners typically track the status of all open CORs and approved change orders by way of a change order log. See Exhibit 41 for an example of a Change Order Log. A contractor's typical change order log assigns a change order number, references any related RFIs, Design Bulletins, or other project communications, provides a brief description of the change, includes relevant dates of notice, submission, and any owner response, and identifies whether and in what amount the change order is approved. Supporting the change order log are COR files, which include underlying documentation, responses, estimates, and cost data for each of the CORs. The change order log is a quick reference guide or index that summarizes the status of every known potential change on the project.

A similar process takes place at the lower tiers of the construction process. General contractors may pass down or issue their own RFPs and change directives to the subcontractors and subcontractors submit change order requests to the general contractor. The general contractor's change order requests to the owner may incorporate these subcontractor change order requests as "pass-through" claims. On occasion, the general contractor may bear the cost of the subcontractor's extra costs if the contractor fails to include the scope of work in the subcontract, often called a scope "bust." The subcontract may have a flow-down provision incorporating the general contract's change order processes but may also contain provisions related to general contractor-initiated changes that do not involve the owner. General contractors and subcontractors typically track proposed changes in the same manner as the general contractor's CORs although some subcontractors may lack the sophistication in project management and administration to thoroughly document, quantify, and track their own CORs.

The owner is typically the party responsible for memorializing a written "change order" that describes the proposed change, its cost, and time impact. If the general contractor concurs with the terms of a change order as drafted, it signs the change order and returns it to the owner for counter-execution. The contractor may reject a change order as proposed and negotiate further with the owner to reach an acceptable resolution or pursue a formal claim if negotiations fail to reach a resolution. If the owner rejects the contractor's requested pricing, either the contractor does not perform the proposed additional work, or the general contractor performs the work under a CCD, described above. If a disputed change is time-sensitive work and the parties cannot reach an agreement quickly, a CCD allows the work to proceed leaving the dispute over cost and time impact for a later date. Once accepted, a change order becomes a formal modification to the contract.

d. Claims

Claims on a construction project are commonplace. The large number of separate, yet interdependent parties involved in a typical construction project, along with the complex nature of the work itself, leaves the potential for disputes that may evolve into formal claims if unresolved. Disputes that arise directly between the contracting parties cause most construction claims, but some involve more remote parties including subcontractor pass-through claims and general contractor and subcontractor design defect claims against the owner resulting from design team professionals' errors and/or omissions.

(i) Types of Claims

A general contractor's claims against an owner arise from disputes over the scope of work, the origin of project delays, assessment of delay damages, disruption, lack of payment or untimely payment, assessment of various backcharges, contract termination, or other issues related to the owner's performance of its contractual obligations or lack thereof. A general contractor may seek additional compensation from the owner for work that exceeds the scope of the contract. The general contractor may also seek compensation for owner-caused delay damages. In addition, the contractor may demand the release of contract funds that the owner has wrongfully withheld, contest owner-asserted backcharges, or challenge the propriety of a default termination of its contract.

Owner claims against general contractors arise from costs and expenses incurred to repair or replace defective or non-conforming work or to finish incomplete contract work. Depending on the terms of the contract, an owner's claim may also include liquidated or actual damages arising from the contractor's untimely performance. Where there are sufficient funds remaining in unpaid contract balances, and if not otherwise barred by the contract, the owner will normally offset or backcharge its alleged damages from the contract balance.

Claims can also flow in other directions, including subcontractor against general contractor and vice versa, one prime contractor against another contractor on a multi-prime contraction project, owner and/or general contractor against architect/design team, or other combinations including all parties involved in the construction project. Under many construction contracts (and particularly the widely used AIA contract forms), the architect is intended to play a key role beyond just design by serving as the initial decision maker in disputes between the owner and the general contractor, in addition to reviewing and giving initial approval of the contractor's progress payment applications.

Because claims often arise from contested change orders, the areas of dispute remain the same: entitlement and quantum. The parties may dispute one or both components. Entitlement disputes have their basis in potential discrepancies between the parties as to what work was part of the original scope and what constitutes change order work or what constitutes a failure to meet contractual obligations. In contrast, a pure quantum dispute assumes a right to compensation but challenges the appropriate amount of compensation.

Claims must comply with contractual notice requirements and include adequate documentation supporting both entitlement and quantum. Given the complexity of many construction projects, early identification of actual or potential issues, continuous monitoring of the impact of such issues, preparation of contemporaneous cost impact documentation, and following contractual notice procedures are all required elements to successfully pursue a claim. When pursuing claims, the parties must also consider factors external to the contractual claim processes, including the potential negative impact on the parties' future business relationship, the time that claims prosecution and defense take away from other work obligations, and legal/other costs, among others. All parties should undertake a cost-benefit analysis before deciding to pursue a claim and should re-evaluate at each step in the claim process.

(ii) Contractual Requirements

The parties to a written contract primarily handle claims between themselves in accordance with the terms and conditions of that contract. The party bringing a claim must follow the relevant procedures set out in the contract for notice and pursuit of a claim. These procedural requirements vary widely with the contract itself plus any incorporated general conditions, bids, exhibits, and/or addendums setting forth these requirements.

Contract terms may require the owner's representative, often the architect, to review the claim and make a preliminary determination of the propriety of the claim. The architect may have the option to accept the claim, reject it, or seek additional information from the claimant. To contest the architect's decision on a rejected claim or reduced claim, the objecting party may have a deadline to elect to continue to the next phase of the dispute resolution process.

Alternatively, the owner and the general contractor may be contractually required to engage in good faith negotiation of the claim through a meeting of senior management representatives. When such negotiation fails, the owner may direct the contractor to perform (or not perform) in a certain manner. If the matter remains unresolved, the parties may avail themselves of contractual dispute resolution provisions such as mediation and, ultimately, litigation or arbitration. The contract may dictate the ultimate dispute resolution forum, or the forum might be left to the party initiating the claim, subject to local legal rules related to jurisdiction and venue.

e. Payment Processes

The payment process can vary substantially from project to project or owner to owner and is subject to applicable law, especially prompt payment statutes, which may apply to only public construction or both public and private construction. Generally, all construction contracts have provisions that delineate the payment process and link periodic payments to the progress of the work, including explicit milestones. In addition, the amount of underlying or supporting documentation necessary to approve or process a payment can vary widely between a lump sum and a cost-plus contract.

(i) General Contractor/Subcontractor Preparation of Schedule of Values

The first step in the payment process is typically for the owner and general contractor to establish or agree upon a schedule of values (SOV), which breaks down the entire contract value into specific components for invoicing purposes. The parties then use this SOV as a basis for preparing periodic (usually monthly) invoices (i.e., requisition or application for payment based on an estimated percentage of completion for each of the specific line items included in the SOV). The parties often use the Construction Specifications Institute Master Format list of Divisions as the basis for their SOV. See Exhibit 2. As the project advances toward completion, payment applications incorporate approved change orders that will alter the total value of the contract. For a unit price type of contract, the contractor may seek a progress payment based on the estimated or actual quantity of units delivered to date.

Most general contractors utilize subcontractors and vendors who invoice the general contractor for specific tasks. In conjunction with the owner/general contractor payment process, the general contractor and each subcontractor may establish or agree on a separate SOV pertaining to the subcontractor's specific work on the project. Typically, the underlying SOV becomes the basis for the subcontractor's invoicing to the general contractor. A subcontractor's schedule of values may be different than the general contractor's SOV.

(ii) General Contractor/Subcontractor Preparation of Payment Requisition and General Contractor/Owner Review/Approval of Requisition

The contract payment provisions usually contain a timeline that details the steps involved in processing periodic payment requests. The first step customarily involves the general contractor preparing a "pencil copy" or initial draft of the payment requisition reflecting what work the general contractor has performed during the specific period and submitting it to the owner by a specific date (e.g., the 21st day of each month). An owner's representative or the architect performing construction administration services usually reconciles the completed work to date against the progress completion percentage reflected in the pencil copy of the payment requisition. Thereafter, the owner accepts the percentage designated or modifies (usually by way of reduction) the percentages completed. Using the approved percentages, the general contractor calculates the current amount to bill and submits the formal payment requisition, commonly referred to as a "pay app." The architect and/or owner then approve the payment requisition and the owner releases payment within the period established in the contract or required by applicable law. In the absence of any governing contract term or prompt payment law, the owner should arguably pay an approved payment requisition with reasonable promptness. Often, in private construction, there is an additional tier of approval from the construction lender. The lender will have a third-party inspector who will review the work in place compared to the percentages that the contractor billed and will recommend payment based on its review.

Once the general contractor receives payment from the owner, the subcontractors and suppliers should receive payment for their applicable portion of the approved work performed during the period for which payment was received. In some instances, a contractual or statutory prompt payment or construction trust fund provision may apply and dictate the specific timing of when the general contractor must issue payment to subcontractors and vendors following the general contractor's receipt of payment from the owner. In some instances, the subcontractor and vendor invoices do not track with specific line items contained in the general contractor's application for payment, thereby creating inequities and confusion in determining the amount due to a specific subcontractor. Moreover, the contract payment terms in subcontracts or purchase orders may differ from the general contract terms (i.e., payment terms of net 30 or on the flip side, pay-when-paid or pay-if-paid provisions) causing further confusion and disputes as to how much the general contractor owes to a specific subcontractor or vendor each billing cycle. Other factors that may affect the subcontractor/vendor payment process include untimely performance, assessment of backcharges, unresolved CORs, incomplete invoice documentation, withholding of retainage, scope disputes, quality of work issues, and notice of claims from lower-tier subcontractors or suppliers.

(iii) Retainage Procedures

Many contracts and subcontracts contain some type of retainage clause within the payment provisions. Retainage is a percentage that the owner withholds from progress payments earned throughout the project. The owner ultimately releases the retainage after completion. Retainage is an incentive for the general contractor and/or subcontractors to complete the work but, more importantly, is security for the owner or performance bond surety in the case of a default. Retainage amounts usually range between 2% and 10% and the owner may adjust and/or reduce the retainage as the project progresses toward successful completion. Owners usually withhold some amount of retainage until the project is complete, including all punch list work and closeout documentation. Some contracts or statutory provisions allow interest-bearing escrow accounts for retainage.

(iv) Required Payment Requisition Supporting Documentation

The payment process may require the general contractor to provide a substantial amount of underlying documentation supporting progress with the periodic requisitions. Documentation can include releases from the general contractor and subcontractors (see Exhibit 29 for examples of subcontractors' releases), subcontractor and material invoices, certified payrolls, updated schedules, minority reports, and evidence of prior payments and anticipated payments to subcontractors and suppliers. This type of documentation can provide the owner with contemporaneous information necessary to evaluate the project's progress and determine compliance with applicable contractual and statutory requirements as well as provide advance notice of potential problems with the project and the ability of the contractor to complete the work.

The purpose of requiring execution of a conditional release prior to payment is to protect the owner from unexpected or untimely claims in a later stage of the construction project. A release requires a contractor or subcontractor to identify or otherwise waive any claims (including, as applicable, mechanic's lien and payment bond claims) for additional compensation for the specific work or period of work identified in the release. During the project, the release form will request a "partial" release, usually up to a certain date or amount. At project close-out, the general contractor and its subcontractors will execute final releases of all claims. A release generally identifies the specific contractor or subcontractor, the project, and the amount being paid. A release may also require the general contractor or subcontractor to represent that it has paid all its subcontractors and suppliers and has followed applicable laws.

f. Time Processes

While it occasionally happens that a contractor is required to detail the time requirement for completing a project, it is much more likely that the owner places the time constraints on the contractor in the bid documents and contract itself. Preparation of schedules, however, almost universally falls on the contractor during the project. The owner may require CPM schedules, cost-loaded schedules, manpower-loaded schedules, two-week or monthly "look ahead" schedules, and/or baseline schedules. The most common schedule used in the construction process is the CPM schedule.

(i) Project Schedules

A CPM schedule attempts to identify each activity by area or discipline in a construction project and logically sequences them recognizing that some activities are interdependent, and places reasonable completion times (typically by day) on each of the activities. A CPM schedule identifies what activities are critical to project progress, what activities have "float," and how much. CPM schedules are also useful in determining the causes of project delays.

Cost-loaded schedules show the cash flow on a project. A general contractor may prepare such a schedule to demonstrate to the owner the amount of money due once the general contractor completes or makes progress on each identified component of the project.

Manpower-loaded schedules are those in which a general contractor identifies the number of manpower units required to complete a task, thus permitting the owner to monitor the manpower at any point in time and to determine how efficiently the general contractor is using that manpower. It is much more likely to see manpower-loaded schedules on time and material projects than hard dollar contract projects because of the owner's interest in monitoring costs.

A baseline schedule serves as a control on the project. It is the baseline schedule that typically is included as a contract exhibit or contract document and requires the joint approval of the owner and the general contractor, with input from subcontractors.

(ii) Schedule Updates

In nearly every instance, major projects require periodic schedule updates (usually monthly). In a perfect world, the as-planned schedule remains accurate, the conditions of the site are as anticipated, contractors, subcontractors, and material suppliers perform as expected, the weather follows typical patterns, and the project is completed with no modification to the schedule. On construction projects, the perfect world rarely exists. Contracts typically require the general contractor to submit schedule updates at each progress meeting between the owner and the general contractor or with each progress payment application. The differences between the original schedule and the updated schedule determine whether the project is on time, ahead of schedule, or behind schedule. These schedules and updates allow assessment of the amount of delay, the cause of delay, and the impact of delay.

There is no issue in the construction industry quite as volatile or as disputed as delay and the damages arising therefrom. The owner's position typically is that if the contractor does not complete on time and does not receive approved time extensions or permission for delay, the contractor is required to pay damages and is not entitled to recover its own delay damages. Contractors must document every delay beyond their control, promptly apply for extensions of time in accordance with the contract documents, demand timely responses from the owner, and dispute any owner decision that is not fair to both parties.

g. Default and Termination Processes

Nearly every construction contract contains one or more provisions addressing the issue of default. Default provisions are often one-sided. In other words, because the owner generally drafts the general contract and the general contractor drafts the subcontract, the default provisions rarely address what constitutes an owner default under the general contract or what constitutes a general contractor default under a subcontract (e.g., failure to make payment or timely payment). This issue is usually left to the courts or other outside arbiters to decide under contract law principles.

(i) Owner-Initiated Notice of Default to General Contractor or General Contractor-Initiated Notice of Default to Subcontractor

Default provisions address what events, acts, or omissions constitute a default, notice requirements, how the contractor can remedy the default, and what remedies and damages are available to the non-defaulting party. Events of default typically include failure to complete the work properly, failure to supply enough properly skilled workers or proper materials, failure to maintain the project work schedule, failure to pay lower-tier subcontractors or suppliers, and failure to comply with applicable laws and regulations.

Some parties try to avoid disputes over what constitutes a default or what remedies are available upon default by providing highly detailed default provisions in their contracts. Others take the opposite approach and leave the provisions deliberately vague to ensure maximum flexibility for the non-defaulting party. No matter what type of provision applies, in many cases, the determination that a default has occurred is subjective and often results in claims and ensuing litigation.

(ii) Opportunity to Cure

Not every default results in immediate contract termination. Many construction contracts provide the alleged defaulting contractor with an opportunity to cure the default. An "opportunity to cure" provision allows the alleged defaulting contractor a certain amount of time to cure the default. The cure period commences with a written "notice to cure" letter sent to the alleged defaulting contractor describing the alleged default. Failure to allow the contractually required time period for cure to expire may nullify any resulting termination. Even in the absence of such a written cure provision, it is well-accepted in the industry that a contractor should be given notice and an opportunity to cure a default prior to termination.

Frequently, disputes arise over whether the contractor has cured the default. Likewise, arguments are often raised that the non-defaulting party has waived a default by failing to communicate further on the issue, leading the defaulting contractor to believe that the default has been adequately cured, and by not terminating the defaulting contractor promptly after the expiration of the cure period.

(iii) Contract/Subcontract Termination

If a general contractor or subcontractor cannot or will not cure a default or disputes the existence of such a default, the contract default provisions usually provide for several remedies, the most drastic of which is the termination of the contract. The party seeking to terminate the contract must abide by any contractual notice provisions regarding termination. After a default termination, the owner/general contractor makes no further progress payments and dedicates any unpaid contract funds to completing the remaining work and paying any other damages. Some contractual default provisions also permit the owner or general contractor to use any of the defaulted party's material, equipment, or tools to complete the work and assign any lower-tier subcontracts or purchase orders to the owner or general contractor in order to complete the remaining work.

Terminations do not always arise because of a default. On occasion, due to a change in circumstances, an owner may decide that it is no longer in its best interest to complete a project. This happens most frequently in the case of public contracts and often relates to funding problems. Because of this phenomenon, most construction contracts also contain a provision allowing for a termination "for convenience." Such provisions expressly authorize a termination without fault and define what compensation is available to the party terminated for convenience. Subcontracts contain "flow down" provisions that also allow the general contractor to terminate the subcontractor for convenience in the event the owner terminates the general contractor for convenience.

(iv) Surety Involvement following Default or Termination

On a bonded contract, a surety usually becomes involved whenever there is a default and subsequent termination. Often, the bond obligee (typically the owner or general contractor) notifies the surety when problems start to arise to avoid a default and potential termination.

Depending on the form of the performance bond, the bond itself may contain specific provisions separate and apart from the construction contract default provisions with which the obligee must comply to trigger an obligation on the surety's part to respond to a default or termination. These requirements may include notice to the surety, a certain cure period, a meeting of the parties, or similar provisions. For example, see section three of the AIA A312 performance bond. Depending on the circumstances and the various alternates set forth in the performance bond, the surety may elect to remedy the default or otherwise arrange for the completion of the remaining work.

D. Processes During Project Close-Out

1. Processes Involving Performance or Scope of Work

a. Substantial Completion

Substantial completion is a term of art in the construction industry that means that the work is sufficiently complete that the owner may now use the work or occupy the building for its intended purpose. The contract may expressly define substantial completion, citing the achievement of specific milestones. Various statutes around the country also may define substantial completion. Many contracts provide that the owner or architect must issue a certificate containing the date that the contractor accomplished substantial completion. This certificate usually involves a thorough inspection of the completed work and the generation of one or more punch lists of work for the contractor to complete or correct to achieve final completion and owner acceptance. The owner's representative (usually the architect) generates the punch list, but a general contractor may prepare its own punch list for itself and its subcontractors to complete before calling in the owner's representative for a substantial completion inspection. Once the contractor completes the punch list work, the owner's representative returns for a re-inspection and "signs off" of the punch list, signifying that the contractor has satisfactorily completed the work.

Substantial completion is a significant milestone. In the absence of a contrary provision in the contract, it requires the owner to pay the remaining contract balance less some reasonable sum withheld for incomplete or non-conforming work. Case law generally prohibits a party from recovering liquidated damages or certain other delay damages after the date of substantial completion unless the contract contains explicit language focusing on final completion. Various contractual or statutory notice or limitations provisions may commence or are otherwise connected to the date of substantial completion (i.e. warranties).

b. Final Completion

Final completion occurs after the general contractor has completed or corrected all of the work, has provided all required documentation, and the owner accepts the project as fully completed. It triggers the owner's obligation to pay the entire remaining contract balance, including retainage, to the general contractor. As in the case of substantial completion, there may be a contract provision requiring the owner or architect to issue a certificate of final completion. Usually, this process involves further inspections to ensure that the contractor has satisfactorily completed all the punch list work. Various contractual or statutory notice or limitations provisions (such as warranty obligations) may commence upon final completion.

Specific contractual requirements may require the general contractor (often through its subcontractors or suppliers) to provide warranties for certain aspects of the work, often for large equipment and roofing. The warranty period may commence on the date of substantial completion or final completion. Upon discovering a problem with the materials or equipment during the warranty period, the owner will contact the general contractor and request correction or replacement pursuant to the warranty. If a manufacturer provided the warranty, the general contractor would contact the manufacturer to make the required repair or replacement.

The owner may also discover latent defects in the work performed, not otherwise covered by a warranty, after final completion. Depending on their severity, the general contractor or its subcontractors may need to return to the project to make repairs. Damage to finished areas arising from a latent defect may trigger a claim against the general contractor's or a subcontractor's insurance coverage. It can be difficult at times to get a general contractor or subcontractor to return to a project to correct its defective work. If the contractor at issue is bonded, the owner may call upon the performance bond surety to exert additional pressure on the contractor to return to the project to repair the work or pay someone else to repair the work. If the contractor is unavailable, the surety may be the entity that ultimately bears the cost of the repair work. To the extent that the owner has not yet released the final payment on the contract, outstanding warranty, and latent defect claims may impact its release.

c. Required Close-Out Documentation Process

In addition to completing all construction work, most contracts require the general contractor to submit additional paperwork to the owner at the end of the project. Often this additional paperwork is submitted electronically using submittal software required by the contract. What documentation is required depends on the nature of the project and is set forth in the contract documents. Generally, the contract requires the contractor to provide as-built drawings that accurately reflect the work as it was actually built (incorporating all changes made during construction), O&M (Operation and Maintenance) manuals for various equipment and systems that the general contractor and its subcontractors installed to allow the owner or other intended occupants of the project to operate, service, and maintain the equipment and controls in the future, and any written warranties or guarantees (for equipment, roofing, or other items) that the contract requires.

2. Final Payment Processes

After the general contractor has completed all the work and turned over the required close-out documentation to the owner and the owner has executed certifications and signoffs, the parties can finalize the remaining financial aspects of the project. Customarily, the final application for payment is comprised of the remaining retainage balance that the owner has been holding. However, the final application may also include money withheld for punch list work and late-resolved change orders and claims.

More than likely, before the owner or general contractor processes the final pay application, the parties will perform a reconciliation of the contract funds. Again, the owner may require full and final releases from the contractor, subcontractors, and major vendors. If the project is bonded, a "consent of surety" is often required from the general contractor's surety for the owner to release the final payment. See Exhibit 30 for an example of a consent of surety. The consent of surety provides the bonding company an opportunity to raise any issues or concerns related to unpaid vendors, claims filed, or other underlying issues associated with the project (i.e., labor and tax liabilities) before the surety's principal receives the remaining contract funds.

3. Dispute Resolution Processes involving Final Payment or Unresolved Change Orders/Claims

Some construction disputes need outside intervention for resolution. When efforts to resolve open claims prior to final completion fail, the parties may "carve out" unresolved claims during the final payment process and manage them separately. Sometimes, the owner refuses to issue final payment based on pending owner claims and/or disputed backcharges.

a. Contractual Requirements/Limitations

Disputing parties to a construction contract may file lawsuits against one another to enforce their rights; however, many construction contracts contain language mandating binding arbitration. A court is likely to dismiss or stay any litigation filed in contravention of an applicable contractual arbitration provision pending the outcome of arbitration. Occasionally, due to conflicting contract provisions, an unfortunate owner or contractor may find itself in litigation with one party and in arbitration with another party over the same issues on the project.

Lack of contractual privity between the parties to a dispute, for example, the architect and general contractor, has made it difficult for the general contractor to seek recovery for lost time and/or money directly from the architect based on defective plans and specifications. More recently, courts in a variety of states are now permitting contractors to seek monetary damages from architects whose negligence has caused economic loss to the contractor. Because there is no contract between the architect and the general contractor, absent a subsequent agreement to engage in alternative dispute resolution, there is no other means of resolving this type of claim other than litigation.

Subcontractors also frequently have claims or unresolved/rejected change orders against the owner or architect but cannot assert direct claims due to a lack of contractual privity. The subcontractor must instead assert the claim against the general contractor who then pursues the claim against the owner as a "pass-through" claim. In appropriate circumstances, the owner may then bring the architect into litigation or arbitration. Frequently, general contractors and subcontractors enter into liquidation agreements to pursue and resolve these "pass-through" claims.

b. Alternative Sources or Means of Recovery

The general contractor and subcontractors may also seek recovery of any unpaid contract balance or other damages by filing a mechanic's lien against the project's real property. The process and procedure for properly and timely bringing a mechanic's lien are state-specific and vary widely. Frequently, even slight technical failings in this process can cause the mechanic's lien action to fail. As a general rule, public owners have sovereign immunity from mechanic's lien claims, so this right typically only exists on private projects.

Owners, subcontractors, and suppliers may also claim recovery from surety bonds. In the instance where an owner default terminates the general contractor and asserts damages exceeding the remaining contract balance, the owner may seek recovery from the general contractor's performance bond if the general contractor has provided one for the project. Likewise, a general contractor may seek recovery from its defaulted subcontractor's performance bond for costs incurred in completing the subcontractor's work. Some larger general contractors obtain subcontractor default insurance for the same purpose, to protect them from the costs incurred in completing the subcontractor's work.

Where there is a dispute between the general contractor and its subcontractor(s) or supplier(s) and the general contractor has posted a payment bond, the subcontractor(s) or supplier(s) may also seek payment of their claims from the general contractor's payment bond surety. The first step in this process is for the claimant to identify the surety and secure a copy of the payment bond. The most direct method of doing this is by requesting a copy of the bond from the general contractor and/or the owner. Some states also provide for the filing of bonds at the initiation of a project.

Both performance and payment bonds contain various notice provisions, time limitations, or other obligations with which a claimant may need to comply in order to bring a claim. In public works projects, such as a school district or the military, certain statutes may apply and include notice provisions, time limitations, and other obligations with which a claimant will need to comply. In the federal context, that statute is called the Miller Act and, in the states, such statutes are often known as "Little Miller Acts." As noted above, while the minimum requirements for giving notice of a payment bond claim to a surety varies by jurisdiction and bond form, a simple letter to the surety, on the claimant's letterhead, identifying the project, the general contractor, the bond number (if available), the service provided, the outstanding debt, and advising the surety that the claimant is bringing a claim under the bond, is normally sufficient to initiate the claims process.

APPENDIX

Exhibit 1

Project Design Criteria

Space program provided by Owner may be altered in consultations between Owner and Architect during Design Phases.

4. Parking Structure

4 levels of parking structure from the ground with 307± parking stalls.

- 13 parking stalls for each 1-bedroom unit
- 35 parking stalls for each 2-bedroom unit
- parking stall for each 444 SF of commercial area
- parking stall for 889 SF of musicians' facility

*One parking stall for bedroom is desirable.
*345 (total number of bedrooms) + 23 + 8 = 376 parking stalls

5. Unit Quantity

- One-bedroom unit (625 - 650 SF) = 107 units
- Two-bedroom unit (950 SF) = 107 units
- Three-bedroom unit (1500 SF±) = 8 units

6. Unit Location

Level 4 (Recreation Deck Level)

- 3 one-bedroom units
- 4 two-bedroom units

Level 530

- 4 one-bedroom units per level
- 4 two-bedroom units per level

Level 3 132

- 3 three-bedroom units per level
- 2 two-bedroom units per level

Exhibit 2

Work Breakdown Structure/Division System

MasterFormat®

PROCUREMENT AND CONTRACTING REQUIREMENTS GROUP

- Division 00 — Procurement and Contracting Requirements

SPECIFICATIONS GROUP

- General Requirements Subgroup
  - Division 01 — General Requirements
- Facility Construction Subgroup
  - Division 02 — Existing Conditions
  - Division 03 — Concrete
  - Division 04 — Masonry
  - Division 05 — Metals
  - Division 06 — Wood, Plastics and Composites
  - Division 07 — Thermal and Moisture Protection
  - Division 08 — Openings
  - Division 09 — Finishes
  - Division 10 — Specialties
  - Division 11 — Equipment
  - Division 12 — Furnishings
  - Division 13 — Special Construction
  - Division 14 — Conveying Equipment
- Facility Services Subgroup
  - Division 21 — Fire Suppression
  - Division 22 — Plumbing
  - Division 23 — Heating, Ventilating and Air Conditioning (HVAC)
  - Division 25 — Integrated Automation
  - Division 26 — Electrical
  - Division 27 — Communications
  - Division 28 — Electronic Safety and Security
- Site and Infrastructure Subgroup
  - Division 31 — Earthwork
  - Division 32 — Exterior Improvements
  - Division 33 — Utilities
  - Division 34 — Transportation

- Division 35 — Waterway and Marine Construction
- Process Equipment Subgroup
  - Division 40 — Process Interconnections
  - Division 41 — Material Processing and Handling Equipment
  - Division 42 — Process Heating, Cooling and Drying Equipment
  - Division 43 — Process Gas and Liquid Handling, Purification and Storage Equipment
  - Division 44 — Pollution and Waste Control Equipment
  - Division 45 — Industry-Specific Manufacturing Equipment
  - Division 46 — Water and Wastewater Equipment
  - Division 48 — Electrical Power Generation

By Construction Specifications Institute, https://en.wikipedia.org/wiki/MasterFormat

Exhibit 3

Advertisement for Bids

New Auditorium/Administration Building.

XYX Joint Union High School District is receiving General Contractor bids for the furnishing of all services necessary for construction of the project entitled "ABC High School, New Auditorium /Administration Building" in the City of DEF, State of GHI.

The project consists of construction of a new 25,000 sf 2-story steel-frame auditorium/administration building. Estimated construction value of $25,000,000 to $30,000,000.

Drawings and Specifications may be viewed and downloaded from the following site:

https://XYXJointUnionDistrictProject.website

Password: XYXProject

A non-mandatory pre-bid walk-through will be held at 1:30 p.m. on Wednesday, July 19, 2023, at PQR High School at 805 Lakeview Drive, DEF, GHI 00003.

All offers must be submitted electronically to the below website by 1:30 p.m on Wednesday, August 16, 2023, at which time they will be publicly opened and read:

https://XYXJointUnionDistrictProjectBidSubmission.website

Exhibit 4

Bid Addendum

Addendum Number 1

[Date]

This Addendum forms a part of Contract Documents and modifies the original Bidding Documents as noted below. Please acknowledge receipt of this Addendum in the space provided on the Bid Proposal. Failure to do so may be sufficient cause for the Department to reject the bid. This Addendum consists of 4 items.

Item Number	Page Drawing Reference	Description
General		
1		Attached are the agenda, handouts and sign-in list from the pre-bid meeting held at 2:45 pm on Tuesday, August 28, 2023, at the ABC Auditorium. Also included are the questions raised at the pre-bid meeting along with the answers to those questions.
Changes to the Specifications (In Sequence)		
2	08400-3	Delete Subparagraph 1.5 A. I in its entirety.
3	I 0685-2	At Subparagraph 4.6 D.2, add the following subparagraph: "D.2 - Fire extinguisher (bracket mounted) with Simpson bracket."

Exhibit 5

Bid Bond—AIA Document A310™ - 2010

AIA® Document A310™ – 2010

Bid Bond

CONTRACTOR:
(Name, legal status and address)

SURETY:
(Name, legal status and principal place of business)

OWNER:
(Name, legal status and address)

This document has important legal consequences. Consultation with an attorney is encouraged with respect to its completion or modification.

Any singular reference to Contractor, Surety, Owner or other party shall be considered plural where applicable.

BOND AMOUNT: $

PROJECT:
(Name, location or address, and Project number, if any)

The Contractor and Surety are bound to the Owner in the amount set forth above, for the payment of which the Contractor and Surety bind themselves, their heirs, executors, administrators, successors and assigns, jointly and severally, as provided herein. The conditions of this Bond are such that if the Owner accepts the bid of the Contractor within the time specified in the bid documents, or within such time period as may be agreed to by the Owner and Contractor, and the Contractor either (1) enters into a contract with the Owner in accordance with the terms of such bid, and gives such bond or bonds as may be specified in the bidding or Contract Documents, with a surety admitted in the jurisdiction of the Project and otherwise acceptable to the Owner, for the faithful performance of such Contract and for the prompt payment of labor and material furnished in the prosecution thereof; or (2) pays to the Owner the difference, not to exceed the amount of this Bond, between the amount specified in said bid and such larger amount for which the Owner may in good faith contract with another party to perform the work covered by said bid, then this obligation shall be null and void, otherwise to remain in full force and effect. The Surety hereby waives any notice of an agreement between the Owner and Contractor to extend the time in which the Owner may accept the bid. Waiver of notice by the Surety shall not apply to any extension exceeding sixty (60) days in the aggregate beyond the time for acceptance of bids specified in the bid documents, and the Owner and Contractor shall obtain the Surety's consent for an extension beyond sixty (60) days.

If this Bond is issued in connection with a subcontractor's bid to a Contractor, the term Contractor in this Bond shall be deemed to be Subcontractor and the term Owner shall be deemed to be Contractor.

When this Bond has been furnished to comply with a statutory or other legal requirement in the location of the Project, any provision in this Bond conflicting with said statutory or legal requirement shall be deemed deleted herefrom and provisions conforming to such statutory or other legal requirement shall be deemed incorporated herein. When so furnished, the intent is that this Bond shall be construed as a statutory bond and not as a common law bond.

Signed and sealed this day of

	(Contractor as Principal)	*(Seal)*
(Witness)	*(Title)*	
	(Surety)	*(Seal)*
(Witness)	*(Title)*	

Init.
/

Exhibit 6

Notice of Award

Construction Award Notice

Additions / Alterations to the ABC Elementary School Center / Renovations to Existing Training Building and Organizational Maintenance Shop/Unheated Storage Building, DEF, GHI

General Information

Document Type: Award Notice
Solicitation Number: R64 1 BK-82-S-002
Posted Date: August 1, 2023
Original Archive Date: August 28, 2023
Current Archive Date: August 28, 2023
Classification Code: 72 - Construction & Building Materials
NAICS Code 427113 - Commercial and Institutional Building Construction

Contracting Office Address

ABC Elementary Headquarters, JKL, 546 Textbook Dr., Room 212, JKL, GHI 00004

Description

Contract Award Date: September 29, 2023
Contract Award Number: R64 1 BK-82-S-00
Contract Award Amount: $19,264,502.
Contract Line Item Number: 0001, 0002, 0003
Contractor: No Excuse Contractors, Inc. 5472 Bridgewater Way, Crane, CA 92222

Point of Contact

Rock P. Bridges, 676/429-1367
Email your questions to ABC Elementary Headquarters, JKL, GHI at rock.p.bridges@reh.edu

Exhibit 7

AIA Document A201™ – 2017

General Conditions of the Contract for Construction

AIA Document A201® – 2017

General Conditions of the Contract for Construction

for the following PROJECT:
(Name and location or address)

THE OWNER:
(Name, legal status and address)

THE ARCHITECT:
(Name, legal status and address)

This document has important legal consequences. Consultation with an attorney is encouraged with respect to its completion or modification.

For guidance in modifying this document to include supplementary conditions, see AIA Document A503™, Guide for Supplementary Conditions.

TABLE OF ARTICLES

Init.
/

INDEX
(Topics and numbers in bold are Section headings.)

Init.

/

Init.
/

Init.

/

Init.
/

ARTICLE 1 GENERAL PROVISIONS
§ 1.1 Basic Definitions
§ 1.1.1 The Contract Documents
The Contract Documents are enumerated in the Agreement between the Owner and Contractor (hereinafter the Agreement) and consist of the Agreement, Conditions of the Contract (General, Supplementary and other Conditions), Drawings, Specifications, Addenda issued prior to execution of the Contract, other documents listed in the Agreement, and Modifications issued after execution of the Contract. A Modification is (1) a written amendment to the Contract signed by both parties, (2) a Change Order, (3) a Construction Change Directive, or (4) a written order for a minor change in the Work issued by the Architect. Unless specifically enumerated in the Agreement, the Contract Documents do not include the advertisement or invitation to bid, Instructions to Bidders, sample forms, other information furnished by the Owner in anticipation of receiving bids or proposals, the Contractor's bid or proposal, or portions of Addenda relating to bidding or proposal requirements.

§ 1.1.2 The Contract
The Contract Documents form the Contract for Construction. The Contract represents the entire and integrated agreement between the parties hereto and supersedes prior negotiations, representations, or agreements, either written or oral. The Contract may be amended or modified only by a Modification. The Contract Documents shall not be construed to create a contractual relationship of any kind (1) between the Contractor and the Architect or the Architect's consultants, (2) between the Owner and a Subcontractor or a Sub-subcontractor, (3) between the Owner and the Architect or the Architect's consultants, or (4) between any persons or entities other than the Owner and the Contractor. The Architect shall, however, be entitled to performance and enforcement of obligations under the Contract intended to facilitate performance of the Architect's duties.

§ 1.1.3 The Work
The term "Work" means the construction and services required by the Contract Documents, whether completed or partially completed, and includes all other labor, materials, equipment, and services provided or to be provided by the Contractor to fulfill the Contractor's obligations. The Work may constitute the whole or a part of the Project.

§ 1.1.4 The Project
The Project is the total construction of which the Work performed under the Contract Documents may be the whole or a part and which may include construction by the Owner and by Separate Contractors.

§ 1.1.5 The Drawings
The Drawings are the graphic and pictorial portions of the Contract Documents showing the design, location and dimensions of the Work, generally including plans, elevations, sections, details, schedules, and diagrams.

§ 1.1.6 The Specifications
The Specifications are that portion of the Contract Documents consisting of the written requirements for materials, equipment, systems, standards and workmanship for the Work, and performance of related services.

§ 1.1.7 Instruments of Service
Instruments of Service are representations, in any medium of expression now known or later developed, of the tangible and intangible creative work performed by the Architect and the Architect's consultants under their respective professional services agreements. Instruments of Service may include, without limitation, studies, surveys, models, sketches, drawings, specifications, and other similar materials.

§ 1.1.8 Initial Decision Maker
The Initial Decision Maker is the person identified in the Agreement to render initial decisions on Claims in accordance with Section 15.2. The Initial Decision Maker shall not show partiality to the Owner or Contractor and shall not be liable for results of interpretations or decisions rendered in good faith.

§ 1.2 Correlation and Intent of the Contract Documents
§ 1.2.1 The intent of the Contract Documents is to include all items necessary for the proper execution and completion of the Work by the Contractor. The Contract Documents are complementary, and what is required by one shall be as binding as if required by all; performance by the Contractor shall be required only to the extent consistent with the Contract Documents and reasonably inferable from them as being necessary to produce the indicated results.

§ 1.2.1.1 The invalidity of any provision of the Contract Documents shall not invalidate the Contract or its remaining provisions. If it is determined that any provision of the Contract Documents violates any law, or is otherwise invalid or unenforceable, then that provision shall be revised to the extent necessary to make that provision legal and enforceable. In such case the Contract Documents shall be construed, to the fullest extent permitted by law, to give effect to the parties' intentions and purposes in executing the Contract.

§ 1.2.2 Organization of the Specifications into divisions, sections and articles, and arrangement of Drawings shall not control the Contractor in dividing the Work among Subcontractors or in establishing the extent of Work to be performed by any trade.

§ 1.2.3 Unless otherwise stated in the Contract Documents, words that have well-known technical or construction industry meanings are used in the Contract Documents in accordance with such recognized meanings.

§ 1.3 Capitalization
Terms capitalized in these General Conditions include those that are (1) specifically defined, (2) the titles of numbered articles, or (3) the titles of other documents published by the American Institute of Architects.

§ 1.4 Interpretation
In the interest of brevity the Contract Documents frequently omit modifying words such as "all" and "any" and articles such as "the" and "an," but the fact that a modifier or an article is absent from one statement and appears in another is not intended to affect the interpretation of either statement.

§ 1.5 Ownership and Use of Drawings, Specifications, and Other Instruments of Service
§ 1.5.1 The Architect and the Architect's consultants shall be deemed the authors and owners of their respective Instruments of Service, including the Drawings and Specifications, and retain all common law, statutory, and other reserved rights in their Instruments of Service, including copyrights. The Contractor, Subcontractors, Sub-subcontractors, and suppliers shall not own or claim a copyright in the Instruments of Service. Submittal or distribution to meet official regulatory requirements or for other purposes in connection with the Project is not to be construed as publication in derogation of the Architect's or Architect's consultants' reserved rights.

§ 1.5.2 The Contractor, Subcontractors, Sub-subcontractors, and suppliers are authorized to use and reproduce the Instruments of Service provided to them, subject to any protocols established pursuant to Sections 1.7 and 1.8, solely and exclusively for execution of the Work. All copies made under this authorization shall bear the copyright notice, if any, shown on the Instruments of Service. The Contractor, Subcontractors, Sub-subcontractors, and suppliers may not use the Instruments of Service on other projects or for additions to the Project outside the scope of the Work without the specific written consent of the Owner, Architect, and the Architect's consultants.

§ 1.6 Notice
§ 1.6.1 Except as otherwise provided in Section 1.6.2, where the Contract Documents require one party to notify or give notice to the other party, such notice shall be provided in writing to the designated representative of the party to whom the notice is addressed and shall be deemed to have been duly served if delivered in person, by mail, by courier, or by electronic transmission if a method for electronic transmission is set forth in the Agreement.

§ 1.6.2 Notice of Claims as provided in Section 15.1.3 shall be provided in writing and shall be deemed to have been duly served only if delivered to the designated representative of the party to whom the notice is addressed by certified or registered mail, or by courier providing proof of delivery.

§ 1.7 Digital Data Use and Transmission
The parties shall agree upon protocols governing the transmission and use of Instruments of Service or any other information or documentation in digital form. The parties will use AIA Document E203™–2013, Building Information Modeling and Digital Data Exhibit, to establish the protocols for the development, use, transmission, and exchange of digital data.

§ 1.8 Building Information Models Use and Reliance
Any use of, or reliance on, all or a portion of a building information model without agreement to protocols governing the use of, and reliance on, the information contained in the model and without having those protocols set forth in AIA Document E203™–2013, Building Information Modeling and Digital Data Exhibit, and the requisite AIA Document G202™–2013, Project Building Information Modeling Protocol Form, shall be at the using or relying party's sole risk and without liability to the other party and its contractors or consultants, the authors of, or contributors to, the building

information model, and each of their agents and employees.

ARTICLE 2 OWNER

§ 2.1 General

§ 2.1.1 The Owner is the person or entity identified as such in the Agreement and is referred to throughout the Contract Documents as if singular in number. The Owner shall designate in writing a representative who shall have express authority to bind the Owner with respect to all matters requiring the Owner's approval or authorization. Except as otherwise provided in Section 4.2.1, the Architect does not have such authority. The term "Owner" means the Owner or the Owner's authorized representative.

§ 2.1.2 The Owner shall furnish to the Contractor, within fifteen days after receipt of a written request, information necessary and relevant for the Contractor to evaluate, give notice of, or enforce mechanic's lien rights. Such information shall include a correct statement of the record legal title to the property on which the Project is located, usually referred to as the site, and the Owner's interest therein.

§ 2.2 Evidence of the Owner's Financial Arrangements

§ 2.2.1 Prior to commencement of the Work and upon written request by the Contractor, the Owner shall furnish to the Contractor reasonable evidence that the Owner has made financial arrangements to fulfill the Owner's obligations under the Contract. The Contractor shall have no obligation to commence the Work until the Owner provides such evidence. If commencement of the Work is delayed under this Section 2.2.1, the Contract Time shall be extended appropriately.

§ 2.2.2 Following commencement of the Work and upon written request by the Contractor, the Owner shall furnish to the Contractor reasonable evidence that the Owner has made financial arrangements to fulfill the Owner's obligations under the Contract only if (1) the Owner fails to make payments to the Contractor as the Contract Documents require; (2) the Contractor identifies in writing a reasonable concern regarding the Owner's ability to make payment when due; or (3) a change in the Work materially changes the Contract Sum. If the Owner fails to provide such evidence, as required, within fourteen days of the Contractor's request, the Contractor may immediately stop the Work and, in that event, shall notify the Owner that the Work has stopped. However, if the request is made because a change in the Work materially changes the Contract Sum under (3) above, the Contractor may immediately stop only that portion of the Work affected by the change until reasonable evidence is provided. If the Work is stopped under this Section 2.2.2, the Contract Time shall be extended appropriately and the Contract Sum shall be increased by the amount of the Contractor's reasonable costs of shutdown, delay and start-up, plus interest as provided in the Contract Documents.

§ 2.2.3 After the Owner furnishes evidence of financial arrangements under this Section 2.2, the Owner shall not materially vary such financial arrangements without prior notice to the Contractor.

§ 2.2.4 Where the Owner has designated information furnished under this Section 2.2 as "confidential," the Contractor shall keep the information confidential and shall not disclose it to any other person. However, the Contractor may disclose "confidential" information, after seven (7) days' notice to the Owner, where disclosure is required by law, including a subpoena or other form of compulsory legal process issued by a court or governmental entity, or by court or arbitrator(s) order. The Contractor may also disclose "confidential" information to its employees, consultants, sureties, Subcontractors and their employees, Sub-subcontractors, and others who need to know the content of such information solely and exclusively for the Project and who agree to maintain the confidentiality of such information.

§ 2.3 Information and Services Required of the Owner

§ 2.3.1 Except for permits and fees that are the responsibility of the Contractor under the Contract Documents, including those required under Section 3.7.1, the Owner shall secure and pay for necessary approvals, easements, assessments and charges required for construction, use or occupancy of permanent structures or for permanent changes in existing facilities.

§ 2.3.2 The Owner shall retain an architect lawfully licensed to practice architecture, or an entity lawfully practicing architecture, in the jurisdiction where the Project is located. That person or entity is identified as the Architect in the Agreement and is referred to throughout the Contract Documents as if singular in number.

§ 2.3.3 If the employment of the Architect terminates, the Owner shall employ a successor to whom the Contractor has no reasonable objection and whose status under the Contract Documents shall be that of the Architect.

§ 2.3.4 The Owner shall furnish surveys describing physical characteristics, legal limitations and utility locations for the

Init.

/

site of the Project, and a legal description of the site. The Contractor shall be entitled to rely on the accuracy of information furnished by the Owner but shall exercise proper precautions relating to the safe performance of the Work.

§ 2.3.5 The Owner shall furnish information or services required of the Owner by the Contract Documents with reasonable promptness. The Owner shall also furnish any other information or services under the Owner's control and relevant to the Contractor's performance of the Work with reasonable promptness after receiving the Contractor's written request for such information or services.

§ 2.3.6 Unless otherwise provided in the Contract Documents, the Owner shall furnish to the Contractor one copy of the Contract Documents for purposes of making reproductions pursuant to Section 1.5.2.

§ 2.4 Owner's Right to Stop the Work
If the Contractor fails to correct Work that is not in accordance with the requirements of the Contract Documents as required by Section 12.2 or repeatedly fails to carry out Work in accordance with the Contract Documents, the Owner may issue a written order to the Contractor to stop the Work, or any portion thereof, until the cause for such order has been eliminated; however, the right of the Owner to stop the Work shall not give rise to a duty on the part of the Owner to exercise this right for the benefit of the Contractor or any other person or entity, except to the extent required by Section 6.1.3.

§ 2.5 Owner's Right to Carry Out the Work
If the Contractor defaults or neglects to carry out the Work in accordance with the Contract Documents and fails within a ten-day period after receipt of notice from the Owner to commence and continue correction of such default or neglect with diligence and promptness, the Owner may, without prejudice to other remedies the Owner may have, correct such default or neglect. Such action by the Owner and amounts charged to the Contractor are both subject to prior approval of the Architect and the Architect may, pursuant to Section 9.5.1, withhold or nullify a Certificate for Payment in whole or in part, to the extent reasonably necessary to reimburse the Owner for the reasonable cost of correcting such deficiencies, including Owner's expenses and compensation for the Architect's additional services made necessary by such default, neglect, or failure. If current and future payments are not sufficient to cover such amounts, the Contractor shall pay the difference to the Owner. If the Contractor disagrees with the actions of the Owner or the Architect, or the amounts claimed as costs to the Owner, the Contractor may file a Claim pursuant to Article 15.

ARTICLE 3 CONTRACTOR
§ 3.1 General
§ 3.1.1 The Contractor is the person or entity identified as such in the Agreement and is referred to throughout the Contract Documents as if singular in number. The Contractor shall be lawfully licensed, if required in the jurisdiction where the Project is located. The Contractor shall designate in writing a representative who shall have express authority to bind the Contractor with respect to all matters under this Contract. The term "Contractor" means the Contractor or the Contractor's authorized representative.

§ 3.1.2 The Contractor shall perform the Work in accordance with the Contract Documents.

§ 3.1.3 The Contractor shall not be relieved of its obligations to perform the Work in accordance with the Contract Documents either by activities or duties of the Architect in the Architect's administration of the Contract, or by tests, inspections or approvals required or performed by persons or entities other than the Contractor.

§ 3.2 Review of Contract Documents and Field Conditions by Contractor
§ 3.2.1 Execution of the Contract by the Contractor is a representation that the Contractor has visited the site, become generally familiar with local conditions under which the Work is to be performed, and correlated personal observations with requirements of the Contract Documents.

§ 3.2.2 Because the Contract Documents are complementary, the Contractor shall, before starting each portion of the Work, carefully study and compare the various Contract Documents relative to that portion of the Work, as well as the information furnished by the Owner pursuant to Section 2.3.4, shall take field measurements of any existing conditions related to that portion of the Work, and shall observe any conditions at the site affecting it. These obligations are for the purpose of facilitating coordination and construction by the Contractor and are not for the purpose of discovering errors, omissions, or inconsistencies in the Contract Documents; however, the Contractor shall promptly report to the Architect any errors, inconsistencies or omissions discovered by or made known to the Contractor as a request for information in such form as the Architect may require. It is recognized that the Contractor's review is made in the Contractor's

Init.
/

capacity as a contractor and not as a licensed design professional, unless otherwise specifically provided in the Contract Documents.

§ 3.2.3 The Contractor is not required to ascertain that the Contract Documents are in accordance with applicable laws, statutes, ordinances, codes, rules and regulations, or lawful orders of public authorities, but the Contractor shall promptly report to the Architect any nonconformity discovered by or made known to the Contractor as a request for information in such form as the Architect may require.

§ 3.2.4 If the Contractor believes that additional cost or time is involved because of clarifications or instructions the Architect issues in response to the Contractor's notices or requests for information pursuant to Sections 3.2.2 or 3.2.3, the Contractor shall submit Claims as provided in Article 15. If the Contractor fails to perform the obligations of Sections 3.2.2 or 3.2.3, the Contractor shall pay such costs and damages to the Owner, subject to Section 15.1.7, as would have been avoided if the Contractor had performed such obligations. If the Contractor performs those obligations, the Contractor shall not be liable to the Owner or Architect for damages resulting from errors, inconsistencies or omissions in the Contract Documents, for differences between field measurements or conditions and the Contract Documents, or for nonconformities of the Contract Documents to applicable laws, statutes, ordinances, codes, rules and regulations, and lawful orders of public authorities.

§ 3.3 Supervision and Construction Procedures

§ 3.3.1 The Contractor shall supervise and direct the Work, using the Contractor's best skill and attention. The Contractor shall be solely responsible for, and have control over, construction means, methods, techniques, sequences, and procedures, and for coordinating all portions of the Work under the Contract. If the Contract Documents give specific instructions concerning construction means, methods, techniques, sequences, or procedures, the Contractor shall evaluate the jobsite safety thereof and shall be solely responsible for the jobsite safety of such means, methods, techniques, sequences, or procedures. If the Contractor determines that such means, methods, techniques, sequences or procedures may not be safe, the Contractor shall give timely notice to the Owner and Architect, and shall propose alternative means, methods, techniques, sequences, or procedures. The Architect shall evaluate the proposed alternative solely for conformance with the design intent for the completed construction. Unless the Architect objects to the Contractor's proposed alternative, the Contractor shall perform the Work using its alternative means, methods, techniques, sequences, or procedures.

§ 3.3.2 The Contractor shall be responsible to the Owner for acts and omissions of the Contractor's employees, Subcontractors and their agents and employees, and other persons or entities performing portions of the Work for, or on behalf of, the Contractor or any of its Subcontractors.

§ 3.3.3 The Contractor shall be responsible for inspection of portions of Work already performed to determine that such portions are in proper condition to receive subsequent Work.

§ 3.4 Labor and Materials

§ 3.4.1 Unless otherwise provided in the Contract Documents, the Contractor shall provide and pay for labor, materials, equipment, tools, construction equipment and machinery, water, heat, utilities, transportation, and other facilities and services necessary for proper execution and completion of the Work, whether temporary or permanent and whether or not incorporated or to be incorporated in the Work.

§ 3.4.2 Except in the case of minor changes in the Work approved by the Architect in accordance with Section 3.12.8 or ordered by the Architect in accordance with Section 7.4, the Contractor may make substitutions only with the consent of the Owner, after evaluation by the Architect and in accordance with a Change Order or Construction Change Directive.

§ 3.4.3 The Contractor shall enforce strict discipline and good order among the Contractor's employees and other persons carrying out the Work. The Contractor shall not permit employment of unfit persons or persons not properly skilled in tasks assigned to them.

§ 3.5 Warranty

§ 3.5.1 The Contractor warrants to the Owner and Architect that materials and equipment furnished under the Contract will be of good quality and new unless the Contract Documents require or permit otherwise. The Contractor further warrants that the Work will conform to the requirements of the Contract Documents and will be free from defects, except for those inherent in the quality of the Work the Contract Documents require or permit. Work, materials, or equipment not conforming to these requirements may be considered defective. The Contractor's warranty excludes remedy for damage or defect caused by abuse, alterations to the Work not executed by the Contractor, improper or insufficient maintenance, improper operation, or normal wear and tear and normal usage. If required by the Architect, the Contractor shall furnish satisfactory evidence as to the kind and quality of materials and equipment.

§ 3.5.2 All material, equipment, or other special warranties required by the Contract Documents shall be issued in the name of the Owner, or shall be transferable to the Owner, and shall commence in accordance with Section 9.8.4.

§ 3.6 Taxes
The Contractor shall pay sales, consumer, use and similar taxes for the Work provided by the Contractor that are legally enacted when bids are received or negotiations concluded, whether or not yet effective or merely scheduled to go into effect.

§ 3.7 Permits, Fees, Notices and Compliance with Laws
§ 3.7.1 Unless otherwise provided in the Contract Documents, the Contractor shall secure and pay for the building permit as well as for other permits, fees, licenses, and inspections by government agencies necessary for proper execution and completion of the Work that are customarily secured after execution of the Contract and legally required at the time bids are received or negotiations concluded.

§ 3.7.2 The Contractor shall comply with and give notices required by applicable laws, statutes, ordinances, codes, rules and regulations, and lawful orders of public authorities applicable to performance of the Work.

§ 3.7.3 If the Contractor performs Work knowing it to be contrary to applicable laws, statutes, ordinances, codes, rules and regulations, or lawful orders of public authorities, the Contractor shall assume appropriate responsibility for such Work and shall bear the costs attributable to correction.

§ 3.7.4 Concealed or Unknown Conditions
If the Contractor encounters conditions at the site that are (1) subsurface or otherwise concealed physical conditions that differ materially from those indicated in the Contract Documents or (2) unknown physical conditions of an unusual nature that differ materially from those ordinarily found to exist and generally recognized as inherent in construction activities of the character provided for in the Contract Documents, the Contractor shall promptly provide notice to the Owner and the Architect before conditions are disturbed and in no event later than 14 days after first observance of the conditions. The Architect will promptly investigate such conditions and, if the Architect determines that they differ materially and cause an increase or decrease in the Contractor's cost of, or time required for, performance of any part of the Work, will recommend that an equitable adjustment be made in the Contract Sum or Contract Time, or both. If the Architect determines that the conditions at the site are not materially different from those indicated in the Contract Documents and that no change in the terms of the Contract is justified, the Architect shall promptly notify the Owner and Contractor, stating the reasons. If either party disputes the Architect's determination or recommendation, that party may submit a Claim as provided in Article 15.

§ 3.7.5 If, in the course of the Work, the Contractor encounters human remains or recognizes the existence of burial markers, archaeological sites or wetlands not indicated in the Contract Documents, the Contractor shall immediately suspend any operations that would affect them and shall notify the Owner and Architect. Upon receipt of such notice, the Owner shall promptly take any action necessary to obtain governmental authorization required to resume the operations. The Contractor shall continue to suspend such operations until otherwise instructed by the Owner but shall continue with all other operations that do not affect those remains or features. Requests for adjustments in the Contract Sum and Contract Time arising from the existence of such remains or features may be made as provided in Article 15.

§ 3.8 Allowances
§ 3.8.1 The Contractor shall include in the Contract Sum all allowances stated in the Contract Documents. Items covered by allowances shall be supplied for such amounts and by such persons or entities as the Owner may direct, but the Contractor shall not be required to employ persons or entities to whom the Contractor has reasonable objection.

§ 3.8.2 Unless otherwise provided in the Contract Documents,

.1 allowances shall cover the cost to the Contractor of materials and equipment delivered at the site and all required taxes, less applicable trade discounts;

.2 Contractor's costs for unloading and handling at the site, labor, installation costs, overhead, profit, and other expenses contemplated for stated allowance amounts shall be included in the Contract Sum but not in the allowances; and

Init.

/

.3 whenever costs are more than or less than allowances, the Contract Sum shall be adjusted accordingly by Change Order. The amount of the Change Order shall reflect (1) the difference between actual costs and the allowances under Section 3.8.2.1 and (2) changes in Contractor's costs under Section 3.8.2.2.

§ 3.8.3 Materials and equipment under an allowance shall be selected by the Owner with reasonable promptness.

§ 3.9 Superintendent
§ 3.9.1 The Contractor shall employ a competent superintendent and necessary assistants who shall be in attendance at the Project site during performance of the Work. The superintendent shall represent the Contractor, and communications given to the superintendent shall be as binding as if given to the Contractor.

§ 3.9.2 The Contractor, as soon as practicable after award of the Contract, shall notify the Owner and Architect of the name and qualifications of a proposed superintendent. Within 14 days of receipt of the information, the Architect may notify the Contractor, stating whether the Owner or the Architect (1) has reasonable objection to the proposed superintendent or (2) requires additional time for review. Failure of the Architect to provide notice within the 14-day period shall constitute notice of no reasonable objection.

§ 3.9.3 The Contractor shall not employ a proposed superintendent to whom the Owner or Architect has made reasonable and timely objection. The Contractor shall not change the superintendent without the Owner's consent, which shall not unreasonably be withheld or delayed.

§ 3.10 Contractor's Construction and Submittal Schedules
§ 3.10.1 The Contractor, promptly after being awarded the Contract, shall submit for the Owner's and Architect's information a Contractor's construction schedule for the Work. The schedule shall contain detail appropriate for the Project, including (1) the date of commencement of the Work, interim schedule milestone dates, and the date of Substantial Completion; (2) an apportionment of the Work by construction activity; and (3) the time required for completion of each portion of the Work. The schedule shall provide for the orderly progression of the Work to completion and shall not exceed time limits current under the Contract Documents. The schedule shall be revised at appropriate intervals as required by the conditions of the Work and Project.

§ 3.10.2 The Contractor, promptly after being awarded the Contract and thereafter as necessary to maintain a current submittal schedule, shall submit a submittal schedule for the Architect's approval. The Architect's approval shall not be unreasonably delayed or withheld. The submittal schedule shall (1) be coordinated with the Contractor's construction schedule, and (2) allow the Architect reasonable time to review submittals. If the Contractor fails to submit a submittal schedule, or fails to provide submittals in accordance with the approved submittal schedule, the Contractor shall not be entitled to any increase in Contract Sum or extension of Contract Time based on the time required for review of submittals.

§ 3.10.3 The Contractor shall perform the Work in general accordance with the most recent schedules submitted to the Owner and Architect.

§ 3.11 Documents and Samples at the Site
The Contractor shall make available, at the Project site, the Contract Documents, including Change Orders, Construction Change Directives, and other Modifications, in good order and marked currently to indicate field changes and selections made during construction, and the approved Shop Drawings, Product Data, Samples, and similar required submittals. These shall be in electronic form or paper copy, available to the Architect and Owner, and delivered to the Architect for submittal to the Owner upon completion of the Work as a record of the Work as constructed.

§ 3.12 Shop Drawings, Product Data and Samples
§ 3.12.1 Shop Drawings are drawings, diagrams, schedules, and other data specially prepared for the Work by the Contractor or a Subcontractor, Sub-subcontractor, manufacturer, supplier, or distributor to illustrate some portion of the Work.

§ 3.12.2 Product Data are illustrations, standard schedules, performance charts, instructions, brochures, diagrams, and other information furnished by the Contractor to illustrate materials or equipment for some portion of the Work.

§ 3.12.3 Samples are physical examples that illustrate materials, equipment, or workmanship, and establish standards by which the Work will be judged.

Init.

/

§ 3.12.4 Shop Drawings, Product Data, Samples, and similar submittals are not Contract Documents. Their purpose is to demonstrate how the Contractor proposes to conform to the information given and the design concept expressed in the Contract Documents for those portions of the Work for which the Contract Documents require submittals. Review by the Architect is subject to the limitations of Section 4.2.7. Informational submittals upon which the Architect is not expected to take responsive action may be so identified in the Contract Documents. Submittals that are not required by the Contract Documents may be returned by the Architect without action.

§ 3.12.5 The Contractor shall review for compliance with the Contract Documents, approve, and submit to the Architect, Shop Drawings, Product Data, Samples, and similar submittals required by the Contract Documents, in accordance with the submittal schedule approved by the Architect or, in the absence of an approved submittal schedule, with reasonable promptness and in such sequence as to cause no delay in the Work or in the activities of the Owner or of Separate Contractors.

§ 3.12.6 By submitting Shop Drawings, Product Data, Samples, and similar submittals, the Contractor represents to the Owner and Architect that the Contractor has (1) reviewed and approved them, (2) determined and verified materials, field measurements and field construction criteria related thereto, or will do so, and (3) checked and coordinated the information contained within such submittals with the requirements of the Work and of the Contract Documents.

§ 3.12.7 The Contractor shall perform no portion of the Work for which the Contract Documents require submittal and review of Shop Drawings, Product Data, Samples, or similar submittals, until the respective submittal has been approved by the Architect.

§ 3.12.8 The Work shall be in accordance with approved submittals except that the Contractor shall not be relieved of responsibility for deviations from the requirements of the Contract Documents by the Architect's approval of Shop Drawings, Product Data, Samples, or similar submittals, unless the Contractor has specifically notified the Architect of such deviation at the time of submittal and (1) the Architect has given written approval to the specific deviation as a minor change in the Work, or (2) a Change Order or Construction Change Directive has been issued authorizing the deviation. The Contractor shall not be relieved of responsibility for errors or omissions in Shop Drawings, Product Data, Samples, or similar submittals, by the Architect's approval thereof.

§ 3.12.9 The Contractor shall direct specific attention, in writing or on resubmitted Shop Drawings, Product Data, Samples, or similar submittals, to revisions other than those requested by the Architect on previous submittals. In the absence of such notice, the Architect's approval of a resubmission shall not apply to such revisions.

§ 3.12.10 The Contractor shall not be required to provide professional services that constitute the practice of architecture or engineering unless such services are specifically required by the Contract Documents for a portion of the Work or unless the Contractor needs to provide such services in order to carry out the Contractor's responsibilities for construction means, methods, techniques, sequences, and procedures. The Contractor shall not be required to provide professional services in violation of applicable law.

§ 3.12.10.1 If professional design services or certifications by a design professional related to systems, materials, or equipment are specifically required of the Contractor by the Contract Documents, the Owner and the Architect will specify all performance and design criteria that such services must satisfy. The Contractor shall be entitled to rely upon the adequacy and accuracy of the performance and design criteria provided in the Contract Documents. The Contractor shall cause such services or certifications to be provided by an appropriately licensed design professional, whose signature and seal shall appear on all drawings, calculations, specifications, certifications, Shop Drawings, and other submittals prepared by such professional. Shop Drawings, and other submittals related to the Work, designed or certified by such professional, if prepared by others, shall bear such professional's written approval when submitted to the Architect. The Owner and the Architect shall be entitled to rely upon the adequacy and accuracy of the services, certifications, and approvals performed or provided by such design professionals, provided the Owner and Architect have specified to the Contractor the performance and design criteria that such services must satisfy. Pursuant to this Section 3.12.10, the Architect will review and approve or take other appropriate action on submittals only for the limited purpose of checking for conformance with information given and the design concept expressed in the Contract Documents.

§ 3.12.10.2 If the Contract Documents require the Contractor's design professional to certify that the Work has been performed in accordance with the design criteria, the Contractor shall furnish such certifications to the Architect at the time and in the form specified by the Architect.

§ 3.13 Use of Site
The Contractor shall confine operations at the site to areas permitted by applicable laws, statutes, ordinances, codes, rules and regulations, lawful orders of public authorities, and the Contract Documents and shall not unreasonably encumber the site with materials or equipment.

§ 3.14 Cutting and Patching
§ 3.14.1 The Contractor shall be responsible for cutting, fitting, or patching required to complete the Work or to make its parts fit together properly. All areas requiring cutting, fitting, or patching shall be restored to the condition existing prior to the cutting, fitting, or patching, unless otherwise required by the Contract Documents.

§ 3.14.2 The Contractor shall not damage or endanger a portion of the Work or fully or partially completed construction of the Owner or Separate Contractors by cutting, patching, or otherwise altering such construction, or by excavation. The Contractor shall not cut or otherwise alter construction by the Owner or a Separate Contractor except with written consent of the Owner and of the Separate Contractor. Consent shall not be unreasonably withheld. The Contractor shall not unreasonably withhold, from the Owner or a Separate Contractor, its consent to cutting or otherwise altering the Work.

§ 3.15 Cleaning Up
§ 3.15.1 The Contractor shall keep the premises and surrounding area free from accumulation of waste materials and rubbish caused by operations under the Contract. At completion of the Work, the Contractor shall remove waste materials, rubbish, the Contractor's tools, construction equipment, machinery, and surplus materials from and about the Project.

§ 3.15.2 If the Contractor fails to clean up as provided in the Contract Documents, the Owner may do so and the Owner shall be entitled to reimbursement from the Contractor.

§ 3.16 Access to Work
The Contractor shall provide the Owner and Architect with access to the Work in preparation and progress wherever located.

§ 3.17 Royalties, Patents and Copyrights
The Contractor shall pay all royalties and license fees. The Contractor shall defend suits or claims for infringement of copyrights and patent rights and shall hold the Owner and Architect harmless from loss on account thereof, but shall not be responsible for defense or loss when a particular design, process, or product of a particular manufacturer or manufacturers is required by the Contract Documents, or where the copyright violations are contained in Drawings, Specifications, or other documents prepared by the Owner or Architect. However, if an infringement of a copyright or patent is discovered by, or made known to, the Contractor, the Contractor shall be responsible for the loss unless the information is promptly furnished to the Architect.

§ 3.18 Indemnification
§ 3.18.1 To the fullest extent permitted by law, the Contractor shall indemnify and hold harmless the Owner, Architect, Architect's consultants, and agents and employees of any of them from and against claims, damages, losses, and expenses, including but not limited to attorneys' fees, arising out of or resulting from performance of the Work, provided that such claim, damage, loss, or expense is attributable to bodily injury, sickness, disease or death, or to injury to or destruction of tangible property (other than the Work itself), but only to the extent caused by the negligent acts or omissions of the Contractor, a Subcontractor, anyone directly or indirectly employed by them, or anyone for whose acts they may be liable, regardless of whether or not such claim, damage, loss, or expense is caused in part by a party indemnified hereunder. Such obligation shall not be construed to negate, abridge, or reduce other rights or obligations of indemnity that would otherwise exist as to a party or person described in this Section 3.18.

§ 3.18.2 In claims against any person or entity indemnified under this Section 3.18 by an employee of the Contractor, a Subcontractor, anyone directly or indirectly employed by them, or anyone for whose acts they may be liable, the indemnification obligation under Section 3.18.1 shall not be limited by a limitation on amount or type of damages, compensation, or benefits payable by or for the Contractor or a Subcontractor under workers' compensation acts, disability benefit acts, or other employee benefit acts.

Init.
/

ARTICLE 4 ARCHITECT

§ 4.1 General

§ 4.1.1 The Architect is the person or entity retained by the Owner pursuant to Section 2.3.2 and identified as such in the Agreement.

§ 4.1.2 Duties, responsibilities, and limitations of authority of the Architect as set forth in the Contract Documents shall not be restricted, modified, or extended without written consent of the Owner, Contractor, and Architect. Consent shall not be unreasonably withheld.

§ 4.2 Administration of the Contract

§ 4.2.1 The Architect will provide administration of the Contract as described in the Contract Documents and will be an Owner's representative during construction until the date the Architect issues the final Certificate for Payment. The Architect will have authority to act on behalf of the Owner only to the extent provided in the Contract Documents.

§ 4.2.2 The Architect will visit the site at intervals appropriate to the stage of construction, or as otherwise agreed with the Owner, to become generally familiar with the progress and quality of the portion of the Work completed, and to determine in general if the Work observed is being performed in a manner indicating that the Work, when fully completed, will be in accordance with the Contract Documents. However, the Architect will not be required to make exhaustive or continuous on-site inspections to check the quality or quantity of the Work. The Architect will not have control over, charge of, or responsibility for the construction means, methods, techniques, sequences or procedures, or for the safety precautions and programs in connection with the Work, since these are solely the Contractor's rights and responsibilities under the Contract Documents.

§ 4.2.3 On the basis of the site visits, the Architect will keep the Owner reasonably informed about the progress and quality of the portion of the Work completed, and promptly report to the Owner (1) known deviations from the Contract Documents, (2) known deviations from the most recent construction schedule submitted by the Contractor, and (3) defects and deficiencies observed in the Work. The Architect will not be responsible for the Contractor's failure to perform the Work in accordance with the requirements of the Contract Documents. The Architect will not have control over or charge of, and will not be responsible for acts or omissions of, the Contractor, Subcontractors, or their agents or employees, or any other persons or entities performing portions of the Work.

§ 4.2.4 Communications

The Owner and Contractor shall include the Architect in all communications that relate to or affect the Architect's services or professional responsibilities. The Owner shall promptly notify the Architect of the substance of any direct communications between the Owner and the Contractor otherwise relating to the Project. Communications by and with the Architect's consultants shall be through the Architect. Communications by and with Subcontractors and suppliers shall be through the Contractor. Communications by and with Separate Contractors shall be through the Owner. The Contract Documents may specify other communication protocols.

§ 4.2.5 Based on the Architect's evaluations of the Contractor's Applications for Payment, the Architect will review and certify the amounts due the Contractor and will issue Certificates for Payment in such amounts.

§ 4.2.6 The Architect has authority to reject Work that does not conform to the Contract Documents. Whenever the Architect considers it necessary or advisable, the Architect will have authority to require inspection or testing of the Work in accordance with Sections 13.4.2 and 13.4.3, whether or not the Work is fabricated, installed or completed. However, neither this authority of the Architect nor a decision made in good faith either to exercise or not to exercise such authority shall give rise to a duty or responsibility of the Architect to the Contractor, Subcontractors, suppliers, their agents or employees, or other persons or entities performing portions of the Work.

§ 4.2.7 The Architect will review and approve, or take other appropriate action upon, the Contractor's submittals such as Shop Drawings, Product Data, and Samples, but only for the limited purpose of checking for conformance with information given and the design concept expressed in the Contract Documents. The Architect's action will be taken in accordance with the submittal schedule approved by the Architect or, in the absence of an approved submittal schedule, with reasonable promptness while allowing sufficient time in the Architect's professional judgment to permit adequate review. Review of such submittals is not conducted for the purpose of determining the accuracy and completeness of other details such as dimensions and quantities, or for substantiating instructions for installation or performance of equipment or systems, all of which remain the responsibility of the Contractor as required by the Contract Documents. The Architect's review of the Contractor's submittals shall not relieve the Contractor of the obligations under

Init.
/

Sections 3.3, 3.5, and 3.12. The Architect's review shall not constitute approval of safety precautions or of any construction means, methods, techniques, sequences, or procedures. The Architect's approval of a specific item shall not indicate approval of an assembly of which the item is a component.

§ 4.2.8 The Architect will prepare Change Orders and Construction Change Directives, and may order minor changes in the Work as provided in Section 7.4. The Architect will investigate and make determinations and recommendations regarding concealed and unknown conditions as provided in Section 3.7.4.

§ 4.2.9 The Architect will conduct inspections to determine the date or dates of Substantial Completion and the date of final completion; issue Certificates of Substantial Completion pursuant to Section 9.8; receive and forward to the Owner, for the Owner's review and records, written warranties and related documents required by the Contract and assembled by the Contractor pursuant to Section 9.10; and issue a final Certificate for Payment pursuant to Section 9.10.

§ 4.2.10 If the Owner and Architect agree, the Architect will provide one or more Project representatives to assist in carrying out the Architect's responsibilities at the site. The Owner shall notify the Contractor of any change in the duties, responsibilities and limitations of authority of the Project representatives.

§ 4.2.11 The Architect will interpret and decide matters concerning performance under, and requirements of, the Contract Documents on written request of either the Owner or Contractor. The Architect's response to such requests will be made in writing within any time limits agreed upon or otherwise with reasonable promptness.

§ 4.2.12 Interpretations and decisions of the Architect will be consistent with the intent of, and reasonably inferable from, the Contract Documents and will be in writing or in the form of drawings. When making such interpretations and decisions, the Architect will endeavor to secure faithful performance by both Owner and Contractor, will not show partiality to either, and will not be liable for results of interpretations or decisions rendered in good faith.

§ 4.2.13 The Architect's decisions on matters relating to aesthetic effect will be final if consistent with the intent expressed in the Contract Documents.

§ 4.2.14 The Architect will review and respond to requests for information about the Contract Documents. The Architect's response to such requests will be made in writing within any time limits agreed upon or otherwise with reasonable promptness. If appropriate, the Architect will prepare and issue supplemental Drawings and Specifications in response to the requests for information.

ARTICLE 5 SUBCONTRACTORS

§ 5.1 Definitions

§ 5.1.1 A Subcontractor is a person or entity who has a direct contract with the Contractor to perform a portion of the Work at the site. The term "Subcontractor" is referred to throughout the Contract Documents as if singular in number and means a Subcontractor or an authorized representative of the Subcontractor. The term "Subcontractor" does not include a Separate Contractor or the subcontractors of a Separate Contractor.

§ 5.1.2 A Sub-subcontractor is a person or entity who has a direct or indirect contract with a Subcontractor to perform a portion of the Work at the site. The term "Sub-subcontractor" is referred to throughout the Contract Documents as if singular in number and means a Sub-subcontractor or an authorized representative of the Sub-subcontractor.

§ 5.2 Award of Subcontracts and Other Contracts for Portions of the Work

§ 5.2.1 Unless otherwise stated in the Contract Documents, the Contractor, as soon as practicable after award of the Contract, shall notify the Owner and Architect of the persons or entities proposed for each principal portion of the Work, including those who are to furnish materials or equipment fabricated to a special design. Within 14 days of receipt of the information, the Architect may notify the Contractor whether the Owner or the Architect (1) has reasonable objection to any such proposed person or entity or (2) requires additional time for review. Failure of the Architect to provide notice within the 14-day period shall constitute notice of no reasonable objection.

§ 5.2.2 The Contractor shall not contract with a proposed person or entity to whom the Owner or Architect has made reasonable and timely objection. The Contractor shall not be required to contract with anyone to whom the Contractor has made reasonable objection.

§ 5.2.3 If the Owner or Architect has reasonable objection to a person or entity proposed by the Contractor, the

Init.

/

Contractor shall propose another to whom the Owner or Architect has no reasonable objection. If the proposed but rejected Subcontractor was reasonably capable of performing the Work, the Contract Sum and Contract Time shall be increased or decreased by the difference, if any, occasioned by such change, and an appropriate Change Order shall be issued before commencement of the substitute Subcontractor's Work. However, no increase in the Contract Sum or Contract Time shall be allowed for such change unless the Contractor has acted promptly and responsively in submitting names as required.

§ 5.2.4 The Contractor shall not substitute a Subcontractor, person, or entity for one previously selected if the Owner or Architect makes reasonable objection to such substitution.

§ 5.3 Subcontractual Relations
By appropriate written agreement, the Contractor shall require each Subcontractor, to the extent of the Work to be performed by the Subcontractor, to be bound to the Contractor by terms of the Contract Documents, and to assume toward the Contractor all the obligations and responsibilities, including the responsibility for safety of the Subcontractor's Work that the Contractor, by these Contract Documents, assumes toward the Owner and Architect. Each subcontract agreement shall preserve and protect the rights of the Owner and Architect under the Contract Documents with respect to the Work to be performed by the Subcontractor so that subcontracting thereof will not prejudice such rights, and shall allow to the Subcontractor, unless specifically provided otherwise in the subcontract agreement, the benefit of all rights, remedies, and redress against the Contractor that the Contractor, by the Contract Documents, has against the Owner. Where appropriate, the Contractor shall require each Subcontractor to enter into similar agreements with Sub-subcontractors. The Contractor shall make available to each proposed Subcontractor, prior to the execution of the subcontract agreement, copies of the Contract Documents to which the Subcontractor will be bound, and, upon written request of the Subcontractor, identify to the Subcontractor terms and conditions of the proposed subcontract agreement that may be at variance with the Contract Documents. Subcontractors will similarly make copies of applicable portions of such documents available to their respective proposed Sub-subcontractors.

§ 5.4 Contingent Assignment of Subcontracts
§ 5.4.1 Each subcontract agreement for a portion of the Work is assigned by the Contractor to the Owner, provided that

- **.1** assignment is effective only after termination of the Contract by the Owner for cause pursuant to Section 14.2 and only for those subcontract agreements that the Owner accepts by notifying the Subcontractor and Contractor; and
- **.2** assignment is subject to the prior rights of the surety, if any, obligated under bond relating to the Contract.

When the Owner accepts the assignment of a subcontract agreement, the Owner assumes the Contractor's rights and obligations under the subcontract.

§ 5.4.2 Upon such assignment, if the Work has been suspended for more than 30 days, the Subcontractor's compensation shall be equitably adjusted for increases in cost resulting from the suspension.

§ 5.4.3 Upon assignment to the Owner under this Section 5.4, the Owner may further assign the subcontract to a successor contractor or other entity. If the Owner assigns the subcontract to a successor contractor or other entity, the Owner shall nevertheless remain legally responsible for all of the successor contractor's obligations under the subcontract.

ARTICLE 6 CONSTRUCTION BY OWNER OR BY SEPARATE CONTRACTORS
§ 6.1 Owner's Right to Perform Construction and to Award Separate Contracts
§ 6.1.1 The term "Separate Contractor(s)" shall mean other contractors retained by the Owner under separate agreements. The Owner reserves the right to perform construction or operations related to the Project with the Owner's own forces, and with Separate Contractors retained under Conditions of the Contract substantially similar to those of this Contract, including those provisions of the Conditions of the Contract related to insurance and waiver of subrogation.

§ 6.1.2 When separate contracts are awarded for different portions of the Project or other construction or operations on the site, the term "Contractor" in the Contract Documents in each case shall mean the Contractor who executes each separate Owner-Contractor Agreement.

§ 6.1.3 The Owner shall provide for coordination of the activities of the Owner's own forces and of each Separate

Contractor with the Work of the Contractor, who shall cooperate with them. The Contractor shall participate with any Separate Contractors and the Owner in reviewing their construction schedules. The Contractor shall make any revisions to its construction schedule deemed necessary after a joint review and mutual agreement. The construction schedules shall then constitute the schedules to be used by the Contractor, Separate Contractors, and the Owner until subsequently revised.

§ 6.1.4 Unless otherwise provided in the Contract Documents, when the Owner performs construction or operations related to the Project with the Owner's own forces or with Separate Contractors, the Owner or its Separate Contractors shall have the same obligations and rights that the Contractor has under the Conditions of the Contract, including, without excluding others, those stated in Article 3, this Article 6, and Articles 10, 11, and 12.

§ 6.2 Mutual Responsibility
§ 6.2.1 The Contractor shall afford the Owner and Separate Contractors reasonable opportunity for introduction and storage of their materials and equipment and performance of their activities, and shall connect and coordinate the Contractor's construction and operations with theirs as required by the Contract Documents.

§ 6.2.2 If part of the Contractor's Work depends for proper execution or results upon construction or operations by the Owner or a Separate Contractor, the Contractor shall, prior to proceeding with that portion of the Work, promptly notify the Architect of apparent discrepancies or defects in the construction or operations by the Owner or Separate Contractor that would render it unsuitable for proper execution and results of the Contractor's Work. Failure of the Contractor to notify the Architect of apparent discrepancies or defects prior to proceeding with the Work shall constitute an acknowledgment that the Owner's or Separate Contractor's completed or partially completed construction is fit and proper to receive the Contractor's Work. The Contractor shall not be responsible for discrepancies or defects in the construction or operations by the Owner or Separate Contractor that are not apparent.

§ 6.2.3 The Contractor shall reimburse the Owner for costs the Owner incurs that are payable to a Separate Contractor because of the Contractor's delays, improperly timed activities or defective construction. The Owner shall be responsible to the Contractor for costs the Contractor incurs because of a Separate Contractor's delays, improperly timed activities, damage to the Work or defective construction.

§ 6.2.4 The Contractor shall promptly remedy damage that the Contractor wrongfully causes to completed or partially completed construction or to property of the Owner or Separate Contractor as provided in Section 10.2.5.

§ 6.2.5 The Owner and each Separate Contractor shall have the same responsibilities for cutting and patching as are described for the Contractor in Section 3.14.

§ 6.3 Owner's Right to Clean Up
If a dispute arises among the Contractor, Separate Contractors, and the Owner as to the responsibility under their respective contracts for maintaining the premises and surrounding area free from waste materials and rubbish, the Owner may clean up and the Architect will allocate the cost among those responsible.

ARTICLE 7 CHANGES IN THE WORK
§ 7.1 General
§ 7.1.1 Changes in the Work may be accomplished after execution of the Contract, and without invalidating the Contract, by Change Order, Construction Change Directive or order for a minor change in the Work, subject to the limitations stated in this Article 7 and elsewhere in the Contract Documents.

§ 7.1.2 A Change Order shall be based upon agreement among the Owner, Contractor, and Architect. A Construction Change Directive requires agreement by the Owner and Architect and may or may not be agreed to by the Contractor. An order for a minor change in the Work may be issued by the Architect alone.

§ 7.1.3 Changes in the Work shall be performed under applicable provisions of the Contract Documents. The Contractor shall proceed promptly with changes in the Work, unless otherwise provided in the Change Order, Construction Change Directive, or order for a minor change in the Work.

§ 7.2 Change Orders
§ 7.2.1 A Change Order is a written instrument prepared by the Architect and signed by the Owner, Contractor, and Architect stating their agreement upon all of the following:

Init.
/

.1 The change in the Work;
.2 The amount of the adjustment, if any, in the Contract Sum; and
.3 The extent of the adjustment, if any, in the Contract Time.

§ 7.3 Construction Change Directives
§ 7.3.1 A Construction Change Directive is a written order prepared by the Architect and signed by the Owner and Architect, directing a change in the Work prior to agreement on adjustment, if any, in the Contract Sum or Contract Time, or both. The Owner may by Construction Change Directive, without invalidating the Contract, order changes in the Work within the general scope of the Contract consisting of additions, deletions, or other revisions, the Contract Sum and Contract Time being adjusted accordingly.

§ 7.3.2 A Construction Change Directive shall be used in the absence of total agreement on the terms of a Change Order.

§ 7.3.3 If the Construction Change Directive provides for an adjustment to the Contract Sum, the adjustment shall be based on one of the following methods:

.1 Mutual acceptance of a lump sum properly itemized and supported by sufficient substantiating data to permit evaluation;
.2 Unit prices stated in the Contract Documents or subsequently agreed upon;
.3 Cost to be determined in a manner agreed upon by the parties and a mutually acceptable fixed or percentage fee; or
.4 As provided in Section 7.3.4.

§ 7.3.4 If the Contractor does not respond promptly or disagrees with the method for adjustment in the Contract Sum, the Architect shall determine the adjustment on the basis of reasonable expenditures and savings of those performing the Work attributable to the change, including, in case of an increase in the Contract Sum, an amount for overhead and profit as set forth in the Agreement, or if no such amount is set forth in the Agreement, a reasonable amount. In such case, and also under Section 7.3.3.3, the Contractor shall keep and present, in such form as the Architect may prescribe, an itemized accounting together with appropriate supporting data. Unless otherwise provided in the Contract Documents, costs for the purposes of this Section 7.3.4 shall be limited to the following:

.1 Costs of labor, including applicable payroll taxes, fringe benefits required by agreement or custom, workers' compensation insurance, and other employee costs approved by the Architect;
.2 Costs of materials, supplies, and equipment, including cost of transportation, whether incorporated or consumed;
.3 Rental costs of machinery and equipment, exclusive of hand tools, whether rented from the Contractor or others;
.4 Costs of premiums for all bonds and insurance, permit fees, and sales, use, or similar taxes, directly related to the change; and
.5 Costs of supervision and field office personnel directly attributable to the change.

§ 7.3.5 If the Contractor disagrees with the adjustment in the Contract Time, the Contractor may make a Claim in accordance with applicable provisions of Article 15.

§ 7.3.6 Upon receipt of a Construction Change Directive, the Contractor shall promptly proceed with the change in the Work involved and advise the Architect of the Contractor's agreement or disagreement with the method, if any, provided in the Construction Change Directive for determining the proposed adjustment in the Contract Sum or Contract Time.

§ 7.3.7 A Construction Change Directive signed by the Contractor indicates the Contractor's agreement therewith, including adjustment in Contract Sum and Contract Time or the method for determining them. Such agreement shall be effective immediately and shall be recorded as a Change Order.

§ 7.3.8 The amount of credit to be allowed by the Contractor to the Owner for a deletion or change that results in a net decrease in the Contract Sum shall be actual net cost as confirmed by the Architect. When both additions and credits covering related Work or substitutions are involved in a change, the allowance for overhead and profit shall be figured on the basis of net increase, if any, with respect to that change.

§ 7.3.9 Pending final determination of the total cost of a Construction Change Directive to the Owner, the Contractor may request payment for Work completed under the Construction Change Directive in Applications for Payment. The

Init.
/

Architect will make an interim determination for purposes of monthly certification for payment for those costs and certify for payment the amount that the Architect determines, in the Architect's professional judgment, to be reasonably justified. The Architect's interim determination of cost shall adjust the Contract Sum on the same basis as a Change Order, subject to the right of either party to disagree and assert a Claim in accordance with Article 15.

§ 7.3.10 When the Owner and Contractor agree with a determination made by the Architect concerning the adjustments in the Contract Sum and Contract Time, or otherwise reach agreement upon the adjustments, such agreement shall be effective immediately and the Architect will prepare a Change Order. Change Orders may be issued for all or any part of a Construction Change Directive.

§ 7.4 Minor Changes in the Work
The Architect may order minor changes in the Work that are consistent with the intent of the Contract Documents and do not involve an adjustment in the Contract Sum or an extension of the Contract Time. The Architect's order for minor changes shall be in writing. If the Contractor believes that the proposed minor change in the Work will affect the Contract Sum or Contract Time, the Contractor shall notify the Architect and shall not proceed to implement the change in the Work. If the Contractor performs the Work set forth in the Architect's order for a minor change without prior notice to the Architect that such change will affect the Contract Sum or Contract Time, the Contractor waives any adjustment to the Contract Sum or extension of the Contract Time.

ARTICLE 8 TIME
§ 8.1 Definitions
§ 8.1.1 Unless otherwise provided, Contract Time is the period of time, including authorized adjustments, allotted in the Contract Documents for Substantial Completion of the Work.

§ 8.1.2 The date of commencement of the Work is the date established in the Agreement.

§ 8.1.3 The date of Substantial Completion is the date certified by the Architect in accordance with Section 9.8.

§ 8.1.4 The term "day" as used in the Contract Documents shall mean calendar day unless otherwise specifically defined.

§ 8.2 Progress and Completion
§ 8.2.1 Time limits stated in the Contract Documents are of the essence of the Contract. By executing the Agreement, the Contractor confirms that the Contract Time is a reasonable period for performing the Work.

§ 8.2.2 The Contractor shall not knowingly, except by agreement or instruction of the Owner in writing, commence the Work prior to the effective date of insurance required to be furnished by the Contractor and Owner.

§ 8.2.3 The Contractor shall proceed expeditiously with adequate forces and shall achieve Substantial Completion within the Contract Time.

§ 8.3 Delays and Extensions of Time
§ 8.3.1 If the Contractor is delayed at any time in the commencement or progress of the Work by (1) an act or neglect of the Owner or Architect, of an employee of either, or of a Separate Contractor; (2) by changes ordered in the Work; (3) by labor disputes, fire, unusual delay in deliveries, unavoidable casualties, adverse weather conditions documented in accordance with Section 15.1.6.2, or other causes beyond the Contractor's control; (4) by delay authorized by the Owner pending mediation and binding dispute resolution; or (5) by other causes that the Contractor asserts, and the Architect determines, justify delay, then the Contract Time shall be extended for such reasonable time as the Architect may determine.

§ 8.3.2 Claims relating to time shall be made in accordance with applicable provisions of Article 15.

§ 8.3.3 This Section 8.3 does not preclude recovery of damages for delay by either party under other provisions of the Contract Documents.

ARTICLE 9 PAYMENTS AND COMPLETION
§ 9.1 Contract Sum
§ 9.1.1 The Contract Sum is stated in the Agreement and, including authorized adjustments, is the total amount payable

by the Owner to the Contractor for performance of the Work under the Contract Documents.

§ 9.1.2 If unit prices are stated in the Contract Documents or subsequently agreed upon, and if quantities originally contemplated are materially changed so that application of such unit prices to the actual quantities causes substantial inequity to the Owner or Contractor, the applicable unit prices shall be equitably adjusted.

§ 9.2 Schedule of Values
Where the Contract is based on a stipulated sum or Guaranteed Maximum Price, the Contractor shall submit a schedule of values to the Architect before the first Application for Payment, allocating the entire Contract Sum to the various portions of the Work. The schedule of values shall be prepared in the form, and supported by the data to substantiate its accuracy, required by the Architect. This schedule, unless objected to by the Architect, shall be used as a basis for reviewing the Contractor's Applications for Payment. Any changes to the schedule of values shall be submitted to the Architect and supported by such data to substantiate its accuracy as the Architect may require, and unless objected to by the Architect, shall be used as a basis for reviewing the Contractor's subsequent Applications for Payment.

§ 9.3 Applications for Payment
§ 9.3.1 At least ten days before the date established for each progress payment, the Contractor shall submit to the Architect an itemized Application for Payment prepared in accordance with the schedule of values, if required under Section 9.2, for completed portions of the Work. The application shall be notarized, if required, and supported by all data substantiating the Contractor's right to payment that the Owner or Architect require, such as copies of requisitions, and releases and waivers of liens from Subcontractors and suppliers, and shall reflect retainage if provided for in the Contract Documents.

§ 9.3.1.1 As provided in Section 7.3.9, such applications may include requests for payment on account of changes in the Work that have been properly authorized by Construction Change Directives, or by interim determinations of the Architect, but not yet included in Change Orders.

§ 9.3.1.2 Applications for Payment shall not include requests for payment for portions of the Work for which the Contractor does not intend to pay a Subcontractor or supplier, unless such Work has been performed by others whom the Contractor intends to pay.

§ 9.3.2 Unless otherwise provided in the Contract Documents, payments shall be made on account of materials and equipment delivered and suitably stored at the site for subsequent incorporation in the Work. If approved in advance by the Owner, payment may similarly be made for materials and equipment suitably stored off the site at a location agreed upon in writing. Payment for materials and equipment stored on or off the site shall be conditioned upon compliance by the Contractor with procedures satisfactory to the Owner to establish the Owner's title to such materials and equipment or otherwise protect the Owner's interest, and shall include the costs of applicable insurance, storage, and transportation to the site, for such materials and equipment stored off the site.

§ 9.3.3 The Contractor warrants that title to all Work covered by an Application for Payment will pass to the Owner no later than the time of payment. The Contractor further warrants that upon submittal of an Application for Payment all Work for which Certificates for Payment have been previously issued and payments received from the Owner shall, to the best of the Contractor's knowledge, information, and belief, be free and clear of liens, claims, security interests, or encumbrances, in favor of the Contractor, Subcontractors, suppliers, or other persons or entities that provided labor, materials, and equipment relating to the Work.

§ 9.4 Certificates for Payment
§ 9.4.1 The Architect will, within seven days after receipt of the Contractor's Application for Payment, either (1) issue to the Owner a Certificate for Payment in the full amount of the Application for Payment, with a copy to the Contractor; or (2) issue to the Owner a Certificate for Payment for such amount as the Architect determines is properly due, and notify the Contractor and Owner of the Architect's reasons for withholding certification in part as provided in Section 9.5.1; or (3) withhold certification of the entire Application for Payment, and notify the Contractor and Owner of the Architect's reason for withholding certification in whole as provided in Section 9.5.1.

§ 9.4.2 The issuance of a Certificate for Payment will constitute a representation by the Architect to the Owner, based on the Architect's evaluation of the Work and the data in the Application for Payment, that, to the best of the Architect's knowledge, information, and belief, the Work has progressed to the point indicated, the quality of the Work is in accordance with the Contract Documents, and that the Contractor is entitled to payment in the amount certified. The

Init.
/

foregoing representations are subject to an evaluation of the Work for conformance with the Contract Documents upon Substantial Completion, to results of subsequent tests and inspections, to correction of minor deviations from the Contract Documents prior to completion, and to specific qualifications expressed by the Architect. However, the issuance of a Certificate for Payment will not be a representation that the Architect has (1) made exhaustive or continuous on-site inspections to check the quality or quantity of the Work; (2) reviewed construction means, methods, techniques, sequences, or procedures; (3) reviewed copies of requisitions received from Subcontractors and suppliers and other data requested by the Owner to substantiate the Contractor's right to payment; or (4) made examination to ascertain how or for what purpose the Contractor has used money previously paid on account of the Contract Sum.

§ 9.5 Decisions to Withhold Certification

§ 9.5.1 The Architect may withhold a Certificate for Payment in whole or in part, to the extent reasonably necessary to protect the Owner, if in the Architect's opinion the representations to the Owner required by Section 9.4.2 cannot be made. If the Architect is unable to certify payment in the amount of the Application, the Architect will notify the Contractor and Owner as provided in Section 9.4.1. If the Contractor and Architect cannot agree on a revised amount, the Architect will promptly issue a Certificate for Payment for the amount for which the Architect is able to make such representations to the Owner. The Architect may also withhold a Certificate for Payment or, because of subsequently discovered evidence, may nullify the whole or a part of a Certificate for Payment previously issued, to such extent as may be necessary in the Architect's opinion to protect the Owner from loss for which the Contractor is responsible, including loss resulting from acts and omissions described in Section 3.3.2, because of

.1 defective Work not remedied;
.2 third party claims filed or reasonable evidence indicating probable filing of such claims, unless security acceptable to the Owner is provided by the Contractor;
.3 failure of the Contractor to make payments properly to Subcontractors or suppliers for labor, materials or equipment;
.4 reasonable evidence that the Work cannot be completed for the unpaid balance of the Contract Sum;
.5 damage to the Owner or a Separate Contractor;
.6 reasonable evidence that the Work will not be completed within the Contract Time, and that the unpaid balance would not be adequate to cover actual or liquidated damages for the anticipated delay; or
.7 repeated failure to carry out the Work in accordance with the Contract Documents.

§ 9.5.2 When either party disputes the Architect's decision regarding a Certificate for Payment under Section 9.5.1, in whole or in part, that party may submit a Claim in accordance with Article 15.

§ 9.5.3 When the reasons for withholding certification are removed, certification will be made for amounts previously withheld.

§ 9.5.4 If the Architect withholds certification for payment under Section 9.5.1.3, the Owner may, at its sole option, issue joint checks to the Contractor and to any Subcontractor or supplier to whom the Contractor failed to make payment for Work properly performed or material or equipment suitably delivered. If the Owner makes payments by joint check, the Owner shall notify the Architect and the Contractor shall reflect such payment on its next Application for Payment.

§ 9.6 Progress Payments

§ 9.6.1 After the Architect has issued a Certificate for Payment, the Owner shall make payment in the manner and within the time provided in the Contract Documents, and shall so notify the Architect.

§ 9.6.2 The Contractor shall pay each Subcontractor, no later than seven days after receipt of payment from the Owner, the amount to which the Subcontractor is entitled, reflecting percentages actually retained from payments to the Contractor on account of the Subcontractor's portion of the Work. The Contractor shall, by appropriate agreement with each Subcontractor, require each Subcontractor to make payments to Sub-subcontractors in a similar manner.

§ 9.6.3 The Architect will, on request, furnish to a Subcontractor, if practicable, information regarding percentages of completion or amounts applied for by the Contractor and action taken thereon by the Architect and Owner on account of portions of the Work done by such Subcontractor.

§ 9.6.4 The Owner has the right to request written evidence from the Contractor that the Contractor has properly paid Subcontractors and suppliers amounts paid by the Owner to the Contractor for subcontracted Work. If the Contractor fails to furnish such evidence within seven days, the Owner shall have the right to contact Subcontractors and suppliers

Init.
/

to ascertain whether they have been properly paid. Neither the Owner nor Architect shall have an obligation to pay, or to see to the payment of money to, a Subcontractor or supplier, except as may otherwise be required by law.

§ 9.6.5 The Contractor's payments to suppliers shall be treated in a manner similar to that provided in Sections 9.6.2, 9.6.3 and 9.6.4.

§ 9.6.6 A Certificate for Payment, a progress payment, or partial or entire use or occupancy of the Project by the Owner shall not constitute acceptance of Work not in accordance with the Contract Documents.

§ 9.6.7 Unless the Contractor provides the Owner with a payment bond in the full penal sum of the Contract Sum, payments received by the Contractor for Work properly performed by Subcontractors or provided by suppliers shall be held by the Contractor for those Subcontractors or suppliers who performed Work or furnished materials, or both, under contract with the Contractor for which payment was made by the Owner. Nothing contained herein shall require money to be placed in a separate account and not commingled with money of the Contractor, create any fiduciary liability or tort liability on the part of the Contractor for breach of trust, or entitle any person or entity to an award of punitive damages against the Contractor for breach of the requirements of this provision.

§ 9.6.8 Provided the Owner has fulfilled its payment obligations under the Contract Documents, the Contractor shall defend and indemnify the Owner from all loss, liability, damage or expense, including reasonable attorney's fees and litigation expenses, arising out of any lien claim or other claim for payment by any Subcontractor or supplier of any tier. Upon receipt of notice of a lien claim or other claim for payment, the Owner shall notify the Contractor. If approved by the applicable court, when required, the Contractor may substitute a surety bond for the property against which the lien or other claim for payment has been asserted.

§ 9.7 Failure of Payment
If the Architect does not issue a Certificate for Payment, through no fault of the Contractor, within seven days after receipt of the Contractor's Application for Payment, or if the Owner does not pay the Contractor within seven days after the date established in the Contract Documents, the amount certified by the Architect or awarded by binding dispute resolution, then the Contractor may, upon seven additional days' notice to the Owner and Architect, stop the Work until payment of the amount owing has been received. The Contract Time shall be extended appropriately and the Contract Sum shall be increased by the amount of the Contractor's reasonable costs of shutdown, delay and start-up, plus interest as provided for in the Contract Documents.

§ 9.8 Substantial Completion
§ 9.8.1 Substantial Completion is the stage in the progress of the Work when the Work or designated portion thereof is sufficiently complete in accordance with the Contract Documents so that the Owner can occupy or utilize the Work for its intended use.

§ 9.8.2 When the Contractor considers that the Work, or a portion thereof which the Owner agrees to accept separately, is substantially complete, the Contractor shall prepare and submit to the Architect a comprehensive list of items to be completed or corrected prior to final payment. Failure to include an item on such list does not alter the responsibility of the Contractor to complete all Work in accordance with the Contract Documents.

§ 9.8.3 Upon receipt of the Contractor's list, the Architect will make an inspection to determine whether the Work or designated portion thereof is substantially complete. If the Architect's inspection discloses any item, whether or not included on the Contractor's list, which is not sufficiently complete in accordance with the Contract Documents so that the Owner can occupy or utilize the Work or designated portion thereof for its intended use, the Contractor shall, before issuance of the Certificate of Substantial Completion, complete or correct such item upon notification by the Architect. In such case, the Contractor shall then submit a request for another inspection by the Architect to determine Substantial Completion.

§ 9.8.4 When the Work or designated portion thereof is substantially complete, the Architect will prepare a Certificate of Substantial Completion that shall establish the date of Substantial Completion; establish responsibilities of the Owner and Contractor for security, maintenance, heat, utilities, damage to the Work and insurance; and fix the time within which the Contractor shall finish all items on the list accompanying the Certificate. Warranties required by the Contract Documents shall commence on the date of Substantial Completion of the Work or designated portion thereof unless otherwise provided in the Certificate of Substantial Completion.

Init.
/

§ 9.8.5 The Certificate of Substantial Completion shall be submitted to the Owner and Contractor for their written acceptance of responsibilities assigned to them in the Certificate. Upon such acceptance, and consent of surety if any, the Owner shall make payment of retainage applying to the Work or designated portion thereof. Such payment shall be adjusted for Work that is incomplete or not in accordance with the requirements of the Contract Documents.

§ 9.9 Partial Occupancy or Use

§ 9.9.1 The Owner may occupy or use any completed or partially completed portion of the Work at any stage when such portion is designated by separate agreement with the Contractor, provided such occupancy or use is consented to by the insurer and authorized by public authorities having jurisdiction over the Project. Such partial occupancy or use may commence whether or not the portion is substantially complete, provided the Owner and Contractor have accepted in writing the responsibilities assigned to each of them for payments, retainage, if any, security, maintenance, heat, utilities, damage to the Work and insurance, and have agreed in writing concerning the period for correction of the Work and commencement of warranties required by the Contract Documents. When the Contractor considers a portion substantially complete, the Contractor shall prepare and submit a list to the Architect as provided under Section 9.8.2. Consent of the Contractor to partial occupancy or use shall not be unreasonably withheld. The stage of the progress of the Work shall be determined by written agreement between the Owner and Contractor or, if no agreement is reached, by decision of the Architect.

§ 9.9.2 Immediately prior to such partial occupancy or use, the Owner, Contractor, and Architect shall jointly inspect the area to be occupied or portion of the Work to be used in order to determine and record the condition of the Work.

§ 9.9.3 Unless otherwise agreed upon, partial occupancy or use of a portion or portions of the Work shall not constitute acceptance of Work not complying with the requirements of the Contract Documents.

§ 9.10 Final Completion and Final Payment

§ 9.10.1 Upon receipt of the Contractor's notice that the Work is ready for final inspection and acceptance and upon receipt of a final Application for Payment, the Architect will promptly make such inspection. When the Architect finds the Work acceptable under the Contract Documents and the Contract fully performed, the Architect will promptly issue a final Certificate for Payment stating that to the best of the Architect's knowledge, information and belief, and on the basis of the Architect's on-site visits and inspections, the Work has been completed in accordance with the Contract Documents and that the entire balance found to be due the Contractor and noted in the final Certificate is due and payable. The Architect's final Certificate for Payment will constitute a further representation that conditions listed in Section 9.10.2 as precedent to the Contractor's being entitled to final payment have been fulfilled.

§ 9.10.2 Neither final payment nor any remaining retained percentage shall become due until the Contractor submits to the Architect (1) an affidavit that payrolls, bills for materials and equipment, and other indebtedness connected with the Work for which the Owner or the Owner's property might be responsible or encumbered (less amounts withheld by Owner) have been paid or otherwise satisfied, (2) a certificate evidencing that insurance required by the Contract Documents to remain in force after final payment is currently in effect, (3) a written statement that the Contractor knows of no reason that the insurance will not be renewable to cover the period required by the Contract Documents, (4) consent of surety, if any, to final payment, (5) documentation of any special warranties, such as manufacturers' warranties or specific Subcontractor warranties, and (6) if required by the Owner, other data establishing payment or satisfaction of obligations, such as receipts and releases and waivers of liens, claims, security interests, or encumbrances arising out of the Contract, to the extent and in such form as may be designated by the Owner. If a Subcontractor refuses to furnish a release or waiver required by the Owner, the Contractor may furnish a bond satisfactory to the Owner to indemnify the Owner against such lien, claim, security interest, or encumbrance. If a lien, claim, security interest, or encumbrance remains unsatisfied after payments are made, the Contractor shall refund to the Owner all money that the Owner may be compelled to pay in discharging the lien, claim, security interest, or encumbrance, including all costs and reasonable attorneys' fees.

§ 9.10.3 If, after Substantial Completion of the Work, final completion thereof is materially delayed through no fault of the Contractor or by issuance of Change Orders affecting final completion, and the Architect so confirms, the Owner shall, upon application by the Contractor and certification by the Architect, and without terminating the Contract, make payment of the balance due for that portion of the Work fully completed, corrected, and accepted. If the remaining balance for Work not fully completed or corrected is less than retainage stipulated in the Contract Documents, and if bonds have been furnished, the written consent of the surety to payment of the balance due for that portion of the Work fully completed and accepted shall be submitted by the Contractor to the Architect prior to certification of such payment. Such payment shall be made under terms and conditions governing final payment, except that it shall not constitute a waiver of Claims.

§ 9.10.4 The making of final payment shall constitute a waiver of Claims by the Owner except those arising from

- **.1** liens, Claims, security interests, or encumbrances arising out of the Contract and unsettled;
- **.2** failure of the Work to comply with the requirements of the Contract Documents;
- **.3** terms of special warranties required by the Contract Documents; or
- **.4** audits performed by the Owner, if permitted by the Contract Documents, after final payment.

§ 9.10.5 Acceptance of final payment by the Contractor, a Subcontractor, or a supplier, shall constitute a waiver of claims by that payee except those previously made in writing and identified by that payee as unsettled at the time of final Application for Payment.

ARTICLE 10 PROTECTION OF PERSONS AND PROPERTY

§ 10.1 Safety Precautions and Programs

The Contractor shall be responsible for initiating, maintaining, and supervising all safety precautions and programs in connection with the performance of the Contract.

§ 10.2 Safety of Persons and Property

§ 10.2.1 The Contractor shall take reasonable precautions for safety of, and shall provide reasonable protection to prevent damage, injury, or loss to

- **.1** employees on the Work and other persons who may be affected thereby;
- **.2** the Work and materials and equipment to be incorporated therein, whether in storage on or off the site, under care, custody, or control of the Contractor, a Subcontractor, or a Sub-subcontractor; and
- **.3** other property at the site or adjacent thereto, such as trees, shrubs, lawns, walks, pavements, roadways, structures, and utilities not designated for removal, relocation, or replacement in the course of construction.

§ 10.2.2 The Contractor shall comply with, and give notices required by applicable laws, statutes, ordinances, codes, rules and regulations, and lawful orders of public authorities, bearing on safety of persons or property or their protection from damage, injury, or loss.

§ 10.2.3 The Contractor shall implement, erect, and maintain, as required by existing conditions and performance of the Contract, reasonable safeguards for safety and protection, including posting danger signs and other warnings against hazards; promulgating safety regulations; and notifying the owners and users of adjacent sites and utilities of the safeguards.

§ 10.2.4 When use or storage of explosives or other hazardous materials or equipment, or unusual methods are necessary for execution of the Work, the Contractor shall exercise utmost care and carry on such activities under supervision of properly qualified personnel.

§ 10.2.5 The Contractor shall promptly remedy damage and loss (other than damage or loss insured under property insurance required by the Contract Documents) to property referred to in Sections 10.2.1.2 and 10.2.1.3 caused in whole or in part by the Contractor, a Subcontractor, a Sub-subcontractor, or anyone directly or indirectly employed by any of them, or by anyone for whose acts they may be liable and for which the Contractor is responsible under Sections 10.2.1.2 and 10.2.1.3. The Contractor may make a Claim for the cost to remedy the damage or loss to the extent such damage or loss is attributable to acts or omissions of the Owner or Architect or anyone directly or indirectly employed by either of them, or by anyone for whose acts either of them may be liable, and not attributable to the fault or negligence of the Contractor. The foregoing obligations of the Contractor are in addition to the Contractor's obligations under Section 3.18.

§ 10.2.6 The Contractor shall designate a responsible member of the Contractor's organization at the site whose duty shall be the prevention of accidents. This person shall be the Contractor's superintendent unless otherwise designated by the Contractor in writing to the Owner and Architect.

§ 10.2.7 The Contractor shall not permit any part of the construction or site to be loaded so as to cause damage or create an unsafe condition.

§ 10.2.8 Injury or Damage to Person or Property
If either party suffers injury or damage to person or property because of an act or omission of the other party, or of others for whose acts such party is legally responsible, notice of the injury or damage, whether or not insured, shall be given to the other party within a reasonable time not exceeding 21 days after discovery. The notice shall provide sufficient detail to enable the other party to investigate the matter.

§ 10.3 Hazardous Materials and Substances
§ 10.3.1 The Contractor is responsible for compliance with any requirements included in the Contract Documents regarding hazardous materials or substances. If the Contractor encounters a hazardous material or substance not addressed in the Contract Documents and if reasonable precautions will be inadequate to prevent foreseeable bodily injury or death to persons resulting from a material or substance, including but not limited to asbestos or polychlorinated biphenyl (PCB), encountered on the site by the Contractor, the Contractor shall, upon recognizing the condition, immediately stop Work in the affected area and notify the Owner and Architect of the condition.

§ 10.3.2 Upon receipt of the Contractor's notice, the Owner shall obtain the services of a licensed laboratory to verify the presence or absence of the material or substance reported by the Contractor and, in the event such material or substance is found to be present, to cause it to be rendered harmless. Unless otherwise required by the Contract Documents, the Owner shall furnish in writing to the Contractor and Architect the names and qualifications of persons or entities who are to perform tests verifying the presence or absence of the material or substance or who are to perform the task of removal or safe containment of the material or substance. The Contractor and the Architect will promptly reply to the Owner in writing stating whether or not either has reasonable objection to the persons or entities proposed by the Owner. If either the Contractor or Architect has an objection to a person or entity proposed by the Owner, the Owner shall propose another to whom the Contractor and the Architect have no reasonable objection. When the material or substance has been rendered harmless, Work in the affected area shall resume upon written agreement of the Owner and Contractor. By Change Order, the Contract Time shall be extended appropriately and the Contract Sum shall be increased by the amount of the Contractor's reasonable additional costs of shutdown, delay, and start-up.

§ 10.3.3 To the fullest extent permitted by law, the Owner shall indemnify and hold harmless the Contractor, Subcontractors, Architect, Architect's consultants, and agents and employees of any of them from and against claims, damages, losses, and expenses, including but not limited to attorneys' fees, arising out of or resulting from performance of the Work in the affected area if in fact the material or substance presents the risk of bodily injury or death as described in Section 10.3.1 and has not been rendered harmless, provided that such claim, damage, loss, or expense is attributable to bodily injury, sickness, disease or death, or to injury to or destruction of tangible property (other than the Work itself), except to the extent that such damage, loss, or expense is due to the fault or negligence of the party seeking indemnity.

§ 10.3.4 The Owner shall not be responsible under this Section 10.3 for hazardous materials or substances the Contractor brings to the site unless such materials or substances are required by the Contract Documents. The Owner shall be responsible for hazardous materials or substances required by the Contract Documents, except to the extent of the Contractor's fault or negligence in the use and handling of such materials or substances.

§ 10.3.5 The Contractor shall reimburse the Owner for the cost and expense the Owner incurs (1) for remediation of hazardous materials or substances the Contractor brings to the site and negligently handles, or (2) where the Contractor fails to perform its obligations under Section 10.3.1, except to the extent that the cost and expense are due to the Owner's fault or negligence.

§ 10.3.6 If, without negligence on the part of the Contractor, the Contractor is held liable by a government agency for the cost of remediation of a hazardous material or substance solely by reason of performing Work as required by the Contract Documents, the Owner shall reimburse the Contractor for all cost and expense thereby incurred.

§ 10.4 Emergencies
In an emergency affecting safety of persons or property, the Contractor shall act, at the Contractor's discretion, to prevent threatened damage, injury, or loss. Additional compensation or extension of time claimed by the Contractor on account of an emergency shall be determined as provided in Article 15 and Article 7.

ARTICLE 11 INSURANCE AND BONDS
§ 11.1 Contractor's Insurance and Bonds
§ 11.1.1 The Contractor shall purchase and maintain insurance of the types and limits of liability, containing the

Init.
/

endorsements, and subject to the terms and conditions, as described in the Agreement or elsewhere in the Contract Documents. The Contractor shall purchase and maintain the required insurance from an insurance company or insurance companies lawfully authorized to issue insurance in the jurisdiction where the Project is located. The Owner, Architect, and Architect's consultants shall be named as additional insureds under the Contractor's commercial general liability policy or as otherwise described in the Contract Documents.

§ 11.1.2 The Contractor shall provide surety bonds of the types, for such penal sums, and subject to such terms and conditions as required by the Contract Documents. The Contractor shall purchase and maintain the required bonds from a company or companies lawfully authorized to issue surety bonds in the jurisdiction where the Project is located.

§ 11.1.3 Upon the request of any person or entity appearing to be a potential beneficiary of bonds covering payment of obligations arising under the Contract, the Contractor shall promptly furnish a copy of the bonds or shall authorize a copy to be furnished.

§ 11.1.4 Notice of Cancellation or Expiration of Contractor's Required Insurance. Within three (3) business days of the date the Contractor becomes aware of an impending or actual cancellation or expiration of any insurance required by the Contract Documents, the Contractor shall provide notice to the Owner of such impending or actual cancellation or expiration. Upon receipt of notice from the Contractor, the Owner shall, unless the lapse in coverage arises from an act or omission of the Owner, have the right to stop the Work until the lapse in coverage has been cured by the procurement of replacement coverage by the Contractor. The furnishing of notice by the Contractor shall not relieve the Contractor of any contractual obligation to provide any required coverage.

§ 11.2 Owner's Insurance

§ 11.2.1 The Owner shall purchase and maintain insurance of the types and limits of liability, containing the endorsements, and subject to the terms and conditions, as described in the Agreement or elsewhere in the Contract Documents. The Owner shall purchase and maintain the required insurance from an insurance company or insurance companies lawfully authorized to issue insurance in the jurisdiction where the Project is located.

§ 11.2.2 Failure to Purchase Required Property Insurance. If the Owner fails to purchase and maintain the required property insurance, with all of the coverages and in the amounts described in the Agreement or elsewhere in the Contract Documents, the Owner shall inform the Contractor in writing prior to commencement of the Work. Upon receipt of notice from the Owner, the Contractor may delay commencement of the Work and may obtain insurance that will protect the interests of the Contractor, Subcontractors, and Sub-Subcontractors in the Work. When the failure to provide coverage has been cured or resolved, the Contract Sum and Contract Time shall be equitably adjusted. In the event the Owner fails to procure coverage, the Owner waives all rights against the Contractor, Subcontractors, and Sub-subcontractors to the extent the loss to the Owner would have been covered by the insurance to have been procured by the Owner. The cost of the insurance shall be charged to the Owner by a Change Order. If the Owner does not provide written notice, and the Contractor is damaged by the failure or neglect of the Owner to purchase or maintain the required insurance, the Owner shall reimburse the Contractor for all reasonable costs and damages attributable thereto.

§ 11.2.3 Notice of Cancellation or Expiration of Owner's Required Property Insurance. Within three (3) business days of the date the Owner becomes aware of an impending or actual cancellation or expiration of any property insurance required by the Contract Documents, the Owner shall provide notice to the Contractor of such impending or actual cancellation or expiration. Unless the lapse in coverage arises from an act or omission of the Contractor: (1) the Contractor, upon receipt of notice from the Owner, shall have the right to stop the Work until the lapse in coverage has been cured by the procurement of replacement coverage by either the Owner or the Contractor; (2) the Contract Time and Contract Sum shall be equitably adjusted; and (3) the Owner waives all rights against the Contractor, Subcontractors, and Sub-subcontractors to the extent any loss to the Owner would have been covered by the insurance had it not expired or been cancelled. If the Contractor purchases replacement coverage, the cost of the insurance shall be charged to the Owner by an appropriate Change Order. The furnishing of notice by the Owner shall not relieve the Owner of any contractual obligation to provide required insurance.

§ 11.3 Waivers of Subrogation

§ 11.3.1 The Owner and Contractor waive all rights against (1) each other and any of their subcontractors, sub-subcontractors, agents, and employees, each of the other; (2) the Architect and Architect's consultants; and (3) Separate Contractors, if any, and any of their subcontractors, sub-subcontractors, agents, and employees, for damages caused by fire, or other causes of loss, to the extent those losses are covered by property insurance required by the Agreement or other property insurance applicable to the Project, except such rights as they have to proceeds of such insurance. The

Owner or Contractor, as appropriate, shall require similar written waivers in favor of the individuals and entities identified above from the Architect, Architect's consultants, Separate Contractors, subcontractors, and sub-subcontractors. The policies of insurance purchased and maintained by each person or entity agreeing to waive claims pursuant to this section 11.3.1 shall not prohibit this waiver of subrogation. This waiver of subrogation shall be effective as to a person or entity (1) even though that person or entity would otherwise have a duty of indemnification, contractual or otherwise, (2) even though that person or entity did not pay the insurance premium directly or indirectly, or (3) whether or not the person or entity had an insurable interest in the damaged property.

§ 11.3.2 If during the Project construction period the Owner insures properties, real or personal or both, at or adjacent to the site by property insurance under policies separate from those insuring the Project, or if after final payment property insurance is to be provided on the completed Project through a policy or policies other than those insuring the Project during the construction period, to the extent permissible by such policies, the Owner waives all rights in accordance with the terms of Section 11.3.1 for damages caused by fire or other causes of loss covered by this separate property insurance.

§ 11.4 Loss of Use, Business Interruption, and Delay in Completion Insurance
The Owner, at the Owner's option, may purchase and maintain insurance that will protect the Owner against loss of use of the Owner's property, or the inability to conduct normal operations, due to fire or other causes of loss. The Owner waives all rights of action against the Contractor and Architect for loss of use of the Owner's property, due to fire or other hazards however caused.

§11.5 Adjustment and Settlement of Insured Loss
§ 11.5.1 A loss insured under the property insurance required by the Agreement shall be adjusted by the Owner as fiduciary and made payable to the Owner as fiduciary for the insureds, as their interests may appear, subject to requirements of any applicable mortgagee clause and of Section 11.5.2. The Owner shall pay the Architect and Contractor their just shares of insurance proceeds received by the Owner, and by appropriate agreements the Architect and Contractor shall make payments to their consultants and Subcontractors in similar manner.

§ 11.5.2 Prior to settlement of an insured loss, the Owner shall notify the Contractor of the terms of the proposed settlement as well as the proposed allocation of the insurance proceeds. The Contractor shall have 14 days from receipt of notice to object to the proposed settlement or allocation of the proceeds. If the Contractor does not object, the Owner shall settle the loss and the Contractor shall be bound by the settlement and allocation. Upon receipt, the Owner shall deposit the insurance proceeds in a separate account and make the appropriate distributions. Thereafter, if no other agreement is made or the Owner does not terminate the Contract for convenience, the Owner and Contractor shall execute a Change Order for reconstruction of the damaged or destroyed Work in the amount allocated for that purpose. If the Contractor timely objects to either the terms of the proposed settlement or the allocation of the proceeds, the Owner may proceed to settle the insured loss, and any dispute between the Owner and Contractor arising out of the settlement or allocation of the proceeds shall be resolved pursuant to Article 15. Pending resolution of any dispute, the Owner may issue a Construction Change Directive for the reconstruction of the damaged or destroyed Work.

ARTICLE 12 UNCOVERING AND CORRECTION OF WORK
§ 12.1 Uncovering of Work
§ 12.1.1 If a portion of the Work is covered contrary to the Architect's request or to requirements specifically expressed in the Contract Documents, it must, if requested in writing by the Architect, be uncovered for the Architect's examination and be replaced at the Contractor's expense without change in the Contract Time.

§ 12.1.2 If a portion of the Work has been covered that the Architect has not specifically requested to examine prior to its being covered, the Architect may request to see such Work and it shall be uncovered by the Contractor. If such Work is in accordance with the Contract Documents, the Contractor shall be entitled to an equitable adjustment to the Contract Sum and Contract Time as may be appropriate. If such Work is not in accordance with the Contract Documents, the costs of uncovering the Work, and the cost of correction, shall be at the Contractor's expense.

§ 12.2 Correction of Work
§ 12.2.1 Before Substantial Completion
The Contractor shall promptly correct Work rejected by the Architect or failing to conform to the requirements of the Contract Documents, discovered before Substantial Completion and whether or not fabricated, installed or completed. Costs of correcting such rejected Work, including additional testing and inspections, the cost of uncovering and replacement, and compensation for the Architect's services and expenses made necessary thereby, shall be at the

Init.
/

Contractor's expense.

§ 12.2.2 After Substantial Completion
§ 12.2.2.1 In addition to the Contractor's obligations under Section 3.5, if, within one year after the date of Substantial Completion of the Work or designated portion thereof or after the date for commencement of warranties established under Section 9.9.1, or by terms of any applicable special warranty required by the Contract Documents, any of the Work is found to be not in accordance with the requirements of the Contract Documents, the Contractor shall correct it promptly after receipt of notice from the Owner to do so, unless the Owner has previously given the Contractor a written acceptance of such condition. The Owner shall give such notice promptly after discovery of the condition. During the one-year period for correction of Work, if the Owner fails to notify the Contractor and give the Contractor an opportunity to make the correction, the Owner waives the rights to require correction by the Contractor and to make a claim for breach of warranty. If the Contractor fails to correct nonconforming Work within a reasonable time during that period after receipt of notice from the Owner or Architect, the Owner may correct it in accordance with Section 2.5.

§ 12.2.2.2 The one-year period for correction of Work shall be extended with respect to portions of Work first performed after Substantial Completion by the period of time between Substantial Completion and the actual completion of that portion of the Work.

§ 12.2.2.3 The one-year period for correction of Work shall not be extended by corrective Work performed by the Contractor pursuant to this Section 12.2.

§ 12.2.3 The Contractor shall remove from the site portions of the Work that are not in accordance with the requirements of the Contract Documents and are neither corrected by the Contractor nor accepted by the Owner.

§ 12.2.4 The Contractor shall bear the cost of correcting destroyed or damaged construction of the Owner or Separate Contractors, whether completed or partially completed, caused by the Contractor's correction or removal of Work that is not in accordance with the requirements of the Contract Documents.

§ 12.2.5 Nothing contained in this Section 12.2 shall be construed to establish a period of limitation with respect to other obligations the Contractor has under the Contract Documents. Establishment of the one-year period for correction of Work as described in Section 12.2.2 relates only to the specific obligation of the Contractor to correct the Work, and has no relationship to the time within which the obligation to comply with the Contract Documents may be sought to be enforced, nor to the time within which proceedings may be commenced to establish the Contractor's liability with respect to the Contractor's obligations other than specifically to correct the Work.

§ 12.3 Acceptance of Nonconforming Work
If the Owner prefers to accept Work that is not in accordance with the requirements of the Contract Documents, the Owner may do so instead of requiring its removal and correction, in which case the Contract Sum will be reduced as appropriate and equitable. Such adjustment shall be effected whether or not final payment has been made.

ARTICLE 13 MISCELLANEOUS PROVISIONS
§ 13.1 Governing Law
The Contract shall be governed by the law of the place where the Project is located, excluding that jurisdiction's choice of law rules. If the parties have selected arbitration as the method of binding dispute resolution, the Federal Arbitration Act shall govern Section 15.4.

§ 13.2 Successors and Assigns
§ 13.2.1 The Owner and Contractor respectively bind themselves, their partners, successors, assigns, and legal representatives to covenants, agreements, and obligations contained in the Contract Documents. Except as provided in Section 13.2.2, neither party to the Contract shall assign the Contract as a whole without written consent of the other. If either party attempts to make an assignment without such consent, that party shall nevertheless remain legally responsible for all obligations under the Contract.

§ 13.2.2 The Owner may, without consent of the Contractor, assign the Contract to a lender providing construction financing for the Project, if the lender assumes the Owner's rights and obligations under the Contract Documents. The Contractor shall execute all consents reasonably required to facilitate the assignment.

Init.
/

§ 13.3 Rights and Remedies
§ 13.3.1 Duties and obligations imposed by the Contract Documents and rights and remedies available thereunder shall be in addition to and not a limitation of duties, obligations, rights, and remedies otherwise imposed or available by law.

§ 13.3.2 No action or failure to act by the Owner, Architect, or Contractor shall constitute a waiver of a right or duty afforded them under the Contract, nor shall such action or failure to act constitute approval of or acquiescence in a breach thereunder, except as may be specifically agreed upon in writing.

§ 13.4 Tests and Inspections
§ 13.4.1 Tests, inspections, and approvals of portions of the Work shall be made as required by the Contract Documents and by applicable laws, statutes, ordinances, codes, rules, and regulations or lawful orders of public authorities. Unless otherwise provided, the Contractor shall make arrangements for such tests, inspections, and approvals with an independent testing laboratory or entity acceptable to the Owner, or with the appropriate public authority, and shall bear all related costs of tests, inspections, and approvals. The Contractor shall give the Architect timely notice of when and where tests and inspections are to be made so that the Architect may be present for such procedures. The Owner shall bear costs of tests, inspections, or approvals that do not become requirements until after bids are received or negotiations concluded. The Owner shall directly arrange and pay for tests, inspections, or approvals where building codes or applicable laws or regulations so require.

§ 13.4.2 If the Architect, Owner, or public authorities having jurisdiction determine that portions of the Work require additional testing, inspection, or approval not included under Section 13.4.1, the Architect will, upon written authorization from the Owner, instruct the Contractor to make arrangements for such additional testing, inspection, or approval, by an entity acceptable to the Owner, and the Contractor shall give timely notice to the Architect of when and where tests and inspections are to be made so that the Architect may be present for such procedures. Such costs, except as provided in Section 13.4.3, shall be at the Owner's expense.

§ 13.4.3 If procedures for testing, inspection, or approval under Sections 13.4.1 and 13.4.2 reveal failure of the portions of the Work to comply with requirements established by the Contract Documents, all costs made necessary by such failure, including those of repeated procedures and compensation for the Architect's services and expenses, shall be at the Contractor's expense.

§ 13.4.4 Required certificates of testing, inspection, or approval shall, unless otherwise required by the Contract Documents, be secured by the Contractor and promptly delivered to the Architect.

§ 13.4.5 If the Architect is to observe tests, inspections, or approvals required by the Contract Documents, the Architect will do so promptly and, where practicable, at the normal place of testing.

§ 13.4.6 Tests or inspections conducted pursuant to the Contract Documents shall be made promptly to avoid unreasonable delay in the Work.

§ 13.5 Interest
Payments due and unpaid under the Contract Documents shall bear interest from the date payment is due at the rate the parties agree upon in writing or, in the absence thereof, at the legal rate prevailing from time to time at the place where the Project is located.

ARTICLE 14 TERMINATION OR SUSPENSION OF THE CONTRACT
§ 14.1 Termination by the Contractor
§ 14.1.1 The Contractor may terminate the Contract if the Work is stopped for a period of 30 consecutive days through no act or fault of the Contractor, a Subcontractor, a Sub-subcontractor, their agents or employees, or any other persons or entities performing portions of the Work, for any of the following reasons:

.1 Issuance of an order of a court or other public authority having jurisdiction that requires all Work to be stopped;
.2 An act of government, such as a declaration of national emergency, that requires all Work to be stopped;
.3 Because the Architect has not issued a Certificate for Payment and has not notified the Contractor of the reason for withholding certification as provided in Section 9.4.1, or because the Owner has not made payment on a Certificate for Payment within the time stated in the Contract Documents; or
.4 The Owner has failed to furnish to the Contractor reasonable evidence as required by Section 2.2.

Init.
/

§ 14.1.2 The Contractor may terminate the Contract if, through no act or fault of the Contractor, a Subcontractor, a Sub-subcontractor, their agents or employees, or any other persons or entities performing portions of the Work, repeated suspensions, delays, or interruptions of the entire Work by the Owner as described in Section 14.3, constitute in the aggregate more than 100 percent of the total number of days scheduled for completion, or 120 days in any 365-day period, whichever is less.

§ 14.1.3 If one of the reasons described in Section 14.1.1 or 14.1.2 exists, the Contractor may, upon seven days' notice to the Owner and Architect, terminate the Contract and recover from the Owner payment for Work executed, as well as reasonable overhead and profit on Work not executed, and costs incurred by reason of such termination.

§ 14.1.4 If the Work is stopped for a period of 60 consecutive days through no act or fault of the Contractor, a Subcontractor, a Sub-subcontractor, or their agents or employees or any other persons or entities performing portions of the Work because the Owner has repeatedly failed to fulfill the Owner's obligations under the Contract Documents with respect to matters important to the progress of the Work, the Contractor may, upon seven additional days' notice to the Owner and the Architect, terminate the Contract and recover from the Owner as provided in Section 14.1.3.

§ 14.2 Termination by the Owner for Cause
§ 14.2.1 The Owner may terminate the Contract if the Contractor

.1 repeatedly refuses or fails to supply enough properly skilled workers or proper materials;
.2 fails to make payment to Subcontractors or suppliers in accordance with the respective agreements between the Contractor and the Subcontractors or suppliers;
.3 repeatedly disregards applicable laws, statutes, ordinances, codes, rules and regulations, or lawful orders of a public authority; or
.4 otherwise is guilty of substantial breach of a provision of the Contract Documents.

§ 14.2.2 When any of the reasons described in Section 14.2.1 exist, and upon certification by the Architect that sufficient cause exists to justify such action, the Owner may, without prejudice to any other rights or remedies of the Owner and after giving the Contractor and the Contractor's surety, if any, seven days' notice, terminate employment of the Contractor and may, subject to any prior rights of the surety:

.1 Exclude the Contractor from the site and take possession of all materials, equipment, tools, and construction equipment and machinery thereon owned by the Contractor;
.2 Accept assignment of subcontracts pursuant to Section 5.4; and
.3 Finish the Work by whatever reasonable method the Owner may deem expedient. Upon written request of the Contractor, the Owner shall furnish to the Contractor a detailed accounting of the costs incurred by the Owner in finishing the Work.

§ 14.2.3 When the Owner terminates the Contract for one of the reasons stated in Section 14.2.1, the Contractor shall not be entitled to receive further payment until the Work is finished.

§ 14.2.4 If the unpaid balance of the Contract Sum exceeds costs of finishing the Work, including compensation for the Architect's services and expenses made necessary thereby, and other damages incurred by the Owner and not expressly waived, such excess shall be paid to the Contractor. If such costs and damages exceed the unpaid balance, the Contractor shall pay the difference to the Owner. The amount to be paid to the Contractor or Owner, as the case may be, shall be certified by the Initial Decision Maker, upon application, and this obligation for payment shall survive termination of the Contract.

§ 14.3 Suspension by the Owner for Convenience
§ 14.3.1 The Owner may, without cause, order the Contractor in writing to suspend, delay or interrupt the Work, in whole or in part for such period of time as the Owner may determine.

§ 14.3.2 The Contract Sum and Contract Time shall be adjusted for increases in the cost and time caused by suspension, delay, or interruption under Section 14.3.1. Adjustment of the Contract Sum shall include profit. No adjustment shall be made to the extent

.1 that performance is, was, or would have been, so suspended, delayed, or interrupted, by another cause for which the Contractor is responsible; or
.2 that an equitable adjustment is made or denied under another provision of the Contract.

Init.
/

§ 14.4 Termination by the Owner for Convenience
§ 14.4.1 The Owner may, at any time, terminate the Contract for the Owner's convenience and without cause.

§ 14.4.2 Upon receipt of notice from the Owner of such termination for the Owner's convenience, the Contractor shall
- **.1** cease operations as directed by the Owner in the notice;
- **.2** take actions necessary, or that the Owner may direct, for the protection and preservation of the Work; and
- **.3** except for Work directed to be performed prior to the effective date of termination stated in the notice, terminate all existing subcontracts and purchase orders and enter into no further subcontracts and purchase orders.

§ 14.4.3 In case of such termination for the Owner's convenience, the Owner shall pay the Contractor for Work properly executed; costs incurred by reason of the termination, including costs attributable to termination of Subcontracts; and the termination fee, if any, set forth in the Agreement.

ARTICLE 15 CLAIMS AND DISPUTES
§ 15.1 Claims
§ 15.1.1 Definition
A Claim is a demand or assertion by one of the parties seeking, as a matter of right, payment of money, a change in the Contract Time, or other relief with respect to the terms of the Contract. The term "Claim" also includes other disputes and matters in question between the Owner and Contractor arising out of or relating to the Contract. The responsibility to substantiate Claims shall rest with the party making the Claim. This Section 15.1.1 does not require the Owner to file a Claim in order to impose liquidated damages in accordance with the Contract Documents.

§ 15.1.2 Time Limits on Claims
The Owner and Contractor shall commence all Claims and causes of action against the other and arising out of or related to the Contract, whether in contract, tort, breach of warranty or otherwise, in accordance with the requirements of the binding dispute resolution method selected in the Agreement and within the period specified by applicable law, but in any case not more than 10 years after the date of Substantial Completion of the Work. The Owner and Contractor waive all Claims and causes of action not commenced in accordance with this Section 15.1.2.

§ 15.1.3 Notice of Claims
§ 15.1.3.1 Claims by either the Owner or Contractor, where the condition giving rise to the Claim is first discovered prior to expiration of the period for correction of the Work set forth in Section 12.2.2, shall be initiated by notice to the other party and to the Initial Decision Maker with a copy sent to the Architect, if the Architect is not serving as the Initial Decision Maker. Claims by either party under this Section 15.1.3.1 shall be initiated within 21 days after occurrence of the event giving rise to such Claim or within 21 days after the claimant first recognizes the condition giving rise to the Claim, whichever is later.

§ 15.1.3.2 Claims by either the Owner or Contractor, where the condition giving rise to the Claim is first discovered after expiration of the period for correction of the Work set forth in Section 12.2.2, shall be initiated by notice to the other party. In such event, no decision by the Initial Decision Maker is required.

§ 15.1.4 Continuing Contract Performance
§ 15.1.4.1 Pending final resolution of a Claim, except as otherwise agreed in writing or as provided in Section 9.7 and Article 14, the Contractor shall proceed diligently with performance of the Contract and the Owner shall continue to make payments in accordance with the Contract Documents.

§ 15.1.4.2 The Contract Sum and Contract Time shall be adjusted in accordance with the Initial Decision Maker's decision, subject to the right of either party to proceed in accordance with this Article 15. The Architect will issue Certificates for Payment in accordance with the decision of the Initial Decision Maker.

§ 15.1.5 Claims for Additional Cost
If the Contractor wishes to make a Claim for an increase in the Contract Sum, notice as provided in Section 15.1.3 shall be given before proceeding to execute the portion of the Work that is the subject of the Claim. Prior notice is not required for Claims relating to an emergency endangering life or property arising under Section 10.4.

§ 15.1.6 Claims for Additional Time
§ 15.1.6.1 If the Contractor wishes to make a Claim for an increase in the Contract Time, notice as provided in Section

15.1.3 shall be given. The Contractor's Claim shall include an estimate of cost and of probable effect of delay on progress of the Work. In the case of a continuing celay, only one Claim is necessary.

§ 15.1.6.2 If adverse weather conditions are the basis for a Claim for additional time, such Claim shall be documented by data substantiating that weather conditions were abnormal for the period of time, could not have been reasonably anticipated, and had an adverse effect on the scheculed construction.

§ 15.1.7 Waiver of Claims for Consequential Damages
The Contractor and Owner waive Claims against each other for consequential damages arising out of or relating to this Contract. This mutual waiver includes

.1 damages incurred by the Owner for rental expenses, for losses of use, income, profit, financing, business and reputation, and for loss of management or employee productivity or of the services of such persons; and

.2 damages incurred by the Contractor for principal office expenses including the compensation of personnel stationed there, for losses of financing, business and reputation, and for loss of profit, except anticipated profit arising directly from the Work.

This mutual waiver is applicable, without limitation, to all consequential damages due to either party's termination in accordance with Article 14. Nothing contained in this Section 15.1.7 shall be deemed to preclude assessment of liquidated damages, when applicable, in accordance with the requirements of the Contract Documents.

§ 15.2 Initial Decision
§ 15.2.1 Claims, excluding those where the condition giving rise to the Claim is first discovered after expiration of the period for correction of the Work set forth in Section 12.2.2 or arising under Sections 10.3, 10.4, and 11.5, shall be referred to the Initial Decision Maker for initial decision. The Architect will serve as the Initial Decision Maker, unless otherwise indicated in the Agreement. Except for those Claims excluded by this Section 15.2.1, an initial decision shall be required as a condition precedent to mediation of any Claim. If an initial decision has not been rendered within 30 days after the Claim has been referred to the Initial Decision Maker, the party asserting the Claim may demand mediation and binding dispute resolution without a decision having been rendered. Unless the Initial Decision Maker and all affected parties agree, the Initial Decision Maker will not decide disputes between the Contractor and persons or entities other than the Owner.

§ 15.2.2 The Initial Decision Maker will review Claims and within ten days of the receipt of a Claim take one or more of the following actions: (1) request additional supporting data from the claimant or a response with supporting data from the other party, (2) reject the Claim in whole or in part, (3) approve the Claim, (4) suggest a compromise, or (5) advise the parties that the Initial Decision Maker is unable to resolve the Claim if the Initial Decision Maker lacks sufficient information to evaluate the merits of the Claim or if the Initial Decision Maker concludes that, in the Initial Decision Maker's sole discretion, it would be inappropriate for the Initial Decision Maker to resolve the Claim.

§ 15.2.3 In evaluating Claims, the Initial Decision Maker may, but shall not be obligated to, consult with or seek information from either party or from persons with special knowledge or expertise who may assist the Initial Decision Maker in rendering a decision. The Initial Decision Maker may request the Owner to authorize retention of such persons at the Owner's expense.

§ 15.2.4 If the Initial Decision Maker requests a party to provide a response to a Claim or to furnish additional supporting data, such party shall respond, within ten days after receipt of the request, and shall either (1) provide a response on the requested supporting data, (2) advise the Initial Decision Maker when the response or supporting data will be furnished, or (3) advise the Initial Decision Maker that no supporting data will be furnished. Upon receipt of the response or supporting data, if any, the Initial Decision Maker will either reject or approve the Claim in whole or in part.

§ 15.2.5 The Initial Decision Maker will render an initial decision approving or rejecting the Claim, or indicating that the Initial Decision Maker is unable to resolve the Claim. This initial decision shall (1) be in writing; (2) state the reasons therefor; and (3) notify the parties and the Architect, if the Architect is not serving as the Initial Decision Maker, of any change in the Contract Sum or Contract Time or both. The initial decision shall be final and binding on the parties but subject to mediation and, if the parties fail to resolve their dispute through mediation, to binding dispute resolution.

§ 15.2.6 Either party may file for mediation of an initial decision at any time, subject to the terms of Section 15.2.6.1.

Init.

/

4.1"

§ 15.2.6.1 Either party may, within 30 days from the date of receipt of an initial decision, demand in writing that the other party file for mediation. If such a demand is made and the party receiving the demand fails to file for mediation within 30 days after receipt thereof, then both parties waive their rights to mediate or pursue binding dispute resolution proceedings with respect to the initial decision.

§ 15.2.7 In the event of a Claim against the Contractor, the Owner may, but is not obligated to, notify the surety, if any, of the nature and amount of the Claim. If the Claim relates to a possibility of a Contractor's default, the Owner may, but is not obligated to, notify the surety and request the surety's assistance in resolving the controversy.

§ 15.2.8 If a Claim relates to or is the subject of a mechanic's lien, the party asserting such Claim may proceed in accordance with applicable law to comply with the lien notice or filing deadlines.

§ 15.3 Mediation
§ 15.3.1 Claims, disputes, or other matters in controversy arising out of or related to the Contract, except those waived as provided for in Sections 9.10.4, 9.10.5, and 15.1.7, shall be subject to mediation as a condition precedent to binding dispute resolution.

§ 15.3.2 The parties shall endeavor to resolve their Claims by mediation which, unless the parties mutually agree otherwise, shall be administered by the American Arbitration Association in accordance with its Construction Industry Mediation Procedures in effect on the date of the Agreement. A request for mediation shall be made in writing, delivered to the other party to the Contract, and filed with the person or entity administering the mediation. The request may be made concurrently with the filing of binding dispute resolution proceedings but, in such event, mediation shall proceed in advance of binding dispute resolution proceedings, which shall be stayed pending mediation for a period of 60 days from the date of filing, unless stayed for a longer period by agreement of the parties or court order. If an arbitration is stayed pursuant to this Section 15.3.2, the parties may nonetheless proceed to the selection of the arbitrator(s) and agree upon a schedule for later proceedings.

§ 15.3.3 Either party may, within 30 days from the date that mediation has been concluded without resolution of the dispute or 60 days after mediation has been demanded without resolution of the dispute, demand in writing that the other party file for binding dispute resolution. If such a demand is made and the party receiving the demand fails to file for binding dispute resolution within 60 days after receipt thereof, then both parties waive their rights to binding dispute resolution proceedings with respect to the initial decision.

§ 15.3.4 The parties shall share the mediator's fee and any filing fees equally. The mediation shall be held in the place where the Project is located, unless another location is mutually agreed upon. Agreements reached in mediation shall be enforceable as settlement agreements in any court having jurisdiction thereof.

§ 15.4 Arbitration
§ 15.4.1 If the parties have selected arbitration as the method for binding dispute resolution in the Agreement, any Claim subject to, but not resolved by, mediation shall be subject to arbitration which, unless the parties mutually agree otherwise, shall be administered by the American Arbitration Association in accordance with its Construction Industry Arbitration Rules in effect on the date of the Agreement. The Arbitration shall be conducted in the place where the Project is located, unless another location is mutually agreed upon. A demand for arbitration shall be made in writing, delivered to the other party to the Contract, and filed with the person or entity administering the arbitration. The party filing a notice of demand for arbitration must assert in the demand all Claims then known to that party on which arbitration is permitted to be demanded.

§ 15.4.1.1 A demand for arbitration shall be made no earlier than concurrently with the filing of a request for mediation, but in no event shall it be made after the date when the institution of legal or equitable proceedings based on the Claim would be barred by the applicable statute of limitations. For statute of limitations purposes, receipt of a written demand for arbitration by the person or entity administering the arbitration shall constitute the institution of legal or equitable proceedings based on the Claim.

§ 15.4.2 The award rendered by the arbitrator or arbitrators shall be final, and judgment may be entered upon it in accordance with applicable law in any court having jurisdiction thereof.

§ 15.4.3 The foregoing agreement to arbitrate and other agreements to arbitrate with an additional person or entity duly

Init.
/

consented to by parties to the Agreement, shall be specifically enforceable under applicable law in any court having jurisdiction thereof.

§ 15.4.4 Consolidation or Joinder

§ 15.4.4.1 Subject to the rules of the American Arbitration Association or other applicable arbitration rules, either party may consolidate an arbitration conducted under this Agreement with any other arbitration to which it is a party provided that (1) the arbitration agreement governing the other arbitration permits consolidation, (2) the arbitrations to be consolidated substantially involve common questions of law or fact, and (3) the arbitrations employ materially similar procedural rules and methods for selecting arbitrator(s).

§ 15.4.4.2 Subject to the rules of the American Arbitration Association or other applicable arbitration rules, either party may include by joinder persons or entities substantially involved in a common question of law or fact whose presence is required if complete relief is to be accorded in arbitration, provided that the party sought to be joined consents in writing to such joinder. Consent to arbitration involving an additional person or entity shall not constitute consent to arbitration of any claim, dispute or other matter in question not described in the written consent.

§ 15.4.4.3 The Owner and Contractor grant to any person or entity made a party to an arbitration conducted under this Section 15.4, whether by joinder or consolidation, the same rights of joinder and consolidation as those of the Owner and Contractor under this Agreement.

Exhibit 8

Notice Inviting Bids to Subcontractors

NOTICE IS HEREBY GIVEN that PROPOSALS will be received at the office of XYZ General Contractor, up to the hour of 2:00 p.m., September 15, 2023, at which time they will be opened and read, in the Contractor's Conference Room, for performing the work as follows:

No bid will be accepted unless it is made on the Bidder's Proposal form furnished by the Contractor. Certificates of Insurance shall be submitted to Contractor, no later than ten (10) calendar days after the date of receipt of notice of award of the Contract, but in all events PRIOR TO commencement of any work under the Contract that was awarded.

A Performance and Payment Bond, if required by Contractor, shall: (a) be provided in an amount equal to 100 percent (100%) of the total contract amount of the contract; (b) be provided concurrently with execution of the contract; and (c) be in the form set forth in the Construction Contract Documents.

Although this Project is a private works development, Contractor has elected to incorporate certain limited provisions of the Public Contract Code of the State of California, into the contract between itself and the successful bidder. By doing so, Contractor does not intend, and it shall not be inferred that, by such use of various limited Public Contract Code provisions, this development and/or the contract is anything other than a private works contract. In strict reliance upon the literal interpretation of the above statement, Contractor does hereby state that the contract to be awarded, shall contain provisions: (i) the right of the successful bidder to substitute securities for any monies withheld by the Contractor at the expense of the successful bidder; (ii) the obligation of the successful subcontractor to adopt the general prevailing rate of per diem wages and the general prevailing rate for holiday and overtime work in the locality where the work will be conducted (said rates are on file with the City Clerk and will be made available to any interested party on request), and the Subcontractor to whom the Contract is awarded, and all sub-subcontractors, must pay said rates; (iii) all bids are to be compared on the basis of the Bid Schedule's estimate of quantities of work to be done, subject to adjustment as provided within the Contract

Documents; and (iv) no bid will be accepted from a Subcontractor who is not: (a) licensed in accordance with provisions of the Business and Professions Code of the State of California on the date and at the time of submittal of the Bidder's Proposal; and (b) in possession of a valid and current Class 'A' or Class 'B' (whichever Contractor shall require in the Invitation-To-Bid letter) Contractor's License or a combination of specialty Class 'C' licenses sufficient to cover all of the work to be performed by them.

Contract Documents, including Plans and Specifications may be obtained from the Contractor at ________________.

The Contractor reserves the right to reject any and all bids, to waive any irregularity or informality in any bid to the extent permitted by law, or to award the contract to other than the lowest bidder. Bidders may not withdraw their bids for sixty (60) days after the bid opening.

For technical information relating to the details of the proposed project and/or bidding requirements, please contact __________.

Dated: ________________

Exhibit 9

AIA Document G703-1992

Pay Application and Continuation Sheet

AIA® Document G702™ – 1992

Application and Certificate for Payment

TO OWNER: PROJECT: APPLICATION NO: **Distribution to:**

PERIOD TO: OWNER ☐

CONTRACT FOR: ARCHITECT ☐

FROM CONTRACTOR: VIA ARCHITECT: CONTRACT DATE: CONTRACTOR ☐

PROJECT NOS: FIELD ☐

OTHER ☐

CONTRACTOR'S APPLICATION FOR PAYMENT

Application is made for payment, as shown below, in connection with the Contract. AIA Document G703™, Continuation Sheet, is attached.

1. ORIGINAL CONTRACT SUM .... $______
2. NET CHANGE BY CHANGE ORDERS .... $______
3. CONTRACT SUM TO DATE *(Line 1 + 2)* .... $______
4. TOTAL COMPLETED & STORED TO DATE *(Column G on G703)* .... $______
5. RETAINAGE:
   a. ____% of Completed Work *(Columns D + E on G703)* $______
   b. ____% of Stored Material *(Column F on G703)* $______

   Total Retainage *(Lines 5a + 5b, or Total in Column I of G703)* .... $______
6. TOTAL EARNED LESS RETAINAGE .... $______ *(Line 4 minus Line 5 Total)*
7. LESS PREVIOUS CERTIFICATES FOR PAYMENT .... $______ *(Line 6 from prior Certificate)*
8. CURRENT PAYMENT DUE .... $______
9. BALANCE TO FINISH, INCLUDING RETAINAGE *(Line 3 minus Line 6)* $______

CHANGE ORDER SUMMARY	ADDITIONS	DEDUCTIONS
Total changes approved in previous months by Owner	$	$
Total approved this month	$	$
TOTAL	$	$
NET CHANGES by Change Order	$	

The undersigned Contractor certifies that to the best of the Contractor's knowledge, information and belief the Work covered by this Application for Payment has been completed in accordance with the Contract Documents, that all amounts have been paid by the Contractor for Work for which previous Certificates for Payment were issued and payments received from the Owner, and that current payment shown herein is now due.

CONTRACTOR:

By: ______ Date: ______

State of:

County of:

Subscribed and sworn to before me this day of

Notary Public:

My commission expires:

ARCHITECT'S CERTIFICATE FOR PAYMENT

In accordance with the Contract Documents, based on on-site observations and the data comprising this application, the Architect certifies to the Owner that to the best of the Architect's knowledge, information and belief the Work has progressed as indicated, the quality of the Work is in accordance with the Contract Documents, and the Contractor is entitled to payment of the AMOUNT CERTIFIED.

AMOUNT CERTIFIED .... $______

(Attach explanation if amount certified differs from the amount applied. Initial all figures on this Application and on the Continuation Sheet that are changed to conform with the amount certified.)

ARCHITECT:

By: ______ Date: ______

This Certificate is not negotiable. The AMOUNT CERTIFIED is payable only to the Contractor named herein. Issuance, payment and acceptance of payment are without prejudice to any rights of the Owner or Contractor under this Contract.

CAUTION: You should sign an original AIA Contract Document, on which this text appears in RED. An original assures that changes will not be obscured.

AIA® Document G703® – 1992

Continuation Sheet

AIA Document G702®, Application and Certificate for Payment, or G732™, Application and Certificate for Payment, Construction Manager as Adviser Edition, containing Contractor's signed certification is attached.
Use Column I on Contracts where variable retainage for line items may apply.

APPLICATION NO:
APPLICATION DATE:
PERIOD TO:
ARCHITECT'S PROJECT NO:

A	B	C	D	E	F	G		H	I
			WORK COMPLETED						
ITEM NO.	DESCRIPTION OF WORK	SCHEDULED VALUE	FROM PREVIOUS APPLICATION *(D + E)*	THIS PERIOD	MATERIALS PRESENTLY STORED *(Not in D or E)*	TOTAL COMPLETED AND STORED TO DATE *(D+E+F)*	% *(G ÷ C)*	BALANCE TO FINISH *(C – G)*	RETAINAGE *(If variable rate)*
	GRAND TOTAL								

Exhibit 10

Bid Summary

Project: Bid Date:	Base Bid Estimate	Ded. Alt. 1	Ded. Alt. 2	Ded. Alt. 3	Ded. Alt. 4	Ded. Alt. 5

Exhibit 11

AIA Document B101™ – 2017

Standard Form Agreement Between Owner and Architect

AIA Document B101® – 2017

Standard Form of Agreement Between Owner and Architect

AGREEMENT made as of the ________ day of ________ in the year ________
(In words, indicate day, month and year.)

BETWEEN the Architect's client identified as the Owner:
(Name, legal status, address and other information)

This document has important legal consequences. Consultation with an attorney is encouraged with respect to its completion or modification.

and the Architect:
(Name, legal status, address and other information)

for the following Project:
(Name, location and detailed description)

The Owner and Architect agree as follows.

 1

TABLE OF ARTICLES

ARTICLE 1 INITIAL INFORMATION

§ 1.1 This Agreement is based on the Initial Information set forth in this Section 1.1.
(For each item in this section, insert the information or a statement such as "not applicable" or "unknown at time of execution.")

§ 1.1.1 The Owner's program for the Project:
(Insert the Owner's program, identify documentation that establishes the Owner's program, or state the manner in which the program will be developed.)

§ 1.1.2 The Project's physical characteristics:
(Identify or describe pertinent information about the Project's physical characteristics, such as size; location; dimensions; geotechnical reports; site boundaries; topographic surveys; traffic and utility studies; availability of public and private utilities and services; legal description of the site, etc.)

§ 1.1.3 The Owner's budget for the Cost of the Work, as defined in Section 6.1:
(Provide total and, if known, a line item breakdown.)

§ 1.1.4 The Owner's anticipated design and construction milestone dates:

.1 Design phase milestone dates, if any:

Init.
/

.2 Construction commencement date:

.3 Substantial Completion date or dates:

.4 Other milestone dates:

§ 1.1.5 The Owner intends the following procurement and delivery method for the Project:
(Identify method such as competitive bid or negotiated contract, as well as any requirements for accelerated or fast-track design and construction, multiple bid packages, or phased construction.)

§ 1.1.6 The Owner's anticipated Sustainable Objective for the Project:
(Identify and describe the Owner's Sustainable Objective for the Project, if any.)

§ 1.1.6.1 If the Owner identifies a Sustainable Objective, the Owner and Architect shall complete and incorporate AIA Document E204™–2017, Sustainable Projects Exhibit, into this Agreement to define the terms, conditions and services related to the Owner's Sustainable Objective. If E204–2017 is incorporated into this agreement, the Owner and Architect shall incorporate the completed E204–2017 into the agreements with the consultants and contractors performing services or Work in any way associated with the Sustainable Objective.

§ 1.1.7 The Owner identifies the following representative in accordance with Section 5.3:
(List name, address, and other contact information.)

§ 1.1.8 The persons or entities, in addition to the Owner's representative, who are required to review the Architect's submittals to the Owner are as follows:
(List name, address, and other contact information.)

§ 1.1.9 The Owner shall retain the following consultants and contractors:
(List name, legal status, address, and other contact information.)

.1 Geotechnical Engineer:

Init.

/

.2 Civil Engineer:

.3 Other, if any:
(List any other consultants and contractors retained by the Owner.)

§ 1.1.10 The Architect identifies the following representative in accordance with Section 2.3:
(List name, address, and other contact information.)

§ 1.1.11 The Architect shall retain the consultants identified in Sections 1.1.11.1 and 1.1.11.2:
(List name, legal status, address, and other contact information.)

§ 1.1.11.1 Consultants retained under Basic Services:
.1 Structural Engineer:

.2 Mechanical Engineer:

.3 Electrical Engineer:

§ 1.1.11.2 Consultants retained under Supplemental Services:

§ 1.1.12 Other Initial Information on which the Agreement is based:

Init.
/

§ 1.2 The Owner and Architect may rely on the Initial Information. Both parties, however, recognize that the Initial Information may materially change and, in that event, the Owner and the Architect shall appropriately adjust the Architect's services, schedule for the Architect's services, and the Architect's compensation. The Owner shall adjust the Owner's budget for the Cost of the Work and the Owner's anticipated design and construction milestones, as necessary, to accommodate material changes in the Initial Information.

§ 1.3 The parties shall agree upon protocols governing the transmission and use of Instruments of Service or any other information or documentation in digital form. The parties will use AIA Document E203™–2013, Building Information Modeling and Digital Data Exhibit, to establish the protocols for the development, use, transmission, and exchange of digital data.

§ 1.3.1 Any use of, or reliance on, all or a portion of a building information model without agreement to protocols governing the use of, and reliance on, the information contained in the model and without having those protocols set forth in AIA Document E203™–2013, Building Information Modeling and Digital Data Exhibit, and the requisite AIA Document G202™–2013, Project Building Information Modeling Protocol Form, shall be at the using or relying party's sole risk and without liability to the other party and its contractors or consultants, the authors of, or contributors to, the building information model, and each of their agents and employees.

ARTICLE 2 ARCHITECT'S RESPONSIBILITIES

§ 2.1 The Architect shall provide professional services as set forth in this Agreement. The Architect represents that it is properly licensed in the jurisdiction where the Project is located to provide the services required by this Agreement, or shall cause such services to be performed by appropriately licensed design professionals.

§ 2.2 The Architect shall perform its services consistent with the professional skill and care ordinarily provided by architects practicing in the same or similar locality under the same or similar circumstances. The Architect shall perform its services as expeditiously as is consistent with such professional skill and care and the orderly progress of the Project.

§ 2.3 The Architect shall identify a representative authorized to act on behalf of the Architect with respect to the Project.

§ 2.4 Except with the Owner's knowledge and consent, the Architect shall not engage in any activity, or accept any employment, interest or contribution that would reasonably appear to compromise the Architect's professional judgment with respect to this Project.

§ 2.5 The Architect shall maintain the following insurance until termination of this Agreement. If any of the requirements set forth below are in addition to the types and limits the Architect normally maintains, the Owner shall pay the Architect as set forth in Section 11.9.

§ 2.5.1 Commercial General Liability with policy limits of not less than ($) for each occurrence and ($) in the aggregate for bodily injury and property damage.

§ 2.5.2 Automobile Liability covering vehicles owned, and non-owned vehicles used, by the Architect with policy limits of not less than ($) per accident for bodily injury, death of any person, and property damage arising out of the ownership, maintenance and use of those motor vehicles, along with any other statutorily required automobile coverage.

§ 2.5.3 The Architect may achieve the required limits and coverage for Commercial General Liability and Automobile Liability through a combination of primary and excess or umbrella liability insurance, provided such primary and excess or umbrella liability insurance policies result in the same or greater coverage as the coverages required under Sections 2.5.1 and 2.5.2, and in no event shall any excess or umbrella liability insurance provide narrower coverage than the primary policy. The excess policy shall not require the exhaustion of the underlying limits only through the actual payment by the underlying insurers.

§ 2.5.4 Workers' Compensation at statutory limits.

§ 2.5.5 Employers' Liability with policy limits not less than ($) each accident, ($) each employee, and ($) policy limit.

§ 2.5.6 Professional Liability covering negligent acts, errors and omissions in the performance of professional services with policy limits of not less than ($) per claim and ($) in the aggregate.

§ 2.5.7 Additional Insured Obligations. To the fullest extent permitted by law, the Architect shall cause the primary and excess or umbrella polices for Commercial General Liability and Automobile Liability to include the Owner as an additional insured for claims caused in whole or in part by the Architect's negligent acts or omissions. The additional insured coverage shall be primary and non-contributory to any of the Owner's insurance policies and shall apply to both ongoing and completed operations.

§ 2.5.8 The Architect shall provide certificates of insurance to the Owner that evidence compliance with the requirements in this Section 2.5.

ARTICLE 3 SCOPE OF ARCHITECT'S BASIC SERVICES

§ 3.1 The Architect's Basic Services consist of those described in this Article 3 and include usual and customary structural, mechanical, and electrical engineering services. Services not set forth in this Article 3 are Supplemental or Additional Services.

§ 3.1.1 The Architect shall manage the Architect's services, research applicable design criteria, attend Project meetings, communicate with members of the Project team, and report progress to the Owner.

§ 3.1.2 The Architect shall coordinate its services with those services provided by the Owner and the Owner's consultants. The Architect shall be entitled to rely on, and shall not be responsible for, the accuracy, completeness, and timeliness of, services and information furnished by the Owner and the Owner's consultants. The Architect shall provide prompt written notice to the Owner if the Architect becomes aware of any error, omission, or inconsistency in such services or information.

§ 3.1.3 As soon as practicable after the date of this Agreement, the Architect shall submit for the Owner's approval a schedule for the performance of the Architect's services. The schedule initially shall include anticipated dates for the commencement of construction and for Substantial Completion of the Work as set forth in the Initial Information. The schedule shall include allowances for periods of time required for the Owner's review, for the performance of the Owner's consultants, and for approval of submissions by authorities having jurisdiction over the Project. Once approved by the Owner, time limits established by the schedule shall not, except for reasonable cause, be exceeded by the Architect or Owner. With the Owner's approval, the Architect shall adjust the schedule, if necessary, as the Project proceeds until the commencement of construction.

§ 3.1.4 The Architect shall not be responsible for an Owner's directive or substitution, or for the Owner's acceptance of non-conforming Work, made or given without the Architect's written approval.

§ 3.1.5 The Architect shall contact governmental authorities required to approve the Construction Documents and entities providing utility services to the Project. The Architect shall respond to applicable design requirements imposed by those authorities and entities.

§ 3.1.6 The Architect shall assist the Owner in connection with the Owner's responsibility for filing documents required for the approval of governmental authorities having jurisdiction over the Project.

§ 3.2 Schematic Design Phase Services

§ 3.2.1 The Architect shall review the program and other information furnished by the Owner, and shall review laws, codes, and regulations applicable to the Architect's services.

§ 3.2.2 The Architect shall prepare a preliminary evaluation of the Owner's program, schedule, budget for the Cost of the Work, Project site, the proposed procurement and delivery method, and other Initial Information, each in terms of the other, to ascertain the requirements of the Project. The Architect shall notify the Owner of (1) any inconsistencies discovered in the information, and (2) other information or consulting services that may be reasonably needed for the Project.

§ 3.2.3 The Architect shall present its preliminary evaluation to the Owner and shall discuss with the Owner alternative approaches to design and construction of the Project. The Architect shall reach an understanding with the Owner regarding the requirements of the Project.

§ 3.2.4 Based on the Project requirements agreed upon with the Owner, the Architect shall prepare and present, for the Owner's approval, a preliminary design illustrating the scale and relationship of the Project components.

§ 3.2.5 Based on the Owner's approval of the preliminary design, the Architect shall prepare Schematic Design Documents for the Owner's approval. The Schematic Design Documents shall consist of drawings and other documents including a site plan, if appropriate, and preliminary building plans, sections and elevations; and may include some combination of study models, perspective sketches, or digital representations. Preliminary selections of major building systems and construction materials shall be noted on the drawings or described in writing.

§ 3.2.5.1 The Architect shall consider sustainable design alternatives, such as material choices and building orientation, together with other considerations based on program and aesthetics, in developing a design that is consistent with the Owner's program, schedule and budget for the Cost of the Work. The Owner may obtain more advanced sustainable design services as a Supplemental Service under Section 4.1.1.

§ 3.2.5.2 The Architect shall consider the value of alternative materials, building systems and equipment, together with other considerations based on program and aesthetics, in developing a design for the Project that is consistent with the Owner's program, schedule, and budget for the Cost of the Work.

§ 3.2.6 The Architect shall submit to the Owner an estimate of the Cost of the Work prepared in accordance with Section 6.3.

§ 3.2.7 The Architect shall submit the Schematic Design Documents to the Owner, and request the Owner's approval.

§ 3.3 Design Development Phase Services

§ 3.3.1 Based on the Owner's approval of the Schematic Design Documents, and on the Owner's authorization of any adjustments in the Project requirements and the budget for the Cost of the Work, the Architect shall prepare Design Development Documents for the Owner's approval. The Design Development Documents shall illustrate and describe the development of the approved Schematic Design Documents and shall consist of drawings and other documents including plans, sections, elevations, typical construction details, and diagrammatic layouts of building systems to fix and describe the size and character of the Project as to architectural, structural, mechanical and electrical systems, and other appropriate elements. The Design Development Documents shall also include outline specifications that identify major materials and systems and establish, in general, their quality levels.

§ 3.3.2 The Architect shall update the estimate of the Cost of the Work prepared in accordance with Section 6.3.

§ 3.3.3 The Architect shall submit the Design Development Documents to the Owner, advise the Owner of any adjustments to the estimate of the Cost of the Work, and request the Owner's approval.

§ 3.4 Construction Documents Phase Services

§ 3.4.1 Based on the Owner's approval of the Design Development Documents, and on the Owner's authorization of any adjustments in the Project requirements and the budget for the Cost of the Work, the Architect shall prepare Construction Documents for the Owner's approval. The Construction Documents shall illustrate and describe the further development of the approved Design Development Documents and shall consist of Drawings and Specifications setting forth in detail the quality levels and performance criteria of materials and systems and other requirements for the construction of the Work. The Owner and Architect acknowledge that, in order to perform the Work, the Contractor will provide additional information, including Shop Drawings, Product Data, Samples and other similar submittals, which the Architect shall review in accordance with Section 3.6.4.

§ 3.4.2 The Architect shall incorporate the design requirements of governmental authorities having jurisdiction over the Project into the Construction Documents.

§ 3.4.3 During the development of the Construction Documents, the Architect shall assist the Owner in the development and preparation of (1) procurement information that describes the time, place, and conditions of bidding, including bidding or proposal forms; (2) the form of agreement between the Owner and Contractor; and (3) the Conditions of the Contract for Construction (General, Supplementary and other Conditions). The Architect shall also compile a project manual that includes the Conditions of the Contract for Construction and Specifications, and may include bidding requirements and sample forms.

Init.

/

§ 3.4.4 The Architect shall update the estimate for the Cost of the Work prepared in accordance with Section 6.3.

§ 3.4.5 The Architect shall submit the Construction Documents to the Owner, advise the Owner of any adjustments to the estimate of the Cost of the Work, take any action required under Section 6.5, and request the Owner's approval.

§ 3.5 Procurement Phase Services
§ 3.5.1 General
The Architect shall assist the Owner in establishing a list of prospective contractors. Following the Owner's approval of the Construction Documents, the Architect shall assist the Owner in (1) obtaining either competitive bids or negotiated proposals; (2) confirming responsiveness of bids or proposals; (3) determining the successful bid or proposal, if any; and, (4) awarding and preparing contracts for construction.

§ 3.5.2 Competitive Bidding
§ 3.5.2.1 Bidding Documents shall consist of bidding requirements and proposed Contract Documents.

§ 3.5.2.2 The Architect shall assist the Owner in bidding the Project by:
- .1 facilitating the distribution of Bidding Documents to prospective bidders;
- .2 organizing and conducting a pre-bid conference for prospective bidders;
- .3 preparing responses to questions from prospective bidders and providing clarifications and interpretations of the Bidding Documents to the prospective bidders in the form of addenda; and,
- .4 organizing and conducting the opening of the bids, and subsequently documenting and distributing the bidding results, as directed by the Owner.

§ 3.5.2.3 If the Bidding Documents permit substitutions, upon the Owner's written authorization, the Architect shall, as an Additional Service, consider requests for substitutions and prepare and distribute addenda identifying approved substitutions to all prospective bidders.

§ 3.5.3 Negotiated Proposals
§ 3.5.3.1 Proposal Documents shall consist of proposal requirements and proposed Contract Documents.

§ 3.5.3.2 The Architect shall assist the Owner in obtaining proposals by:
- .1 facilitating the distribution of Proposal Documents for distribution to prospective contractors and requesting their return upon completion of the negotiation process;
- .2 organizing and participating in selection interviews with prospective contractors;
- .3 preparing responses to questions from prospective contractors and providing clarifications and interpretations of the Proposal Documents to the prospective contractors in the form of addenda; and,
- .4 participating in negotiations with prospective contractors, and subsequently preparing a summary report of the negotiation results, as directed by the Owner.

§ 3.5.3.3 If the Proposal Documents permit substitutions, upon the Owner's written authorization, the Architect shall, as an Additional Service, consider requests for substitutions and prepare and distribute addenda identifying approved substitutions to all prospective contractors.

§ 3.6 Construction Phase Services
§ 3.6.1 General
§ 3.6.1.1 The Architect shall provide administration of the Contract between the Owner and the Contractor as set forth below and in AIA Document A201™–2017, General Conditions of the Contract for Construction. If the Owner and Contractor modify AIA Document A201–2017, those modifications shall not affect the Architect's services under this Agreement unless the Owner and the Architect amend this Agreement.

§ 3.6.1.2 The Architect shall advise and consult with the Owner during the Construction Phase Services. The Architect shall have authority to act on behalf of the Owner only to the extent provided in this Agreement. The Architect shall not have control over, charge of, or responsibility for the construction means, methods, techniques, sequences or procedures, or for safety precautions and programs in connection with the Work, nor shall the Architect be responsible for the Contractor's failure to perform the Work in accordance with the requirements of the Contract Documents. The Architect shall be responsible for the Architect's negligent acts or omissions, but shall not have control over or charge of, and shall not be responsible for, acts or omissions of the Contractor or of any other persons or entities performing portions of the Work.

§ 3.6.1.3 Subject to Section 4.2 and except as provided in Section 3.6.6.5, the Architect's responsibility to provide Construction Phase Services commences with the award of the Contract for Construction and terminates on the date the Architect issues the final Certificate for Payment.

§ 3.6.2 Evaluations of the Work

§ 3.6.2.1 The Architect shall visit the site at intervals appropriate to the stage of construction, or as otherwise required in Section 4.2.3, to become generally familiar with the progress and quality of the portion of the Work completed, and to determine, in general, if the Work observed is being performed in a manner indicating that the Work, when fully completed, will be in accordance with the Contract Documents. However, the Architect shall not be required to make exhaustive or continuous on-site inspections to check the quality or quantity of the Work. On the basis of the site visits, the Architect shall keep the Owner reasonably informed about the progress and quality of the portion of the Work completed, and promptly report to the Owner (1) known deviations from the Contract Documents, (2) known deviations from the most recent construction schedule submitted by the Contractor, and (3) defects and deficiencies observed in the Work.

§ 3.6.2.2 The Architect has the authority to reject Work that does not conform to the Contract Documents. Whenever the Architect considers it necessary or advisable, the Architect shall have the authority to require inspection or testing of the Work in accordance with the provisions of the Contract Documents, whether or not the Work is fabricated, installed or completed. However, neither this authority of the Architect nor a decision made in good faith either to exercise or not to exercise such authority shall give rise to a duty or responsibility of the Architect to the Contractor, Subcontractors, suppliers, their agents or employees, or other persons or entities performing portions of the Work.

§ 3.6.2.3 The Architect shall interpret and decide matters concerning performance under, and requirements of, the Contract Documents on written request of either the Owner or Contractor. The Architect's response to such requests shall be made in writing within any time limits agreed upon or otherwise with reasonable promptness.

§ 3.6.2.4 Interpretations and decisions of the Architect shall be consistent with the intent of, and reasonably inferable from, the Contract Documents and shall be in writing or in the form of drawings. When making such interpretations and decisions, the Architect shall endeavor to secure faithful performance by both Owner and Contractor, shall not show partiality to either, and shall not be liable for results of interpretations or decisions rendered in good faith. The Architect's decisions on matters relating to aesthetic effect shall be final if consistent with the intent expressed in the Contract Documents.

§ 3.6.2.5 Unless the Owner and Contractor designate another person to serve as an Initial Decision Maker, as that term is defined in AIA Document A201–2017, the Architect shall render initial decisions on Claims between the Owner and Contractor as provided in the Contract Documents.

§ 3.6.3 Certificates for Payment to Contractor

§ 3.6.3.1 The Architect shall review and certify the amounts due the Contractor and shall issue certificates in such amounts. The Architect's certification for payment shall constitute a representation to the Owner, based on the Architect's evaluation of the Work as provided in Section 3.6.2 and on the data comprising the Contractor's Application for Payment, that, to the best of the Architect's knowledge, information and belief, the Work has progressed to the point indicated, the quality of the Work is in accordance with the Contract Documents, and that the Contractor is entitled to payment in the amount certified. The foregoing representations are subject to (1) an evaluation of the Work for conformance with the Contract Documents upon Substantial Completion, (2) results of subsequent tests and inspections, (3) correction of minor deviations from the Contract Documents prior to completion, and (4) specific qualifications expressed by the Architect.

§ 3.6.3.2 The issuance of a Certificate for Payment shall not be a representation that the Architect has (1) made exhaustive or continuous on-site inspections to check the quality or quantity of the Work, (2) reviewed construction means, methods, techniques, sequences or procedures, (3) reviewed copies of requisitions received from Subcontractors and suppliers and other data requested by the Owner to substantiate the Contractor's right to payment, or (4) ascertained how or for what purpose the Contractor has used money previously paid on account of the Contract Sum.

§ 3.6.3.3 The Architect shall maintain a record of the Applications and Certificates for Payment.

Init.

/

4.1"

§ 3.6.4 Submittals
§ 3.6.4.1 The Architect shall review the Contractor's submittal schedule and shall not unreasonably delay or withhold approval of the schedule. The Architect's action in reviewing submittals shall be taken in accordance with the approved submittal schedule or, in the absence of an approved submittal schedule, with reasonable promptness while allowing sufficient time, in the Architect's professional judgment, to permit adequate review.

§ 3.6.4.2 The Architect shall review and approve, or take other appropriate action upon, the Contractor's submittals such as Shop Drawings, Product Data and Samples, but only for the limited purpose of checking for conformance with information given and the design concept expressed in the Contract Documents. Review of such submittals is not for the purpose of determining the accuracy and completeness of other information such as dimensions, quantities, and installation or performance of equipment or systems, which are the Contractor's responsibility. The Architect's review shall not constitute approval of safety precautions or construction means, methods, techniques, sequences or procedures. The Architect's approval of a specific item shall not indicate approval of an assembly of which the item is a component.

§ 3.6.4.3 If the Contract Documents specifically require the Contractor to provide professional design services or certifications by a design professional related to systems, materials, or equipment, the Architect shall specify the appropriate performance and design criteria that such services must satisfy. The Architect shall review and take appropriate action on Shop Drawings and other submittals related to the Work designed or certified by the Contractor's design professional, provided the submittals bear such professional's seal and signature when submitted to the Architect. The Architect's review shall be for the limited purpose of checking for conformance with information given and the design concept expressed in the Contract Documents. The Architect shall be entitled to rely upon, and shall not be responsible for, the adequacy and accuracy of the services, certifications, and approvals performed or provided by such design professionals.

§ 3.6.4.4 Subject to Section 4.2, the Architect shall review and respond to requests for information about the Contract Documents. The Architect shall set forth, in the Contract Documents, the requirements for requests for information. Requests for information shall include, at a minimum, a detailed written statement that indicates the specific Drawings or Specifications in need of clarification and the nature of the clarification requested. The Architect's response to such requests shall be made in writing within any time limits agreed upon, or otherwise with reasonable promptness. If appropriate, the Architect shall prepare and issue supplemental Drawings and Specifications in response to the requests for information.

§ 3.6.4.5 The Architect shall maintain a record of submittals and copies of submittals supplied by the Contractor in accordance with the requirements of the Contract Documents.

§ 3.6.5 Changes in the Work
§ 3.6.5.1 The Architect may order minor changes in the Work that are consistent with the intent of the Contract Documents and do not involve an adjustment in the Contract Sum or an extension of the Contract Time. Subject to Section 4.2, the Architect shall prepare Change Orders and Construction Change Directives for the Owner's approval and execution in accordance with the Contract Documents.

§ 3.6.5.2 The Architect shall maintain records relative to changes in the Work.

§ 3.6.6 Project Completion
§ 3.6.6.1 The Architect shall:

.1 conduct inspections to determine the date or dates of Substantial Completion and the date of final completion;
.2 issue Certificates of Substantial Completion;
.3 forward to the Owner, for the Owner's review and records, written warranties and related documents required by the Contract Documents and received from the Contractor; and,
.4 issue a final Certificate for Payment based upon a final inspection indicating that, to the best of the Architect's knowledge, information, and belief, the Work complies with the requirements of the Contract Documents.

§ 3.6.6.2 The Architect's inspections shall be conducted with the Owner to check conformance of the Work with the requirements of the Contract Documents and to verify the accuracy and completeness of the list submitted by the Contractor of Work to be completed or corrected.

Init.
/

§ 3.6.6.3 When Substantial Completion has been achieved, the Architect shall inform the Owner about the balance of the Contract Sum remaining to be paid the Contractor, including the amount to be retained from the Contract Sum, if any, for final completion or correction of the Work.

§ 3.6.6.4 The Architect shall forward to the Owner the following information received from the Contractor: (1) consent of surety or sureties, if any, to reduction in or partial release of retainage or the making of final payment; (2) affidavits, receipts, releases and waivers of liens, or bonds indemnifying the Owner against liens; and (3) any other documentation required of the Contractor under the Contract Documents.

§ 3.6.6.5 Upon request of the Owner, and prior to the expiration of one year from the date of Substantial Completion, the Architect shall, without additional compensation, conduct a meeting with the Owner to review the facility operations and performance.

ARTICLE 4 SUPPLEMENTAL AND ADDITIONAL SERVICES
§ 4.1 Supplemental Services
§ 4.1.1 The services listed below are not included in Basic Services but may be required for the Project. The Architect shall provide the listed Supplemental Services only if specifically designated in the table below as the Architect's responsibility, and the Owner shall compensate the Architect as provided in Section 11.2. Unless otherwise specifically addressed in this Agreement, if neither the Owner nor the Architect is designated, the parties agree that the listed Supplemental Service is not being provided for the Project.
(Designate the Architect's Supplemental Services and the Owner's Supplemental Services required for the Project by indicating whether the Architect or Owner shall be responsible for providing the identified Supplemental Service. Insert a description of the Supplemental Services in Section 4.1.2 below or attach the description of services as an exhibit to this Agreement.)

Supplemental Services	Responsibility *(Architect, Owner, or not provided)*
§ 4.1.1.1 Programming	
§ 4.1.1.2 Multiple preliminary designs	
§ 4.1.1.3 Measured drawings	
§ 4.1.1.4 Existing facilities surveys	
§ 4.1.1.5 Site evaluation and planning	
§ 4.1.1.6 Building Information Model management responsibilities	
§ 4.1.1.7 Development of Building Information Models for post construction use	
§ 4.1.1.8 Civil engineering	
§ 4.1.1.9 Landscape design	
§ 4.1.1.10 Architectural interior design	
§ 4.1.1.11 Value analysis	
§ 4.1.1.12 Detailed cost estimating beyond that required in Section 6.3	
§ 4.1.1.13 On-site project representation	
§ 4.1.1.14 Conformed documents for construction	
§ 4.1.1.15 As-designed record drawings	
§ 4.1.1.16 As-constructed record drawings	
§ 4.1.1.17 Post-occupancy evaluation	
§ 4.1.1.18 Facility support services	
§ 4.1.1.19 Tenant-related services	
§ 4.1.1.20 Architect's coordination of the Owner's consultants	
§ 4.1.1.21 Telecommunications/data design	

Init.
/

Supplemental Services	**Responsibility** *(Architect, Owner, or not provided)*
§ 4.1.1.22 Security evaluation and planning	
§ 4.1.1.23 Commissioning	
§ 4.1.1.24 Sustainable Project Services pursuant to Section 4.1.3	
§ 4.1.1.25 Fast-track design services	
§ 4.1.1.26 Multiple bid packages	
§ 4.1.1.27 Historic preservation	
§ 4.1.1.28 Furniture, furnishings, and equipment design	
§ 4.1.1.29 Other services provided by specialty Consultants	
§ 4.1.1.30 Other Supplemental Services	

§ 4.1.2 Description of Supplemental Services

§ 4.1.2.1 A description of each Supplemental Service identified in Section 4.1.1 as the Architect's responsibility is provided below.
(Describe in detail the Architect's Supplemental Services identified in Section 4.1.1 or, if set forth in an exhibit, identify the exhibit. The AIA publishes a number of Standard Form of Architect's Services documents that can be included as an exhibit to describe the Architect's Supplemental Services.)

§ 4.1.2.2 A description of each Supplemental Service identified in Section 4.1.1 as the Owner's responsibility is provided below.
(Describe in detail the Owner's Supplemental Services identified in Section 4.1.1 or, if set forth in an exhibit, identify the exhibit.)

§ 4.1.3 If the Owner identified a Sustainable Objective in Article 1, the Architect shall provide, as a Supplemental Service, the Sustainability Services required in AIA Document E204™–2017, Sustainable Projects Exhibit, attached to this Agreement. The Owner shall compensate the Architect as provided in Section 11.2.

§ 4.2 Architect's Additional Services

The Architect may provide Additional Services after execution of this Agreement without invalidating the Agreement. Except for services required due to the fault of the Architect, any Additional Services provided in accordance with this Section 4.2 shall entitle the Architect to compensation pursuant to Section 11.3 and an appropriate adjustment in the Architect's schedule.

§ 4.2.1 Upon recognizing the need to perform the following Additional Services, the Architect shall notify the Owner with reasonable promptness and explain the facts and circumstances giving rise to the need. The Architect shall not proceed to provide the following Additional Services until the Architect receives the Owner's written authorization:

.1 Services necessitated by a change in the Initial Information, previous instructions or approvals given by the Owner, or a material change in the Project including size, quality, complexity, the Owner's schedule or budget for Cost of the Work, or procurement or delivery method;

.2 Services necessitated by the enactment or revision of codes, laws, or regulations, including changing or editing previously prepared Instruments of Service;

.3 Changing or editing previously prepared Instruments of Service necessitated by official interpretations of applicable codes, laws or regulations that are either (a) contrary to specific interpretations by the applicable authorities having jurisdiction made prior to the issuance of the building permit, or (b) contrary to requirements of the Instruments of Service when those Instruments of Service were prepared in accordance with the applicable standard of care;

Init.

/

.4 Services necessitated by decisions of the Owner not rendered in a timely manner or any other failure of performance on the part of the Owner or the Owner's consultants or contractors;
.5 Preparing digital models or other design documentation for transmission to the Owner's consultants and contractors, or to other Owner-authorized recipients;
.6 Preparation of design and documentation for alternate bid or proposal requests proposed by the Owner;
.7 Preparation for, and attendance at, a public presentation, meeting or hearing;
.8 Preparation for, and attendance at, a dispute resolution proceeding or legal proceeding, except where the Architect is party thereto;
.9 Evaluation of the qualifications of entities providing bids or proposals;
.10 Consultation concerning replacement of Work resulting from fire or other cause during construction; or,
.11 Assistance to the Initial Decision Maker, if other than the Architect.

§ 4.2.2 To avoid delay in the Construction Phase, the Architect shall provide the following Additional Services, notify the Owner with reasonable promptness, and explain the facts and circumstances giving rise to the need. If, upon receipt of the Architect's notice, the Owner determines that all or parts of the services are not required, the Owner shall give prompt written notice to the Architect of the Owner's determination. The Owner shall compensate the Architect for the services provided prior to the Architect's receipt of the Owner's notice.
.1 Reviewing a Contractor's submittal out of sequence from the submittal schedule approved by the Architect;
.2 Responding to the Contractor's requests for information that are not prepared in accordance with the Contract Documents or where such information is available to the Contractor from a careful study and comparison of the Contract Documents, field conditions, other Owner-provided information, Contractor-prepared coordination drawings, or prior Project correspondence or documentation;
.3 Preparing Change Orders and Construction Change Directives that require evaluation of Contractor's proposals and supporting data, or the preparation or revision of Instruments of Service;
.4 Evaluating an extensive number of Claims as the Initial Decision Maker; or,
.5 Evaluating substitutions proposed by the Owner or Contractor and making subsequent revisions to Instruments of Service resulting therefrom.

§ 4.2.3 The Architect shall provide Construction Phase Services exceeding the limits set forth below as Additional Services. When the limits below are reached, the Architect shall notify the Owner:
.1 ( ) reviews of each Shop Drawing, Product Data item, sample and similar submittals of the Contractor
.2 ( ) visits to the site by the Architect during construction
.3 ( ) inspections for any portion of the Work to determine whether such portion of the Work is substantially complete in accordance with the requirements of the Contract Documents
.4 ( ) inspections for any portion of the Work to determine final completion.

§ 4.2.4 Except for services required under Section 3.6.6.5 and those services that do not exceed the limits set forth in Section 4.2.3, Construction Phase Services provided more than 60 days after (1) the date of Substantial Completion of the Work or (2) the initial date of Substantial Completion identified in the agreement between the Owner and Contractor, whichever is earlier, shall be compensated as Additional Services to the extent the Architect incurs additional cost in providing those Construction Phase Services.

§ 4.2.5 If the services covered by this Agreement have not been completed within ( ) months of the date of this Agreement, through no fault of the Architect, extension of the Architect's services beyond that time shall be compensated as Additional Services.

ARTICLE 5 OWNER'S RESPONSIBILITIES
§ 5.1 Unless otherwise provided for under this Agreement, the Owner shall provide information in a timely manner regarding requirements for and limitations on the Project, including a written program, which shall set forth the Owner's objectives; schedule; constraints and criteria, including space requirements and relationships; flexibility; expandability; special equipment; systems; and site requirements.

§ 5.2 The Owner shall establish the Owner's budget for the Project, including (1) the budget for the Cost of the Work as defined in Section 6.1; (2) the Owner's other costs; and, (3) reasonable contingencies related to all of these costs. The Owner shall update the Owner's budget for the Project as necessary throughout the duration of the Project until final completion. If the Owner significantly increases or decreases the Owner's budget for the Cost of the Work, the Owner shall notify the Architect. The Owner and the Architect shall thereafter agree to a corresponding change in the Project's scope and quality.

§ 5.3 The Owner shall identify a representative authorized to act on the Owner's behalf with respect to the Project. The Owner shall render decisions and approve the Architect's submittals in a timely manner in order to avoid unreasonable delay in the orderly and sequential progress of the Architect's services.

§ 5.4 The Owner shall furnish surveys to describe physical characteristics, legal limitations and utility locations for the site of the Project, and a written legal description of the site. The surveys and legal information shall include, as applicable, grades and lines of streets, alleys, pavements and adjoining property and structures; designated wetlands; adjacent drainage; rights-of-way, restrictions, easements, encroachments, zoning, deed restrictions, boundaries and contours of the site; locations, dimensions, and other necessary data with respect to existing buildings, other improvements and trees; and information concerning available utility services and lines, both public and private, above and below grade, including inverts and depths. All the information on the survey shall be referenced to a Project benchmark.

§ 5.5 The Owner shall furnish services of geotechnical engineers, which may include test borings, test pits, determinations of soil bearing values, percolation tests, evaluations of hazardous materials, seismic evaluation, ground corrosion tests and resistivity tests, including necessary operations for anticipating subsoil conditions, with written reports and appropriate recommendations.

§ 5.6 The Owner shall provide the Supplemental Services designated as the Owner's responsibility in Section 4.1.1.

§ 5.7 If the Owner identified a Sustainable Objective in Article 1, the Owner shall fulfill its responsibilities as required in AIA Document E204™–2017, Sustainable Projects Exhibit, attached to this Agreement.

§ 5.8 The Owner shall coordinate the services of its own consultants with those services provided by the Architect. Upon the Architect's request, the Owner shall furnish copies of the scope of services in the contracts between the Owner and the Owner's consultants. The Owner shall furnish the services of consultants other than those designated as the responsibility of the Architect in this Agreement, or authorize the Architect to furnish them as an Additional Service, when the Architect requests such services and demonstrates that they are reasonably required by the scope of the Project. The Owner shall require that its consultants and contractors maintain insurance, including professional liability insurance, as appropriate to the services or work provided.

§ 5.9 The Owner shall furnish tests, inspections and reports required by law or the Contract Documents, such as structural, mechanical, and chemical tests, tests for air and water pollution, and tests for hazardous materials.

§ 5.10 The Owner shall furnish all legal, insurance and accounting services, including auditing services, that may be reasonably necessary at any time for the Project to meet the Owner's needs and interests.

§ 5.11 The Owner shall provide prompt written notice to the Architect if the Owner becomes aware of any fault or defect in the Project, including errors, omissions or inconsistencies in the Architect's Instruments of Service.

§ 5.12 The Owner shall include the Architect in all communications with the Contractor that relate to or affect the Architect's services or professional responsibilities. The Owner shall promptly notify the Architect of the substance of any direct communications between the Owner and the Contractor otherwise relating to the Project. Communications by and with the Architect's consultants shall be through the Architect.

§ 5.13 Before executing the Contract for Construction, the Owner shall coordinate the Architect's duties and responsibilities set forth in the Contract for Construction with the Architect's services set forth in this Agreement. The Owner shall provide the Architect a copy of the executed agreement between the Owner and Contractor, including the General Conditions of the Contract for Construction.

§ 5.14 The Owner shall provide the Architect access to the Project site prior to commencement of the Work and shall obligate the Contractor to provide the Architect access to the Work wherever it is in preparation or progress.

§ 5.15 Within 15 days after receipt of a written request from the Architect, the Owner shall furnish the requested information as necessary and relevant for the Architect to evaluate, give notice of, or enforce lien rights.

ARTICLE 6 COST OF THE WORK

§ 6.1 For purposes of this Agreement, the Cost of the Work shall be the total cost to the Owner to construct all elements of the Project designed or specified by the Architect and shall include contractors' general conditions costs, overhead and profit. The Cost of the Work also includes the reasonable value of labor, materials, and equipment, donated to, or otherwise furnished by, the Owner. The Cost of the Work does not include the compensation of the Architect; the costs of the land, rights-of-way, financing, or contingencies for changes in the Work; or other costs that are the responsibility of the Owner.

§ 6.2 The Owner's budget for the Cost of the Work is provided in Initial Information, and shall be adjusted throughout the Project as required under Sections 5.2, 6.4 and 6.5. Evaluations of the Owner's budget for the Cost of the Work, and the preliminary estimate of the Cost of the Work and updated estimates of the Cost of the Work, prepared by the Architect, represent the Architect's judgment as a design professional. It is recognized, however, that neither the Architect nor the Owner has control over the cost of labor, materials, or equipment; the Contractor's methods of determining bid prices; or competitive bidding, market, or negotiating conditions. Accordingly, the Architect cannot and does not warrant or represent that bids or negotiated prices will not vary from the Owner's budget for the Cost of the Work, or from any estimate of the Cost of the Work, or evaluation, prepared or agreed to by the Architect.

§ 6.3 In preparing estimates of the Cost of Work, the Architect shall be permitted to include contingencies for design, bidding, and price escalation; to determine what materials, equipment, component systems, and types of construction are to be included in the Contract Documents; to recommend reasonable adjustments in the program and scope of the Project; and to include design alternates as may be necessary to adjust the estimated Cost of the Work to meet the Owner's budget. The Architect's estimate of the Cost of the Work shall be based on current area, volume or similar conceptual estimating techniques. If the Owner requires a detailed estimate of the Cost of the Work, the Architect shall provide such an estimate, if identified as the Architect's responsibility in Section 4.1.1, as a Supplemental Service.

§ 6.4 If, through no fault of the Architect, the Procurement Phase has not commenced within 90 days after the Architect submits the Construction Documents to the Owner, the Owner's budget for the Cost of the Work shall be adjusted to reflect changes in the general level of prices in the applicable construction market.

§ 6.5 If at any time the Architect's estimate of the Cost of the Work exceeds the Owner's budget for the Cost of the Work, the Architect shall make appropriate recommendations to the Owner to adjust the Project's size, quality, or budget for the Cost of the Work, and the Owner shall cooperate with the Architect in making such adjustments.

§ 6.6 If the Owner's budget for the Cost of the Work at the conclusion of the Construction Documents Phase Services is exceeded by the lowest bona fide bid or negotiated proposal, the Owner shall

- **.1** give written approval of an increase in the budget for the Cost of the Work;
- **.2** authorize rebidding or renegotiating of the Project within a reasonable time;
- **.3** terminate in accordance with Section 9.5;
- **.4** in consultation with the Architect, revise the Project program, scope, or quality as required to reduce the Cost of the Work; or,
- **.5** implement any other mutually acceptable alternative.

§ 6.7 If the Owner chooses to proceed under Section 6.6.4, the Architect shall modify the Construction Documents as necessary to comply with the Owner's budget for the Cost of the Work at the conclusion of the Construction Documents Phase Services, or the budget as adjusted under Section 6.6.1. If the Owner requires the Architect to modify the Construction Documents because the lowest bona fide bid or negotiated proposal exceeds the Owner's budget for the Cost of the Work due to market conditions the Architect could not reasonably anticipate, the Owner shall compensate the Architect for the modifications as an Additional Service pursuant to Section 11.3; otherwise the Architect's services for modifying the Construction Documents shall be without additional compensation. In any event, the Architect's modification of the Construction Documents shall be the limit of the Architect's responsibility under this Article 6.

ARTICLE 7 COPYRIGHTS AND LICENSES

§ 7.1 The Architect and the Owner warrant that in transmitting Instruments of Service, or any other information, the transmitting party is the copyright owner of such information or has permission from the copyright owner to transmit such information for its use on the Project.

§ 7.2 The Architect and the Architect's consultants shall be deemed the authors and owners of their respective Instruments of Service, including the Drawings and Specifications, and shall retain all common law, statutory and other reserved rights, including copyrights. Submission or distribution of Instruments of Service to meet official regulatory requirements or for similar purposes in connection with the Project is not to be construed as publication in derogation of the reserved rights of the Architect and the Architect's consultants.

§ 7.3 The Architect grants to the Owner a nonexclusive license to use the Architect's Instruments of Service solely and exclusively for purposes of constructing, using, maintaining, altering and adding to the Project, provided that the Owner substantially performs its obligations under this Agreement, including prompt payment of all sums due pursuant to Article 9 and Article 11. The Architect shall obtain similar nonexclusive licenses from the Architect's consultants consistent with this Agreement. The license granted under this section permits the Owner to authorize the Contractor, Subcontractors, Sub-subcontractors, and suppliers, as well as the Owner's consultants and separate contractors, to reproduce applicable portions of the Instruments of Service, subject to any protocols established pursuant to Section 1.3, solely and exclusively for use in performing services or construction for the Project. If the Architect rightfully terminates this Agreement for cause as provided in Section 9.4, the license granted in this Section 7.3 shall terminate.

§ 7.3.1 In the event the Owner uses the Instruments of Service without retaining the authors of the Instruments of Service, the Owner releases the Architect and Architect's consultant(s) from all claims and causes of action arising from such uses. The Owner, to the extent permitted by law, further agrees to indemnify and hold harmless the Architect and its consultants from all costs and expenses, including the cost of defense, related to claims and causes of action asserted by any third person or entity to the extent such costs and expenses arise from the Owner's use of the Instruments of Service under this Section 7.3.1. The terms of this Section 7.3.1 shall not apply if the Owner rightfully terminates this Agreement for cause under Section 9.4.

§ 7.4 Except for the licenses granted in this Article 7, no other license or right shall be deemed granted or implied under this Agreement. The Owner shall not assign, delegate, sublicense, pledge or otherwise transfer any license granted herein to another party without the prior written agreement of the Architect. Any unauthorized use of the Instruments of Service shall be at the Owner's sole risk and without liability to the Architect and the Architect's consultants.

§ 7.5 Except as otherwise stated in Section 7.3, the provisions of this Article 7 shall survive the termination of this Agreement.

ARTICLE 8 CLAIMS AND DISPUTES

§ 8.1 General

§ 8.1.1 The Owner and Architect shall commence all claims and causes of action against the other and arising out of or related to this Agreement, whether in contract, tort, or otherwise, in accordance with the requirements of the binding dispute resolution method selected in this Agreement and within the period specified by applicable law, but in any case not more than 10 years after the date of Substantial Completion of the Work. The Owner and Architect waive all claims and causes of action not commenced in accordance with this Section 8.1.1.

§ 8.1.2 To the extent damages are covered by property insurance, the Owner and Architect waive all rights against each other and against the contractors, consultants, agents, and employees of the other for damages, except such rights as they may have to the proceeds of such insurance as set forth in AIA Document A201–2017, General Conditions of the Contract for Construction. The Owner or the Architect, as appropriate, shall require of the contractors, consultants, agents, and employees of any of them, similar waivers in favor of the other parties enumerated herein.

§ 8.1.3 The Architect and Owner waive consequential damages for claims, disputes, or other matters in question, arising out of or relating to this Agreement. This mutual waiver is applicable, without limitation, to all consequential damages due to either party's termination of this Agreement, except as specifically provided in Section 9.7.

§ 8.2 Mediation

§ 8.2.1 Any claim, dispute or other matter in question arising out of or related to this Agreement shall be subject to mediation as a condition precedent to binding dispute resolution. If such matter relates to or is the subject of a lien arising out of the Architect's services, the Architect may proceed in accordance with applicable law to comply with the lien notice or filing deadlines prior to resolution of the matter by mediation or by binding dispute resolution.

§ 8.2.2 The Owner and Architect shall endeavor to resolve claims, disputes and other matters in question between them by mediation, which, unless the parties mutually agree otherwise, shall be administered by the American Arbitration Association in accordance with its Construction Industry Mediation Procedures in effect on the date of this Agreement. A request for mediation shall be made in writing, delivered to the other party to this Agreement, and filed with the

Init.

/

person or entity administering the mediation. The request may be made concurrently with the filing of a complaint or other appropriate demand for binding dispute resolution but, in such event, mediation shall proceed in advance of binding dispute resolution proceedings, which shall be stayed pending mediation for a period of 60 days from the date of filing, unless stayed for a longer period by agreement of the parties or court order. If an arbitration proceeding is stayed pursuant to this section, the parties may nonetheless proceed to the selection of the arbitrator(s) and agree upon a schedule for later proceedings.

§ 8.2.3 The parties shall share the mediator's fee and any filing fees equally. The mediation shall be held in the place where the Project is located, unless another location is mutually agreed upon. Agreements reached in mediation shall be enforceable as settlement agreements in any court having jurisdiction thereof.

§ 8.2.4 If the parties do not resolve a dispute through mediation pursuant to this Section 8.2, the method of binding dispute resolution shall be the following:
(Check the appropriate box.)

☐ Arbitration pursuant to Section 8.3 of this Agreement

☐ Litigation in a court of competent jurisdiction

☐ Other: *(Specify)*

If the Owner and Architect do not select a method of binding dispute resolution, or do not subsequently agree in writing to a binding dispute resolution method other than litigation, the dispute will be resolved in a court of competent jurisdiction.

§ 8.3 Arbitration
§ 8.3.1 If the parties have selected arbitration as the method for binding dispute resolution in this Agreement, any claim, dispute or other matter in question arising out of or related to this Agreement subject to, but not resolved by, mediation shall be subject to arbitration, which, unless the parties mutually agree otherwise, shall be administered by the American Arbitration Association in accordance with its Construction Industry Arbitration Rules in effect on the date of this Agreement. A demand for arbitration shall be made in writing, delivered to the other party to this Agreement, and filed with the person or entity administering the arbitration.

§ 8.3.1.1 A demand for arbitration shall be made no earlier than concurrently with the filing of a request for mediation, but in no event shall it be made after the date when the institution of legal or equitable proceedings based on the claim, dispute or other matter in question would be barred by the applicable statute of limitations. For statute of limitations purposes, receipt of a written demand for arbitration by the person or entity administering the arbitration shall constitute the institution of legal or equitable proceedings based on the claim, dispute or other matter in question.

§ 8.3.2 The foregoing agreement to arbitrate, and other agreements to arbitrate with an additional person or entity duly consented to by parties to this Agreement, shall be specifically enforceable in accordance with applicable law in any court having jurisdiction thereof.

§ 8.3.3 The award rendered by the arbitrator(s) shall be final, and judgment may be entered upon it in accordance with applicable law in any court having jurisdiction thereof.

§ 8.3.4 Consolidation or Joinder
§ 8.3.4.1 Either party, at its sole discretion, may consolidate an arbitration conducted under this Agreement with any other arbitration to which it is a party provided that (1) the arbitration agreement governing the other arbitration permits consolidation; (2) the arbitrations to be consolidated substantially involve common questions of law or fact; and (3) the arbitrations employ materially similar procedural rules and methods for selecting arbitrator(s).

§ 8.3.4.2 Either party, at its sole discretion, may include by joinder persons or entities substantially involved in a common question of law or fact whose presence is required if complete relief is to be accorded in arbitration, provided that the party sought to be joined consents in writing to such joinder. Consent to arbitration involving an additional

Init.
/

person or entity shall not constitute consent to arbitration of any claim, dispute or other matter in question not described in the written consent.

§ 8.3.4.3 The Owner and Architect grant to any person or entity made a party to an arbitration conducted under this Section 8.3, whether by joinder or consolidation, the same rights of joinder and consolidation as the Owner and Architect under this Agreement.

§ 8.4 The provisions of this Article 8 shall survive the termination of this Agreement.

ARTICLE 9 TERMINATION OR SUSPENSION

§ 9.1 If the Owner fails to make payments to the Architect in accordance with this Agreement, such failure shall be considered substantial nonperformance and cause for termination or, at the Architect's option, cause for suspension of performance of services under this Agreement. If the Architect elects to suspend services, the Architect shall give seven days' written notice to the Owner before suspending services. In the event of a suspension of services, the Architect shall have no liability to the Owner for delay or damage caused the Owner because of such suspension of services. Before resuming services, the Owner shall pay the Architect all sums due prior to suspension and any expenses incurred in the interruption and resumption of the Architect's services. The Architect's fees for the remaining services and the time schedules shall be equitably adjusted.

§ 9.2 If the Owner suspends the Project, the Architect shall be compensated for services performed prior to notice of such suspension. When the Project is resumed, the Architect shall be compensated for expenses incurred in the interruption and resumption of the Architect's services. The Architect's fees for the remaining services and the time schedules shall be equitably adjusted.

§ 9.3 If the Owner suspends the Project for more than 90 cumulative days for reasons other than the fault of the Architect, the Architect may terminate this Agreement by giving not less than seven days' written notice.

§ 9.4 Either party may terminate this Agreement upon not less than seven days' written notice should the other party fail substantially to perform in accordance with the terms of this Agreement through no fault of the party initiating the termination.

§ 9.5 The Owner may terminate this Agreement upon not less than seven days' written notice to the Architect for the Owner's convenience and without cause.

§ 9.6 If the Owner terminates this Agreement for its convenience pursuant to Section 9.5, or the Architect terminates this Agreement pursuant to Section 9.3, the Owner shall compensate the Architect for services performed prior to termination, Reimbursable Expenses incurred, and costs attributable to termination, including the costs attributable to the Architect's termination of consultant agreements.

§ 9.7 In addition to any amounts paid under Section 9.6, if the Owner terminates this Agreement for its convenience pursuant to Section 9.5, or the Architect terminates this Agreement pursuant to Section 9.3, the Owner shall pay to the Architect the following fees:
(Set forth below the amount of any termination or licensing fee, or the method for determining any termination or licensing fee.)

.1 Termination Fee:

.2 Licensing Fee if the Owner intends to continue using the Architect's Instruments of Service:

§ 9.8 Except as otherwise expressly provided herein, this Agreement shall terminate one year from the date of Substantial Completion.

§ 9.9 The Owner's rights to use the Architect's Instruments of Service in the event of a termination of this Agreement are set forth in Article 7 and Section 9.7.

Init.
/

ARTICLE 10 MISCELLANEOUS PROVISIONS

§ 10.1 This Agreement shall be governed by the law of the place where the Project is located, excluding that jurisdiction's choice of law rules. If the parties have selected arbitration as the method of binding dispute resolution, the Federal Arbitration Act shall govern Section 8.3.

§ 10.2 Terms in this Agreement shall have the same meaning as those in AIA Document A201–2017, General Conditions of the Contract for Construction.

§ 10.3 The Owner and Architect, respectively, bind themselves, their agents, successors, assigns, and legal representatives to this Agreement. Neither the Owner nor the Architect shall assign this Agreement without the written consent of the other, except that the Owner may assign this Agreement to a lender providing financing for the Project if the lender agrees to assume the Owner's rights and obligations under this Agreement, including any payments due to the Architect by the Owner prior to the assignment.

§ 10.4 If the Owner requests the Architect to execute certificates, the proposed language of such certificates shall be submitted to the Architect for review at least 14 days prior to the requested dates of execution. If the Owner requests the Architect to execute consents reasonably required to facilitate assignment to a lender, the Architect shall execute all such consents that are consistent with this Agreement, provided the proposed consent is submitted to the Architect for review at least 14 days prior to execution. The Architect shall not be required to execute certificates or consents that would require knowledge, services, or responsibilities beyond the scope of this Agreement.

§ 10.5 Nothing contained in this Agreement shall create a contractual relationship with, or a cause of action in favor of, a third party against either the Owner or Architect.

§ 10.6 Unless otherwise required in this Agreement, the Architect shall have no responsibility for the discovery, presence, handling, removal or disposal of, or exposure of persons to, hazardous materials or toxic substances in any form at the Project site.

§ 10.7 The Architect shall have the right to include photographic or artistic representations of the design of the Project among the Architect's promotional and professional materials. The Architect shall be given reasonable access to the completed Project to make such representations. However, the Architect's materials shall not include the Owner's confidential or proprietary information if the Owner has previously advised the Architect in writing of the specific information considered by the Owner to be confidential or proprietary. The Owner shall provide professional credit for the Architect in the Owner's promotional materials for the Project. This Section 10.7 shall survive the termination of this Agreement unless the Owner terminates this Agreement for cause pursuant to Section 9.4.

§ 10.8 If the Architect or Owner receives information specifically designated as "confidential" or "business proprietary," the receiving party shall keep such information strictly confidential and shall not disclose it to any other person except as set forth in Section 10.8.1. This Section 10.8 shall survive the termination of this Agreement.

§ 10.8.1 The receiving party may disclose "confidential" or "business proprietary" information after 7 days' notice to the other party, when required by law, arbitrator's order, or court order, including a subpoena or other form of compulsory legal process issued by a court or governmental entity, or to the extent such information is reasonably necessary for the receiving party to defend itself in any dispute. The receiving party may also disclose such information to its employees, consultants, or contractors in order to perform services or work solely and exclusively for the Project, provided those employees, consultants and contractors are subject to the restrictions on the disclosure and use of such information as set forth in this Section 10.8.

§ 10.9 The invalidity of any provision of the Agreement shall not invalidate the Agreement or its remaining provisions. If it is determined that any provision of the Agreement violates any law, or is otherwise invalid or unenforceable, then that provision shall be revised to the extent necessary to make that provision legal and enforceable. In such case the Agreement shall be construed, to the fullest extent permitted by law, to give effect to the parties' intentions and purposes in executing the Agreement.

Init.

/

ARTICLE 11 COMPENSATION

§ 11.1 For the Architect's Basic Services described under Article 3, the Owner shall compensate the Architect as follows:

.1 Stipulated Sum
(Insert amount)

.2 Percentage Basis
(Insert percentage value)

( ) % of the Owner's budget for the Cost of the Work, as calculated in accordance with Section 11.6.

.3 Other
(Describe the method of compensation)

§ 11.2 For the Architect's Supplemental Services designated in Section 4.1.1 and for any Sustainability Services required pursuant to Section 4.1.3, the Owner shall compensate the Architect as follows:
(Insert amount of, or basis for, compensation. If necessary, list specific services to which particular methods of compensation apply.)

§ 11.3 For Additional Services that may arise during the course of the Project, including those under Section 4.2, the Owner shall compensate the Architect as follows:
(Insert amount of, or basis for, compensation.)

§ 11.4 Compensation for Supplemental and Additional Services of the Architect's consultants when not included in Section 11.2 or 11.3, shall be the amount invoiced to the Architect plus percent (%), or as follows:
(Insert amount of, or basis for computing, Architect's consultants' compensation for Supplemental or Additional Services.)

§ 11.5 When compensation for Basic Services is based on a stipulated sum or a percentage basis, the proportion of compensation for each phase of services shall be as follows:

Schematic Design Phase		percent (		%)
Design Development Phase		percent (		%)
Construction Documents Phase		percent (		%)
Procurement Phase		percent (		%)
Construction Phase		percent (		%)
Total Basic Compensation	one hundred	percent (	100	%)

§ 11.6 When compensation identified in Section 11.1 is on a percentage basis, progress payments for each phase of Basic Services shall be calculated by multiplying the percentages identified in this Article by the Owner's most recent budget for the Cost of the Work. Compensation paid in previous progress payments shall not be adjusted based on subsequent updates to the Owner's budget for the Cost of the Work.

§ 11.6.1 When compensation is on a percentage basis and any portions of the Project are deleted or otherwise not constructed, compensation for those portions of the Project shall be payable to the extent services are performed on those portions. The Architect shall be entitled to compensation in accordance with this Agreement for all services performed whether or not the Construction Phase is commenced.

§ 11.7 The hourly billing rates for services of the Architect and the Architect's consultants are set forth below. The rates shall be adjusted in accordance with the Architect's and Architect's consultants' normal review practices.
(If applicable, attach an exhibit of hourly billing rates or insert them below.)

Employee or Category	Rate ($0.00)

§ 11.8 Compensation for Reimbursable Expenses
§ 11.8.1 Reimbursable Expenses are in addition to compensation for Basic, Supplemental, and Additional Services and include expenses incurred by the Architect and the Architect's consultants directly related to the Project, as follows:

.1 Transportation and authorized out-of-town travel and subsistence;
.2 Long distance services, dedicated data and communication services, teleconferences, Project web sites, and extranets;
.3 Permitting and other fees required by authorities having jurisdiction over the Project;
.4 Printing, reproductions, plots, and standard form documents;
.5 Postage, handling, and delivery;
.6 Expense of overtime work requiring higher than regular rates, if authorized in advance by the Owner;
.7 Renderings, physical models, mock-ups, professional photography, and presentation materials requested by the Owner or required for the Project;
.8 If required by the Owner, and with the Owner's prior written approval, the Architect's consultants' expenses of professional liability insurance dedicated exclusively to this Project, or the expense of additional insurance coverage or limits in excess of that normally maintained by the Architect's consultants;
.9 All taxes levied on professional services and on reimbursable expenses;
.10 Site office expenses;
.11 Registration fees and any other fees charged by the Certifying Authority or by other entities as necessary to achieve the Sustainable Objective; and,
.12 Other similar Project-related expenditures.

§ 11.8.2 For Reimbursable Expenses the compensation shall be the expenses incurred by the Architect and the Architect's consultants plus percent (%) of the expenses incurred.

§ 11.9 Architect's Insurance. If the types and limits of coverage required in Section 2.5 are in addition to the types and limits the Architect normally maintains, the Owner shall pay the Architect for the additional costs incurred by the Architect for the additional coverages as set forth below:
(Insert the additional coverages the Architect is required to obtain in order to satisfy the requirements set forth in Section 2.5, and for which the Owner shall reimburse the Architect.)

§ 11.10 Payments to the Architect
§ 11.10.1 Initial Payments
§ 11.10.1.1 An initial payment of ($) shall be made upon execution of this Agreement and is the minimum payment under this Agreement. It shall be credited to the Owner's account in the final invoice.

§ 11.10.1.2 If a Sustainability Certification is part of the Sustainable Objective, an initial payment to the Architect of ($) shall be made upon execution of this Agreement for registration fees and other fees payable to the Certifying Authority and necessary to achieve the Sustainability Certification. The Architect's payments to the Certifying Authority shall be credited to the Owner's account at the time the expense is incurred.

Init.
/

§ 11.10.2 Progress Payments
§ 11.10.2.1 Unless otherwise agreed, payments for services shall be made monthly in proportion to services performed. Payments are due and payable upon presentation of the Architect's invoice. Amounts unpaid ( ) days after the invoice date shall bear interest at the rate entered below, or in the absence thereof at the legal rate prevailing from time to time at the principal place of business of the Architect.
(Insert rate of monthly or annual interest agreed upon.)

%

§ 11.10.2.2 The Owner shall not withhold amounts from the Architect's compensation to impose a penalty or liquidated damages on the Architect, or to offset sums requested by or paid to contractors for the cost of changes in the Work, unless the Architect agrees or has been found liable for the amounts in a binding dispute resolution proceeding.

§ 11.10.2.3 Records of Reimbursable Expenses, expenses pertaining to Supplemental and Additional Services, and services performed on the basis of hourly rates shall be available to the Owner at mutually convenient times.

ARTICLE 12 SPECIAL TERMS AND CONDITIONS
Special terms and conditions that modify this Agreement are as follows:
(Include other terms and conditions applicable to this Agreement.)

ARTICLE 13 SCOPE OF THE AGREEMENT
§ 13.1 This Agreement represents the entire and integrated agreement between the Owner and the Architect and supersedes all prior negotiations, representations or agreements, either written or oral. This Agreement may be amended only by written instrument signed by both the Owner and Architect.

§ 13.2 This Agreement is comprised of the following documents identified below:
.1 AIA Document B101™–2017, Standard Form Agreement Between Owner and Architect
.2 AIA Document E203™–2013, Building Information Modeling and Digital Data Exhibit, dated as indicated below:
(Insert the date of the E203-2013 incorporated into this agreement.)

.3 Exhibits:
(Check the appropriate box for any exhibits incorporated into this Agreement.)

☐ AIA Document E204™–2017, Sustainable Projects Exhibit, dated as indicated below:
(Insert the date of the E204-2017 incorporated into this agreement.)

☐ Other Exhibits incorporated into this Agreement:
(Clearly identify any other exhibits incorporated into this Agreement, including any exhibits and scopes of services identified as exhibits in Section 4.1.2.)

.4 Other documents:
(List other documents, if any, forming part of the Agreement.)

This Agreement entered into as of the day and year first written above.

OWNER *(Signature)*	**ARCHITECT** *(Signature)*
(Printed name and title)	*(Printed name, title, and license number, if required)*

Init.

/

Exhibit 12

AIA Document A101^{TM} – 2017

Standard Form Agreement Between Owner and Contractor Where the Basis for Payment Is a Stipulated Sum

AIA Document A101® – 2017

***Standard Form of Agreement Between Owner and Contractor** where the basis of payment is a Stipulated Sum*

AGREEMENT made as of the ________ day of ________ in the year ________
(In words, indicate day, month and year.)

BETWEEN the Owner:
(Name, legal status, address and other information)

and the Contractor:
(Name, legal status, address and other information)

for the following Project:
(Name, location and detailed description)

The Architect:
(Name, legal status, address and other information)

This document has important legal consequences. Consultation with an attorney is encouraged with respect to its completion or modification.

The parties should complete A101®–2017, Exhibit A, Insurance and Bonds, contemporaneously with this Agreement.

AIA Document A201®–2017, General Conditions of the Contract for Construction, is adopted in this document by reference. Do not use with other general conditions unless this document is modified.

The Owner and Contractor agree as follows.

Init.

/

TABLE OF ARTICLES

ARTICLE 1 THE CONTRACT DOCUMENTS
The Contract Documents consist of this Agreement, Conditions of the Contract (General, Supplementary, and other Conditions), Drawings, Specifications, Addenda issued prior to execution of this Agreement, other documents listed in this Agreement, and Modifications issued after execution of this Agreement, all of which form the Contract, and are as fully a part of the Contract as if attached to this Agreement or repeated herein. The Contract represents the entire and integrated agreement between the parties hereto and supersedes prior negotiations, representations, or agreements, either written or oral. An enumeration of the Contract Documents, other than a Modification, appears in Article 9.

ARTICLE 2 THE WORK OF THIS CONTRACT
The Contractor shall fully execute the Work described in the Contract Documents, except as specifically indicated in the Contract Documents to be the responsibility of others.

ARTICLE 3 DATE OF COMMENCEMENT AND SUBSTANTIAL COMPLETION
§ 3.1 The date of commencement of the Work shall be:
(Check one of the following boxes.)

☐ The date of this Agreement.

☐ A date set forth in a notice to proceed issued by the Owner.

☐ Established as follows:
(Insert a date or a means to determine the date of commencement of the Work.)

If a date of commencement of the Work is not selected, then the date of commencement shall be the date of this Agreement.

§ 3.2 The Contract Time shall be measured from the date of commencement of the Work.

§ 3.3 Substantial Completion
§ 3.3.1 Subject to adjustments of the Contract Time as provided in the Contract Documents, the Contractor shall achieve Substantial Completion of the entire Work:
(Check one of the following boxes and complete the necessary information.)

☐ Not later than ( ) calendar days from the date of commencement of the Work.

Init.
/

☐ By the following date:

§ 3.3.2 Subject to adjustments of the Contract Time as provided in the Contract Documents, if portions of the Work are to be completed prior to Substantial Completion of the entire Work, the Contractor shall achieve Substantial Completion of such portions by the following dates:

Portion of Work	Substantial Completion Date

§ 3.3.3 If the Contractor fails to achieve Substantial Completion as provided in this Section 3.3, liquidated damages, if any, shall be assessed as set forth in Section 4.5.

ARTICLE 4 CONTRACT SUM

§ 4.1 The Owner shall pay the Contractor the Contract Sum in current funds for the Contractor's performance of the Contract. The Contract Sum shall be ($), subject to additions and deductions as provided in the Contract Documents.

§ 4.2 Alternates

§ 4.2.1 Alternates, if any, included in the Contract Sum:

Item	Price

§ 4.2.2 Subject to the conditions noted below, the following alternates may be accepted by the Owner following execution of this Agreement. Upon acceptance, the Owner shall issue a Modification to this Agreement.
(Insert below each alternate and the conditions that must be met for the Owner to accept the alternate.)

Item	Price	Conditions for Acceptance

§ 4.3 Allowances, if any, included in the Contract Sum:
(Identify each allowance.)

Item	Price

§ 4.4 Unit prices, if any:
(Identify the item and state the unit price and quantity limitations, if any, to which the unit price will be applicable.)

Item	Units and Limitations	Price per Unit ($0.00)

§ 4.5 Liquidated damages, if any:
(Insert terms and conditions for liquidated damages, if any.)

§ 4.6 Other:
(Insert provisions for bonus or other incentives, if any, that might result in a change to the Contract Sum.)

ARTICLE 5 PAYMENTS

§ 5.1 Progress Payments

§ 5.1.1 Based upon Applications for Payment submitted to the Architect by the Contractor and Certificates for Payment issued by the Architect, the Owner shall make progress payments on account of the Contract Sum to the Contractor as provided below and elsewhere in the Contract Documents.

§ 5.1.2 The period covered by each Application for Payment shall be one calendar month ending on the last day of the month, or as follows:

§ 5.1.3 Provided that an Application for Payment is received by the Architect not later than the day of a month, the Owner shall make payment of the amount certified to the Contractor not later than the day of the month. If an Application for Payment is received by the Architect after the application date fixed above, payment of the amount certified shall be made by the Owner not later than ( ) days after the Architect receives the Application for Payment.

(Federal, state or local laws may require payment within a certain period of time.)

§ 5.1.4 Each Application for Payment shall be based on the most recent schedule of values submitted by the Contractor in accordance with the Contract Documents. The schedule of values shall allocate the entire Contract Sum among the various portions of the Work. The schedule of values shall be prepared in such form, and supported by such data to substantiate its accuracy, as the Architect may require. This schedule of values shall be used as a basis for reviewing the Contractor's Applications for Payment.

§ 5.1.5 Applications for Payment shall show the percentage of completion of each portion of the Work as of the end of the period covered by the Application for Payment.

§ 5.1.6 In accordance with AIA Document A201™–2017, General Conditions of the Contract for Construction, and subject to other provisions of the Contract Documents, the amount of each progress payment shall be computed as follows:

§ 5.1.6.1 The amount of each progress payment shall first include:

.1 That portion of the Contract Sum properly allocable to completed Work;

.2 That portion of the Contract Sum properly allocable to materials and equipment delivered and suitably stored at the site for subsequent incorporation in the completed construction, or, if approved in advance by the Owner, suitably stored off the site at a location agreed upon in writing; and

.3 That portion of Construction Change Directives that the Architect determines, in the Architect's professional judgment, to be reasonably justified.

§ 5.1.6.2 The amount of each progress payment shall then be reduced by:

.1 The aggregate of any amounts previously paid by the Owner;

.2 The amount, if any, for Work that remains uncorrected and for which the Architect has previously withheld a Certificate for Payment as provided in Article 9 of AIA Document A201–2017;

.3 Any amount for which the Contractor does not intend to pay a Subcontractor or material supplier, unless the Work has been performed by others the Contractor intends to pay;

.4 For Work performed or defects discovered since the last payment application, any amount for which the Architect may withhold payment, or nullify a Certificate of Payment in whole or in part, as provided in Article 9 of AIA Document A201–2017; and

.5 Retainage withheld pursuant to Section 5.1.7.

§ 5.1.7 Retainage

§ 5.1.7.1 For each progress payment made prior to Substantial Completion of the Work, the Owner may withhold the following amount, as retainage, from the payment otherwise due:

(Insert a percentage or amount to be withheld as retainage from each Application for Payment. The amount of retainage may be limited by governing law.)

Init.

/

§ 5.1.7.1.1 The following items are not subject to retainage:
(Insert any items not subject to the withholding of retainage, such as general conditions, insurance, etc.)

§ 5.1.7.2 Reduction or limitation of retainage, if any, shall be as follows:
(If the retainage established in Section 5.1.7.1 is to be modified prior to Substantial Completion of the entire Work, including modifications for Substantial Completion of portions of the Work as provided in Section 3.3.2, insert provisions for such modifications.)

§ 5.1.7.3 Except as set forth in this Section 5.1.7.3, upon Substantial Completion of the Work, the Contractor may submit an Application for Payment that includes the retainage withheld from prior Applications for Payment pursuant to this Section 5.1.7. The Application for Payment submitted at Substantial Completion shall not include retainage as follows:
(Insert any other conditions for release of retainage upon Substantial Completion.)

§ 5.1.8 If final completion of the Work is materially delayed through no fault of the Contractor, the Owner shall pay the Contractor any additional amounts in accordance with Article 9 of AIA Document A201–2017.

§ 5.1.9 Except with the Owner's prior approval, the Contractor shall not make advance payments to suppliers for materials or equipment which have not been delivered and stored at the site.

§ 5.2 Final Payment
§ 5.2.1 Final payment, constituting the entire unpaid balance of the Contract Sum, shall be made by the Owner to the Contractor when

- **.1** the Contractor has fully performed the Contract except for the Contractor's responsibility to correct Work as provided in Article 12 of AIA Document A201–2017, and to satisfy other requirements, if any, which extend beyond final payment; and
- **.2** a final Certificate for Payment has been issued by the Architect.

§ 5.2.2 The Owner's final payment to the Contractor shall be made no later than 30 days after the issuance of the Architect's final Certificate for Payment, or as follows:

§ 5.3 Interest
Payments due and unpaid under the Contract shall bear interest from the date payment is due at the rate stated below, or in the absence thereof, at the legal rate prevailing from time to time at the place where the Project is located.
(Insert rate of interest agreed upon, if any.)

______ %

ARTICLE 6 DISPUTE RESOLUTION
§ 6.1 Initial Decision Maker
The Architect will serve as the Initial Decision Maker pursuant to Article 15 of AIA Document A201–2017, unless the parties appoint below another individual, not a party to this Agreement, to serve as the Initial Decision Maker.
(If the parties mutually agree, insert the name, address and other contact information of the Initial Decision Maker, if other than the Architect.)

Init.
/

§ 6.2 Binding Dispute Resolution
For any Claim subject to, but not resolved by, mediation pursuant to Article 15 of AIA Document A201–2017, the method of binding dispute resolution shall be as follows:
(Check the appropriate box.)

- [ ] Arbitration pursuant to Section 15.4 of AIA Document A201–2017
- [ ] Litigation in a court of competent jurisdiction
- [ ] Other *(Specify)*

If the Owner and Contractor do not select a method of binding dispute resolution, or do not subsequently agree in writing to a binding dispute resolution method other than litigation, Claims will be resolved by litigation in a court of competent jurisdiction.

ARTICLE 7 TERMINATION OR SUSPENSION
§ 7.1 The Contract may be terminated by the Owner or the Contractor as provided in Article 14 of AIA Document A201–2017.

§ 7.1.1 If the Contract is terminated for the Owner's convenience in accordance with Article 14 of AIA Document A201–2017, then the Owner shall pay the Contractor a termination fee as follows:
(Insert the amount of, or method for determining, the fee, if any, payable to the Contractor following a termination for the Owner's convenience.)

§ 7.2 The Work may be suspended by the Owner as provided in Article 14 of AIA Document A201–2017.

ARTICLE 8 MISCELLANEOUS PROVISIONS
§ 8.1 Where reference is made in this Agreement to a provision of AIA Document A201–2017 or another Contract Document, the reference refers to that provision as amended or supplemented by other provisions of the Contract Documents.

§ 8.2 The Owner's representative:
(Name, address, email address, and other information)

§ 8.3 The Contractor's representative:
(Name, address, email address, and other information)

§ 8.4 Neither the Owner's nor the Contractor's representative shall be changed without ten days' prior notice to the other party.

§ 8.5 Insurance and Bonds
§ 8.5.1 The Owner and the Contractor shall purchase and maintain insurance as set forth in AIA Document A101™–2017, Standard Form of Agreement Between Owner and Contractor where the basis of payment is a Stipulated Sum, Exhibit A, Insurance and Bonds, and elsewhere in the Contract Documents.

§ 8.5.2 The Contractor shall provide bonds as set forth in AIA Document A101™–2017 Exhibit A, and elsewhere in the Contract Documents.

§ 8.6 Notice in electronic format, pursuant to Article 1 of AIA Document A201–2017, may be given in accordance with AIA Document E203™–2013, Building Information Modeling and Digital Data Exhibit, if completed, or as otherwise set forth below:
(If other than in accordance with AIA Document E203–2013, insert requirements for delivering notice in electronic format such as name, title, and email address of the recipient and whether and how the system will be required to generate a read receipt for the transmission.)

§ 8.7 Other provisions:

ARTICLE 9 ENUMERATION OF CONTRACT DOCUMENTS
§ 9.1 This Agreement is comprised of the following documents:

.1 AIA Document A101™–2017, Standard Form of Agreement Between Owner and Contractor
.2 AIA Document A101™–2017, Exhibit A, Insurance and Bonds
.3 AIA Document A201™–2017, General Conditions of the Contract for Construction
.4 AIA Document E203™–2013, Building Information Modeling and Digital Data Exhibit, dated as indicated below:
(Insert the date of the E203-2013 incorporated into this Agreement.)

.5 Drawings

Number	Title	Date

.6 Specifications

Section	Title	Date	Pages

.7 Addenda, if any:

Number	Date	Pages

Portions of Addenda relating to bidding or proposal requirements are not part of the Contract Documents unless the bidding or proposal requirements are also enumerated in this Article 9.

.8 Other Exhibits:
(Check all boxes that apply and include appropriate information identifying the exhibit where required.)

☐ AIA Document E204™–2017, Sustainable Projects Exhibit, dated as indicated below:
(Insert the date of the E204-2017 incorporated into this Agreement.)

☐ The Sustainability Plan:

Title	Date	Pages

☐ Supplementary and other Conditions of the Contract:

Document	Title	Date	Pages

.9 Other documents, if any, listed below:
(List here any additional documents that are intended to form part of the Contract Documents. AIA Document A201™–2017 provides that the advertisement or invitation to bid, Instructions to Bidders, sample forms, the Contractor's bid or proposal, portions of Addenda relating to bidding or proposal requirements, and other information furnished by the Owner in anticipation of receiving bids or proposals, are not part of the Contract Documents unless enumerated in this Agreement. Any such documents should be listed here only if intended to be part of the Contract Documents.)

This Agreement entered into as of the day and year first written above.

OWNER *(Signature)*	**CONTRACTOR** *(Signature)*
(Printed name and title)	*(Printed name and title)*

Init.
/

 8

Exhibit 13

ConsensusDocs 200

Standard Form of Agreement and General Conditions between Owner and Contractor (Lump Sum)

ConsensusDocs®
BUILDING A BETTER WAY

ConsensusDocs® 200
STANDARD AGREEMENT AND GENERAL CONDITIONS BETWEEN OWNER AND CONSTRUCTOR (Lump Sum)

This page is solely for the information and convenience of ConsensusDocs users, and is not a part of the contract. Gray boxes indicate where you should click and type in your project information. The yellow shading is a Word® default function that displays editable text. Shading can be turned off by going to the Review tab, select "Restrict Editing" button and uncheck "Highlight the regions I can edit". In Word 2003 you will find this option under the Tools tab, Options, Security tab, Protect Document button.

EMBEDDED INSTRUCTIONS are provided solely to help you complete the document. To display or hide instructions select the "¶" button under the "Home" tab to show all formatting marks.

Red Boxes: Instructions for fields that are typically required to complete contract.
Blue Boxes: Instructions for fields that may or may not be required for a complete contract.
Green Boxes: Provide general instructions or ConsensusDocs Coalition Guidebook comments, which can be found at www.ConsensusDocs.org/guidebook.

This document was developed through a collaborative effort of organizations representing a wide cross-section of the design and construction industry. This document has important legal and insurance consequences, and it is not intended as a substitute for competent professional services and advice. This document must be reviewed and adapted to meet your project-specific needs. Federal, State and Local laws may vary with respect to the applicability or enforceability of specific provisions in this document. CONSENSUSDOCS SPECIFICALLY DISCLAIMS ALL WARRANTIES, EXPRESS OR IMPLIED, INCLUDING ANY WARRANTY OF MERCHANTABILITY OR FITNESS FOR A PARTICULAR PURPOSE. PURCHASER ASSUMES ALL LIABILITY WITH RESPECT TO THE USE OF THIS DOCUMENT, AND CONSENSUSDOCS AND ANY OF THE ORGANIZATIONS SHALL NOT BE LIABLE FOR ANY DIRECT, INDIRECT OR CONSEQUENTIAL DAMAGES RESULTING FROM SUCH USE. For additional information, please contact ConsensusDocs, 2300 Wilson Blvd, Suite 300, Arlington, VA 22201, 866-925-DOCS (3627), support@consensusdocs.org or www.ConsensusDocs.org.

1

ConsensusDocs® 200

STANDARD AGREEMENT AND GENERAL CONDITIONS BETWEEN OWNER AND CONSTRUCTOR (Lump Sum)

TABLE OF ARTICLES

ARTICLE 1 AGREEMENT

Job Number: [ ] Account Code: [ ]

This Agreement is made this [ ] day of [ ] in the year [ ],

by and between the

OWNER, [ ]

and the

CONSTRUCTOR, [ ]

Tax identification number (TIN) [ ]
Contractor License No., if applicable [ ]

for construction and services in connection with the following

PROJECT [ ]

Design Professional is [ ].

ARTICLE 2 GENERAL PROVISIONS

2.1 PARTIES' RELATIONSHIP Each Party agrees to act on the basis of mutual trust, good faith, and fair dealing, and perform in an economical and timely manner. The Parties shall each endeavor to promote harmony and cooperation among all Project participants.

2.1.1 Neither Constructor nor any of its agents or employees shall act on behalf of or in the name of Owner.

2.2 ETHICS Each Party shall perform with integrity. Each shall: (a) avoid conflicts of interest; and (b) promptly disclose to the other Party any conflicts that may arise. Each Party warrants it has not and shall not pay or receive any contingent fees or gratuities to or from the other Party, including its agents, officers, employees, Subcontractors, Subsubcontractors, Suppliers, or Others to secure preferential treatment.

2.3 DESIGN PROFESSIONAL Owner, through its Design Professional, shall provide all architectural and engineering design services necessary for the completion of the Work excluding, however, (a) design services delegated to Constructor in accordance with §3.15, and (b) services within the construction means, methods, techniques, sequences, and procedures employed by Constructor, its Subcontractors and Subsubcontractors in connection with their construction operations.

2.3.1 Owner shall obtain from Design Professional either a license for Constructor and Subcontractors to use the design documents prepared by Design Professional or ownership of the copyrights for such design documents. Owner shall indemnify and hold harmless Constructor against any suits or claims of infringement of any copyrights or licenses arising out of the use of the design documents for the Project.

2.4 DEFINITIONS

2.4.1 "Agreement" means this ConsensusDocs 200 Standard Agreement and General Conditions Between Owner and Constructor (Lump Sum), as modified, and exhibits and attachments made part of this agreement upon its execution.

2.4.1.1 The following exhibits are part of this Agreement:
Exhibit A: Schedule of the Work, [_____] pages.
Exhibit B: Labor Relations, if applicable.

2.4.2 "Business Day" means all Days, except weekends and official federal or state holidays where the Project is located.

2.4.3 A "Change Order" is a written order signed by the Parties after execution of this Agreement, indicating a change in the scope of the Work, Contract Price, or Contract Time, including substitutions proposed by Constructor and accepted by Owner.

2.4.4 The "Contract Documents" consist of (a) this Agreement; (b) documents listed in §14.1 as existing contract documents; (c) drawings, specifications, addenda issued and acknowledged before execution of this Agreement; (d) information furnished by Owner pursuant to §3.13.4; and (e) Change Orders, Interim Directives, and amendments issued in accordance with this Agreement.

2.4.5 "Contract Price" is the amount indicated in §7.1 and represents full compensation for performance by the Constructor of the Work in conformance with the Contract Documents.

2.4.6 "Contract Time" is the period between the Date of Commencement and the total time authorized to achieve Final Completion in §6.1.1.

2.4.7 "Constructor" is the person or entity identified in ARTICLE 1. References to General Contractor or Contractor in the Contract Documents may be a reference to Constructor.

2.4.8 "Cost of the Work" means the costs and discounts specified in §8.3.4.

2.4.9 "Date of Commencement" is as set forth in §6.1.

2.4.10 "Day" means a calendar day.

2.4.11 "Defective Work" is any portion of the Work that does not conform to the requirements of the Contract Documents.

2.4.12 "Design Professional" means the licensed architect or engineer, and its consultants, retained by Owner to perform design services for the Project.

2.4.13 "Final Completion" occurs on the date when Constructor's obligations under this Agreement are complete and accepted by Owner and final payment becomes due and payable. This date shall be confirmed by a Certificate of Final Completion signed by Parties.

2.4.14 "Hazardous Material" is any substance or material identified now or in the future as hazardous under the Law, or any other substance or material that may be considered hazardous or otherwise subject to statutory or regulatory requirement governing handling, disposal, or cleanup.

2.4.15 "Law" means federal, state, or local law, ordinance, code, rule, and regulations applicable to the Work with which Constructor must comply that are enacted as of the Agreement date.

2.4.16 "Interim Directive" is a written order containing Work instructions directed by Owner pursuant to §8.2 and that is signed by Owner after execution of this Agreement and before Substantial Completion.

2.4.17 "Others" means Owner's other: (a) contractors/constructors, (b) suppliers, (c) subcontractors, subsubcontractors, or suppliers of (a) and (b); and others employed directly or indirectly by (a), (b), or (c) or any by any of them or for whose acts any of them may be liable.

2.4.18 "Overhead" means (a) payroll costs, burden, and other compensation of Constructor's employees in Constructor's principal and branch offices; (b) general and administrative expenses of Constructor's principal and branch offices including charges against Constructor for delinquent payments; and (c) Constructor's capital expenses, including interest on capital used for the Work.

2.4.19 "Owner" is the person or entity identified in ARTICLE 1.

2.4.20 The "Parties" are collectively Owner and Constructor.

2.4.21 The "Project," as identified in ARTICLE 1, is the building, facility, or other improvements for which Constructor is to perform Work under this Agreement. It may also include construction by Owner or Others.

2.4.22 The "Schedule of the Work" is the document prepared by Constructor that specifies the dates on which Constructor plans to begin and complete various parts of the Work, including dates on which information and approvals are required from Owner.

2.4.23 A "Subcontractor" is a person or entity retained by Constructor as an independent contractor to provide the labor, materials, equipment, or services necessary to complete a specific portion of the Work. The term Subcontractor does not include Design Professional or Others.

2.4.24 "Substantial Completion" of the Work, or of a designated portion, occurs on the date when the Work is sufficiently complete in accordance with the Contract Documents so that Owner may occupy or utilize the Project, or a designated portion, for the use for which it is intended, without unapproved disruption. The issuance of a certificate of occupancy is not a prerequisite for Substantial Completion if the certificate of occupancy cannot be obtained due to factors beyond Constructor's control. This date shall be confirmed by a Certificate of Substantial Completion signed by the Parties.

2.4.25 A "Subsubcontractor" is a person or entity who has an agreement with a Subcontractor, another subsubcontractor, or Supplier to perform a portion of the Work or to supply material or equipment.

2.4.26 A "Supplier" is a person or entity retained by Constructor to provide material or equipment for the Work.

2.4.27 "Terrorism" means a violent act, or an act that is dangerous to human life, property, or infrastructure, that is committed by an individual or individuals and that appears to be part of an effort to coerce a civilian population or to influence the policy or affect the conduct of any government by coercion. Terrorism includes, but is not limited to, any act certified by the United States government as an act of terrorism pursuant to the Terrorism Risk Insurance Act, as amended.

2.4.28 "Work" means the construction and services necessary or incidental to fulfill Constructor's obligations for the Project in accordance with and reasonably inferable from the Contract Documents. The Work may refer to the whole Project or only a part of the Project if work is also being performed by Owner or Others.

2.4.29 "Worksite" means the area of the Project location identified in ARTICLE 1 where the Work is to be performed.

ARTICLE 3 CONSTRUCTOR'S RESPONSIBILITIES

Constructor shall use its diligent efforts to perform the Work in an expeditious manner consistent with the Contract Documents. Such Work includes furnishing construction administration and management services.

3.1 GENERAL RESPONSIBILITIES

3.1.1 Constructor shall provide all labor, materials, equipment, and services necessary to complete the Work, all of which shall be provided in full accord with the Contract Documents and shall include any Work reasonably inferable from the Contract Documents.

3.1.2 Constructor represents that it is an independent contractor and that it is familiar with the type of work required by this Agreement.

3.1.3 Unless the Contract Documents instruct otherwise, Constructor shall be responsible for the supervision and coordination of the Work, including the construction means, methods, techniques, sequences, and procedures utilized. When following construction means, methods, techniques, sequences, or procedures instructed by the Contract Documents, Constructor is not liable to Owner for damages resulting from compliance with such instructions unless (a) Constructor recognized and (b) failed to timely report to Owner any error, inconsistency, omission, or unsafe practice that it discovered in such requirements.

3.1.4 Constructor shall perform Work only within locations allowed by the Contract Documents, Law, and applicable permits.

3.2 COOPERATION WITH WORK OF OWNER AND OTHERS

3.2.1 Owner may perform work at the Worksite directly or by Others. Any agreements with Others to perform construction or operations related to the Project shall include provisions pertaining to insurance, indemnification, waiver of subrogation, consequential damages, coordination, interference, cleanup, and safety that are substantively the same as the corresponding provisions of this Agreement.

3.2.2 If Owner elects to perform work at the Worksite directly or by Others, the Parties shall coordinate the activities of all forces at the Worksite and agree upon fair and reasonable schedules and operational procedures for Worksite activities. Owner shall require each separate contractor to cooperate with Constructor and to assist with the coordination of activities and the review of construction schedules and operations. In accordance with §6.3, Contract Price and Contract Time may be equitably adjusted for changes resulting from the coordination of construction activities, and the Schedule of the Work shall be revised accordingly.

3.2.3 With regard to the work of Owner and Others, Constructor shall: (a) proceed with the Work in a manner that does not hinder, delay, or interfere with the work of Owner or Others or cause the work of Owner or Others to become defective; (b) afford Owner and Others reasonable access for introduction and storage of their materials and equipment and performance of their activities; and (c) coordinate Constructor's Work with theirs.

3.2.4 Before proceeding with any portion of the Work affected by the construction or operations of Owner or Others, Constructor shall give Owner prompt written notification of any defects Constructor discovers in their work which will prevent the proper execution of the Work. Constructor's obligations in this subsection do not create a responsibility for the work of Owner or Others, but are for the purpose of facilitating the Work. If Constructor does not notify Owner of defects interfering with the performance of the Work, Constructor acknowledges that the work of Owner or Others is not defective and is acceptable for the proper execution of the Work. Following receipt of written notice from Constructor of defects, Owner shall promptly issue an Interim Directive informing Constructor what action, if any, Constructor shall take with regard to the defects.

3.3 CONTRACT DOCUMENT REVIEW

3.3.1 Before commencing the Work, Constructor shall examine and compare the drawings and specifications with information furnished in the Contract Documents, relevant field measurements made by Constructor, and any visible conditions at the Worksite affecting the Work.

3.3.2 Should Constructor discover any errors, omissions, or inconsistencies in the Contract Documents, Constructor shall promptly report them to Owner. It is recognized, however, that Constructor is not acting in the capacity of a licensed design professional, and that Constructor's examination is to facilitate construction and does not create an affirmative responsibility to detect errors, omissions, or inconsistencies or to ascertain compliance with a Law, building code, or regulation. Following receipt of written notice from Constructor of errors, omissions, or inconsistencies, Owner shall promptly inform Constructor what action, if any, Constructor shall take with regard to the errors, omissions, or inconsistencies.

3.3.3 In accordance with this Agreement, Constructor may be entitled to adjustments of the Contract Price or Contract Time because of clarifications or instructions arising out of Constructor's reports described in this §3.3.

3.3.4 Nothing in §3.3 shall relieve Constructor of responsibility for its own errors, inconsistencies, or omissions.

3.4 CONSTRUCTION PERSONNEL AND SUPERVISION

3.4.1 Constructor shall provide competent supervision for the performance of the Work. Before commencing the Work, Constructor shall notify Owner in writing of the name and qualifications of its proposed superintendent(s) and project manager so Owner may review their qualifications. If, for reasonable cause, Owner refuses to approve an individual, or withdraws its approval after once giving it, Constructor shall name a different superintendent or project manager for Owner's review. Any disapproved superintendent shall not perform in that capacity thereafter at the Worksite.

3.4.2 Constructor shall be responsible to Owner for acts or omissions of a person or entity performing on behalf of Constructor or any of its Subcontractors and Suppliers.

3.4.3 Constructor shall permit only qualified persons to perform the Work. Constructor shall enforce safety procedures, strict discipline, and good order among persons performing the Work. If Owner determines that a particular person does not follow safety procedures, or is unfit or unskilled for the assigned Work, Constructor shall immediately reassign the person upon receipt of Owner's Interim Directive to do so.

3.4.4 CONSTRUCTOR'S REPRESENTATIVE Constructor's authorized representative is [ ]. Constructor's Representative shall possess full authority to receive instructions from Owner and to act on those instructions. If Constructor changes its representative or the representative's authority, Constructor shall immediately notify Owner in writing.

3.5 WORKMANSHIP The Work shall be executed in accordance with the Contract Documents in a workmanlike manner. All materials used in the Work shall be furnished in sufficient quantities to facilitate the proper and expeditious execution of the Work and shall be new except as otherwise provided in the Contract Documents.

3.6 MATERIALS FURNISHED BY OWNER OR OTHERS If the Work includes installation of materials or equipment furnished by Owner or Others, it shall be the responsibility of Constructor to examine the items so provided and thereupon handle, store, and install the items, unless otherwise provided in the Contract Documents, with such skill and care as to provide a satisfactory and proper installation. Loss or damage due to acts or omissions of Constructor shall be the responsibility of Constructor and may be deducted from any amounts due or to become due Constructor. Any defects discovered in such materials or equipment shall be reported at once to Owner. Following receipt of written notice from Constructor of defects, Owner shall promptly inform Constructor what action, if any, Constructor shall take with regard to the defects.

3.7 TESTS AND INSPECTIONS

3.7.1 Constructor shall schedule all required tests, approvals, and inspections of the Work or portions thereof at appropriate times so as not to delay the progress of the Work or other work related to the Project. Constructor shall give proper notice to all required parties of such tests, approvals, and inspections. If feasible, Owner and Others may timely observe the tests at the normal place of testing. Except as provided in §3.7.3, Owner shall bear all expenses associated with tests, inspections, and approvals required by the Contract Documents, which shall be conducted by an independent testing laboratory or entity retained by Owner. Unless otherwise required by the Contract Documents, required certificates of testing, approval, or inspection shall be secured by Constructor and promptly delivered to Owner.

3.7.2 If Owner or appropriate authorities determine that tests, inspections, or approvals in addition to those required by the Contract Documents will be necessary, Constructor shall arrange for the procedures and give timely notice to Owner and Others who may observe the procedures. Costs of the additional tests, inspections, or approvals are at Owner's expense except as provided in the subsection below.

3.7.3 If the procedures described in the two subsections immediately above indicate that portions of the Work fail to comply with the Contract Documents, Constructor shall be responsible for costs of correction and retesting.

3.8 WARRANTY

3.8.1 Constructor warrants that all materials and equipment shall be new unless otherwise specified, of good quality, in conformance with the Contract Documents, and free from defective workmanship and materials. At Owner's request, Constructor shall furnish satisfactory evidence of the quality and type of materials and equipment furnished. Constructor further warrants that the Work shall be free from material defects not intrinsic in the design or materials required in the Contract Documents. Constructor's warranty does not include remedies for defects or damages caused by normal wear and tear during normal usage, use for a purpose for which the Project was not intended, improper or insufficient maintenance, modifications performed by Owner or others, or abuse. Constructor's warranty shall commence on the Date of Substantial Completion of the Work, or of a designated portion.

3.8.2 To the extent products, equipment, systems, or materials incorporated in the Work are specified and purchased by Owner, they shall be covered exclusively by the warranty of the manufacturer. There are no warranties which extend beyond the description on the face of any such warranty. For such incorporated items, ALL OTHER WARRANTIES EXPRESSED OR IMPLIED INCLUDING THE WARRANTY OF MERCHANTABILITY AND THE WARRANTY OF FITNESS FOR A PARTICULAR PURPOSE ARE EXPRESSLY DISCLAIMED.

3.8.3 Constructor shall obtain from its Subcontractors and Suppliers any special or extended warranties required by the Contract Documents. Constructor's liability for such warranties shall be limited to the one-year correction period as provided in the section below. After that period, Constructor shall provide reasonable assistance to Owner in enforcing the obligations of Subcontractors or Suppliers for such extended warranties.

3.9 CORRECTION OF WORK WITHIN ONE YEAR

3.9.1 Before Substantial Completion and within one year after the date of Substantial Completion of the Work, if any Defective Work is found, Owner shall promptly notify Constructor in writing. Unless Owner provides written acceptance of the condition, Constructor shall promptly correct the Defective Work at its own cost and time and bear the expense of additional services required for correction of any Defective Work for which it is responsible. If within the one-year correction period Owner discovers and does not promptly notify Constructor or give Constructor an opportunity to test or correct Defective Work as reasonably requested by Constructor, Owner waives Constructor's obligation to correct that Defective Work as well as Owner's right to claim a breach of the warranty with respect to that Defective Work.

3.9.2 With respect to any portion of Work first performed after Substantial Completion, the one-year correction period shall commence when that portion of the Work is substantially complete. Correction periods shall not be extended by corrective work performed by Constructor.

3.9.3 If Constructor fails to correct Defective Work within a reasonable time after receipt of written notice from Owner before final payment, Owner may correct it in accordance with Owner's right to carry out the Work. In such case, an appropriate Change Order shall be issued deducting the cost of correcting the Defective Work from payments then or thereafter due Constructor. If payments then or thereafter due Constructor are not sufficient to cover such amounts, Constructor shall pay the difference to Owner.

3.9.4 Constructor's obligations and liability, if any, with respect to any Defective Work discovered after the one-year correction period shall be determined by the Law. If, after the one-year correction period but before the applicable limitation period has expired, Owner discovers any Work which Owner considers Defective Work, Owner shall, unless the Defective Work requires emergency correction, promptly notify Constructor and allow Constructor an opportunity to correct the Work if Constructor elects to do so. If Constructor elects to correct the Work, it shall provide written notice of such intent within fourteen (14) Days of its receipt of notice from Owner and shall complete the correction of Work within a mutually agreed timeframe. If Constructor does not elect to correct the Work, Owner may have the Work corrected by itself or others, and, if Owner intends to seek recovery of those costs from Constructor, Owner shall promptly provide Constructor with an accounting of actual correction costs.

3.9.5 If Constructor's correction or removal of Defective Work causes damage to or destroys other completed or partially completed Work or existing buildings, Constructor shall be responsible for the cost of correcting the destroyed or damaged property.

3.9.6 The one-year period for correction of Defective Work does not constitute a limitation period with respect to the enforcement of Constructor's other obligations under the Contract Documents.

3.9.7 Before final payment, at Owner's option and with Constructor's agreement, Owner may elect to accept Defective Work rather than require its removal and correction. In such case, the Contract Price shall be equitably adjusted for any diminution in the value of the Project caused by such Defective Work.

3.10 CORRECTION OF COVERED WORK

3.10.1 Upon issuance of an Interim Directive, Work that has been covered without a requirement that it be inspected before being covered shall be uncovered for Owner's inspection. Owner shall pay for the costs of uncovering and replacement if the Work proves to be in conformance with the Contract Documents, or if the defective condition was caused by Owner or Others. If the uncovered Work proves to be defective, Constructor shall pay the costs of uncovering and replacement.

3.10.2 If any Work is covered contrary to requirements in the Contract Documents, Owner may issue an Interim Directive to uncover the Work for Owner's observation and recover the Work all at Constructor's expense and with no Contract Time adjustment.

3.11 SAFETY

3.11.1 SAFETY PROGRAMS Constructor holds overall responsibility for safety programs. However, such obligation does not relieve Subcontractors their safety responsibilities and to comply with the Law. Constructor shall prevent against injury, loss, or damage to persons or property by taking reasonable steps to protect: (a) its employees and other persons at the Worksite; (b) materials and equipment stored onsite or offsite for use in the Work; and (c) property located at the Worksite and adjacent to work areas.

3.11.2 CONSTRUCTOR'S SAFETY REPRESENTATIVE Constructor shall designate an individual at the Worksite in its employ as its safety representative. Unless otherwise identified by Constructor in writing to Owner, Constructor's project superintendent shall serve as its safety representative. Constructor shall report promptly in writing to Owner all recordable accidents and injuries occurring at the Worksite. When Constructor is required to file an accident report with a public authority, Constructor shall furnish a copy of the report to Owner.

3.11.3 Constructor shall provide Owner with copies of all notices required of Constructor by Law. Constructor's safety program shall comply with the requirements of authorities having jurisdiction.

3.11.4 Damage or loss not insured under property insurance which may arise from the Work, to the extent caused by the negligent or intentionally wrongful acts or omissions of Constructor, or anyone for whose acts Constructor may be liable, shall be promptly remedied by Constructor.

3.11.5 If Owner deems any part of the Work or Worksite unsafe, Owner, without assuming responsibility for Constructor's safety program, may require by Interim Directive, Constructor to stop performance of the Work, take corrective measures satisfactory to Owner, or both. If Constructor does not adopt corrective measures, Owner may perform them and deduct their cost from the Contract Price. Constructor agrees to make no claim for damages, for an increase in the Contract Price or Contract Time based on Constructor's compliance with Owner's reasonable request.

3.12 EMERGENCIES

3.12.1 In an emergency affecting the safety of persons or property, Constructor shall act in a reasonable manner to prevent threatened damage, injury, or loss. Any change in the Contract Price or Contract Time resulting from the actions of Constructor in an emergency situation shall be determined as provided in ARTICLE 8.

3.13 HAZARDOUS MATERIALS

3.13.1 Constructor shall not be obligated to commence Work until any Hazardous Material discovered at the Worksite has been removed, rendered, or determined to be harmless by Owner as certified by an independent testing laboratory and approved by the appropriate governmental agency.

3.13.2 If after commencing the Work, Hazardous Material is discovered at the Worksite, Constructor shall be entitled to immediately stop Work in the affected area. Constructor shall promptly report the condition to Owner, Design Professional, and, if required, the governmental agency with jurisdiction.

3.13.3 Constructor shall not resume nor be required to continue any Work affected by any Hazardous Material without written mutual agreement between the Parties after the Hazardous Material has been removed or rendered harmless and only after approval, if necessary, of the governmental agency with jurisdiction.

3.13.4 Owner shall be responsible for retaining an independent testing laboratory to determine the nature of the material encountered and whether the material requires corrective measures or remedial action. Such measures shall be the sole responsibility of Owner, and shall be performed in a manner minimizing any adverse effect upon the Work.

3.13.5 If Constructor incurs additional costs or is delayed due to the presence or remediation of Hazardous Material, Constructor shall be entitled to an equitable adjustment in the Contract Price or the Contract Time in accordance with this Agreement.

3.13.6 To the extent permitted by §6.6 and to the extent not caused by the negligent or intentionally wrongful acts or omissions of Constructor, its Subcontractors and Subsubcontractors, and the agents, officers, directors, and employees of each of them, Owner shall defend, indemnify, and hold harmless Constructor, its Subcontractors and Subsubcontractors, and the agents, officers, directors, and employees of each of them, from and against all claims, damages, losses, costs, and expenses, including but not limited to reasonable attorneys' fees, costs, and expenses incurred in connection with any dispute resolution procedure, arising out of or relating to the performance of the Work in any area affected by Hazardous Material.

3.13.7 MATERIALS BROUGHT TO THE WORKSITE

3.13.7.1 Safety Data Sheets (SDS) as required by Law and pertaining to materials or substances used or consumed in the performance of the Work, whether obtained by Constructor, Subcontractors, Owner, or Others, shall be maintained at the Worksite by Constructor and made available to Owner, Subcontractors, and Others.

3.13.7.2 Constructor shall be responsible for the proper delivery, handling, application, storage, removal, and disposal of all materials and substances brought to the Worksite by Constructor and used or consumed in the performance of the Work. Upon the issuance of the Certificate of Substantial Completion, Owner shall be responsible for materials and substances brought to the Worksite by Constructor if such materials or substances are required by the Contract Documents.

3.13.7.3 To the extent caused by the negligent or intentionally wrongful acts or omissions of Constructor, its agents, officers, directors, and employees, Constructor shall indemnify and hold harmless Owner, its agents, officers, directors, and employees, from and against any and all claims, damages, losses, costs, and expenses, including but not limited to attorneys' fees, costs, and expenses incurred in connection with any dispute resolution procedure, arising out of or relating to the delivery, handling, application, storage, removal, and disposal of all materials and substances brought to the Worksite by Constructor.

3.13.8 §3.13 in its entirety shall survive the completion of the Work or Agreement termination.

3.14 SUBMITTALS

3.14.1 Constructor shall submit to Owner and Design Professional all shop drawings, samples, product data, and similar submittals required by the Contract Documents for review and approval. Submittals shall be submitted in electronic form if required by §4.6.1. Constructor shall be responsible for the accuracy and conformity of its submittals to the Contract Documents. At no additional cost, Constructor shall prepare and deliver its submittals in a manner consistent with the Schedule of the Work and in such time and sequence so as not to delay the performance of the Work or the work of Owner and Others. Constructor submittals shall identify in writing for each submittal all changes, deviations, or substitutions from the requirements of the Contract Documents. The approval of any Constructor submittal shall not be deemed to authorize changes, deviations, or substitutions from the requirements of the Contract Documents unless a Change Order or Interim Directive specifically authorizes such deviation, substitution, or change. To the extent a change, deviation, or substitution causes an impact to the Contract Price or Contract Time, such approval shall be memorialized in a Change Order no later than seven (7) Days following approval by Owner. Neither Design Professional nor Owner shall make any change, deviation, or substitution through the submittal process without specifically identifying and authorizing such deviation to Constructor. If the Contract Documents do not contain submittal requirements pertaining to the Work, Constructor agrees upon request to submit in a timely fashion to Design Professional and Owner for review any shop drawings, samples, product data, manufacturers' literature, or similar submittals as may reasonably be required by Owner.

3.14.2 Owner shall be responsible for review and approval of submittals with reasonable promptness to avoid causing delay.

3.14.3 Constructor shall perform all Work strictly in accordance with approved submittals. Approval of shop drawings is not an authorization to perform changed work, unless the procedures of ARTICLE 8 are followed. Approval does not relieve Constructor from responsibility for Defective Work resulting from errors or omissions on the approved shop drawings.

3.14.4 Record copies of the following, incorporating field changes and selections made during construction, shall be accessible at the Worksite and available to Owner upon request: drawings, specifications, addenda, Change Order and other modifications, and required submittals including product data, samples, and shop drawings.

3.14.5 Constructor shall prepare and submit to Owner:

☐ Final marked-up as-built drawings;
☐ Updated electronic data, in accordance with §4.6.1; or
☐ Other documentation required by the Contract Documents that specifies how various elements of the Work were actually constructed or installed.

3.15 DESIGN DELEGATION If the Contract Documents specify that Constructor is responsible for the design of a particular system or component to be incorporated into the Project, then Owner shall specify all required performance and design criteria. Constructor shall not be responsible for the adequacy of such performance and design criteria.

As required by the Law, Constructor shall procure design services and certifications necessary to satisfactorily complete the Work from a licensed design professional. The signature and seal of Constructor's design professional shall appear on all drawings, calculations, specifications, certifications, shop drawings, and other submittals related to the Work designed or certified by Constructor's design professional.

3.16 WORKSITE CONDITIONS

3.16.1 WORKSITE VISIT Constructor acknowledges that it has visited, or has had the opportunity to visit, the Worksite to visually inspect the general and local conditions which could affect the Work.

3.16.2 CONCEALED OR UNKNOWN SITE CONDITIONS If a condition encountered at the Worksite is (a) subsurface or other physical condition materially different from those indicated in the Contract Documents, or (b) unusual and unknown physical condition materially different from conditions ordinarily encountered and generally recognized as inherent in Work provided for in the Contract Documents, Constructor shall stop affected Work after the concealed or unknown condition is first observed and give prompt written notice of the condition to Owner and Design Professional. Owner shall investigate and then issue an Interim Directive specifying the extent to which Owner agrees that a concealed or unknown condition exists and directing how Constructor is to proceed. Constructor shall not be required to perform any Work relating to the condition without the written mutual agreement of the Parties. Any change in the Contract Price or the Contract Time as a result of the condition, including any dispute about its existence or nature, shall be determined as provided in ARTICLE 8.

3.17 PERMITS AND TAXES

3.17.1 Constructor shall give public authorities all notices required by Law and, except for permits and fees that are the responsibility of Owner, shall obtain and pay for all necessary permits, licenses, and renewals pertaining to the Work. Constructor shall provide to Owner copies of all notices, permits, licenses, and renewals required under this Agreement.

3.17.2 Constructor shall pay applicable taxes for the Work provided by Constructor.

3.17.3 If, in accordance with Owner's direction, Constructor claims an exemption for taxes, Owner shall indemnify and hold Constructor harmless from any liability, penalty, interest, fine, tax assessment, attorneys' fees, or other expense or cost incurred by Constructor as a result of any such claim.

3.18 CUTTING, FITTING, AND PATCHING

3.18.1 Constructor shall perform cutting, fitting, and patching necessary to coordinate the various parts of the Work and to prepare its Work for the work of Owner or Others.

3.18.2 Cutting, patching, or altering the work of Owner or Others shall be done with the prior written approval of Owner. Such approval shall not be unreasonably withheld.

3.19 CLEAN UP

3.19.1 Constructor shall regularly remove debris and waste materials at the Worksite resulting from the Work. Before discontinuing Work in an area, Constructor shall clean the area and remove all rubbish and its construction equipment, tools, machinery, waste, and surplus materials. Constructor shall minimize and confine dust and debris resulting from construction activities. At the completion of the Work, Constructor shall remove from the Worksite all construction equipment, tools, surplus materials, waste materials, and debris.

3.19.2 If Constructor fails to commence compliance with cleanup duties within two (2) Business Days after written notification from Owner of non-compliance, Owner may implement appropriate cleanup measures without further notice and shall deduct the reasonable costs from any amounts due or to become due to Constructor in the next payment period.

3.20 ACCESS TO WORK Constructor shall facilitate the access of Owner, Design Professional, and Others to Work in progress.

3.21 COMPLIANCE WITH THE LAW Constructor shall comply with the Law at its own cost. Constructor shall be liable to Owner for all loss, cost, or expense attributable to any acts or omissions by Constructor, its employees, subcontractors, suppliers, and agents for failure to comply with the Law, including fines, penalties, or corrective measures. However, liability under this subsection shall not apply if prior approval by appropriate authorities and Owner is received.

3.21.1 The Contract Price or Contract Time shall be equitably adjusted by Change Order for additional costs or time needed resulting from any change in Law, including increased taxes, enacted after the date of this Agreement.

3.22 CONFIDENTIALITY Constructor shall treat as confidential and not disclose to third-persons, nor use for its own benefit ("Treat as Confidential"), any of Owner's confidential information, know-how, discoveries, production methods, and the like disclosed to Constructor or which Constructor may acquire in performing the Work. To the extent necessary to perform the Work, Constructor's confidentiality obligations do not apply to disclosures to Subcontractors, Subsubcontractors, and Suppliers. Owner shall

Treat as Confidential information all of Constructor's estimating systems and historical and parameter cost data disclosed to Owner in performing the Work. Each Party shall specify and mark confidential items as "Confidential." Confidentiality obligations do not supersede compulsion by Law, a governmental agency or authority, an order of a court of competent jurisdiction, or a validly issued subpoena. In such event, a Party shall promptly notify the other Party to permit that Party's legal objection.

ARTICLE 4 OWNER'S RESPONSIBILITIES

4.1 INFORMATION AND SERVICES Owner's responsibilities under this article shall be fulfilled with reasonable detail and in a timely manner.

4.2 FINANCIAL INFORMATION Before commencing the Work and thereafter, at the written request of Constructor, Owner shall provide Constructor with evidence of Project financing. Evidence of such financing shall be a condition precedent to Constructor's commencing or continuing the Work. Constructor shall be notified before any material change in Project financing.

4.3 WORKSITE INFORMATION To the extent Owner has obtained, or is required to obtain the following Worksite information, then Owner shall provide Constructor the following:

4.3.1 information describing the physical characteristics of the Worksite, including surveys, Worksite evaluations, legal descriptions, data or drawings depicting existing conditions, subsurface conditions, and environmental studies, reports, and investigations;

4.3.2 tests, inspections, and other reports dealing with environmental matters, Hazardous Material and other existing conditions, including structural, mechanical, and chemical tests, required by the Contract Documents or by Law;

4.3.3 the limits of Pollution Liability Insurance covering the Worksite held by Owner; and

4.3.4 any other information or services requested in writing by Constructor which are required for Constructor's performance of the Work and under Owner's control.

4.4 BUILDING PERMIT, FEES, AND APPROVALS Except for those permits and fees related to the Work which are the responsibility of Constructor, Owner shall secure and pay for all other permits, approvals, easements, assessments, and fees required for the development, construction, use, or occupancy of permanent structures or for permanent changes in existing facilities, including the building permit.

4.5 MECHANICS AND CONSTRUCTION LIEN INFORMATION Within seven (7) Days after receiving Constructor's written request, Owner shall provide Constructor with the information necessary to give notice of or enforce mechanics lien rights and, where applicable, stop notices. This information shall include Owner's real property interests in the Worksite and the record legal title.

4.6 CONTRACT DOCUMENTS Unless otherwise specified, Owner shall provide [_____] ([_____]) hard copies of the Contract Documents to Constructor without cost.

4.6.1 ELECTRONIC DOCUMENTS If Owner requires that Owner, Design Professional, and Constructor exchange documents and data in electronic or digital form, before any such exchange, Owner, Design Professional, and Constructor shall agree on and follow a written protocol governing all exchanges in ConsensusDocs 200.2 or a separate addenda, which, at a minimum, shall specify: (a) the definition of documents and data to be accepted in electronic or digital form or to be transmitted electronically or digitally; (b) management and coordination responsibilities; (c) necessary equipment, software, and services; (d) acceptable formats, transmission methods, and verification procedures; (e) methods for maintaining version control; (f) privacy and security requirements; and (g) storage and retrieval requirements. Except as otherwise agreed to by the Parties in writing, each Party shall bear its own costs as identified in the protocol. In the absence of a written protocol, use of documents and data in electronic or digital form shall be at the sole risk of the recipient.

4.7 OWNER'S REPRESENTATIVE Owner's Representative is [ ]. Owner's Representative shall be fully acquainted with the Project, and shall have authority to bind Owner in all matters requiring Owner's approval, authorization, or written notice. If Owner changes its Representative or its Representative's authority, Owner shall immediately notify Constructor in writing.

4.8 OWNER'S CUTTING AND PATCHING Cutting, patching, or altering the Work by Owner or Others shall be done with the prior written approval of Constructor, which approval shall not be unreasonably withheld.

4.9 OWNER'S RIGHT TO CLEAN UP In case of a dispute between Constructor and Others with regard to respective responsibilities for clean up at the Worksite, Owner may implement appropriate cleanup measures after two (2) Business Days' notice and allocate the cost among those responsible during the following pay period.

4.10 COST OF CORRECTING DAMAGED OR DESTROYED WORK With regard to damage or loss attributable to the acts or omissions of Owner or Others and not to Constructor, Owner shall either (a) promptly remedy the damage or loss (and assume affected warranty responsibilities), (b) accept the damage or loss, or (c) issue an Interim Directive or Change Order to remedy the damage or loss. If Constructor incurs costs or is delayed due to such loss or damage, Constructor may seek an equitable adjustment in the Contract Price or Contract Time under this Agreement.

ARTICLE 5 SUBCONTRACTS

5.1 AWARD OF SUBCONTRACTS AND OTHER CONTRACTS FOR PORTIONS OF THE WORK

5.1.1 Promptly after executing this Agreement, Constructor shall provide Owner and, if directed, Design Professional with a written list of the proposed Subcontractors and significant Suppliers. If Owner has a reasonable objection to any proposed Subcontractor or Supplier, Owner shall notify Constructor in writing. Failure to promptly object shall constitute acceptance.

5.1.2 If Owner has reasonably and promptly objected, Constructor shall not contract with the proposed Subcontractor or Supplier, and Constructor shall propose another acceptable Subcontractor or Supplier to Owner. An appropriate Change Order shall reflect any increase or decrease in the Contract Price or Contract Time because of the substitution.

5.2 BINDING OF SUBCONTRACTORS AND SUPPLIERS Constructor agrees to bind every Subcontractor and Supplier (and require each Subcontractor to so bind its subcontractors and significant suppliers) to the Contract Document's applicable provisions to that portion of the Work.

5.3 CONTINGENT ASSIGNMENT OF SUBCONTRACTS

If this Agreement is terminated, each subcontract and supply agreement shall be assigned by Constructor to Owner, subject to the prior rights of any surety, provided that: (a) this Agreement is terminated by Owner pursuant to §11.3 or §11.4; and

(b) Owner accepts such assignment after termination by notifying Constructor and Subcontractor or Constructor and Supplier in writing, and assumes all rights and obligations of Constructor pursuant to each subcontract or supply agreement.

5.3.1 If Owner accepts such an assignment, and the Work has been suspended for more than thirty (30) consecutive Days, following termination, if appropriate, Subcontractor's or Supplier's compensation shall be equitably adjusted as a result of the suspension.

ARTICLE 6 TIME

6.1 DATE OF COMMENCEMENT The Date of Commencement is the Agreement date in ARTICLE 1 unless otherwise set forth below: [ ]

6.1.1 SUBSTANTIAL/FINAL COMPLETION Substantial Completion of the Work shall be achieved in [ ] ([ ]) Days from the Date of Commencement. Unless otherwise specified in the Certificate of Substantial Completion, Constructor shall achieve Final Completion within [ ] ([ ]) Days after the date of Substantial Completion. The deadlines for Substantial and Final Completion are subject to adjustments as provided for in the Contract Documents.

6.1.2 Time is of the essence with regard to the obligations of the Contract Documents.

6.1.3 Unless instructed by Owner in writing, Constructor shall not knowingly commence the Work before the effective date of Constructor's required insurance.

6.2 SCHEDULE OF THE WORK

6.2.1 Before submitting its first application for payment, Constructor shall submit to Owner, and if directed, to Design Professional, a Schedule of the Work showing the dates on which Constructor plans to begin and complete various parts of the Work, including dates on which information and approvals are required from Owner. Except as otherwise directed by Owner, Constructor shall comply with the approved Schedule of the Work. Unless otherwise agreed, the Schedule of the Work shall be formatted in a detailed precedence-style critical path method that (a) provides a graphic representation of all activities and events, including float values that will affect the critical path of the Work, and (b) identifies dates that are critical to ensure timely and orderly completion of the Work. Constructor shall update the Schedule of the Work on a monthly basis or as mutually agreed by the Parties.

6.2.2 Owner may determine the sequence in which the Work shall be performed, provided it does not unreasonably interfere with the Schedule of the Work. Owner may require Constructor to make reasonable changes in the sequence at any time during the performance of the Work in order to facilitate the performance of work by Owner or Others. If Constructor consequently incurs costs or is delayed, or both, Constructor may seek an equitable adjustment in the Contract Price or Contract Time under ARTICLE 8.

6.3 DELAYS AND EXTENSIONS OF TIME

6.3.1 If Constructor is delayed at any time in the commencement or progress of the Work by any cause beyond the control of Constructor, Constructor shall be entitled to an equitable extension of the Contract Time. Examples of causes beyond the control of Constructor include, but are not limited to, the following: (a) acts or omissions of Owner, Design Professional, or Others; (b) changes in the Work or the sequencing of the Work ordered by Owner, or arising from decisions of Owner that impact the time of performance of the Work; (c) encountering Hazardous Materials, or concealed or unknown conditions; (d) delay authorized by Owner pending dispute resolution or suspension by Owner under §11.1; (e) transportation delays not reasonably foreseeable; (f) labor disputes not involving Constructor; (g) general labor disputes impacting the Project but not specifically related to the Worksite; (h) fire; (i) Terrorism; (j) epidemics; (k) adverse governmental actions; (l) unavoidable accidents or circumstances; (m) adverse weather conditions not reasonably anticipated. Constructor shall submit any requests for equitable extensions of Contract Time in accordance with ARTICLE 8.

6.3.2 In addition, if Constructor incurs additional costs as a result of a delay that is caused by items (a) through (d) immediately above, Constructor shall be entitled to an equitable adjustment in the Contract Price subject to §6.6.

6.3.3 NOTICE OF DELAYS If delays to the Work are encountered for any reason, Constructor shall provide prompt written notice to Owner of the cause of such delays after Constructor first recognizes the delay. The Parties each agree to take reasonable steps to mitigate the effect of such delays.

6.4 NOTICE OF DELAY CLAIMS If Constructor requests an equitable extension of the Contract Time or an equitable adjustment in the Contract Price as a result of a delay described in §6.3, Constructor shall give Owner written notice of the claim in accordance with §8.4. If Constructor causes delay in the completion of the Work, Owner shall be entitled to recover its additional costs subject to §6.6. Owner shall process any such claim against Constructor in accordance with ARTICLE 8.

6.5 LIQUIDATED DAMAGES

6.5.1 SUBSTANTIAL COMPLETION Liquidated damages based on Substantial Completion date ☐shall/ ☐shall not apply.

6.5.1.1 Owner will suffer damages which are difficult to determine and accurately specify if the Substantial Completion date, which may be amended by Change Order, is not attained. Constructor shall pay Owner [_____] dollars ($[_____]) as liquidated damages and not as a penalty for each Day that Substantial Completion extends beyond the Substantial Completion date. These liquidated damages are in lieu of all liability for all extra costs, losses, expenses, claims, penalties, and any other damages of any nature incurred by Owner resulting from not attaining the Substantial Completion date.

6.5.2 FINAL COMPLETION Liquidated damages based on the Final Completion date ☐ shall/ ☐ shall not apply.

6.5.3 Owner will suffer damages which are difficult to determine and accurately specify if the Final Completion date, as may be amended by subsequent Change Order, is not attained. Constructor shall pay Owner [_____] dollars ($[_____]) as liquidated damages and not as a penalty for each Day that Final Completion extends beyond the Final Completion date. These liquidated damages are in lieu of all liability for any extra costs, losses, expenses, claims, penalties, and any other damages of any nature incurred by Owner resulting from not attaining Final Completion date.

6.5.4 Other applicable liquidated damages shall be included as Agreement exhibit.

6.6 LIMITED MUTUAL WAIVER OF CONSEQUENTIAL DAMAGES Except for damages mutually agreed upon by the Parties as liquidated damages in §6.5 and excluding losses covered by insurance required by the Contract Documents, the Parties agree to waive all claims against each other for any consequential damages that may arise out of or relate to this Agreement, except for those specific items of damages excluded from this waiver as mutually agreed upon by the Parties and identified below. Owner agrees to waive damages, including but not limited to Owner's loss of use of the Project, any rental expenses incurred, loss of income, profit, or financing related to the Project, as well as the loss of business, loss of financing, loss of profits not related to this Project, loss of reputation, or insolvency. Constructor agrees to waive damages, including but not limited to loss of business, loss of financing, loss of profits not related to this Project, loss of bonding capacity, loss of reputation, or insolvency. The provisions of this section shall also apply to the termination of this Agreement and shall survive such termination. The following are excluded from this mutual waiver: [ ].

6.6.1 The Parties shall each require similar waivers in contracts with Subcontractors and Others retained for the Project.

ARTICLE 7 PRICE

7.1 LUMP SUM Lump sum is the Contract Price of [ ] dollars ($[ ]) subject to adjustment as provided in this Agreement.

7.2 ALLOWANCES

7.2.1 All allowances stated in the Contract Documents shall be included in the Contract Price. While Owner may direct the amounts of, and the particular Suppliers or Subcontractors to supply specific allowance items, if Constructor reasonably objects to a Supplier or Subcontractor, it shall not be required to contract with them. Owner shall select allowance items in a timely manner so as not to delay the Work.

7.2.2 Allowances shall include the costs of materials, supplies, and equipment delivered to the Worksite, less applicable trade discounts and including requisite taxes, unloading and handling at the Worksite, and labor and installation, unless specifically stated otherwise. Constructor's Overhead and profit for the allowances is included in the Contract Price, not in the allowances. If incurred costs are greater or less than the allowances, a Party may seek an equitable adjustment in the Contract Price or Contract Time under ARTICLE 8.

ARTICLE 8 CHANGES

Changes in the Work that are within the general scope of this Agreement shall be accomplished, without invalidating this Agreement, by Change Order and Interim Directive.

8.1 CHANGE ORDER

8.1.1 Constructor may request or Owner may order changes in the Work or the timing or sequencing of the Work that impact the Contract Price or the Contract Time. All such changes in the Work that affect Contract Time or Contract Price shall be formalized in a Change Order and processed in accordance with this article.

8.1.2 For changes in the Work, the Parties shall negotiate an appropriate adjustment to the Contract Price or the Contract Time in good faith and conclude negotiations as expeditiously as possible. Acceptance of the Change Order and any adjustment in the Contract Price or Contract Time shall not be unreasonably withheld.

8.1.3 NO OBLIGATION TO PERFORM Constructor shall not be obligated to perform changes in the Work without a Change Order or Interim Directive.

8.2 INTERIM DIRECTIVES

8.2.1 Owner may issue an Interim Directive directing a change in the Work before agreeing on an adjustment to Contract Price or Contract Time, or directing Constructor to perform Work that Owner believes is not a change. If the Parties disagree that the Interim Directed work is within the scope of the Work, Constructor shall perform the disputed Work and furnish Owner with an estimate of the costs to perform the disputed work in accordance with Owner's interpretations.

8.2.2 The Parties shall negotiate expeditiously and in good faith for appropriate adjustments, as applicable, to the Contract Price or the Contract Time arising out of an Interim Directive. As the directed Work is performed, Constructor shall submit its costs for such Work with its application for payment beginning with the next application for payment within thirty (30) Days of the issuance of the Interim Directive. If there is a dispute as to the cost to Owner, Owner shall pay Constructor fifty percent (50%) of its actual (incurred or committed) cost to perform such Work. In such event, the Parties reserve their rights as to the disputed amount, subject to the requirements of ARTICLE 12. Owner's payment does not prejudice its right to be reimbursed should it be determined that the disputed work was within the scope of the Work. Constructor's receipt of payment for the disputed work does not prejudice its right to receive full payment for the disputed work should it be determined that the disputed work is not within the scope of the Work. Undisputed amounts may be included in applications for payment and shall be paid by Owner in accordance with this Agreement.

8.2.3 When the Parties agree upon the adjustment in the Contract Price or the Contract Time, for a change in the Work directed by an Interim Directive, such agreement shall be the subject of a Change Order. The Change Order shall include all outstanding Interim Directives on which The Parties have reached agreement on Contract Price or Contract Time issued since the last Change Order.

8.3 DETERMINATION OF COST

8.3.1 An increase or decrease in the Contract Price resulting from a change in the Work shall be determined by one or more of the following methods:

8.3.2 unit prices set forth in this Agreement or as subsequently agreed;

8.3.3 a mutually accepted, itemized lump sum; or

8.3.4 COST OF THE WORK Cost of the Work as defined by this §8.3.4 plus [   ]% for Overhead and [   ]% for profit. "Cost of the Work" shall include the following costs reasonably incurred to perform a change in the Work:

8.3.4.1 Labor wages directly employed by Constructor performing the Work;

8.3.4.2 Salaries of Constructor's employees when stationed at the field office to the extent necessary to complete the applicable Work, employees engaged on the road expediting the production or transportation of material and equipment, and supervisory employees from the principal or branch office as mutually agreed by the Parties in writing;

8.3.4.3 Cost of applicable employee benefits and taxes, including but not limited to, workers' compensation, unemployment compensation, social security, health, welfare, retirement, and other fringe benefits as required by law, labor agreements, or paid under Constructor's standard personnel policy, insofar as such costs are paid to employees of Constructor who are included in the Cost of the Work in §8.3.4.1 and §8.3.4.2;

8.3.4.4 Reasonable transportation, travel, and hotel expenses of Constructor's personnel incurred in connection with the Work;

8.3.4.5 Cost of all materials, supplies, and equipment incorporated in the Work, including costs of inspection and testing if not provided by Owner, transportation, storage, and handling;

8.3.4.6 Payments made by Constructor to Subcontractors for performed Work;

8.3.4.7 Cost, including transportation and maintenance of all materials, supplies, equipment, temporary facilities, and hand tools not owned by the workers that are used or consumed in the performance of the Work, less salvage value or residual value; and cost less salvage value of such items used, but not consumed that remain the property of Constructor;

8.3.4.8 Rental charges of all necessary machinery and equipment, exclusive of hand tools owned by workers, used at the Worksite, whether rented from Constructor or others, including installation, repair and replacement, dismantling, removal, maintenance, transportation, and delivery costs. Rental from unrelated third parties shall be reimbursed at actual cost. Rentals from Constructor or its affiliates, subsidiaries, or related parties shall be reimbursed at the prevailing rates in the locality of the Worksite up to eighty-five percent (85%) of the value of the piece of equipment;

8.3.4.9 Cost of the premiums for all insurance and surety bonds which Constructor is required to procure or deems necessary, and approved by Owner including any additional premium incurred as a result of any increase in the cost of the Work;

8.3.4.10 Sales, use, gross receipts, or other taxes, tariffs, or duties related to the Work for which Constructor is liable;

8.3.4.11 Permits, fees, licenses, tests, and royalties;

8.3.4.12 Losses, expenses, or damages to the extent not compensated by insurance or otherwise, and the cost of corrective work, provided that such did not arise from Constructor's negligence.

8.3.4.13 Water, power, and fuel costs necessary for the changed Work;

8.3.4.14 Cost of removal of all nonhazardous substances, debris, and waste materials;

8.3.4.15 Costs directly incurred to perform a change in the Work which are reasonably inferable from the Contract Documents for the changed Work;

8.3.4.16 DISCOUNTS All discounts for prompt payment shall accrue to Owner to the extent such payments are made directly by Owner. To the extent payments are made with funds of Constructor, all cash discounts shall accrue to Constructor. All trade discounts, rebates, and refunds, and all returns from sale of surplus materials and equipment, shall be credited to the Cost of the Work;

8.3.4.17 COST REPORTING Constructor shall maintain complete and current records that comply with generally accepted accounting principles and calculate the Cost of Work. Owner shall be afforded access to Constructor's records, books, correspondence, instructions, drawings, receipts, vouchers, memoranda, and similar data relating to requested payment for Cost of the Work. Constructor shall preserve all such records for a period of three years after the final payment or longer where required by Law;

8.3.4.18 COST AND SCHEDULE ESTIMATES Constructor shall use reasonable skill and judgment in the preparation of a cost estimate or schedule for a change to the Work, but does not warrant or guarantee their accuracy.

8.3.4.19 Cost of the Work pursuant to §8.3.4 is determined net of savings from the change. Constructor's Overhead and profit shall be added to any net increase in Cost of the Work. No Overhead and profit shall be applied to any net decrease in the Cost of the Work that is less than ten (10) percent of the Contract Price. Overhead and profit shall be applied to any net decrease of ten (10) percent or more. Constructor shall maintain a documented, itemized accounting evidencing expenses and savings.

8.3.5 If unit prices are set forth in the Contract Documents or the Parties subsequently agree, but the character or quantity of such unit items as originally contemplated is so different in a proposed Change Order that the original unit prices will cause substantial inequity to either Party, such unit prices shall be equitably adjusted.

8.4 CHANGES NOTICE Except as provided in §6.3.2 and §6.4 for any claim for an increase in the Contract Price or the Contract Time, Constructor shall give Owner written notice of the claim within fourteen (14) Days after the occurrence giving rise to the claim or within fourteen (14) Days after Constructor first recognizes the condition giving rise to the claim, whichever is later. Except in an emergency, notice shall be given before proceeding with the Work. Thereafter, Constructor shall submit written documentation of its claim, including appropriate supporting documentation, within twenty-one (21) Days after giving notice, unless the Parties mutually agree upon a longer period of time. Owner shall respond in writing denying or approving Constructor's claim no later than fourteen (14) Days after receipt of Constructor's claim. Owner's failure to so respond shall be deemed a denial of the claim. Any change in the Contract Price or the Contract Time resulting from such claim shall be authorized by Change Order.

8.5 INCIDENTAL CHANGES Owner may direct Constructor to perform incidental changes in the Work, upon concurrence with Constructor that such changes do not involve adjustments in the Contract Price or Contract Time. Incidental changes shall be consistent with the scope and intent of the Contract Documents. Owner shall initiate an incidental change in the Work by issuing an Interim Directive.

ARTICLE 9 PAYMENT

9.1 SCHEDULE OF VALUES Within twenty-one (21) Days from the date of execution of this Agreement, Constructor shall prepare and submit to Owner and, if directed, Design Professional, a schedule of values apportioned to the various divisions or phases of the Work. Each line item contained in the schedule of values shall be assigned a value such that the total of all items shall equal the Contract Price.

9.2 PROGRESS PAYMENTS

9.2.1 APPLICATIONS Constructor shall submit to Owner, and if directed, Design Professional a monthly application for payment no later than the [_____] Day of the calendar month for the preceding calendar month. Constructor's applications for payment shall be itemized and supported by Constructor's schedule of values based on a percentage of completion and shall include any other substantiating data as required by this Agreement. Applications for payment shall include payment requests on account of properly authorized Change Orders or Interim Directives. Owner shall pay the amount due on a payment application, no later than fifteen (15) Days after accepting such application. Owner may deduct from any progress payment amounts that may be retained pursuant to §9.2.4.

9.2.2 STORED MATERIALS AND EQUIPMENT Unless otherwise provided in the Contract Documents, applications for payment may include materials and equipment not yet incorporated into the Work but delivered to and suitably stored onsite or offsite including applicable insurance, storage, and costs incurred transporting the materials to an offsite storage facility. Approval of payment applications for stored materials and equipment stored offsite shall be conditioned on a submission by Constructor of bills of sale and proof of required insurance, or such other documentation satisfactory to Owner to establish the proper valuation of the stored materials and equipment, Owner's title to such materials and equipment, and to otherwise protect Owner's interests therein, including transportation to the Worksite.

9.2.3 LIEN WAIVERS AND LIENS

9.2.3.1 PARTIAL LIEN WAIVERS AND AFFIDAVITS If required by Owner as a prerequisite for payment, Constructor shall provide a partial lien and claim waiver in the amount of the application for payment and affidavits from its Subcontractors and Suppliers for the completed Work. Such waivers shall be conditional upon payment. Constructor shall not be required to sign an unconditional waiver of lien or claim, before receiving payment or in an amount in excess of what it has been paid.

9.2.3.2 REMOVING LIENS If Owner has made payments in the time required by this ARTICLE 9, Constructor shall, within thirty (30) Days after filing, remove any liens filed against the premises or public improvement fund by any party or parties performing labor or services or supplying materials in connection with the Work. If Constructor fails to take such action on a lien, Owner may cause the lien to be removed at Constructor's expense, including bond costs and reasonable attorneys' fees. This subsection shall not apply if there is a dispute pursuant to ARTICLE 12 relating to the subject matter of the lien.

9.2.4 RETAINAGE From each progress payment made before Substantial Completion, Owner may retain [____] percent ([____]%) of the amount otherwise due after deduction of any amounts as provided in §9.3, provided such percentage doesn't exceed the Law. If Owner chooses to use this retainage provision:

9.2.4.1 after the Work is fifty percent (50%) complete, Owner shall withhold no additional retainage and shall pay Constructor the full amount due on account of subsequent progress payments;

9.2.4.2 Owner may, in its sole discretion, reduce the amount to be retained at any time;

9.2.4.3 Owner may release retainage on that portion of the Work a Subcontractor has completed in whole or in part, and which Owner has accepted. In lieu of retainage, Constructor may furnish a retention bond or other security interest acceptable to Owner, to be held by Owner.

9.3 ADJUSTMENT OF CONSTRUCTOR'S PAYMENT APPLICATION Owner may adjust or reject a payment application or nullify a previously approved payment application, in whole or in part, as may reasonably be necessary to protect Owner from loss or damage based upon the following, to the extent that Constructor is responsible under this Agreement:

9.3.1 Constructor's repeated failure to perform the Work as required by the Contract Documents;

9.3.2 Except as accepted by the insurer providing Builder's Risk or other property insurance covering the project, loss or damage arising out of or relating to this Agreement and caused by Constructor to Owner or to others to whom Owner may be liable;

9.3.3 Constructor's failure to properly pay either Subcontractors or Suppliers following receipt of payment from Owner for that portion of the Work or for supplies, provided that Owner is making payments to Constructor in accordance with this Agreement;

9.3.4 rejected or Defective Work not corrected in a timely fashion;

9.3.5 reasonable evidence of delay in performance of the Work such that the Work will not be completed within the Contract Time;

9.3.6 reasonable evidence demonstrating that the unpaid balance of the Contract Price is insufficient to fund the cost to complete the Work; and

9.3.7 uninsured third-party claims involving Constructor, or reasonable evidence demonstrating that third-party claims are likely to be filed unless and until Constructor furnishes Owner with adequate security in the form of a surety bond, letter of credit, or other collateral or commitment sufficient to discharge such claims if established.

No later than seven (7) Days after receipt of an application for payment, Owner shall give written notice to Constructor, at the time of disapproving or nullifying all or part of an application for payment, stating its specific reasons for such disapproval or nullification, and the remedial actions to be taken by Constructor in order to receive payment. When the above reasons for disapproving or nullifying an application for payment are removed, payment will be promptly made for the amount previously withheld.

9.4 ACCEPTANCE OF WORK Neither Owner's payment of progress payments nor its partial or full use or occupancy of the Project constitutes acceptance of Work not complying with the Contract Documents.

9.5 PAYMENT DELAY If for any reason not the fault of Constructor, Constructor does not receive a progress payment from Owner within seven (7) Days after the time such payment is due, then Constructor, upon giving seven (7) Days' written notice to Owner, and without prejudice to and in addition to any other legal remedies, may stop Work until payment of the full amount owing to Constructor has been received, including interest for late payment. If Constructor incurs costs or is delayed resulting from shutdown, delay, and start-up, Constructor may seek an equitable adjustment in the Contract Price or Contract Time under ARTICLE 8.

9.6 SUBSTANTIAL COMPLETION

9.6.1 Constructor shall notify Owner and, if directed, Design Professional, when it considers Substantial Completion of the Work or a designated portion to have been achieved. Owner, with the assistance of its Design Professional, shall promptly conduct an inspection to determine whether the Work or designated portion can be occupied or used for its intended use by Owner without excessive interference in completing any remaining unfinished Work. If Owner determines that the Work or designated portion has not reached Substantial Completion, Owner shall promptly compile a list of items to be completed or corrected so Owner may occupy or use the Work or designated portion for its intended use. Constructor shall promptly complete all items on the list.

9.6.2 When Substantial Completion of the Work or a designated portion is achieved, Constructor shall prepare a Certificate of Substantial Completion establishing the date of Substantial Completion and the respective responsibilities of each Party for interim items such as security, maintenance, utilities, insurance, and damage to the Work. In the absence of a clear delineation of responsibilities, Owner shall assume all responsibilities for items such as security, maintenance, utilities, insurance, and damage to the Work. The Certificate of Substantial Completion shall also list any items to be completed or corrected, and establish the time for their completion or correction. The Certificate of Substantial Completion shall be submitted by Constructor to Owner and, if directed, to Design Professional for written acceptance of responsibilities assigned in the Certificate of Substantial Completion.

9.6.3 Unless otherwise provided in the Certificate of Substantial Completion, warranties required by the Contract Documents shall commence on the date of Substantial Completion of the Work or a designated portion.

9.6.4 Upon Owner's written acceptance of the Certificate of Substantial Completion, Owner shall pay to Constructor the remaining retainage held by Owner for the Work described in the Certificate of Substantial Completion, less a sum equal to one hundred fifty percent (150%) of the estimated cost of completing or correcting remaining items on that part of the Work, as agreed to by the Parties as necessary to achieve Final Completion. Uncompleted items shall be completed by Constructor in a mutually agreed upon timeframe. Owner shall pay Constructor monthly the amount retained for unfinished items as each item is completed.

9.7 PARTIAL OCCUPANCY OR USE

9.7.1 Owner may occupy or use completed or partially completed portions of the Work when (a) the portion of the Work is designated in a Certificate of Substantial Completion, (b) appropriate insurer(s) consent to the occupancy or use, and (c) appropriate public authorities authorize the occupancy or use. Such partial occupancy or use shall constitute Substantial Completion of that portion of the Work.

9.8 FINAL COMPLETION AND FINAL PAYMENT

9.8.1 Upon notification from Constructor that the Work is complete and ready for final inspection and acceptance, Owner with the assistance of its Design Professional shall promptly conduct an inspection to determine if the Work has been completed and is acceptable under the Contract Documents.

9.8.2 When Final Completion has been achieved, Constructor shall prepare for Owner's written acceptance a final application for payment stating that to the best of Constructor's knowledge, and based on Owner's inspections, the Work has reached Final Completion in accordance with the Contract Documents.

9.8.3 Final payment of the balance of the Contract Price shall be made to Constructor within twenty (20) Days after Constructor has submitted a complete and accurate application for final payment, including submissions required under §9.8.4, and a Certificate of Final Completion has been executed by the Parties.

9.8.4 Final payment is due upon Constructor's submission to Owner of the following:

9.8.4.1 An affidavit declaring any indebtedness connected with the Work to have been paid, satisfied, or to be paid with the proceeds of final payment, so as not to encumber Owner's property;

9.8.4.2 As-built drawings, manuals, copies of warranties, and all other close-out documents required by the Contract Documents;

9.8.4.3 Release of any liens, conditioned on final payment being received;

9.8.4.4 Consent of any surety; and

9.8.4.5 Any outstanding known and unreported accidents or injuries experienced by Constructor or its Subcontractors at the Worksite.

9.8.5 If, after Substantial Completion of the Work, the Final Completion of a portion of the Work is materially delayed through no fault of Constructor, Owner shall pay the balance due for any portion of the Work fully completed and accepted. If the remaining contract balance for Work not fully completed and accepted is less than the retained amount before payment, Constructor shall submit to Owner, and if directed, Design Professional, the written consent of any surety to payment of the balance due for portions of the Work that are fully completed and accepted. Such payment shall not constitute a waiver of claims, but otherwise shall be governed by these final payment provisions.

9.8.6 OWNER'S CLAIMS RESERVATION Owner's claims not reserved in writing with final payment are waived except for claims relating to liens or similar encumbrances, warranties, Defective Work, and latent defects.

9.8.7 CONSTRUCTOR ACCEPTANCE OF FINAL PAYMENT Unless Constructor provides written identification of unsettled claims with an application for final payment, its acceptance of final payment constitutes a waiver of such claims.

9.9 LATE PAYMENT Payments due but unpaid shall bear interest from the date payment is due at the statutory rate at the place of the Project.

ARTICLE 10 INDEMNITY, INSURANCE, AND BONDS

10.1 INDEMNITY

10.1.1 To the fullest extent permitted by law, Constructor shall indemnify and hold harmless Owner, Owner's officers, directors, members, consultants, agents, and employees, Design Professional, and Others (the Indemnitees) from all claims for bodily injury and property damage, other than to the Work itself and other property insured, including reasonable attorneys' fees, costs and expenses, that may arise from the performance of the Work, but only to the extent caused by the negligent or intentionally wrongful acts or omissions of Constructor, Subcontractors, Suppliers, Subsubcontractors, or anyone employed directly or indirectly by any of them or by anyone for whose acts any of them may be liable. Constructor shall be entitled to reimbursement of any defense costs paid above Constructor's percentage of liability for the underlying claim to the extent provided for by §10.1.2.

10.1.2 To the fullest extent permitted by law, Owner shall indemnify and hold harmless Constructor, its officers, directors, members, consultants, agents, and employees, Subcontractors, Suppliers, or anyone employed directly or indirectly by any of them or anyone for whose acts any of them may be liable from all claims for bodily injury and property damage, other than property insured, including reasonable attorneys' fees, costs, and expenses, that may arise from the performance of work by Owner, Design Professional, or Others, but only to the extent caused by the negligent or intentionally wrongful acts or omissions of Owner, Design Professional, or Others. Owner shall be entitled to reimbursement of any defense costs paid above Owner's percentage of liability for the underlying claim to the extent provided for by §10.1.1.

10.1.3 NO LIMITATION ON LIABILITY In any and all claims against the Indemnitees by any employee of Constructor, anyone directly or indirectly employed by Constructor or anyone for whose acts Constructor may be liable, the indemnification obligation shall not be limited in any way by any limitation on the amount or type of damages, compensation, or benefits payable by or for Constructor under workers' compensation acts, disability benefit acts, or other employment benefit acts.

10.2 INSURANCE

10.2.1 Before starting the Work and as a condition precedent to payment, Constructor shall procure and maintain in force Workers' Compensation Insurance, Employers' Liability Insurance, Business Automobile Liability Insurance, and Commercial General Liability Insurance (CGL). The CGL policy shall include coverage for liability arising from premises, operations, independent contractors, products-completed operations, personal injury and advertising injury, contractual liability, and broad form property damage. Constructor shall maintain completed operations liability insurance for one year after Substantial Completion, or as required by the Contract Documents, whichever is longer. Constructor's Employers' Liability, Business Automobile Liability, and CGL policies, shall be written with at least the following limits of liability:

10.2.1.1 Employers' Liability Insurance
(a) $[ ] bodily injury by accident per accident.
(b) $[ ] bodily injury by disease policy limit.
(c) $[ ] bodily injury by disease per employee.

10.2.1.2 Business Automobile Liability Insurance $[ ] per accident.

10.2.1.3 Commercial General Liability Insurance
(a) $[ ] per occurrence.
(b) $[ ] general aggregate.
(c) $[ ] products/completed operations aggregate.
(d) $[ ] personal and advertising injury limit.

10.2.2 Employers' Liability, Business Automobile Liability, and CGL coverage required under §10.2.1 may be provided by a single policy for the full limits required or by a combination of underlying policies with the balance provided by excess or umbrella liability policies.

10.2.3 Constructor shall maintain in effect all insurance coverage required under §10.2.1 with insurance companies lawfully authorized to do business in the jurisdiction in which the Project is located. If Constructor fails to obtain or maintain any insurance coverage required under this Agreement, Owner may purchase such coverage and charge the expense to Constructor, or terminate this Agreement.

10.2.4 To the extent commercially available to Constructor from its current insurance company, insurance policies required under §10.2.1 shall contain a provision that the insurance company or its designee must give Owner written notice transmitted in paper or electronic format: (a) 30 Days before coverage is nonrenewed by the insurance company and (b) within 10 Business Days after cancelation of coverage by the insurance company. Before commencing the Work and upon renewal or replacement of the insurance policies, Constructor shall furnish Owner with certificates of insurance until one year after Substantial Completion or longer if required by the Contract Documents. In addition, if any insurance policy required under §10.2.1 is not to be immediately replaced without lapse in coverage when it expires, exhausts its limits, or is to be cancelled, Constructor shall give Owner prompt written notice upon actual or constructive knowledge of such condition.

10.3 PROPERTY INSURANCE

10.3.1 Unless otherwise directed in writing by Owner, before starting the Work, Constructor shall obtain and maintain a Builder's Risk Policy upon the entire Project for the full cost of replacement at the time of loss, including existing structures. This insurance shall also: (a) name Constructor, Subcontractors, Subsubcontractors, Suppliers, and Design Professional as insureds; (b) be written in such form as to cover all risks of physical loss except those specifically excluded by the policy; and (c) insure at least against and not exclude:

10.3.1.1 the perils of fire, lightning, explosion, windstorm, hail, smoke, aircraft (except aircraft, including helicopter, operated by or on behalf of the Contractor) and vehicles, riot and civil commotion, theft, vandalism, malicious mischief, debris removal, flood, earthquake, earth movement, water damage, wind damage, testing if applicable, collapse however caused;

10.3.1.2 damage resulting from defective design, workmanship, or material;

10.3.1.3 coverage extension for damage to existing buildings, plant, or other structures at the Worksite, when the Project is contained within or attached to such existing buildings, plant, or structures. Coverage shall be to the extent loss or damage arises out of Constructor's activities or operations at the Project;

10.3.1.4 equipment breakdown, including mechanical breakdown, electrical injury to electrical devices, explosion of steam equipment, and damage to steam equipment caused by a condition within the equipment;

10.3.1.5 testing coverage for running newly installed machinery and equipment at or beyond the specified limits of their capacity to determine whether they are fit for their intended use; and

10.3.1.6 physical loss resulting from Terrorism.

10.3.2 The Party that is the primary cause of a Builder's Risk Policy claim shall be responsible for any deductible amounts or coinsurance payments. If no Party is the primary cause of a claim, then the Party obtaining and maintaining the Builder's Risk Policy pursuant to §10.3.1 shall be responsible for the deductible amounts or coinsurance payments. This policy shall provide for a waiver of subrogation. This insurance shall remain in effect until final payment has been made or until no person or entity other than Owner has an insurable interest in the property to be covered by this insurance, whichever is sooner. Partial occupancy or use of the Work shall not commence until Constructor has secured the consent of the insurance company or companies providing the coverage required in this subsection. Before commencing the Work, Constructor shall provide a copy of the property policy or policies obtained in compliance with §10.3.1

10.3.3 If Owner elects to purchase the property insurance required by this Agreement, including all of the same coverages and deductibles for the same duration specified in §10.3.1, then Owner shall give written notice to Constructor and the Design Professional before the Work is commenced and provide a copy of the property policy or policies obtained in compliance with §10.3.1. Owner may then provide insurance to protect its interests and the interests of the Constructor, Subcontractors, Suppliers, and Subsubcontractors. The cost of this insurance shall be paid by Owner in a Change Order. If Owner gives written notice of its intent to purchase property insurance required by this Agreement and fails to purchase or maintain such insurance, Owner shall be responsible for costs reasonably attributed to such failure.

10.3.4 The Parties each waive all rights against each other and their respective employees, agents, contractors, subcontractors, suppliers, subsubcontractors, and design professionals for damages caused by risks covered by the property insurance except such rights as they may have to the proceeds of the insurance.

10.3.5 To the extent of the limits of Constructor's CGL specified in §10.2.1 or [______] dollars ($[______]), whichever is more, Constructor shall indemnify and hold harmless Owner against any and all liability, claims, demands, damages, losses, and expenses, including attorneys' fees, in connection with or arising out of any damage or alleged damage to any of Owner's existing adjacent property that may arise from the performance of the Work, to the extent caused by the negligent or intentionally wrongful acts or omissions of Constructor, Subcontractor, Supplier, Subsubcontractor, or anyone employed directly or indirectly by any of them or by anyone for whose acts any of them may be liable.

10.3.6 RISK OF LOSS Except to the extent a loss is covered by applicable insurance, risk of loss from damage to the Work shall be upon the Party obtaining and maintaining the Builder's Risk Policy pursuant to section 10.3.1 until the Date of Final Completion.

10.3.7 POLLUTION LIABILITY INSURANCE Constructor ☐is/ ☐is not required to maintain pollution liability insurance. Unless indicated affirmatively, the obligation to procure such insurance is not triggered.

10.3.7.1 If applicable: in the following amounts: [ ] per occurrence, and shall apply for [ ] year(s) after Final Completion. The policy shall cover Constructor's liability during construction, removal, storage, encapsulation, transport, and disposal of hazardous waste and contaminated soil, and asbestos abatement. The policy shall include coverage for on-site and off-site bodily injury and loss of damage to, or loss of use of property, directly or indirectly arising out of the discharge, dispersal, release, or escape of smoke, vapors, soot, fumes, acids, alkalis, toxic chemicals, liquids or gas, waste materials, or other irritants, contaminants, or pollutants into or upon the land, the atmosphere or any water body, whether it be gradual or sudden and accidental. The policy shall not have exclusions for mold or asbestos.

10.4 ADDITIONAL GENERAL LIABILITY COVERAGE Owner ☐shall/ ☐shall not require Constructor to purchase and maintain additional liability coverage. If required, Constructor shall provide:

10.4.1 ☐ Additional Insured. Owner shall be named as an additional insured on Constructor's CGL specified for on-going operations and completed operations, excess/umbrella liability, commercial automobile liability, and any required pollution liability, but only with respect to liability for bodily injury, property damage, or personal and advertising injury to the extent caused by the negligent acts or omissions of Constructor, or those acting on Constructor's behalf, in the performance of Constructor's Work for Owner at the Worksite. The insurance (both primary and excess) of the Constructor and its Subcontractors shall be primary and non-contributory to any insurance available to the Additional Insureds.

10.4.2 ☐ OCP. Constructor shall provide an Owners' and Contractors' Protective Liability Insurance ("OCP") policy with limits equal to the limits on CGL specified, or limits as otherwise required by Owner.

Any documented additional cost in the form of a surcharge associated with procuring the additional general liability coverage in accordance with this subsection shall be paid by Owner directly or the costs may be reimbursed by Owner to Constructor by increasing the Contract Price to correspond to the actual cost required to purchase and maintain the coverage. Before commencing the Work, Constructor shall provide either a copy of the OCP policy, or a certificate and endorsement evidencing that Owner has been named as an additional insured, as applicable.

10.5 ROYALTIES, PATENTS, AND COPYRIGHTS Constructor shall pay all royalties and license fees which may be due on the inclusion of any patented or copyrighted materials, methods, or systems selected by Constructor and incorporated in the Work. Constructor shall defend, indemnify, and hold Owner harmless from all suits or claims for infringement of any patent rights or copyrights arising out of such selection. Owner agrees to defend, indemnify, and hold Constructor harmless from any suits or claims of infringement of any patent rights or copyrights arising out of any patented or copyrighted materials, methods, or systems specified by Owner or Design Professional.

10.6 BONDS Performance and Payments bonds ☐are/ ☐are not required. Such bonds shall be issued by a surety admitted in the state in which the Project is located and must be acceptable to Owner. Owner's acceptance shall not be withheld without reasonable cause. The penal sum of the bonds shall each be one hundred percent (100%) of the original Contract Price. Constructor shall endeavor to keep its surety advised of changes potentially impacting the Contract Time and Contract Price, though Constructor shall require that its surety waives any requirement to be notified of any alteration or extension of time.

10.7 PROFESSIONAL LIABILITY INSURANCE To the extent Constructor is required to procure design services in accordance with §3.15, Constructor shall require its design professional to obtain professional liability insurance for claims arising from the negligent performance of design services under this Agreement, with a company reasonably satisfactory to Owner, including coverage for all professional liability caused by any consultants to Constructor's design professional, written for not less than [_____] dollars ($[\_\_\_\_\_]) per claim and in the aggregate with the deductible not to exceed [\_\_\_\_\_] dollars ($[_____]). The Professional Liability Insurance shall contain a retroactive date providing prior acts coverage sufficient to cover all Services performed by the Constructor's design professional for this Project. Coverage shall be continued in effect for [_____] ([_____]) year(s) following Substantial Completion. Constructor's design professional shall pay the self-insured retention and deductible. The combined total deductible and self-insured retention maximum shall be [_____] dollars ($[_____]).

ARTICLE 11 SUSPENSION, NOTICE TO CURE, AND TERMINATION

11.1 SUSPENSION BY OWNER FOR CONVENIENCE

11.1.1 OWNER SUSPENSION Should Owner order Constructor in writing to suspend, delay, or interrupt the performance of the Work for the convenience of Owner and not due to any act or omission of Constructor or any person or entity for whose acts or omissions Constructor may be liable, then Constructor shall immediately suspend, delay, or interrupt that portion of the Work for the time period ordered by Owner.

11.1.2 Any action taken by Owner that is permitted by any other provision of the Contract Documents and that results in a suspension of part or all of the Work does not constitute a suspension of Work under this section.

11.2 NOTICE TO CURE A DEFAULT If Constructor persistently fails to supply enough qualified workers, proper materials, or equipment to maintain the approved Schedule of the Work, or fails to make prompt payment to its workers, Subcontractors, or Suppliers, disregards a Law or orders of any public authority having jurisdiction, or is otherwise guilty of a material breach of a provision of this Agreement, Constructor may be deemed in default.

11.2.1 After receiving Owner's written notice, if Constructor fails within seven (7) Days after receipt of written notice from Owner to commence and continue satisfactory correction of such default with diligence and promptness, then Owner shall give Constructor a second notice to correct the default within three (3) Business Days after receipt. The second notice to Constructor, and if applicable, the surety, may include, that Owner intends to terminate this Agreement for default absent appropriate corrective action.

11.2.2 If Constructor fails to promptly commence and continue satisfactory correction of the default following receipt of such second notice, Owner without prejudice to any other rights or remedies may: (a) take possession of the Worksite; (b) complete the Work utilizing reasonable means; (c) withhold payment due to Constructor; and (d) as Owner deems necessary, supply workers and materials, equipment, and other facilities for the satisfactory correction of the default, and charge Constructor the costs and expenses, including reasonable Overhead, profit, and attorneys' fees.

11.2.3 In the event of an emergency affecting the safety of persons or property, Owner may immediately commence and continue satisfactory correction of such default without first giving written notice to Constructor, but shall give Constructor prompt written notice.

11.3 OWNER'S RIGHT TO TERMINATE FOR DEFAULT

11.3.1 TERMINATION BY OWNER FOR DEFAULT Upon expiration of the second notice period to cure pursuant to §11.2 and absent appropriate corrective action, Owner may terminate this Agreement by written notice. Termination for default is in addition to any other remedies available to Owner under §11.2. If Owner's costs arising out of Constructor's failure to cure, including the costs of completing the Work and reasonable attorneys' fees, exceed the unpaid Contract Price, Constructor shall be liable to Owner for such excess costs. If Owner's costs are less than the unpaid Contract Price, Owner shall pay the difference to Constructor. If Owner exercises its rights under this section, upon the request of Constructor, Owner shall furnish to Constructor a detailed accounting of the costs incurred by Owner.

11.3.2 USE OF CONSTRUCTOR'S MATERIALS, SUPPLIES, AND EQUIPMENT If Owner or Others perform work under §11.3, Owner shall have the right to take and use any materials and supplies for which Owner has paid and located at the Worksite for the purpose of completing any remaining Work. Owner and others performing work under §11.3 shall also have the right to use construction tools and equipment located on the Worksite and belonging to the Constructor or Subsubcontractors for the purpose of completing the remaining Work, but only after Constructor's written consent. If Owner uses Constructor's construction tools and equipment in accordance with this subsection, then Owner shall indemnify and hold harmless Constructor and applicable Subcontractors and the agents, officers, directors, and employees of each of them, from and against all claims, damages, losses, costs, and expenses, including but not limited to reasonable attorneys' fees, costs, and expenses incurred in connection with Owner's use of Constructor's or applicable subcontractor's construction tools and equipment. Immediately upon completion of the Work, any remaining materials, supplies, or equipment not consumed or incorporated in the Work shall be returned to Constructor in substantially the same condition as when they were taken, reasonable wear and tear excepted.

11.3.3 If Constructor files a petition under the Bankruptcy Code, this Agreement shall terminate if: (a) Constructor or Constructor's trustee rejects the Agreement; (b) a default occurred and Constructor is unable to give adequate assurance of required performance; or (c) Constructor is otherwise unable to comply with the requirements for assuming this Agreement under the applicable provisions of the Bankruptcy Code.

11.3.4 Owner shall make reasonable efforts to mitigate damages arising from Constructor default, and shall promptly invoice Constructor for all amounts due pursuant to §11.2 and §11.3.

11.4 TERMINATION BY OWNER FOR CONVENIENCE

11.4.1 Upon Constructor's receipt of Owner's written notice from Owner, Owner may, without cause, terminate this Agreement. Constructor shall immediately stop the Work, follow Owner's instructions regarding shutdown and termination procedures, and strive to minimize any further costs.

11.4.2 If Owner terminates this Agreement for convenience, Constructor shall be paid: (a) for the Work performed to date including Overhead and profit; (b) for all demobilization costs and costs incurred resulting from termination, but not including Overhead or profit on Work not performed; (c) reasonable attorneys' fees and costs related to termination; and (d) a premium as follows: [ ].

11.4.3 If Owner terminates this Agreement, Constructor shall:

11.4.3.1 execute and deliver to Owner all papers and take all action required to assign, transfer, and vest in Owner the rights of Constructor to all materials, supplies, and equipment for which payment has been or will be made in accordance with the Contract Documents and all subcontracts, orders, and commitments which have been made in accordance with the Contract Documents;

11.4.3.2 exert reasonable effort to reduce to a minimum Owner's liability for subcontracts, orders, and commitments that have not been fulfilled at the time of the termination;

11.4.3.3 cancel any subcontracts, orders, and commitments as Owner directs; and

11.4.3.4 sell at prices approved by Owner any materials, supplies, and equipment as Owner directs, with all proceeds paid or credited to Owner.

11.5 CONSTRUCTOR'S RIGHT TO TERMINATE

11.5.1 Seven (7) Days' after Owner's receipt of written notice from Constructor, Constructor may terminate this Agreement if the Work has been stopped for a thirty (30) Day period through no fault of Constructor for any of the following reasons:

(a) under court order or order of other governmental authorities having jurisdiction;
(b) as a result of the declaration of a national emergency or other governmental act during which, through no act or fault of Constructor, materials are not available; or
(c) suspension by Owner for convenience pursuant to §11.1.

11.5.2 In addition, upon seven (7) Days' written notice to Owner and an opportunity to cure within three (3) Days, Constructor may terminate this Agreement if Owner:

11.5.2.1 fails to furnish reasonable evidence pursuant to §4.2 that sufficient funds are available and committed for Project financing; or

11.5.2.2 assigns this Agreement over Constructor's reasonable objection; or

11.5.2.3 fails to pay Constructor in accordance with this Agreement and Constructor has stopped Work in compliance with §9.5; or

11.5.2.4 otherwise materially breaches this Agreement.

11.5.3 Upon termination by Constructor in accordance with §11.5.2, Constructor is entitled to recover from Owner payment for all Work executed and for any proven loss, cost, or expense in connection with the Work, including all demobilization costs plus reasonable Overhead and profit on Work not performed.

11.6 OBLIGATIONS ARISING BEFORE TERMINATION Even after termination, the provisions of this Agreement still apply to any Work performed, payments made, events occurring, costs charged or incurred, or obligations arising before the termination date.

ARTICLE 12 DISPUTE MITIGATION AND RESOLUTION

12.1 WORK CONTINUANCE AND PAYMENT Constructor shall continue the Work and maintain the Schedule of the Work during any dispute mitigation or resolution procedure. If Constructor continues to perform, Owner shall continue to make payments in accordance with this Agreement.

12.2 DIRECT DISCUSSIONS If the Parties cannot reach resolution on a matter relating to or arising out of this Agreement, the Parties shall endeavor to reach resolution through good faith direct discussions between the Parties' representatives, who shall possess the necessary authority to resolve such matter and who shall record the date of first discussions. If the Parties' representatives are not able to resolve such matter within five (5) Business Days from the date of first discussion, the Parties' representatives shall immediately inform senior executives of the Parties in writing that a resolution could not be reached. Upon receipt of such notice, the senior executives of the Parties shall meet within five (5) Business Days to endeavor to reach resolution. If the dispute remains unresolved after fifteen (15) Days from the date of first discussion, the Parties shall submit such matter to the dispute mitigation and dispute resolution procedures selected below.

12.3 MITIGATION If the Parties select one of the dispute mitigation procedures below, disputes remaining unresolved after direct discussions shall be directed to the selected mitigation procedure. The dispute mitigation procedure shall result in a nonbinding finding on the matter, which may be introduced as evidence at a subsequent binding adjudication of the matter, as designated in §12.5. The Parties agree that the dispute mitigation procedure shall be:

- ☐ Project Neutral ("Neutral"); or
- ☐ Dispute Review Board ("DRB").

12.3.1 MITIGATION PROCEDURES As soon as practicable after the execution of this Agreement, the Neutral or DRB shall be mutually selected and appointed by the Parties and shall execute a retainer agreement with the Parties establishing the scope of responsibilities, including requirements for nonbinding findings. Costs and expenses of Neutral or DRB shall be shared equally by the Parties. A Neutral or DRB shall be available to either Party, upon request, throughout the course of the Project, and shall make regular visits to the Project so as to maintain an up-to-date understanding of the Project progress and issues and to enable the Neutral or DRB to address matters in dispute between the Parties promptly and knowledgeably.

12.3.2 If the matter remains unresolved following the issuance of the nonbinding findings or such findings are not made within five (5) Business Days of the referral, the Parties shall submit the matter to the binding dispute resolution procedure designated in §12.5.

12.3.3 If the Parties execute a DRB Addendum, then the dispute mitigation procedures and time requirements in §12.3.1 and §12.3.2 shall be governed by that DRB Addendum.

12.4 MEDIATION If direct discussions pursuant to §12.2 do not result in resolution of the matter and no dispute mitigation procedure is selected under §12.3, the Parties shall endeavor to resolve the matter by mediation. The mediation shall be convened within thirty (30) Business Days of the matter first being discussed and shall conclude within forty-five (45) Business Days of the matter first being discussed. Either Party may terminate the mediation at any time after the first session by written notice to the non-terminating Party and mediator. The costs of the mediation shall be shared equally by the Parties. The Parties choose mediation through:

- ☐ the current Construction Industry Mediation Rules of the American Arbitration Association (AAA), and administered by AAA.
- ☐ the current Mediation Guidelines of JAMS and administered by JAMS.
- ☐ the current rules and administration by [_____].

If no box is checked the default is AAA rules and administration.

12.5 BINDING DISPUTE RESOLUTION If the matter is unresolved after submission of the matter to a mitigation procedure or to mediation, the Parties shall submit the matter to the binding dispute resolution procedure selected below:

12.5.1 ARBITRATION

☐ The Parties choose binding arbitration for any claim or dispute arising out of or relating to this Agreement. **EACH PARTY WAIVES THEIR RIGHT TO BE HEARD IN A COURT OF LAW**, with or without a jury. Arbitration does not involve a judge or jury. Instead, an arbitrator with the power to award damages and other appropriate relief will decide claims and disputes. An arbitrator's award shall be final and binding upon the Parties, and judgment may be entered upon it in any court having jurisdiction.

12.5.1.1 Neither Party may commence arbitration if the claim or cause of action would be barred by the applicable statute of limitations had the claim or cause of action been filed in a state or federal court. Receipt of a demand for arbitration by the person or entity administering the arbitration shall constitute the commencement of legal proceedings for the purposes of determining whether a claim or cause of action is barred by the applicable statute of limitations. If, however, a state or federal court exercising jurisdiction over a timely filed claim or cause of action orders that the claim or cause of action be submitted to arbitration, the arbitration proceeding shall be deemed commenced as of the date the court action was filed, provided that the Party asserting the claim or cause of action files its demand for arbitration with the person or entity administering the arbitration within thirty (30) Days after the entry of such order.

12.5.1.2 The arbitration shall use the following rules:

☐ the current AAA Construction Industry Arbitration Rules and AAA administration. AAA Construction Fast Track Rules shall apply to all two-party cases when neither Party's disclosed claim or counterclaim exceeds $250,000. If arbitration is selected but no rules are selected, then this subsection shall apply by default;
☐ the current JAMS Engineering and Construction Arbitration Rules and Procedures and administered by JAMS; or
☐ the current arbitration rules of [ ] and administered by [ ].

12.5.2 LITIGATION

☐ Litigation in either the state or federal court having jurisdiction of the matter in the location of the Project.

If not indicated, then litigation is the default and not arbitration.

12.5.3 COSTS The costs of any binding dispute resolution procedures and reasonable attorneys' fees shall be borne by the non-prevailing Party, as determined by the adjudicator of the dispute.

12.5.4 VENUE The Project location shall serve as the venue.

12.6 MULTIPARTY PROCEEDING All parties necessary to resolve a matter agree to be parties to the same dispute resolution proceeding, if possible. Appropriate provisions shall be included in all other contracts relating to the Work to provide for the joinder or consolidation of such dispute resolution procedures.

12.7 LIEN RIGHTS Nothing in this article shall limit any rights or remedies not expressly waived by Constructor that Constructor may have under lien laws.

ARTICLE 13 MISCELLANEOUS

13.1 EXTENT OF AGREEMENT Except as expressly provided, this Agreement is for the exclusive benefit of the Parties, and not for the benefit of any third party. This Agreement represents the entire and integrated agreement between the Parties, and supersedes all prior negotiations, representations, or agreements, either written or oral.

13.2 ASSIGNMENT Except as to the assignment of proceeds, the Parties shall not assign their interest in this Agreement without the written consent of the other. The terms and conditions of this Agreement shall be binding upon both Parties, their partners, successors, assigns, and legal representatives. Neither Party shall assign the Agreement as a whole without written consent of the other except that Owner may assign the Agreement to a wholly owned subsidiary of Owner when Owner has fully indemnified Constructor or to an institutional lender providing construction financing for the Project as long as the assignment is no less favorable to Constructor than this Agreement. If such assignment occurs, Constructor shall execute any consent reasonably required. In such event, the wholly owned subsidiary or lender shall assume Owner's rights and obligations under the Contract Documents. If either Party attempts to make such an assignment, that Party shall nevertheless remain legally responsible for all obligations under this Agreement, unless otherwise agreed by the other Party.

13.3 GOVERNING LAW The law in effect at the location of the Project shall govern this Agreement.

13.4 SEVERABILITY The partial or complete invalidity of any one or more provisions of this Agreement shall not affect the validity or continuing force and effect of any other provision.

13.5 NOTICE Unless changed in writing, a Party's address indicated in Article 1 shall be used when delivering notice to a physical address. Except for Agreement termination and as otherwise specified in the Contract Documents, notice is effective upon transmission by any effective means, including U.S. postal service and overnight delivery service.

13.6 NO WAIVER OF PERFORMANCE Either Party's failure to insist upon any, in any one or more instances, on the performance of any of the terms, covenants, or conditions of this Agreement, or to exercise any of its rights, shall not be construed as a waiver or relinquishment of such term, covenant, condition, or right with respect to further performance or any other term, covenant, condition, or right.

13.7 TITLES The titles given to the articles are for ease of reference only and shall not be relied upon or cited for any other purpose.

13.8 JOINT DRAFTING The Parties expressly agree that this Agreement was jointly drafted, and that both had opportunity to negotiate its terms and to obtain the assistance of counsel in reviewing its terms before execution. Therefore, this Agreement shall be construed neither against nor in favor of either Party, but shall be construed in a neutral manner.

ARTICLE 14 CONTRACT DOCUMENTS

14.1 EXISTING CONTRACT DOCUMENTS

14.1.1 The Contract Documents in existence at the time of execution of this Agreement are as follows:

(a) Drawings: [ ]
(b) Specifications: [ ]
(c) Addenda: [ ]
(d) Owner Provided information: [ ]
(e) Other: [ ]

14.2 INTERPRETATION OF CONTRACT DOCUMENTS

14.2.1 The drawings and specifications are complementary. If Work is shown only on one but not on the other, Constructor shall perform the Work as though fully described on both.

14.2.2 In case of conflicts between the drawings and specifications, the specifications shall govern. In any case of omissions or errors in figures, drawings, or specifications, Constructor shall immediately submit the matter to Owner for clarification. Subject to an equitable adjustment in Contract Time or Contract Price pursuant to ARTICLE 8, or a dispute mitigation and resolution, Owner's clarifications are final and binding.

14.2.3 Where figures are given, they shall be preferred to scaled dimensions.

14.2.4 Unless otherwise specifically defined in this Agreement, any terms that have well-known technical or trade meanings shall be interpreted in accordance with their well-known meanings.

14.3 ORDER OF PRECEDENCE In case of any inconsistency, conflict, or ambiguity among the Contract Documents, the documents shall govern in the following order: (a) Change Orders and written amendments to this Agreement; (b) this Agreement; (c) subject to §14.2.2 the drawings (large scale governing over small scale), specifications, and addenda issued and acknowledged before Agreement execution or signed by both Parties; (d) information furnished by Owner pursuant to §3.13.4 or designated as a Contract Document in §14.1; (e) other Contract Documents listed in this Agreement. Among categories of documents having the same order of precedence, the term or provision that includes the latest date shall control.

OWNER: [ ]

BY: ____________________ NAME: ____________________ TITLE: ____________________

WITNESS: ____________________ NAME: ____________________ TITLE: ____________________

CONSTRUCTOR: [ ]

BY: ____________________ NAME: ____________________ TITLE: ____________________

WITNESS: ____________________ NAME: ____________________ TITLE: ____________________

END OF DOCUMENT.

Exhibit 14

AIA Document A102™ – 2017

Standard Form Agreement Between Owner and Contractor Where the Basis for Payment Is the Cost of the Work Plus a Fee with a Negotiated Guaranteed Maximum Price

AIA Document A102® – 2017

***Standard Form of Agreement Between Owner and Contractor** where the basis of payment is the Cost of the Work Plus a Fee with a Guaranteed Maximum Price*

AGREEMENT made as of the _______ day of _______ in the year _______
(In words, indicate day, month and year.)

BETWEEN the Owner:
(Name, legal status, address and other information)

and the Contractor:
(Name, legal status, address and other information)

for the following Project:
(Name, location and detailed description)

The Architect:
(Name, legal status, address and other information)

This document has important legal consequences. Consultation with an attorney is encouraged with respect to its completion or modification.

The parties should complete A102™–2017, Exhibit A, Insurance and Bonds, contemporaneously with this Agreement.

AIA Document A201™–2017, General Conditions of the Contract for Construction, is adopted in this document by reference. Do not use with other general conditions unless this document is modified.

The Owner and Contractor agree as follows.

Init.
/

TABLE OF ARTICLES

ARTICLE 1 THE CONTRACT DOCUMENTS
The Contract Documents consist of this Agreement, Conditions of the Contract (General, Supplementary, and other Conditions), Drawings, Specifications, Addenda issued prior to execution of this Agreement, other documents listed in this Agreement and Modifications issued after execution of this Agreement, all of which form the Contract, and are as fully a part of the Contract as if attached to this Agreement or repeated herein. The Contract represents the entire and integrated agreement between the parties hereto and supersedes prior negotiations, representations, or agreements, either written or oral. If anything in the other Contract Documents, other than a Modification, is inconsistent with this Agreement, this Agreement shall govern. An enumeration of the Contract Documents, other than a Modification, appears in Article 16.

ARTICLE 2 THE WORK OF THIS CONTRACT
The Contractor shall fully execute the Work described in the Contract Documents, except as specifically indicated in the Contract Documents to be the responsibility of others.

ARTICLE 3 RELATIONSHIP OF THE PARTIES
The Contractor accepts the relationship of trust and confidence established by this Agreement and covenants with the Owner to cooperate with the Architect and exercise the Contractor's skill and judgment in furthering the interests of the Owner; to furnish efficient business administration and supervision; to furnish at all times an adequate supply of workers and materials; and to perform the Work in an expeditious and economical manner consistent with the Owner's interests. The Owner agrees to furnish and approve, in a timely manner, information required by the Contractor and to make payments to the Contractor in accordance with the requirements of the Contract Documents.

ARTICLE 4 DATE OF COMMENCEMENT AND SUBSTANTIAL COMPLETION
§ 4.1 The date of commencement of the Work shall be:
(Check one of the following boxes.)

☐ The date of this Agreement

☐ A date set forth in a notice to proceed issued by the Owner.

☐ Established as follows:
(Insert a date or a means to determine the date of commencement of the Work.)

If a date of commencement of the Work is not selected, then the date of commencement shall be the date of this Agreement.

§ 4.2 The Contract Time shall be measured from the date of commencement of the Work.

§ 4.3 Substantial Completion
§ 4.3.1 Subject to adjustments of the Contract Time as provided in the Contract Documents, the Contractor shall achieve Substantial Completion of the entire Work:
(Check one of the following boxes and complete the necessary information.)

☐ Not later than ________ (__) calendar days from the date of commencement of the Work.

☐ By the following date:

§ 4.3.2 Subject to adjustments of the Contract Time as provided in the Contract Documents, if portions of the Work are to be completed prior to Substantial Completion of the entire Work, the Contractor shall achieve Substantial Completion of such portions by the following dates:

Portion of Work	Substantial Completion Date

§ 4.3.3 If the Contractor fails to achieve Substantial Completion as provided in this Section 4.3, liquidated damages, if any, shall be assessed as set forth in Section 5.1.6.

ARTICLE 5 CONTRACT SUM
§ 5.1 The Owner shall pay the Contractor the Contract Sum in current funds for the Contractor's performance of the Contract. The Contract Sum is the Cost of the Work as defined in Article 7 plus the Contractor's Fee.

§ 5.1.1 The Contractor's Fee:
(State a lump sum, percentage of Cost of the Work, or other provision for determining the Contractor's Fee.)

§ 5.1.2 The method of adjustment of the Contractor's Fee for changes in the Work:

§ 5.1.3 Limitations, if any, on a Subcontractor's overhead and profit for increases in the cost of its portion of the Work:

§ 5.1.4 Rental rates for Contractor-owned equipment shall not exceed ________ percent (__ %) of the standard rental rate paid at the place of the Project.

Init.
/

§ 5.1.5 Unit prices, if any:
(Identify the item and state the unit price and quantity limitations, if any, to which the unit price will be applicable.)

Item	Units and Limitations	Price Per Unit ($0.00)

§ 5.1.6 Liquidated damages, if any:
(Insert terms and conditions for liquidated damages, if any.)

§ 5.1.7 Other:
(Insert provisions for bonus, cost savings or other incentives, if any, that might result in a change to the Contract Sum.)

§ 5.2 Guaranteed Maximum Price
§ 5.2.1 The Contract Sum is guaranteed by the Contractor not to exceed ________ ($__), subject to additions and deductions by Change Order as provided in the Contract Documents. This maximum sum is referred to in the Contract Documents as the Guaranteed Maximum Price. Costs which would cause the Guaranteed Maximum Price to be exceeded shall be paid by the Contractor without reimbursement by the Owner.

§ 5.2.2 Alternates
§ 5.2.2.1 Alternates, if any, included in the Guaranteed Maximum Price:

Item	Price

§ 5.2.2.2 Subject to the conditions noted below, the following alternates may be accepted by the Owner following execution of this Agreement. Upon acceptance, the Owner shall issue a Modification to this Agreement.
(Insert below each alternate and the conditions that must be met for the Owner to accept the alternate.)

Item	Price	Conditions for Acceptance

§ 5.2.3 Allowances, if any, included in the Guaranteed Maximum Price:
(Identify each allowance.)

Item	Price

§ 5.2.4 Assumptions, if any, upon which the Guaranteed Maximum Price is based:
(Identify each assumption.)

§ 5.2.5 To the extent that the Contract Documents are anticipated to require further development, the Guaranteed Maximum Price includes the costs attributable to such further development consistent with the Contract Documents and reasonably inferable therefrom. Such further development does not include changes in scope, systems, kinds and quality of materials, finishes or equipment, all of which, if required, shall be incorporated by Change Order.

§ 5.2.6 The Owner shall authorize preparation of revisions to the Contract Documents that incorporate the agreed-upon assumptions contained in Section 5.2.4. The Owner shall promptly furnish such revised Contract Documents to the

Init.
/

Contractor. The Contractor shall notify the Owner and Architect of any inconsistencies between the agreed-upon assumptions contained in Section 5.2.4 and the revised Contract Documents.

ARTICLE 6 CHANGES IN THE WORK

§ 6.1 Adjustments to the Guaranteed Maximum Price on account of changes in the Work may be determined by any of the methods listed in Article 7 of AIA Document A201™–2017, General Conditions of the Contract for Construction.

§ 6.2 Adjustments to subcontracts awarded on the basis of a stipulated sum shall be determined in accordance with Article 7 of A201–2017, as they refer to "cost" and "fee," and not by Articles 5, 7 and 8 of this Agreement. Adjustments to subcontracts awarded with the Owner's prior written consent on the basis of cost plus a fee shall be calculated in accordance with the terms of those subcontracts.

§ 6.3 In calculating adjustments to the Guaranteed Maximum Price, the terms "cost" and "costs" as used in Article 7 of AIA Document A201–2017 shall mean the Cost of the Work as defined in Article 7 of this Agreement and the term "fee" shall mean the Contractor's Fee as defined in Section 5.1.1 of this Agreement.

§ 6.4 If no specific provision is made in Article 5 for adjustment of the Contractor's Fee in the case of changes in the Work, or if the extent of such changes is such, in the aggregate, that application of the adjustment provisions of Article 5 will cause substantial inequity to the Owner or Contractor, the Contractor's Fee shall be equitably adjusted on the same basis that was used to establish the Fee for the original Work, and the Guaranteed Maximum Price shall be adjusted accordingly.

ARTICLE 7 COSTS TO BE REIMBURSED

§ 7.1 Cost of the Work

§ 7.1.1 The term Cost of the Work shall mean costs necessarily incurred by the Contractor in the proper performance of the Work. The Cost of the Work shall include only the items set forth in this Article 7.

§ 7.1.2 Where, pursuant to the Contract Documents, any cost is subject to the Owner's prior approval, the Contractor shall obtain such approval in writing prior to incurring the cost.

§ 7.1.3 Costs shall be at rates not higher than the standard paid at the place of the Project, except with prior approval of the Owner.

§ 7.2 Labor Costs

§ 7.2.1 Wages or salaries of construction workers directly employed by the Contractor to perform the construction of the Work at the site or, with the Owner's prior approval, at off-site workshops.

§ 7.2.2 Wages or salaries of the Contractor's supervisory and administrative personnel when stationed at the site and performing Work, with the Owner's prior approval.

§ 7.2.2.1 Wages or salaries of the Contractor's supervisory and administrative personnel when performing Work and stationed at a location other than the site, but only for that portion of time required for the Work, and limited to the personnel and activities listed below:
(Identify the personnel, type of activity and, if applicable, any agreed upon percentage of time to be devoted to the Work.)

§ 7.2.3 Wages or salaries of the Contractor's supervisory or administrative personnel engaged at factories, workshops or while traveling, in expediting the production or transportation of materials or equipment required for the Work, but only for that portion of their time required for the Work.

§ 7.2.4 Costs paid or incurred by the Contractor, as required by law or collective bargaining agreements, for taxes, insurance, contributions, assessments, and benefits and, for personnel not covered by collective bargaining agreements, customary benefits such as sick leave, medical and health benefits, holidays, vacations and pensions, provided such costs are based on wages and salaries included in the Cost of the Work under Sections 7.2.1 through 7.2.3.

§ 7.2.5 If agreed rates for labor costs, in lieu of actual costs, are provided in this Agreement, the rates shall remain unchanged throughout the duration of this Agreement, unless the parties execute a Modification.

§ 7.3 Subcontract Costs
Payments made by the Contractor to Subcontractors in accordance with the requirements of the subcontracts and this Agreement.

§ 7.4 Costs of Materials and Equipment Incorporated in the Completed Construction
§ 7.4.1 Costs, including transportation and storage at the site, of materials and equipment incorporated, or to be incorporated, in the completed construction.

§ 7.4.2 Costs of materials described in the preceding Section 7.4.1 in excess of those actually installed to allow for reasonable waste and spoilage. Unused excess materials, if any, shall become the Owner's property at the completion of the Work or, at the Owner's option, shall be sold by the Contractor. Any amounts realized from such sales shall be credited to the Owner as a deduction from the Cost of the Work.

§ 7.5 Costs of Other Materials and Equipment, Temporary Facilities and Related Items
§ 7.5.1 Costs of transportation, storage, installation, dismantling, maintenance, and removal of materials, supplies, temporary facilities, machinery, equipment and hand tools not customarily owned by construction workers that are provided by the Contractor at the site and fully consumed in the performance of the Work. Costs of materials, supplies, temporary facilities, machinery, equipment, and tools, that are not fully consumed, shall be based on the cost or value of the item at the time it is first used on the Project site less the value of the item when it is no longer used at the Project site. Costs for items not fully consumed by the Contractor shall mean fair market value.

§ 7.5.2 Rental charges for temporary facilities, machinery, equipment, and hand tools not customarily owned by construction workers that are provided by the Contractor at the site, and the costs of transportation, installation, dismantling, minor repairs, and removal of such temporary facilities, machinery, equipment, and hand tools. Rates and quantities of equipment owned by the Contractor, or a related party as defined in Section 7.8, shall be subject to the Owner's prior approval. The total rental cost of any such equipment may not exceed the purchase price of any comparable item.

§ 7.5.3 Costs of removal of debris from the site of the Work and its proper and legal disposal.

§ 7.5.4 Costs of the Contractor's site office, including general office equipment and supplies.

§ 7.5.5 Costs of materials and equipment suitably stored off the site at a mutually acceptable location, subject to the Owner's prior approval.

§ 7.6 Miscellaneous Costs
§ 7.6.1 Premiums for that portion of insurance and bonds required by the Contract Documents that can be directly attributed to this Contract.

§ 7.6.1.1 Costs for self-insurance, for either full or partial amounts of the coverages required by the Contract Documents, with the Owner's prior approval.

§ 7.6.1.2 Costs for insurance through a captive insurer owned or controlled by the Contractor, with the Owner's prior approval.

§ 7.6.2 Sales, use, or similar taxes, imposed by a governmental authority, that are related to the Work and for which the Contractor is liable.

§ 7.6.3 Fees and assessments for the building permit, and for other permits, licenses, and inspections, for which the Contractor is required by the Contract Documents to pay.

§ 7.6.4 Fees of laboratories for tests required by the Contract Documents, except those related to defective or nonconforming Work for which reimbursement is excluded under Article 13 of AIA Document A201–2017 or by other provisions of the Contract Documents, and which do not fall within the scope of Section 7.7.3.

§ 7.6.5 Royalties and license fees paid for the use of a particular design, process, or product, required by the Contract Documents.

§ 7.6.5.1 The cost of defending suits or claims for infringement of patent rights arising from requirements of the Contract Documents, payments made in accordance with legal judgments against the Contractor resulting from such suits or claims, and payments of settlements made with the Owner's consent, unless the Contractor had reason to believe that the required design, process or product was an infringement of a copyright or a patent, and the Contractor failed to promptly furnish such information to the Architect as required by Article 3 of AIA Document A201–2017. The costs of legal defenses, judgments, and settlements, shall not be included in the Cost of the Work used to calculate the Contractor's Fee or subject to the Guaranteed Maximum Price.

§ 7.6.6 Costs for communications services, electronic equipment, and software, directly related to the Work and located at the site, with the Owner's prior approval.

§ 7.6.7 Costs of document reproductions and delivery charges.

§ 7.6.8 Deposits lost for causes other than the Contractor's negligence or failure to fulfill a specific responsibility in the Contract Documents.

§ 7.6.9 Legal, mediation and arbitration costs, including attorneys' fees, other than those arising from disputes between the Owner and Contractor, reasonably incurred by the Contractor after the execution of this Agreement in the performance of the Work and with the Owner's prior approval, which shall not be unreasonably withheld.

§ 7.6.10 Expenses incurred in accordance with the Contractor's standard written personnel policy for relocation and temporary living allowances of the Contractor's personnel required for the Work, with the Owner's prior approval.

§ 7.6.11 That portion of the reasonable expenses of the Contractor's supervisory or administrative personnel incurred while traveling in discharge of duties connected with the Work.

§ 7.7 Other Costs and Emergencies
§ 7.7.1 Other costs incurred in the performance of the Work, with the Owner's prior approval.

§ 7.7.2 Costs incurred in taking action to prevent threatened damage, injury, or loss, in case of an emergency affecting the safety of persons and property, as provided in Article 10 of AIA Document A201–2017.

§ 7.7.3 Costs of repairing or correcting damaged or nonconforming Work executed by the Contractor, Subcontractors, or suppliers, provided that such damaged or nonconforming Work was not caused by the negligence of, or failure to fulfill a specific responsibility by, the Contractor, and only to the extent that the cost of repair or correction is not recovered by the Contractor from insurance, sureties, Subcontractors, suppliers, or others.

§ 7.8 Related Party Transactions
§ 7.8.1 For purposes of this Section 7.8, the term "related party" shall mean (1) a parent, subsidiary, affiliate, or other entity having common ownership of, or sharing common management with, the Contractor; (2) any entity in which any stockholder in, or management employee of, the Contractor holds an equity interest in excess of ten percent in the aggregate; (3) any entity which has the right to control the business or affairs of the Contractor; or (4) any person, or any member of the immediate family of any person, who has the right to control the business or affairs of the Contractor.

§ 7.8.2 If any of the costs to be reimbursed arise from a transaction between the Contractor and a related party, the Contractor shall notify the Owner of the specific nature of the contemplated transaction, including the identity of the related party and the anticipated cost to be incurred, before any such transaction is consummated or cost incurred. If the Owner, after such notification, authorizes the proposed transaction in writing, then the cost incurred shall be included as a cost to be reimbursed, and the Contractor shall procure the Work, equipment, goods, or service, from the related party, as a Subcontractor, according to the terms of Article 10. If the Owner fails to authorize the transaction in writing, the Contractor shall procure the Work, equipment, goods, or service from some person or entity other than a related party according to the terms of Article 10.

ARTICLE 8 COSTS NOT TO BE REIMBURSED
§ 8.1 The Cost of the Work shall not include the items listed below:

.1 Salaries and other compensation of the Contractor's personnel stationed at the Contractor's principal office or offices other than the site office, except as specifically provided in Section 7.2, or as may be provided in Article 15;

Init.
/

.2 Bonuses, profit sharing, incentive compensation, and any other discretionary payments, paid to anyone hired by the Contractor or paid to any Subcontractor or vendor, unless the Owner has provided prior approval;
.3 Expenses of the Contractor's principal office and offices other than the site office;
.4 Overhead and general expenses, except as may be expressly included in Article 7;
.5 The Contractor's capital expenses, including interest on the Contractor's capital employed for the Work;
.6 Except as provided in Section 7.7.3 of this Agreement, costs due to the negligence of, or failure to fulfill a specific responsibility of the Contract by, the Contractor, Subcontractors, and suppliers, or anyone directly or indirectly employed by any of them or for whose acts any of them may be liable;
.7 Any cost not specifically and expressly described in Article 7; and
.8 Costs, other than costs included in Change Orders approved by the Owner, that would cause the Guaranteed Maximum Price to be exceeded.

ARTICLE 9 DISCOUNTS, REBATES AND REFUNDS
§ 9.1 Cash discounts obtained on payments made by the Contractor shall accrue to the Owner if (1) before making the payment, the Contractor included the amount to be paid, less such discount, in an Application for Payment and received payment from the Owner, or (2) the Owner has deposited funds with the Contractor with which to make payments; otherwise, cash discounts shall accrue to the Contractor. Trade discounts, rebates, refunds, and amounts received from sales of surplus materials and equipment shall accrue to the Owner, and the Contractor shall make provisions so that they can be obtained.

§ 9.2 Amounts that accrue to the Owner in accordance with the provisions of Section 9.1 shall be credited to the Owner as a deduction from the Cost of the Work.

ARTICLE 10 SUBCONTRACTS AND OTHER AGREEMENTS
§ 10.1 Those portions of the Work that the Contractor does not customarily perform with the Contractor's own personnel shall be performed under subcontracts or other appropriate agreements with the Contractor. The Owner may designate specific persons from whom, or entities from which, the Contractor shall obtain bids. The Contractor shall obtain bids from Subcontractors, and from suppliers of materials or equipment fabricated especially for the Work, who are qualified to perform that portion of the Work in accordance with the requirements of the Contract Documents. The Contractor shall deliver such bids to the Architect and Owner with an indication as to which bids the Contractor intends to accept. The Owner then has the right to review the Contractor's list of proposed subcontractors and suppliers in consultation with the Architect and, subject to Section 10.1.1, to object to any subcontractor or supplier. Any advice of the Architect, or approval or objection by the Owner, shall not relieve the Contractor of its responsibility to perform the Work in accordance with the Contract Documents. The Contractor shall not be required to contract with anyone to whom the Contractor has reasonable objection.

§ 10.1.1 When a specific subcontractor or supplier (1) is recommended to the Owner by the Contractor; (2) is qualified to perform that portion of the Work; and (3) has submitted a bid that conforms to the requirements of the Contract Documents without reservations or exceptions, but the Owner requires that another bid be accepted, then the Contractor may require that a Change Order be issued to adjust the Guaranteed Maximum Price by the difference between the bid of the person or entity recommended to the Owner by the Contractor and the amount of the subcontract or other agreement actually signed with the person or entity designated by the Owner.

§ 10.2 Subcontracts or other agreements shall conform to the applicable payment provisions of this Agreement, and shall not be awarded on the basis of cost plus a fee without the Owner's prior written approval. If a subcontract is awarded on the basis of cost plus a fee, the Contractor shall provide in the subcontract for the Owner to receive the same audit rights with regard to the Subcontractor as the Owner receives with regard to the Contractor in Article 11.

ARTICLE 11 ACCOUNTING RECORDS
The Contractor shall keep full and detailed records and accounts related to the Cost of the Work, and exercise such controls, as may be necessary for proper financial management under this Contract and to substantiate all costs incurred. The accounting and control systems shall be satisfactory to the Owner. The Owner and the Owner's auditors shall, during regular business hours and upon reasonable notice, be afforded access to, and shall be permitted to audit and copy, the Contractor's records and accounts, including complete documentation supporting accounting entries, books, job cost reports, correspondence, instructions, drawings, receipts, subcontracts, Subcontractor's proposals, Subcontractor's invoices, purchase orders, vouchers, memoranda, and other data relating to this Contract. The Contractor shall preserve these records for a period of three years after final payment, or for such longer period as may be required by law.

ARTICLE 12 PAYMENTS

§ 12.1 Progress Payments

§ 12.1.1 Based upon Applications for Payment submitted to the Architect by the Contractor, and Certificates for Payment issued by the Architect, the Owner shall make progress payments on account of the Contract Sum, to the Contractor, as provided below and elsewhere in the Contract Documents.

§ 12.1.2 The period covered by each Application for Payment shall be one calendar month ending on the last day of the month, or as follows:

§ 12.1.3 Provided that an Application for Payment is received by the Architect not later than the ________ day of a month, the Owner shall make payment of the amount certified to the Contractor not later than the ________ day of the ________ month. If an Application for Payment is received by the Architect after the application date fixed above, payment of the amount certified shall be made by the Owner not later than ________ (___) days after the Architect receives the Application for Payment.
(Federal, state or local laws may require payment within a certain period of time.)

§ 12.1.4 With each Application for Payment, the Contractor shall submit payrolls, petty cash accounts, receipted invoices or invoices with check vouchers attached, and any other evidence required by the Owner or Architect to demonstrate that payments already made by the Contractor on account of the Cost of the Work equal or exceed progress payments already received by the Contractor plus payrolls for the period covered by the present Application for Payment, less that portion of the progress payments attributable to the Contractor's Fee.

§ 12.1.5 Each Application for Payment shall be based on the most recent schedule of values submitted by the Contractor in accordance with the Contract Documents. The schedule of values shall allocate the entire Guaranteed Maximum Price among: (1) the various portions of the Work; (2) any contingency for costs that are included in the Guaranteed Maximum Price but not otherwise allocated to another line item or included in a Change Order; and (3) the Contractor's Fee.

§ 12.1.5.1 The schedule of values shall be prepared in such form and supported by such data to substantiate its accuracy as the Architect may require. The schedule of values shall be used as a basis for reviewing the Contractor's Applications for Payment.

§ 12.1.5.2 The allocation of the Guaranteed Maximum Price under this Section 12.1.5 shall not constitute a separate guaranteed maximum price for the Cost of the Work of each individual line item in the schedule of values.

§ 12.1.5.3 When the Contractor allocates costs from a contingency to another line item in the schedule of values, the Contractor shall submit supporting documentation to the Architect.

§ 12.1.6 Applications for Payment shall show the percentage of completion of each portion of the Work as of the end of the period covered by the Application for Payment. The percentage of completion shall be the lesser of (1) the percentage of that portion of the Work which has actually been completed; or (2) the percentage obtained by dividing (a) the expense that has actually been incurred by the Contractor on account of that portion of the Work and for which the Contractor has made payment or intends to make payment prior to the next Application for Payment, by (b) the share of the Guaranteed Maximum Price allocated to that portion of the Work in the schedule of values.

§ 12.1.7 In accordance with AIA Document A201–2017 and subject to other provisions of the Contract Documents, the amount of each progress payment shall be computed as follows:

§ 12.1.7.1 The amount of each progress payment shall first include:

- **.1** That portion of the Guaranteed Maximum Price properly allocable to completed Work as determined by multiplying the percentage of completion of each portion of the Work by the share of the Guaranteed Maximum Price allocated to that portion of the Work in the most recent schedule of values;
- **.2** That portion of the Guaranteed Maximum Price properly allocable to materials and equipment delivered and suitably stored at the site for subsequent incorporation in the completed construction or, if approved in writing in advance by the Owner, suitably stored off the site at a location agreed upon in writing;

.3 That portion of Construction Change Directives that the Architect determines, in the Architect's professional judgment, to be reasonably justified; and

.4 The Contractor's Fee, computed upon the Cost of the Work described in the preceding Sections 12.1.7.1.1 and 12.1.7.1.2 at the rate stated in Section 5.1.1 or, if the Contractor's Fee is stated as a fixed sum in that Section, an amount that bears the same ratio to that fixed-sum fee as the Cost of the Work included in Sections 12.1.7.1.1 and 12.1.7.1.2 bears to a reasonable estimate of the probable Cost of the Work upon its completion.

§ 12.1.7.2 The amount of each progress payment shall then be reduced by:

.1 The aggregate of any amounts previously paid by the Owner;

.2 The amount, if any, for Work that remains uncorrected and for which the Architect has previously withheld a Certificate for Payment as provided in Article 9 of AIA Document A201–2017;

.3 Any amount for which the Contractor does not intend to pay a Subcontractor or material supplier, unless the Work has been performed by others the Contractor intends to pay;

.4 For Work performed or defects discovered since the last payment application, any amount for which the Architect may withhold payment, or nullify a Certificate of Payment in whole or in part, as provided in Article 9 of AIA Document A201–2017;

.5 The shortfall, if any, indicated by the Contractor in the documentation required by Section 12.1.4 to substantiate prior Applications for Payment, or resulting from errors subsequently discovered by the Owner's auditors in such documentation; and

.6 Retainage withheld pursuant to Section 12.1.8.

§ 12.1.8 Retainage

§ 12.1.8.1 For each progress payment made prior to Substantial Completion of the Work, the Owner may withhold the following amount, as retainage, from the payment otherwise due:

(Insert a percentage or amount to be withheld as retainage from each Application for Payment. The amount of retainage may be limited by governing law.)

§ 12.1.8.1.1 The following items are not subject to retainage:

(Insert any items not subject to the withholding of retainage, such as general conditions, insurance, etc.)

§ 12.1.8.2 Reduction or limitation of retainage, if any, shall be as follows:

(If the retainage established in Section 12.1.8.1 is to be modified prior to Substantial Completion of the entire Work, insert provisions for such modification.)

§ 12.1.8.3 Except as set forth in this Section 12.1.8.3, upon Substantial Completion of the Work, the Contractor may submit an Application for Payment that includes the retainage withheld from prior Applications for Payment pursuant to this Section 12.1.8. The Application for Payment submitted at Substantial Completion shall not include retainage as follows:

(Insert any other conditions for release of retainage, such as upon completion of the Owner's audit and reconciliation, upon Substantial Completion.)

§ 12.1.9 If final completion of the Work is materially delayed through no fault of the Contractor, the Owner shall pay the Contractor any additional amounts in accordance with Article 9 of AIA Document A201–2017.

§ 12.1.10 Except with the Owner's prior written approval, the Contractor shall not make advance payments to suppliers for materials or equipment which have not been delivered and suitably stored at the site.

§ 12.1.11 The Owner and the Contractor shall agree upon a mutually acceptable procedure for review and approval of payments to Subcontractors, and the percentage of retainage held on Subcontracts, and the Contractor shall execute subcontracts in accordance with those agreements.

Init.

/

§ 12.1.12 In taking action on the Contractor's Applications for Payment the Architect shall be entitled to rely on the accuracy and completeness of the information furnished by the Contractor, and such action shall not be deemed to be a representation that (1) the Architect has made a detailed examination, audit, or arithmetic verification, of the documentation submitted in accordance with Section 12.1.4 or other supporting data; (2) that the Architect has made exhaustive or continuous on-site inspections; or (3) that the Architect has made examinations to ascertain how or for what purposes the Contractor has used amounts previously paid on account of the Contract. Such examinations, audits, and verifications, if required by the Owner, will be performed by the Owner's auditors acting in the sole interest of the Owner.

§ 12.2 Final Payment

§ 12.2.1 Final payment, constituting the entire unpaid balance of the Contract Sum, shall be made by the Owner to the Contractor when

- **.1** the Contractor has fully performed the Contract, except for the Contractor's responsibility to correct Work as provided in Article 12 of AIA Document A201–2017, and to satisfy other requirements, if any, which extend beyond final payment;
- **.2** the Contractor has submitted a final accounting for the Cost of the Work and a final Application for Payment; and
- **.3** a final Certificate for Payment has been issued by the Architect in accordance with Section 12.2.2.

§ 12.2.2 Within 30 days of the Owner's receipt of the Contractor's final accounting for the Cost of the Work, the Owner shall conduct an audit of the Cost of the Work or notify the Architect that it will not conduct an audit.

§ 12.2.2.1 If the Owner conducts an audit of the Cost of the Work, the Owner shall, within 10 days after completion of the audit, submit a written report based upon the auditors' findings to the Architect.

§ 12.2.2.2 Within seven days after receipt of the written report described in Section 12.2.2.1, or receipt of notice that the Owner will not conduct an audit, and provided that the other conditions of Section 12.2.1 have been met, the Architect will either issue to the Owner a final Certificate for Payment with a copy to the Contractor, or notify the Contractor and Owner in writing of the Architect's reasons for withholding a certificate as provided in Article 9 of AIA Document A201–2017. The time periods stated in this Section 12.2.2 supersede those stated in Article 9 of AIA Document A201–2017. The Architect is not responsible for verifying the accuracy of the Contractor's final accounting.

§ 12.2.2.3 If the Owner's auditors' report concludes that the Cost of the Work, as substantiated by the Contractor's final accounting, is less than claimed by the Contractor, the Contractor shall be entitled to request mediation of the disputed amount without seeking an initial decision pursuant to Article 15 of AIA Document A201–2017. A request for mediation shall be made by the Contractor within 30 days after the Contractor's receipt of a copy of the Architect's final Certificate for Payment. Failure to request mediation within this 30-day period shall result in the substantiated amount reported by the Owner's auditors becoming binding on the Contractor. Pending a final resolution of the disputed amount, the Owner shall pay the Contractor the amount certified in the Architect's final Certificate for Payment.

§ 12.2.3 The Owner's final payment to the Contractor shall be made no later than 30 days after the issuance of the Architect's final Certificate for Payment, or as follows:

§ 12.2.4 If, subsequent to final payment, and at the Owner's request, the Contractor incurs costs, described in Article 7 and not excluded by Article 8, to correct defective or nonconforming Work, the Owner shall reimburse the Contractor for such costs, and the Contractor's Fee applicable thereto, on the same basis as if such costs had been incurred prior to final payment, but not in excess of the Guaranteed Maximum Price. If adjustments to the Contract Sum are provided for in Section 5.1.7, the amount of those adjustments shall be recalculated, taking into account any reimbursements made pursuant to this Section 12.2.4 in determining the net amount to be paid by the Owner to the Contractor.

§ 12.3 Interest

Payments due and unpaid under the Contract shall bear interest from the date payment is due at the rate stated below, or in the absence thereof, at the legal rate prevailing from time to time at the place where the Project is located.
(Insert rate of interest agreed upon, if any.)

________ % ________

Init.

/

ARTICLE 13 DISPUTE RESOLUTION
§ 13.1 Initial Decision Maker
The Architect will serve as Initial Decision Maker pursuant to Article 15 of AIA Document A201–2017, unless the parties appoint below another individual, not a party to the Agreement, to serve as Initial Decision Maker.
(If the parties mutually agree, insert the name, address and other contact information of the Initial Decision Maker, if other than the Architect.)

§ 13.2 Binding Dispute Resolution
For any Claim subject to, but not resolved by mediation pursuant to Article 15 of AIA Document A201–2017, the method of binding dispute resolution shall be as follows:
(Check the appropriate box.)

☐ Arbitration pursuant to Section 15 of AIA Document A201–2017

☐ Litigation in a court of competent jurisdiction

☐ Other *(Specify)*

If the Owner and Contractor do not select a method of binding dispute resolution, or do not subsequently agree in writing to a binding dispute resolution method other than litigation, Claims will be resolved by litigation in a court of competent jurisdiction.

ARTICLE 14 TERMINATION OR SUSPENSION
§ 14.1 Termination
§ 14.1.1 The Contract may be terminated by the Owner or the Contractor as provided in Article 14 of AIA Document A201–2017.

§ 14.1.2 Termination by the Owner for Cause
§ 14.1.2.1 If the Owner terminates the Contract for cause as provided in Article 14 of AIA Document A201–2017, the amount, if any, to be paid to the Contractor under Article 14 of AIA Document A201–2017 shall not cause the Guaranteed Maximum Price to be exceeded, nor shall it exceed an amount calculated as follows:

.1 Take the Cost of the Work incurred by the Contractor to the date of termination;
.2 Add the Contractor's Fee, computed upon the Cost of the Work to the date of termination at the rate stated in Section 5.1.1 or, if the Contractor's Fee is stated as a fixed sum in that Section, an amount that bears the same ratio to that fixed-sum Fee as the Cost of the Work at the time of termination bears to a reasonable estimate of the probable Cost of the Work upon its completion;
.3 Subtract the aggregate of previous payments made by the Owner; and
.4 Subtract the costs and damages incurred, or to be incurred, by the Owner under Article 14 of AIA Document A201–2017.

§ 14.1.2.2 The Owner shall also pay the Contractor fair compensation, either by purchase or rental at the election of the Owner, for any equipment owned by the Contractor that the Owner elects to retain and that is not otherwise included in the Cost of the Work under Section 14.1.2.1.1. To the extent that the Owner elects to take legal assignment of subcontracts and purchase orders (including rental agreements), the Contractor shall, as a condition of receiving the payments referred to in this Article 14, execute and deliver all such papers and take all such steps, including the legal assignment of such subcontracts and other contractual rights of the Contractor, as the Owner may require for the purpose of fully vesting in the Owner the rights and benefits of the Contractor under such subcontracts or purchase orders.

§ 14.1.3 Termination by the Owner for Convenience
If the Owner terminates the Contract for convenience in accordance with Article 14 of AIA Document A201–2017, then the Owner shall pay the Contractor a termination fee as follows:
(Insert the amount of or method for determining the fee, if any, payable to the Contractor following a termination for the Owner's convenience.)

§ 14.2 Suspension
The Work may be suspended by the Owner as provided in Article 14 of AIA Document A201–2017; in such case, the Guaranteed Maximum Price and Contract Time shall be increased as provided in Article 14 of AIA Document A201–2017, except that the term "profit" shall be understood to mean the Contractor's Fee as described in Article 5 and Section 6.4 of this Agreement.

ARTICLE 15 MISCELLANEOUS PROVISIONS
§ 15.1 Where reference is made in this Agreement to a provision of AIA Document A201–2017 or another Contract Document, the reference refers to that provision as amended or supplemented by other provisions of the Contract Documents.

§ 15.2 The Owner's representative:
(Name, address, email address and other information)

§ 15.3 The Contractor's representative:
(Name, address, email address and other information)

§ 15.4 Neither the Owner's nor the Contractor's representative shall be changed without ten days' prior notice to the other party.

§ 15.5 Insurance and Bonds
§ 15.5.1 The Owner and the Contractor shall purchase and maintain insurance as set forth in AIA Document A102™–2017, Standard Form of Agreement Between Owner and Contractor where the basis of payment is the Cost of the Work Plus a Fee with a Guaranteed Maximum Price, Exhibit A, Insurance and Bonds, and elsewhere in the Contract Documents.

§ 15.5.2 The Contractor shall provide bonds as set forth in AIA Document A102™–2017 Exhibit A, and elsewhere in the Contract Documents.

§ 15.6 Notice in electronic format, pursuant to Article 1 of AIA Document A201–2017, may be given in accordance with AIA Document E203™–2013, Building Information Modeling and Digital Data Exhibit, if completed, or as otherwise set forth below:
(If other than in accordance with AIA Document E203–2013, insert requirements for delivering notice in electronic format such as name, title, and email address of the recipient and whether and how the system will be required to generate a read receipt for the transmission.)

Init.
/

§ 15.7 Other provisions:

ARTICLE 16 ENUMERATION OF CONTRACT DOCUMENTS

§ 16.1 This Agreement is comprised of the following documents:

.1 AIA Document A102™–2017, Standard Form of Agreement Between Owner and Contractor

.2 AIA Document A102™–2017, Exhibit A, Insurance and Bonds

.3 AIA Document A201™–2017, General Conditions of the Contract for Construction

.4 AIA Document E203™–2013, Building Information Modeling and Digital Data Exhibit, dated as indicated below:
(Insert the date of the E203-2013 incorporated into this Agreement.)

.5 Drawings

Number	Title	Date

.6 Specifications

Section	Title	Date	Pages

.7 Addenda, if any:

Number	Date	Pages

Portions of Addenda relating to bidding or proposal requirements are not part of the Contract Documents unless the bidding or proposal requirements are also enumerated in this Article 16.

.8 Other Exhibits:
(Check all boxes that apply.)

☐ AIA Document E204™–2017, Sustainable Projects Exhibit, dated as indicated below:
(Insert the date of the E204-2017 incorporated into this Agreement.)

☐ The Sustainability Plan:

Title	Date	Pages

☐ Supplementary and other Conditions of the Contract:

Document	Title	Date	Pages

.9 Other documents, if any, listed below:
(List here any additional documents that are intended to form part of the Contract Documents. AIA Document A201–2017 provides that the advertisement or invitation to bid, Instructions to Bidders, sample forms, the Contractor's bid or proposal, portions of Addenda relating to bidding or proposal requirements, and other information furnished by the Owner in anticipation of receiving bids or proposals, are not part of the Contract Documents unless enumerated in this Agreement. Any such documents should be listed here only if intended to be part of the Contract Documents.)

This Agreement entered into as of the day and year first written above.

OWNER *(Signature)*	**CONTRACTOR** *(Signature)*
(Printed name and title)	*(Printed name and title)*

Exhibit 15

ConsensusDocs 230

Standard Form of Agreement and General Conditions between Owner and Contractor (Cost of Work Plus a Fee with GMP)

ConsensusDocs®
BUILDING A BETTER WAY

ConsensusDocs® 230
STANDARD AGREEMENT AND GENERAL CONDITIONS BETWEEN OWNER AND CONSTRUCTOR (Cost of the Work Plus a Fee with GMP)

This page is solely for the information and convenience of ConsensusDocs users, and is not a part of the contract. Gray boxes indicate where you should click and type in your project information. The yellow shading is a Word® default function that displays editable text. Shading can be turned off by going to the Review tab, select "Restrict Editing" button and uncheck "Highlight the regions I can edit". In Word 2003 you will find this option under the Tools tab, Options, Security tab, Protect Document button.

EMBEDDED INSTRUCTIONS are provided solely to help you complete the document. To display or hide instructions select the "¶" button under the "Home" tab to show all formatting marks.

Red Boxes: Instructions for fields that are typically required to complete contract.
Blue Boxes: Instructions for fields that may or may not be required for a complete contract.
Green Boxes: Provide general instructions or ConsensusDocs Coalition Guidebook comments, which can be found at www.ConsensusDocs.org/guidebook

This document was developed through a collaborative effort of organizations representing a wide cross-section of the design and construction industry. This document has important legal and insurance consequences, and it is not intended as a substitute for competent professional services and advice. This document must be reviewed and adapted to meet your project-specific needs. Federal, State and Local laws may vary with respect to the applicability or enforceability of specific provisions in this document. CONSENSUSDOCS SPECIFICALLY DISCLAIMS ALL WARRANTIES, EXPRESS OR IMPLIED, INCLUDING ANY WARRANTY OF MERCHANTABILITY OR FITNESS FOR A PARTICULAR PURPOSE. PURCHASER ASSUMES ALL LIABILITY WITH RESPECT TO THE USE OF THIS DOCUMENT, AND CONSENSUSDOCS AND ANY OF THE ORGANIZATIONS SHALL NOT BE LIABLE FOR ANY DIRECT, INDIRECT OR CONSEQUENTIAL DAMAGES RESULTING FROM SUCH USE. For additional information, please contact ConsensusDocs, 2300 Wilson Blvd, Suite 300, Arlington, VA 22201, 866-925-DOCS (3627), support@consensusdocs.org or www.ConsensusDocs.org

ConsensusDocs® 230
STANDARD AGREEMENT AND GENERAL CONDITIONS BETWEEN OWNER AND CONSTRUCTOR (Cost of the Work Plus a Fee with GMP)

TABLE OF ARTICLES

ARTICLE 1 AGREEMENT

Job Number: [_____] Account Code: [_____]

This Agreement is made this [_____] day of [_____] in the year [_____],

by and between the

OWNER [_____]

and the

CONSTRUCTOR [_____]

Tax identification number (TIN) [_____]
Contractor License No., if applicable [_____]

for construction and services in connection with the following

PROJECT [_____].

Design Professional is [_____].

ARTICLE 2 GENERAL PROVISIONS

2.1 PARTIES' RELATIONSHIP Each Party agrees to act on the basis of mutual trust, good faith, and fair dealing, and perform in an economical and timely manner. The Parties shall each endeavor to promote harmony and cooperation among all Project participants.

2.1.1 Neither Constructor nor any of its agents or employees shall act on behalf of or in the name of Owner.

2.2 ETHICS Each Party shall perform with integrity. Each shall (a) avoid conflicts of interest; and (b) promptly disclose to the other Party any conflicts that may arise. Each Party warrants it has not and shall not pay or receive any contingent fees or gratuities to or from the other Party, including agents, officers, employees, Subcontractors, Subsubcontractors, Suppliers, or Others to secure preferential treatment.

2.3 DESIGN PROFESSIONAL Owner, through its Design Professional, shall provide all architectural and engineering design services necessary for the completion of the Work, excluding, however, (a) design services delegated to Constructor in accordance with §3.16, and (b) services within the construction means, methods, techniques, sequences, and procedures employed by Constructor, its Subcontractors and Subsubcontractors in connection with their construction operations.

2.3.1 Owner shall obtain from Design Professional either a license for Constructor and Subcontractors to use the design documents prepared for the Project by Design Professional or ownership of the copyrights for such design documents, and Owner shall indemnify and hold harmless Constructor against any suits or claims of infringement of any copyrights or licenses arising out of the use of such design documents.

2.4 DEFINITIONS

2.4.1 "Agreement" means this ConsensusDocs 230 Standard Agreement and General Conditions Between Owner and Constructor (Basis of Payment is Cost of the Work Plus a Fee with GMP), as modified by the Parties, and exhibits and attachments made part of this agreement upon its execution.

2.4.1.1 The following exhibits are part of this Agreement:
Exhibit A: Schedule of the Work, [_____] pages.
Exhibit B: Labor Relations, if applicable.

2.4.2 "Business Day" means all Days, except weekends and official federal or state holidays where the Project is located.

2.4.3 A "Change Order" is a written order signed by the Parties after execution of this Agreement, indicating a change in the scope of Work, GMP, or Contract Time, including substitutions proposed by Constructor and accepted by Owner.

2.4.4 "Constructor" is the person or entity identified in ARTICLE 1. References to General Contractor or Contractor in the Contract Documents may be a reference to Constructor.

2.4.5 "Constructor's Contingency" is the difference between the GMP and the estimated Cost of the Work plus the Constructor's Fee.

2.4.6 "Constructor's Fee" is the compensation paid to Constructor for salaries and other mandatory or customary compensation of Constructor's employees at its principal and branch offices except employees listed in §8.1.2, general and administrative expenses of Constructor's principal and branch offices other than the field office, and Constructor's capital expenses, including interest on Constructor's capital employed for the Work, and profit.

2.4.7 "Contract Documents" consist of (a) this Agreement, (b) documents listed in §15.1 as existing contract documents, (c) drawing, specifications, addenda issued and acknowledged before execution of this Agreement, (d) information furnished by Owner pursuant to §3.14.4, and (e) Change Orders, Interim Directives, and amendments issued in accordance with this Agreement.

2.4.8 "Contract Price" is the amount indicated in ARTICLE 8 and represents full compensation for performance by Constructor of the Work in conformance with the Contract Documents.

2.4.9 "Contract Time" is the period between the Date of Commencement and Final Completion.

2.4.10 "Cost of the Work" means the costs and discounts specified in ARTICLE 8.

2.4.11 "Date of Commencement" is as set forth in §6.1.

2.4.12 "Day" means a calendar day.

2.4.13 "Defective Work" is any portion of the Work that does not conform to the requirements of the Contract Documents.

2.4.14 "Design Professional" means the licensed architect or engineer, and its consultants, retained by Owner to perform design services for the Project.

2.4.15 "Final Completion" occurs on the date when Constructor's obligations under this Agreement are complete and accepted by Owner and final payment becomes due and payable. This date shall be confirmed by a Certificate of Final Completion signed by the Parties.

2.4.16 "Hazardous Material" is any substance of material identified now or in the future as hazardous under the Law, or any other substance or material that may be considered hazardous or otherwise subject to statutory or regulatory requirement governing handling, disposal, or cleanup.

2.4.17 "Interim Directive" is a written order containing Work instructions directed by Owner pursuant to §9.2 and that is signed by Owner after execution of this Agreement and before Substantial Completion.

2.4.18 "Law" means federal, state, or local law, ordinance, code, rule, and regulation applicable to the Work with which Constructor must comply that are enacted as of the Agreement date.

2.4.19 "Others" means Owner's other (a) contractors, (b) suppliers, (c) subcontractors, subsubcontractors, or suppliers of (a) and (b); and others employed directly or indirectly by (a), (b), or (c) or any by any of them or for whose acts any of them may be liable.

2.4.20 "Overhead" means (a) payroll costs, burden, and other compensation of Constructor's employees in Constructor's principal and branch offices; (b) general and administrative expenses of Constructor's principal and branch offices including charges against Constructor for delinquent payments, and (c) Constructor's capital expenses, including interest on capital used for the Work.

2.4.21 "Owner" is the person or entity identified in ARTICLE 1.

2.4.22 "Parties" are collectively Owner and Constructor.

2.4.23 "Project," as identified in ARTICLE 1, is the building, facility, or other improvements for which Constructor is to perform Work under this Agreement. It may also include construction by Owner or Others.

2.4.24 "Schedule of the Work" is the document prepared by Constructor that specifies the dates on which Constructor plans to begin and complete various parts of the Work, including dates on which information and approvals are required from Owner.

2.4.25 "Subcontractor" is a person or entity retained by Constructor as an independent contractor to provide the labor, materials, equipment, or services necessary to complete a specific portion of the Work. Subcontractor does not include Design Professional or Others.

2.4.26 "Substantial Completion of the Work," or of a designated portion, occurs on the date when the Work is sufficiently complete in accordance with the Contract Documents so that Owner may occupy or utilize the Project, or a designated portion, for the use for which it is intended, without unapproved disruption. The issuance of a certificate of occupancy is not a prerequisite for Substantial Completion if the certificate of occupancy cannot be obtained due to factors beyond Constructor's control. This date shall be confirmed by a certificate of Substantial Completion signed by the Parties.

2.4.27 "Subsubcontractor" is a person or entity who has an agreement with a Subcontractor, another subsubcontractor, or Supplier to perform any portion of the Work or to supply material or equipment.

2.4.28 "Supplier" is a person or entity retained by Constructor to provide material or equipment for the Work.

2.4.29 "Terrorism" means a violent act, or an act that is dangerous to human life, property, or infrastructure, that is committed by an individual or individuals and that appears to be part of an effort to coerce a civilian population or to influence the policy or affect the conduct of any government by coercion. Terrorism includes, but is not limited to, any act certified by the United States government as an act of terrorism pursuant to the Terrorism Risk Insurance Act, as amended.

2.4.30 "Work" means the construction and services necessary or incidental to fulfill Constructor's obligations for the Project in accordance with and reasonably inferable from the Contract Documents. Work may refer to the whole Project or only a part of the Project if work is also being performed by Owner or Others.

2.4.31 "Worksite" means the area of the Project location identified in ARTICLE 1 where the Work is to be performed.

ARTICLE 3 CONSTRUCTOR'S RESPONSIBILITIES

Constructor shall use its diligent efforts to perform the Work in an expeditious manner consistent with the Contract Documents. Such Work includes furnishing construction administration and management services.

3.1 GENERAL RESPONSIBILITIES

3.1.1 Constructor shall provide all labor, materials, equipment, and services necessary to complete the Work, all of which shall be provided in full accord with the Contract Documents and shall include any Work reasonably inferable from the Contract Documents.

3.1.2 Constructor represents that it is an independent contractor and that it is familiar with the type of work required by this Agreement.

3.1.3 Unless the Contract Documents instruct otherwise, Constructor shall be responsible for the supervision and coordination of the Work, including the construction means, methods, techniques, sequences, and procedures utilized. When following construction means, methods, techniques, sequences, or procedures instructed by the Contract Documents, Constructor is not liable to Owner for damages resulting from compliance with such instructions unless (a) Constructor recognized and (b) failed to timely report to Owner any error, inconsistency, omission, or unsafe practice that it discovered in such requirements.

3.1.4 Constructor shall perform Work only within locations allowed by the Contract Documents, Law, and applicable permits.

3.2 COOPERATION WITH WORK OF OWNER AND OTHERS

3.2.1 Owner may perform work at the Worksite directly or by Others. Any agreements with Others to perform construction or operations related to the Project shall include provisions pertaining to insurance, indemnification, waiver of subrogation, consequential damages, coordination, interference, cleanup, and safety that are substantively the same as the corresponding provisions of this Agreement.

3.2.2 If Owner elects to perform work at the Worksite directly or by Others, the Parties shall coordinate the activities of all forces at the Worksite and agree upon fair and reasonable schedules and operational procedures for Worksite activities. Owner shall require each separate contractor to cooperate with Constructor and to assist with the coordination of activities and the review of construction schedules and operations. In accordance with §6.3, Contract Price and Contract Time may be equitably adjusted for changes resulting from the coordination of construction activities, and the Schedule of the Work shall be revised accordingly.

3.2.3 With regard to the work of Owner and Others, Constructor shall: (a) proceed with the Work in a manner that does not hinder, delay, or interfere with the work of Owner or Others or cause the work of Owner or Others to become defective; (b) afford Owner and Others reasonable access for introduction and storage of their materials and equipment and performance of their activities; and (c) coordinate Constructor's Work with theirs.

3.2.4 Before proceeding with any portion of the Work affected by the construction or operations of Owner or Others, Constructor shall give Owner prompt written notification of any defects Constructor discovers in their work which will prevent the proper execution of the Work. Constructor's obligations in this subsection do not create a responsibility for the work of Owner or Others, but are for the purpose of facilitating the Work. If Constructor does not notify Owner of defects interfering with the performance of the Work, Constructor acknowledges that the work of Owner or Others is not defective and is acceptable for the proper execution of the Work. Following receipt of written notice from Constructor of defects, Owner shall promptly issue an Interim Directive informing Constructor what action, if any, Constructor shall take with regard to the defects.

3.3 CONTRACT DOCUMENT REVIEW

3.3.1 Before commencing the Work, Constructor shall examine and compare the drawings and specifications with information furnished in the Contract Documents, relevant field measurements made by Constructor, and any visible conditions at the Worksite affecting the Work.

3.3.2 Should Constructor discover any errors, omissions, or inconsistencies in the Contract Documents, Constructor shall promptly report them to Owner. It is recognized, however, that Constructor is not acting in the capacity of a licensed design professional, and that Constructor's examination is to facilitate construction and does not create an affirmative responsibility to detect errors, omissions, or inconsistencies or to ascertain compliance with a Law, building code, or regulation. Following receipt of written notice from Constructor of errors, omissions, or inconsistencies, Owner shall promptly inform Constructor what action, if any, Constructor shall take with regard to the errors, omissions, or inconsistencies.

3.3.3 In accordance with this Agreement, Constructor may be entitled to adjustments of the Contract Price or Contract Time because of clarifications or instructions arising out of Constructor's reports described in this §3.3.

3.3.4 Nothing in §3.3 shall relieve Constructor of responsibility for its own errors, inconsistencies, or omissions.

3.4 CONSTRUCTION PERSONNEL AND SUPERVISION

3.4.1 Constructor shall provide competent supervision for the performance of the Work. Before commencing the Work, Constructor shall notify Owner in writing of the name and qualifications of its proposed superintendent(s) and project manager so Owner may review their qualifications. If, for reasonable cause, Owner refuses to approve an individual, or withdraws its approval after once giving it, Constructor shall name a different superintendent or project manager for Owner's review. Any disapproved superintendent shall not perform in that capacity thereafter at the Worksite.

3.4.2 Constructor shall be responsible to Owner for acts or omissions of a person or entity performing on behalf of Constructor or any of its Subcontractors and Suppliers.

3.4.3 Constructor shall permit only qualified persons to perform the Work. Constructor shall enforce safety procedures, strict discipline, and good order among persons performing the Work. If Owner determines that a particular person does not follow safety procedures, or is unfit or unskilled for the assigned Work, Constructor shall immediately reassign the person upon receipt of Owner's Interim Directive to do so.

3.4.4 CONSTRUCTOR'S REPRESENTATIVE Constructor's authorized representative is [_____]. Constructor's Representative shall possess full authority to receive instructions from Owner and to act on those instructions. If Constructor changes its representative or the representative's authority, Constructor shall immediately notify Owner in writing.

3.5 GUARANTEED MAXIMUM PRICE (GMP)

3.5.1 The GMP is the maximum amount Owner shall pay to Constructor for the performance of the Work and shall include the estimated Cost of the Work as defined in ARTICLE 8 and Constructor's Fee as defined in ARTICLE 7. The GMP shall be subject to modification as provided in ARTICLE 9. Constructor does not guarantee any specific line item provided as part of the GMP, but agrees that it will be responsible for paying all costs of completing the Work that exceed the GMP, as adjusted in accordance with this Agreement. Owner and Constructor agree that the GMP

_____ is identified in an amendment attached hereto or

_____ shall be determined in accordance with §3.5.2 below.

3.5.2 BASIS OF GUARANTEED MAXIMUM PRICE If the GMP has not been established prior to execution of this Agreement as identified in §3.5.1 above, Constructor shall prepare for Owner a GMP Proposal. Constructor shall include as part of the GMP Proposal a written statement of its basis, which, to the extent deemed necessary by Owner or Constructor, shall include:

3.5.2.1 list of the drawings and specifications, including all addenda, which were used in preparation of the GMP Proposal;

3.5.2.2 list of allowances and a statement of their basis;

3.5.2.3 list of the assumptions and clarifications made by Constructor in the preparation of the GMP Proposal to supplement the information contained in the drawings and specifications;

3.5.2.4 Date of Substantial Completion and Date of Final Completion upon which the GMP is based, and the Schedule of Work upon which Date of Substantial Completion and Date of Final Completion are based;

3.5.2.5 schedule of applicable alternate prices;

3.5.2.6 schedule of applicable unit prices;

3.5.2.7 statement of Additional Services included, if any;

3.5.2.8 statement of Constructor's Contingency, if any, as either a lump sum or as a percentage of the initial estimated Cost of the Work;

3.5.2.9 statement of any work to be self-performed by Constructor; and

3.5.2.10 statement identifying all patented or copyrighted materials, methods, or systems selected by Constructor and incorporated in the Work that are likely to require the payment of royalties or license fees.

3.5.3 Constructor shall meet with Owner and Design Professional to review the GMP Proposal. If Owner or Design Professional discovers any inconsistencies, inaccuracies, or omissions in the information presented, they shall promptly notify Constructor, who shall make appropriate adjustments to the GMP. Owner shall then give prompt written approval of the GMP Proposal at which time it becomes an amendment to this Agreement.

3.5.4 Owner shall cause Design Professional to revise the drawings and specifications to the extent necessary to reflect the clarifications, assumptions, and allowances on which the GMP is based. Revised drawings and specifications shall be furnished to Constructor in accordance with the current Schedule of the Work, unless otherwise agreed by Owner and Constructor. Constructor shall promptly notify Owner and Design Professional if the revised drawings and specifications are inconsistent with the GMP's clarifications, assumptions, and allowances.

3.5.5 If the Contract Documents are not complete at the time the GMP Proposal is submitted to Owner, Constructor shall provide in the GMP for further development of the Contract Documents. Such further development does not include changes in scope, systems, kinds and quality of materials, finishes, or equipment, all of which, if required, shall be incorporated by Change Order.

3.5.6 Allowances shall include the costs of materials, supplies, and equipment delivered to the Worksite less applicable trade discounts and including requisite taxes, unloading and handling at the Worksite, and labor and installation, unless specifically stated otherwise. Constructor's overhead and profit for the allowances shall be included in the GMP, but not in the allowances. The GMP shall be adjusted by Change Order to reflect the actual costs when they are greater than or less than the allowances.

3.5.7 FAILURE TO ACCEPT THE GMP PROPOSAL Unless Owner accepts the GMP Proposal in writing on or before the date specified in the GMP Proposal for such acceptance and so notifies Constructor, the GMP Proposal shall not be effective. If Owner fails to accept the GMP Proposal, or rejects the GMP Proposal, Owner shall have the right to:

3.5.7.1 suggest modifications to the GMP Proposal. If such modifications are accepted in writing by Constructor, the GMP Proposal shall be deemed accepted in accordance with §3.5.3 at which time it becomes an amendment to this Agreement. If such modifications are not accepted, Constructor may either offer a new GMP Proposal, or terminate the Agreement with the Parties to bear their own costs except as otherwise provided in §12.4.2, or

3.5.7.2 terminate the Agreement for convenience in accordance with §12.4.

3.5.8 If Owner does not either (a) accept the GMP Proposal in writing, (b) suggest modifications in accordance with §3.5.7.1, or (c) terminate the Agreement for convenience as contemplated by §3.5.7.2 on or before the date specified in the GMP Proposal for such acceptance, Constructor may terminate the Agreement with the Parties to bear their own costs except as otherwise provided in §12.4.2.

3.5.9 PRE-GMP WORK Prior to Owner's acceptance of the GMP Proposal, Constructor shall not incur any cost to be reimbursed as part of the Cost of the Work, except as provided in this Agreement or as Owner may specifically authorize in writing.

3.6 WORKMANSHIP The Work shall be executed in accordance with the Contract Documents in a workmanlike manner. All materials used in the Work shall be furnished in sufficient quantities to facilitate the proper and expeditious execution of the Work and shall be new except as may be otherwise provided in the Contract Documents.

3.7 MATERIALS FURNISHED BY OWNER OR OTHERS If the Work includes installation of materials or equipment furnished by Owner or Others, it shall be the responsibility of Constructor to examine the items so provided and thereupon handle, store, and install the items, unless otherwise provided in the Contract Documents, with such skill and care as to provide a satisfactory and proper installation. Loss or damage due to acts or omissions of Constructor shall be the responsibility of Constructor and may be deducted from any amounts due or to become due Constructor. Any defects discovered in such materials or equipment shall be reported at once to Owner. Following receipt of written notice from Constructor of defects, Owner shall promptly inform Constructor what action, if any, Constructor shall take with regard to the defects.

3.8 TESTS AND INSPECTIONS

3.8.1 Constructor shall schedule all required tests, approvals, and inspections of the Work or portions thereof at appropriate times so as not to delay the progress of the Work or other work related to the Project. Constructor shall give proper notice to all required parties of such tests, approvals, and inspections. If feasible, Owner and Others may timely observe the tests at the normal place of testing. Except as provided in §3.8.3, Owner shall bear all expenses associated with tests, inspections, and approvals required by the Contract Documents, which, unless otherwise agreed to, shall be conducted by an independent testing laboratory or entity retained by Owner. Unless otherwise required by the Contract Documents, required certificates of testing, approval, or inspection shall be secured by Constructor and promptly delivered to Owner.

3.8.2 If Owner or appropriate authorities determine that tests, inspections, or approvals in addition to those required by the Contract Documents will be necessary, Constructor shall arrange for the procedures and give timely notice to Owner and Others who may observe the procedures. Costs of the additional tests, inspections, or approvals are at Owner's expense except as provided in the subsection below.

3.8.3 If the procedures described in §3.8.1—§3.8.2 indicate that portions of the Work fail to comply with the Contract Documents, Constructor shall be responsible for the costs of correction and retesting.

3.9 WARRANTY

3.9.1 Constructor warrants that all materials and equipment shall be new unless otherwise specified, of good quality, in conformance with the Contract Documents, and free from defective workmanship and materials. At Owner's request, Constructor shall furnish satisfactory evidence of the quality and type of materials and equipment furnished. Constructor further warrants that the Work shall be free from material defects not intrinsic in the design or materials required in the Contract Documents. Constructor's warranty does not include remedies for defects or damages caused by normal wear and tear during normal usage, use for a purpose for which the Project was not intended, improper or insufficient maintenance, modifications performed by Owner or others, or abuse. Constructor's warranty shall commence on the Date of Substantial Completion of the Work or of a designated portion.

3.9.2 To the extent products, equipment, systems, or materials incorporated in the Work are specified and purchased by Owner, they shall be covered exclusively by the warranty of the manufacturer. There are no warranties which extend beyond the description on the face of any such warranty. For such incorporated items, ALL OTHER WARRANTIES EXPRESSED OR IMPLIED INCLUDING THE WARRANTY OF MERCHANTABILITY AND THE WARRANTY OF FITNESS FOR A PARTICULAR PURPOSE ARE EXPRESSLY DISCLAIMED.

3.9.3 Constructor shall obtain from its Subcontractors and Suppliers any special or extended warranties required by the Contract Documents. Constructor's liability for such warranties shall be limited to the one-year correction period as provided in the section below. After that period, Constructor shall provide reasonable assistance to Owner in enforcing the obligations of Subcontractors or Suppliers for such extended warranties.

3.10 CORRECTION OF WORK WITHIN ONE YEAR

3.10.1 Before Substantial Completion and within one year after the date of Substantial Completion of the Work, if any Defective Work is found, Owner shall promptly notify Constructor in writing. Unless Owner provides written acceptance of the condition, Constructor shall promptly correct the Defective Work at its own cost and time and bear the expense of additional services required for correction of any Defective Work for which it is responsible. If within the one-year correction period Owner discovers and does not promptly notify Constructor or give Constructor an opportunity to test or correct Defective Work as reasonably requested by Constructor, Owner waives Constructor's obligation to correct that Defective Work, as well as Owner's right to claim a breach of the warranty with respect to that Defective Work.

3.10.2 With respect to any portion of Work first performed after Substantial Completion, the one-year correction period shall commence when that portion of the Work is substantially complete. Correction periods shall not be extended by corrective work performed by Constructor.

3.10.3 If Constructor fails to correct Defective Work within a reasonable time after receipt of written notice from Owner before final payment, Owner may correct it in accordance with Owner's right to carry out the Work. In such case, an appropriate Change Order shall be issued deducting the cost of correcting the Defective Work from payments then or thereafter due Constructor. If payments then or thereafter due Constructor are not sufficient to cover such amounts, Constructor shall pay the difference to Owner.

3.10.4 Constructor's obligations and liability, if any, with respect to any Defective Work discovered after the one-year correction period shall be determined by the Law. If, after the one-year correction period but before the applicable limitation period has expired, Owner discovers any Work which Owner considers Defective Work, Owner shall, unless the Defective Work requires emergency correction, promptly notify Constructor and allow Constructor an opportunity to correct the Work if Constructor elects to do so. If Constructor elects to correct the Work, it shall provide written notice of such intent within fourteen (14) Days of its receipt of notice from Owner and shall complete the correction of Work within a mutually agreed timeframe. If Constructor does not elect to correct the Work, Owner may have the Work corrected by itself or others, and, if Owner intends to seek recovery of those costs from Constructor, Owner shall promptly provide Constructor with an accounting of the actual correction costs.

3.10.5 If Constructor's correction or removal of Defective Work causes damage to or destroys other completed or partially completed Work or existing buildings, Constructor shall be responsible for the cost of correcting such damage.

3.10.6 The one-year period for correction of Defective Work does not constitute a limitation period with respect to the enforcement of Constructor's other obligations under the Contract Documents.

3.10.7 Before final payment, at Owner's option and with Constructor's agreement, Owner may elect to accept Defective Work rather than require its removal and correction. In such case, the GMP shall be equitably adjusted for any diminution in the value of the Project caused by such Defective Work.

3.11 CORRECTION OF COVERED WORK

3.11.1 Upon issuance of an Interim Directive, Work that has been covered without a requirement that it be inspected before being covered shall be uncovered for Owner's inspection. Owner shall pay for the costs of uncovering and replacement if the Work proves to be in conformance with the Contract Documents, or if the defective condition was caused by Owner or Others. If the uncovered Work proves to be defective, Constructor shall pay the costs of uncovering and replacement.

3.11.2 If any Work is covered contrary to requirements in the Contract Documents, Owner may issue an Interim Directive to uncover the Work for Owner's observation and recover the Work all at Constructor's expense and with Contract Time adjustment.

3.12 SAFETY

3.8

3.12.1 SAFETY PROGRAMS Constructor holds overall responsibility for safety. However, such obligation does not relieve Subcontractors of their safety responsibilities nor to comply with the Law. Constructor shall prevent against injury, loss, or damage to persons or property by taking reasonable steps to protect: (a) its employees and other persons at the Worksite; (b) materials and equipment stored onsite or offsite for use in the Work; and (c) property located at the Worksite and adjacent to work areas.

3.12.2 CONSTRUCTOR'S SAFETY REPRESENTATIVE Constructor shall designate an individual at the Worksite in its employ as its safety representative. Unless otherwise identified by Constructor in writing to Owner, Constructor's project superintendent shall serve as its safety representative. Constructor shall report promptly in writing to Owner all recordable accidents and injuries occurring at the Worksite. When Constructor is required to file an accident report with a public authority, Constructor shall furnish a copy of the report to Owner.

3.12.3 Constructor shall provide Owner with copies of all notices required of Constructor by Law. Constructor's safety program shall comply with the requirements of authorities having jurisdiction.

3.12.4 Damage or loss not insured under property insurance which may arise from the Work, to the extent caused by the negligent or intentionally wrongful acts or omissions of Constructor, or anyone for whose acts Constructor may be liable, shall be promptly remedied by Constructor.

3.12.5 If Owner deems any part of the Work or Worksite unsafe, Owner, without assuming responsibility for Constructor's safety program, may require by Interim Directive, Constructor to stop performance of the Work, take corrective measures satisfactory to Owner, or both. If Constructor does not adopt corrective measures, Owner may perform them and reduce the amount of the GMP by the cost of the corrective measures. Constructor agrees to make no claim for damages, for an increase in the GMP or for a change in the Contract Time based on Constructor's compliance with Owner's reasonable request.

3.13 EMERGENCIES

3.13.1 In an emergency affecting the safety of persons or property, Constructor shall act in a reasonable manner to prevent threatened damage, injury, or loss. Any change in the GMP, estimated Cost of the Work, Constructor's Fee, or Contract Time resulting from the actions of Constructor in an emergency situation shall be determined as provided for in ARTICLE 9.

3.14 HAZARDOUS MATERIALS

3.14.1 Constructor shall not be obligated to commence Work until any Hazardous Material discovered at the Worksite has been removed, rendered, or determined to be harmless by Owner as certified by an independent testing laboratory and approved by the appropriate government agency.

3.14.2 If after commencing Work, Hazardous Material is discovered at the Worksite, Constructor shall be entitled to immediately stop Work in the affected area. Constructor shall report the condition to Owner, Design Professional, and, if required, the governmental agency with jurisdiction.

3.14.3 Constructor shall not resume nor be required to continue any Work affected by any Hazardous Material without written mutual agreement between the Parties after the Hazardous Material has been removed or rendered harmless and only after approval, if necessary, of the governmental agency with jurisdiction.

3.14.4 Owner shall be responsible for retaining an independent testing laboratory to determine the nature of the material encountered and whether the material requires corrective measures or remedial action. Such measures shall be the sole responsibility of Owner, and shall be performed in a manner minimizing any adverse effect upon the Work.

3.14.5 If Constructor incurs additional costs or is delayed due to the presence or remediation of Hazardous Material, Constructor shall be entitled to an equitable adjustment in GMP or Contract Time in accordance with this Agreement.

3.14.6 To the extent permitted by §6.6 and to the extent not caused by the negligent or intentionally wrongful acts or omissions of Constructor, its Subcontractors and Subsubcontractors, and the agents, officers, directors, and employees of each of them, Owner shall defend, indemnify, and hold harmless Constructor, its Subcontractors and Subsubcontractors, and the agents, officers, directors, and employees of each of them, from and against all claims, damages, losses, costs, and expenses, including but not limited to reasonable attorneys' fees, costs, and expenses incurred in connection with any dispute resolution procedure, arising out of or relating to the performance of the Work in any area affected by Hazardous Material.

3.14.7 MATERIALS BROUGHT TO THE WORKSITE

3.14.7.1 Safety Data Sheets (SDS) as required by Law and pertaining to materials or substances used or consumed in the performance of the Work, whether obtained by Constructor, Subcontractors, Owner, or Others, shall be maintained at the Worksite by Constructor and made available to Owner, Subcontractors, and Others.

3.14.7.2 Constructor shall be responsible for the proper delivery, handling, application, storage, removal, and disposal of all materials and substances brought to the Worksite by Constructor and used or consumed in the performance of the Work. Upon the issuance of the Certificate of Substantial Completion, Owner shall be responsible for materials and substances brought to the Worksite by Constructor if such materials or substances are required by the Contract Documents.

3.14.7.3 To the extent caused by the negligent or intentionally wrongful acts or omissions of Constructor, its agents, officers, directors, and employees, Constructor shall defend, indemnify, and hold harmless Owner, its agents, officers, directors, and employees from and against claims, damages, losses, costs, and expenses, including but not limited to reasonable attorneys' fees, costs, and expenses incurred in connection with any dispute resolution procedure, arising out of or relating to the delivery, handling, application, storage, removal, and disposal of all materials and substances brought to the Worksite by Constructor]

3.14.8 §3.14 in its entirety shall survive the completion of the Work or Agreement termination.

3.15 SUBMITTALS

3.15.1 Constructor shall submit to Owner and, if directed, to its Design Professional for review and Owner's approval all shop drawings, samples, product data, and similar submittals required by the Contract Documents. Submittals shall be submitted in electronic form if required by §4.6.1. Constructor shall be responsible to Owner for the accuracy and conformity of its submittals to the Contract Documents. Constructor shall prepare and deliver its submittals to Owner in such time and sequence so as not to delay the performance of the Work or the work of the Owner and Others. When Constructor delivers its submittals to Owner, Constructor shall identify in writing for each submittal all changes, deviations, or substitutions from the requirements of the Contract Documents.

The approval of any Constructor submittal shall not be deemed to authorize changes, deviations, or substitutions from the requirements of the Contact Documents unless a Change Order or Interim Directive specifically authorizes such deviation, substitution, or change. To the extent a change, deviation, or substitution causes an impact to the Constructor's Fee, GMP, or Contract Time, such approval shall be memorialized in a Change Order no later than seven (7) Days following approval by Owner. Neither Design Professional nor Owner shall make any change, deviation, or substitution through the submittal process without specifically identifying and authorizing such deviation to Constructor. If the Contract Documents do not contain submittal requirements pertaining to the Work, Constructor agrees upon request to submit in a timely fashion to Design Professional and Owner for review any shop drawings, samples, product data, manufacturers' literature, or similar submittals as may reasonably be required by Owner.

3.15.2 Owner shall be responsible for review and approval of submittals with reasonable promptness to avoid causing delay.

3.15.3 Constructor shall perform all Work strictly in accordance with approved submittals. Approval of shop drawings is not an authorization to perform Changed Work, unless the procedures of ARTICLE 9 are followed. Approval does not relieve Constructor from responsibility for Defective Work resulting from errors or omissions on the approved shop drawings.

3.15.4 Record copies of the following, incorporating field changes and selections made during construction, shall be accessible at the Worksite and available to Owner upon request: drawings, specifications, addenda, Change Orders, and other modifications, and required submittals including product data, samples, and shop drawings.

3.15.5 Constructor shall prepare and submit to Owner:

[_____] Final marked-up as-built drawings;
[_____] Updated electronic data, in accordance with §4.6.1; or
[_____] Other documentation required by the Contract Documents that specifies how various elements of the Work were actually constructed or installed.

3.16 DESIGN DELEGATION If the Contract Documents specify that Constructor is responsible for the design of a particular system or component to be incorporated into the Project, then Owner shall specify all required performance and design criteria. Constructor shall not be responsible for the adequacy of such performance and design criteria.

As required by the Law, Constructor shall procure design services and certifications necessary to satisfactorily complete the Work from a licensed design professional. The signature and seal of Constructor's design professional shall appear on all drawings, calculations, specifications, certifications, shop drawings, and other submittals related to the Work designed or certified by Constructor's design professional.

3.17 WORKSITE CONDITIONS

3.17.1 WORKSITE VISIT Constructor acknowledges that it has visited, or has had the opportunity to visit, the Worksite to visually inspect the general and local conditions which could affect the Work.

3.17.2 CONCEALED OR UNKNOWN WORKSITE CONDITIONS If a condition encountered at the Worksite is (a) subsurface or other physical condition materially different from those indicated in the Contract Documents, or (b) unusual and unknown physical condition materially different from conditions ordinarily encountered and generally recognized as inherent in Work provided for in the Contract Documents, Constructor shall stop affected Work after the concealed or unknown condition is first observed and give prompt written notice of the condition to Owner and Design Professional. Owner shall investigate and then issue an Interim Directive specifying the extent to which Owner agrees that a concealed or unknown condition exists and directing how Constructor is to proceed. Constructor shall not be required to perform any Work relating to the condition without the written mutual agreement of the Parties. Any change in the Constructor's Fee, GMP, or Contract Time as a result of the condition, including any dispute about its existence or nature, shall be determined as provided in ARTICLE 9.

3.18 PERMITS AND TAXES

3.18.1 Constructor shall give public authorities all notices required by Law and, except for permits and fees that are the responsibility of Owner, shall obtain and pay for all necessary permits, licenses, and renewals pertaining to the Work. Constructor shall provide to Owner copies of all notices, permits, licenses, and renewals required under this Agreement.

3.18.2 Constructor shall pay applicable taxes for the Work provided by Constructor.

3.18.3 If, in accordance with Owner's direction, Constructor claims an exemption for taxes, Owner shall indemnify and hold Constructor harmless from any liability, penalty, interest, fine, tax assessment, attorneys' fees, or other expense or cost incurred by Constructor as a result of any such claim.

3.19 CUTTING, FITTING, AND PATCHING

3.19.1 Constructor shall perform cutting, fitting, and patching necessary to coordinate the various parts of the Work and to prepare its Work for the work of Owner or Others.

3.19.2 Cutting, patching, or altering the work of Owner or Others shall be done with the prior written approval of Owner. Such approval shall not be unreasonably withheld.

3.20 CLEAN UP

3.20.1 Constructor shall regularly remove debris and waste materials at the Worksite resulting from the Work. Before discontinuing Work in an area, Constructor shall clean the area and remove all rubbish and its construction equipment, tools, machinery, waste, and surplus materials. Constructor shall minimize and confine dust and debris resulting from construction activities. At the completion of the Work, Constructor shall remove from the Worksite all construction equipment, tools, surplus materials, waste materials, and debris.

3.20.2 If Constructor fails to commence compliance with cleanup duties within two (2) Business Days after written notification from Owner of non-compliance, Owner may implement appropriate cleanup measures without further notice and shall deduct the reasonable costs from any amounts due or to become due to Constructor in the next payment period.

3.21 CONSTRUCTOR'S CONTINGENCY Constructor's Contingency is for Constructor's exclusive use to cover costs and expenses incurred by Constructor in its performance of the Work. Constructor's Contingency is not intended to be used for changes in scope or for any item that would be the basis for an increase in the GMP. Constructor shall provide Owner with a contemporaneous accounting of charges against Constructor's Contingency, if applicable, with each application for payment.

3.22 CONSTRUCTION SERVICES AND ADMINISTRATION

3.22.1 COST REPORTING Constructor shall maintain in conformance with generally accepted accounting principles a complete and current set of records that are prepared or used by Constructor to calculate the Cost of Work. Owner shall be afforded access to Constructor's records, books, correspondence, instructions, drawings, receipts, vouchers, memoranda, and similar data relating to requested payment for Cost of the Work. Constructor shall preserve all such records for a period of three (3) years after the final payment or longer where required by Law.

3.22.2 Constructor agrees to use reasonable skill and judgment in the preparation of cost estimates and Schedule of the Work, but does not warrant or guarantee them, except to the extent of the GMP.

3.22.3 CONSTRUCTION PERSONNEL AND SUPERVISION

3.22.3.1 Constructor shall provide competent supervision for the performance of the Work. Before commencing the Work Constructor shall notify Owner in writing of the name and qualifications of its proposed superintendent(s) and project manager, so Owner may review the individual's qualifications. If, for reasonable cause, Owner refuses to approve the individual, or withdraws its approval after once giving it, Constructor shall name a different superintendent or project manager for Owner's review. Any disapproved superintendent shall not perform in that capacity thereafter at the Worksite.

3.22.3.2 Constructor shall be responsible to Owner for acts or omissions of persons or entities supplying materials or equipment or performing portions of the Work for or on behalf of Constructor.

3.22.3.3 Constructor shall permit only qualified persons to perform the Work. Constructor shall enforce safety procedures, strict discipline, and good order among persons performing the Work. If Owner determines that a particular person does not follow safety procedures, or is unfit or unskilled for the assigned work, Constructor shall immediately reassign the person upon receipt of Owner's written notice to do so.

3.22.4 COOPERATION WITH WORK OF OWNER AND OTHERS

3.22.4.1 Owner may perform work at the Worksite directly or by Others. Any agreements with Others to perform construction or operations related to the Project shall include provisions pertaining to insurance, indemnification, waiver of subrogation, consequential damages, coordination, interference, clean up, and safety that are substantively the same as the corresponding provisions of this Agreement.

3.22.4.2 If Owner elects to perform work at the Worksite directly or by Others, Constructor and Owner shall coordinate the activities of all forces at the Worksite and agree upon fair and reasonable schedules and operational procedures for Worksite activities. Owner shall require each separate contractor to cooperate with Constructor and assist with the coordination of activities and the review of construction schedules and operations. The GMP and Contract Time shall be equitably adjusted, as mutually agreed by the Parties, for changes made necessary by the coordination of construction activities, and the Schedule of the Work shall be revised accordingly. Constructor, Owner, and Others shall adhere to the revised construction schedule.

3.22.4.3 With regard to the work of Owner and Others, Constructor shall (a) proceed with the Work in a manner which does not hinder, delay, or interfere with the work of Owner or Others or cause the work of Owner or Others to become defective; (b) afford Owner or

Others reasonable access for introduction and storage of their materials and equipment and performance of their activities; and (c) cooperate with Owner's efforts to coordinate Constructor's Work with theirs.

3.22.4.4 Before proceeding with any portion of the Work affected by the construction or operations of Owner or Others, Constructor shall give Owner prompt written notification of any defects Constructor discovers in their work which will prevent the proper execution of the Work. Constructor's obligations in this subsection do not create a responsibility for the work of Owner or Others, but are for the purpose of facilitating the Work. If Constructor does not notify Owner of patent defects interfering with the performance of the Work, Constructor acknowledges that the work of Owner or Others is not patently defective and is acceptable for the proper execution of the Work. Following receipt of written notice from Constructor of defects, Owner shall promptly inform Constructor what action, if any, Constructor shall take with regard to the defects.

3.22.5 MATERIALS, FIXTURES, OR EQUIPMENT FURNISHED BY OWNER OR OTHERS If the Work includes installation of materials, fixtures, or equipment furnished by Owner or Others and incorporated into the Work, it shall be the responsibility of Constructor to examine the items so provided and thereupon handle, store, and install the items, unless otherwise provided in the Contract Documents, with such skill and care as to provide a satisfactory and proper installation. Loss or damage due to acts or omissions of Constructor shall be the responsibility of Constructor and may be deducted from any amounts due or to become due Constructor. Any defects discovered in such materials, fixtures, or equipment shall be reported at once to Owner. Following receipt of written notice from Constructor of defects, Owner shall promptly inform Constructor what action, if any, Constructor shall take with regard to the defects.

3.23 ACCESS TO WORK Constructor shall facilitate the access of Owner, Design Professional, and Others to Work in progress.

3.24 COMPLIANCE WITH THE LAW Constructor shall comply with the Law at its own cost. Constructor shall be liable to Owner for all loss, cost, or expense attributable to any acts or omissions by Constructor, its employees, subcontractors, suppliers, and agents for failure to comply with Law, including fines, penalties, or corrective measures. However, liability under this subsection shall not apply if prior approval by appropriate authorities and Owner is received.

3.24.1 Constructor's Fee, GMP, or Contract Time shall be equitably adjusted by Change Order for additional costs or time needed resulting from any change in Law, including increased taxes enacted after the date of this Agreement.

3.25 CONFIDENTIALITY Constructor shall treat as confidential and not disclose to third-persons, nor use for its own benefit ("Treat as Confidential"), any of Owner's confidential information, know-how, discoveries, production methods, and the like disclosed to Constructor or which Constructor may acquire in performing the Work. To the extent necessary to perform the Work, Constructor's confidentiality obligations do not apply to disclosures to Subcontractors, Subsubcontractors, and Suppliers. Owner shall Treat as Confidential information all of Constructor's estimating systems and historical and parameter cost data disclosed to Owner in performing the Work. Each Party shall specify and mark confidential items to as "Confidential." Confidentiality obligations do not supersede compulsion by Law, a governmental agency or authority, an order of a court of competent jurisdiction, or a validly issued subpoena. In such event, a Party shall promptly notify the other Party to permit that Party's legal objection.

ARTICLE 4 OWNER'S RESPONSIBILITIES

4.1 INFORMATION AND SERVICES Owner's responsibilities under this article shall be fulfilled with reasonable detail and in a timely manner.

4.2 FINANCIAL INFORMATION Before commencing the Work and thereafter, at the written request of Constructor, Owner shall provide Constructor with evidence of Project financing. Evidence of such financing shall be a condition precedent to Constructor's commencing or continuing the Work. Constructor shall be notified before any material change in Project financing.

4.3 WORKSITE INFORMATION To the extent Owner has obtained, or is required in the Contract Documents to obtain, then Owner shall provide the following:

4.3.1 information describing the physical characteristics of the Worksite, including surveys, Worksite evaluations, legal descriptions, data or drawings depicting existing conditions, subsurface conditions and environmental studies, reports, and investigations;

4.3.2 tests, inspections, and other reports dealing with environmental matters, Hazardous Material and other existing conditions, including structural, mechanical, and chemical tests, required by the Contract Documents or by Law;

4.3.3 the limits of Pollution Liability Insurance covering the Worksite held by Owner; and

4.3.4 any other information or services requested in writing by Constructor which are required for Constructor's performance of the Work and under Owner's control.

4.4 BUILDING PERMIT, FEES, AND APPROVALS Except for those permits and fees related to the Work which are the responsibility of Constructor, Owner shall secure and pay for all other permits, approvals, easements, assessments, and fees required for the development, construction, use, or occupancy of permanent structures or for permanent changes in existing facilities, including the building permit.

4.5 MECHANIC'S AND CONSTRUCTION LIEN INFORMATION Within seven (7) Days after receiving Constructor's written request, Owner shall provide Constructor with the information necessary to give notice of or enforce mechanic's lien rights and, where applicable, stop notices. This information shall include Owner's real property interests in the Worksite and the record legal title.

4.6 CONTRACT DOCUMENTS Unless otherwise specified, Owner shall provide [_____] ([_____]) copies of the Contract Documents to Constructor without cost.

4.6.1 ELECTRONIC DOCUMENTS If Owner requires that Owner, Design Professional, and Constructor exchange documents and data in electronic or digital form, before any such exchange, Owner, Design Professional, and Constructor shall agree on and follow a written protocol governing all exchanges in ConsensusDocs 200.2 or a separate addenda, which, at a minimum, shall specify: (a) the definition of documents and data to be accepted in electronic or digital form or to be transmitted electronically or digitally; (b) management and coordination responsibilities; (c) necessary equipment, software, and services; (d) acceptable formats, transmission methods, and verification procedures; (e) methods for maintaining version control; (f) privacy and security requirements; and (g) storage and retrieval requirements. Except as otherwise agreed to by the Parties in writing, each Party shall bear its own costs as identified in the protocol. In the absence of a written protocol, use of documents and data in electronic or digital form shall be at the sole risk of the recipient.

4.7 OWNER'S REPRESENTATIVE Owner's Representative is [_____]. Owner's Representative shall be fully acquainted with the Project, and shall have authority to bind Owner in all matters requiring Owner's approval, authorization, or written notice. If Owner changes its Representative or its Representative's authority, Owner shall immediately notify Constructor in writing.

4.8 OWNER'S CUTTING AND PATCHING Cutting, patching, or altering the Work by Owner or Others shall be done with the prior written approval of Constructor, which approval shall not be unreasonably withheld.

4.9 OWNER'S RIGHT TO CLEAN UP In case of a dispute between Constructor and Others with regard to respective responsibilities for clean up at the Worksite, Owner may implement appropriate cleanup measures after two (2) Business Days' notice and allocate the cost among those responsible during the following pay period.

4.10 COST OF CORRECTING DAMAGED OR DESTROYED WORK With regard to damage or loss attributable to the acts or omissions of Owner or Others and not to Constructor, Owner shall either (a) promptly remedy the damage or loss and assume affected warranty responsibilities, (b) accept the damage or loss, or (c) issue an Interim Directive or Change Order to Remedy the damage or loss. If Constructor incurs costs or is delayed due to such loss or damage, Constructor may seek an equitable adjustment in GMP or Contract Time under this Agreement.

ARTICLE 5 SUBCONTRACTS

5.1 AWARD OF SUBCONTRACTS AND OTHER CONTRACTS FOR PORTIONS OF THE WORK

5.1.1 Promptly after executing this Agreement, Constructor shall provide Owner, and if directed, Design Professional with a written list of the proposed Subcontractors and significant Suppliers. If Owner has a reasonable objection to any proposed Subcontractor or Supplier, Owner shall notify Constructor in writing. Failure to promptly object shall constitute acceptance.

5.1.2 If Owner has reasonably and promptly objected, Constructor shall not contract with the proposed Subcontractor or Supplier, and Constructor shall propose another acceptable to Owner. An appropriate Change Order shall reflect any increase or decrease in GMP or Contract Time because of the substitution.

5.2 BINDING OF SUBCONTRACTORS AND SUPPLIERS Constructor agrees to bind every Subcontractor and Supplier (and require each Subcontractor to so bind its Subsubcontractors and significant suppliers) to the Contract Document's applicable provisions to that portion of the Work.

5.3 CONTINGENT ASSIGNMENT OF SUBCONTRACTS

5.3.1 If this Agreement is terminated, each subcontract and supply agreement shall be assigned by Constructor to Owner, subject to the prior rights of any surety, provided that: (a) this Agreement is terminated by Owner pursuant to §12.3 or §12.4; and (b) Owner accepts such assignment after termination by notifying Constructor and Subcontractor or Constructor and Supplier in writing, and assumes all rights and obligations of Constructor pursuant to each subcontract or supply agreement.

5.3.2 If Owner accepts such an assignment, and the Work has been suspended for more than thirty (30) consecutive Days, following termination, if appropriate, Subcontractor's or Supplier's compensation shall be equitably adjusted as a result of the suspension.

ARTICLE 6 TIME

6.1 DATE OF COMMENCEMENT The Date of Commencement is the Agreement date in ARTICLE 1 unless otherwise set forth below: [_____]

6.1.1 SUBSTANTIAL/FINAL COMPLETION Substantial Completion of the Work shall be achieved in [_____] ([_____]) Days from the Date of Commencement. Unless otherwise specified in the Certificate of Substantial Completion, Constructor shall achieve Final Completion within [_____] ([_____]) Days after the date of Substantial Completion. The deadlines for Substantial and Final Completion are subject to adjustments as provided for in the Contract Documents.

6.1.2 Time is of the essence with regard to the obligations of the Contract Documents.

6.1.3 Unless instructed by Owner in writing, Constructor shall not knowingly commence the Work before the effective date of Constructor's required insurance.

6.2 SCHEDULE OF THE WORK

6.2.1 Before submitting its first application for payment, Constructor shall submit to Owner, and if directed, to Design Professional, a Schedule of the Work showing the dates on which Constructor plans to begin and complete various parts of the Work, including dates on which information and approvals are required from Owner. Except as otherwise directed by Owner, Constructor shall comply with the approved Schedule of the Work. Unless otherwise agreed, the Schedule of the Work shall be formatted in a detailed precedence-style critical path method that (a) provides a graphic representation of all activities and events, including float values that will affect the critical path of the Work, and (b) identifies dates that are critical to ensure timely and orderly completion of the Work. Constructor shall update the Schedule of the Work on a monthly basis or as mutually agreed by the Parties.

6.2.2 Owner may determine the sequence in which the Work shall be performed, provided it does not unreasonably interfere with the Schedule of the Work. Owner may require Constructor to make reasonable changes in the sequence at any time during the performance of the Work in order to facilitate the performance of work by Owner or Others. If Constructor consequently incurs costs or is delayed, or both, Constructor may seek an equitable adjustment in Constructor's Fee, GMP Price, or Contract Time under ARTICLE 9.

6.3 DELAYS AND EXTENSIONS OF TIME

6.3.1 If Constructor is delayed at any time in the commencement or progress of the Work by any cause beyond the control of Constructor, Constructor shall be entitled to an equitable extension of the Contract Time. Examples of causes beyond the control of Constructor include, but are not limited to, the following: (a) acts or omissions of Owner, Design Professional, or Others; (b) changes in the Work or the sequencing of the Work ordered by Owner, or arising from decisions of Owner that impact the time of performance of the Work; (c) encountering Hazardous Materials, or concealed or unknown conditions; (d) delay authorized by Owner pending dispute resolution or suspension by Owner under §12.1; (e) transportation delays not reasonably foreseeable; (f) labor disputes not involving Constructor; (g) general labor disputes impacting the Project but not specifically related to the Worksite; (h) fire; (i) Terrorism; (j) epidemics; (k) adverse governmental actions; (l) unavoidable accidents or circumstances; (m) adverse weather conditions not reasonably anticipated. Constructor shall submit any requests for equitable extensions of Contract Time in accordance with ARTICLE 9.

6.3.2 In addition, if Constructor incurs additional costs as a result of a delay that is caused by items (a) through (d) immediately above, Constructor may be entitled to an equitable adjustment in Constructor's Fee or GMP pursuant to ARTICLE 9 and subject to §6.6.

6.3.3 NOTICE OF DELAYS If delays to the Work are encountered for any reason, Constructor shall provide prompt written notice to Owner of the cause of such delays after Constructor first recognizes the delay. The Parties each agree to take reasonable steps to mitigate the effect of such delays.

6.4 NOTICE OF DELAY CLAIMS If Constructor requests an equitable extension of the Contract Time or an equitable adjustment in the GMP as a result of a delay described §6.3, Constructor shall give Owner written notice of the claim in accordance with §9.4. If Constructor causes delay in the completion of the Work, Owner shall be entitled to recover its additional costs subject to §6.6. Owner shall process any such claim against Constructor in accordance with ARTICLE 9.

6.5 LIQUIDATED DAMAGES

6.5.1 SUBSTANTIAL COMPLETION Liquidated damages based on Substantial Completion date __ ☐shall/ ☐shall not apply.

6.5.1.1 Owner will suffer damages which are difficult to determine and accurately specify if the Substantial Completion date, which may be amended by Change Order, is not attained. Constructor shall pay Owner [_____] dollars ($[_____]) as liquidated damages and not as a penalty for each Day that Substantial Completion extends beyond the Substantial Completion date. These liquidated damages are in lieu of all liability for all extra costs, losses, expenses, claims, penalties, and any other damages of any nature incurred by Owner resulting from not attaining the Substantial Completion date.

6.5.2 FINAL COMPLETION Liquidated damages based on the Final Completion date ☐shall/ ☐shall not apply.

6.5.3 Owner will suffer damages which are difficult to determine and accurately specify. Constructor agrees that if the Final Completion date, as may be amended by subsequent Change Order, is not attained, Constructor shall pay Owner [_____] dollars ($[_____]) as liquidated damages and not as a penalty for each Day that Final Completion extends beyond the Final Completion date. These liquidated damages are in lieu of all liability for all extra costs, losses, expenses, claims, penalties, and any other damages of any nature incurred by Owner resulting from not attaining Final Completion date.

6.5.4 Other applicable liquidated damages shall be included as Agreement exhibit.

6.6 LIMITED MUTUAL WAIVER OF CONSEQUENTIAL DAMAGES Except for damages mutually agreed upon by the Parties as liquidated damages in §6.5 and excluding losses covered by insurance required by the Contract Documents, Parties agree to waive all claims against each other for any consequential damages that may arise out of or relate to this Agreement, except for those specific items of damages excluded from this waiver as mutually agreed upon by the Parties and identified below. Owner agrees to waive damages, including but not limited to Owner's loss of use of the Project, any rental expenses incurred, loss of income, profit, or financing related to the Project, as well as the loss of business, loss of financing, loss of profits not related to this Project, loss of reputation, or insolvency. Constructor agrees to waive damages, including but not limited to loss of business, loss of financing, loss of profits not related to this Project, loss of bonding capacity, loss of reputation, or insolvency. The provisions of this section shall also apply to the termination of this Agreement and shall survive such termination. The following are excluded from this mutual waiver: [_____].

6.6.1 Parties shall each require similar waivers in contracts with Subcontractors and Others retained for the Project.

ARTICLE 7 COMPENSATION

7.1 Owner shall compensate Constructor for Work performed on the following basis:

7.1.1 Cost of the Work as allowed in ARTICLE 8; and

7.1.2 Constructor's Fee paid in proportion to Work performed subject to adjustment as provided in §7.4.

7.1.3 If at Final Completion, Cost of the Work plus Constructor's Fee is less than the GMP, the difference shall be shared as follows: The savings, if any, shall accrue _____ percent (_____%) to Owner and _____ percent (_____%) to Constructor. The shared savings shall be calculated and paid as part of final payment. Constructor shall not be entitled to any portion of the shared savings if either Party terminates this Agreement except for a termination for convenience pursuant to section §12.4, Constructor's termination pursuant to §12.5, or, in the case of a termination for default under §12.3, if §12.3.4 applies.

7.2 Payment for Work performed shall be as set forth in ARTICLE 10.

7.3 CONSTRUCTOR'S FEE Constructor's Fee shall be as follows, subject to adjustment as provided in §7.4:

_____ % of the Cost of the Work, or;

$_____, a lump sum amount.

7.4 ADJUSTMENT IN CONSTRUCTOR'S FEE Adjustment in Constructor's Fee shall be made as follows:

7.4.1 if Constructor performs changed work pursuant to ARTICLE 9 and if Constructor's Fee is a lump sum amount, §9.1.2 shall appy.

7.4.2 if Constructor performs changed work pursuant to ARTICLE 9 and if Constructor's Fee is a percentage of the Cost of the Work, Constructor's Fees shall be calculated as a percentage of the total Cost of the Work, including changed work pursuant to ARTICLE 9.

7.4.3 if Constructor is placed in charge of managing the replacement of an insured or uninsured loss, Constructor shall be paid an additional fee in the same proportion that Constructor's Fee bears to the estimated cost of the work for the replacement.

ARTICLE 8 COST OF THE WORK

8.1 Owner agrees to pay Constructor for Cost of the Work as defined in this article. This payment shall be in addition to Constructor's Fee in §7.3. The Cost of the Work includes:

8.1.1 Labor wages directly employed by Constructor in the performing the Work.

8.1.2 Salaries of Constructor's employees when stationed at the field office to the extent necessary to complete the applicable Work, employees engaged on the road expediting the production or transportation of material and equipment, and supervisory employees from the principal or branch office as mutually agreed by the Parties in writing;

8.1.3 Cost of all employee benefits and taxes including but not limited to Workers' Compensation, unemployment compensation, Social Security, health, welfare, retirement, and other fringe benefits as required by Laws, labor agreements, or paid under Constructor's standard personnel policy, insofar as such costs are paid to employees of Constructor who are included in the Cost of the Work above;

8.1.4 Reasonable transportation, travel, hotel, and moving expenses of Constructor's personnel incurred in connection with Work;

8.1.5 Cost of all materials, supplies, and equipment incorporated in the Work, including costs of inspection and testing if not provided by Owner, transportation, storage and handling;

8.1.6 Payments properly made by Constructor to Subcontractors for performed Work;

8.1.7 Cost, including transportation and maintenance of all materials, supplies, equipment, temporary facilities, and hand tools not owned by the workers that are used or consumed in the performance of Work, less salvage value or residual value; and cost less salvage value on such items used, but not consumed, that remain the property of Constructor;

8.1.8 Rental charges of all necessary machinery and equipment, exclusive of hand tools owned by workers, used at Worksite, whether rented from Constructor or others, including installation, repair and replacement, dismantling, removal, maintenance, transportation, and delivery costs. Rental from unrelated third parties shall be reimbursed at actual cost. Rentals from Constructor or its affiliates, subsidiaries, or related parties shall be reimbursed at the prevailing rates in the locality of Worksite up to eighty-five percent (85%) of the value of the piece of equipment;

8.1.9 Cost for the premiums for all insurance and surety bonds, which Constructor is required to procure, pay or deems necessary, and approved by Owner, including any additional premium incurred as a result of any increase in the Cost of the Work;

8.1.10 Sales, use, gross receipts or other taxes, tariffs, or duties related to Work for which Constructor is liable;

8.1.11 Permits, fees, licenses, tests, and royalties;

8.1.12 Losses, expenses or damages to the extent not compensated by insurance or otherwise, and the cost of corrective work before expiration of the one-year period following the Date of Substantial Completion, provided that such losses, expenses, damages, or corrective work did not arise from Constructor's negligence;

8.1.13 Costs associated with establishing, equipping, operating, maintaining, and demobilizing the field office;

8.1.14 Water, power, and fuel costs necessary for the Work;

8.1.15 Cost of removal of all nonhazardous substances, debris, and waste materials;

8.1.16 Costs incurred due to an emergency affecting the safety of persons or property;

8.1.17 Legal, mediation, and arbitration fees and costs, other than those arising from disputes between the Parties, reasonably and properly needed in Constructor's performance of Work; and

8.1.18 Costs directly incurred in performing the Work, or in connection with the Project, and not included in Constructor's Fee as set forth in ARTICLE 7, which are reasonably inferable from the Contract Documents.

8.1.19 DISCOUNTS All discounts for prompt payment shall accrue to Owner to the extent such payments are made directly by Owner. To the extent payments are made with funds of Constructor, all cash discounts shall accrue to Constructor. All trade discounts, rebates, and refunds, and all returns from sale of surplus materials and equipment, shall be credited to Cost of the Work.

8.1.20 FINANCIAL RECORDS Constructor shall maintain complete, accurate, and current records that comply with generally accepted accounting principles and calculate the proper financial management with respect to the Project. Owner shall be afforded access to all of Constructor's records, books, correspondence, instructions, drawing, receipts, vouchers, memoranda, and similar data relating to this Agreement. Constructor shall preserve all such records for a period of three years after the final payment or longer where required by Law. Constructor agrees to use reasonable skill and judgment in the preparation of cost estimates, but does not warrant or guarantee them.

ARTICLE 9 CHANGES

Changes in the Work which are within the general scope of this Agreement may be accomplished, without invalidating this Agreement, by Change Order and Interim Directive.

9.1 CHANGE ORDER

9.1.1 Constructor may request or Owner may order changes in Work or the timing or sequencing of Work that impact the GMP, Constructor's Fee, or Contract Time. All such changes in Work that affect GMP, Constructor's Fee, or Contract Time shall be formalized in a Change Order, and processed in accordance with this article.

9.1.2 Each adjustment in GMP resulting from a Change Order shall clearly separate the amount attributable to Cost of the Work and Constructor's Fee, with Constructor's Fee not to exceed [_____] percent ([_____] %) of Cost of the Work.

9.1.3 For changes in the Work, the Parties shall negotiate an appropriate adjustment to GMP, Constructor's Fee, or the Contract Time in good faith and conclude negotiations as expeditiously as possible. Acceptance of Change Orders and any adjustment in GMP, Constructor's Fee, or Contract Time shall not be unreasonably withheld.

9.1.4 NO OBLIGATION TO PERFORM Constructor shall not be obligated to perform changes in Work without a Change Order or Interim Directive.

9.2 INTERIM DIRECTIVES

9.2.1 Owner may issue an Interim Directive directing a change in Work before agreeing on an adjustment to the GMP, Constructor's Fee, or Contract Time, directing Constructor to perform Work that Owner believes is not a change. If the Parties disagree that the interim Director work is within the scope of the Work, Constructor shall perform the disputed Work and furnish Owner with an estimate of the costs to perform the disputed work in accordance with Owner's interpretations.

9.2.2 The Parties shall negotiate expeditiously and in good faith for appropriate adjustments, as applicable, to the Contract Price or the Contract Time arising out of an Interim Directive. As the directed Work is performed, Constructor shall submit its costs for such Work with its application for payment beginning with the next application for payment within thirty (30) Days of the issuance of the Interim Directive. If there is a dispute as to the cost to Owner, Owner shall pay Constructor fifty percent (50%) of its actual (incurred or committed) cost to perform such Work. In such event, the Parties reserve their rights as to the disputed amount, subject to the requirements of ARTICLE 12. Owner's payment does not prejudice its right to be reimbursed should it be determined that the disputed work was within the scope of the Work. Constructor's receipt of payment for the disputed work does not prejudice its right to receive full payment for the disputed work should it be determined that the disputed work is not within the scope of the Work. Undisputed amounts may be included in applications for payment and shall be paid by Owner in accordance with this Agreement.

9.2.3 When the Parties agree upon the adjustment in GMP, Constructor's Fee, or Contract Time, for a change in Work directed by an Interim Directive, such agreement shall be the subject of a Change Order. The Change Order shall include all outstanding Interim Directives on which the Parties have reached agreement on GMP, Constructor's Fee, or Contract Time issued since the last Change Order.

9.3 DETERMINATION OF COST

9.3.1 An increase or decrease in GMP resulting from a change in the Work shall be determined pursuant to §9.1.3 and Constructor's Fee shall be determined pursuant to §7.4; or

9.3.2 If an increase or decrease in GMP or Contract Time cannot be agreed to as set forth in the subsection above, and Owner issues an Interim Directive, the change in GMP shall be determined by the reasonable actual expense incurred and savings realized in the performance of the Work resulting from the change. If there is a net increase in GMP, Constructor's Fee shall be adjusted as set forth in §7.4. In case of a net decrease in GMP, Constructor's Fee shall not be adjusted unless ten percent (10%) or more of the Project is deleted. Constructor shall maintain a documented, itemized accounting evidencing the expenses and savings.

9.4 CLAIMS FOR ADDITIONAL COST OR TIME For any claim for an increase in GMP, Constructor's Fee, Date of Substantial Completion, or Date of Final Completion, Constructor shall give Owner written notice of the claim within twenty-one (21) Days after the occurrence giving rise to the claim or within twenty-one (21) Days after Constructor first recognizes the condition giving rise to the claim, whichever is later. Except in an emergency, notice shall be given before proceeding with the Work. Claims for estimated costs incurred in connection with possible changes requested by Owner, but which do not proceed, shall be made within twenty-one (21) Days after the decision is made not to proceed. Thereafter, Constructor shall submit written documentation of its claim, including appropriate supporting documentation, within twenty-one (21) Days after giving notice, unless the Parties mutually agree upon a longer period of time. Owner shall respond in writing denying or approving Constructor's claim no later than fourteen (14) Days after receipt of Constructor's documentation of claim. Owner's failure to so respond shall be deemed a denial of Constructor's claim. Any change in GMP, Constructor's Fee, Date of Substantial Completion, or Date of Final Completion resulting from such claim shall be authorized by Change Order.

9.5 INCIDENTAL CHANGES Owner may direct Constructor to perform incidental changes in the Work upon concurrence with Constructor that such changes do not involve adjustments in the Cost of the Work or Contract Time. Incidental changes shall be consistent with the scope and intent of the Contract Documents. Owner shall initiate an incidental change in the Work by issuing an Interim Directive.

ARTICLE 10 PAYMENT

10.1 SCHEDULE OF VALUES Within twenty-one (21) Days from the date of execution of this Agreement, Constructor shall prepare and submit to Owner a schedule of values apportioned to the various divisions or phases of the Work. Each line item contained in the schedule of values shall be assigned a value such that the total of all items shall equal the Contract Price.

10.2 PROGRESS PAYMENTS

10.2.1 APPLICATIONS Constructor shall submit to Owner and, if directed, Design Professional a monthly application for payment no later than the [_____] day of the calendar month for the preceding calendar month. Constructor's applications for payment shall consist of the Cost of the Work performed up to the [_____] day of the month, along with a proportionate share of Constructor's Fee. Constructor shall include an estimate of the additional costs necessary to complete the Work. Applications for payment may include materials and equipment not yet incorporated into the Work, but delivered to and suitably stored onsite or offsite, including applicable insurance, storage, and costs incurred transporting the materials to an offsite storage facility. Approval of payment applications for such stored materials stored off-site shall be conditioned upon submission by Constructor of bills of sale and applicable insurance or such other procedures satisfactory to Owner to establish Owner's title to such materials, or otherwise to protect Owner's interest, including transportation to the Worksite. Before submitting the next application for payment, Constructor shall furnish to Owner a statement accounting for the disbursement of funds received under the previous application. The extent of such statement shall be as agreed upon between the Parties.

10.2.2 STORED MATERIALS AND EQUIPMENT Unless otherwise provided in the Contract Documents, applications for payment may include materials and equipment not yet incorporated into the Work but delivered to and suitably stored onsite or offsite including applicable insurance, storage, and costs incurred transporting the materials to an offsite storage facility. Approval of payment applications for stored materials and equipment stored offsite shall be conditioned on a submission by Constructor of bills of sale and proof of required insurance, or such other documentation satisfactory to Owner to establish the proper valuation of the stored materials and equipment, Owner's title to such materials and equipment, and to otherwise protect Owner's interests therein, including transportation to the Worksite

10.2.3 LIEN WAIVERS AND LIENS

10.2.3.1 PARTIAL LIEN WAIVERS AND AFFIDAVITS If required by Owner, as a prerequisite for payment, Constructor shall provide a partial lien and claim waiver in the amount of the application for payment and affidavits from its Subcontractors and Suppliers for the completed Work. Such waivers shall be conditional upon payment. Constructor shall not be required to sign an unconditional waiver of lien or claim, before receiving payment or in an amount in excess of what it has been paid.

10.2.3.2 REMOVING LIENS If Owner has made payments in the time required by this ARTICLE 10, Constructor shall, within thirty (30) Days after filing, remove any liens filed against the premises or public improvement fund by any party or parties performing labor or services or supplying materials in connection with the Work. If Constructor fails to take such action on a lien, Owner may cause the lien to be removed at Constructor's expense, including bond costs and reasonable attorneys' fees. This subsection shall not apply if there is a dispute pursuant to ARTICLE 13 relating to the subject matter of the lien.

10.2.4 RETAINAGE From each progress payment made before Substantial Completion, Owner may retain [_____] percent ([_____]%) of the amount otherwise due after deduction of any amounts as provided in §10.3, provided such percentage doesn't exceed the Law. If Owner chooses to use this retainage provision:

10.2.4.1 after the Work is fifty percent (50%) complete, Owner shall withhold no additional retainage and shall pay Constructor the full amount due on account of subsequent progress payments;

10.2.4.2 Owner may, in its sole discretion, reduce the amount to be retained at any time;

10.2.4.3 Owner may release retainage on that portion of the Work a Subcontractor has completed in whole or in part, and which Owner has accepted. In lieu of retainage, Constructor may furnish a retention bond or other security interest acceptable to Owner, to be held by Owner.

10.3 ADJUSTMENT OF CONSTRUCTOR'S PAYMENT APPLICATION Owner may adjust or reject a payment application or nullify a previously approved payment application, in whole or in part, as may reasonably be necessary to protect Owner from loss or damage based upon the following, to the extent that Constructor is responsible under this Agreement:

10.3.1 Constructor's repeated failure to perform the Work as required by the Contract Documents;

10.3.2 Except as accepted by the insurer providing Builder's Risk or other property insurance covering the Project, loss or damage arising out of or relating to this Agreement and caused by Constructor to Owner or others to whom Owner may be liable;

10.3.3 Constructor's failure to properly pay either Subcontractors or Suppliers following receipt of payment from Owner for that portion of the Work or for supplies, provided that Owner is making payments to Constructor in accordance with this Agreement;

10.3.4 rejected Defective Work not corrected in a timely fashion;

10.3.5 reasonable evidence of delay in performance of the Work such that the Work will not be completed within the Contract Time;

10.3.6 reasonable evidence demonstrating that the unpaid balance of the GMP is insufficient to fund the cost to complete the Work; and

10.3.7 uninsured third-party claims involving Constructor, or reasonable evidence demonstrating that third-party claims are likely to be filed unless and until Constructor furnishes Owner with adequate security in the form of a surety bond, letter of credit, or other collateral or commitment sufficient to discharge such claims if established.

No later than seven (7) Days after receipt of an application for payment, Owner shall give written notice to Constructor, at the time of disapproving or nullifying all or part of an application for payment, stating its specific reasons for such disapproval or nullification, and the remedial actions to be taken by Constructor in order to receive payment. When the above reasons for disapproving or nullifying an application for payment are removed, payment will be promptly made for the amount previously withheld.

10.4 ACCEPTANCE OF WORK Neither Owner's payment of progress payments nor its partial or full use or occupancy of the Project constitutes acceptance of Work not complying with the Contract Documents.

10.5 PAYMENT DELAY If for any reason not the fault of Constructor, Constructor does not receive a progress payment from Owner within seven (7) Days after the time such payment is due, then Constructor, upon giving seven (7) Days written notice to Owner, and without prejudice to and in addition to any other legal remedies, may stop Work until payment of the full amount owing to Constructor has been received, including interest for late payment. If Constructor incurs costs or is delayed resulting from shutdown, delay, and start-up, Constructor may seek an equitable adjustment in GMP, Constructor's Fee or Contract Time under ARTICLE 9.

10.6 SUBSTANTIAL COMPLETION

10.6.1 Constructor shall notify Owner and, if directed, Design Professional when it considers that Substantial Completion of the Work or a designated portion to have been achieved. Owner, with the assistance of Design Professional, shall promptly conduct an inspection to determine whether the Work or designated portion can be occupied or used for its intended use by Owner without excessive interference in completing any remaining unfinished Work. If Owner determines that the Work or designated portion has not reached Substantial Completion, Owner shall promptly compile a list of items to be completed or corrected so Owner may occupy or use the Work or designated portion for its intended use. Constructor shall promptly complete all items on the list.

10.6.2 When Substantial Completion of the Work or a designated portion is achieved, Constructor shall prepare a Certificate of Substantial Completion establishing the date of Substantial Completion and the respective responsibilities of each Party for interim items such as security, maintenance, utilities, insurance, and damage to the Work. In the absence of a clear delineation of responsibilities, Owner shall assume all responsibilities for items such as security, maintenance, utilities, insurance, and damage to the Work. The Certificate of Substantial Completion shall also list any items to be completed or corrected, and establish the time for their completion or correction. The Certificate of Substantial Completion shall be submitted by Constructor to Owner, and, if directed, to Design Professional, for written acceptance of responsibilities assigned in the Certificate of Substantial Completion.

10.6.3 Unless otherwise provided in the Certificate of Substantial Completion, warranties required by the Contract Documents shall commence on the date of Substantial Completion of the Work or a designated portion.

10.6.4 Upon Owner's written acceptance of the Certificate of Substantial Completion, Owner shall pay to Constructor the remaining retainage held by Owner for the Work described in the Certificate of Substantial Completion, less a sum equal to one hundred fifty percent (150%) of the estimated cost of completing or correcting remaining items on that part of the Work, as agreed to by the Parties as necessary to achieve Final Completion. Uncompleted items shall be completed by Constructor in a mutually agreed upon timeframe. Owner shall pay Constructor monthly the amount retained for unfinished items as each item is completed.

10.7 PARTIAL OCCUPANCY OR USE

10.7.1 Owner may occupy or use completed or partially completed portions of the Work when (a) the portion of the Work is designated in a Certificate of Substantial Completion, (b) appropriate insurer(s) consent to the occupancy or use, and (c) appropriate public authorities authorize the occupancy or use. Such partial occupancy or use shall constitute Substantial Completion of that portion of the Work.

10.8 FINAL COMPLETION AND FINAL PAYMENT

10.8.1 Upon notification from Constructor that the Work is complete and ready for final inspection and acceptance, Owner, with the assistance of Design Professional, shall promptly conduct an inspection to determine if the Work has been completed and is acceptable under the Contract Documents.

10.8.2 When Final Completion has been achieved, Constructor shall prepare for Owner's written acceptance a final application for payment stating that to the best of Constructor's knowledge, and based on Owner's inspections, the Work has reached Final Completion in accordance with the Contract Documents.

10.8.3 Final payment of the balance of the Cost of the Work shall be made to Constructor within twenty (20) Days after Constructor has submitted a complete and accurate application for final payment, including submissions required under §10.8.4, and a Certificate of Final Completion has been executed by the Parties.

10.8.4 Final payment is due upon Constructor's submission to Owner of the following:

10.8.4.1 An affidavit declaring any indebtedness connected with the Work to have been paid, satisfied, or to be paid with the proceeds of final payment, so as not to encumber Owner's property;

10.8.4.2 As-built drawings, manuals, copies of warranties, and all other close-out documents required by the Contract Documents;

10.8.4.3 Release of any liens, conditioned on final payment being received;

10.8.4.4 Consent of any surety; and

10.8.4.5 Any outstanding known and unreported accidents or injuries experienced by Constructor or its Subcontractors at the Worksite.

10.8.5 If, after Substantial Completion of the Work, the Final Completion of a portion of the Work is materially delayed through no fault of Constructor, Owner shall pay the balance due for any portion of the Work fully completed and accepted. If the estimated Cost of the Work for Work not fully completed and accepted is less than the retained amount before payment, Constructor shall submit to Owner, and if directed, to Design Professional, the written consent of any surety to payment of the balance due for portions of the Work that are fully completed and accepted. Such payment shall not constitute a waiver of claims, but otherwise shall be governed by §10.8.6 and §10.8.7.

10.8.6 OWNER'S CLAIMS RESERVATION Owner's claims not reserved in writing with final payment are waived except for claims relating to liens or similar encumbrances, warranties, Defective Work.

10.8.7 CONSTRUCTOR ACCEPTANCE OF FINAL PAYMENT Unless Constructor provides written identification of unsettled claims with an application for final payment, its acceptance of final payment constitutes a waiver of such claims.

10.9 LATE PAYMENT Payments due but unpaid shall bear interest from the date payment is due at the rate made applicable by Law.

ARTICLE 11 INDEMNITY, INSURANCE AND BONDS

11.1 INDEMNITY

11.1.1 To the fullest extent permitted by law, Constructor shall indemnify and hold harmless Owner, Owner's officers, directors, members, consultants, agents and employees, Design Professional, and Others (the Indemnitees) from all claims for bodily injury and property damage, other than to the Work itself and other property insured, including reasonable attorneys' fees, costs, and expenses, that may arise from the performance of the Work, but only to the extent caused by the negligent or intentionally wrongful acts or omissions of Constructor, Subcontractors, Suppliers, Subsubcontractors, or anyone employed directly or indirectly by any of them or by anyone for whose acts any of them may be liable. Constructor shall be entitled to reimbursement of any defense costs paid above Constructor's percentage of liability for the underlying claim to the extent provided for by §11.1.2.

11.1.2 To the fullest extent permitted by Law, Owner shall indemnify and hold harmless Constructor, its officers, directors, members, consultants, agents and employees, Subcontractors, Suppliers, or anyone employed directly or indirectly by any of them or anyone for whose acts any of them may be liable from all claims for bodily injury and property damage, other than property insured, including reasonable attorneys' fees, costs and expenses, that may arise from the performance of work by Owner, Design Professional, or Others, but only to the extent caused by the negligent or intentionally wrongful acts or omissions of Owner, Design Professional, or Others. Owner shall be entitled to reimbursement of any defense costs paid above Owner's percentage of liability for the underlying claim to the extent provided for by §11.1.1.

11.1.3 NO LIMITATION ON LIABILITY In any and all claims against the Indemnitees by any employee of Constructor, anyone directly or indirectly employed by Constructor, or anyone for whose acts Constructor may be liable, the indemnification obligation shall not be limited in any way by any limitation on the amount or type of damages, compensation, or benefits payable by or for Constructor under workers' compensation acts, disability benefit acts, or other employment benefit acts.

11.2 INSURANCE

11.2.1 Before starting Work and as a condition precedent to payment, Constructor shall procure and maintain in force Workers' Compensation Insurance, Employers Liability Insurance, Business Automobile Liability Insurance, and Commercial General Liability Insurance (CGL). The CGL policy shall include coverage for liability arising from premises, operations, independent contractors, products-completed operations, personal injury and advertising injury, contractual liability, and broad form property damage. Constructor shall maintain completed operations liability insurance for one year after Substantial Completion, or as required by the Contract Documents, whichever is longer. Constructor's Employers' Liability, Business Automobile Liability, and CGL policies shall be written with at least the following limits of liability:

11.2.1.1 Employers' Liability Insurance

(a) $[_____] bodily injury by accident per accident.
(b) $[_____] bodily injury by disease policy limit.
(c) $[_____] bodily injury by disease per employee.

11.2.1.2 Business Automobile Liability Insurance $[_____] per accident.

11.2.1.3 Commercial General Liability Insurance

(a) $[_____] per occurrence.
(b) $[_____] general aggregate.
(c) $[_____] products/completed operations aggregate.
(d) $[_____] personal and advertising injury limit.

11.2.2 Employers' Liability, Business Automobile Liability, and CGL coverages required under §11.2.1 may be provided by a single policy for the full limits required or by a combination of underlying policies with the balance provided by excess or umbrella liability policies.

11.2.3 Constructor shall maintain in effect all insurance coverage required under §11.2.1 with insurance companies lawfully authorized to do business in the jurisdiction in which the Project is located. If Constructor fails to obtain or maintain any insurance coverage required under this Agreement, Owner may purchase such coverage and charge the expense to Constructor, or terminate this Agreement.

11.2.4 To the extent commercially available to Constructor from its current insurance company, insurance policies required under §11.2.1 shall contain a provision that the insurance company or its designee must give Owner written notice transmitted in paper or electronic format: (a) thirty (30) Days before coverage is nonrenewed by the insurance company and (b) within ten (10) Business Days after cancelation of coverage by the insurance company. Before commencing the Work and upon renewal or replacement of the insurance policies, Constructor shall furnish Owner with certificates of insurance until one year after Substantial Completion or longer if required by the Contract Documents. In addition, if any insurance policy required under §11.2.1 is not to be immediately replaced without lapse in coverage when it expires, exhausts its limits, or is to be cancelled, Constructor shall give Owner prompt written notice upon actual or constructive knowledge of such condition.

11.3 PROPERTY INSURANCE

11.3.1 Unless otherwise directed in writing by Owner, before starting the Work, Constructor shall obtain and maintain a Builder's Risk Policy upon the entire Project for the full cost of replacement at the time of loss, including existing structures. This insurance shall also (a) name Constructor, Subcontractors, Subsubcontractors, Suppliers, and Design Professional as insureds; (b) be written in such form as to cover all risks of physical loss except those specifically excluded by the policy. In addition, this insurance shall insure at least against and not exclude:

11.3.1.1 the perils of fire, lightning, explosion, windstorm, hail, smoke, aircraft (except aircraft, including helicopter, operated by or on behalf of Constructor) and vehicles, riot and civil commotion, theft, vandalism, malicious mischief, debris removal, flood, earthquake, earth movement, water damage, wind damage, testing if applicable, collapse however caused;

11.3.1.2 damage resulting from defective design, workmanship, or material;

11.3.1.3 coverage extension for damage to existing buildings, plan, or other structures at the Worksite, when the Project is contained within or attached to such existing buildings, plant, or structure. Coverage shall be to the extent loss or damage arises out of Constructor's activities or operations at the Projects;

11.3.1.4 equipment breakdown, including mechanical breakdown, electrical injury to electrical devices, explosion of steam equipment, and damage to steam equipment caused by a condition within the equipment;

11.3.1.5 testing coverage for running newly installed machinery and equipment at or beyond the specified limits of their capacity to determine whether they are fit for their intended use; and

11.3.1.6 physical loss resulting from Terrorism.

11.3.2 The Party that is the primary cause of a Builder's Risk Policy claim shall be responsible for any deductible amounts or coinsurance payments. If no Party is the primary cause of a claim, then the Party obtaining and maintaining the Builder's Risk Policy pursuant to §11.3.1 shall be responsible for the deductible amounts or coinsurance payments. This policy shall provide for a waiver of subrogation. This insurance shall remain in effect until final payment has been made or until no person or entity other than Owner has an insurable interest in the property to be covered by this insurance, whichever is sooner. Partial occupancy or use of the Work shall not commence until Constructor has secured the consent of the insurance company or companies providing the coverage required in this subsection. Before commencing the Work, Constructor shall provide a copy of the property policy or policies obtained in compliance with this §11.3.

11.3.3 If Owner elects to purchase the property insurance required by this Agreement, including all of the same coverages and deductibles for the same duration specified in this §11.3, then Owner shall give written notice to Constructor and Design Professional before the Work is commenced, and provide a copy of the property policy or policies obtained in compliance with this §11.3. Owner may then provide insurance to protect its interests and the interests of Constructor, Subcontractors, Suppliers, and Subsubcontractors. The cost of this insurance shall be paid by Owner in a Change Order. If Owner gives written notice of its intent to purchase property insurance required by this Agreement and fails to purchase or maintain such insurance, Owner shall be responsible for costs reasonably attributed to such failure.

11.3.4 The Parties each waive all rights against each other and their respective employees, agents, contractors, subcontractors, suppliers subsubcontractors and Design Professional for damages caused by risks covered by the property insurance, except such rights as they may have to the proceeds of the insurance.

11.3.5 To the extent of the limits of Constructor's CGL specified in §11.2.1 or [_____] dollars ($[_____]), whichever is more, Constructor shall indemnify and hold harmless Owner against any and all liability, claims, demands, damages, losses, and expenses, including attorneys' fees, in connection with or arising out of any damage or alleged damage to any of Owner's existing adjacent property that may arise from the performance of the Work, to the extent caused by the negligent or intentionally wrongful acts or omissions of Constructor, Subcontractor, Supplier, Subsubcontractor, or anyone employed directly or indirectly by any of them or by anyone for whose acts any of them may be liable.

11.3.6 POLLUTION LIABILITY INSURANCE Constructor ☐ is / ☐ is not required to maintain pollution liability insurance. Unless indicated affirmatively, the obligation to procure such insurance is not triggered.

> 11.3.6.1 If applicable: in the following amounts: [_____] per occurrence, and shall apply for [_____] year(s) after Final Completion. The policy shall cover Constructor's liability during construction, removal, storage, encapsulation, transport, and disposal of hazardous waste and contaminated soil, and asbestos abatement. The policy shall include coverage for on-site and off-site bodily injury and loss of damage to, or loss of use of property, directly or indirectly arising out of the discharge, dispersal, release, or escape of smoke, vapors, soot, fumes, acids, alkalis, toxic chemicals, liquids or gas, waste materials, or other irritants, contaminants, or pollutants into or upon the land, the atmosphere or any water body, whether it be gradual or sudden and accidental. The policy shall not have exclusions for mold or asbestos.

11.4 ADDITIONAL GENERAL LIABILITY COVERAGE Owner [_____] shall/ [_____] shall not require Constructor to purchase and maintain additional liability coverage. If required, Constructor shall provide:

11.4.1 ☐ Additional Insured. Owner shall be named as an additional insured on Constructor's CGL specified for on-going operations and completed operations, excess/umbrella liability, commercial automobile liability, and any required pollution liability, but only with respect to liability for bodily injury, property damage, or personal and advertising injury to the extent caused by the negligent acts or omissions of Constructor, or those acting on Constructor's behalf, in the performance of Constructor's Work for Owner at the Worksite. The insurance (both primary and excess) of the Constructor and its Subcontractors shall be primary and non-contributory to any insurance available to the Additional Insureds.

11.4.2 ☐ OCP. Constructor shall provide an Owners' and Contractors' Protective Liability Insurance ("OCP") policy with limits equal to the limits on CGL specified, or limits as otherwise required by Owner.

Any documented additional cost in the form of a surcharge associated with procuring the additional general liability coverage in accordance with this subsection shall be paid by Owner directly, or the costs may be reimbursed by Owner to Constructor by increasing the GMP to correspond to the actual cost required to purchase and maintain the coverage. Before commencing Work, Constructor shall provide either a copy of the OCP policy, or a certificate and endorsement evidencing that Owner has been named as an additional insured, as applicable.

11.5 ROYALTIES, PATENTS AND COPYRIGHTS Constructor shall pay all royalties and license fees which may be due on the inclusion of any patented or copyrighted materials, methods, or systems selected by Constructor and incorporated in the Work. Constructor shall defend, indemnify, and hold Owner harmless from all suits or claims for infringement of any patent rights or copyrights arising out of such selection. Owner agrees to defend, indemnify, and hold Constructor harmless from any suits or claims of infringement of any patent rights or copyrights arising out of any patented or copyrighted materials, methods, or systems specified by Owner or Design Professional.

11.6 BONDS Performance and Payment Bonds are [_____]/ are not [_____] required of Constructor. Such bonds shall be issued by a surety admitted in the state in which the Project is located and must be acceptable to Owner. Owner's acceptance shall not be withheld without reasonable cause. The penal sum of the bonds shall each be one hundred percent (100%) of the original GMP. Constructor shall endeavor to keep its surety advised of changes potentially impacting the Contract Time and GMP, though Constructor shall require that its surety waives any requirement to be notified of any alteration or extension of time.

11.7 PROFESSIONAL LIABILITY INSURANCE To the extent Constructor is required to procure design services in accordance with §3.16, Constructor shall require its design professional to obtain professional liability insurance for claims arising from the negligent performance of design services under this Agreement, with a company reasonably satisfactory to Owner, including coverage for all professional liability caused by any consultants to Constructor's design professional, written for not less than [_____] dollars ($[_____]) per claim and in the aggregate with the deductible not to exceed [_____] dollars ($[_____]). The Professional Liability Insurance shall contain a retroactive date providing prior acts coverage sufficient to cover all Services performed by the Constructor's design professional for this Project. Coverage shall be continued in effect for [_____] ([_____]) year(s) following Substantial Completion. Constructor's design professional shall pay the self-insured retention and deductible. The combined total deductible and self-insured retention maximum shall be [_____] dollars ($[_____]).

ARTICLE 12 SUSPENSION, NOTICE TO CURE, AND TERMINATION OF AGREEMENT

12.1 SUSPENSION BY OWNER FOR CONVENIENCE

12.1.1 OWNER SUSPENSION Should Owner order Constructor in writing to suspend, delay, or interrupt the performance of the Work for the convenience of Owner and not due to any act or omission of Constructor or any person or entity for whose acts or omissions Constructor may be liable, then Constructor shall immediately suspend, delay, or interrupt that portion of the Work for the time period ordered by Owner.

12.1.2 Any action taken by Owner that is permitted by any other provision of the Contract Documents and that results in a suspension of part or all of the Work does not constitute a suspension of Work under this section.

12.2 NOTICE TO CURE A DEFAULT If Constructor persistently fails to supply enough qualified workers, proper materials, or equipment to maintain the approved Schedule of the Work, or fails to make prompt payment to its workers, Subcontractors, or Suppliers, disregards a Law or orders of any public authority having jurisdiction, or is otherwise guilty of a material breach of a provision of this Agreement, Constructor may be deemed in default.

12.2.1 After receiving Owner's written notice, if Constructor fails within seven (7) Days after receipt of written notice from Owner to commence and continue satisfactory correction of such default with diligence and promptness, then Owner shall give Constructor a second notice to correct the default within three (3) Business Days after receipt. The second notice to Constructor, and if applicable, the surety, may include, that Owner intends to terminate this Agreement for default absent appropriate corrective action.

12.2.2 If Constructor fails to promptly commence and continue satisfactory correction of the default following receipt of such second notice, Owner without prejudice to any other rights or remedies may: (a) take possession of the Worksite; (b) complete the Work utilizing reasonable means; (c) withhold payment due to Constructor; and (d) as Owner deems necessary, supply workers and materials, equipment, and other facilities for the satisfactory correction of the default, and charge Constructor the costs and expenses, including reasonable Overhead, profit, and attorneys' fees.

12.2.3 In the event of an emergency affecting the safety of persons or property, Owner may immediately commence and continue satisfactory correction of such default without first giving written notice to Constructor, but shall give Constructor prompt written notice.

12.3 OWNER'S RIGHT TO TERMINATE FOR DEFAULT

12.3.1 TERMINATION BY OWNER FOR DEFAULT Upon expiration of the second notice period to cure pursuant to §12.2 and absent appropriate corrective action, Owner may terminate this Agreement by written notice. Termination for default is in addition to any other remedies available to Owner under §12.2. If Owner's costs arising out of Constructor's failure to cure, including the costs of completing the Work and reasonable attorneys' fees, exceed the unpaid GMP, Constructor shall be liable to Owner for such excess costs. If Owner's costs are less than the unpaid GMP, Owner shall pay the difference to Constructor. If Owner exercises its rights under this section, upon the request of Constructor, Owner shall furnish to Constructor a detailed accounting of the costs incurred by Owner.

12.3.2 USE OF CONSTRUCTOR'S MATERIALS, SUPPLIES, AND EQUIPMENT If Owner or Others perform work under §12.2, Owner shall have the right to take and use any materials and supplies for which Owner has paid and located at the Worksite for the purpose of completing any remaining Work. Owner and others performing work under this §12.3 shall also have the right to use construction tools and equipment located on the Worksite and belonging to the Constructor or Subsubcontractors for the purpose of completing the remaining Work, but only after Constructor's written consent. If Owner uses Constructor's construction tools and equipment in accordance with this subsection, then Owner shall indemnify and hold harmless Constructor and applicable Subcontractors and the agents, officers, directors, and employees of each of them, from and against all claims, damages, losses, costs, and expenses, including but not limited to reasonable attorneys' fees, costs, and expenses incurred in connection with Owner's use of Constructor's or applicable subcontractor's construction tools and equipment. Immediately upon completion of the Work, any remaining materials, supplies, or equipment not consumed or incorporated in the Work shall be returned to Constructor in substantially the same condition as when they were taken, reasonable wear and tear excepted.

12.3.3 If Constructor files a petition under the Bankruptcy Code, this Agreement shall terminate if (a) Constructor or Constructor's trustee rejects the Agreement; (b) a default occurred and Constructor is unable to give adequate assurance of required performance; or (c) Constructor is otherwise unable to comply with the requirements for assuming this Agreement under the applicable provisions of the Bankruptcy Code.

12.3.4 Owner shall make reasonable efforts to mitigate damages arising from Constructor's default, and shall promptly invoice Constructor for all amounts due pursuant to §12.2 and §12.3.

12.4 TERMINATION BY OWNER FOR CONVENIENCE

12.4.1 Upon Constructor's receipt of Owner's written notice from Owner, Owner may, without cause, terminate this Agreement. Constructor shall immediately stop the Work, follow Owner's instructions regarding shutdown and termination procedures, and strive to minimize any further costs.

12.4.2 If Owner terminates this Agreement for convenience, Constructor shall be paid: (a) for the Work performed to date including Overhead and profit; (b) for all demobilization costs and costs incurred resulting from termination, but not including Overhead or profit on Work not performed; (c) reasonable attorneys' fees and costs related to termination; and (d) a premium as follows: [_____].

12.4.3 If Owner terminates this Agreement, Constructor shall:

12.4.3.1 execute and deliver to Owner all papers and take all action required to assign, transfer, and vest in Owner the rights of Constructor to all materials, supplies, and equipment for which payment has been or will be made in accordance with the Contract Documents and all subcontracts, orders, and commitments which have been made in accordance with the Contract Documents;

12.4.3.2 exert reasonable effort to reduce to a minimum Owner's liability for subcontracts, orders, and commitments that have not been fulfilled at the time of the termination;

12.4.3.3 cancel any subcontracts, orders, and commitments as Owner directs; and

12.4.3.4 sell at prices approved by Owner any materials, supplies, and equipment as Owner directs, with all proceeds paid or credited to Owner.

12.5 CONSTRUCTOR'S RIGHT TO TERMINATE

12.5.1 Seven (7) Days after Owner's receipt of written notice from Constructor, Constructor may terminate this Agreement if the Work has been stopped for a thirty (30) Day period through no fault of Constructor for any of the following reasons:

(a) under court order or order of other governmental authorities having jurisdiction;
(b) as a result of the declaration of a national emergency or other governmental act during which, through no act or fault of Constructor, materials are not available; or
(c) suspension by Owner for convenience pursuant to §12.1.

12.5.2 In addition, upon seven (7) Days written notice to Owner, and an opportunity to cure within three (3) Days, Constructor may terminate the Agreement if Owner:

12.5.2.1 fails to furnish reasonable evidence pursuant to §4.2 that sufficient funds are available and committed for Project financing; or

12.5.2.2 assigns this Agreement over Constructor's reasonable objection; or

12.5.2.3 fails to pay Constructor in accordance with this Agreement and Constructor stopped Work in compliance with §10.5; or

12.5.2.4 otherwise materially breaches this Agreement.

12.5.3 Upon termination by Constructor in accordance with this §12.5, Constructor is entitled to recover from Owner payment for all Work executed and for any proven loss, cost, or expense in connection with the Work, including all demobilization costs plus reasonable Overhead and profit on Work not performed.

12.6 OBLIGATIONS ARISING BEFORE TERMINATION Even after termination, the provisions of this Agreement still apply to any Work performed, payments made, events occurring, costs charged or incurred, or obligations arising before the termination date.

ARTICLE 13 DISPUTE MITIGATION AND RESOLUTION

13.1 WORK CONTINUANCE AND PAYMENT Constructor shall continue the Work and maintain the Schedule of the Work during any dispute mitigation or resolution procedure. If Constructor continues to perform, Owner shall continue to make payments in accordance with this Agreement.

13.2 DIRECT DISCUSSIONS If the Parties cannot reach resolution on a matter relating to or arising out of this Agreement, the Parties shall endeavor to reach resolution through good faith direct discussions between the Parties' representatives, who shall possess the necessary authority to resolve such matter and who shall record the date of first discussions. If the Parties' representatives are not able to resolve such matter within five (5) Business Days from the date of first discussion, the Parties' representatives shall immediately inform senior executives of the Parties in writing that a resolution could not be reached. Upon receipt of such notice, the senior executives of the Parties shall meet within five (5) Business Days to endeavor to reach resolution. If the dispute remains unresolved after fifteen (15) Days from the date of first discussion, the Parties shall submit such matter to the dispute mitigation and dispute resolution procedures selected below.

13.3 MITIGATION If the Parties select one of the dispute mitigation procedures below, disputes remaining unresolved after direct discussions shall be directed to the selected mitigation procedure. The dispute mitigation procedure shall result in a nonbinding finding on the matter, which may be introduced as evidence at a subsequent binding adjudication of the matter, as designated in §13.5. The Parties agree that the dispute mitigation procedure shall be:

☐ Project Neutral ("Neutral")

☐ Dispute Review Board ("DRB")

13.3.1 MITIGATION PROCEDURES As soon as practicable after the execution of this Agreement, the Neutral or DRB shall be mutually selected and appointed by the Parties and shall execute a retainer agreement with the Parties establishing the scope of responsibilities, including requirements for nonbinding findings. Costs and expenses of Neutral or DRB shall be shared equally by the Parties. A Neutral or DRB shall be available to either Party, upon request, throughout the course of the Project, and shall make regular visits to the Project so as to maintain an up-to-date understanding of the Project progress and issues and to enable the Neutral or DRB to address matters in dispute between the Parties promptly and knowledgeably.

13.3.2 If the matter remains unresolved following the issuance of the nonbinding findings or such findings are not made within five (5) Business Days of the referral, the Parties shall submit the matter to the binding dispute resolution procedure designated in §13.5.

13.3.3 If the Parties execute a DRB Addendum, then the dispute mitigation procedures and time requirements in §13.3.1 and §13.3.2 shall be governed by that DRB Addendum.

13.4 MEDIATION If direct discussions pursuant to §13.2 do not result in resolution of the matter and no dispute mitigation procedure is selected under §13.3, the Parties shall endeavor to resolve the matter by mediation. The mediation shall be convened within thirty (30) Business Days of the matter first being discussed and shall conclude within forty-five (45) Business Days of the matter first being discussed. Either Party may terminate the mediation at any time after the first session by written notice to the non-terminating Party and mediator. The costs of the mediation shall be shared equally by the Parties. The Parties choose mediation through:

☐ the current Construction Industry Mediation Rules of the American Arbitration Association (AAA), and administered by AAA.
☐ the current Mediation Guidelines of JAMS and administered by JAMS.
☐ the current rules and administration by [_____].

If no box is checked the default is AAA rules and administration.

13.5 BINDING DISPUTE RESOLUTION If the matter is unresolved after submission of the matter to a mitigation procedure or to mediation, the Parties shall submit the matter to the binding dispute resolution procedure selected below:

13.5.1 ARBITRATION

☐ The Parties choose binding arbitration for any claim or dispute arising out of or relating to this Agreement. EACH PARTY WAIVES THEIR RIGHT TO BE HEARD IN A COURT OF LAW, with or without a jury. Arbitration does not involve a judge or jury. Instead, an arbitrator with the power to award damages and other appropriate relief will decide claims and disputes. An arbitrator's award shall be final and binding upon the Parties, and judgment may be entered upon it in any court having jurisdiction.

13.5.1.1 Neither Party may commence arbitration if the claim or cause of action would be barred by the applicable statute of limitations had the claim or cause of action been filed in a state or federal court. Receipt of a demand for arbitration by the person or entity administering the arbitration shall constitute the commencement of legal proceedings for the purposes of determining whether a claim or cause of action is barred by the applicable statute of limitations. If, however, a state or federal court exercising jurisdiction over a timely filed claim or cause of action orders that the claim or cause of action be submitted to arbitration, the arbitration proceeding shall be deemed commenced as of the date the court action was filed, provided that the Party asserting the claim or cause of action files its demand for arbitration with the person or entity administering the arbitration within thirty (30) Days after the entry of such order.

13.5.1.2 The arbitration shall use the following rules:

☐ the current AAA Construction Industry Arbitration Rules and AAA administration. AAA Construction Fast Track Rules shall apply to all two-party cases when neither Party's disclosed claim or counterclaim exceeds $250,000. If arbitration is selected but no rules are selected, then this subsection shall apply by default;
☐ the current JAMS Engineering and Construction Arbitration Rules and Procedures and administered by JAMS; or
☐ the current arbitration rules of [_____] and administered by [_____].

13.5.2 LITIGATION

☐ Litigation in either the state or federal court having jurisdiction of the matter in the location of the Project.

If not indicated, then litigation is the default and not arbitration.

13.5.3 COSTS The costs of any binding dispute resolution procedures and reasonable attorneys' fees shall be borne by the non-prevailing Party, as determined by the adjudicator of the dispute.

13.5.4 VENUE The Project location shall serve as the venue.

13.6 MULTIPARTY PROCEEDING All parties necessary to resolve a matter agree to be parties to the same dispute resolution proceeding, if possible. Appropriate provisions shall be included in all other contracts relating to the Work to provide for the joinder or consolidation of such dispute resolution procedures.

13.7 LIEN RIGHTS Nothing in this article shall limit any rights or remedies not expressly waived by the Constructor.

ARTICLE 14 MISCELLANEOUS

14.1 EXTENT OF AGREEMENT Except as expressly provided, this Agreement is for the exclusive benefit of the Parties, and not for the benefit of any third party. This Agreement represents the entire and integrated agreement between the Parties, and supersedes all prior negotiations, representations, or agreements, either written or oral.

14.2 ASSIGNMENT Except as to the assignment of proceeds, the Parties shall not assign their interest in this Agreement without the written consent of the other. The terms and conditions of this Agreement shall be binding upon both Parties, their partners, successors, assigns, and legal representatives. Neither Party shall assign the Agreement as a whole without written consent of the other except that Owner may assign the Agreement to a wholly owned subsidiary of Owner when Owner has fully indemnified Constructor or to an institutional lender providing construction financing for the Project as long as the assignment is no less favorable to Constructor than this Agreement. If such assignment occurs, Constructor shall execute any consent reasonably required. In such event, the wholly owned subsidiary or lender shall assume Owner's rights and obligations under the Contract Documents. If either Party attempts to make such an assignment, that Party shall nevertheless remain legally responsible for all obligations under this Agreement, unless otherwise agreed by the other Party.

14.3 GOVERNING LAW The Law in effect at the location of the Project shall govern this Agreement.

14.4 SEVERABILITY The partial or complete invalidity of any one or more provisions of this Agreement shall not affect the validity or continuing force and effect of any other provision.

14.5 NOTICE Unless changed in writing, a Party's address indicated in ARTICLE 1 shall be used when delivering notice to a physical address. Except for Agreement termination and as otherwise specified in the Contract Documents, notice is effective upon transmission by any effective means, including U.S. postal service and overnight delivery service.

14.6 NO WAIVER OF PERFORMANCE Either Party's failure to insist, in any one or more instances, on the performance of any of the terms, covenants, or conditions of this Agreement, or to exercise any of its rights, shall not be construed as a waiver or relinquishment of such term, covenant, condition, or right with respect to further performance or any other term, covenant, condition, or right.

14.7 TITLES The titles given to the articles are for ease of reference only and shall not be relied upon or cited for any other purpose.

14.8 JOINT DRAFTING The Parties expressly agree that this Agreement was jointly drafted, and that both had opportunity to negotiate its terms and to obtain the assistance of counsel in reviewing its terms before execution. Therefore, this Agreement shall be construed neither against nor in favor of either Party, but shall be construed in a neutral manner.

ARTICLE 15 CONTRACT DOCUMENTS

15.1 EXISTING CONTRACT DOCUMENTS

15.1.1 The Contract Documents in existence at the time of execution of this Agreement are as follows:

(a) Drawings: [____]
(b) Specifications: [____]
(c) Addenda: [____]
(d) Owner Provided information: [____].
(e) GMP written statement
(f) Other: [____]

15.2 INTERPRETATION OF CONTRACT DOCUMENTS

15.2.1 The drawings and specifications are complementary. If Work is shown only on one but not on the other, Constructor shall perform the Work as though fully described on both.

15.2.2 In case of conflicts between the drawings and specifications, the specifications shall govern. In any case of omissions or errors in figures, drawings, or specifications, Constructor shall immediately submit the matter to Owner for clarification. Subject to an equitable adjustment in Contract Time or GMP pursuant to ARTICLE 9, or a dispute mitigation and resolution, Owner's clarifications are final and binding.

15.2.3 Where figures are given, they shall be preferred to scaled dimensions.

15.2.4 Unless otherwise specifically defined in this Agreement, any terms that have well-known technical or trade meanings shall be interpreted in accordance with their well-known meanings.

15.3 ORDER OF PRECEDENCE In case of any inconsistency, conflict, or ambiguity among the Contract Documents, the documents shall govern in the following order: (a) Change Orders and written amendments to this Agreement; (b) this Agreement; (c) subject to §15.2.2 the drawings (large scale governing over small scale), specifications, and addenda issued and acknowledged before Agreement execution or signed by both Parties; (d) information furnished by Owner pursuant to §3.14.4 or designated as a Contract Document in §15.1; (e) other Contract Documents listed in this Agreement. Among categories of documents having the same order of precedence, the term or provision that includes the latest date shall control.

OWNER: [____]
BY: ____________________ NAME: ____________________ TITLE: ____________
WITNESS: ________________ NAME: ____________________ TITLE: ____________

CONSTRUCTOR: [____]
BY: ____________________ NAME: ____________________ TITLE: ____________
WITNESS: ________________ NAME: ____________________ TITLE: ____________

END OF DOCUMENT.

Exhibit 16

ConsensusDocs 301

BIM Addendum

ConsensusDocs®
BUILDING A BETTER WAY

ConsensusDocs® 301
BUILDING INFORMATION MODELING (BIM) ADDENDUM

This page is solely for the information and convenience of ConsensusDocs users, and is not a part of the contract. Gray boxes indicate where you should click and type in your project information. The yellow shading is a Word® default function that displays editable text. Shading can be turned off by going to the Review tab, select "Restrict Editing" button and uncheck "Highlight the regions I can edit". In Word 2003 you will find this option under the Tools tab, Options, Security tab, Protect Document button.

EMBEDDED INSTRUCTIONS are provided solely to help you complete the document. To display or hide instructions select the "¶" button under the "Home" tab to show all formatting marks.

Red Boxes: Instructions for fields that are typically required to complete contract.
Blue Boxes: Instructions for fields that may or may not be required for a complete contract.
Green Boxes: Provide general instructions or ConsensusDocs Coalition Guidebook comments, which can be found at www.ConsensusDocs.org/guidebook.

This document was developed through a collaborative effort of organizations representing a wide cross-section of the design and construction industry. This document has important legal and insurance consequences, and it is not intended as a substitute for competent professional services and advice. This document must be reviewed and adapted to meet your project-specific needs. Federal, State and Local laws may vary with respect to the applicability or enforceability of specific provisions in this document. CONSENSUSDOCS SPECIFICALLY DISCLAIMS ALL WARRANTIES, EXPRESS OR IMPLIED, INCLUDING ANY WARRANTY OF MERCHANTABILITY OR FITNESS FOR A PARTICULAR PURPOSE. PURCHASER ASSUMES ALL LIABILITY WITH RESPECT TO THE USE OF THIS DOCUMENT, AND CONSENSUSDOCS AND ANY OF THE ENDORSING ORGANIZATIONS SHALL NOT BE LIABLE FOR ANY DIRECT, INDIRECT OR CONSEQUENTIAL DAMAGES RESULTING FROM SUCH USE. For additional information, please contact ConsensusDocs, 2300 Wilson Blvd, Suite 300, Arlington, VA 22201, 866-925-DOCS (3627), support@consensusdocs.org or www.ConsensusDocs.org.

ConsensusDocs® 301

BUILDING INFORMATION MODELING (BIM) ADDENDUM

TABLE OF ARTICLES

ARTICLE 1 GENERAL PRINCIPLES

1.1 This Addendum identifies rights and responsibilities of Project Participants related to the use of BIM on this Project. It is not intended to create privity of contract among any Project Participants beyond that which otherwise exists at law or by the terms of the Governing Contracts or Affiliated Contracts.

1.2 This Addendum and its Exhibits shall be appended to or incorporated by reference in the Governing Contracts and all Affiliated Contracts of Contributors, as well as any contracts of others having rights or obligations under this Addendum, as needed.

1.3 Nothing in this Addendum shall relieve the Design Professional from any design obligations under its Governing Contract, including responsibility for its Contributions to comply with applicable codes, regulations, or laws. No Contributor may require the Design Professional to provide designs inconsistent with these obligations or may modify another Contributor's Contribution without that Contributor's consent.

1.4 Nothing in this Addendum shall diminish or expand the extent to which, under applicable law, Owner confirms or warrants the adequacy, sufficiency, or both of any Model.

1.5 Except to the extent required under the Constructor's Governing Contract, Constructor's and its Subcontractors' and Suppliers' Contributions or participation in modeling activities shall not constitute the performance of design services.

1.6 If any Project Participant becomes aware of a discrepancy between a Model and another Model or Contract Document, that Project Participant shall promptly notify the other affected Model Contributors and the BIM Manager.

1.7 Except as expressly provided in this Addendum, this Addendum shall take precedence over any conflicting or inconsistent Governing Contract or Affiliated Contract terms.

ARTICLE 2 DEFINITIONS

2.1 Capitalized terms not otherwise defined in this Addendum shall have definitions as set forth in the most current edition at the time of execution to the Governing Contract of the ConsensusDocs 200 Standard Agreement and General Conditions between Owner and Constructor.

2.2 "4D" means integrating time or schedule information, including phase planning modeling into a Model.

2.3 "5D" means integrating quantity or cost data, including cost estimation modeling and cost control analysis into a Model.

2.4 "Affiliated Contract" means any Project contract to which this Addendum is attached or into which it is incorporated by reference, other than the Governing Contracts.

2.5 "As-Built Construction Model" is a Construction Model modified to reflect as-built conditions of the Work as constructed during Construction Phase, including facility Geometric data, fabrication, and coordination modeling.

2.6 "Building Information Modeling" or BIM, means the collaborative development of a three-dimensional digital representation that is Intelligent and Parametric, depicting the physical and functional characteristics of a structure or site for use as a shared knowledge resource; it may also include generation of Geometric and non-graphic Information, and related processes, analysis, and deliverables for use over the lifecycle of the structure or site depicted.

2.7 "BIM Execution Plan" means a plan that enumerates the goals, implementation processes, metrics, and deliverables that will be used to develop BIM for the Project, which also may be referred to as a PxP or project execution plan.

2.8 "BIM Manager" means the Project Participant or parties responsible for the information management program for the Project.

2.9 "CIM" or civil information modeling, means the digital representation of the physical and functional characteristics of a site, including topography and location of structures on the site, usable as a shared knowledge resource.

2.10 "Conformed Design Model" means a Design Model that reflects all final changes to physical conditions of the modeled structure and other as-built updates to the design that occurred throughout the construction Phase, including Intelligent attributes, and may include related deliverables.

2.11 "Construction Model" is a Model that utilizes data imported from a Design Model or Drawings containing the equivalent of shop drawings and other information useful for construction.

2.12 "Contract Documents" is as defined in a Governing Contract, but is hereby modified to include the Full Design Model, this Addendum, as modified and agreed to by the parties, and the BIM Execution Plan adopted by the parties pursuant to this Agreement.

2.13 "Constructor" is identified in the Governing Contract with Owner as the responsible entity to provide or coordinate construction Work for the Project, and may be referred to as the General Contractor, Contractor, Prime Contractor, Constructor, Design-Builder, or Construction Manager.

2.14 "Contribution" means the expression, design, data or information created or prepared for the Project that is incorporated, distributed, transmitted, communicated by, or shared with Project Participants through or in connection with a Model.

2.15 "Contributor" is any Project Participant who makes a Contribution.

2.16 "Coordinated Construction Model" is: (a) a discipline-specific Shop Model; (b) updated to incorporate the changes and updates approved during the digital design coordination process and before commencement of the Work; (c) that is modeled to a Level of Granularity; and (d) is delivered in the format and with the file extension specified in Attachment A to the BIM Execution Plan.

2.17 "Design Model" is a discipline-specific Model prepared by a Design Professional to illustrate the architectural, structural, mechanical electrical and plumbing (MEP), or other specialty design requirements of the Project, exclusive of analysis undertaken by other Contributors to that Model.

2.18 "Design Professional" is responsible for the development and delivery of design services for the Project, and may be referred to as the architect/engineer, architect, engineer, or Design Professional in their Governing Contract with Owner.

2.19 "Digital Fabrication" means the process by which machine technology is used to prefabricate Elements used in construction directly from Model data, including spooling into appropriate sections and inputting into fabrication equipment for production of system assemblies to be used in construction of the Project.

2.20 "Dimensional Accuracy" means the expected content of a Model and its prescribed reliability at each milestone or Model Phase established in the BIM Execution Plan.

2.21 "Drawings" are (1) two-dimensional projections derived from a Model, which may be supplemented with independent graphics and annotations and (2) two-dimensional plans, sketches, or other graphic depictions created separately and not derived from a Model.

2.22 "Element" means a self-contained, uniquely identified object in a Model representing a building component, system, or assembly within a structure or on the Project site.

2.23 "Federated Model" is a Model that links distinct component Models, Drawings, analysis, and other data sources that do not lose their identity or integrity by being so linked, such that a change to one component Model does not change another component Model in the Federated Model.

2.24 "Full Design Model" is a Model consisting of linked component Design Models that illustrate the construction-ready designs as designated in the BIM Execution Plan.

2.25 "Geometric" means rectilinear or curvilinear points, lines, and surfaces developed using BIM.

2.26 "Geospatial" means three dimensional objects developed using BIM.

2.27 "Governing Contract" means an agreement between the Project Owner and Design Professional or between Owner and Constructor, to which this Addendum is to be attached or incorporated by reference.

2.28 "Granularity" means the level of accuracy of Geometric representation of a Model Element needed to support a specific BIM use.

2.29 "Intelligent" means the imbedded specifications, sizes, material definitions, characteristics, manufacturer properties, identification numbers, and other data describing the attributes and configuration of an Element that are readable directly within the Model.

2.30 "Interoperability" means the capability of different software programs to exchange data via a common set of exchange formats, to read and write in those formats, and to use the same protocols so that Model data is not dropped, repurposed, or reformatted.

2.31 "Level of Detail" means the input detail, information maturity, and richness of a Model Element.

2.32 "Level of Development (LOD)" specifies the completeness of a Model Element or reliability of Model output at various stages in the design and construction process, and the minimum requirements for its expression.

2.33 The "LOD Specification," unless otherwise defined in the Contract Documents, is as defined or incorporated into the BIM Forum's Levels of Development Specification as published at https://bimforum.org/lod/ on the Governing Contract's effective date.

2.34 "Level of Granularity (LOG)" means the level of dimensional accuracy of Model data.

2.35 "Model" means an electronic, three-dimensional representation of building Elements representing solid objects with true-to-scale Geospatial relationships and dimensions, which may include additional attribute information, or data, and 4D, 5D, sustainability, or other analyses.

2.36 "Model Use" is the deliverable that is derived from a specific Model or an intended use of a Model.

2.37 "Model Phase" means any of the following phases of development or anticipated use of a Model over the lifecycle of a Project, including conceptual planning, design development, construction, commissioning, turnover, facility operation & maintenance, enterprise management, and decommissioning and recycling.

2.38 "Parametric" means that attributes of construction materials, equipment, and assemblies are linked and consistently coordinated and maintained in all Model views and schedules such that a change to a Model Element or other data in any view or schedule is automatically similarly modified in all views and schedules where it appears in the Model.

2.39 "Project Model" means a Model consisting of the federation of a Full Design Model and one or more Construction Models designated to be produced in the BIM Execution Plan.

2.40 "Project Participants" means all parties to a Governing Contract or Affiliated Contract for the Project.

2.41 Record Model" means a separate, discipline-specific Model that accurately reflects clarifications and changes made during Project construction to the Geospatial and Geometric attributes that comprise Elements of a Design Model, but which does not modify the original Design Model or require creation of new Design Model Elements beyond the LOG established in the BIM Execution Plan. If required under § 4.5.4 as a data collection protocol, a Record Model may require the addition of new, or refinement of existing, non-graphic Information.

2.42 "Shop Model" means a digital Model created from data derived from one or more Design Models or a Full Design Model and prepared by a Constructor, Subcontractor, or Supplier to illustrate some portion of their Work and its conformity to Project specifications and other design requirements.

2.43 "UniFormat™" means the UniFormat Classification System used to arrange construction information for Elements of a structure characterized by their functions without regard to the materials and methods used to complete these systems or assemblies, often for 5D costing analysis.

ARTICLE 3 BIM MANAGER

3.1 Owner designates the following BIM Manager to undertake overall responsibility for the use, implementation, and creation of BIM for the Project:

- ☐ Constructor
- ☐ Design Professional
- ☐ Other: [ ].

Unless otherwise agreed in the BIM Execution Plan, all compensation and related costs for the BIM Manager shall be paid by Owner. Owner may replace the BIM Manager at its own discretion.

3.2 The BIM Manager shall perform, or procure from third parties approved by Owner, the following functions:

3.2.1 Develop and oversee Contributor compliance with the BIM Execution Plan for the Project;

3.2.2 Schedule and manage BIM-related meetings with Contributor BIM technicians and coordinators to assist them in their development of their respective Contributions;

3.2.3 Create, delete, modify, and maintain individual user accounts, including confirming Contributor use of hardware, software, formatting, file exchange, maintenance, archiving, and other technology protocols specified in the BIM Execution Plan;

3.2.4 Assign, delete, and modify access rights to Contributors, including coordinating necessary access training, and facilitating proper export and data extraction from BIM to support the Model Uses;

3.2.5 Develop system access controls so that only authorized Contributors to the Model can access Model data, and so they may only access the data they are authorized to access;

3.2.6 Establish and maintain encryption and access security measures selected;

3.2.7 Maintain Model Element continuity, and coordinate Geospatial coordination, clash resolution, and Model quality control processes;

3.2.8 Backup and restore Model data, as appropriate, including developing protocols for versioning, storage, access rights, and availability;

3.2.9 Undertake information system scans to maintain Model security;

3.2.10 Maintain and monitor information system logs documenting access to the Models and resolving functional problems associated with Model access;

3.2.11 Determine measures needed to achieve Interoperability of Model applications and resolve documented Model Interoperability issues;

3.2.12 Document and report any incident relating to the Model, including but not limited to an incident originating outside the Model that results in the Model data loss, corruption, or unauthorized access, and take action to protect the Model;

3.2.13 Provide authorized users with system hardware configuration and software and related version requirements, and access instructions;

3.2.14 Respond to requests by authorized users for assistance in maintaining access;

3.2.15 Review all deliverables for compliance with submittal requirements developed pursuant to § 4.3, § 4.4, and § 4.5 for the BIM Execution Plan adopted for the Project;

3.2.16 Confirm that changes made during the Project design and construction are updated in the Model; and

3.2.17 Perform any and all other responsibilities or functions as required of the BIM Manager in the BIM Execution Plan.

3.3 BIM Manager shall transfer unconditionally to a successor BIM Manager, as directed by Owner, all tangible and intangible property and information in the BIM Manager's possession, custody, or control related to the Project.

ARTICLE 4 BIM EXECUTION PLAN

BIM EXECUTION PLAN DEVELOPMENT The BIM addendum assumes that Owner, Design Professional, and Contractor may not be able to meet, confer and agree on issues relating to the BIM Execution Plan until after Owner-Design Professional and Owner-Contractor agreements are negotiated. Ideally, if possible, the details of the BIM Execution Plan should be resolved prior to execution of the agreements, so that the compensation for such agreements can accurately reflect the scope of services to be provided. As additional Project Participants join the Project, it is necessary to convene another meeting to consider whether the addition of other Project Participants requires any modification of the BIM Execution Plan. Such a meeting could easily occur as part of a regular meeting.

4.1 No later than thirty (30) calendar days after execution of the first Governing Contract for the Project, the parties to that Governing Contract, together with any other anticipated or actual Contributors that have then been identified, shall develop a BIM Execution Plan for the Project. When completed, the BIM Execution Plan shall become an Exhibit to this Addendum. The BIM Execution Plan may be revised by mutual agreement of Owner, Constructor, and Design Professional as additional Contributors whose Contributions require modification of the Plan are identified.

4.2 The BIM Manager shall schedule and manage all meetings necessary for development of the BIM Execution Plan.

4.3 MODEL USES AND DELIVERABLES The BIM Execution Plan shall address, at a minimum, the following Model Uses and deliverables:

4.3.1 Identify and prioritize desired goals and objectives for BIM;

4.3.2 Maximize structure lifecycle best value and develop a list of Model Uses; and

4.3.3 Determine required Geometric modeling, related deliverables, process and Model deliverable requirements, including:

4.3.3.1 Identify by Model Phase the Models needed to achieve each Model Use;

4.3.3.2 Identify the parties responsible for each Model deliverable;

4.3.3.3 Determine which Models will be Contract Documents;

4.3.3.4 Create a schedule for Model deliverables, including dates for completion of Model Phases and interim coordination milestones within Model Phases, as necessary; and

4.3.3.5 Determine a process to preserve versions of each Federated Model and its constituent Models, and scheduling for such process.

4.4 BIM PROCESS EXECUTION: GEOMETRIC MODELING Specific Models and their development sequence shall be identified. This shall include (a) Project areas to be depicted in each Model; (b) the Geospatial portions or Project areas not to be modeled; (c) the process of collaborative information exchanges; and (d) the sequence and required development of required Models at each of the following Model Phases in order to achieve the Project Model Uses:

4.4.1 Conceptual Planning

4.4.1.1 Project budget development.

4.4.1.2 Project schedule development.

4.4.1.3 CIM or civil survey, master planning, and analysis – geolocation, boundary, topography, geographic information system and map (GIS) development, including necessary surface and subsurface data.

4.4.1.4 Site utilization, demolition, space, and phase planning.

4.4.1.5 Existing conditions modeling – laser scan and manual measurement-based.

4.4.1.6 Programming review – Geospatial or adjacency analysis and confirmation.

4.4.2 Design

4.4.2.1 Design authoring and related schedule development – specifying required disciplines.

4.4.2.2 Design review, audit, and analysis – including quality control, lean coordination and resolution requirements, and building systems performance analysis – structural, MEP, fire protection, etc.

4.4.2.3 Constructability and life-cycle value engineering analysis.

4.4.2.4 Shop modeling and fabrication modeling, including any 3D printed objects or components to be derived from Model data (specify individual disciplines and coordination requirements).

4.4.2.5 Planning approval and regulatory permitting designs.

4.4.2.6 Digital Fabrication modeling and tolerance requirements.

4.4.2.7 Energy and sustainability massing or other modeling for simulation and analysis, including energy distribution and consumption, temperature control, solar radiation, shading and wind analysis, seismic, CO^2 emissions, carbon footprint, thermal, lighting and water usage, acoustics, and airflow studies.

4.4.2.8 Geospatial coordination and clash resolution – identifying Design Models and Coordinated Construction Models to be compared at each Model Phase.

4.4.2.9 Life safety and other code analysis and validation.

4.4.2.10 Record Model and Conformed Design Model development; source of changes and updates will be derived from:

- ☐ annotated 2D Drawings
- ☐ annotated Construction Model
- ☐ scaled dimensions of the as-built Work field measured at the Project site
- ☐ electronic scan or laser point cloud of the as-built Work at the Project site
- ☐ other (specify): [_____]

4.4.3 Construction

4.4.3.1 Construction management – site utilization, Geospatial coordination, phasing, layout and Work control and sequencing for Intelligent and automated construction site activities.

4.4.3.2 Assembly and Work sequence training simulations for construction systems.

4.4.3.3 Construction quality control.

4.4.3.4 Timeframes and milestones for model updating during construction.

4.4.3.5 Safety planning.

4.4.3.6 Site logistics and security controls.

4.4.3.7 Digital Fabrication – searchable and indexed pre-assembly, modularization and prefabrication processes and production of any 3D printed objects and building components.

4.4.3.8 Construction waste management and reduction.

4.4.3.9 Material supply and RFID or other smart tagging.

4.4.3.10 Model-based request for information (RFI) and Change Order management.

4.4.3.11 As-Built Construction Model development.

4.4.3.12 Work completion Model deliverables.

4.4.4 Commissioning and Turnover

4.4.4.1 Building system performance confirmation.

4.4.4.2 Model documentation of commissioning performance levels.

4.4.4.3 Operation and maintenance staff training using Model simulations.

4.4.4.4 Identification of specific data, software (current and planned), systems, and databases which will be exchange information. Chart A below specifies the purpose (for As-Built Construction Models, Record Models, or both), information type (Geometric, non-graphical, or both), exchange dynamic (one-way or reciprocal), Participant responsible for the deliverable, and the schedule for doing so: *(Chart A on the next page)*

Chart A								
Owner System	As-Built Construction Models	As-Built Construction Models			Record Models	Record Models		
		Geometric Data	Related deliverables (specify)	One-way or reciprocal?		Geometric Data	Related deliverables (specify)	One-way or reciprocal?
☐ **Project Management**	☐	☐	☐	**Specify**	☐	☐	☐	**Specify**
☐ **Project Document Management** (Drawings)	☐	☐	☐	**Specify**	☐	☐	☐	**Specify**
☐ **Project Document Management** (Non-Drawings)	☐	☐	☐	**Specify**	☐	☐	☐	**Specify**
☐ **Project Collaboration** (if separate or distinct from above)	☐	☐	☐	**Specify**	☐	☐	☐	**Specify**
☐ **As-Built Repository** (Drawings)	☐	☐	☐	**Specify**	☐	☐	☐	**Specify**
☐ **Preventative Maintenance** (a/k/a CMMS)	☐	☐	☐	**Specify**	☐	☐	☐	**Specify**
☐ **Building Automation and Controls** (a/k/a BAS or BMS)	☐	☐	☐	**Specify**	☐	☐	☐	**Specify**
☐ **Life Safety Management and Reporting**	☐	☐	☐	**Specify**	☐	☐	☐	**Specify**
☐ **Space and Lease Management** (a/k/a CAFM)	☐	☐	☐	**Specify**	☐	☐	☐	**Specify**
☐ **Furniture and Equipment Management**	☐	☐	☐	**Specify**	☐	☐	☐	**Specify**
☐ **Finance, Accounting and Tax – Any & All Programs used**	☐	☐	☐	**Specify**	☐	☐	☐	**Specify**
☐ **Other:**	☐	☐	☐	**Specify**	☐	☐	☐	**Specify**

4.4.5 Facility Operation & Maintenance (O&M) and Enterprise Management

4.4.5.1 Facility operation and management – Model-embedded O&M manual and warranty data requirements for intelligent or smart building, self-maintaining, and reporting operational facilities within a structure.

4.4.5.2 Maintenance – scheduling, job planning, training processes.

4.4.5.3 Asset management

(a) Furniture Fixtures & Equipment (FF&E) – fixed and moveable – RFID or other smart tagging and management.

(b) Installed Building Equipment (IBE) – performance monitoring of Project equipment.

(c) Inventory – tracking and location monitoring.

(d) Exterior Assets – performance monitoring of Project equipment and fixtures located outside of structures (transformers, light and utility poles, etc.).

4.4.5.4 Space and lease management and tracking and related computer-aided facility management (CAFM) or integrated workplace management system (IWMS).

4.4.5.5 Building systems analysis – energy management and comparison of as planned and actual energy use, equipment, and systems functionality.

4.4.5.6 Building automation system, building management system (BAS/BMS), and related controls.

4.4.5.7 Disaster planning – dynamic automation and static building information, and routing, access, and evacuation protocol development.

4.4.5.8 Access and security monitoring.

4.4.5.9 CIM data, site, and auxiliary systems management.

4.4.5.10 Record Model - repository and updating, including As-Built Construction Model and Record Model requirements, with one-way and two-way integration; related deliverables documentation, and delivery format and file extension development.

4.4.5.11 Expansion and renovation planning.

4.4.5.12 Decommissioning and recycling.

4.5 BIM EXECUTION: RELATED DELIVERABLES Determine related non-Model deliverables, such as Drawings, reports, records, performance data, diagrams, and analyses and activities, including schedule of information sharing and required development milestones to achieve the Model Uses, including:

4.5.1 Drawings – Two-dimensional documents, including details, sections, elevations, plans, permitting sets, and diagrammatic RFI responses:

4.5.1.1 2D Drawings will be derived from:

☐ 3D Model data; or
☐ Non-Model, computer-assisted design data (CAD) or other non-computerized sources.

4.5.1.2 If there is a conflict between a Model Contribution and a portion of the design generated in a 2-dimensional medium then:

☐ The Model Contribution shall take precedence over the dimensions called for in or reasonably inferred from the Drawings; or
☐ Dimensions called for in or reasonably inferred from the Drawings shall take precedence over a Model Contribution.

4.5.2 4D scheduling – Model-based or Model-embedded Project and Work schedule sequencing and phase planning, including fixed chart and simulation sequencing; quantity take off by location (material type, work area, floor, structure, type of amenity, corners); on-site production control (as planned vs. as-built, forecasting by trade, location, or assembly).

4.5.3 5D estimating – Model-based or Parametric Project and Work cost estimating and quantity planning, including unit pricing by location and Element type; budget tracking (as planned vs. as-built); target cost analysis for value engineering and design changes; cash flow projection; and sustainability feature valuation.

4.5.4 Data collection protocols – determine Construction Operations Building Information Exchange (COBie) or other Owner-specific Element data spreadsheet requirements by Project Model Phase, Contributor and deliverable type and format for all data collection protocol requirements, including identifying Element listings by location, identification number, space type, manufacturer, model number, serial number, O&M requirements and any other data fields required for the Project. Identify any Governing or Affiliated Contract provisions that will be amended to reflect the use of the selected data collection protocol, including submittal schedules, submittal review, review of information and Final Completion, As-Built Drawings, commissioning, and final payment.

4.5.5 Sustainability analyses – energy analysis, use and performance; lighting and daylighting studies; airflow (computational fluid analysis), HVAC, and thermal comfort analysis; lifecycle impact; materials performance modeling; and LEED®, Energy Star®, Green Globes®, GreenMark®, or other environmental evaluation and certification testing, including formats and required content of written reports from analysis derived from Model data.

4.5.6 Other Related Deliverables – any other related deliverables, including spreadsheets, reports, photographic documentation, .pdf deliverables, RFI and Change Order management logs and lists.

4.6 TECHNOLOGY INFRASTRUCTURE & INFORMATION EXCHANGE After determination of the necessary Model Geometric and related deliverables as provided in § 4.4 and § 4.5, develop necessary technology infrastructure and information exchange processes and protocols to support the Model Uses, including determination of the following:

4.6.1 Hardware – configuration specifications (processor, operating system, memory storage, random access memory, graphics, network card, etc.) for computers and related peripherals (printers, scanners, screens, etc.) and mobile devices (tablets, smart phones, slates, etc.);

4.6.2 Software – proprietary and open source authoring and file sharing platforms and applications including version (and version upgrade process, if applicable);

4.6.3 Physical workspaces – mobile, fixed and collaborative, co-located, including furniture, power, connectivity and interactivity tools, and lighting needs;

4.6.4 Access – permitted users, including security protocols and training, collaboration and communication process requirements, priority of access, and data transfer interoperability and patching obligations;

4.6.5 Model sharing and networking infrastructure;

4.6.6 Meeting scheduling – including frequency, participants and locations, decision documentation for each Phase of Model development;

4.6.7 Model management and content, including:

4.6.7.1 data formatting (font, dimension, line styles, unit conventions, levels, etc.);

4.6.7.2 file- and element-naming and file size, protocols – including project identification number, discipline designation, model number, revision number, Element name and type, layer, sharing status, and related information;

4.6.7.3 measurement system;

4.6.7.4 Geospatial coordinate system (geo-referenced, origin point);

4.6.7.5 permitted native file types;

4.6.7.6 model Element and facility data accuracy requirements – minimum Geometric and Geospatial data, Element property, Element constitution, space holder parameters for cost and schedule data, and authoritative source information;

4.6.7.7 model partitioning; and

4.6.7.8 submission procedures and protocols – electronic stamping, approval process for designating a Model as a Design Model or Full Design Model, version and change tracking requirements, and system for notification of action on a request for approval of a Model or portion of it.

4.6.8 Model precision requirements – use of Level of Development, Granularity, and Level of Detail measurement tools by Phase and milestone.

4.6.9 DIMENSIONAL ACCURACY A Contribution of or to a Model shall be:

☐ dimensionally accurate and take precedence over the dimensions called out in the Drawings or inferred from the Drawings; details and components that are not represented in a Contribution to a Model must be retrieved from the Drawings; or
☐ accurate to the extent the LOD specified in the BIM Execution Plan requires dimensions to be accurate, and all other dimensions must be retrieved from the Drawings; or
☐ not dimensionally accurate; the Model can be used for reference only and all dimensions must be retrieved from the Drawings; or
☐ Other (*specify*): [_____].

4.6.10 Model reliability standards and quality control measures – visual, interference, standards, model integrity for accuracy and completeness of information, eliminating undefined, incorrectly defined and duplicated Elements. Paper and other non-electronic documentation requirements, including drawing set sizes, title sheet and sheet block designation formats, and content.

4.6.11 Utilization of BIM for RFI and Change Order processes, response protocols and timing, incorporation of responses into Models.

4.6.12 Workflow and revision management – process and approval, and validation tracking mechanisms.

4.6.13 Archiving, and data legacy integration and reuse rights – version, Record Model, Conformed Design Model control.

4.7 BIM STAFFING

4.7.1 Identify contact information for each Contributor and any other authorized users of Project BIM.

4.7.2 Determine roles and responsibilities – by Contributor organization and individually, including contact information sharing.

4.7.3 Develop training requirements for all Contributors.

4.7.4 Decision hierarchies – develop preferred sequence of information management and Model access, including identifying required decision makers for various aspects of Model development.

ARTICLE 5 RISK ALLOCATION

5.1 Each Model Contributor shall be responsible for the Contributions it makes to a Model or the data that is developed as a result of that Contributor's access to a Model. A Model Contributor is also responsible for any Contribution or access to a Model by a Project Participant in privity with, and of a lower tier contractually than, that Contributor.

5.2 With respect to waiver of consequential damages:

5.2.1 The applicable Governing Contract shall govern, as between the parties to that Governing Contract, for any waiver of consequential damages by or in favor of Constructor or Design Professional arising from their respective Contribution; and

5.2.2 Each Affiliated Contract Contributor waives claims against the other Project Contributors for consequential damages arising out of or relating to the use of, or access to, a Model, including, but not limited to, damages for loss of use of the Project, rental expenses, loss of income or profit, costs of financing, loss of business, principal office overhead and expenses, loss of reputation, or insolvency.

5.3 The standard of care applicable to a Contributor's Contributions to, or use of, a Model shall be governed by a Contributor's Governing Contract or Affiliated Contract, or, if no such standard is stated, then pursuant to common law, as applicable.

5.4 Each Model Contributor shall use its best efforts to minimize the risk of claims and liability arising from that Contributor's use of, or access to, its Model or any other Project Models. Such efforts shall include promptly reporting to affected Contributors any errors, inconsistencies, or omissions the Contributor discovers in its Model or other Project Models; however, nothing in this section shall relieve any Contributor of liability it would otherwise bear under § 5.1.

5.5 To the extent that any Design Models are included as Contract Documents under the BIM Execution Plan adopted for the Project or otherwise in this Addendum, Project Participants may rely upon the accuracy of information in those Design Models; provided, however, the selection in § 4.6.9 shall control a Project Participant's right to rely on the Dimensional Accuracy of a Contribution, Model, or Model Elements.

5.6 No Contributor shall be responsible for costs, expenses, liabilities, or damages that may result from use of its Model by other Contributors beyond the uses set forth in this Addendum, as may be amended.

5.7 Model use beyond the permitted uses set forth in this Addendum, as may be amended, is at the sole risk of the user; provided, however, nothing in this Addendum conveys any right to use a Model or other Contribution for a purpose other than for this Project to the extent provided herein.

5.8 Unless agreed otherwise in the BIM Execution Plan, and in addition to any insurance required by a Governing Contract or Affiliated Contract, Contributors shall procure and maintain the following insurance coverage, with at least the following aggregate limits:

5.8.1 For the BIM Manager:

(a) Professional liability insurance with a policy definition of covered "professional services" including either "BIM model management," "technical consulting," or similar wording covering the BIM Manager services required under this Addendum: $[   ]

(b) Electronic data processing insurance: $[   ]

5.8.2 For any Contributor that is a Constructor, or a Subcontractor or Supplier having a direct contractual relationship with a Constructor:

(a) Constructor's professional liability insurance having a policy definition of covered "professional services" that includes "BIM model management," "technical consulting," or similar wording: $[   ]

5.8.3 For any Contributor that is a Design Professional or that furnishes a Design Model for the Project:

(a) professional liability insurance with a policy definition of covered "professional services" that includes "BIM model management," "technical consulting," or similar wording: $[   ]

5.8.4 For all Contributors:

(a) technology or cyber liability insurance, including liability for exposures that include electronic security breaches, mistakes, and unauthorized employee acts, virus attacks, hacking, identity theft or private information loss, and infringing or disparaging content: $[   ]

5.8.5 For any Project Participant providing hosting services:

(a) electronic data processing insurance, including coverage for electronic data processing (EDP), including media replacement cost coverage and EDP data coverage: $[   ]

5.9 A defect in the software used in the creation, modification, federation, or other use of a Model shall entitle a Contributor to a reasonable time extension or other excuse from performance, provided the Contributor could not have reasonably avoided the delay or loss resulting from the defect and the Contributor uses reasonable diligence to mitigate such delay or loss.

ARTICLE 6 MODEL INTELLECTUAL PROPERTY RIGHTS

6.1 LICENSE GRANT In addition to any other copyright or other intellectual property licenses that may be granted under a Governing Contract, each Contributor grants to Owner and the other Contributors limited, non-exclusive licenses (Copyright Licenses) to reproduce, distribute, display, make derivative works of, and otherwise use the following for purposes of this Project only:

6.1.1 That Contributor's Contributions;

6.1.2 The Contributions of those other Project Participants who have granted that Contributor an identical license; and

6.1.3 Any Model relating to the Project to which that Contributor has intellectual property rights.

6.2 LICENSE LIMITATIONS

6.2.1 Unless otherwise provided in the BIM Execution Plan, the Copyright License will: (a) remain in effect as permitted by law and as required under this Addendum; and (b) after final completion of construction of the Project, be limited to retention of an archival copy of the Contributor's Project-related Contributions, and any additional Owner licenses as provided in § 6.6.

6.3 OWNERSHIP AND LICENSING Each Contributor warrants to the Project Participants that the Contributor is the copyright owner of, possesses a valid copyright license for, or is otherwise authorized by the copyright owner to use its Contribution, including the right to grant licenses to other Project Participants to use such data or the software used to create it as needed to fulfill duties or Model Uses established in the BIM Execution Plan for the Project. Subject to waiver of subrogation in a Governing Contract or Affiliated Contract applicable to Contributions, each Contributor agrees to defend, indemnify, and hold the other Project Participants harmless, including for costs, expenses of defense, and attorneys' fees, for claims of, and causes of action by, third parties arising out of, or relating to, infringement or alleged infringement of expression by that Contributor's Contribution.

6.4 COLLABORATION IMPACT ON IP

6.4.1 CONTRIBUTOR MODEL RIGHTS No Contributor possesses rights in a Model greater than those of its own Contribution to that Model or to a joint work on a Model or Element(s) therein, if any, and those granted by the Copyright License provided in this Addendum.

6.4.2 NO JOINT WORK Project Participants, Contributors, and other persons or entities involved in the Project are not co-authors or co-owners in the Contributions of other Contributors, except as provided in § 6.4.3.

6.4.3 Collaborative work on Models by Contributors:

☐ will not result in the creation of joint work; or
☐ will result in the creation of joint work as follows: [____].

6.5 NO TRANSFER OR DEPRIVATION OF RIGHTS Except as expressly granted by this Addendum, this Addendum is not intended to limit, transfer, deprive, dispossess, or otherwise affect any intellectual property rights that a Contributor has with respect to its respective Contribution.

6.6 ADDITIONAL OWNER LICENSES Owner's entitlement, if any, to use the Models developed for this Project for purposes other than this Project is as provided in the Governing Contract between Owner and Design Professional, and the Governing Contract between Owner and Constructor.

6.6.1 This entire subsection:

☐ does
☐ does not

take precedence over any terms in the Governing Contract pertaining to non-payment by Owner:

6.6.1.1 Except as provided in subsection 6.6.1.2 immediately below, the Copyright License granted to Owner in this Addendum to reproduce, distribute, display, or otherwise reuse the Contributions and Models for this Project shall be for the entire lifecycle of the Project.

6.6.1.2 If Owner fails to make Project-related payments to a Contributor when due under a Governing Contract, and that material failure is so adjudged against Owner by the final decision of the court of law, or alternative dispute resolution forum identified in that Governing Contract, or via such other forum mutually agreed by Owner and affected Contributor(s) (an "Adjudication"), then any Copyright Licenses granted to Owner from that Contributor shall be suspended as of the time of such Adjudication and reinstated upon satisfaction of the Adjudication.

6.6.1.3 Contributors waive any rights against other Contributors who are not found liable in an Adjudication (for failure to pay or otherwise) to:

6.6.1.3.1 claim contributory, direct, or vicarious copyright infringement;

6.6.1.3.2 to assert claims of misappropriation or like claims;

6.6.1.3.3 to revoke licenses granted in this Addendum; or

6.6.1.3.4 to pursue equitable remedies under the US Copyright Act, 17 U.S.C. §§ 101 et seq., or under applicable law, including their respective Model Use obligations, if any, to the Contributor unpaid by Owner.

6.6.1.4 The non-liable Contributor's licenses granted in this Addendum shall not be affected by the suspension of Owner's license due to an Adjudication.

Exhibit 17

Material Submittal

SUBMITTAL #49.32-rev.01 ASPHALT & BASE

ABC Materials Company
P.O. Box 123
Happy Town, XX
(800) 555-1234

August 1, 2023

XYZ Paving Company
P.O. Box 789
Sadtown, XX
Attn: Subcontractor Superintendent

Reference: Happy Town Shopping Center

Subject: State Caltrans C1 II Aggregate Base

The C1 II aggregate base material being proposed for delivery to your project, or being delivered to your project, meets specifications for Caltrans Class II Aggregate Base, Section 26; Standard Specifications for Public Works Construction, Section 200-2.4 for Crushed Miscellaneous Base specifications.

Our stockpiles are sampled periodically by Caltrans and others to assure our conformance.

Please find attached the latest test results. If you require further information, please advise.

Sincerely,

ABC Materials Company

Exhibit 18

Notice to Proceed

Owner/Development LLC
P.O. Box 10000
Jolly Town, XX

August 1, 2023

General Contractor, Inc.
P.O. Box 567
Happy Town, XX
(800) 555-1234

Reference: Project: Happy Town Shopping Center

Subject: Notice to Proceed

This letter shall serve as authorization by Owner/Development LLC ("Owner") for General Contractor, Inc. ("Contractor") to commence work within 10 days of the date of this notice and to provide necessary services in connection with the Project. Contractor covenants and agrees that it shall maintain all of the insurance, and comply with all of the provisions required by the Contract and will provide Owner with certificates of insurance before commencing work.

Contractor covenants and agrees that in performing the work it shall abide by all applicable laws and regulations.

Contractor covenants and agrees to arrange for the release any and all lien claims of subcontractors or suppliers arising out of or in connection with the Project.

Sincerely,

Owner/Development LLC

Exhibit 19

Performance Bond—AIA Document A312™ - 2010

AIA® Document A312® – 2010

Performance Bond

CONTRACTOR:
(Name, legal status and address)

SURETY:
(Name, legal status and principal place of business)

This document has important legal consequences. Consultation with an attorney is encouraged with respect to its completion or modification.

Any singular reference to Contractor, Surety, Owner or other party shall be considered plural where applicable.

OWNER:
(Name, legal status and address)

CONSTRUCTION CONTRACT
Date:

Amount:

Description:
(Name and location)

BOND
Date:
(Not earlier than Construction Contract Date)

Amount:

Modifications to this Bond: ☐ None ☐ See Section 16

CONTRACTOR AS PRINCIPAL
Company: *(Corporate Seal)*

Signature: ______________________
Name
and Title:

SURETY
Company: *(Corporate Seal)*

Signature: ______________________
Name
and Title:

(Any additional signatures appear on the last page of this Performance Bond.)

(FOR INFORMATION ONLY — Name, address and telephone)

AGENT or **BROKER:**

OWNER'S REPRESENTATIVE:
(Architect, Engineer or other party:)

Init.
/

§ 1 The Contractor and Surety, jointly and severally, bind themselves, their heirs, executors, administrators, successors and assigns to the Owner for the performance of the Construction Contract, which is incorporated herein by reference.

§ 2 If the Contractor performs the Construction Contract, the Surety and the Contractor shall have no obligation under this Bond, except when applicable to participate in a conference as provided in Section 3.

§ 3 If there is no Owner Default under the Construction Contract, the Surety's obligation under this Bond shall arise after

.1 the Owner first provides notice to the Contractor and the Surety that the Owner is considering declaring a Contractor Default. Such notice shall indicate whether the Owner is requesting a conference among the Owner, Contractor and Surety to discuss the Contractor's performance. If the Owner does not request a conference, the Surety may, within five (5) business days after receipt of the Owner's notice, request such a conference. If the Surety timely requests a conference, the Owner shall attend. Unless the Owner agrees otherwise, any conference requested under this Section 3.1 shall be held within ten (10) business days of the Surety's receipt of the Owner's notice. If the Owner, the Contractor and the Surety agree, the Contractor shall be allowed a reasonable time to perform the Construction Contract, but such an agreement shall not waive the Owner's right, if any, subsequently to declare a Contractor Default;

.2 the Owner declares a Contractor Default, terminates the Construction Contract and notifies the Surety; and

.3 the Owner has agreed to pay the Balance of the Contract Price in accordance with the terms of the Construction Contract to the Surety or to a contractor selected to perform the Construction Contract.

§ 4 Failure on the part of the Owner to comply with the notice requirement in Section 3.1 shall not constitute a failure to comply with a condition precedent to the Surety's obligations, or release the Surety from its obligations, except to the extent the Surety demonstrates actual prejudice.

§ 5 When the Owner has satisfied the conditions of Section 3, the Surety shall promptly and at the Surety's expense take one of the following actions:

§ 5.1 Arrange for the Contractor, with the consent of the Owner, to perform and complete the Construction Contract;

§ 5.2 Undertake to perform and complete the Construction Contract itself, through its agents or independent contractors;

§ 5.3 Obtain bids or negotiated proposals from qualified contractors acceptable to the Owner for a contract for performance and completion of the Construction Contract, arrange for a contract to be prepared for execution by the Owner and a contractor selected with the Owner's concurrence, to be secured with performance and payment bonds executed by a qualified surety equivalent to the bonds issued on the Construction Contract, and pay to the Owner the amount of damages as described in Section 7 in excess of the Balance of the Contract Price incurred by the Owner as a result of the Contractor Default; or

§ 5.4 Waive its right to perform and complete, arrange for completion, or obtain a new contractor and with reasonable promptness under the circumstances:

.1 After investigation, determine the amount for which it may be liable to the Owner and, as soon as practicable after the amount is determined, make payment to the Owner; or

.2 Deny liability in whole or in part and notify the Owner, citing the reasons for denial.

§ 6 If the Surety does not proceed as provided in Section 5 with reasonable promptness, the Surety shall be deemed to be in default on this Bond seven days after receipt of an additional written notice from the Owner to the Surety demanding that the Surety perform its obligations under this Bond, and the Owner shall be entitled to enforce any remedy available to the Owner. If the Surety proceeds as provided in Section 5.4, and the Owner refuses the payment or the Surety has denied liability, in whole or in part, without further notice the Owner shall be entitled to enforce any remedy available to the Owner.

§ 7 If the Surety elects to act under Section 5.1, 5.2 or 5.3, then the responsibilities of the Surety to the Owner shall not be greater than those of the Contractor under the Construction Contract, and the responsibilities of the Owner to the Surety shall not be greater than those of the Owner under the Construction Contract. Subject to the commitment by the Owner to pay the Balance of the Contract Price, the Surety is obligated, without duplication, for

.1 the responsibilities of the Contractor for correction of defective work and completion of the Construction Contract;

.2 additional legal, design professional and delay costs resulting from the Contractor's Default, and resulting from the actions or failure to act of the Surety under Section 5; and

.3 liquidated damages, or if no liquidated damages are specified in the Construction Contract, actual damages caused by delayed performance or non-performance of the Contractor.

§ 8 If the Surety elects to act under Section 5.1, 5.3 or 5.4, the Surety's liability is limited to the amount of this Bond.

§ 9 The Surety shall not be liable to the Owner or others for obligations of the Contractor that are unrelated to the Construction Contract, and the Balance of the Contract Price shall not be reduced or set off on account of any such unrelated obligations. No right of action shall accrue on this Bond to any person or entity other than the Owner or its heirs, executors, administrators, successors and assigns.

§ 10 The Surety hereby waives notice of any change, including changes of time, to the Construction Contract or to related subcontracts, purchase orders and other obligations.

§ 11 Any proceeding, legal or equitable, under this Bond may be instituted in any court of competent jurisdiction in the location in which the work or part of the work is located and shall be instituted within two years after a declaration of Contractor Default or within two years after the Contractor ceased working or within two years after the Surety refuses or fails to perform its obligations under this Bond, whichever occurs first. If the provisions of this Paragraph are void or prohibited by law, the minimum period of limitation available to sureties as a defense in the jurisdiction of the suit shall be applicable.

§ 12 Notice to the Surety, the Owner or the Contractor shall be mailed or delivered to the address shown on the page on which their signature appears.

§ 13 When this Bond has been furnished to comply with a statutory or other legal requirement in the location where the construction was to be performed, any provision in this Bond conflicting with said statutory or legal requirement shall be deemed deleted herefrom and provisions conforming to such statutory or other legal requirement shall be deemed incorporated herein. When so furnished, the intent is that this Bond shall be construed as a statutory bond and not as a common law bond.

§ 14 Definitions

§ 14.1 Balance of the Contract Price. The total amount payable by the Owner to the Contractor under the Construction Contract after all proper adjustments have been made, including allowance to the Contractor of any amounts received or to be received by the Owner in settlement of insurance or other claims for damages to which the Contractor is entitled, reduced by all valid and proper payments made to or on behalf of the Contractor under the Construction Contract.

§ 14.2 Construction Contract. The agreement between the Owner and Contractor identified on the cover page, including all Contract Documents and changes made to the agreement and the Contract Documents.

§ 14.3 Contractor Default. Failure of the Contractor, which has not been remedied or waived, to perform or otherwise to comply with a material term of the Construction Contract.

§ 14.4 Owner Default. Failure of the Owner, which has not been remedied or waived, to pay the Contractor as required under the Construction Contract or to perform and complete or comply with the other material terms of the Construction Contract.

§ 14.5 Contract Documents. All the documents that comprise the agreement between the Owner and Contractor.

§ 15 If this Bond is issued for an agreement between a Contractor and subcontractor, the term Contractor in this Bond shall be deemed to be Subcontractor and the term Owner shall be deemed to be Contractor.

§ 16 Modifications to this bond are as follows:

(Space is provided below for additional signatures of added parties, other than those appearing on the cover page.)

CONTRACTOR AS PRINCIPAL		**SURETY**	
Company:	*(Corporate Seal)*	Company:	*(Corporate Seal)*
Signature:		Signature:	
Name and Title:		Name and Title:	
Address		Address	

Init.

/

Exhibit 20

Payment Bond—AIA Document A312™ - 2010

AIA® Document A312® – 2010

Payment Bond

CONTRACTOR:
(Name, legal status and address)

SURETY:
(Name, legal status and principal place of business)

This document has important legal consequences. Consultation with an attorney is encouraged with respect to its completion or modification.

Any singular reference to Contractor, Surety, Owner or other party shall be considered plural where applicable.

OWNER:
(Name, legal status and address)

CONSTRUCTION CONTRACT
Date:

Amount:

Description:
(Name and location)

BOND
Date:
(Not earlier than Construction Contract Date)

Amount:

Modifications to this Bond: ☐ None ☐ See Section 18

CONTRACTOR AS PRINCIPAL
Company: *(Corporate Seal)*

Signature: ______________________
Name
and Title:

SURETY
Company: *(Corporate Seal)*

Signature: ______________________
Name
and Title:

(Any additional signatures appear on the last page of this Payment Bond.)

(FOR INFORMATION ONLY — Name, address and telephone)

AGENT or BROKER:

OWNER'S REPRESENTATIVE:
(Architect, Engineer or other party:)

§ 1 The Contractor and Surety, jointly and severally, bind themselves, their heirs, executors, administrators, successors and assigns to the Owner to pay for labor, materials and equipment furnished for use in the performance of the Construction Contract, which is incorporated herein by reference, subject to the following terms.

§ 2 If the Contractor promptly makes payment of all sums due to Claimants, and defends, indemnifies and holds harmless the Owner from claims, demands, liens or suits by any person or entity seeking payment for labor, materials or equipment furnished for use in the performance of the Construction Contract, then the Surety and the Contractor shall have no obligation under this Bond.

§ 3 If there is no Owner Default under the Construction Contract, the Surety's obligation to the Owner under this Bond shall arise after the Owner has promptly notified the Contractor and the Surety (at the address described in Section 13) of claims, demands, liens or suits against the Owner or the Owner's property by any person or entity seeking payment for labor, materials or equipment furnished for use in the performance of the Construction Contract and tendered defense of such claims, demands, liens or suits to the Contractor and the Surety.

§ 4 When the Owner has satisfied the conditions in Section 3, the Surety shall promptly and at the Surety's expense defend, indemnify and hold harmless the Owner against a duly tendered claim, demand, lien or suit.

§ 5 The Surety's obligations to a Claimant under this Bond shall arise after the following:

§ 5.1 Claimants, who do not have a direct contract with the Contractor,

.1 have furnished a written notice of non-payment to the Contractor, stating with substantial accuracy the amount claimed and the name of the party to whom the materials were, or equipment was, furnished or supplied or for whom the labor was done or performed, within ninety (90) days after having last performed labor or last furnished materials or equipment included in the Claim; and

.2 have sent a Claim to the Surety (at the address described in Section 13).

§ 5.2 Claimants, who are employed by or have a direct contract with the Contractor, have sent a Claim to the Surety (at the address described in Section 13).

§ 6 If a notice of non-payment required by Section 5.1.1 is given by the Owner to the Contractor, that is sufficient to satisfy a Claimant's obligation to furnish a written notice of non-payment under Section 5.1.1.

§ 7 When a Claimant has satisfied the conditions of Sections 5.1 or 5.2, whichever is applicable, the Surety shall promptly and at the Surety's expense take the following actions:

§ 7.1 Send an answer to the Claimant, with a copy to the Owner, within sixty (60) days after receipt of the Claim, stating the amounts that are undisputed and the basis for challenging any amounts that are disputed; and

§ 7.2 Pay or arrange for payment of any undisputed amounts.

§ 7.3 The Surety's failure to discharge its obligations under Section 7.1 or Section 7.2 shall not be deemed to constitute a waiver of defenses the Surety or Contractor may have or acquire as to a Claim, except as to undisputed amounts for which the Surety and Claimant have reached agreement. If, however, the Surety fails to discharge its obligations under Section 7.1 or Section 7.2, the Surety shall indemnify the Claimant for the reasonable attorney's fees the Claimant incurs thereafter to recover any sums found to be due and owing to the Claimant.

§ 8 The Surety's total obligation shall not exceed the amount of this Bond, plus the amount of reasonable attorney's fees provided under Section 7.3, and the amount of this Bond shall be credited for any payments made in good faith by the Surety.

§ 9 Amounts owed by the Owner to the Contractor under the Construction Contract shall be used for the performance of the Construction Contract and to satisfy claims, if any, under any construction performance bond. By the Contractor furnishing and the Owner accepting this Bond, they agree that all funds earned by the Contractor in the performance of the Construction Contract are dedicated to satisfy obligations of the Contractor and Surety under this Bond, subject to the Owner's priority to use the funds for the completion of the work.

§ 10 The Surety shall not be liable to the Owner, Claimants or others for obligations of the Contractor that are unrelated to the Construction Contract. The Owner shall not be liable for the payment of any costs or expenses of any Claimant under this Bond, and shall have under this Bond no obligation to make payments to, or give notice on behalf of, Claimants or otherwise have any obligations to Claimants under this Bond.

§ 11 The Surety hereby waives notice of any change, including changes of time, to the Construction Contract or to related subcontracts, purchase orders and other obligations.

§ 12 No suit or action shall be commenced by a Claimant under this Bond other than in a court of competent jurisdiction in the state in which the project that is the subject of the Construction Contract is located or after the expiration of one year from the date (1) on which the Claimant sent a Claim to the Surety pursuant to Section 5.1.2 or 5.2, or (2) on which the last labor or service was performed by anyone or the last materials or equipment were furnished by anyone under the Construction Contract, whichever of (1) or (2) first occurs. If the provisions of this Paragraph are void or prohibited by law, the minimum period of limitation available to sureties as a defense in the jurisdiction of the suit shall be applicable.

§ 13 Notice and Claims to the Surety, the Owner or the Contractor shall be mailed or delivered to the address shown on the page on which their signature appears. Actual receipt of notice or Claims, however accomplished, shall be sufficient compliance as of the date received.

§ 14 When this Bond has been furnished to comply with a statutory or other legal requirement in the location where the construction was to be performed, any provision in this Bond conflicting with said statutory or legal requirement shall be deemed deleted herefrom and provisions conforming to such statutory or other legal requirement shall be deemed incorporated herein. When so furnished, the intent is that this Bond shall be construed as a statutory bond and not as a common law bond.

§ 15 Upon request by any person or entity appearing to be a potential beneficiary of this Bond, the Contractor and Owner shall promptly furnish a copy of this Bond or shall permit a copy to be made.

§ 16 Definitions

§ 16.1 Claim. A written statement by the Claimant including at a minimum:

- **.1** the name of the Claimant;
- **.2** the name of the person for whom the labor was done, or materials or equipment furnished;
- **.3** a copy of the agreement or purchase order pursuant to which labor, materials or equipment was furnished for use in the performance of the Construction Contract;
- **.4** a brief description of the labor, materials or equipment furnished;
- **.5** the date on which the Claimant last performed labor or last furnished materials or equipment for use in the performance of the Construction Contract;
- **.6** the total amount earned by the Claimant for labor, materials or equipment furnished as of the date of the Claim;
- **.7** the total amount of previous payments received by the Claimant; and
- **.8** the total amount due and unpaid to the Claimant for labor, materials or equipment furnished as of the date of the Claim.

§ 16.2 Claimant. An individual or entity having a direct contract with the Contractor or with a subcontractor of the Contractor to furnish labor, materials or equipment for use in the performance of the Construction Contract. The term Claimant also includes any individual or entity that has rightfully asserted a claim under an applicable mechanic's lien or similar statute against the real property upon which the Project is located. The intent of this Bond shall be to include without limitation in the terms "labor, materials or equipment" that part of water, gas, power, light, heat, oil, gasoline, telephone service or rental equipment used in the Construction Contract, architectural and engineering services required for performance of the work of the Contractor and the Contractor's subcontractors, and all other items for which a mechanic's lien may be asserted in the jurisdiction where the labor, materials or equipment were furnished.

§ 16.3 Construction Contract. The agreement between the Owner and Contractor identified on the cover page, including all Contract Documents and all changes made to the agreement and the Contract Documents.

Init.

/

§ 16.4 Owner Default. Failure of the Owner, which has not been remedied or waived, to pay the Contractor as required under the Construction Contract or to perform and complete or comply with the other material terms of the Construction Contract.

§ 16.5 Contract Documents. All the documents that comprise the agreement between the Owner and Contractor.

§ 17 If this Bond is issued for an agreement between a Contractor and subcontractor, the term Contractor in this Bond shall be deemed to be Subcontractor and the term Owner shall be deemed to be Contractor.

§ 18 Modifications to this bond are as follows:

(Space is provided below for additional signatures of added parties, other than those appearing on the cover page.)

CONTRACTOR AS PRINCIPAL		**SURETY**	
Company:	*(Corporate Seal)*	Company:	*(Corporate Seal)*
Signature:	______________________	Signature:	______________________
Name and Title:		Name and Title:	
Address		Address	

Exhibit 21

Miller Act Performance Bond, Standard Form 25

PERFORMANCE BOND *(See instructions on reverse)*	DATE BOND EXECUTED *(Must be same or later than date of contract)*	**OMB Control Number: 9000-0045** **Expiration Date: 8/31/2025**

Paperwork Reduction Act Statement - This information collection meets the requirements of 44 USC § 3507, as amended by section 2 of the Paperwork Reduction Act of 1995. You do not need to answer these questions unless we display a valid Office of Management and Budget (OMB) control number. The OMB control number for this collection is 9000-0045. We estimate that it will take 1 hour to read the instructions, gather the facts, and answer the questions. Send only comments relating to our time estimate, including suggestions for reducing this burden, or any other aspects of this collection of information to: General Services Administration, Regulatory Secretariat Division (M1V1CB), 1800 F Street, NW, Washington, DC 20405.

PRINCIPAL *(Legal name and business address)*	TYPE OF ORGANIZATION *("X" one)* ☐ INDIVIDUAL ☐ PARTNERSHIP ☐ JOINT VENTURE ☐ CORPORATION ☐ OTHER *(Specify)*			
	STATE OF INCORPORATION			
SURETY(IES) *(Name(s) and business address(es))*	PENAL SUM OF BOND			
	MILLION(S)	THOUSAND(S)	HUNDRED(S)	CENTS
	CONTRACT DATE	CONTRACT NUMBER		

OBLIGATION:

We, the Principal and Surety(ies), are firmly bound to the United States of America (hereinafter called the Government) in the above penal sum. For payment of the penal sum, we bind ourselves, our heirs, executors, administrators, and successors, jointly and severally. However, where the Sureties are corporations acting as co-sureties, we, the Sureties, bind ourselves in such sum "jointly and severally" as well as "severally" only for the purpose of allowing a joint action or actions against any or all of us. For all other purposes, each Surety binds itself, jointly and severally with the Principal, for the payment of the sum shown opposite the name of the Surety. If no limit of liability is indicated, the limit of liability is the full amount of the penal sum.

CONDITIONS:

The Principal has entered into the contract identified above.

THEREFORE:

The above obligation is void if the Principal-

(a) (1) Performs and fulfills all the understanding, covenants, terms, conditions, and agreements of the contract during the original term of the contract and any extensions thereof that are granted by the Government, with or without notice of the Surety(ies) and during the life of any guaranty required under the contract, and

(2) Performs and fulfills all the undertakings, covenants, terms, conditions, and agreements of any and all duly authorized modifications of the contract that hereafter are made. Notice of those modifications to the Surety(ies) are waived.

(b) Pays to the Government the full amount of the taxes imposed by the Government, if the said contract is subject to 41 USC Chapter 31, Subchapter III, Bonds, which are collected, deducted, or withheld from wages paid by the Principal in carrying out the construction contract with respect to which this bond is furnished.

WITNESS:

The Principal and Surety(ies) executed this performance bond and affixed their seals on the above date.

PRINCIPAL

SIGNATURE(S)	1. (Seal)	2. (Seal)	3. (Seal)	Corporate Seal
NAME(S) & TITLE(S) *(Typed)*	1.	2.	3.	

INDIVIDUAL SURETY(IES)

SIGNATURE(S)	1. (Seal)	2. (Seal)
NAME(S) *(Typed)*	1.	2.

CORPORATE SURETY(IES)

SURETY A	NAME & ADDRESS		STATE OF INCORPORATION	LIABILITY LIMIT ($)	Corporate Seal
	SIGNATURE(S)	1.	2.		
	NAME(S) & TITLE(S) *(Typed)*	1.	2.		

AUTHORIZED FOR LOCAL REPRODUCTION
Previous edition is NOT usable

STANDARD FORM 25 (REV. 8/2016)
Prescribed by GSA-FAR (48 CFR) 53.228(b)

CORPORATE SURETY(IES) ***(Continued)***

SURETY B	NAME & ADDRESS		STATE OF INCORPORATION	LIABILITY LIMIT ($)	Corporate Seal
	SIGNATURE(S)	1.	2.		
	NAME(S) & TITLE(S) *(Typed)*	1.	2.		
SURETY C	NAME & ADDRESS		STATE OF INCORPORATION	LIABILITY LIMIT ($)	Corporate Seal
	SIGNATURE(S)	1.	2.		
	NAME(S) & TITLE(S) *(Typed)*	1.	2.		
SURETY D	NAME & ADDRESS		STATE OF INCORPORATION	LIABILITY LIMIT ($)	Corporate Seal
	SIGNATURE(S)	1.	2.		
	NAME(S) & TITLE(S) *(Typed)*	1.	2.		
SURETY E	NAME & ADDRESS		STATE OF INCORPORATION	LIABILITY LIMIT ($)	Corporate Seal
	SIGNATURE(S)	1.	2.		
	NAME(S) & TITLE(S) *(Typed)*	1.	2.		
SURETY F	NAME & ADDRESS		STATE OF INCORPORATION	LIABILITY LIMIT ($)	Corporate Seal
	SIGNATURE(S)	1.	2.		
	NAME(S) & TITLE(S) *(Typed)*	1.	2.		
SURETY G	NAME & ADDRESS		STATE OF INCORPORATION	LIABILITY LIMIT ($)	Corporate Seal
	SIGNATURE(S)	1.	2.		
	NAME(S) & TITLE(S) *(Typed)*	1.	2.		

BOND PREMIUM ▶	RATE PER THOUSAND ($)	TOTAL ($)

INSTRUCTIONS

1. This form is authorized for use in connection with Government contracts. Any deviation from this form will require the written approval of the Administrator of General Services.

2. Insert the full legal name and business address of the Principal in the space designated "Principal" on the face of the form. An authorized person shall sign the bond. Any person signing in a representative capacity (e.g., an attorney-in-fact) must furnish evidence of authority if that representative is not a member of the firm, partnership, or joint venture, or an officer of the corporation involved.

3. (a) Corporations executing the bond as sureties must appear on the Department of the Treasury's list of approved sureties and must act within the limitations listed therein. The value put into the LIABILITY LIMIT block is the penal sum (i.e., the face value) of bonds, unless a co-surety arrangement is proposed.

(b) When multiple corporate sureties are involved, their names and addresses shall appear in the spaces (Surety A, Surety B, etc.) headed "CORPORATE SURETY(IES)." In the space designated "SURETY(IES)" on the face of the form, insert only the letter identifier corresponding to each of the sureties. Moreover, when co-surety arrangements exist, the parties may allocate their respective limitations of liability under the bonds, provided that the sum total of their liability equals 100% of the bond penal sum.

(c) When individual sureties are involved, a completed Affidavit of Individual Surety (Standard Form 28) for each individual surety shall accompany the bond. The government may require the surety to furnish additional substantiating information concerning its financial capability.

4. Corporations executing the bond shall affix their corporate seals. Individuals shall execute the bond opposite the words "Corporate Seal", and shall affix an adhesive seal if executed in Maine, New Hampshire, or any other jurisdiction requiring adhesive seals.

5. Type the name and title of each person signing this bond in the space provided.

STANDARD FORM 25 (REV. 8/2016) **BACK**

Exhibit 22

Miller Act Payment Bond, Standard Form 25

PAYMENT BOND *(See instructions on reverse)*	DATE BOND EXECUTED *(Must be same or later than date of contract)*	**OMB Control Number: 9000-0045** **Expiration Date: 8/31/2025**

Paperwork Reduction Act Statement - This information collection meets the requirements of 44 USC § 3507, as amended by section 2 of the Paperwork Reduction Act of 1995. You do not need to answer these questions unless we display a valid Office of Management and Budget (OMB) control number. The OMB control number for this collection is 9000-0045. We estimate that it will take 1 hour to read the instructions, gather the facts, and answer the questions. Send only comments relating to our time estimate, including suggestions for reducing this burden, or any other aspects of this collection of information to: General Services Administration, Regulatory Secretariat Division (M1V1CB), 1800 F Street, NW, Washington, DC 20405.

PRINCIPAL *(Legal name and business address)*	TYPE OF ORGANIZATION *("X" one)* ☐ INDIVIDUAL ☐ PARTNERSHIP ☐ JOINT VENTURE ☐ CORPORATION ☐ OTHER *(Specify)*			
	STATE OF INCORPORATION			
SURETY(IES) *(Name(s) and business address(es))*	PENAL SUM OF BOND			
	MILLION(S)	THOUSAND(S)	HUNDRED(S)	CENTS
	CONTRACT DATE	CONTRACT NUMBER		

OBLIGATION:

We, the Principal and Surety(ies), are firmly bound to the United States of America (hereinafter called the Government) in the above penal sum. For payment of the penal sum, we bind ourselves, our heirs, executors, administrators, and successors, jointly and severally. However, where the Sureties are corporations acting as co-sureties, we, the Sureties, bind ourselves in such sum "jointly and severally" as well as "severally" only for the purpose of allowing a joint action or actions against any or all of us. For all other purposes, each Surety binds itself, jointly and severally with the Principal, for the payment of the sum shown opposite the name of the Surety. If no limit is indicated, the limit of liability is the full amount of the penal sum.

CONDITIONS:

The above obligation is void if the Principal promptly makes payment to all persons having a direct relationship with the Principal or a subcontractor of the Principal for furnishing labor, material or both in the prosecution of the work provided for in the contract identified above, and any authorized modifications of the contract that subsequently are made. Notice of those modifications to the Surety(ies) are waived.

WITNESS:

The Principal and Surety(ies) executed this payment bond and affixed their seals on the above date.

PRINCIPAL				
SIGNATURE(S)	1. (Seal)	2. (Seal)	3. (Seal)	Corporate Seal
NAME(S) & TITLE(S) *(Typed)*	1.	2.	3.	

INDIVIDUAL SURETY(IES)		
SIGNATURE(S)	1. (Seal)	2. (Seal)
NAME(S) *(Typed)*	1.	2.

CORPORATE SURETY(IES)					
SURETY A	NAME & ADDRESS		STATE OF INCORPORATION	LIABILITY LIMIT $	Corporate Seal
	SIGNATURE(S)	1.	2.		
	NAME(S) & TITLE(S) *(Typed)*	1.	2.		

AUTHORIZED FOR LOCAL REPRODUCTION
Previous edition is NOT usable

STANDARD FORM 25A (REV. 8/2016)
Prescribed by GSA-FAR (48 CFR) 53.228(c)

CORPORATE SURETY(IES) *(Continued)*

SURETY B	NAME & ADDRESS		STATE OF INCORPORATION	LIABILITY LIMIT $	Corporate Seal
	SIGNATURE(S)	1.	2.		
	NAME(S) & TITLE(S) *(Typed)*	1.	2.		
SURETY C	NAME & ADDRESS		STATE OF INCORPORATION	LIABILITY LIMIT $	Corporate Seal
	SIGNATURE(S)	1.	2.		
	NAME(S) & TITLE(S) *(Typed)*	1.	2.		
SURETY D	NAME & ADDRESS		STATE OF INCORPORATION	LIABILITY LIMIT $	Corporate Seal
	SIGNATURE(S)	1.	2.		
	NAME(S) & TITLE(S) *(Typed)*	1.	2.		
SURETY E	NAME & ADDRESS		STATE OF INCORPORATION	LIABILITY LIMIT $	Corporate Seal
	SIGNATURE(S)	1.	2.		
	NAME(S) & TITLE(S) *(Typed)*	1.	2.		
SURETY F	NAME & ADDRESS		STATE OF INCORPORATION	LIABILITY LIMIT $	Corporate Seal
	SIGNATURE(S)	1.	2.		
	NAME(S) & TITLE(S) *(Typed)*	1.	2.		
SURETY G	NAME & ADDRESS		STATE OF INCORPORATION	LIABILITY LIMIT $	Corporate Seal
	SIGNATURE(S)	1.	2.		
	NAME(S) & TITLE(S) *(Typed)*	1.	2.		

INSTRUCTIONS

1. This form, for the protection of persons supplying labor and material, is used when a payment bond is required under 40 USC Chapter 31, Subchapter III, Bonds. Any deviation from this form will require the written approval of the Administrator of General Services.

2. Insert the full legal name and business address of the Principal in the space designated "Principal" on the face of the form. An authorized person shall sign the bond. Any person signing in a representative capacity (e.g., an attorney-in-fact) must furnish evidence of authority if that representative is not a member of the firm, partnership, or joint venture, or an officer of the corporation involved.

3. (a) Corporations executing the bond as sureties must appear on the Department of the Treasury's list of approved sureties and must act within the limitations listed therein. The value put into the LIABILITY LIMIT block is the penal sum (i.e., the face value) of the bond, unless a co-surety arrangement is proposed.

(b) When multiple corporate sureties are involved, their names and addresses shall appear in the spaces (Surety A, Surety B, etc.) headed "CORPORATE SURETY(IES)." In the space designated "SURETY(IES)" on the face of the form, insert only the letter identifier corresponding to each of the sureties. Moreover, when co-surety arrangements exist, the parties may allocate their respective limitations of liability under the bonds, provided that the sum total of their liability equals 100% of the bond penal sum.

(c) When individual sureties are involved, a completed Affidavit of Individual Surety (Standard Form 28) for each individual surety shall accompany the bond. The Government may require the surety to furnish additional substantiating information concerning its financial capability.

4. Corporations executing the bond shall affix their corporate seals. Individuals shall execute the bond opposite the words "Corporate Seal", and shall affix an adhesive seal if executed in Maine, New Hampshire, or any other jurisdiction requiring adhesive seals.

5. Type the name and title of each person signing this bond in the space provided.

STANDARD FORM 25A (REV. 8/2016) **BACK**

Exhibit 23

Dual Obligee Rider

THIS DUAL OBLIGEE RIDER IS TO BE ATTACHED AND BECOME PART OF BOND

Bond Principal:____________________

Surety:_________________________

Obligee:_________________________

Obligee:_______________________

Bond No.:______________________

Surety shall not be liable under this bond to Obligees unless said Obligees shall make payments to Principal or to Surety, should it arrange for or undertake the completion of the contract upon Principal's default, in accordance with the terms of said contract; and shall otherwise satisfy all terms and conditions and perform all other obligations set forth in said contract at the time and in the manner provided therein.

In no event shall the aggregate liability of Surety to either or both Obligees exceed the penal sum of this performance Bond, nor shall Surety be liable except for a single payment for each single breach or default.

IT IS FURTHER UNDERSTOOD AND AGREED that nothing herein contained shall be held to change, alter, or vary the terms of the above-described bond except as hereinbefore set forth.

OBLIGEE

____

SURETY

____

PRINCIPAL

____

Exhibit 24

Certificate of Insurance

ACORD® CERTIFICATE OF LIABILITY INSURANCE

DATE (MM/DD/YYYY)

THIS CERTIFICATE IS ISSUED AS A MATTER OF INFORMATION ONLY AND CONFERS NO RIGHTS UPON THE CERTIFICATE HOLDER. THIS CERTIFICATE DOES NOT AFFIRMATIVELY OR NEGATIVELY AMEND, EXTEND OR ALTER THE COVERAGE AFFORDED BY THE POLICIES BELOW. THIS CERTIFICATE OF INSURANCE DOES NOT CONSTITUTE A CONTRACT BETWEEN THE ISSUING INSURER(S), AUTHORIZED REPRESENTATIVE OR PRODUCER, AND THE CERTIFICATE HOLDER.

IMPORTANT: If the certificate holder is an ADDITIONAL INSURED, the policy(ies) must be endorsed. If SUBROGATION IS WAIVED, subject to the terms and conditions of the policy, certain policies may require an endorsement. A statement on this certificate does not confer rights to the certificate holder in lieu of such endorsement(s).

PRODUCER	CONTACT NAME: PHONE (A/C, No, Ext): FAX (A/C, No): E-MAIL ADDRESS:
	INSURER(S) AFFORDING COVERAGE — NAIC #
	INSURER A :
INSURED	INSURER B :
	INSURER C :
	INSURER D :
	INSURER E :
	INSURER F :

COVERAGES **CERTIFICATE NUMBER:** **REVISION NUMBER:**

THIS IS TO CERTIFY THAT THE POLICIES OF INSURANCE LISTED BELOW HAVE BEEN ISSUED TO THE INSURED NAMED ABOVE FOR THE POLICY PERIOD INDICATED. NOTWITHSTANDING ANY REQUIREMENT, TERM OR CONDITION OF ANY CONTRACT OR OTHER DOCUMENT WITH RESPECT TO WHICH THIS CERTIFICATE MAY BE ISSUED OR MAY PERTAIN, THE INSURANCE AFFORDED BY THE POLICIES DESCRIBED HEREIN IS SUBJECT TO ALL THE TERMS, EXCLUSIONS AND CONDITIONS OF SUCH POLICIES. LIMITS SHOWN MAY HAVE BEEN REDUCED BY PAID CLAIMS.

INSR LTR	TYPE OF INSURANCE	ADDL INSR	SUBR WVD	POLICY NUMBER	POLICY EFF (MM/DD/YYYY)	POLICY EXP (MM/DD/YYYY)	LIMITS
	GENERAL LIABILITY COMMERCIAL GENERAL LIABILITY CLAIMS-MADE ☐ OCCUR GEN'L AGGREGATE LIMIT APPLIES PER: POLICY PRO-JECT LOC						EACH OCCURRENCE $ DAMAGE TO RENTED PREMISES (Ea occurrence) $ MED EXP (Any one person) $ PERSONAL & ADV INJURY $ GENERAL AGGREGATE $ PRODUCTS - COMP/OP AGG $ $
	AUTOMOBILE LIABILITY ANY AUTO ALL OWNED AUTOS SCHEDULED AUTOS HIRED AUTOS NON-OWNED AUTOS						COMBINED SINGLE LIMIT (Ea accident) $ BODILY INJURY (Per person) $ BODILY INJURY (Per accident) $ PROPERTY DAMAGE (Per accident) $ $
	UMBRELLA LIAB OCCUR EXCESS LIAB CLAIMS-MADE DED RETENTION $						EACH OCCURRENCE $ AGGREGATE $ $
	WORKERS COMPENSATION AND EMPLOYERS' LIABILITY Y/N ANY PROPRIETOR/PARTNER/EXECUTIVE OFFICER/MEMBER EXCLUDED? ☐ (Mandatory in NH) If yes, describe under DESCRIPTION OF OPERATIONS below	N/A					WC STATU-TORY LIMITS OTH-ER E.L. EACH ACCIDENT $ E.L. DISEASE - EA EMPLOYEE $ E.L. DISEASE - POLICY LIMIT $

DESCRIPTION OF OPERATIONS / LOCATIONS / VEHICLES (Attach ACORD 101, Additional Remarks Schedule, if more space is required)

CERTIFICATE HOLDER	CANCELLATION
	SHOULD ANY OF THE ABOVE DESCRIBED POLICIES BE CANCELLED BEFORE THE EXPIRATION DATE THEREOF, NOTICE WILL BE DELIVERED IN ACCORDANCE WITH THE POLICY PROVISIONS.
	AUTHORIZED REPRESENTATIVE

ACORD 25 (2010/05)

Exhibit 25

Subcontract Agreement—AIA Document A401™ - 2017

AIA Document A401® – 2017

Standard Form of Agreement Between Contractor and Subcontractor

AGREEMENT made as of the ______ day of ______ in the year ______
(In words, indicate day, month and year.)

BETWEEN the Contractor:
(Name, legal status, address and other information)

This document has important l consequences. Consultation w an attorney is encouraged witr respect to its completion or modification.

and the Subcontractor:
(Name, legal status, address and other information)

The Contractor has made a contract for construction (hereinafter, the Prime Contract) dated:

with the Owner:
(Name, legal status, address and other information)

for the following Project:
(Name, location and detailed description)

The Prime Contract provides for the furnishing of labor, materials, equipment and services in connection with the construction of the Project. A copy of the Prime Contract, consisting of the Agreement Between Owner and Contractor (from which compensation amounts may be deleted) and the other Contract Documents enumerated therein, has been made available to the Subcontractor.

The Architect for the Project:
(Name, legal status, address and other information)

The Contractor and the Subcontractor agree as follows.

Init.
/

TABLE OF ARTICLES

ARTICLE 1 THE SUBCONTRACT DOCUMENTS

§ 1.1 The Subcontract Documents consist of (1) this Agreement; (2) the Prime Contract, consisting of the Agreement between the Owner and Contractor and the other Contract Documents enumerated therein; (3) Modifications to the Prime Contract, whether issued before or after the execution of this Agreement, in accordance with the provisions of Article 5; (4) other documents listed in Article 15 of this Agreement; and (5) Modifications to this Subcontract issued after execution of this Agreement, in accordance with the provisions of Article 5. These form the Subcontract, and are as fully a part of the Subcontract as if attached to this Agreement or repeated herein.

§ 1.2 The Subcontract Documents form the Subcontract for Construction. The Subcontract represents the entire and integrated agreement between the parties hereto and supersedes prior negotiations, representations, or agreements, either written or oral. An enumeration of the Subcontract Documents, other than Modifications to the Prime Contract or Modifications to this Subcontract issued subsequent to the execution of this Agreement, appears in Article 15.

§ 1.3 Except to the extent of a conflict with a specific term or condition contained in the Subcontract Documents, the General Conditions governing this Subcontract shall be the AIA Document A201™–2017, General Conditions of the Contract for Construction.

§ 1.4 The Subcontract may be amended or modified only by a Modification to this Subcontract. A Modification to this Subcontract is a written amendment to this Agreement signed by both parties, or as otherwise described in, and in accordance with the provisions of, Article 5.

§ 1.5 The Subcontract Documents shall not be construed to create a contractual relationship of any kind (1) between the Architect and the Subcontractor, (2) between the Owner and the Subcontractor, or (3) between any persons or entities other than the Contractor and Subcontractor.

Init.

/

§ 1.6 The Contractor shall make the Subcontract Documents available to the Subcontractor prior to execution of this Agreement, and thereafter, upon request. The Contractor may charge the Subcontractor for the reasonable cost to reproduce the Subcontract Documents provided to the Subcontractor.

ARTICLE 2 MUTUAL RIGHTS AND RESPONSIBILITIES

The Contractor and Subcontractor shall be mutually bound by the terms of this Agreement and, to the extent that the provisions of AIA Document A201–2017 apply to this Agreement pursuant to Section 1.3 and provisions of the Prime Contract apply to the Work of the Subcontractor, the Contractor shall assume toward the Subcontractor all obligations and responsibilities that the Owner, under such documents, assumes toward the Contractor, and the Subcontractor shall assume toward the Contractor all obligations and responsibilities that the Contractor, under such documents, assumes toward the Owner and the Architect. The Contractor shall have the benefit of all rights, remedies, and redress against the Subcontractor that the Owner, under such documents, has against the Contractor, and the Subcontractor shall have the benefit of all rights, remedies, and redress against the Contractor that the Contractor, under such documents, has against the Owner, insofar as applicable to this Subcontract. Where a provision of such documents is inconsistent with a provision of this Agreement, this Agreement shall govern.

ARTICLE 3 CONTRACTOR

§ 3.1 General

§ 3.1.1 The Contractor is the person or entity identified as such in this Agreement and is referred to throughout the Subcontract Documents as if singular in number. The Contractor shall designate in writing a representative who shall have express authority to bind the Contractor with respect to all Project matters requiring the Contractor's approval or authorization. The term "Contractor" means the Contractor or the Contractor's authorized representative.

§ 3.1.2 The Contractor shall render decisions in a timely manner and in accordance with the Contractor's construction schedule.

§ 3.2 Services Provided by the Contractor

§ 3.2.1 The Contractor shall cooperate with the Subcontractor in scheduling and performing the Contractor's Work to avoid conflicts or interference in the Subcontractor's Work and shall review, and expedite written responses to, submittals made by the Subcontractor in accordance with Section 4.2.3 and Article 5. Promptly after execution of this Agreement, the Contractor shall provide the Subcontractor with copies of the Contractor's construction schedule and schedule of submittals, together with such additional scheduling details as will enable the Subcontractor to plan and perform the Subcontractor's Work properly. The Contractor shall promptly notify the Subcontractor of subsequent changes in the construction and submittal schedules and additional scheduling details.

§ 3.2.2 The Contractor shall provide suitable areas for storage of the Subcontractor's materials and equipment during the course of the Work. Except as previously agreed upon, additional costs to the Subcontractor resulting from relocation of such storage areas at the direction of the Contractor shall be reimbursed by the Contractor.

§ 3.3 Communications

§ 3.3.1 The Contractor shall promptly make available to the Subcontractor information, including information received from the Owner, that affects the performance of this Subcontract and that becomes available to the Contractor subsequent to execution of this Subcontract.

§ 3.3.2 The Contractor shall not give instructions or orders directly to the Subcontractor's employees or to the Subcontractor's Sub-subcontractors or suppliers unless such persons are designated as authorized representatives of the Subcontractor.

§ 3.3.3 The Contractor shall permit the Subcontractor to request information directly from the Architect regarding the percentages of completion and the amount certified on account of Work done by the Subcontractor.

§ 3.3.4 If hazardous materials or substances are being used on the site by the Contractor, a subcontractor, or anyone directly or indirectly employed by them (other than the Subcontractor), and they are a type of hazardous material or substance of which an employer is required by law to notify its employees, the Contractor shall, prior to delivery to the Project site or exposure of the Subcontractor's employees to such material or substance, give notice of the chemical composition thereof to the Subcontractor in sufficient detail and time to permit the Subcontractor's compliance with such laws.

Init.

/

§ 3.3.5 The Contractor shall promptly notify the Subcontractor of any fault or defect in the Work under this Subcontract or nonconformity with the Subcontract Documents.

§ 3.3.6 The Contractor shall furnish to the Subcontractor within 30 days after receipt of a written request, or earlier if so required by law, information necessary and relevant for the Subcontractor to evaluate, give notice of or enforce mechanic's lien rights. Such information shall include a correct statement of the record legal title to the property, usually referred to as the site, on which the Project is located and the Owner's interest therein. If the Contractor does not have such information, the Contractor shall request the information from the Owner in accordance with Article 2 of AIA Document A201-2017 and promptly furnish the information received from the Owner to the Subcontractor.

§ 3.3.7 If the Contractor asserts a Claim against, or defends a Claim by, the Owner that relates to the Work of the Subcontractor, the Contractor shall promptly make available to the Subcontractor all information relating to the portion of the Claim that relates to the Work of the Subcontractor.

§ 3.4 Claims by the Contractor

§ 3.4.1 Liquidated damages, if provided for in the Prime Contract, shall be assessed against the Subcontractor only to the extent caused by the Subcontractor or any person or entity for whose acts the Subcontractor may be liable, and in no case for delays or causes arising outside the scope of this Subcontract.

§ 3.4.2 The Contractor's Claims for the costs of services or materials provided due to the Subcontractor's failure to execute the Work shall require

- **.1** seven days' notice prior to the Contractor's providing services or materials, except in an emergency; and
- **.2** written compilations to the Subcontractor of services and materials provided by the Contractor and charges for such services and materials no later than the fifteenth day of the month following the Contractor's providing such services or materials.

§ 3.5 Contractor's Remedies

If the Subcontractor defaults or neglects to carry out the Work in accordance with this Agreement and fails within five working days after receipt of notice from the Contractor to commence and continue correction of such default or neglect with diligence and promptness, the Contractor may, without prejudice to other remedies the Contractor may have, remedy such default or neglect and withhold, in accordance with Section 11.1.7.2, the reasonable cost thereof from current or future payments due the Subcontractor. If payments due to the Subcontractor are not sufficient to cover such amounts, the Subcontractor shall pay the difference to the Contractor.

ARTICLE 4 SUBCONTRACTOR

§ 4.1 General

The Subcontractor is the person or entity identified as such in this Agreement and is referred to throughout the Subcontract Documents as if singular in number. The Subcontractor shall be lawfully licensed, if required in the jurisdiction where the Project is located. The Subcontractor shall designate in writing a representative who shall have express authority to act on the Subcontractor's behalf with respect to the Project. The term "Subcontractor" means the Subcontractor or the Subcontractor's authorized representative.

§ 4.2 Execution and Progress of the Work

§ 4.2.1 For all Work the Subcontractor intends to subcontract, the Subcontractor shall enter into written agreements with Sub-subcontractors performing portions of the Work of this Subcontract by which the Subcontractor and the Sub-subcontractor are mutually bound, to the extent of the Work to be performed by the Sub-subcontractor, assuming toward each other all obligations and responsibilities that the Contractor and Subcontractor assume toward each other and having the benefit of all rights, remedies and redress each against the other that the Contractor and Subcontractor have by virtue of the provisions of this Agreement.

§ 4.2.2 The Subcontractor shall supervise and direct the Subcontractor's Work, and shall cooperate with the Contractor in scheduling and performing the Subcontractor's Work to avoid conflict, delay in, or interference with the Work of the Contractor, other subcontractors, the Owner, or Separate Contractors.

§ 4.2.3 Submittals
§ 4.2.3.1 The Subcontractor shall submit Shop Drawings, Product Data, Samples, and similar submittals required by the Subcontract Documents with reasonable promptness and in such sequence as to cause no delay in the Work or in the activities of the Contractor or other subcontractors.

§ 4.2.3.2 By submitting Shop Drawings, Product Data, Samples, and similar submittals, the Subcontractor represents to the Contractor that the Subcontractor has (1) reviewed and approved them; (2) determined and verified materials, field measurements, and field construction criteria related thereto, or will do so; and (3) checked and coordinated the information contained within such submittals with the requirements of the Work and of the Subcontract Documents.

§ 4.2.4 The Subcontractor shall furnish to the Contractor periodic progress reports on the Work of this Subcontract as mutually agreed, including information on the status of materials and equipment that may be in the course of preparation, manufacture, or transit.

§ 4.2.5 The Subcontractor agrees that the Contractor and the Architect each have the authority to reject Work of the Subcontractor that does not conform to the Prime Contract. The Architect's decisions on matters relating to aesthetic effect shall be final and binding on the Subcontractor if consistent with the intent expressed in the Prime Contract.

§ 4.2.6 The Subcontractor shall pay for all materials, equipment, and labor used in connection with the performance of this Subcontract through the period covered by previous payments received from the Contractor, and shall furnish satisfactory evidence, when requested by the Contractor, to verify compliance with the above requirements.

§ 4.2.7 The Subcontractor shall take necessary precautions to properly protect the work of the Contractor, Separate Contractors, and other subcontractors from damage caused by operations under this Subcontract.

§ 4.2.8 The Subcontractor shall cooperate with the Contractor, other subcontractors, the Owner, and Separate Contractors whose work might affect the Subcontractor's Work. The Subcontractor shall participate in the preparation of coordinated drawings in areas of congestion, if required by the Prime Contract, specifically noting and advising the Contractor of potential conflicts between the Work of the Subcontractor and that of the Contractor, other subcontractors, the Owner, or Separate Contractors.

§ 4.3 Permits, Fees, Notices, and Compliance with Laws
§ 4.3.1 The Subcontractor shall give notices and comply with applicable laws, statutes, ordinances, codes, rules and regulations, and lawful orders of public authorities bearing on performance of the Work of this Subcontract. The Subcontractor shall secure and pay for permits, fees, licenses, and inspections by government agencies necessary for proper execution and completion of the Subcontractor's Work, the furnishing of which is required of the Contractor by the Prime Contract.

§ 4.3.2 The Subcontractor shall comply with Federal, state, and local tax laws; social security acts; unemployment compensation acts; and workers' compensation acts, insofar as applicable to the performance of this Subcontract.

§ 4.4 Safety Precautions and Procedures
§ 4.4.1 The Subcontractor shall take reasonable safety precautions with respect to performance of this Subcontract. The Subcontractor shall comply with safety measures initiated by the Contractor and with applicable laws, statutes, ordinances, codes, rules and regulations, and lawful orders of public authorities, for the safety of persons and property, in accordance with the requirements of the Prime Contract. The Subcontractor shall notify the Contractor within three days of an injury to an employee or agent of the Subcontractor which occurred at the site.

§ 4.4.2 If hazardous materials or substances are being used on the site by the Subcontractor, the Subcontractor's Sub-subcontractors, or anyone directly or indirectly employed by them, and they are a type of hazardous material or substance of which an employer is required by law to notify its employees, the Subcontractor shall, prior to delivery to the Project site or exposure of the Contractor, other subcontractors, and other employers on the site to such material or substance, give notice of the chemical composition thereof to the Contractor in sufficient detail and time to permit compliance with the laws by the Contractor, other subcontractors, and other employers on the site.

§ 4.4.3 If reasonable precautions will be inadequate to prevent foreseeable bodily injury or death to persons resulting from a hazardous material or substance, including but not limited to asbestos or polychlorinated biphenyl (PCB),

Init.
/

encountered on the site by the Subcontractor, the Subcontractor shall, upon recognizing the condition, immediately stop Work in the affected area and promptly report the condition to the Contractor in writing. When the material or substance has been rendered harmless, the Subcontractor's Work in the affected area shall resume upon written agreement of the Contractor and Subcontractor. The Subcontract Time shall be extended appropriately and the Subcontract Sum shall be increased in the amount of the Subcontractor's reasonable additional costs of demobilization, delay, and remobilization, which adjustments shall be accomplished as provided in Article 5 of this Agreement.

§ 4.4.4 To the fullest extent permitted by law, the Contractor shall indemnify and hold harmless the Subcontractor, the Subcontractor's Sub-subcontractors, and agents and employees of any of them from and against claims, damages, losses, and expenses, including but not limited to attorneys' fees, arising out of or resulting from performance of the Work in the affected area if in fact the material or substance presents the risk of bodily injury or death as described in Section 4.4.3 and has not been rendered harmless, provided that such claim, damage, loss, or expense is attributable to bodily injury, sickness, disease or death, or to injury to or destruction of tangible property (other than the Work itself) except to the extent that such damage, loss, or expense is due to the fault or negligence of the party seeking indemnity.

§ 4.4.5 The Subcontractor shall reimburse the Contractor for the cost and expense the Contractor incurs (1) for remediation of a hazardous material or substance brought to the site and negligently handled by the Subcontractor or (2) where the Subcontractor fails to perform its obligations under Section 4.4.3, except to the extent that the cost and expense are due to the Contractor's fault or negligence.

§ 4.5 Cleaning Up
§ 4.5.1 The Subcontractor shall keep the premises and surrounding area free from accumulation of waste materials or rubbish caused by operations performed under this Subcontract. The Subcontractor shall not be held responsible for conditions caused by other contractors or subcontractors.

§ 4.5.2 As provided under Section 3.4.2, if the Subcontractor fails to clean up as provided in the Subcontract Documents, the Contractor may charge the Subcontractor for the Subcontractor's appropriate share of cleanup costs.

§ 4.6 Warranty
§ 4.6.1 The Subcontractor warrants to the Owner, Architect, and Contractor that materials and equipment furnished under this Subcontract will be of good quality and new unless the Subcontract Documents require or permit otherwise. The Subcontractor further warrants that the Work will conform to the requirements of the Subcontract Documents and will be free from defects, except for those inherent in the quality of the Work the Subcontract Documents require or permit. Work, materials, or equipment not conforming to these requirements may be considered defective. The Subcontractor's warranty excludes remedy for damage or defect caused by abuse, alterations to the Work not executed by the Subcontractor, improper or insufficient maintenance, improper operation, or normal wear and tear under normal usage. If required by the Architect and Contractor, the Subcontractor shall provide satisfactory evidence as to the kind and quality of materials and equipment furnished or to be furnished.

§ 4.6.2 All material, equipment, or other special warranties required by the Subcontract Documents shall be issued in the name of the Owner, or shall be transferable to the Owner, and shall commence in accordance with the Subcontract Documents.

§ 4.7 Indemnification
§ 4.7.1 To the fullest extent permitted by law, the Subcontractor shall indemnify and hold harmless the Owner, Contractor, Architect, Architect's consultants, and agents and employees of any of them from and against claims, damages, losses, and expenses, including but not limited to attorney's fees, arising out of or resulting from performance of the Subcontractor's Work under this Subcontract, provided that any such claim, damage, loss, or expense is attributable to bodily injury, sickness, disease or death, or to injury to or destruction of tangible property (other than the Work itself), but only to the extent caused by the negligent acts or omissions of the Subcontractor, the Subcontractor's Sub-subcontractors, anyone directly or indirectly employed by them, or anyone for whose acts they may be liable, regardless of whether or not such claim, damage, loss, or expense is caused in part by a party indemnified hereunder. Such obligation shall not be construed to negate, abridge, or otherwise reduce other rights or obligations of indemnity which would otherwise exist as to a party or person described in this Section 4.7.

§ 4.7.2 In claims against any person or entity indemnified under this Section 4.7 by an employee of the Subcontractor, the Subcontractor's Sub-subcontractors, anyone directly or indirectly employed by them, or anyone for whose acts they may be liable, the indemnification obligation under Section 4.7.1 shall not be limited by a limitation on the amount or

Init.
/

type of damages, compensation or benefits payable by or for the Subcontractor, or the Subcontractor's Sub-subcontractors under workers' compensation acts, disability benefit acts, or other employee benefit acts.

§ 4.8 Remedies for Nonpayment
If the Contractor does not pay the Subcontractor through no fault of the Subcontractor, within seven days from the time payment should be made as provided in this Agreement, the Subcontractor may, without prejudice to any other available remedies, upon seven additional days' notice to the Contractor, stop the Work of this Subcontract until payment of the amount owing has been received. The Subcontract Sum shall, by appropriate Modification, be increased by the amount of the Subcontractor's reasonable costs of demobilization, delay, and remobilization.

§ 4.9 Professional Services Provided by Subcontractor
§ 4.9.1 The Subcontractor shall not be required to provide professional services that constitute the practice of architecture or engineering unless such services are specifically required by the Subcontract Documents or unless the Subcontractor is required to provide such services in order to carry out the Subcontractor's responsibilities for its own construction means, methods, techniques, sequences, and procedures. The Subcontractor shall not be required to provide professional services in violation of applicable law.

§ 4.9.2 If professional design services or certifications by a design professional related to systems, materials, or equipment are specifically required of the Subcontractor by the Subcontract Documents, the Contractor will provide all performance and design criteria that such services must satisfy to the extent the Contractor has received such performance and design criteria from the Owner and Architect under the terms of the Prime Contract.

§ 4.9.3 If professional design services or certifications by a design professional are required because of means, methods, techniques, sequences, or procedures required by the Contractor and related to the Work of the Subcontractor, the Contractor will provide all performance and design criteria that such services must satisfy.

§ 4.9.4 The Subcontractor shall be entitled to rely upon the adequacy, accuracy, and completeness of the performance and design criteria received from the Contractor under this Section 4.9.

§ 4.9.5 The Subcontractor shall cause the professional services performed under this Section 4.9 to be provided by a properly licensed design professional, whose signature and seal shall appear on all drawings, calculations, specifications, certifications, Shop Drawings, and other submittals prepared by such professional. Shop drawings and other submittals related to the Work designed by such design professional shall bear the professional's written approval when submitted to the Contractor. The Contractor shall be entitled to rely upon the adequacy, accuracy, and completeness of the services, certifications, and approvals performed or provided by the design professionals, provided the Contractor has provided to the Subcontractor all performance and design criteria required by this Section 4.9.

ARTICLE 5 CHANGES IN THE WORK
§ 5.1 The Owner may make changes in the Work by issuing Modifications to the Prime Contract. Upon receipt of a Modification to the Prime Contract issued subsequent to the execution of this Agreement, the Contractor shall promptly notify the Subcontractor of such Modification. Unless otherwise directed by the Contractor, the Subcontractor shall not thereafter order materials or perform Work that would be inconsistent with the changes made by the Modification to the Prime Contract.

§ 5.2 The Subcontractor may be ordered in writing by the Contractor, without invalidating this Subcontract, to make changes in the Work within the general scope of this Subcontract consisting of additions, deletions, or other revisions, including those required by Modifications to the Prime Contract issued subsequent to the execution of this Agreement, with the Subcontract Sum and the Subcontract Time adjusted accordingly. The Subcontractor, prior to the commencement of such changed or revised Work, shall submit promptly to the Contractor written copies of a Claim for adjustment to the Subcontract Sum and Subcontract Time for such revised Work in a manner consistent with requirements of the Subcontract Documents.

§ 5.3 The Subcontractor shall make all Claims promptly to the Contractor for additional cost, extensions of time and damages for delays, or other causes in accordance with the Subcontract Documents. A Claim which will affect or become part of a Claim which the Contractor is required to make under the Prime Contract within a specified time period or in a specified manner shall be made in sufficient time to permit the Contractor to satisfy the requirements of the Prime Contract. Such Claims shall be received by the Contractor not less than two working days preceding the time

Init.
/

by which the Contractor's Claim must be made. Failure of the Subcontractor to make such a timely Claim shall bind the Subcontractor to the same consequences as those to which the Contractor is bound.

ARTICLE 6 CLAIMS AND DISPUTES

§ 6.1 Mediation

§ 6.1.1 Claims, disputes, or other matters in controversy arising out of or related to this Subcontract, except those waived as provided for in Sections 6.4 and 11.3.2, shall be subject to mediation as a condition precedent to binding dispute resolution.

§ 6.1.2 The parties shall endeavor to resolve their Claims by mediation which, unless the parties mutually agree otherwise, shall be administered by the American Arbitration Association in accordance with its Construction Industry Mediation Procedures in effect on the date of the Agreement. A request for mediation shall be made in writing, delivered to the other party to this Subcontract and filed with the person or entity administering the mediation. The request may be made concurrently with the filing of binding dispute resolution proceedings but, in such event, mediation shall proceed in advance of binding dispute resolution proceedings, which shall be stayed pending mediation for a period of 60 days from the date of filing, unless stayed for a longer period by agreement of the parties or court order. If an arbitration is stayed pursuant to this Section 6.1.2, the parties may nonetheless proceed to the selection of the arbitrators(s) and agree upon a schedule for later proceedings.

§ 6.1.3 The parties shall share the mediator's fee and any filing fees equally. The mediation shall be held in the place where the Project is located, unless another location is mutually agreed upon. Agreements reached in mediation shall be enforceable as settlement agreements in any court having jurisdiction thereof.

§ 6.2 Binding Dispute Resolution

For any Claim subject to, but not resolved by mediation pursuant to Section 6.1, the method of binding dispute resolution shall be as follows:
(Check the appropriate box.)

☐ Arbitration pursuant to Section 6.3 of this Agreement

☐ Litigation in a court of competent jurisdiction

☐ Other: *(Specify)*

If the Contractor and Subcontractor do not select a method of binding dispute resolution, or do not subsequently agree in writing to a binding dispute resolution method other than litigation, Claims will be resolved by litigation in a court of competent jurisdiction.

§ 6.3 Arbitration

§ 6.3.1 If the Contractor and Subcontractor have selected arbitration as the method of binding dispute resolution in Section 6.2, any Claim subject to, but not resolved by, mediation shall be subject to arbitration which, unless the parties mutually agree otherwise, shall be administered by the American Arbitration Association in accordance with its Construction Industry Arbitration Rules in effect on the date of this Agreement. The arbitration should be conducted in the place where the Project is located, unless another location is mutually agreed upon. A demand for arbitration shall be made in writing, delivered to the other party to the Subcontract, and filed with the person or entity administering the arbitration. The party filing a notice of demand for arbitration must assert in the demand all Claims then known to that party on which arbitration is permitted to be demanded.

§ 6.3.2 A demand for arbitration shall be made no earlier than concurrently with the filing of a request for mediation but in no event shall it be made after the date when the institution of legal or equitable proceedings based on the Claim would be barred by the applicable statute of limitations. For statute of limitations purposes, receipt of a written demand for arbitration by the person or entity administering the arbitration shall constitute the institution of legal or equitable proceedings based on the Claim.

Init.

/

§ 6.3.3 The award rendered by the arbitrator or arbitrators shall be final, and judgment may be entered upon it in accordance with applicable law in any court having jurisdiction thereof.

§ 6.3.4 The foregoing agreement to arbitrate, and other agreements to arbitrate with an additional person or entity duly consented to by parties to the Agreement, shall be specifically enforceable under applicable law in any court having jurisdiction thereof.

§ 6.3.5 Consolidation or Joinder
§ 6.3.5.1 Subject to the rules of the American Arbitration Association or other applicable arbitration rules, either party may consolidate an arbitration conducted under this Agreement with any other arbitration to which it is a party provided that (1) the arbitration agreement governing the other arbitration permits consolidation; (2) the arbitrations to be consolidated substantially involve common questions of law or fact; and (3) the arbitrations employ materially similar procedural rules and methods for selecting arbitrator(s).

§ 6.3.5.2 Subject to the rules of the American Arbitration Association or other applicable arbitration rules, either party may include by joinder persons or entities substantially involved in a common question of law or fact whose presence is required if complete relief is to be accorded in arbitration, provided that the party sought to be joined consents in writing to such joinder. Consent to arbitration involving an additional person or entity shall not constitute consent to arbitration of a Claim, dispute, or other matter in question not described in the written consent.

§ 6.3.5.3 The Contractor and Subcontractor grant to any person or entity made a party to an arbitration conducted under this Section 6.3, whether by joinder or consolidation, the same rights of joinder and consolidation as the Contractor and Subcontractor under this Agreement.

§ 6.4 Waiver of Claims for Consequential Damages
The Contractor and Subcontractor waive claims against each other for consequential damages arising out of or relating to this Subcontract, including without limitation, any consequential damages due to either party's termination in accordance with Article 7. Nothing contained herein shall be deemed to preclude an award of liquidated damages, when applicable, in accordance with the requirements of this Agreement.

ARTICLE 7 TERMINATION, SUSPENSION OR ASSIGNMENT OF THE SUBCONTRACT
§ 7.1 Termination by the Subcontractor
The Subcontractor may terminate the Subcontract for the same reasons and under the same circumstances and procedures with respect to the Contractor as the Contractor may terminate with respect to the Owner under the Prime Contract, or for nonpayment of amounts due under this Subcontract for 60 days or longer. In the event of such termination by the Subcontractor for any reason which is not the fault of the Subcontractor, the Subcontractor's Sub-subcontractors, or their agents or employees or other persons or entities performing portions of the Work under contract with the Subcontractor, the Subcontractor shall be entitled to recover from the Contractor payment for Work executed and for proven loss with respect to materials, equipment, tools, and construction equipment and machinery, as well as reasonable overhead and profit on work not executed and costs incurred by reason of such termination.

§ 7.2 Termination by the Contractor
§ 7.2.1 Termination for Cause
If the Subcontractor repeatedly fails or neglects to carry out the Work in accordance with the Subcontract Documents or otherwise to perform in accordance with this Subcontract and fails within a ten-day period after receipt of notice to commence and continue correction of such default or neglect with diligence and promptness, the Contractor may, by notice to the Subcontractor and without prejudice to any other remedy the Contractor may have, terminate the Subcontract and finish the Subcontractor's Work by whatever method the Contractor may deem expedient. If the unpaid balance of the Subcontract Sum exceeds the expense of finishing the Subcontractor's Work and other damages incurred by the Contractor and not expressly waived, such excess shall be paid to the Subcontractor. If such expense and damages exceed the unpaid balance of the Subcontract Sum, the Subcontractor shall pay the difference to the Contractor.

§ 7.2.2 Termination for Convenience
§ 7.2.2.1 If the Owner terminates the Prime Contract for the Owner's convenience, the Contractor shall promptly deliver notice to the Subcontractor.

Init.

/

§ 7.2.2.2 In case of such termination for the Owner's convenience, the Subcontractor shall be entitled to receive payment for Work properly executed, costs incurred by reason of the termination, and reasonable overhead and profit on the Work not executed.

§ 7.2.2.3 Upon receipt of notice of termination, the Subcontractor shall

- **.1** cease operations as directed by the Contractor in the notice;
- **.2** take actions necessary, or that the Contractor may direct, for the protection and preservation of the Work; and
- **.3** except for Work directed to be performed prior to the effective date of termination stated in the notice, terminate all existing Sub-subcontracts and purchase orders and enter into no further Sub-subcontracts and purchase orders.

§ 7.3 Suspension by the Contractor for Convenience
§ 7.3.1 The Contractor may, without cause, order the Subcontractor in writing to suspend, delay, or interrupt the Work of this Subcontract in whole or in part for such period of time as the Contractor may determine. In the event of suspension ordered by the Contractor, the Subcontractor shall be entitled to an equitable adjustment of the Subcontract Time and Subcontract Sum.

§ 7.3.2 The Subcontract Time and Subcontract Sum shall be adjusted for increases in the cost and time caused by suspension, delay or interruption as described in Section 7.3.1. Adjustment of the Subcontract Sum shall include profit on the increased cost of performance caused by suspension, delay, or interruption. No adjustment shall be made to the extent that

- **.1** performance is, was or would have been so suspended, delayed, or interrupted by another cause for which the Subcontractor is responsible; or
- **.2** an equitable adjustment is made or denied under another provision of this Subcontract.

§ 7.4 Assignment of the Subcontract
§ 7.4.1 In the event the Owner terminates the Prime Contract for cause, this Subcontract is assigned to the Owner pursuant to Section 5.4 of AIA Document A201–2017 provided the Owner accepts the assignment by notifying the Contractor and Subcontractor.

§ 7.4.2 Without the Contractor's written consent, the Subcontractor shall not assign the Work of this Subcontract, subcontract the whole of this Subcontract, or subcontract portions of this Subcontract.

ARTICLE 8 THE WORK OF THIS SUBCONTRACT
The Subcontractor shall execute the following portion of the Work described in the Subcontract Documents, including all labor, materials, equipment, services and other items required to complete such portion of the Work, except to the extent specifically indicated in the Subcontract Documents to be the responsibility of others.
(Insert a precise description of the Work of this Subcontract, referring where appropriate to numbers of Drawings, sections of Specifications and pages of Addenda, Modifications, and accepted alternates.)

ARTICLE 9 DATE OF COMMENCEMENT AND SUBSTANTIAL COMPLETION
§ 9.1 The date of commencement of the Subcontractor's Work, shall be:
(Check one of the following boxes.)

☐ The date of this Agreement.

☐ A date set forth in a notice to proceed issued by the Contractor.

☐ Established as follows:
(Insert a date or a means to determine the date of commencement of the Subcontractor's Work.)

If a date of commencement of the Subcontractor's Work is not selected, then the date of commencement shall be the date of this Agreement.

§ 9.2 Subcontract Time
§ 9.2.1 The Subcontract Time is the period of time, including authorized adjustments, allotted in the Subcontract Documents for Substantial Completion of the Work described in the Subcontract Documents. The Subcontract Time shall be measured from the date of commencement of the Subcontractor's Work.

§ 9.2.2 Subject to adjustments of the Subcontract Time as provided in the Subcontract Documents, the Subcontractor shall achieve substantial completion of the Subcontractor's Work:
(Check one of the following boxes and complete the necessary information.)

☐ Not later than ( ) calendar days from the date of commencement of the Subcontractor's Work.

☐ By the following date:

§ 9.2.3 Subject to adjustments of the Subcontract Time as provided in the Subcontract Documents, if portions of the Subcontractor's Work are to be completed prior to substantial completion of the Subcontractor's Work, then the Subcontractor shall achieve earlier substantial completion of such portions by the following dates.
(List all portions of the Subcontractor's Work required to achieve substantial completion of the Subcontractor's Portion of the Work.)

Portion of Work	Substantial Completion

§ 9.2.4 If the Subcontractor fails to achieve substantial completion as provided in this Section 9.2, liquidated damages, if any, shall be assessed as set forth in Section 3.4.

§ 9.3 With respect to the obligations of both the Contractor and the Subcontractor, time is of the essence of this Subcontract.

§ 9.4 No extension of time will be valid without the Contractor's written consent after a Claim is made by the Subcontractor in accordance with Section 5.3.

ARTICLE 10 SUBCONTRACT SUM
§ 10.1 The Contractor shall pay the Subcontractor the Subcontract Sum in current funds for the Subcontractor's performance of the Subcontract. The Subcontract Sum shall be ($), subject to additions and deductions as provided in the Subcontract Documents.

§ 10.2 Alternates
§ 10.2.1 Alternates, if any, included in the Subcontract Sum:

Item	Price

§ 10.2.2 Subject to the conditions noted below, the following alternates may be accepted by the Contractor following execution of this Agreement. Upon acceptance, the Contractor shall issue a Modification to this Subcontract:
(Insert below each alternate and the conditions that must be met for the Contractor to accept the alternate.)

Item	Price	Conditions for Acceptance

§ 10.3 Unit prices, if any:
(Identify and state the unit price, and quantity limitations, if any, to which the unit price will be applicable.)

Init.
/

Item	Units and Limitations	Price Per Unit ($0.00)

§ 10.4 Allowances, if any, included in the Subcontract Sum:
(Identify allowance and state exclusions, if any, from the allowance price.)

Item	Price

ARTICLE 11 PAYMENTS
§ 11.1 Progress Payments
§ 11.1.1 Based upon Applications for Payment submitted to the Contractor by the Subcontractor, corresponding to Applications for Payment submitted by the Contractor to the Architect, and Certificates for Payment issued by the Architect, the Contractor shall make progress payments on account of the Subcontract Sum to the Subcontractor as provided below and elsewhere in the Subcontract Documents. Unless the Contractor provides the Owner with a payment bond in the full penal sum of the Contract Sum, payments received by the Contractor and Subcontractor for Work properly performed by their contractors and suppliers shall be held by the Contractor and Subcontractor for those contractors or suppliers who performed Work or furnished materials, or both, under contract with the Contractor or Subcontractor for which payment was made to the Contractor by the Owner or to the Subcontractor by the Contractor, as applicable. Nothing contained herein shall require money to be placed in a separate account and not commingled with money of the Contractor or Subcontractor, shall create any fiduciary liability or tort liability on the part of the Contractor or Subcontractor for breach of trust, or shall entitle any person or entity to an award of punitive damages against the Contractor or Subcontractor for breach of the requirements of this provision.

§ 11.1.2 The period covered by each Application for Payment shall be one calendar month ending on the last day of the month, or as follows:

§ 11.1.3 Provided an Application for Payment is received by the Contractor not later than the day of a month, the Contractor shall include the Subcontractor's Work covered by that application in the next Application for Payment which the Contractor is entitled to submit to the Architect. The Contractor shall pay the Subcontractor each progress payment no later than seven working days after the Contractor receives payment from the Owner. If the Architect does not issue a Certificate for Payment or the Contractor does not receive payment for any cause which is not the fault of the Subcontractor, the Contractor shall pay the Subcontractor, on demand, a progress payment computed as provided in Sections 11.1.7, 11.1.8, 11.1.9 and 11.2.

§ 11.1.4 If the Subcontractor's application for payment is received by the Contractor after the application date fixed above, the Subcontractor's Work covered by it shall be included by the Contractor in the next Application for Payment submitted to the Architect.

§ 11.1.5 The Subcontractor shall submit to the Contractor a schedule of values prior to submitting the Subcontractor's first Application for Payment. Each subsequent Application for Payment shall be based upon the most recent schedule of values submitted by the Subcontractor in accordance with the Subcontract Documents. The schedule of values shall allocate the entire Subcontract Sum among the various portions of the Subcontractor's Work and be prepared in such form and supported by such data to substantiate its accuracy as the Contractor may require, and unless objected to by the Contractor, shall be used as a basis for reviewing the Subcontractor's Applications for Payment.

§ 11.1.6 Applications for Payment submitted by the Subcontractor shall indicate the percentage of completion of each portion of the Subcontractor's Work as of the end of the period covered by the Application for Payment.

§ 11.1.7 Subject to the provisions of the Subcontract Documents, the amount of each progress payment shall be computed as follows:

§ 11.1.7.1 The amount of each progress payment shall first include:
.1 That portion of the Subcontract Sum properly allocable to completed Work;
.2 That portion of the Subcontract Sum properly allocable to materials and equipment delivered

Init.
/

and suitably stored at the site by the Subcontractor for subsequent incorporation in the Subcontractor's Work or, if approved by the Contractor, suitably stored off the site at a location agreed upon in writing; and

.3 The amount, if any, for changes in the Work that are not in dispute and have been properly authorized by the Contractor, to the same extent provided in the Prime Contract, pending a final determination by the Contractor of the cost of changes in the Subcontractor's Work, even though the Subcontract Sum has not yet been adjusted.

§ 11.1.7.2 The amount of each progress payment shall then be reduced by:

.1 The aggregate of previous payments made by the Contractor;

.2 The amount, if any, for Work that remains uncorrected and for which the Contractor has previously withheld a Certificate for Payment as provided in Article 9 of AIA Document A201-2017 for a cause that is the fault of the Subcontractor;

.3 For Work performed or defects discovered since the last payment application, any amount for which the Contractor may withhold payment in whole or in part, as provided in Article 9 of AIA Document A201-2017, for a cause that is the fault of the Subcontractor; and

.4 Retainage withheld pursuant to Section 11.1.8 of this Agreement.

§ 11.1.8 Retainage

§ 11.1.8.1 For each progress payment made prior to substantial completion of the Subcontractor's Work, the Contractor may withhold the following amounts as retainage from the payment otherwise due:
(Insert a percentage or amount to be withheld as retainage from each Application for Payment. The amount of retainage may be limited by governing law.)

§ 11.1.8.1.1 The following items are not subject to retainage:
(Insert any items not subject to the withholding of retainage, such as general conditions, insurance, etc.)

§ 11.1.8.2 Reduction or limitation of retainage, if any, shall be as follows:
(If the retainage established in Section 11.1.8.1 is to be modified prior to substantial completion of the entire Work, including modifications for substantial completion of portions of the Subcontractor's Work as provided in Section 9.2.3, insert provisions for such modification.)

§ 11.1.9 Upon the partial or entire disapproval by the Contractor of the Subcontractor's Application for Payment, the Contractor shall provide notice to the Subcontractor. If the Subcontractor disputes the Contractor's decision regarding a Subcontractor's Application for Payment in whole or in part, the Subcontractor may submit a Claim in accordance with Article 6. When the basis for the disapproval has been remedied, the Subcontractor shall be paid the amounts withheld.

§ 11.1.10 Provided the Contractor has fulfilled its payment obligations under the Subcontract Documents, the Subcontractor shall defend and indemnify the Contractor and Owner from all loss, liability, damage, or expense, including reasonable attorney's fees and litigation expenses, arising out of any lien claim or other claim for payment by any of the Subcontractor's subcontractors, suppliers, or vendors of any tier. Upon receipt of notice of such lien claim or other claim for payment, the Contractor shall notify the Subcontractor. If approved by the applicable court, when required, the Subcontractor may substitute a surety bond for the property against which the lien or other claim for payment has been asserted.

§ 11.2 Substantial Completion

When the Subcontractor's Work or a designated portion thereof is substantially complete and in accordance with the requirements of the Prime Contract, the Contractor shall, upon application by the Subcontractor, make prompt Application for Payment for such Work. Within 30 days following issuance by the Architect of the Certificate for Payment covering such substantially completed Work, the Contractor shall, to the full extent allowed in the Prime Contract, make payment to the Subcontractor, deducting any portion of the funds for the Subcontractor's Work withheld in accordance with the certificate to cover costs of items to be completed or corrected by the Subcontractor. Such

Init.
/

payment to the Subcontractor shall be the entire unpaid balance of the Subcontract Sum if a full release of retainage is allowed under the Prime Contract for the Subcontractor's Work prior to the completion of the entire Project. If the Prime Contract does not allow for a full release of retainage, then such payment shall be an amount which, when added to previous payments to the Subcontractor, will reduce the retainage on the Subcontractor's substantially completed Work to the same percentage of retainage as that on the Contractor's Work covered by the certificate.

§ 11.3 Final Payment

§ 11.3.1 Final payment, constituting the entire unpaid balance of the Subcontract Sum, shall be made by the Contractor to the Subcontractor when the Subcontractor's Work is fully performed in accordance with the requirements of the Subcontract Documents, the Architect has issued a Certificate for Payment covering the Subcontractor's completed Work and the Contractor has received payment from the Owner. If, for any cause which is not the fault of the Subcontractor, a Certificate for Payment is not issued or the Contractor does not receive timely payment or does not pay the Subcontractor within seven days after receipt of payment from the Owner, final payment to the Subcontractor shall be made upon demand.

(Insert provisions for earlier final payment to the Subcontractor, if applicable.)

§ 11.3.2 Before issuance of the final payment, the Subcontractor, if required, shall submit evidence satisfactory to the Contractor that all payrolls, bills for materials and equipment, and all known indebtedness connected with the Subcontractor's Work have been satisfied. Acceptance of final payment by the Subcontractor shall constitute a waiver of claims by the Subcontractor, except those previously made in writing and identified by the Subcontractor as unsettled at the time of final Application for Payment.

§ 11.4 Interest

Payments due and unpaid under this Subcontract shall bear interest from the date payment is due at such rate as the parties may agree upon in writing or, in the absence thereof, at the legal rate prevailing from time to time at the place where the Project is located.

(Insert rate of interest agreed upon, if any.)

________ % ________

ARTICLE 12 INSURANCE AND BONDS

§ 12.1 Subcontractor's Required Insurance Coverage

§ 12.1.1 The Subcontractor shall purchase and maintain the following types and limits of insurance, from a company or companies lawfully authorized to issue insurance in the jurisdiction where the Project is located, as will protect the Subcontractor from claims that may arise out of, or result from, the Subcontractor's operations and completed operations under the Subcontract:

(Specify each type of insurance, such as commercial general liability, automobile, worker's compensation, employers' liability, professional liability, and pollution, required to be carried by the Subcontractor, the limits of coverage for each type of insurance, and any other pertinent requirements.)

Type of Insurance	Limits	Other Pertinent Requirements

§ 12.1.2 Coverages, whether written on an occurrence or claims-made basis, shall be maintained without interruption from the date of commencement of the Subcontractor's Work until the date of final payment and termination of any coverage required to be maintained after final payment to the Subcontractor, and, with respect to the Subcontractor's completed operations coverage, until the expiration of the period for correction of Work or for such other period for maintenance of completed operations coverage as specified in the Prime Contract.

§ 12.1.3 If professional services are required under Section 4.9, the Subcontractor shall provide the professional liability insurance coverage required under this Section 12.1 for the following period after completion of the Work:

§ 12.1.4 Certificates of Insurance. The Subcontractor shall provide certificates of insurance acceptable to the Contractor evidencing compliance with the requirements in this Article 12 at the following times: (1) prior to commencement of the Subcontractor's Work; (2) upon renewal or replacement of each required policy of insurance; and (3) upon the Contractor's written request. An additional certificate evidencing continuation of liability coverage, including coverage for completed operations, shall be submitted with the final Application for Payment and thereafter upon renewal or replacement of such coverage until the expiration of the time required in this Article 12. The certificates shall show the Contractor and the Owner as additional insureds on the Subcontractor's Commercial General Liability and any excess or umbrella liability policy.

§ 12.1.5 Deductibles and Self-Insured Retentions. The Subcontractor shall disclose to the Contractor any deductible or self-insured retentions applicable to any insurance required to be provided by the Subcontractor.

§ 12.1.6 Additional Insured Obligations. To the fullest extent permitted by law, the Subcontractor shall cause its commercial general liability coverage to include: (1) the Contractor, the Owner, the Architect, and the Architect's consultants as additional insureds for claims caused in whole or in part by the Subcontractor's negligent acts or omissions during the Subcontractor's operations; and (2) the Contractor and Owner as additional insureds for claims caused in whole or in part by the Subcontractor's negligent acts or omissions for which loss occurs during the Subcontractor's completed operations. The additional insured coverage shall be primary and non-contributory to any of the Contractor's and Owner's general liability insurance policies and shall apply to both ongoing and completed operations. To the extent commercially available, the additional insured coverage shall be no less than that provided by Insurance Services Office, Inc. (ISO) CG 20 10 07 04, CG 20 37 07 04, and, with respect to the Architect and the Architect's consultants, CG 20 32 07 04.

§ 12.1.7 Notice of Cancellation or Change in Coverage. Within three (3) business days of the date the Subcontractor becomes aware of an impending or actual cancellation or expiration of any insurance required by the Subcontract Documents, the Subcontractor shall provide notice to the Contractor of such impending or actual cancellation or expiration. Upon receipt of notice from the Subcontractor, the Contractor shall, unless the lapse in coverage arises from an act or omission of the Contractor, have the right to suspend the Work in accordance with this Agreement until the lapse in coverage has been cured by the procurement of replacement coverage by the Subcontractor. The furnishing of notice by the Subcontractor shall not relieve the Subcontractor of any contractual obligation to provide any required coverage.

§ 12.2 Subcontractor's Required Performance Bond and Payment Bond

§ 12.2.1 The Subcontractor shall provide surety bonds, from a company or companies lawfully authorized to issue surety bonds in the jurisdiction where the Project is located, as follows:
(Specify type and penal sum of bonds.)

Type	Penal Sum ($0.00)
Payment Bond	
Performance Bond	

Payment and Performance Bonds shall be AIA Document A312™, Payment Bond and Performance Bond, or contain provisions identical to AIA Document A312™, current as of the date of this Agreement.

§ 12.2.2 Upon the request of any person or entity appearing to be a potential beneficiary of bonds covering payment of obligations under this Agreement, the Subcontractor shall promptly furnish a copy of the bonds or shall permit a copy to be made.

§ 12.3 Contractor's Insurance and Bond Obligations

§ 12.3.1 The Contractor shall furnish to the Subcontractor certificates of insurance evidencing insurance coverage required of the Contractor under the Prime Contract.

§ 12.3.2 The Contractor shall promptly, upon request of the Subcontractor, furnish a copy or permit a copy to be made of any bond covering payment of obligations arising under the Subcontract.

§ 12.4 Property Insurance

§ 12.4.1 When requested in writing, the Contractor shall provide the Subcontractor with copies of the property and equipment policies in effect for the Project, to the extent copies of the policies are available to the Contractor. The Contractor shall notify the Subcontractor if the required property insurance policies are not in effect.

§ 12.4.2 If the required property insurance is not in effect for the full value of the Subcontractor's Work, then the Subcontractor shall purchase insurance for the value of the Subcontractor's Work, and the Subcontractor shall be reimbursed for the cost of the insurance by an adjustment in the Subcontract Sum.

§ 12.4.3 Property insurance for the Subcontractor's materials and equipment required for the Subcontractor's Work, stored off site or in transit and not covered by the Project property insurance, shall be paid for through the Application for Payment process.

§ 12.5 Waivers of Subrogation
The Contractor and Subcontractor waive all rights against (1) each other and any of their subcontractors, sub-subcontractors, agents, and employees, each of the other, and (2) the Owner, the Architect, the Architect's consultants, and (3) Separate Contractors, if any, and any of their subcontractors, sub-subcontractors, agents, and employees for damages caused by fire or other causes of loss to the extent those losses are covered by property insurance provided under the Prime Contract or other property insurance applicable to the Work or to property at or adjacent to the Project site, except such rights as they may have to proceeds of such insurance held by the Owner as a fiduciary. The Subcontractor shall require similar written waivers in favor of the individuals and entities enumerated herein from the Subcontractor's Sub-subcontractors, agents, and employees. The policies of insurance purchased and maintained by each person or entity agreeing to waive claims pursuant to this Section 12.5 shall not prohibit this waiver of subrogation, which shall be effective as to a person or entity (1) even though that person or entity would otherwise have a duty of indemnification, contractual or otherwise, (2) even though that person or entity did not pay the insurance premium directly or indirectly, or (3) whether or not the person or entity had an insurable interest in the property damaged.

ARTICLE 13 TEMPORARY FACILITIES, SERVICES, EQUIPMENT AND WORKING CONDITIONS
§ 13.1 The Contractor shall furnish and make the Contractor's temporary facilities and services available to the Subcontractor at no cost, except as noted below:

§ 13.2 The Contractor's equipment will be available to the Subcontractor only at the Contractor's discretion and on mutually satisfactory terms, except as noted below:

§ 13.3 Specific working conditions as noted below:
(Insert any specific arrangements or requirements concerning working conditions and labor matters applicable to the Subcontractor's Work.)

ARTICLE 14 MISCELLANEOUS PROVISIONS
§ 14.1 Where reference is made in this Subcontract to a provision of another Subcontract Document, the reference refers to that provision as amended or supplemented by other provisions of the Subcontract Documents.

§ 14.2 The Contractor's representative:
(Name, address, email address and other information)

§ 14.3 The Subcontractor's representative:
(Name, address, email address and other information)

Init.
/

§ 14.4 Notice
§ 14.4.1 Except as otherwise provided in Section 14.4.2, where the Subcontract Documents require one party to notify or give notice to the other party, such notice shall be provided in writing to the designated representative of the party to whom the notice is addressed and shall be deemed to have been duly served if delivered in person, by mail, by courier, or by electronic transmission if a method for electronic notice is set forth in Section 14.4.3.

§ 14.4.2 Notice of Claims shall be provided in writing and shall be deemed to have been duly served only if delivered to the designated representative of the party to whom the notice is addressed by certified or registered mail, or by courier providing proof of delivery.

§ 14.4.3 Notice in electronic format, pursuant to Section 14.4.1, may be given in accordance with AIA Document E203™–2013, Building Information Modeling and Digital Data Exhibit, if completed, or as otherwise set forth below:
(If other than in accordance with AIA Document E203™–2013, insert requirements for delivering notice in electronic format such as name, title, and email address of the recipient and whether and how the system will be required to generate a read receipt for the transmission.)

§ 14.5 Neither the Contractor's nor the Subcontractor's representative shall be changed without ten days' prior notice to the other party.

§ 14.6 The invalidity of any provision of the Subcontract Documents shall not invalidate the Subcontract or its remaining provisions. If it is determined that any provision of the Subcontract violates any law or is otherwise invalid or unenforceable, then that provision shall be revised to the extent necessary to make that provision legal and enforceable. In such case, the Subcontract shall be construed, to the fullest extent permitted by law, to give effect to the parties' intentions and purposes in executing the Subcontract.

§ 14.7 The parties shall agree upon protocols governing the transmission and use of Instruments of Service or any other information or documentation in digital form. The parties will use AIA Document E203™–2013, Building Information Modeling and Digital Data Exhibit, to establish the protocols for the development, use, transmission, and exchange of digital data.

§ 14.7.1 Any use of, or reliance on, all or a portion of a building information model without agreement to protocols governing the use of, and reliance on, the information contained in the model and without having those protocols set forth in AIA Document E203™–2013, Building Information Modeling and Digital Data Exhibit, and the requisite AIA Document G202™–2013, Project Building Information Modeling Protocol Form, shall be at the using or relying party's sole risk and without liability to the other party and its contractors or consultants, the authors of, or contributors to, the building information model, and each of their agents and employees.

ARTICLE 15 ENUMERATION OF SUBCONTRACT DOCUMENTS
§ 15.1 This Agreement is comprised of the following documents:

.1 AIA Document A401™–2017, Standard Form Agreement Between Contractor and Subcontractor;
.2 Prime Agreement between the Owner and Contractor, including all exhibits thereto, attached as Exhibit A;
.3 AIA Document E203™–2013, Building Information Modeling and Digital Data Exhibit, if not included in the Prime Agreement, dated as indicated below:
(Insert the date of the E203–2013 incorporated into this Agreement.)

.4 Other Exhibits incorporated into this Agreement:
(Clearly identify any other exhibits incorporated into this Agreement.)

Init.
/

.5 Other documents:
(List other documents, if any, forming part of the Agreement.)

This Agreement entered into as of the day and year first written above.

CONTRACTOR *(Signature)*	**SUBCONTRACTOR** *(Signature)*
(Printed name and title)	*(Printed name and title)*

Exhibit 26

Subcontractor Proposal Quote

Proposal Date ______________________________

Proposal Number ______________________________

Name ______________________________

Address ______________________________

Contractor's License # ______________________________

Job Site Address ______________________________

Specifications	Estimate
Subcontractor will machine stock material pertaining to trade, stocking to be done prior to installation of windows and exterior scaffolding. Install 5/8" drywall type X, and GB with screw nails, tape and leave to smooth finish ready for paint. California 1 coat 4' high cmu wall. Metal trim to be cornerbead and J-metal. All bowed/crooked framing, protruding pipes, nails on existing framing must be fixed and proper backing must be provided before installation of drywall. A rough cleanup of all material pertaining to trade will be done and placed in trash bin located near the job site. Trash bin to be provided by general contractor. If no trash bin is provided, all trash will be placed in designated pile. Bid taken per job walk on ________________ [date].	

WE HEREBY PROPOSE TO FURNISH LABOR AND MATERIALS COMPLETE IN ACCORDANCE WITH THE ABOVE SPECIFICATIONS, FOR THE SUM AS LISTED IN THE TOTAL COLUMN BELOW PERIOD.

Terms 40% - stocking 30% - nailing 20% - taping 10% - finish	Total	

All material is guaranteed to be as specified. All work to be completed in a workmanlike manner according to standard practices. Any alteration or deviation from the above specifications, involving extra costs, will be executed only upon a signed Work Change Order, and will become an extra charge over and above this Proposal/Estimate. All Agreements contingent upon strikes, accidents, or delays beyond our control. This proposal is subject to acceptance within sixty (60) days and it is void thereafter at the option of Subcontractor.

Authorized Signature ______________________________

ACCEPTANCE OF PROPOSAL

The above prices, specification, terms and conditions are hereby accepted. Subcontractor is authorized to do the work as specified. Payment will be made as outlined in the terms above or Subcontractor will delay work.

Signature ________________________ Date _________

Exhibit 27

Subcontractor Payment Application

To:

Date: 12/31/23
Progress Estimate Number: 7
Period Ending: 12/20/23
Location:

Invoice Number: 04-06-7
Work Order Number: #H13397

Item #	Description	Contract Quantity	Contract Unit Price		Quantity This Invoice	Amount This Invoice	Quantity To Date	Invoice To Date
6	Remove Existing Grouted Riprap	1	LS	$125,000.00	0.00%	$0.00	100.00%	$125,000.00
16	Grouted Riprap Embankment	4200	CY	$89.00	666.21	$59,292.69	4203.95	$374,151.55
17	Grouted Riprap-Outlet Pads	100	CY	$89.00	110.80	$9,843.40	110.60	$9,843.40
	Change Order Demolition	1	LS	$41,742.00	5.00%	$2,087.10	100.00%	$41,742.00

DATE: 12/31/23
PERIOD ENDING: 12/20/23

$71,233.19	TOTAL EARNED	$550,736.95
$7,122.32	LESS RETENTION	$55,073.70
	LESS PREVIOUS	$431,562.38
$64,100.67	AMOUNT DUE	$64,100.87

PAYMENT CERTIFICATION AND AGREEMENT

The undersigned subcontractor certifies that it has presented truthful information to Contractor and/or its authorized agents to support its request for payment arising from labor performed for or materials supplied to Contractor on the Project, as described above, and that said subcontractor has not previously received payment for any part or portion of the work which forms the basis for any request for payment. Subcontractor acknowledges that Contractor is relying on this certificate at all times when determining whether or not a payment is due for current services performed. In the event that Subcontractor (1) discovers that it has previously been paid for work that forms the basis of any current request for payment, or (2) received an additional payment for the same work for the project owner or others, Subcontractor will immediately notify Contractor of the double payment, and within seven (7) days, return the payment received to Contractor.

Subcontractor's failure to notify Contractor and return any duplicate payment as set forth in this certification will result in a breach of this Subcontract, and entitle Contractor to recover the entirety of any duplicate payment made, along with interest at the maximum allowable rate, and reasonable attorney's fees and costs associated with recovery efforts.
SUBCONTRACTOR

By ____________________________

Name __________________________

Title ___________________________

Date ___________________________

Exhibit 28

Supplier Invoice

Project:

BILL TO:

Name

Street Address

City, State, Zip

ATTN:	**Invoice Date**: 08/28/23
Payment Terms: Net 10 Days	**Invoice Number**: 7920
Method of Shipment: F.O.B.	**F.O.B. Point**:
Purchase Order #:	**Date Order Shipped**: 08/28/23

Tons	Description	United Price	Total
107.60	¼ ton		$1,797.49
37.90	¼ ton		$633.14

145.50 Total Tons

Your Quote: $21.50/ton

Sub-Total	$243.83
Sales Tax (7.75%)	$188.37
Haul	$509.25
Amount Due	**$3,128.25**

Delivery Report

Customer:			**Date**: 08/28/23	
Job Name:			**PO/Job**: 04-06	
Location:			**Quarry**: CPC	
[redacted]				
Load	Ticket #	Truck #	Time	Rock Size ¼ Ton
1	3138	R1	6:34am	16.71
2	3141	R1	8:19am	17.49
3	3143	R1	9:01am	18.32
4	3146	R1	9:48am	18.43
5	3148	R1	10:30am	18.95
6	3153	R1	12:05pm	17.70
7				
8				
9				
10				
11				
12				
13				
14				
15				
16				
17				
18				
19				
20				
21				
22				
23				
24				
25				
			Total	107.60

Customer Detail Summary

Daily Transaction
VinVRS Industries Report

Job #	Material	Trans #	Type	Date/Time	Net Wt.	Units	Charges
	¼ ton	3140	Account	08/28/23 7:37am	17.98 tn	0.00	$0.00
	¼ ton	3152	Account	08/28/23 11:17am	19.92 tn	0.00	$0.00
	¼ ton				37.90 tn	0.00	$0.00
					37.90 tn	0.00	$0.00
					37.90 tn	0.00	$0.00

Terms: Net 30

AP Invoice List
Date: 08/38/23

AP Invoice List
Alpha; by Vendor/Job, with Payments Subs
Vendor in list 450, Job in list #105, Status = 1 and
Record#: 17481

Record #	Invoice #	Due Date	Description	Invoice Total	Retained	Balance
17481	7920	02/28/05		$3,128.25		$3128.25
			Job Totals	$3,128.25		$3128.25
			Vendor Totals	$3,128.25		$3128.25
			Grand Totals	$3,128.25		$3128.25

Exhibit 29

Subcontractor Releases

CONDITIONAL WAIVER AND RELEASE ON PROGRESS PAYMENT

NOTICE: THIS DOCUMENT WAIVES THE CLAIMANT'S LIEN, STOP PAYMENT NOTICE, AND PAYMENT BOND RIGHTS EFFECTIVE ON RECEIPT OF PAYMENT. A PERSON SHOULD NOT RELY ON THIS DOCUMENT UNLESS SATISFIED THAT THE CLAIMANT HAS RECEIVED PAYMENT.

Identifying Information

Name of Claimant:

Name of Customer:

Job Location:

Owner:

Through Date:

Conditional Waiver and Release

This document waives and releases lien, stop payment notice, and payment bond rights the claimant has for labor and service provided, and equipment and material delivered, to the customer on this job through the Through Date of this document. Rights based upon labor or service provided, or equipment or material delivered, pursuant to a written change order that has been fully executed by the parties prior to the date that this document is signed by the claimant, are waived and released by this document, unless listed as an Exception below. This document is effective only on the claimant's receipt of payment from the financial institution on which the following check is drawn:

Maker of Check:

Amount of Check: $

Check Payable to:

Exceptions

This document does not affect any of the following:

(1) Retentions.

(2) Extras for which the claimant has not received payment.

(3) The following progress payments for which the claimant has previously given a conditional waiver and release but has not received payment:

Date(s) of waiver and release:______________________________

Amount(s) of unpaid progress payment(s): $____________________________

(4) Contract rights, including (A) a right based on rescission, abandonment, or breach of contract, and (B) the right to recover compensation for work not compensated by the payment.

Signature

Claimant's Signature:

Claimant's Title:

Date of Signature:

7/1/12

UNCONDITIONAL WAIVER AND RELEASE ON PROGRESS PAYMENT

NOTICE TO CLAIMANT: THIS DOCUMENT WAIVES AND RELEASES LIEN, STOP PAYMENT NOTICE, AND PAYMENT BOND RIGHTS UNCONDITIONALLY AND STATES THAT YOU HAVE BEEN PAID FOR GIVING UP THOSE RIGHTS. THIS DOCUMENT IS ENFORCEABLE AGAINST YOU IF YOU SIGN IT, EVEN IF YOU HAVE NOT BEEN PAID. IF YOU HAVE NOT BEEN PAID, USE A CONDITIONAL WAIVER AND RELEASE FORM.

Identifying Information

Name of Claimant:

Name of Customer:

Job Location:

Owner:

Through Date:

Unconditional Waiver and Release

This document waives and releases lien, stop payment notice, and payment bond rights the claimant has for labor and service provided, and equipment and material delivered, to the customer on this job through the Through Date of this document. Rights based upon labor or service provided, or equipment or material delivered, pursuant to a written change order that has been fully executed by the parties prior to the date that this document is signed by the claimant, are waived and released by this document, unless listed as an Exception below. The claimant has received the following progress payment:

$_______________________________

Exceptions

This document does not affect any of the following:

(1) Retentions.

(2) Extras for which the claimant has not received payment.

(3) Contract rights, including (A) a right based on rescission, abandonment, or breach of contract, and (B) the right to recover compensation for work not compensated by the payment.

Signature

Claimant's Signature:

Claimant's Title:

Date of Signature:

7/1/12

UNCONDITIONAL WAIVER AND RELEASE ON FINAL PAYMENT

NOTICE TO CLAIMANT: THIS DOCUMENT WAIVES AND RELEASES LIEN, STOP PAYMENT NOTICE, AND PAYMENT BOND RIGHTS UNCONDITIONALLY AND STATES THAT YOU HAVE BEEN PAID FOR GIVING UP THOSE RIGHTS. THIS DOCUMENT IS ENFORCEABLE AGAINST YOU IF YOU SIGN IT, EVEN IF YOU HAVE NOT BEEN PAID. IF YOU HAVE NOT BEEN PAID, USE A CONDITIONAL WAIVER AND RELEASE FORM.

Identifying Information

Name of Claimant:

Name of Customer:

Job Location:

Owner:

Unconditional Waiver and Release

This document waives and releases lien, stop payment notice, and payment bond rights the claimant has for all labor and service provided, and equipment and material delivered, to the customer on this job. Rights based upon labor or service provided, or equipment or material delivered, pursuant to a written change order that has been fully executed by the parties prior to the date that this document is signed by the claimant, are waived and released by this document, unless listed as an Exception below. The claimant has been paid in full.

Exceptions

This document does not affect any of the following:
Disputed claims for extras in the amount of: $

Signature

Claimant's Signature:

Claimant's Title:

Date of Signature:

7/1/12

CONDITIONAL WAIVER AND RELEASE ON FINAL PAYMENT

NOTICE: THIS DOCUMENT WAIVES THE CLAIMANT'S LIEN, STOP PAYMENT NOTICE, AND PAYMENT BOND RIGHTS EFFECTIVE ON RECEIPT OF PAYMENT. A PERSON SHOULD NOT RELY ON THIS DOCUMENT UNLESS SATISFIED THAT THE CLAIMANT HAS RECEIVED PAYMENT.

Identifying Information

Name of Claimant:

Name of Customer:

Job Location:

Owner:

Conditional Waiver and Release

This document waives and releases lien, stop payment notice, and payment bond rights the claimant has for labor and service provided, and equipment and material delivered, to the customer on this job. Rights based upon labor or service provided, or equipment or material delivered, pursuant to a written change order that has been fully executed by the parties prior to the date that this document is signed by the claimant, are waived and released by this document, unless listed as an Exception below. This document is effective only on the claimant's receipt of payment from the financial institution on which the following check is drawn:

Maker of Check:

Amount of Check: $

Check Payable to:

Exceptions

This document does not affect any of the following:
Disputed claims for extras in the amount of: $

Signature

Claimant's Signature:

Claimant's Title:

Date of Signature:

7/1/12

Exhibit 30

Consent of Surety Form—Final Payment

Project Name ______________________________
Project Address ______________________________
____
Contract For ______________________________
Contract Date ______________________________
Contractor ______________________________
Owner ______________________________
Surety ______________________________
Bond Number ______________________________

In accordance with the provisions of the Contract between **Owner** and **Contractor** as indicated above, **Surety** hereby approves of the final payment to **Contractor**, and agrees that final payment to **Contractor** shall not relieve **Surety** of any of is obligations to **Owner** as set forth in the Surety's bond.

IN WITNESS, WHEREOF, Surety has hereunto set its hand this ____ day of ______, 20__.

______________________________	______________________________
Attest: (Seal):	Surety
	______________________________
	Signature of Authorized Representative
	______________________________
	Title

Exhibit 31

Preliminary Notice

CALIFORNIA PRELIMINARY NOTICE – PUBLIC WORKS
(Civil Code Section 9300, et seq.)

THIS NOTICE IS REQUIRED TO BE GIVEN UNDER CALIFORNIA LAW

TO:

PUBLIC ENTITY (Name):	**Address:**
DIRECT CONTRACTOR (Name):	**Address:**
SUBCONTRACTOR – FIRST TIER (Name):	**Address:**

YOU ARE HEREBY NOTIFIED THAT

CLAIMANT (Name):	**Address:**
Relationship of Claimant to the parties (e.g. subcontractor to __________, or supplier to __________):	

HAS FURNISHED OR WILL FURNISH WORK, LABOR, SERVICES, EQUIPMENT OR MATERIAL OF THE FOLLOWING GENERAL DESCRIPTION:

TO THE FOLLOWING PERSON OR FIRM:

(Name):	**Address:**

AT THE FOLLOWING SITE OR LOCATION (Address or description sufficient for identification):

THE TOTAL ESTIMATED PRICE OF LABOR, SERVICES, EQUIPMENT AND/OR MATERIALS TO BE FURNISHED IS:

Dated: ______________ **For Claimant, By:** ____________________________

ATTACH PROOF OF NOTICE DECLARATION

VERIFICATION

I, the undersigned, state: I am the ____,
("Agent of", "President of", "A Partner of", "Owner of", etc.)
the owner identified in the foregoing California Preliminary Notice – Public; I have read said document and know the contents thereof, and I certify that the same is true of my own knowledge.

I declare under penalty of perjury under the laws of the State of California that the foregoing is true and correct.

Dated: ____________________ By: ______________________________________

Name (print) ______________________________

> A notary public or other officer completing this certificate verifies only the identity of the individual who signed the document to which this certificate is attached, and not the truthfulness, accuracy, or validity of that document.

State of California
County of ____________________} ss.

(seal)

On ___________________________, ________ (date), before me, ___________________________, notary public (name and title of officer) personally appeared ___________________________, who proved to me on the basis of satisfactory evidence to be the person(s) whose name(s) is/are subscribed to the within instrument and acknowledged to me that he/she/they executed the same in his/her/their authorized capacity(ies), and that by his/her/their signature(s) on the instrument the person(s), or the entity upon behalf of which the person(s) acted, executed the instrument. I certify under PENALTY OF PERJURY under the laws of the State of California that the foregoing paragraph is true and correct.

Witness my hand and official seal. ___________________________
Signature of Notary

PROOF OF MAILING AFFIDAVIT
(Civil Code Section 8416(a)(8) and (c))

I, the undersigned, declare that:

I am a citizen of the United States and am over the age of 18 years. On this date, I caused to be served the following:

CALIFORNIA PRELIMINARY NOTICE – PUBLIC

prepaid, via [check all that apply]:

_______ Certified Mail, Return Receipt Requested

_______ Registered Mail

_______ First Class Mail

_______ Express Service Carrier for Overnight Delivery

_______ Delivery in Person

On the following person or persons [list all persons served]:

Name:

Title (if known):

Address:

I declare under penalty of perjury under the laws of the State of California that the foregoing is true and correct.

Dated: ________________ By: ____________________________________

Print Name: ____________________________

Per California Civil Code section 8118:

(b) If the notice is given by mail, the declaration shall be accompanied by one of the following:

(1) Documentation provided by the United States Postal Service showing that payment was made to mail the notice using registered or certified mail, or express mail.

(2) Documentation provided by an express service carrier showing that payment was made to send the notice using an overnight delivery service.

(3) A return receipt, delivery confirmation, signature confirmation, tracking record, or other proof of delivery or attempted delivery provided by the United States Postal Service, or a photocopy of the record of delivery and receipt maintained by the United States Postal Service, showing the date of delivery and to whom delivered, or in the event of nondelivery, by the returned envelope itself.

(4) A tracking record or other documentation provided by an express service carrier showing delivery or attempted delivery of the notice.

CALIFORNIA PRELIMINARY NOTICE – PRIVATE WORKS

(Civil Code Section 8200 et seq.)

THIS IS NOT A LIEN. THIS NOTICE IS REQUIRED TO BE GIVEN UNDER CALIFORNIA LAW

NOTICE TO PROPERTY OWNER EVEN THOUGHYOU HAVE PAID YOUR CONTRACTOR IN FULL, if the person or firm that has given you this notice is not paid in full for labor, service, equipment, or material provided or to be provided to your construction project, a lien may be placed on your property. Foreclosure of the lien may lead to loss of all or part of your property. You may wish to protect yourself against this by (1) requiring your contractor to provide a signed release by the person or firm that has given you this notice before making payment to your contractor, or (2) any other method that is appropriate under the circumstances. This notice is required by law to be served by the undersigned as a statement of your legal rights. This notice is not intended to reflect upon the financial condition of the contractor or the person employed by you on the construction project. If you record a notice of cessation or completion of your construction project, you must within 10 days after recording, send a copy of the notice of completion to your contractor and the person or firm that has given you this notice. The notice must be sent by registered or certified mail. Failure to send the notice will extend the deadline to record a claim of lien. You are not required to send the notice if you are a residential homeowner of a dwelling containing four or fewer units.

TO:

OWNER **OR REPUTED OWNER (Name):**	**Address:**
DIRECT CONTRACTOR **OR REPUTED DIRECT CONTRACTOR (Name):**	**Address:**
CONSTRUCTION LENDER **OR REPUTED CONSTRUCTION LENDER (Name):**	**Address:**

YOU ARE HEREBY NOTIFIED THAT

CLAIMANT (Name):	**Address:**
Relationship of Claimant to the parties (e.g. subcontractor to __________, or supplier to __________):	

HAS FURNISHED OR WILL FURNISH WORK, LABOR, SERVICES, EQUIPMENT OR MATERIAL OF THE FOLLOWING GENERAL DESCRIPTION:

TO THE FOLLOWING PERSON OR FIRM:

(Name):	**Address:**

AT THE FOLLOWING SITE OR LOCATION (Address or description sufficient for identification):

THE TOTAL ESTIMATED PRICE OF LABOR, SERVICES, EQUIPMENT AND/OR MATERIALS TO BE FURNISHED IS:

Dated: _______________

For Claimant, By:

____

____

ATTACH PROOF OF NOTICE DECLARATION

PROOF OF NOTICE DECLARATION

I, the undersigned, declare that:

I am a citizen of the United States and am over the age of 18 years. On this date, I caused to be served the following:

CALIFORNIA PRELIMINARY NOTICE – PRIVATE WORKS

prepaid, via [check all that apply]:

_______ Certified Mail, Return Receipt Requested

_______ Registered Mail

_______ First Class Mail

_______ Express Service Carrier for Overnight Delivery

_______ Delivery in Person

On the following person or persons [list all persons served]:

Name:

Title (if known):

Address:

I declare under penalty of perjury under the laws of the State of California that the foregoing is true and correct.

Dated: ________________ By: ________________________________

Print Name: ________________________________

Per California Civil Code section 8118:

(b) If the notice is given by mail, the declaration shall be accompanied by one of the following:

(1) Documentation provided by the United States Postal Service showing that payment was made to mail the notice using registered or certified mail, or express mail.

(2) Documentation provided by an express service carrier showing that payment was made to send the notice using an overnight delivery service.

(3) A return receipt, delivery confirmation, signature confirmation, tracking record, or other proof of delivery or attempted delivery provided by the United States Postal Service, or a photocopy of the record of delivery and receipt maintained by the United States Postal Service, showing the date of delivery and to whom delivered, or in the event of nondelivery, by the returned envelope itself.

(4) A tracking record or other documentation provided by an express service carrier showing delivery or attempted delivery of the notice.

Exhibit 32

Delivery Ticket

TICKET # ____________________ Date ____________________

Charge to: ____________________ Day ____________________

Name: ____________________ Your Order # ____________________

Address ____________________ Your Job # ____________________

Job Location ____________________ Truck # __________ Capacity __________

Description ____________________ Fuel ______ gal. Oil ______ qts.

____________________ OFFICE ONLY

____________________ Overtime for Driver Only ________ hrs.

Hourly Rental Rate ____________________ Shift Time ________ hrs.

Travel Time ____________________ Minimum Wage ________ hrs.

Start: ________ am/pm Off Time: Lunch ______ hrs. Total Drivers Time ________ hrs.

Stop: ________ am/pm Down ______ hrs. Total Truck Time ________ hrs.

I agree that all bills are due and payable on the 10th of the month following the date the work was performed. Should collection be necessary by suit or otherwise, I agree to buy collection costs, interest on the unpaid amount, and reasonable attorney's fees.

By ____________________

Exhibit 33

Change Order—AIA Document G701™ - 2017

AIA Document G701® – 2017

Change Order

PROJECT: *(name and address)*	CONTRACT INFORMATION: Contract For: Date:	CHANGE ORDER INFORMATION: Change Order Number: Date:
OWNER: *(name and address)*	ARCHITECT: *(name and address)*	CONTRACTOR: *(name and address)*

THE CONTRACT IS CHANGED AS FOLLOWS:
(Insert a detailed description of the change and, if applicable, attach or reference specific exhibits. Also include agreed upon adjustments attributable to executed Construction Change Directives.)

The original (Contract Sum) (Guaranteed Maximum Price) was	$ ______
The net change by previously authorized Change Orders	$ ______
The (Contract Sum) (Guaranteed Maximum Price) prior to this Change Order was	$ ______
The (Contract Sum) (Guaranteed Maximum Price) will be (increased) (decreased) (unchanged) by this Change Order in the amount of	$ ______
The new (Contract Sum) (Guaranteed Maximum Price), including this Change Order, will be	$ ______
The Contract Time will be (increased) (decreased) (unchanged) by	( ) days.
The new date of Substantial Completion will be	

NOTE: This Change Order does not include adjustments to the Contract Sum or Guaranteed Maximum Price, or the Contract Time, that have been authorized by Construction Change Directive until the cost and time have been agreed upon by both the Owner and Contractor, in which case a Change Order is executed to supersede the Construction Change Directive.

NOT VALID UNTIL SIGNED BY THE ARCHITECT, CONTRACTOR AND OWNER.

ARCHITECT *(Firm name)*	CONTRACTOR *(Firm name)*	OWNER *(Firm name)*
SIGNATURE	SIGNATURE	SIGNATURE
PRINTED NAME AND TITLE	PRINTED NAME AND TITLE	PRINTED NAME AND TITLE
DATE	DATE	DATE

Exhibit 34

Easement of Right-of-Way Agreement

THIS AGREEMENT is made and entered into as of _____, 20__, by and between __________ ("Railroad"); and __________ ("Contractor").

RECITALS:

Contractor has been hired by _______ to perform work relating to the construction of __________ (the "Work"), with all or a portion of such Work to be performed on property of Railroad in the vicinity of __________, which Work is the subject of a contract dated ________ between Contractor and ________.

Contractor needs Railroad to permit Contractor to perform the Work on the portion of property shown on the attached plans marked Exhibit A, attached hereto and hereby made a part hereof, and Railroad is agreeable thereto, subject to the following terms and conditions.

AGREEMENT:

NOW, THEREFORE, it is mutually agreed by and between Railroad and Contractor, as follows:

<u>ARTICLE 1 - DEFINITION OF CONTRACTOR</u>

For purposes of this agreement, all references in this agreement to the contractor shall include Contractor's contractors, subcontractors, officers, agents and employees, and others acting under its or their authority.

<u>ARTICLE 2 - RIGHT GRANTED: PURPOSE</u>

Railroad hereby grants to Contractor the right, during the term hereinafter stated and upon and subject to each and all of the terms, provisions and conditions herein contained, to enter upon and have ingress to and egress from the property described in the Recitals for the purpose of performing the Work described in the Recitals above. The right herein granted to Contractor is limited to those portions of property specifically described herein, or as designated by Railroad.

ARTICLE 3 - TERMS AND CONDITIONS CONTAINED IN EXHIBITS A, B, C ,AND D

The terms and conditions contained in Exhibit A, Exhibit B, Exhibit C, and Exhibit D, attached hereto, are hereby made a part of this agreement.

ARTICLE 4 - ALL EXPENSES TO BE BORNE BY CONTRACTOR

A. Contractor shall bear any and all costs and expenses associated with any Work performed by Contractor, or any costs or expenses incurred by Railroad relating to this agreement.

B. Contractor, at its own expense, shall adequately police and supervise all Work to be performed by Contractor and shall ensure that such Work is performed in a safe manner as set forth in Section 7 of Exhibit B. The responsibility of Contractor for safe conduct and adequate policing and supervision of Contractor's Work shall not be lessened or otherwise affected by the approval of plans and specifications involving the Work, or by the collaboration in performance of any Work, or by the presence at the Work site of Railroad employees, or by compliance by Contractor with any requests or recommendations made by Railroad.

ARTICLE 5 - TERM; TERMINATION

A. The grant of right herein made to Contractor shall commence on the date of this agreement, and continue until ______, unless sooner terminated as herein provided, or at such time as Contractor has completed its Work on the property, whichever is earlier. Contractor agrees to notify Railroad in writing when it has completed its Work on: property.

B. This agreement may be terminated by either party on ten (10) days written notice to the other party.

ARTICLE 6 - CERTIFICATE OF INSURANCE

A. Before commencing any Work, Contractor will provide Railroad with the insurance binders, policies, certificates and/or endorsements set forth in Exhibit C of this agreement.

B. All insurance correspondence, binders, policies, certificates and/or endorsements shall be directed to ______.

ARTICLE 7 - DISMISSAL OF CONTRACTOR /SUBCONTRACTOR EMPLOYEE

At the request of Railroad, Contractor shall remove from Railroad's property any employee of Contractor or any subcontractor who fails to conform to the Railroad's instructions in connection with the Work on the property, and any right of Contractor shall be suspended until such removal has occurred. Contractor shall indemnify against any claims arising from the removal of any such employee from the property.

ARTICLE 8 - ADMINISTRATIVE FEE

Contractor shall pay to Railroad, $_____ as reimbursement for clerical, administrative and handling expenses in connection with the processing of this agreement.

ARTICLE 9 - CROSSINGS

No additional vehicular crossings (including temporary haul roads) or pedestrian crossings over Railroad's trackage shall be installed or used by Contractor without the prior written permission of Railroad,

ARTICLE 10 - EXPLOSIVES

Explosives or other highly flammable substances shall not be stored on property without the prior written approval of Railroad.

IN WITNESS WHEREOF, the parties hereto have duly executed this agreement in duplicate as of the date first herein written.

CONTRACTOR

By: __________

Title: __________

RAILROAD

By: __________

Title: __________

Exhibit 35

Subcontractor Performance Bond

Bond No. ________

Premium: $_______

KNOW ALL MEN BY THESE PRESENTS, that we ___________, as Principal, and ___________, as Surety, are held and firmly bound unto ___________ (hereinafter call the Contractor) in the penal sum of $___________ for which payment well and truly to be made we do bind ourselves, our heirs, executors, successors, administrators, and assigns, jointly and severally, firmly by these presents.

THE CONDITION OF THIS OBJIGATION IS SUCH, that:

WHEREAS, the Principal entered into a certain subcontract with the Contractor, dated ___________ for ___________ [description of subcontract work] at ___________ [location of project], which subcontract shall be deemed a part hereof as fully as if set out herein.

NOW, THEREFORE, if the said Principal shall well and truly perform and fulfill all the undertakings, covenants, terms, conditions, warranties and all other obligations contained in or arising out of said subcontract during the original term of said subcontract including warranty period and any extensions thereof that may be granted by the Contractor, with or without notice to the Surety, shall well and truly perform and fulfill those obligations that by their nature extend beyond the term of subcontract warranty periods ad shall also well and truly perform and fulfill all the undertakings, covenants, terms, conditions, warranties and all other obligations of any and all duly authorized additions to and modifications of said subcontract that may hereafter be made, notice of which additions and modifications to the Surety being hereby waived, then this obligation to be void; otherwise to remain in full force and effect.

PRINCIPAL	SURETY
By ______________________	By ______________________
Its ______________________	Its ______________________
Date ____________________	Date ____________________

Exhibit 36

Subcontractor Payment Bond

Bond No. ________

Premium: $_______

KNOW ALL MEN BY THESE PRESENTS, that we ___________, as Principal, and ___________, as Surety, are held and firmly bound unto ___________ (hereinafter call the Contractor) in the penal sum of $___________ for which payment well and truly to be made we do bind ourselves, our heirs, executors, successors, administrators, and assigns, jointly and severally, firmly by these presents.

THE CONDITION OF THIS OBJIGATION IS SUCH, that:

WHEREAS, the Principal entered into a certain subcontract with the Contractor, dated __________ for __________ [description of subcontract work] at ___________ [location of project], which subcontract shall be deemed a part hereof as fully as if set out herein.

NOW, THEREFORE, if the said Principal shall promptly make payment to all persons or entities providing the Principal directly or indirectly through other tiers with labor, equipment, or material in the prosecution of the work provided for in said subcontract, and any and all duly authorized additions to and modifications of said subcontract that may hereafter by made, and shall promptly pay all other obligations incurred by the Principal in connection with such work, and shall defend, indemnify, and hold harmless the Contractor and Owner from any claims, demands, liens, or suits by any person or entity on account of such labor, equipment, material, or other benefits or obligations, then this obligation to be void; otherwise to remain in full force and effect. Except as otherwise provided herein, the intent of this bond is for claimants to have the status of third party beneficiaries of this bond.

If this bond is furnished in connection with a statutory requirement for the project, this bond shall be considered a statutory bond and shall be governed by the statute that governs it including any terms and conditions required of same that is not otherwise included herein.

PRINCIPAL	SURETY
By ______________________	By ______________________
Its ______________________	Its ______________________
Date ____________________	Date ____________________

Exhibit 37

Certified Payroll Report

U.S. Department of Labor
Wage and Hour Division

PAYROLL
(For Contractor's Optional Use; See Instructions at www.dol.gov/whd/forms/wh347instr.htm)
Persons are not required to respond to the collection of information unless it displays a currently valid OMB control number

U.S. Wage and Hour Division
Rev. Dec. 2008

NAME OF CONTRACTOR ☐ OR SUBCONTRACTOR ☐	ADDRESS	OMB No.: 1235-0008 Expires: 04/30/2021

PAYROLL NO.	FOR WEEK ENDING	PROJECT AND LOCATION	PROJECT OR CONTRACT NO.

(1) NAME AND INDIVIDUAL IDENTIFYING NUMBER (e.g., LAST FOUR DIGITS OF SOCIAL SECURITY NUMBER) OF WORKER	(2) NO. OF WITHHOLDING EXEMPTIONS	(3) WORK CLASSIFICATION	OT. OR ST.	(4) DAY AND DATE / HOURS WORKED EACH DAY							(5) TOTAL HOURS	(6) RATE OF PAY	(7) GROSS AMOUNT EARNED	(8) DEDUCTIONS FICA	WITH-HOLDING TAX			OTHER	TOTAL DEDUCTIONS	(9) NET WAGES PAID FOR WEEK
			O																	
			S																	
			O																	
			S																	
			O																	
			S																	
			O																	
			S																	
			O																	
			S																	
			O																	
			S																	
			O																	
			S																	
			O																	
			S																	

While completion of Form WH-347 is optional, it is mandatory for covered contractors and subcontractors performing work on Federally financed or assisted construction contracts to respond to the information collection contained in 29 C.F.R. §§ 3.3, 5.5(a). The Copeland Act (40 U.S.C. § 3145) contractors and subcontractors performing work on Federally financed or assisted construction contracts to "furnish weekly a statement with respect to the wages paid each employee during the preceding week." U.S. Department of Labor (DOL) regulations at 29 C.F.R. § 5.5(a)(3)(ii) require contractors to submit weekly a copy of all payrolls to the Federal agency contracting for or financing the construction project, accompanied by a signed "Statement of Compliance" indicating that the payrolls are correct and complete and that each laborer or mechanic has been paid not less than the proper Davis-Bacon prevailing wage rate for the work performed. DOL and federal contracting agencies receiving this information review the information to determine that employees have received legally required wages and fringe benefits.

Public Burden Statement

We estimate that is will take an average of 55 minutes to complete this collection, including time for reviewing instructions, searching existing data sources, gathering and maintaining the data needed, and completing and reviewing the collection of information. If you have any comments regarding these estimates or any other aspect of this collection, including suggestions for reducing this burden, send them to the Administrator, Wage and Hour Division, U.S. Department of Labor, Room S3502, 200 Constitution Avenue, N.W. Washington, D.C. 20210

(over)

Date ____________________

I, ______________________________ ______________________________
(Name of Signatory Party) (Title)

do hereby state:

(1) That I pay or supervise the payment of the persons employed by

____ on the
(Contractor or Subcontractor)

______________________________; that during the payroll period commencing on the
(Building or Work)

_______ day of ______________, _______, and ending the _______ day of ______________, _______

all persons employed on said project have been paid the full weekly wages earned, that no rebates have been or will be made either directly or indirectly to or on behalf of said

____ from the full
(Contractor or Subcontractor)

weekly wages earned by any person and that no deductions have been made either directly or indirectly from the full wages earned by any person, other than permissible deductions as defined in Regulations, Part 3 (29 C.F.R. Subtitle A), issued by the Secretary of Labor under the Copeland Act, as amended (48 Stat. 948, 63 Stat. 108, 72 Stat. 967; 76 Stat. 357; 40 U.S.C. § 3145), and described below:

____

____

____

____

(2) That any payrolls otherwise under this contract required to be submitted for the above period are correct and complete, that the wage rates for laborers or mechanics contained therein are not less than the applicable wage rates contained in any wage determination incorporated into the contract, that the classifications set forth therein for each laborer or mechanic conform with the work he performed.

(3) That any apprentices employed in the above period are duly registered in a bona fide apprenticeship program registered with a State apprenticeship agency recognized by the Bureau of Apprenticeship and Training, United States Department of Labor, or if no such recognized agency exists in a State, are registered with the Bureau of Apprenticeship and Training, United States Department of Labor.

(4) That:

(a) WHERE FRINGE BENEFITS ARE PAID TO APPROVED PLANS, FUNDS, OR PROGRAMS

☐ – in addition to the basic hourly wage rates paid to each laborer or mechanic listed in the above referenced payroll, payments of fringe benefits as listed in the contract have been or will be made to appropriate programs for the benefit of such employees, except as noted in section 4(c) below.

(b) WHERE FRINGE BENEFITS ARE PAID IN CASH

☐ – Each laborer or mechanic listed in the above referenced payroll has been paid, as indicated on the payroll, an amount not less than the sum of the applicable basic hourly wage rate plus the amount of the required fringe benefits as listed in the contract, except as noted in section 4(c) below.

(c) EXCEPTIONS

EXCEPTION (CRAFT)	EXPLANATION

REMARKS:

NAME AND TITLE | SIGNATURE

THE WILLFUL FALSIFICATION OF ANY OF THE ABOVE STATEMENTS MAY SUBJECT THE CONTRACTOR OR SUBCONTRACTOR TO CIVIL OR CRIMINAL PROSECUTION. SEE SECTION 1001 OF TITLE 18 AND SECTION 231 OF TITLE 31 OF THE UNITED STATES CODE.

Exhibit 38

Progress Meeting Minutes

Meeting Recap [date]

Attendance:

Submittals/Shop Drawings:

Pending RFI's:

Pending Change Order Requests:

Non-Compliance Reports:

Project Site Conditions:

Schedule:

Payment Status:

Inspection Status:

Miscellaneous:

ACTION ITEMS:

Exhibit 39

Submittal Log

Project Name	High School				
Owner Name	Unified School District	Phone		NTD Proj. Arch.	
Const. Manager	Construction Group	Phone		Job #	
Inspector		Phone		Log Print Date	

Project Division	ID #	Control #	Item Description	Date Received	Consultant's Name	Date to Consultant	Action					Date to Constr. Manager	Contribution					Remarks
							No Revisions Needed	Minor Correction Noted-	Review & Resubmit	Rejected & Resubmit	Resubmit Specific Item		Inspector	Architect Copy	Owner	Const. Manager	Consultant	
5	088-00	81B	05500-Ornamental Iron Fence and Gate	12/11/23	Architect													
10	080-00	123	10522-Fire Extinguisher and Cabinets	12/17/23	Architect													
10	090-0A	123 A	10533-Fire Extinguisher and Cabinet Resubmittal	03/20/23	Architect													
8	091-00	128	05410-Custom Casework	01/23/23	Architect													
12	082-00	131	12820-Library Shelving	01/31/23	Architect													
12	082-0A	131 A	12820-Library Shelving	03/11/23	Architect													
7	083-00	T34	07212-Fiber Glass Insulation	02/28/23	Architect													

Exhibit 40

RFI LOG

#	Subject	Date	Ball in Court	Status	Closed Date
1	Detail drawing for guestroom entry	7/1/23	Arch	Closed	7/10/23
Q: Provide detail drawing for guestroom entry transition					
A: Refer to updated Spec #103 re new transition					
2	Hardware specifications	7/2/23	Owner	Closed	7/12/23
Q:Provide door hardware specs for model rooms #101-102					
A: See attached door hardware schedule extract sheet					
3	Wall finish conflict	7/15/23	Arch	Open	
Q: Millwork finish paint Spec conflicts w/drawings re same					
A:					

Exhibit 41

Change Order Log

					30,500,000
CO #	**Description**	**CO Date**	**CO Amount**	**Status**	**New Contract Amount**
1	**Add Roof Drains**	**7/1/23**	**26,400**	**App'd**	**30,526,400**
2	**Electrical Adds**	**7/15/23**	**380,000**	**App'd**	**30,906,400**
3	**Replace existing cooling tower**	**7/20/23**	**177,950**	**App'd**	**3,084,350**
4	**Plumbing Adds**	**7/22/23**	**124,600**	**App'd**	**31,208,950**
5	**Add to Eco Flex System**	**7/22/23**	**285,500**	**App'd**	**31494.450**
6	**Add Kitchen MEP**	**7/25/23**	**1,449,500**	**Pending**	

Exhibit 42

Notice to Cure Letter

Date

To:

Attn:

From: Name
Street Address
City, State Zip

RE: Project Name
NOTICE TO CURE
Job #:

Dear ,

This is a Notice to Cure to pursuant to Article of the contract. is responsible for all drafting and coordination for its scope of work. Under Article timely and accurate submittal of shop drawings is of the essence of the contract and may not deviate from the contract documents without approval by the owner. [DESCRIPTION OF DEFICIENCIES IN WORK] has breached its obligations to perform drafting and coordination of its work, to perform its work in strict accordance with the contract documents, to examine the contract documents, to timely perform its work, to properly coordinate its work with the work of others, to not make changes in the work without approval, to keep its work free of defects, and to replace/ repair defective work, and to obtain approval of its shop drawings.

Respectfully,

cc: Performance Bond surety (if applicable)

Exhibit 43

Notice to Project Digital Data Protocol Form—AIA Document G201-2013

AIA Document G201™ – 2013

Project Digital Data Protocol Form

PROJECT: *(Name and address)*

PROTOCOL VERSION NUMBER:
DATE:
PREPARED BY:
DISTRIBUTION TO: *(List each individual to whom this protocol is distributed. Include individuals listed in Section 1.2, or reference Section 1.2, along with any additional recipients.)*

This document is intended to be used in conjunction with a project specific AIA Document E203™–2013, Building Information Modeling and Digital Data Exhibit, which the Parties will incorporate into their Agreement for the Project.

TABLE OF ARTICLES

ARTICLE 1 GENERAL PROVISIONS REGARDING USE OF DIGITAL DATA
§ 1.1 List each Project Participant that has incorporated AIA Document E203™–2013, Building Information Modeling and Digital Data Exhibit, dated ________, into its agreement for the Project:

Project Participant	Discipline

§ 1.2 Project Participants. For each Project Participant listed in Section 1.1, identify and provide contact information for the individuals responsible for implementation of the Digital Data protocols.

Project Participant	Individual Responsible	Contact Information

§ 1.3 Terms in this document shall have the same meaning as those in AIA Document E203–2013.

ARTICLE 2 DIGITAL DATA MANAGEMENT PROTOCOLS
§ 2.1.1 Electronic Document Management System. If, pursuant to Section 3.5.1 of the Project specific version of AIA Document E203–2013, the Project Participants indicated an intent to use a centralized electronic document management system on the Project, the requirements for the centralized electronic document management system are as follows:
(The requirements for the system shall address, among other things, access to and security of Digital Data.)

§ 2.1.2 System Startup Requirements. Initial training and other startup requirements to be implemented with respect to the use or management of Digital Data, if any, are as follows:
(Describe in detail any initial training or other startup requirements.)

§ 2.1.3 Ongoing System Requirements. Ongoing training or support programs to be implemented with respect to the use or management of Digital Data, if any, are as follows:
(Describe in detail any ongoing training or support programs to be implemented.)

§ 2.2 Digital Data Storage Requirements. The procedures and requirements for storing Digital Data during the course of the Project, if any, are as follows:
(Describe in detail the procedures and requirements for storing Digital Data during the course of the Project.)

§ 2.3 Digital Data Archiving Requirements. The procedures and requirements for archiving and preserving Digital Data during the course of the Project and following final completion of the Project, if any, are as follows:
(Describe in detail the procedures and requirements for archiving and preserving Digital Data during the course of the Project and following final completion.)

§ 2.4 Other Digital Data Management protocol requirements, if any, are as follows:
(Describe in detail any other requirements.)

ARTICLE 3 TRANSMISSION AND USE OF DIGITAL DATA

§ 3.1 Digital Data Protocol Table. The Project Participants shall comply with the data formats, transmission methods and Authorized Uses set forth in the Digital Data Protocol Table below when transmitting or using Digital Data on the Project.
(Complete the Digital Data Protocol Table by entering information in the spaces below. Adapt the table to the needs of the Project by adding, deleting or modifying the listed Digital Data as necessary. Use Section 3.2 Digital Data Protocol Table Definitions and Notes to define abbreviations placed, and to record notes indicated, in the Digital Data Protocol Table.)

Digital Data		Digital Data Format	Transmission Method	Authorized Uses	Notes *(Enter #)*
§ 3.1.1	Project Agreements and Modifications				
§ 3.1.2	Project communications				
	General communications				
	Meeting notices				
	Agendas				
	Minutes				
	Requests for information				
	Architect's Supplemental Instructions				
§ 3.1.3	Architect's preconstruction submittals				
	Schematic Design Documents				
	Design Development Documents				
	Construction Documents				
§ 3.1.4	Contract Documents				
	Architect's Drawings				
	Architect's Specifications				
§ 3.1.5	Contractor's submittals				
	Product data				
	Submitted by Contractor				
	Returned by Architect				

Digital Data	Digital Data Format	Transmission Method	Authorized Uses	Notes *(Enter #)*
Shop drawings				
Submitted by Contractor				
Returned by Architect				

Digital Data	Digital Data Format	Transmission Method	Authorized Uses	Notes *(Enter #)*
§ 3.1.6 Subcontractor's submittals				
Product data				
Submitted by Subcontractor				
Returned by Contractor				
Shop drawings				
Submitted by Subcontractor				
Returned by Contractor				
§ 3.1.7 Modifications				
Requests for proposal				
Architect's order for a minor change in the Work				
Proposals				
Construction Change Directives				
Change Orders				
§ 3.1.8 Project payment documents				
§ 3.1.9 Notices and Claims				
§ 3.1.10 Closeout documents				
Record documents				
Operations and Maintenance Manual				

§ 3.2 Digital Data Protocol Table Definitions and Notes

Digital Data Format:
(Provide required data format, including software version, if applicable.)

Digital Data Format **Definition**

Transmission Method:
(Below are suggested abbreviations and definitions. Delete, modify or supplement, as necessary.)

Abbreviation	**Definition**
CD	Delivered via Compact Disk
EM	Via e-mail
DMS	Centralized Electronic Document Management System

Authorized Uses of Digital Data:
(Below are suggested abbreviations and definitions. Delete, modify or supplement, as necessary.)

Abbreviation	**Definition**
I	Integrate (incorporate additional digital data without modifying data received)
M	Modify as required to fulfill obligations for the Project
R	Reproduce and distribute
S	Store and view only

Notes:
(List by number shown on table.)

INDEX

Index

P

Q

R

S